HAKIM'S ODYSSEY

FABIEN TOULMÉ

HAKIM'S ODYSSEY

Book 2: From Turkey to Greece

graphic mundi

To all those who help migrants and work to make this world a little bit more humane.

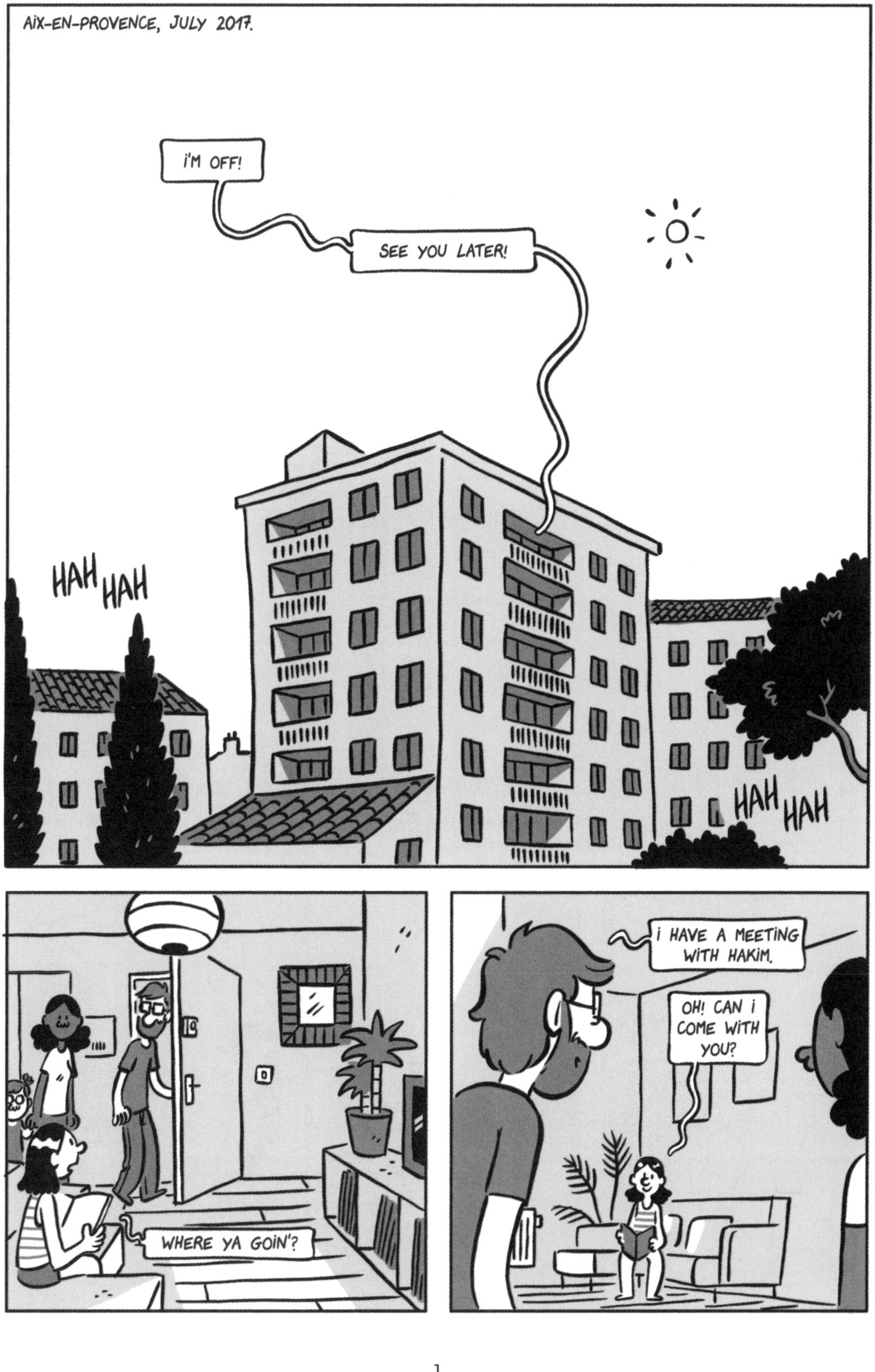
AIX-EN-PROVENCE, JULY 2017.
I'M OFF!
SEE YOU LATER!
HAH HAH
HAH HAH
WHERE YA GOIN'?
I HAVE A MEETING WITH HAKIM.
OH! CAN I COME WITH YOU?

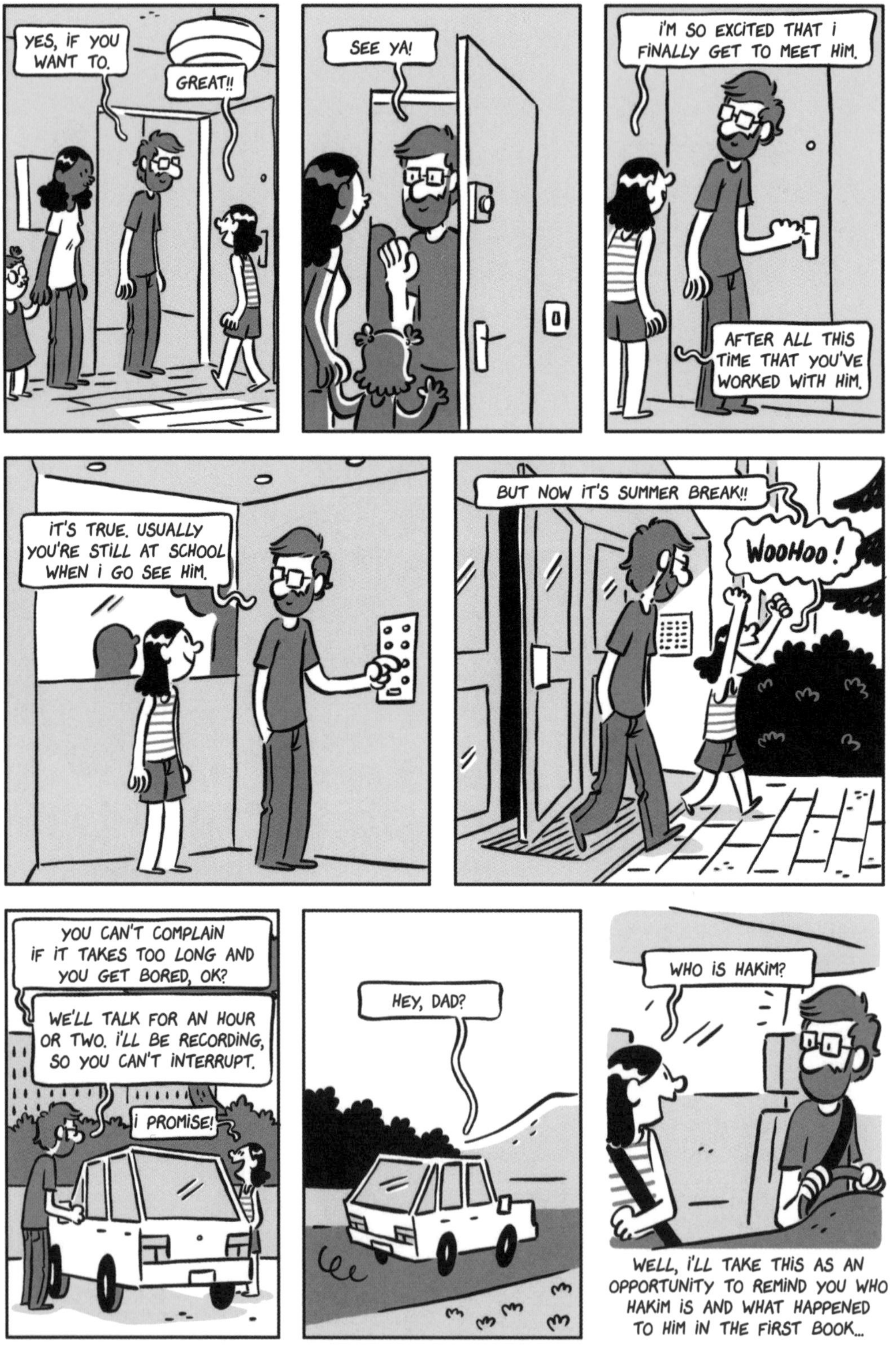
YES, IF YOU WANT TO.
GREAT!!
SEE YA!
I'M SO EXCITED THAT I FINALLY GET TO MEET HIM.
AFTER ALL THIS TIME THAT YOU'VE WORKED WITH HIM.
IT'S TRUE. USUALLY YOU'RE STILL AT SCHOOL WHEN I GO SEE HIM.
BUT NOW IT'S SUMMER BREAK!!
WOOHOO!
YOU CAN'T COMPLAIN IF IT TAKES TOO LONG AND YOU GET BORED, OK?
WE'LL TALK FOR AN HOUR OR TWO. I'LL BE RECORDING, SO YOU CAN'T INTERRUPT.
I PROMISE!
HEY, DAD?
WHO IS HAKIM?
WELL, I'LL TAKE THIS AS AN OPPORTUNITY TO REMIND YOU WHO HAKIM IS AND WHAT HAPPENED TO HIM IN THE FIRST BOOK...

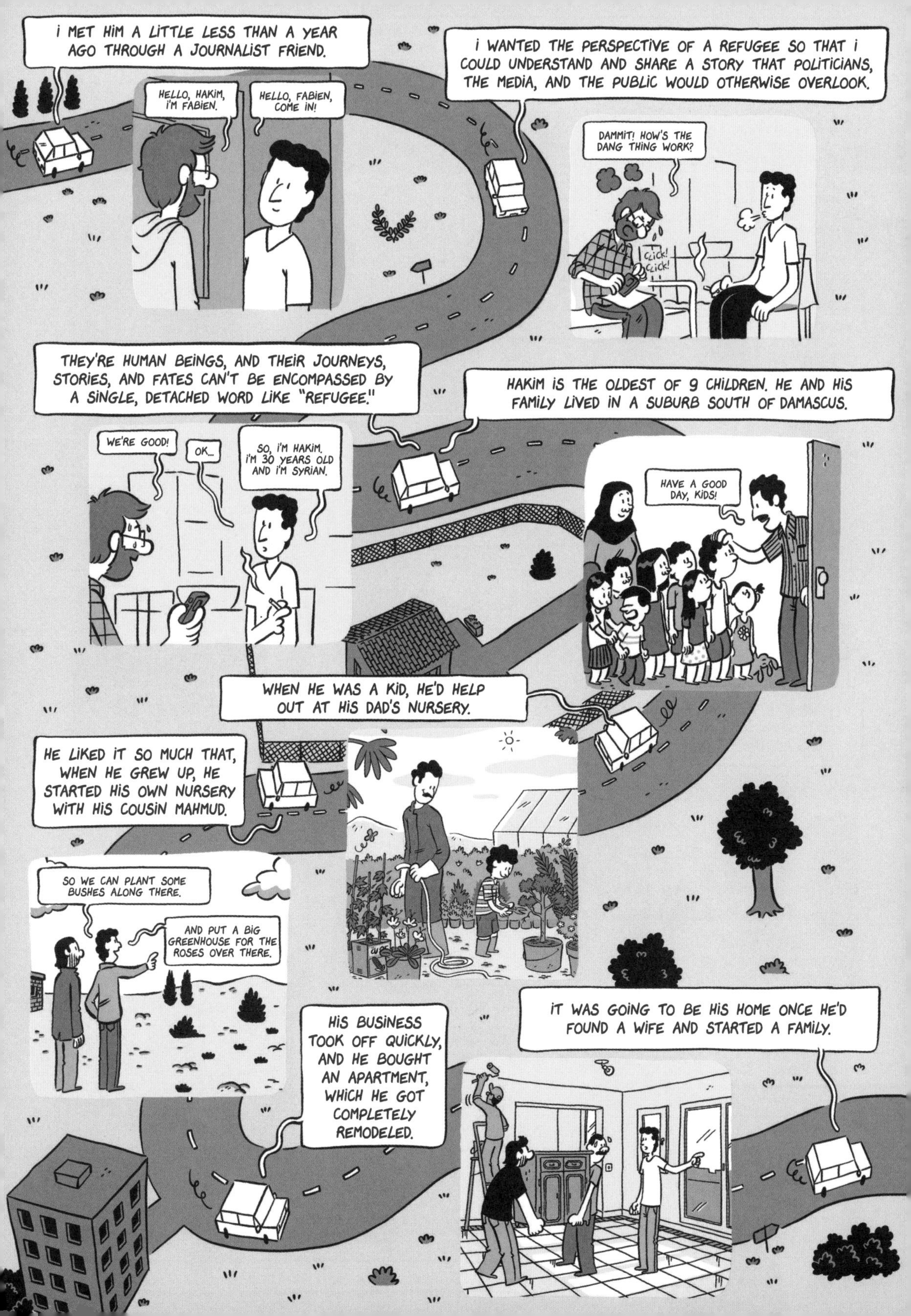
I MET HIM A LITTLE LESS THAN A YEAR AGO THROUGH A JOURNALIST FRIEND.
HELLO, HAKIM, I'M FABIEN.
HELLO, FABIEN, COME IN!
I WANTED THE PERSPECTIVE OF A REFUGEE SO THAT I COULD UNDERSTAND AND SHARE A STORY THAT POLITICIANS, THE MEDIA, AND THE PUBLIC WOULD OTHERWISE OVERLOOK.
DAMMIT! HOW'S THE DANG THING WORK?
CLICK! CLICK!
THEY'RE HUMAN BEINGS, AND THEIR JOURNEYS, STORIES, AND FATES CAN'T BE ENCOMPASSED BY A SINGLE, DETACHED WORD LIKE "REFUGEE."
HAKIM IS THE OLDEST OF 9 CHILDREN. HE AND HIS FAMILY LIVED IN A SUBURB SOUTH OF DAMASCUS.
WE'RE GOOD!
OK...
SO, I'M HAKIM. I'M 30 YEARS OLD AND I'M SYRIAN.
HAVE A GOOD DAY, KIDS!
WHEN HE WAS A KID, HE'D HELP OUT AT HIS DAD'S NURSERY.
HE LIKED IT SO MUCH THAT, WHEN HE GREW UP, HE STARTED HIS OWN NURSERY WITH HIS COUSIN MAHMUD.
SO WE CAN PLANT SOME BUSHES ALONG THERE.
AND PUT A BIG GREENHOUSE FOR THE ROSES OVER THERE.
HIS BUSINESS TOOK OFF QUICKLY, AND HE BOUGHT AN APARTMENT, WHICH HE GOT COMPLETELY REMODELED.
IT WAS GOING TO BE HIS HOME ONCE HE'D FOUND A WIFE AND STARTED A FAMILY.

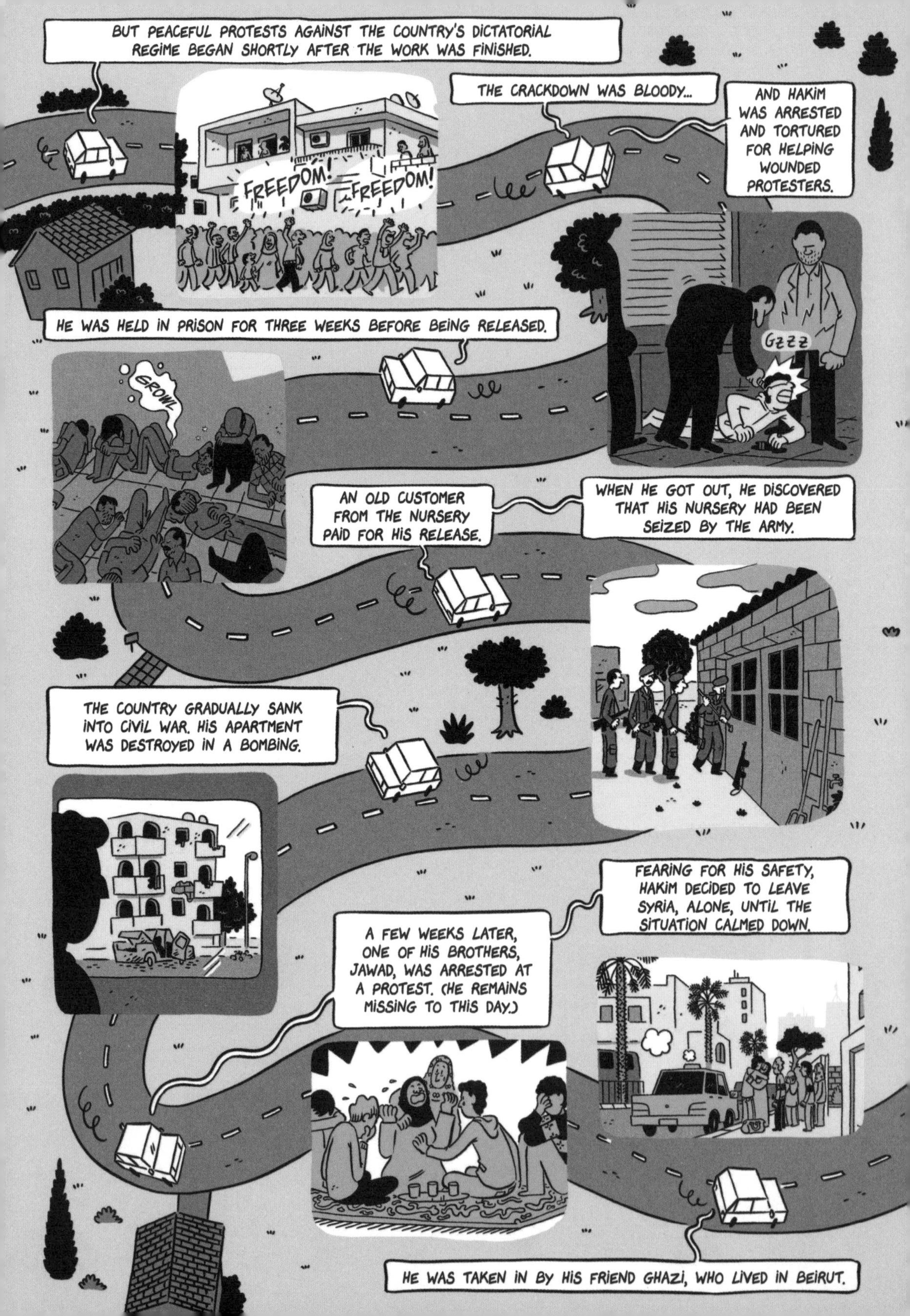
BUT PEACEFUL PROTESTS AGAINST THE COUNTRY'S DICTATORIAL REGIME BEGAN SHORTLY AFTER THE WORK WAS FINISHED.
FREEDOM!
FREEDOM!
THE CRACKDOWN WAS BLOODY...
AND HAKIM WAS ARRESTED AND TORTURED FOR HELPING WOUNDED PROTESTERS.
HE WAS HELD IN PRISON FOR THREE WEEKS BEFORE BEING RELEASED.
GROWL
GZZZ
AN OLD CUSTOMER FROM THE NURSERY PAID FOR HIS RELEASE.
WHEN HE GOT OUT, HE DISCOVERED THAT HIS NURSERY HAD BEEN SEIZED BY THE ARMY.
THE COUNTRY GRADUALLY SANK INTO CIVIL WAR. HIS APARTMENT WAS DESTROYED IN A BOMBING.
FEARING FOR HIS SAFETY, HAKIM DECIDED TO LEAVE SYRIA, ALONE, UNTIL THE SITUATION CALMED DOWN.
A FEW WEEKS LATER, ONE OF HIS BROTHERS, JAWAD, WAS ARRESTED AT A PROTEST. (HE REMAINS MISSING TO THIS DAY.)
HE WAS TAKEN IN BY HIS FRIEND GHAZI, WHO LIVED IN BEIRUT.

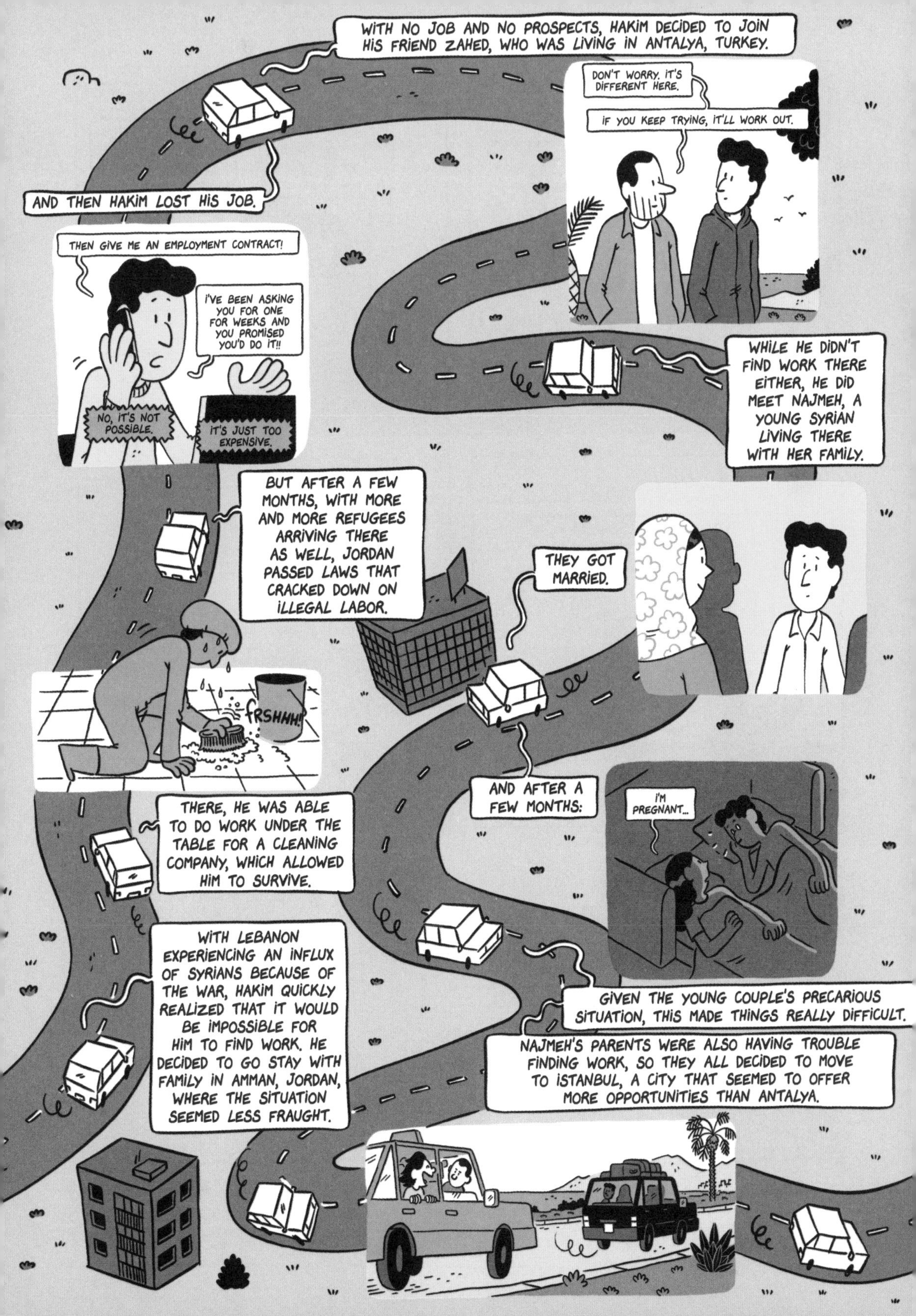
WITH LEBANON EXPERIENCING AN INFLUX OF SYRIANS BECAUSE OF THE WAR, HAKIM QUICKLY REALIZED THAT IT WOULD BE IMPOSSIBLE FOR HIM TO FIND WORK. HE DECIDED TO GO STAY WITH FAMILY IN AMMAN, JORDAN, WHERE THE SITUATION SEEMED LESS FRAUGHT.
THERE, HE WAS ABLE TO DO WORK UNDER THE TABLE FOR A CLEANING COMPANY, WHICH ALLOWED HIM TO SURVIVE.
FRSHHH!
BUT AFTER A FEW MONTHS, WITH MORE AND MORE REFUGEES ARRIVING THERE AS WELL, JORDAN PASSED LAWS THAT CRACKED DOWN ON ILLEGAL LABOR.
THEN GIVE ME AN EMPLOYMENT CONTRACT!
I'VE BEEN ASKING YOU FOR ONE FOR WEEKS AND YOU PROMISED YOU'D DO IT!!
NO, IT'S NOT POSSIBLE.
IT'S JUST TOO EXPENSIVE.
AND THEN HAKIM LOST HIS JOB.
WITH NO JOB AND NO PROSPECTS, HAKIM DECIDED TO JOIN HIS FRIEND ZAHED, WHO WAS LIVING IN ANTALYA, TURKEY.
DON'T WORRY. IT'S DIFFERENT HERE.
IF YOU KEEP TRYING, IT'LL WORK OUT.
WHILE HE DIDN'T FIND WORK THERE EITHER, HE DID MEET NAJMEH, A YOUNG SYRIAN LIVING THERE WITH HER FAMILY.
THEY GOT MARRIED.
AND AFTER A FEW MONTHS:
I'M PREGNANT...
GIVEN THE YOUNG COUPLE'S PRECARIOUS SITUATION, THIS MADE THINGS REALLY DIFFICULT.
NAJMEH'S PARENTS WERE ALSO HAVING TROUBLE FINDING WORK, SO THEY ALL DECIDED TO MOVE TO ISTANBUL, A CITY THAT SEEMED TO OFFER MORE OPPORTUNITIES THAN ANTALYA.

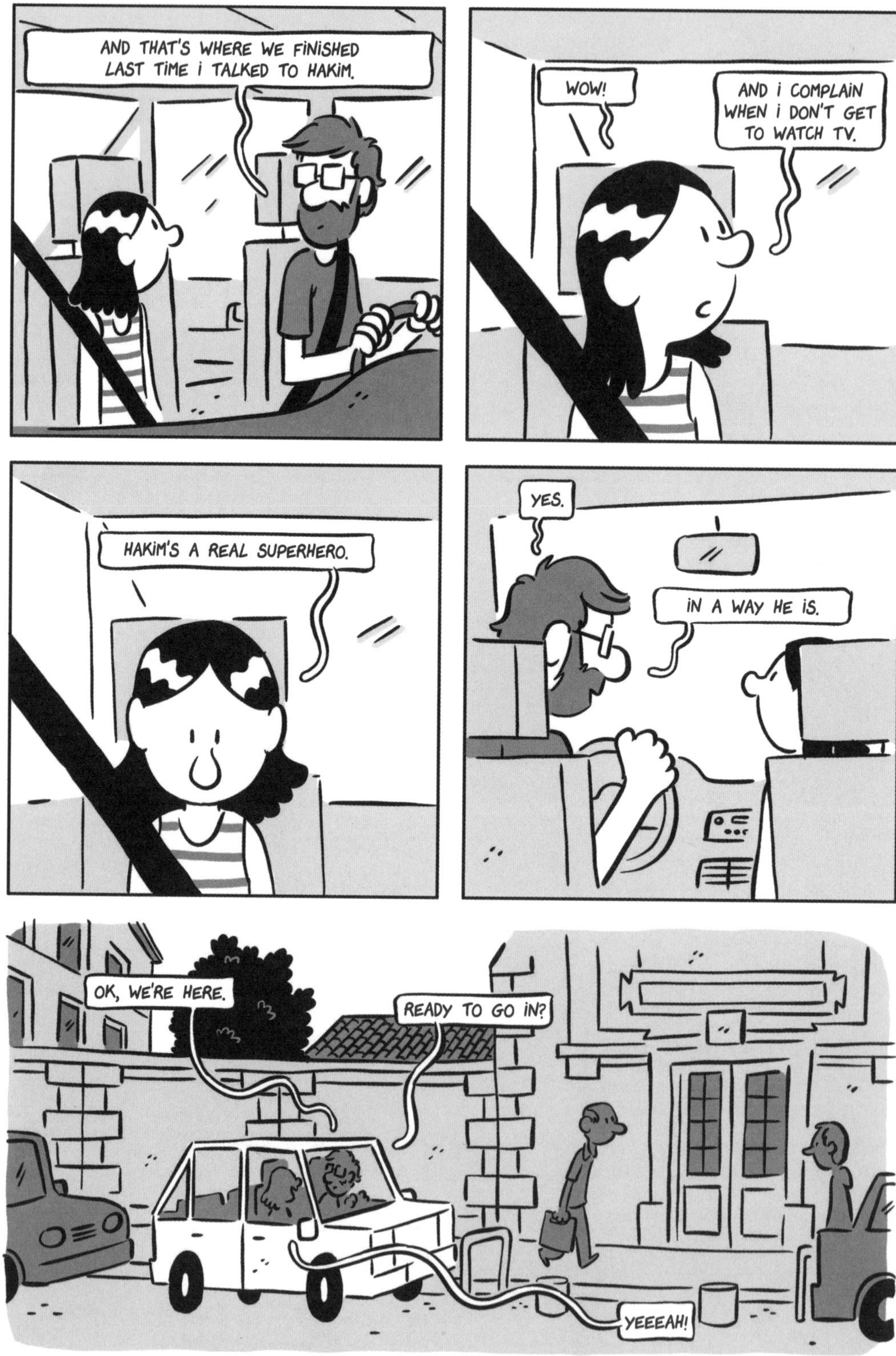
AND THAT'S WHERE WE FINISHED LAST TIME I TALKED TO HAKIM.
WOW!
AND I COMPLAIN WHEN I DON'T GET TO WATCH TV.
HAKIM'S A REAL SUPERHERO.
YES.
IN A WAY HE IS.
OK, WE'RE HERE.
READY TO GO IN?
YEEEAH!

Chapter 9:
Istanbul
(July 2013)

"THIS ISN'T LIVING, IT'S LIKE WE'RE ALREADY DEAD."

RIIING

YES?

IT'S FABIEN.

COME IN!

BZZZ

SO HE LIVES HERE?

YEP.

IT'S NICE.

I GUESS I THOUGHT REFUGEES HAD TO LIVE IN TENTS.

SOME DO, UNFORTUNATELY, BUT EVERY REFUGEE HAS A DIFFERENT STORY. AND THAT'S EXACTLY WHY I WANTED TO TELL ONE OF THESE STORIES.

HELLO!

HELLO, FABIEN.

MM, THAT SMELLS GOOD.

THIS IS MY DAUGHTER LOUISE.

HELLO, LOUISE.

DO YOU LIKE SWEETS?

YEEEAH!

REMEMBER, FABIEN, THE LAST TIME YOU WERE HERE I PROMISED I'D BAKE YOU SOMETHING.

8

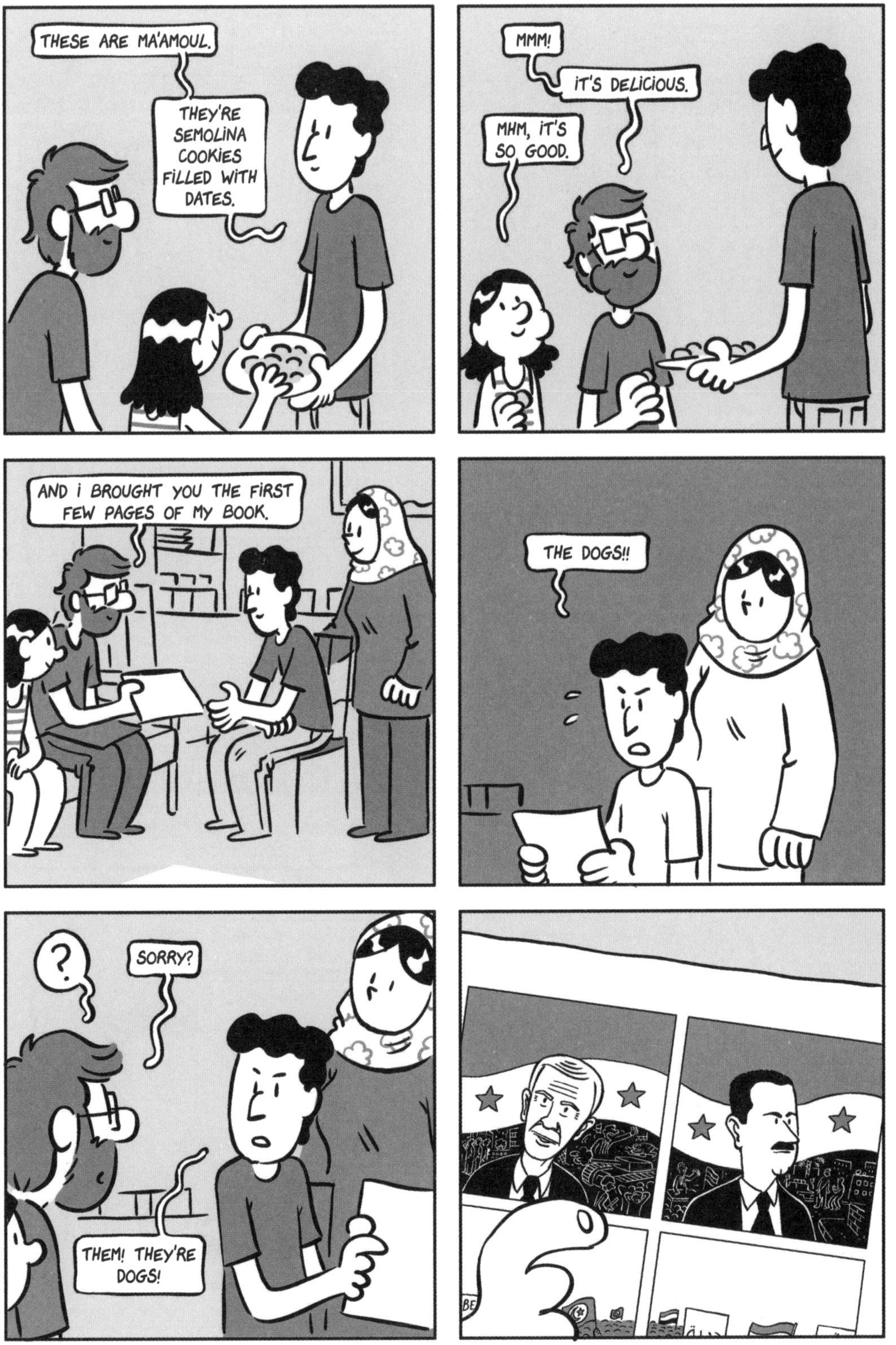
THESE ARE MA'AMOUL.
THEY'RE SEMOLINA COOKIES FILLED WITH DATES.
MMM!
IT'S DELICIOUS.
MHM, IT'S SO GOOD.
AND I BROUGHT YOU THE FIRST FEW PAGES OF MY BOOK.
THE DOGS!!
?
SORRY?
THEM! THEY'RE DOGS!

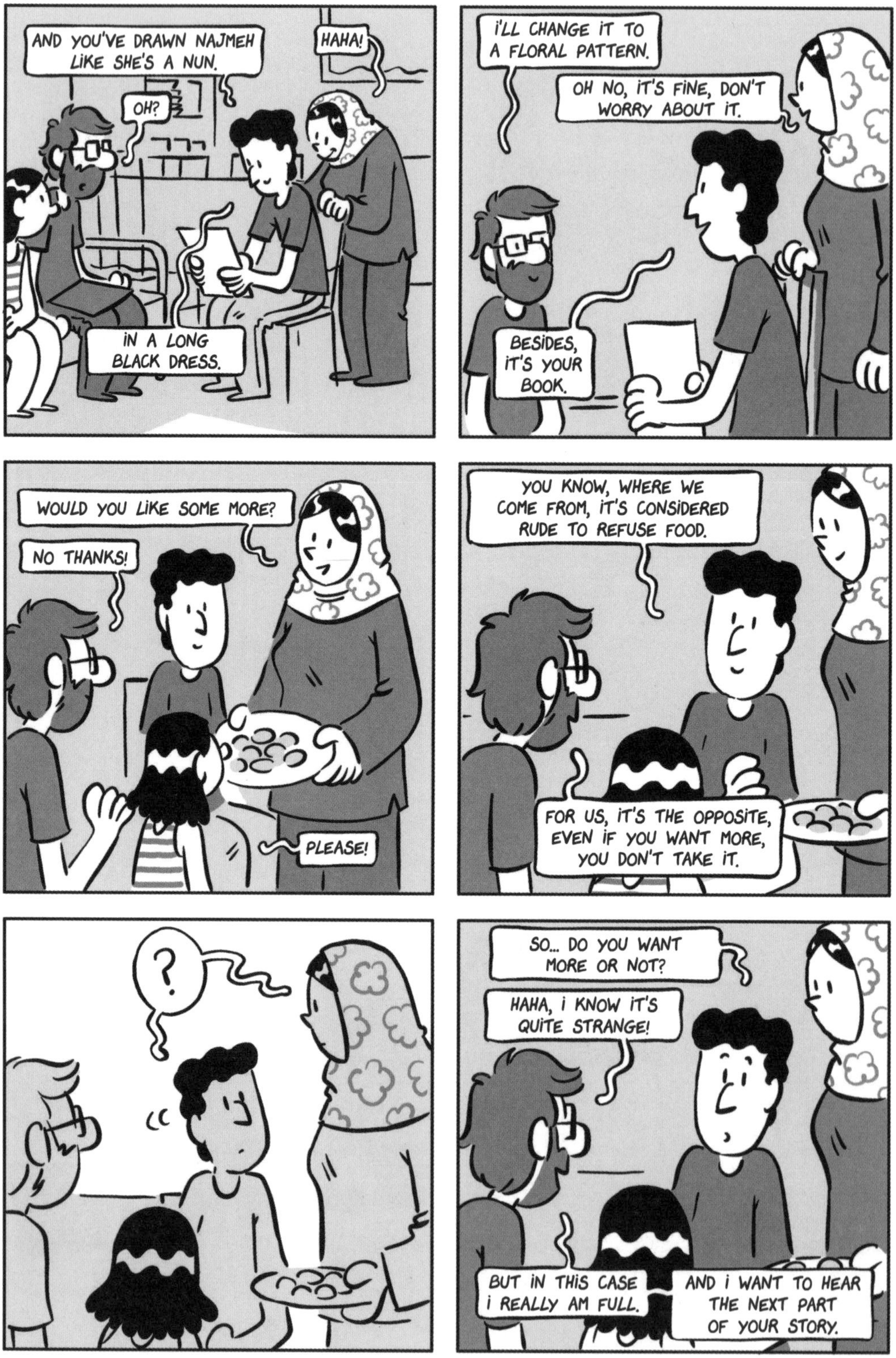
AND YOU'VE DRAWN NAJMEH LIKE SHE'S A NUN.
HAHA!
OH?
IN A LONG BLACK DRESS.
I'LL CHANGE IT TO A FLORAL PATTERN.
OH NO, IT'S FINE, DON'T WORRY ABOUT IT.
BESIDES, IT'S YOUR BOOK.
WOULD YOU LIKE SOME MORE?
NO THANKS!
PLEASE!
YOU KNOW, WHERE WE COME FROM, IT'S CONSIDERED RUDE TO REFUSE FOOD.
FOR US, IT'S THE OPPOSITE, EVEN IF YOU WANT MORE, YOU DON'T TAKE IT.
?
SO... DO YOU WANT MORE OR NOT?
HAHA, I KNOW IT'S QUITE STRANGE!
BUT IN THIS CASE I REALLY AM FULL.
AND I WANT TO HEAR THE NEXT PART OF YOUR STORY.

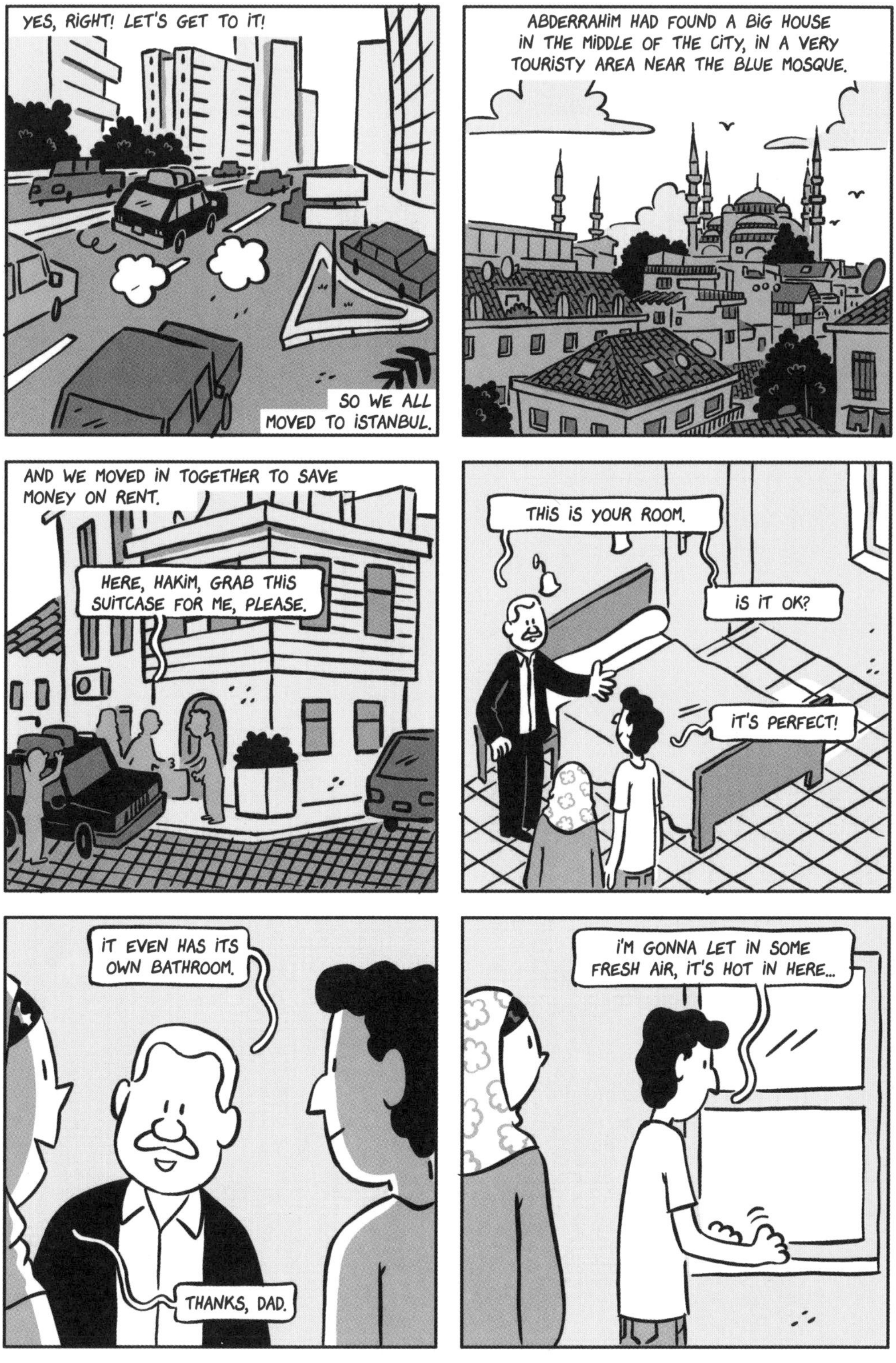
YES, RIGHT! LET'S GET TO IT!
SO WE ALL MOVED TO ISTANBUL.
ABDERRAHIM HAD FOUND A BIG HOUSE IN THE MIDDLE OF THE CITY, IN A VERY TOURISTY AREA NEAR THE BLUE MOSQUE.
AND WE MOVED IN TOGETHER TO SAVE MONEY ON RENT.
HERE, HAKIM, GRAB THIS SUITCASE FOR ME, PLEASE.
THIS IS YOUR ROOM.
IS IT OK?
IT'S PERFECT!
IT EVEN HAS ITS OWN BATHROOM.
THANKS, DAD.
I'M GONNA LET IN SOME FRESH AIR, IT'S HOT IN HERE...

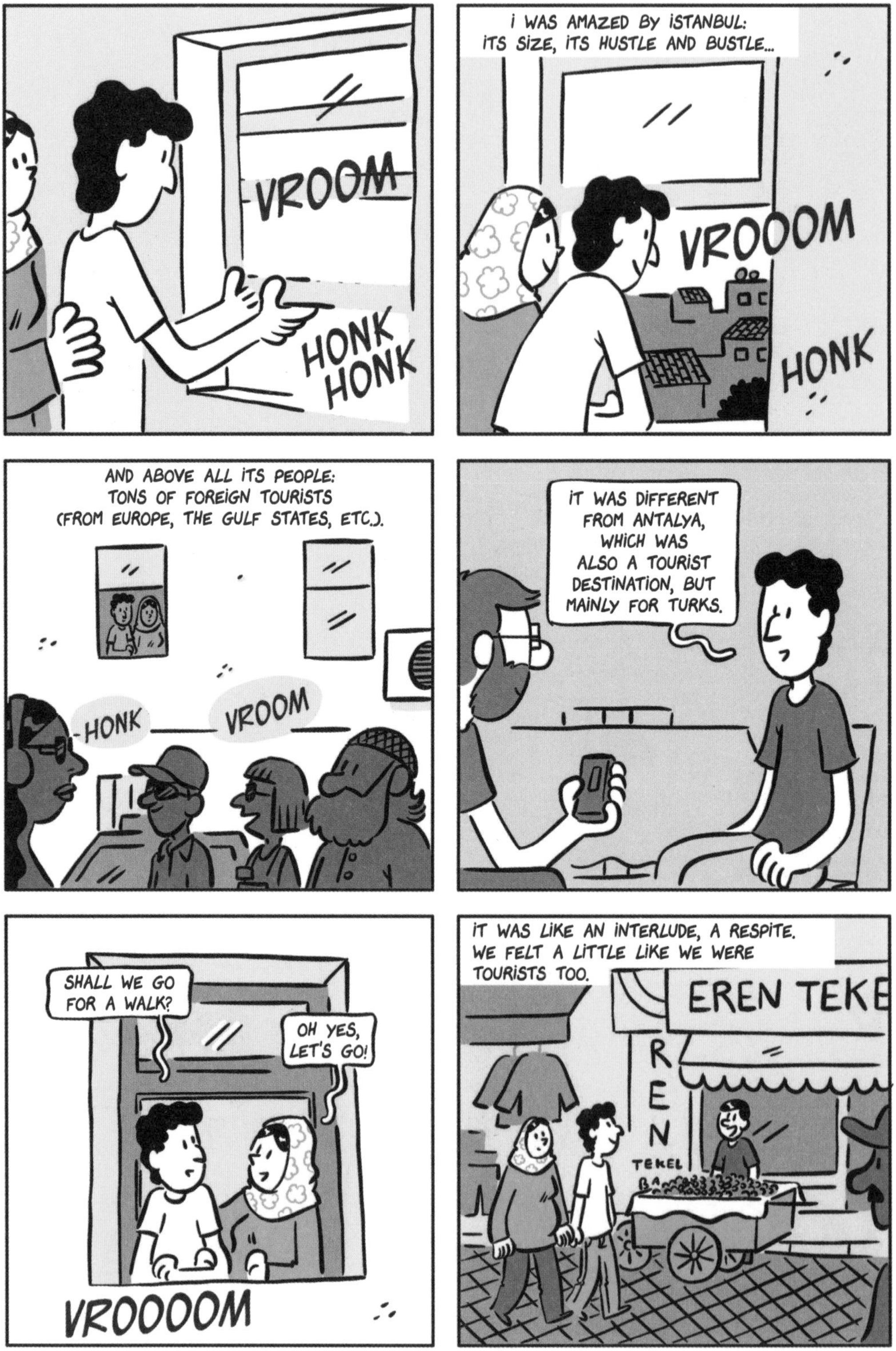
VROOM
HONK HONK
I WAS AMAZED BY ISTANBUL: ITS SIZE, ITS HUSTLE AND BUSTLE...
VROOOM
HONK
AND ABOVE ALL ITS PEOPLE: TONS OF FOREIGN TOURISTS (FROM EUROPE, THE GULF STATES, ETC.).
HONK
VROOM
IT WAS DIFFERENT FROM ANTALYA, WHICH WAS ALSO A TOURIST DESTINATION, BUT MAINLY FOR TURKS.
SHALL WE GO FOR A WALK?
OH YES, LET'S GO!
VROOOOM
IT WAS LIKE AN INTERLUDE, A RESPITE. WE FELT A LITTLE LIKE WE WERE TOURISTS TOO.
EREN TEKE
EREN
TEKEL

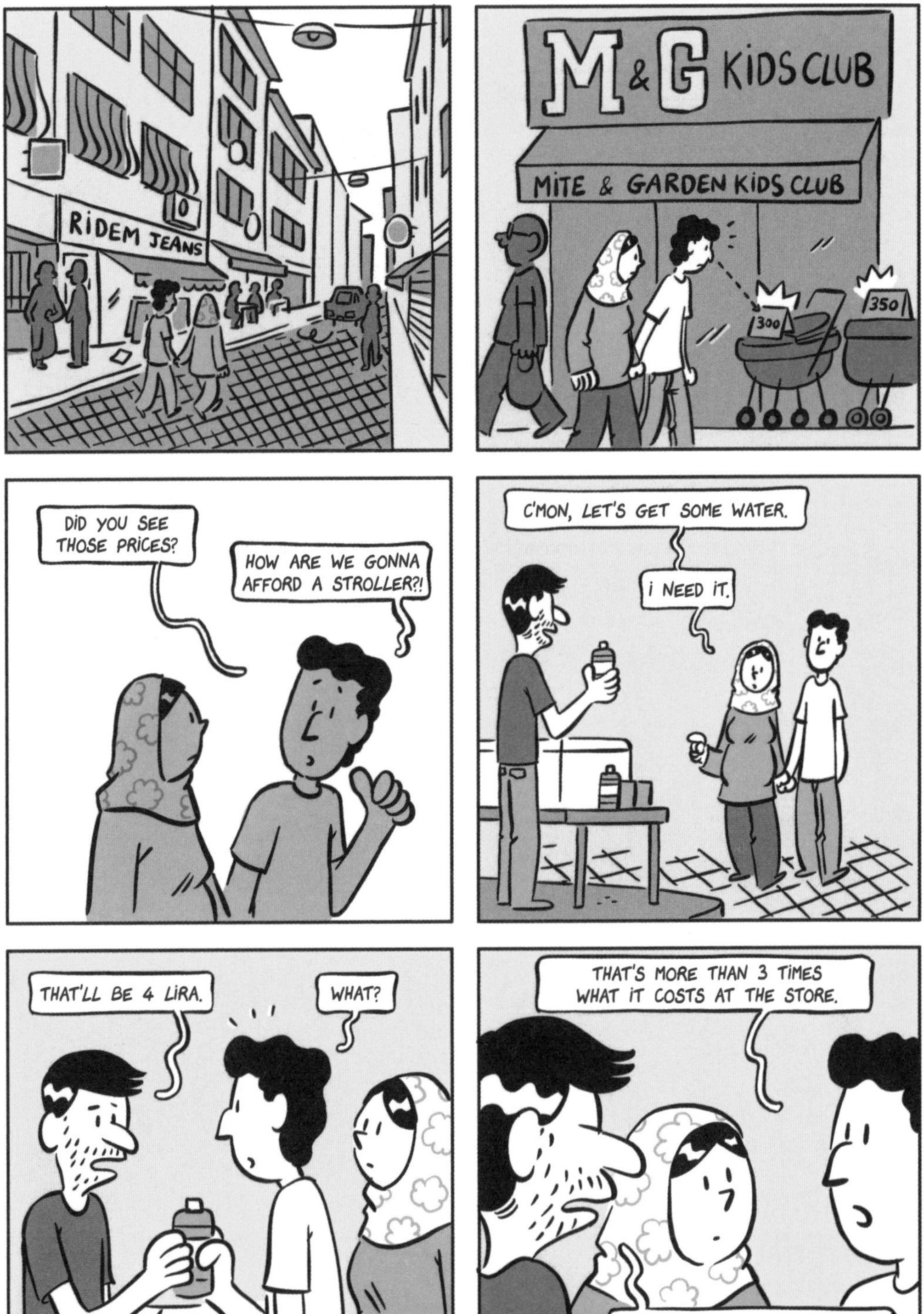
RIDEM JEANS
M & G KIDS CLUB
MITE & GARDEN KIDS CLUB
300
350
DID YOU SEE THOSE PRICES?
HOW ARE WE GONNA AFFORD A STROLLER?!
C'MON, LET'S GET SOME WATER.
I NEED IT.
THAT'LL BE 4 LIRA.
WHAT?
THAT'S MORE THAN 3 TIMES WHAT IT COSTS AT THE STORE.
YEAH, BUT ON THE STREETS THAT'S WHAT WE CHARGE.

I HAVE AN IDEA!!

TO EARN SOME MONEY, I'M GONNA SELL BOTTLED WATER ON THE STREET!

YOU THINK IT'LL WORK, WITH ALL THESE VENDORS ALREADY OUT HERE?

IT DOESN'T SEEM LIKE THE IDEA OF THE CENTURY.

I HAVE TO THINK ABOUT IT.

BUT I THINK IT'LL WORK.

I STILL KIND OF THINK LIKE A BUSINESS OWNER.

SO I DID SOME MARKET RESEARCH...

EMIN İNŞAAT VE EMLAK

I STUDIED THE AREA.

I COMPARED THE CROWDS ON DIFFERENT STREETS.

BAKLAVALARI

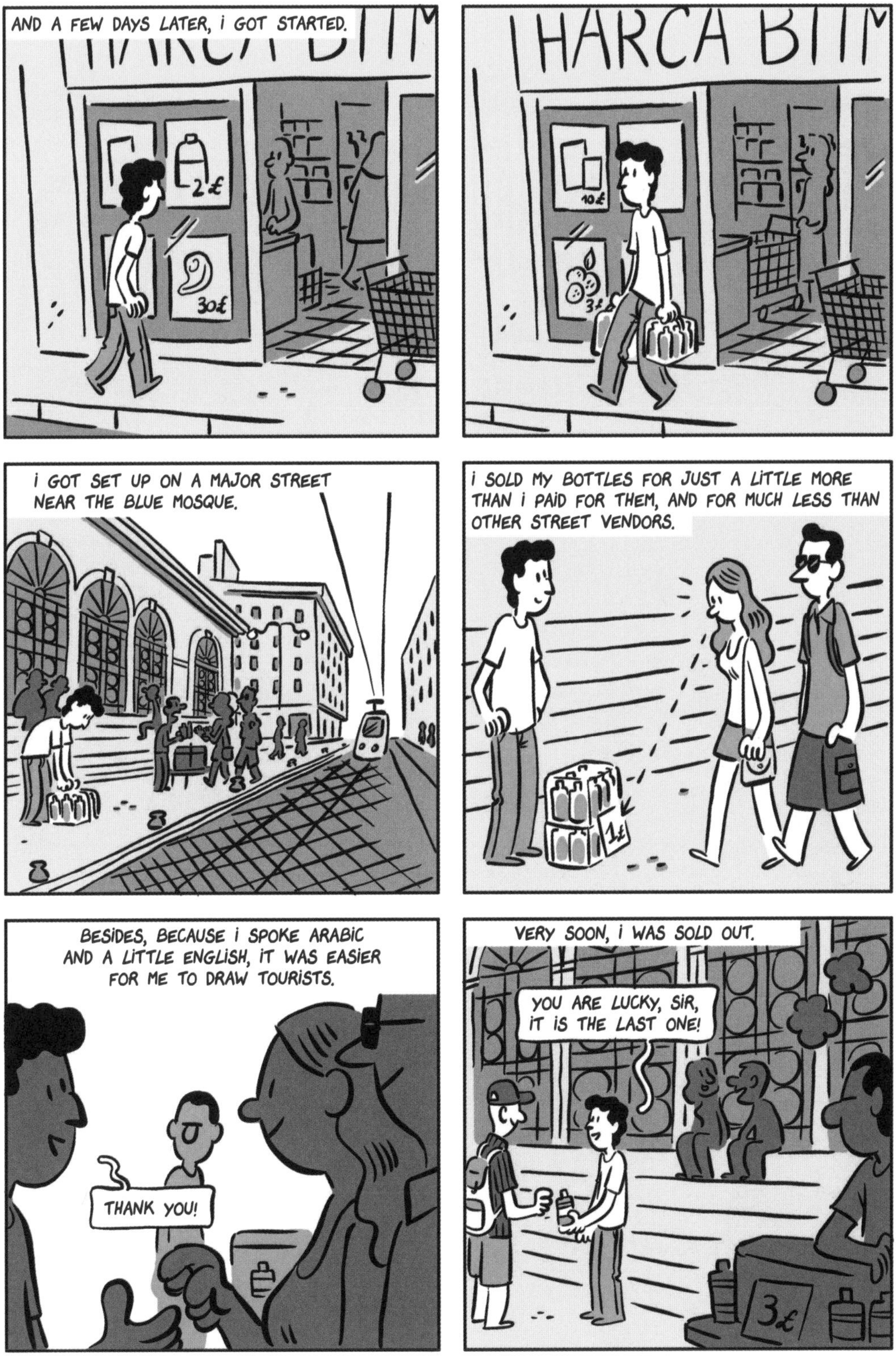
AND A FEW DAYS LATER, I GOT STARTED.
2£
30£
HARCA BIIM
10£
3£
I GOT SET UP ON A MAJOR STREET NEAR THE BLUE MOSQUE.
I SOLD MY BOTTLES FOR JUST A LITTLE MORE THAN I PAID FOR THEM, AND FOR MUCH LESS THAN OTHER STREET VENDORS.
1£
BESIDES, BECAUSE I SPOKE ARABIC AND A LITTLE ENGLISH, IT WAS EASIER FOR ME TO DRAW TOURISTS.
THANK YOU!
VERY SOON, I WAS SOLD OUT.
YOU ARE LUCKY, SIR, IT IS THE LAST ONE!
3£

LOOK!

ALL THIS FROM SELLING BOTTLED WATER?

YEP!

WELL DONE, MR. ENTREPRENEUR!

EVERY DAY AFTER THAT, i WENT BACK.

i COULD TELL i WAS ANNOYING THE OTHER STREET VENDORS, BUT THEY DIDN'T SAY ANYTHING TO ME.

i STARTED MAKING DECENT MONEY.

ENOUGH, AT LEAST, FOR NAJMEH TO BE ABLE TO GO TO THE DOCTOR.

THE BABY IS DOING VERY WELL.

AND IT'S A BOY!

WE WERE HAPPIER TO HEAR THIS THAN WE WERE WHEN WE'D REALIZED NAJMEH WAS PREGNANT.

NOT BECAUSE IT WAS A BOY (BOY OR GIRL, I DIDN'T CARE EITHER WAY) BUT BECAUSE WE WERE NOW IN A BETTER SITUATION.

Medical Center

M & G KIDS CLUB

MITE & GARDEN KIDS CLUB

300   350

OF COURSE, I KNEW OUR SITUATION WAS STILL PRECARIOUS, BUT I TOLD MYSELF WE'D BE ABLE TO PAY FOR THE BIRTH AND HAVE OUR BABY IN SOMEWHAT OK CIRCUMSTANCES.

S CLUB

350

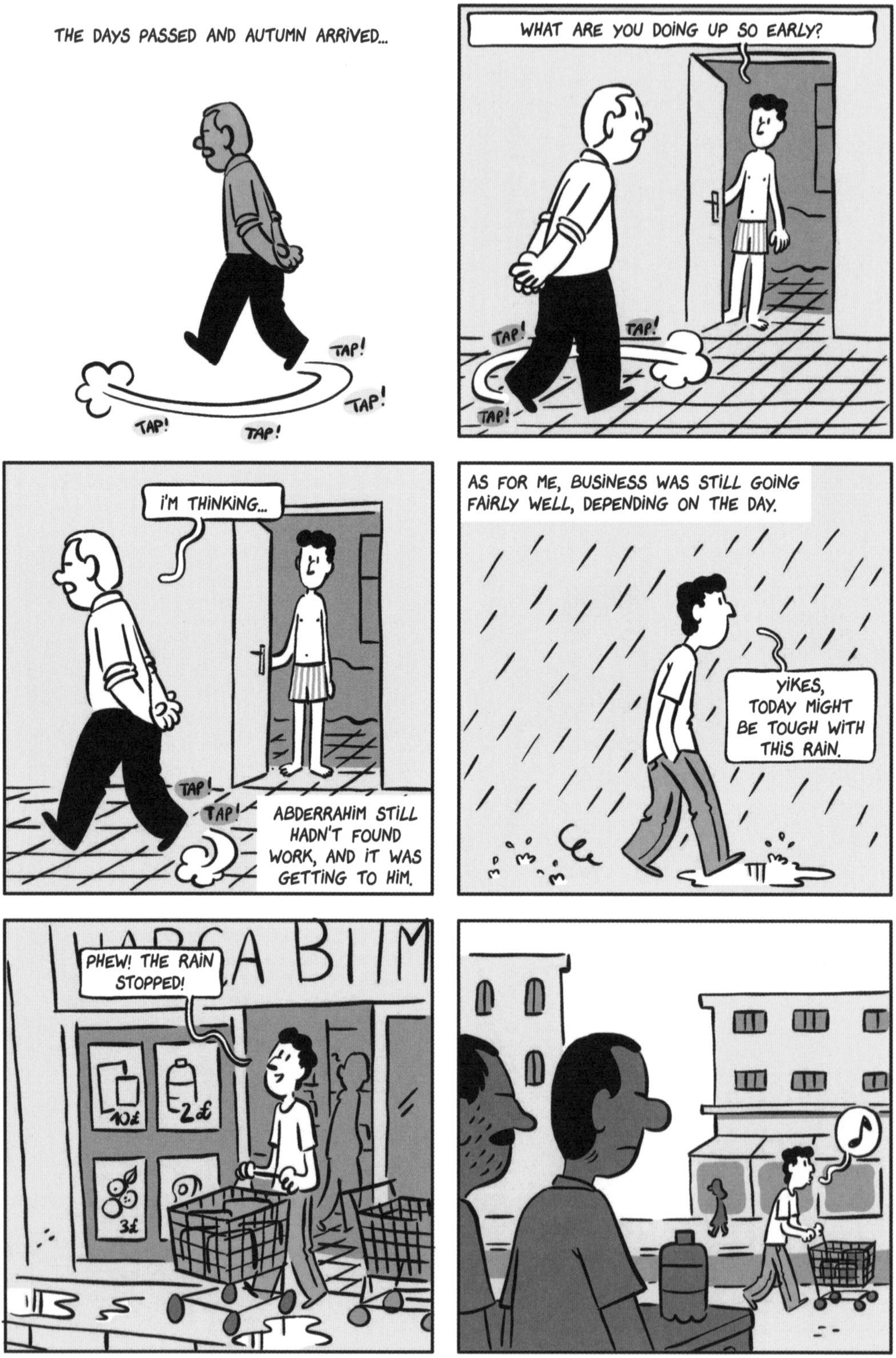
THE DAYS PASSED AND AUTUMN ARRIVED...
TAP!
TAP!
TAP!
TAP!
WHAT ARE YOU DOING UP SO EARLY?
TAP!
TAP!
TAP!
I'M THINKING...
TAP!
TAP!
ABDERRAHIM STILL HADN'T FOUND WORK, AND IT WAS GETTING TO HIM.
AS FOR ME, BUSINESS WAS STILL GOING FAIRLY WELL, DEPENDING ON THE DAY.
YIKES, TODAY MIGHT BE TOUGH WITH THIS RAIN.
PHEW! THE RAIN STOPPED!
10£
2£
3£

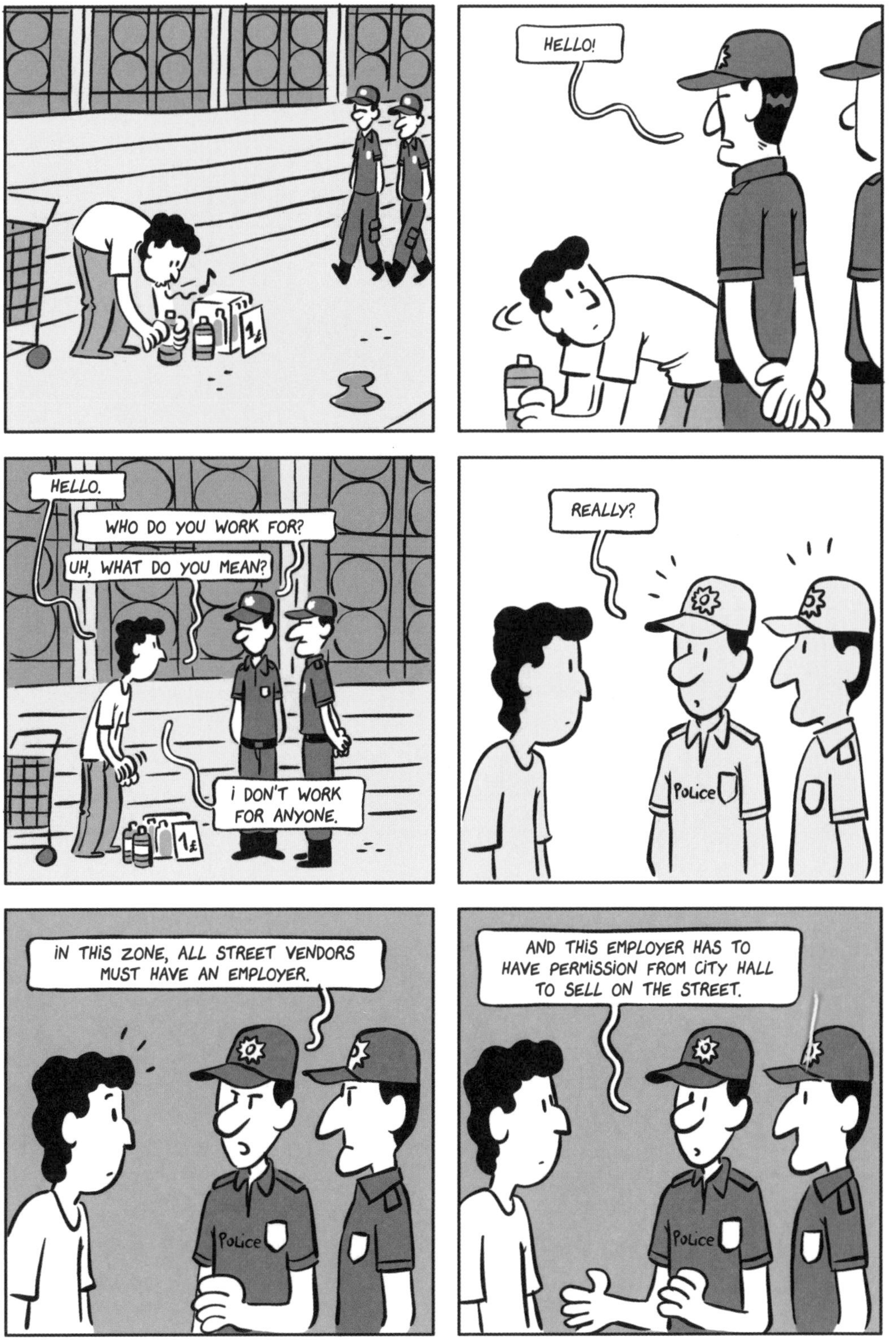
HELLO!
HELLO.
WHO DO YOU WORK FOR?
UH, WHAT DO YOU MEAN?
I DON'T WORK FOR ANYONE.
REALLY?
IN THIS ZONE, ALL STREET VENDORS MUST HAVE AN EMPLOYER.
AND THIS EMPLOYER HAS TO HAVE PERMISSION FROM CITY HALL TO SELL ON THE STREET.

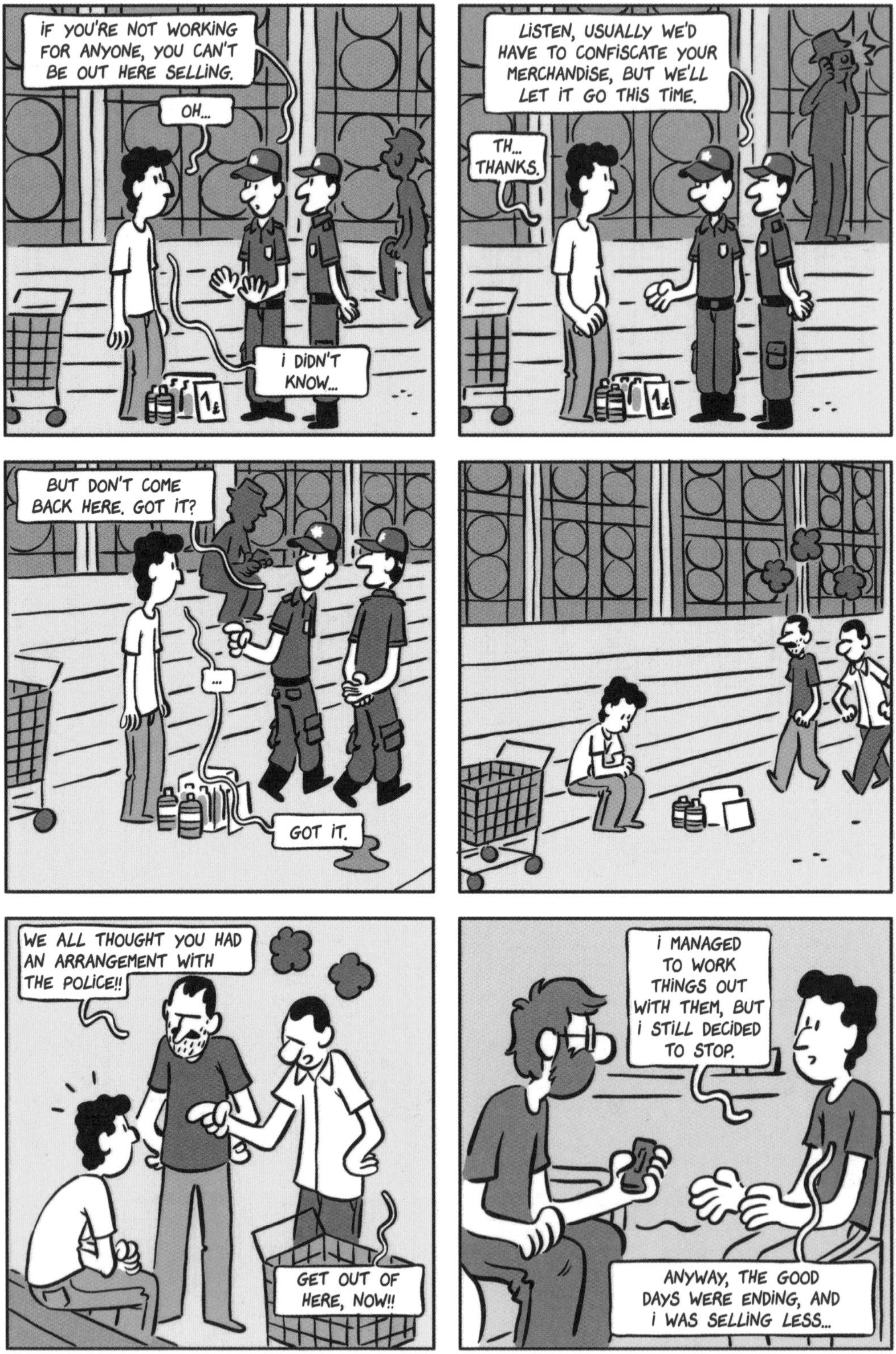
IF YOU'RE NOT WORKING FOR ANYONE, YOU CAN'T BE OUT HERE SELLING.
OH...
I DIDN'T KNOW...
1£
LISTEN, USUALLY WE'D HAVE TO CONFISCATE YOUR MERCHANDISE, BUT WE'LL LET IT GO THIS TIME.
TH... THANKS.
1£
BUT DON'T COME BACK HERE. GOT IT?
...
GOT IT.
WE ALL THOUGHT YOU HAD AN ARRANGEMENT WITH THE POLICE!!
GET OUT OF HERE, NOW!!
I MANAGED TO WORK THINGS OUT WITH THEM, BUT I STILL DECIDED TO STOP.
ANYWAY, THE GOOD DAYS WERE ENDING, AND I WAS SELLING LESS...

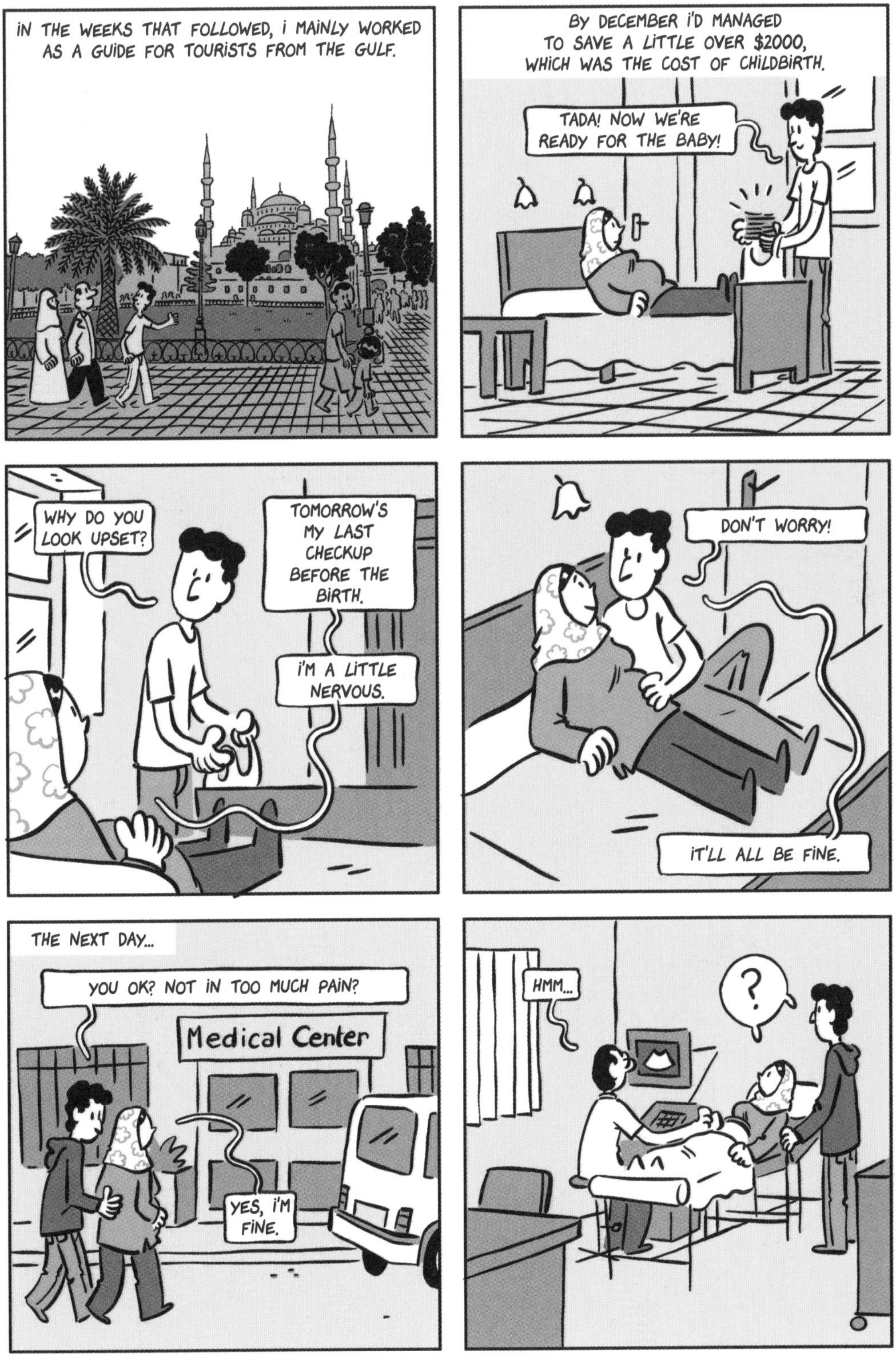
IN THE WEEKS THAT FOLLOWED, I MAINLY WORKED AS A GUIDE FOR TOURISTS FROM THE GULF.
BY DECEMBER I'D MANAGED TO SAVE A LITTLE OVER $2000, WHICH WAS THE COST OF CHILDBIRTH.
TADA! NOW WE'RE READY FOR THE BABY!
WHY DO YOU LOOK UPSET?
TOMORROW'S MY LAST CHECKUP BEFORE THE BIRTH.
I'M A LITTLE NERVOUS.
DON'T WORRY!
IT'LL ALL BE FINE.
THE NEXT DAY...
YOU OK? NOT IN TOO MUCH PAIN?
Medical Center
YES, I'M FINE.
HMM...
?

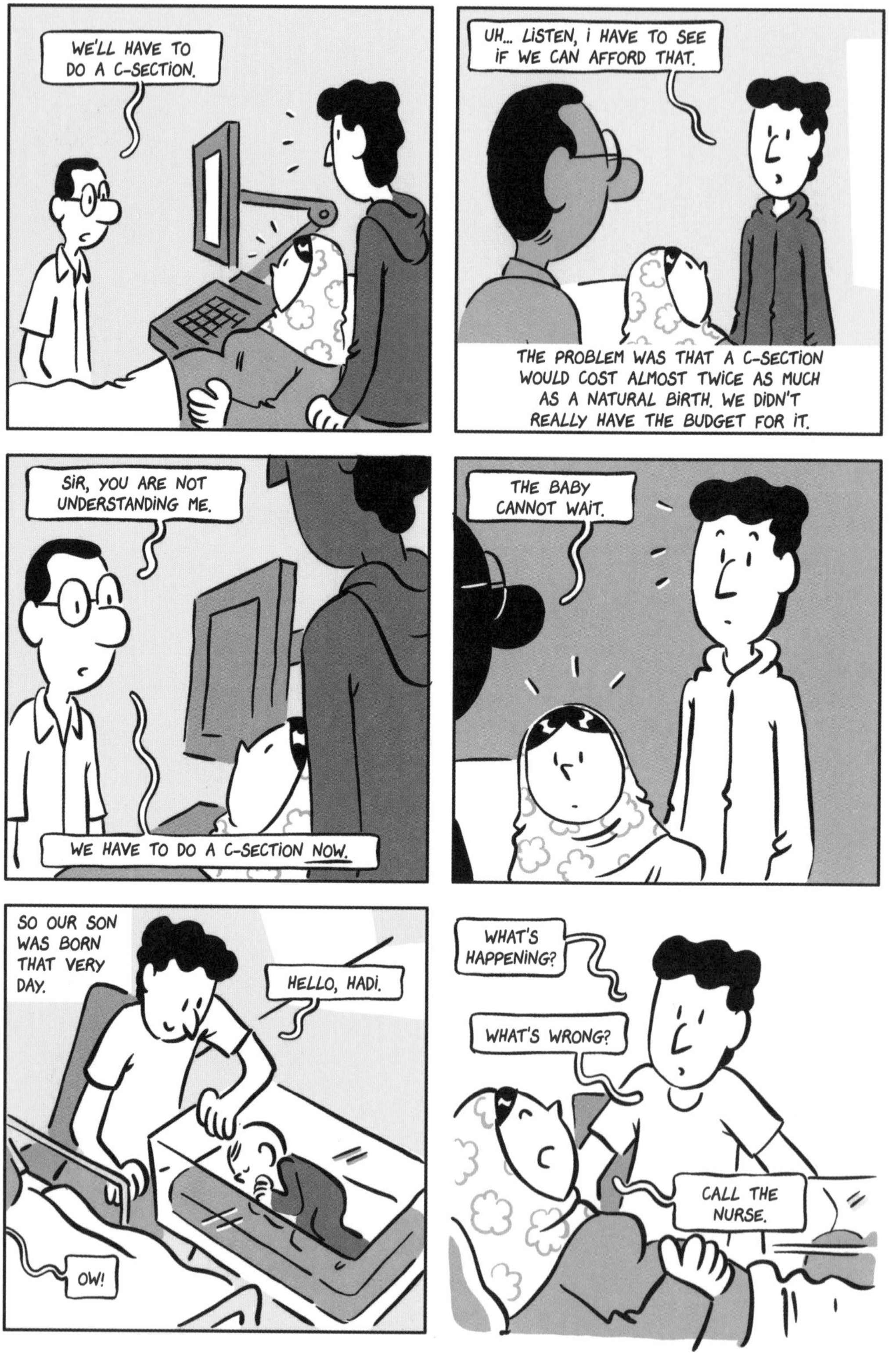
WE'LL HAVE TO DO A C-SECTION.
UH... LISTEN, I HAVE TO SEE IF WE CAN AFFORD THAT.
THE PROBLEM WAS THAT A C-SECTION WOULD COST ALMOST TWICE AS MUCH AS A NATURAL BIRTH. WE DIDN'T REALLY HAVE THE BUDGET FOR IT.
SIR, YOU ARE NOT UNDERSTANDING ME.
WE HAVE TO DO A C-SECTION NOW.
THE BABY CANNOT WAIT.
SO OUR SON WAS BORN THAT VERY DAY.
HELLO, HADI.
OW!
WHAT'S HAPPENING?
WHAT'S WRONG?
CALL THE NURSE.

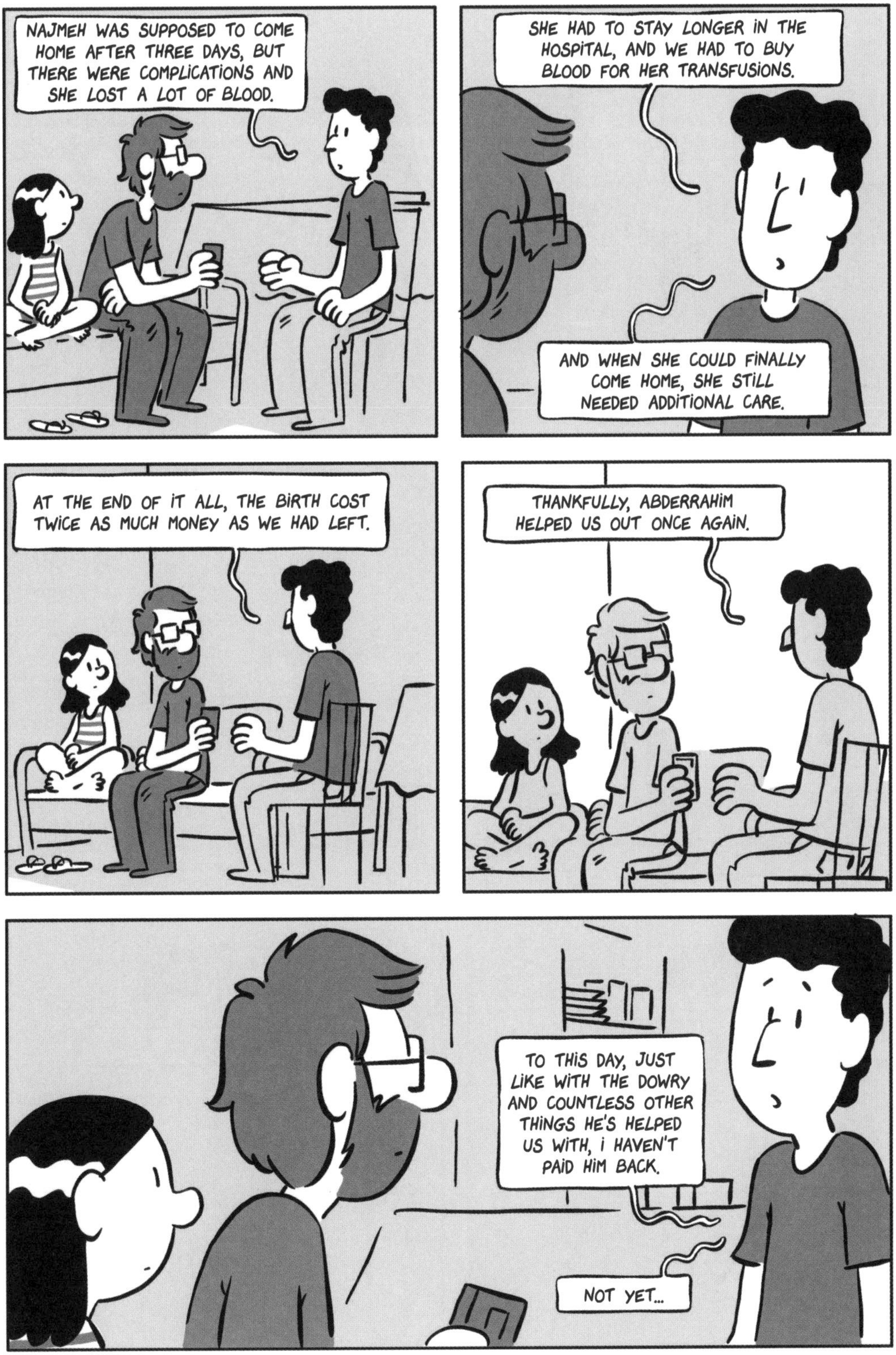
NAJMEH WAS SUPPOSED TO COME HOME AFTER THREE DAYS, BUT THERE WERE COMPLICATIONS AND SHE LOST A LOT OF BLOOD.
SHE HAD TO STAY LONGER IN THE HOSPITAL, AND WE HAD TO BUY BLOOD FOR HER TRANSFUSIONS.
AND WHEN SHE COULD FINALLY COME HOME, SHE STILL NEEDED ADDITIONAL CARE.
AT THE END OF IT ALL, THE BIRTH COST TWICE AS MUCH MONEY AS WE HAD LEFT.
THANKFULLY, ABDERRAHIM HELPED US OUT ONCE AGAIN.
TO THIS DAY, JUST LIKE WITH THE DOWRY AND COUNTLESS OTHER THINGS HE'S HELPED US WITH, I HAVEN'T PAID HIM BACK.
NOT YET...

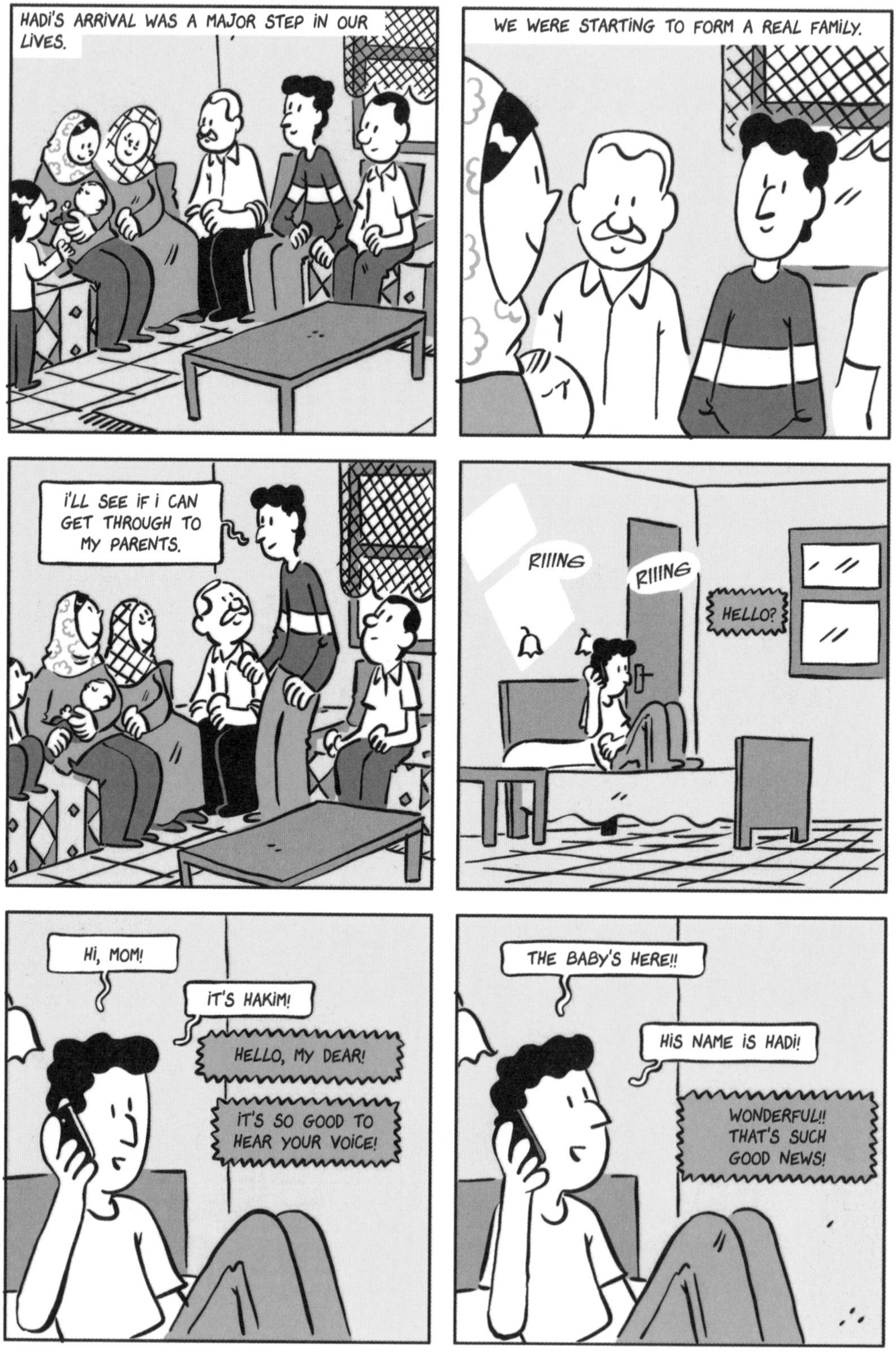
HADI'S ARRIVAL WAS A MAJOR STEP IN OUR LIVES.
WE WERE STARTING TO FORM A REAL FAMILY.
I'LL SEE IF I CAN GET THROUGH TO MY PARENTS.
RIIING
RIIING
HELLO?
HI, MOM!
IT'S HAKIM!
HELLO, MY DEAR!
IT'S SO GOOD TO HEAR YOUR VOICE!
THE BABY'S HERE!!
HIS NAME IS HADI!
WONDERFUL!! THAT'S SUCH GOOD NEWS!

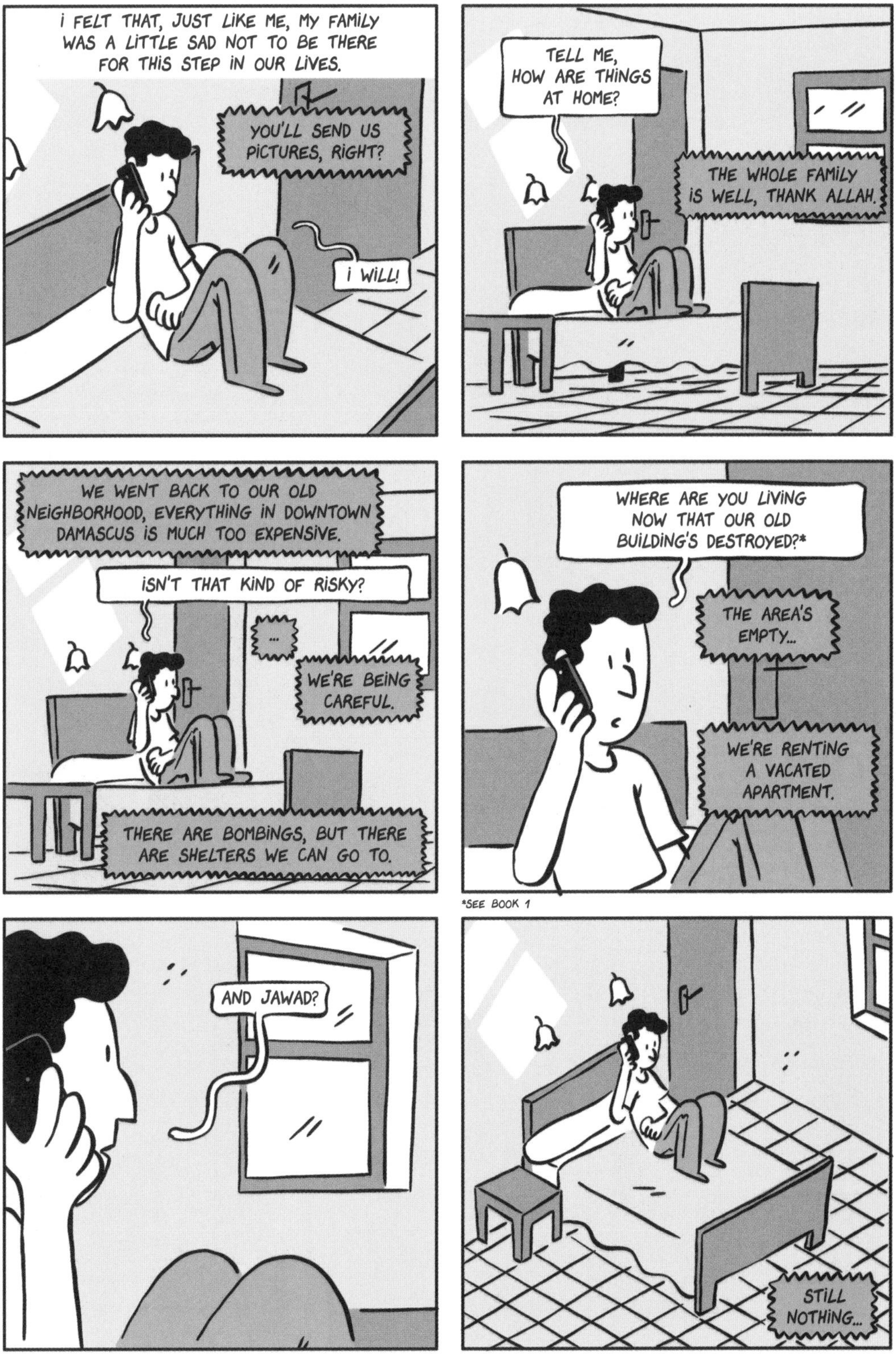
I FELT THAT, JUST LIKE ME, MY FAMILY WAS A LITTLE SAD NOT TO BE THERE FOR THIS STEP IN OUR LIVES.
YOU'LL SEND US PICTURES, RIGHT?
I WILL!
TELL ME, HOW ARE THINGS AT HOME?
THE WHOLE FAMILY IS WELL, THANK ALLAH.
WE WENT BACK TO OUR OLD NEIGHBORHOOD, EVERYTHING IN DOWNTOWN DAMASCUS IS MUCH TOO EXPENSIVE.
ISN'T THAT KIND OF RISKY?
...
WE'RE BEING CAREFUL.
THERE ARE BOMBINGS, BUT THERE ARE SHELTERS WE CAN GO TO.
WHERE ARE YOU LIVING NOW THAT OUR OLD BUILDING'S DESTROYED?*
THE AREA'S EMPTY...
WE'RE RENTING A VACATED APARTMENT.
*SEE BOOK 1
AND JAWAD?
STILL NOTHING...

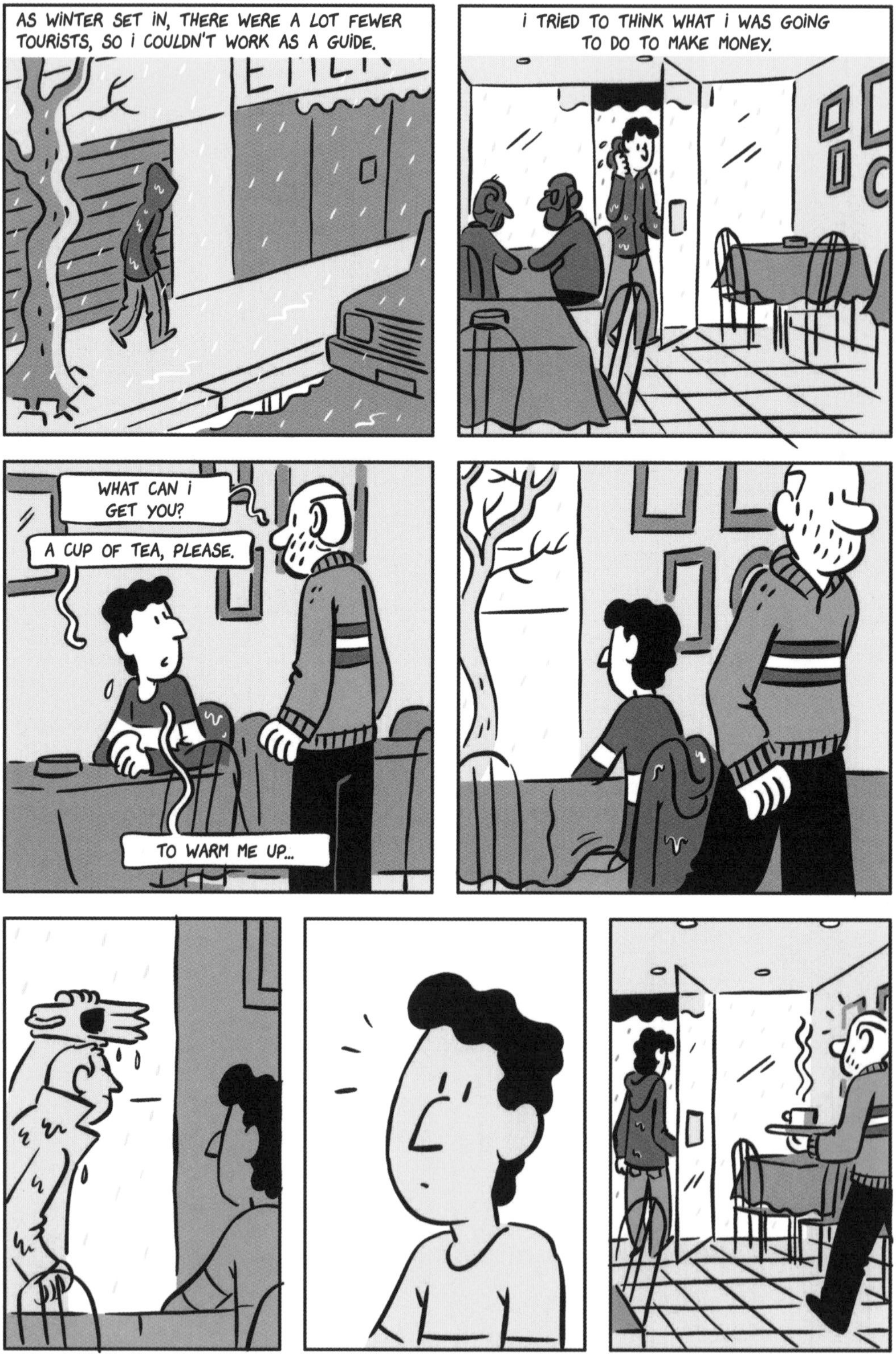
AS WINTER SET IN, THERE WERE A LOT FEWER TOURISTS, SO I COULDN'T WORK AS A GUIDE.
I TRIED TO THINK WHAT I WAS GOING TO DO TO MAKE MONEY.
WHAT CAN I GET YOU?
A CUP OF TEA, PLEASE.
TO WARM ME UP...

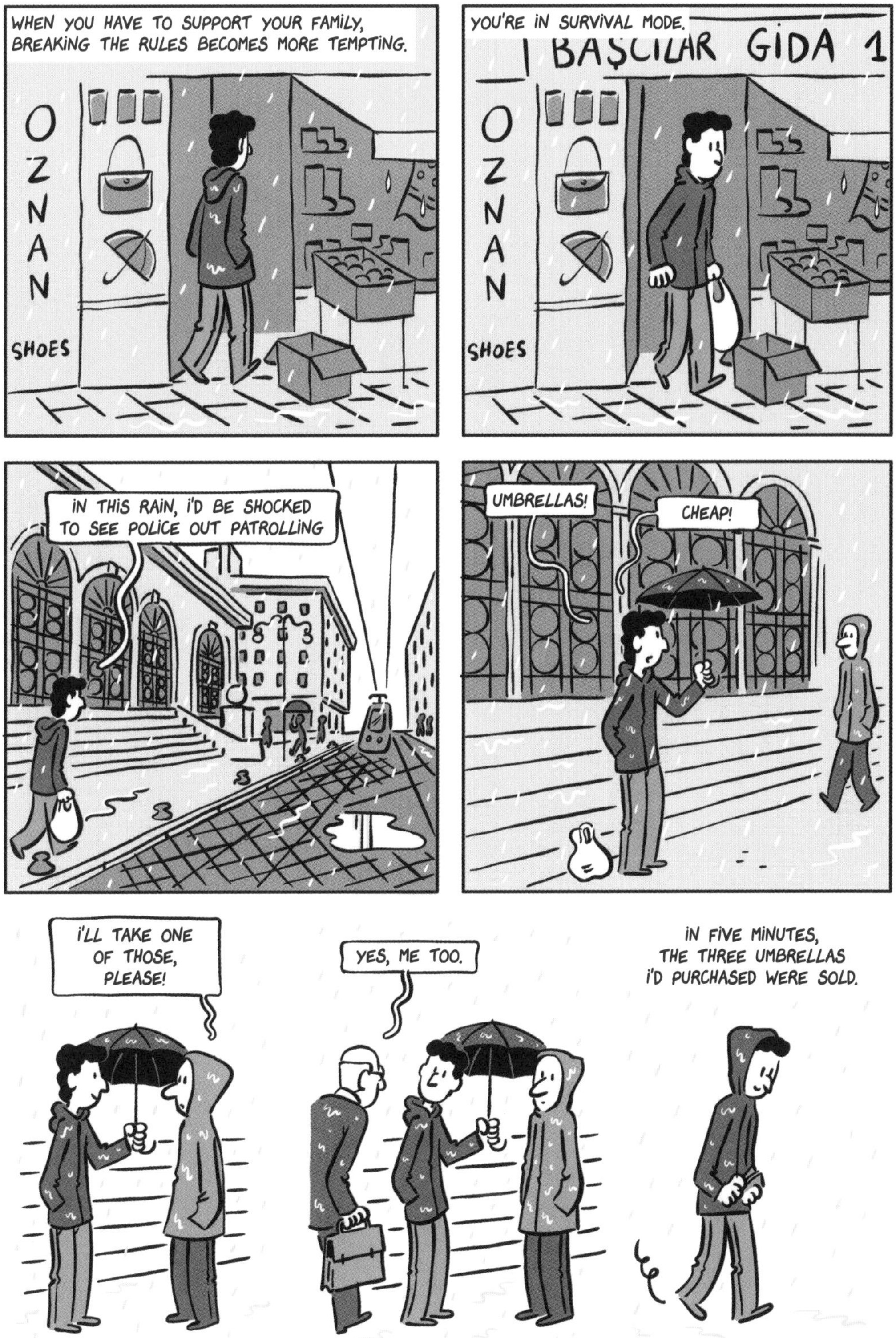
WHEN YOU HAVE TO SUPPORT YOUR FAMILY, BREAKING THE RULES BECOMES MORE TEMPTING.
OZNAN
SHOES
YOU'RE IN SURVIVAL MODE.
BAŞCILAR GIDA 1
OZNAN
SHOES
IN THIS RAIN, I'D BE SHOCKED TO SEE POLICE OUT PATROLLING
UMBRELLAS!
CHEAP!
I'LL TAKE ONE OF THOSE, PLEASE!
YES, ME TOO.
IN FIVE MINUTES, THE THREE UMBRELLAS I'D PURCHASED WERE SOLD.

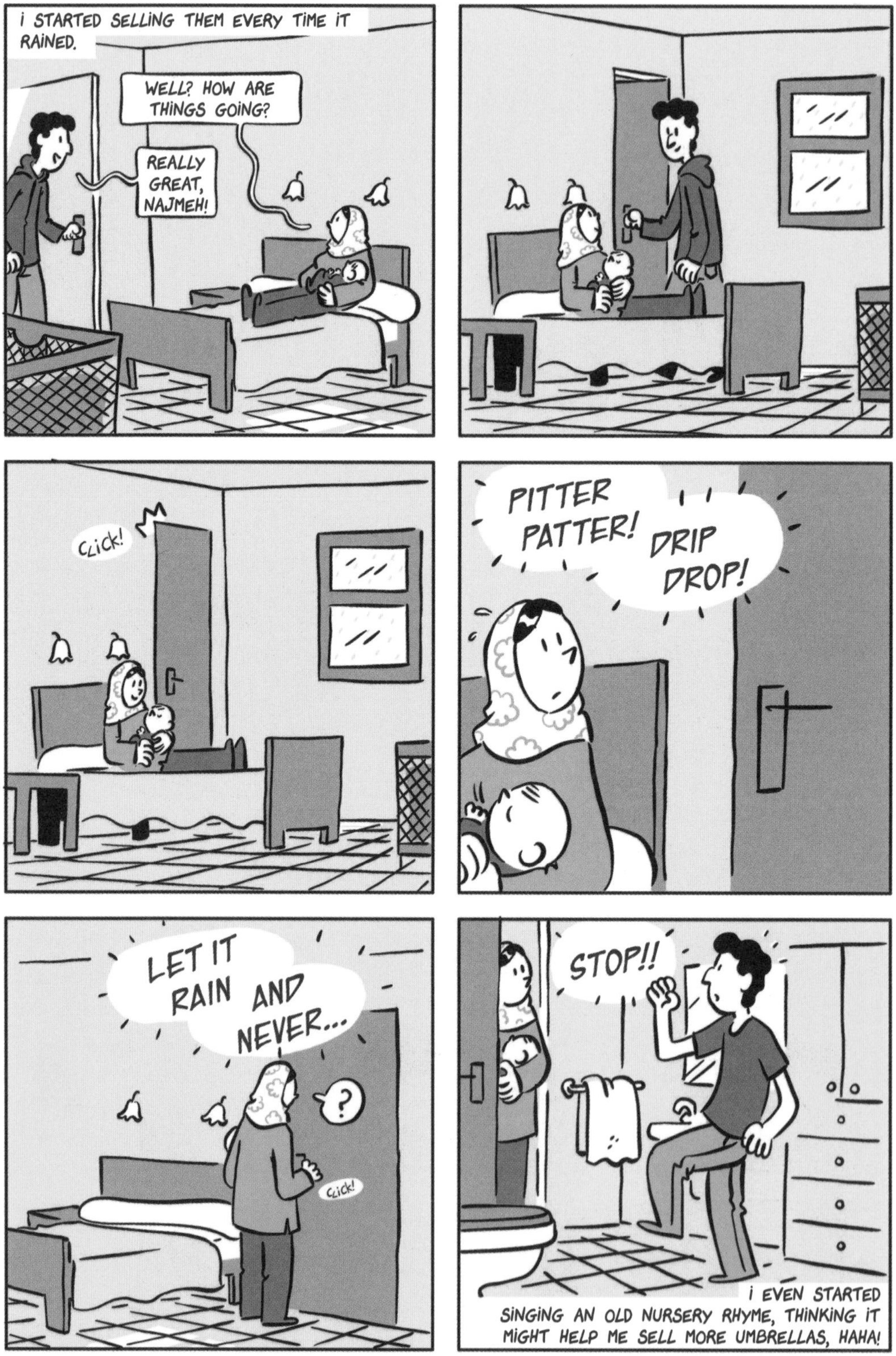
I STARTED SELLING THEM EVERY TIME IT RAINED.
WELL? HOW ARE THINGS GOING?
REALLY GREAT, NAJMEH!
CLICK!
PITTER PATTER!
DRIP DROP!
LET IT RAIN
AND NEVER...
?
CLICK!
STOP!!
I EVEN STARTED SINGING AN OLD NURSERY RHYME, THINKING IT MIGHT HELP ME SELL MORE UMBRELLAS, HAHA!

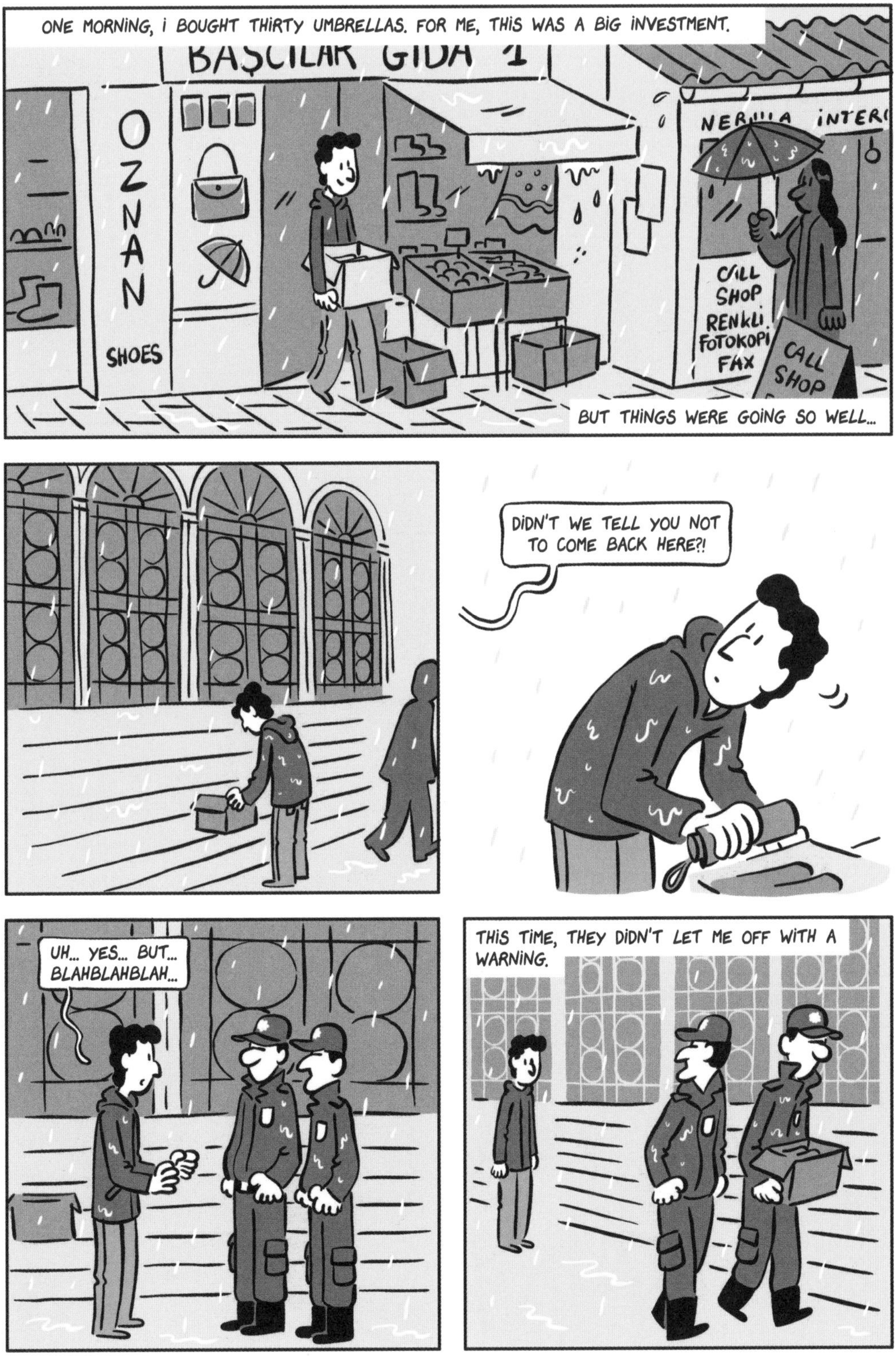
ONE MORNING, i BOUGHT THIRTY UMBRELLAS. FOR ME, THIS WAS A BIG iNVESTMENT.
BAŞCILAR GIDA 1
OZNAN
SHOES
CALL SHOP
RENKLi FOTOKOPi FAX
CALL SHOP
BUT THINGS WERE GOiNG SO WELL...
DiDN'T WE TELL YOU NOT TO COME BACK HERE?!
UH... YES... BUT... BLAHBLAHBLAH...
THiS TiME, THEY DiDN'T LET ME OFF WiTH A WARNiNG.

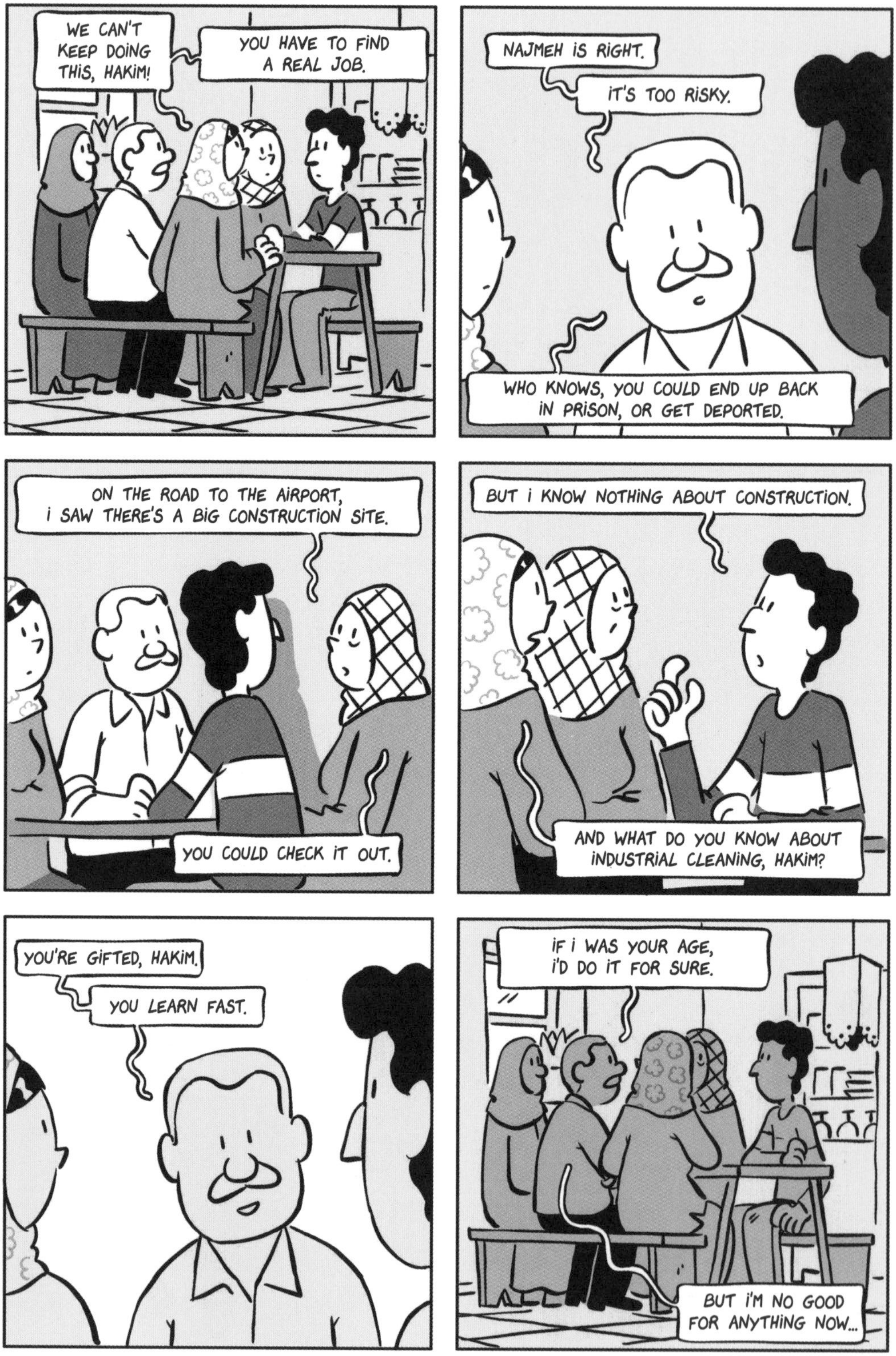
WE CAN'T KEEP DOING THIS, HAKIM!
YOU HAVE TO FIND A REAL JOB.
NAJMEH IS RIGHT.
IT'S TOO RISKY.
WHO KNOWS, YOU COULD END UP BACK IN PRISON, OR GET DEPORTED.
ON THE ROAD TO THE AIRPORT, I SAW THERE'S A BIG CONSTRUCTION SITE.
YOU COULD CHECK IT OUT.
BUT I KNOW NOTHING ABOUT CONSTRUCTION.
AND WHAT DO YOU KNOW ABOUT INDUSTRIAL CLEANING, HAKIM?
YOU'RE GIFTED, HAKIM.
YOU LEARN FAST.
IF I WAS YOUR AGE, I'D DO IT FOR SURE.
BUT I'M NO GOOD FOR ANYTHING NOW...

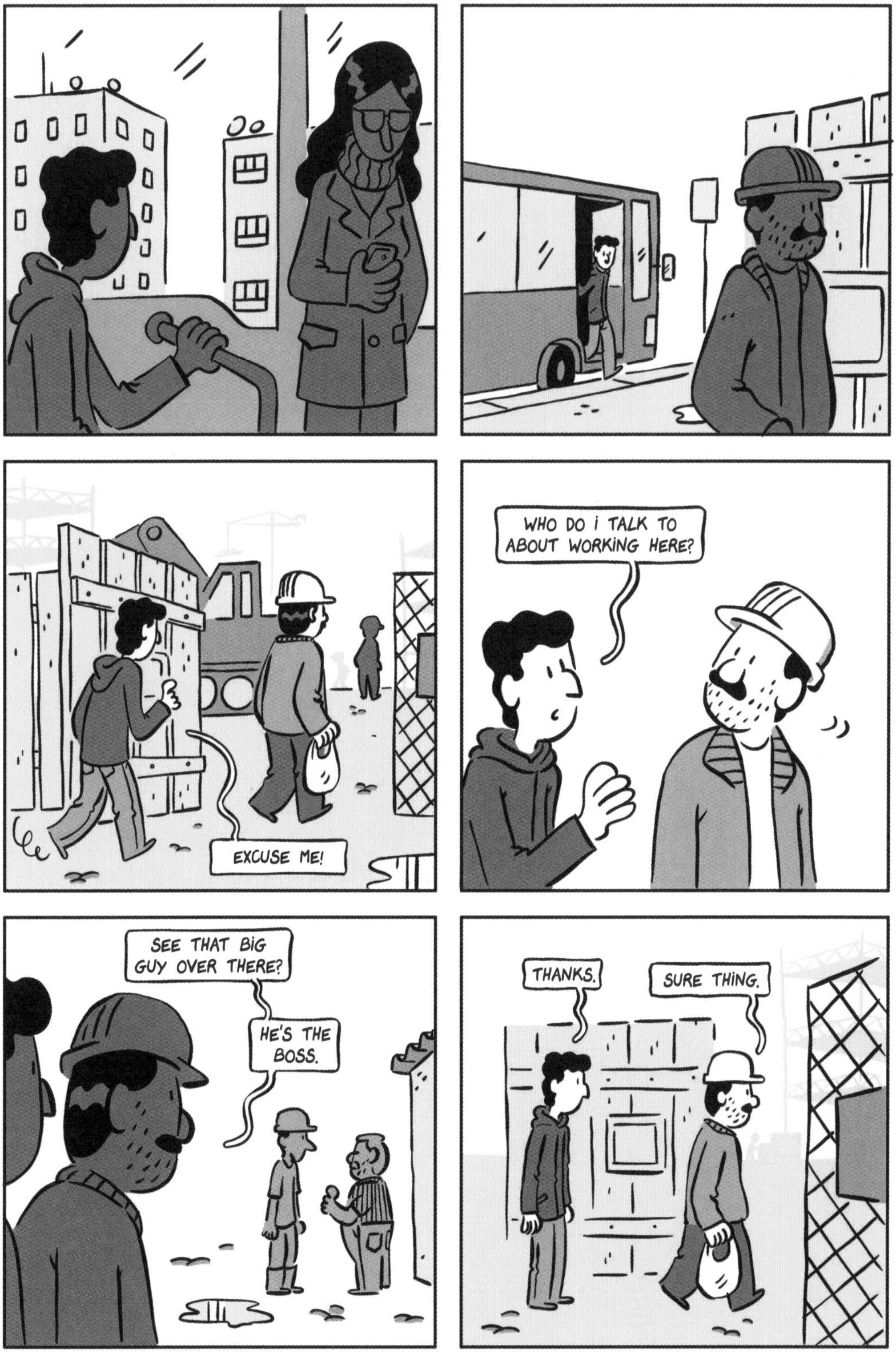
EXCUSE ME!
WHO DO i TALK TO ABOUT WORKiNG HERE?
SEE THAT BiG GUY OVER THERE?
HE'S THE BOSS.
THANKS.
SURE THiNG.

YOU'LL WORK ON FRAMING TODAY. AND SHOW SOME HUSTLE!
OR YOU'RE DONE!!
OK.
GOOD MORNING, SIR.
AND WHAT DO YOU WANT?
I'M LOOKING FOR WORK.
OH, WOW, YOUR TURKISH ISN'T GREAT.
WHERE YOU FROM?
I'M FROM SYRIA.
I SEE...
YOU EVER WORKED IN CONSTRUCTION BEFORE?
NO, NEVER.
HMMM...

COME ON!

HEY! YOU!

HEY!

DEAL WITH THIS GUY.

HE'S A BEGINNER.

TELL ME TONIGHT IF HE'S WORTH KEEPING ON.

THAT FIRST DAY, THEY GAVE ME VERY SIMPLE TASKS TO DO.

HEY!

YOU'RE GOOD, NEW GUY, WE'RE DONE FOR TODAY.

OK, BYE.

HEY!

BE HERE TOMORROW!

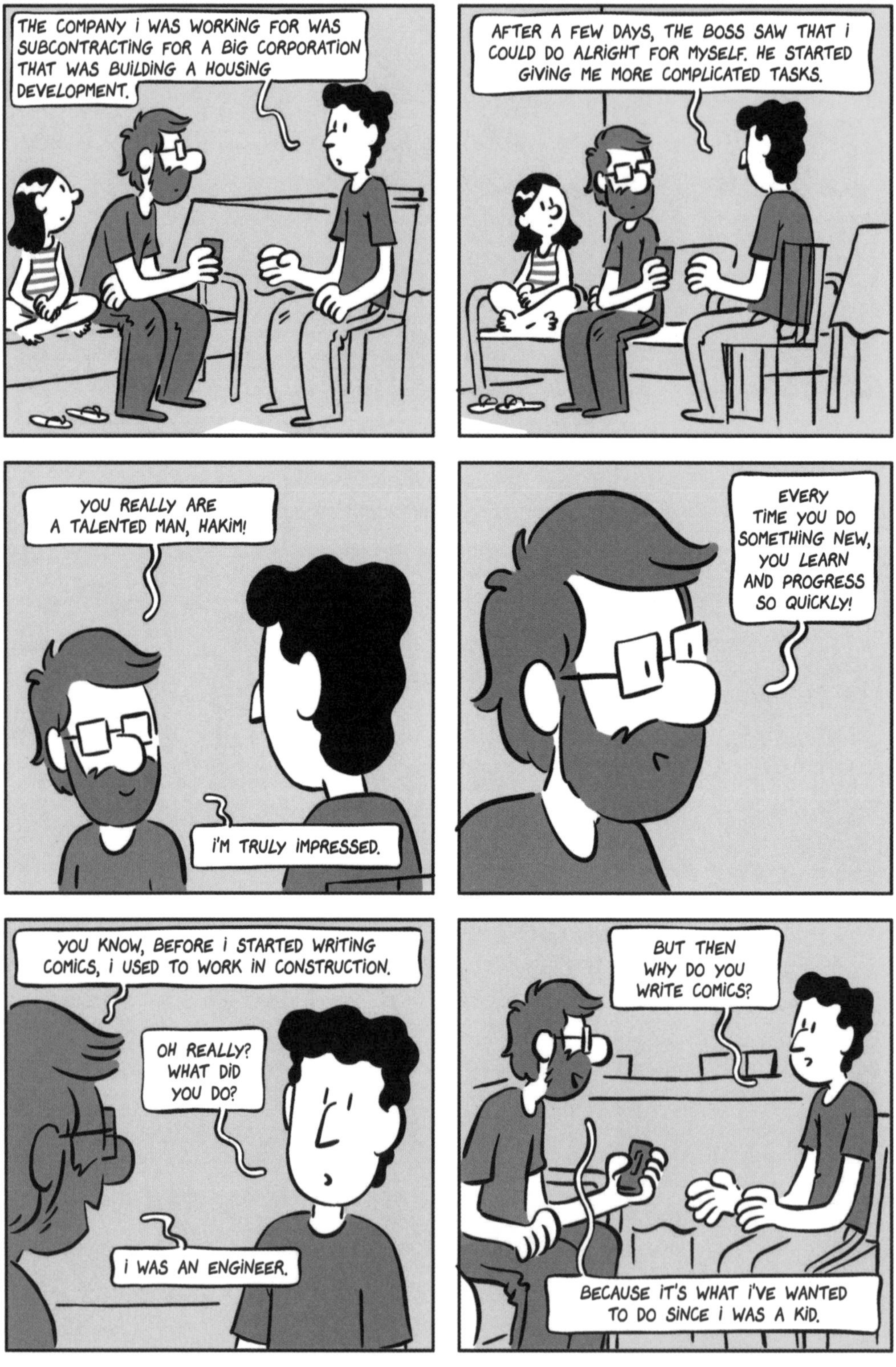
THE COMPANY I WAS WORKING FOR WAS SUBCONTRACTING FOR A BIG CORPORATION THAT WAS BUILDING A HOUSING DEVELOPMENT.
AFTER A FEW DAYS, THE BOSS SAW THAT I COULD DO ALRIGHT FOR MYSELF. HE STARTED GIVING ME MORE COMPLICATED TASKS.
YOU REALLY ARE A TALENTED MAN, HAKIM!
I'M TRULY IMPRESSED.
EVERY TIME YOU DO SOMETHING NEW, YOU LEARN AND PROGRESS SO QUICKLY!
YOU KNOW, BEFORE I STARTED WRITING COMICS, I USED TO WORK IN CONSTRUCTION.
OH REALLY? WHAT DID YOU DO?
I WAS AN ENGINEER.
BUT THEN WHY DO YOU WRITE COMICS?
BECAUSE IT'S WHAT I'VE WANTED TO DO SINCE I WAS A KID.

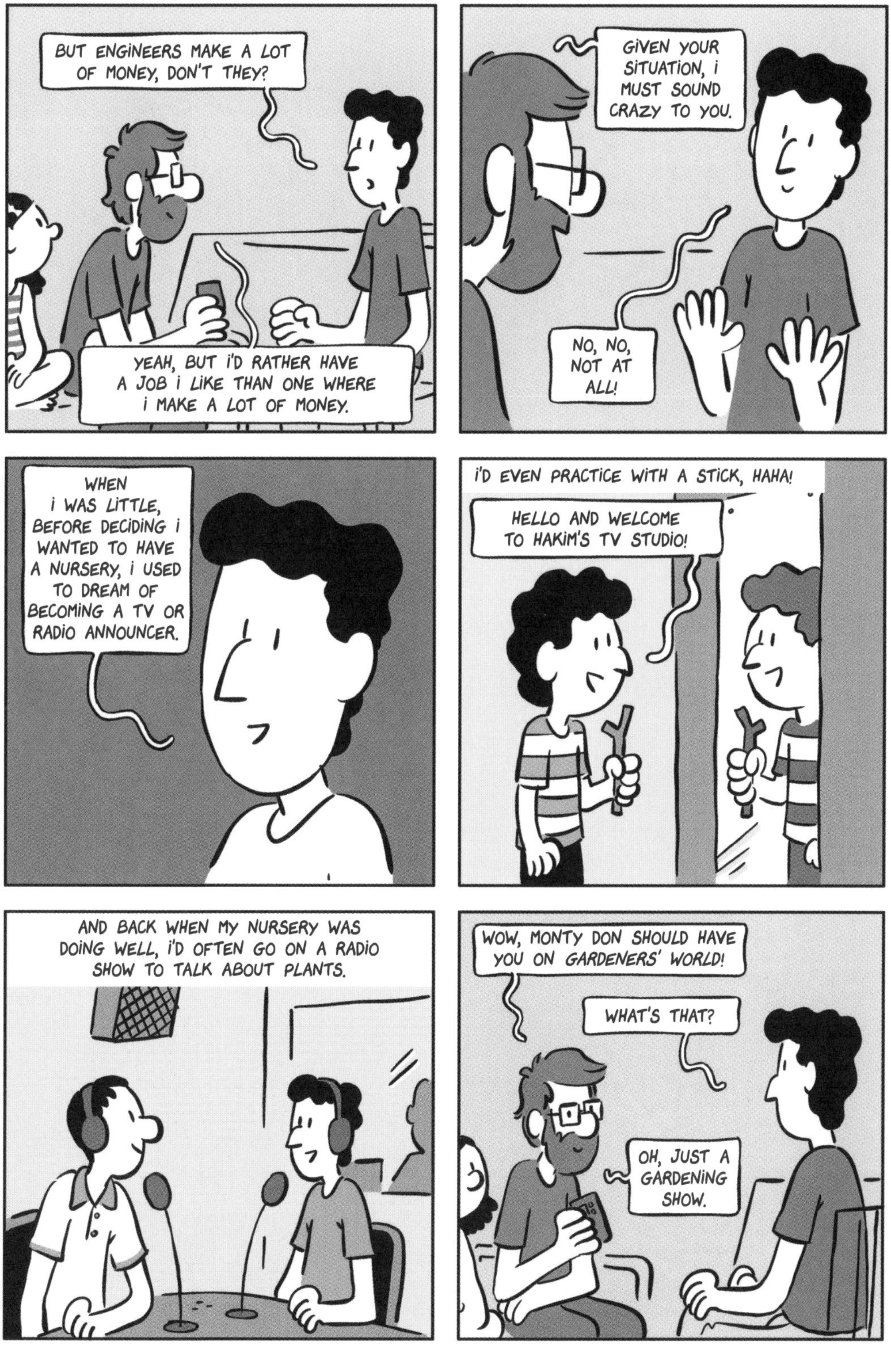
BUT ENGINEERS MAKE A LOT OF MONEY, DON'T THEY?
YEAH, BUT I'D RATHER HAVE A JOB I LIKE THAN ONE WHERE I MAKE A LOT OF MONEY.
GIVEN YOUR SITUATION, I MUST SOUND CRAZY TO YOU.
NO, NO, NOT AT ALL!
WHEN I WAS LITTLE, BEFORE DECIDING I WANTED TO HAVE A NURSERY, I USED TO DREAM OF BECOMING A TV OR RADIO ANNOUNCER.
I'D EVEN PRACTICE WITH A STICK, HAHA!
HELLO AND WELCOME TO HAKIM'S TV STUDIO!
AND BACK WHEN MY NURSERY WAS DOING WELL, I'D OFTEN GO ON A RADIO SHOW TO TALK ABOUT PLANTS.
WOW, MONTY DON SHOULD HAVE YOU ON GARDENERS' WORLD!
WHAT'S THAT?
OH, JUST A GARDENING SHOW.

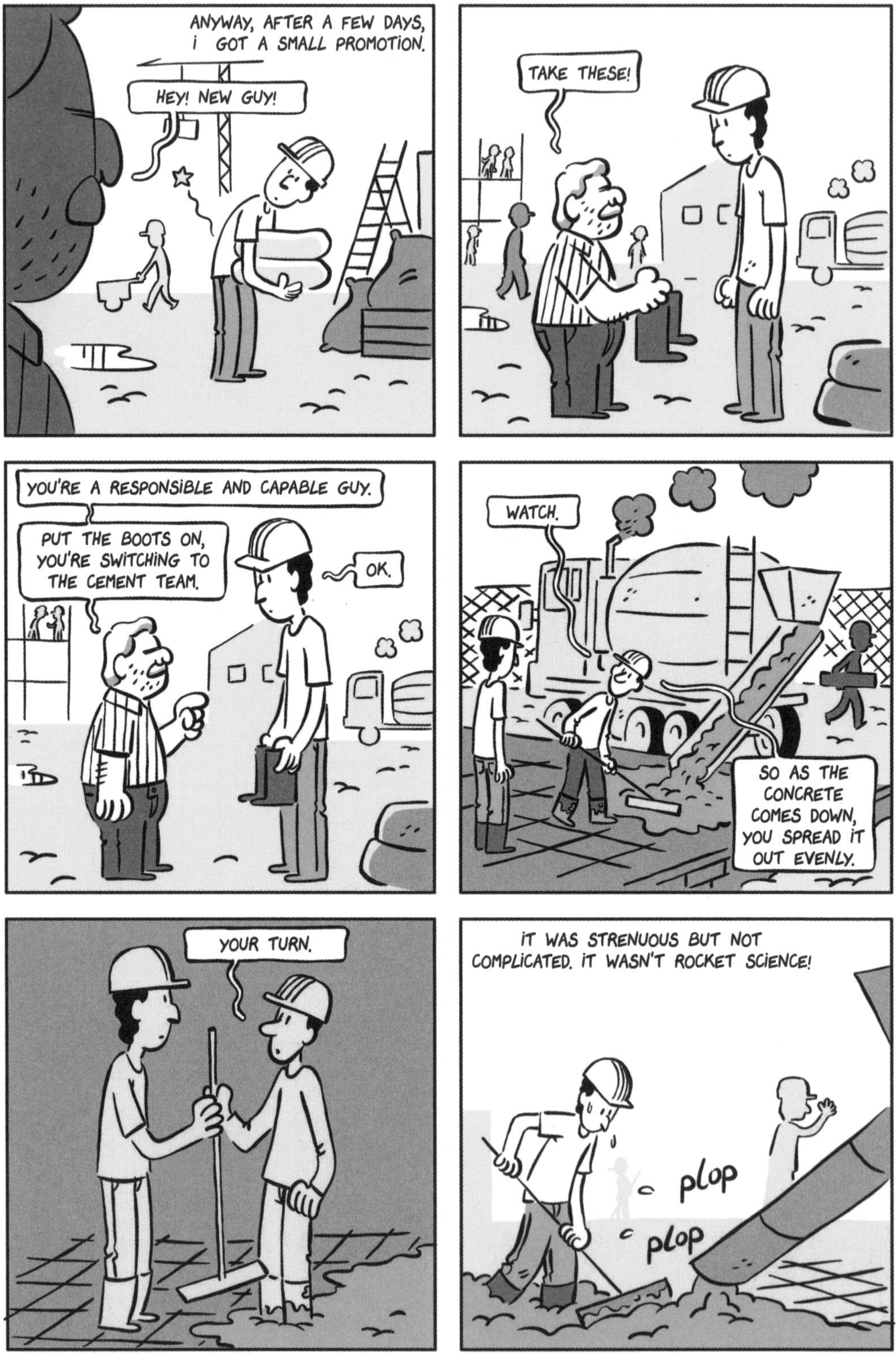
ANYWAY, AFTER A FEW DAYS, I GOT A SMALL PROMOTION.
HEY! NEW GUY!
TAKE THESE!
YOU'RE A RESPONSIBLE AND CAPABLE GUY.
PUT THE BOOTS ON, YOU'RE SWITCHING TO THE CEMENT TEAM.
OK.
WATCH.
SO AS THE CONCRETE COMES DOWN, YOU SPREAD IT OUT EVENLY.
YOUR TURN.
IT WAS STRENUOUS BUT NOT COMPLICATED. IT WASN'T ROCKET SCIENCE!
plop
plop

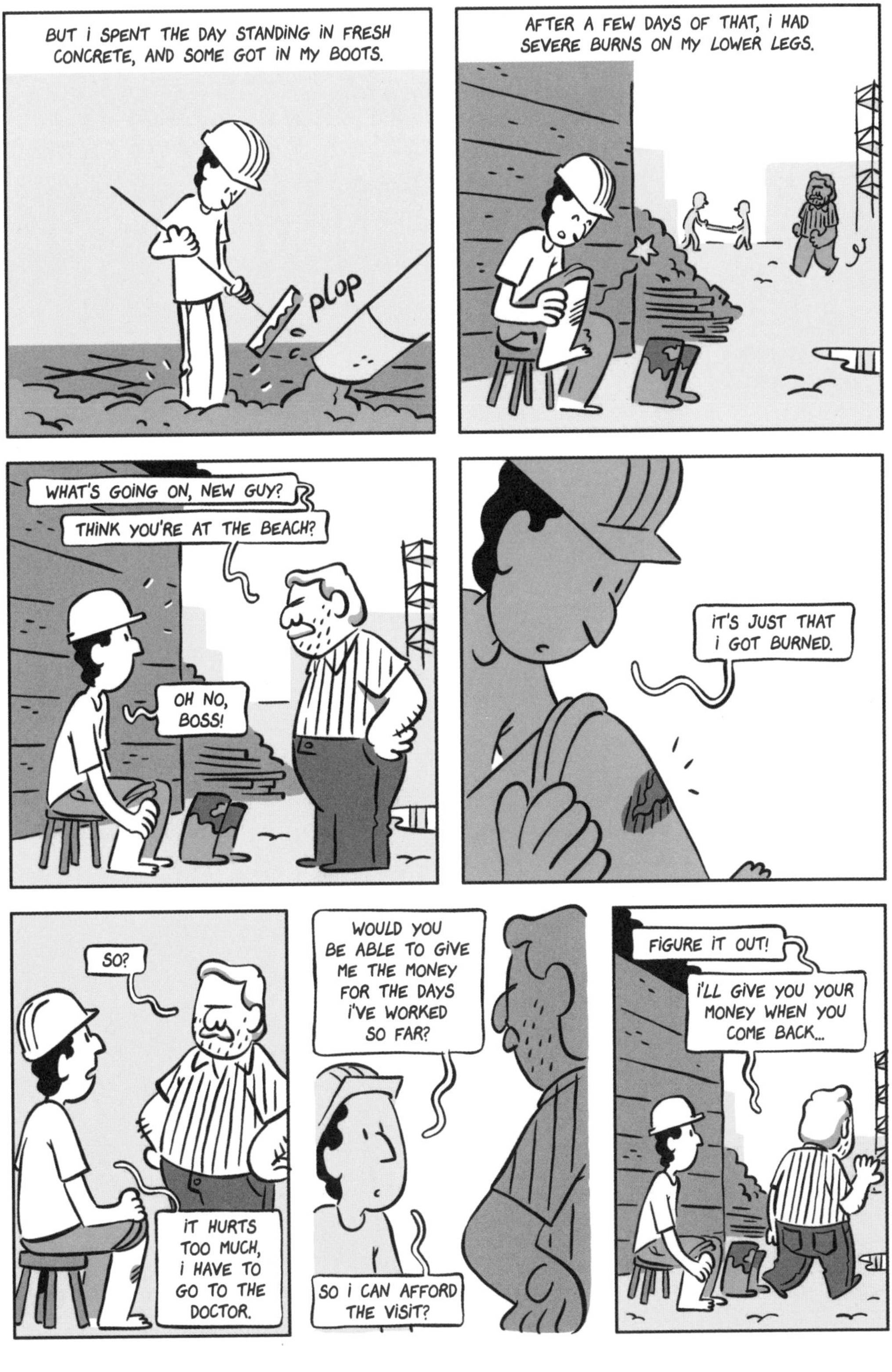
BUT i SPENT THE DAY STANDiNG iN FRESH CONCRETE, AND SOME GOT iN MY BOOTS.
PLOP
AFTER A FEW DAYS OF THAT, i HAD SEVERE BURNS ON MY LOWER LEGS.
WHAT'S GOiNG ON, NEW GUY?
THiNK YOU'RE AT THE BEACH?
OH NO, BOSS!
iT'S JUST THAT i GOT BURNED.
SO?
iT HURTS TOO MUCH, i HAVE TO GO TO THE DOCTOR.
WOULD YOU BE ABLE TO GiVE ME THE MONEY FOR THE DAYS i'VE WORKED SO FAR?
SO i CAN AFFORD THE ViSiT?
FiGURE iT OUT!
i'LL GiVE YOU YOUR MONEY WHEN YOU COME BACK...

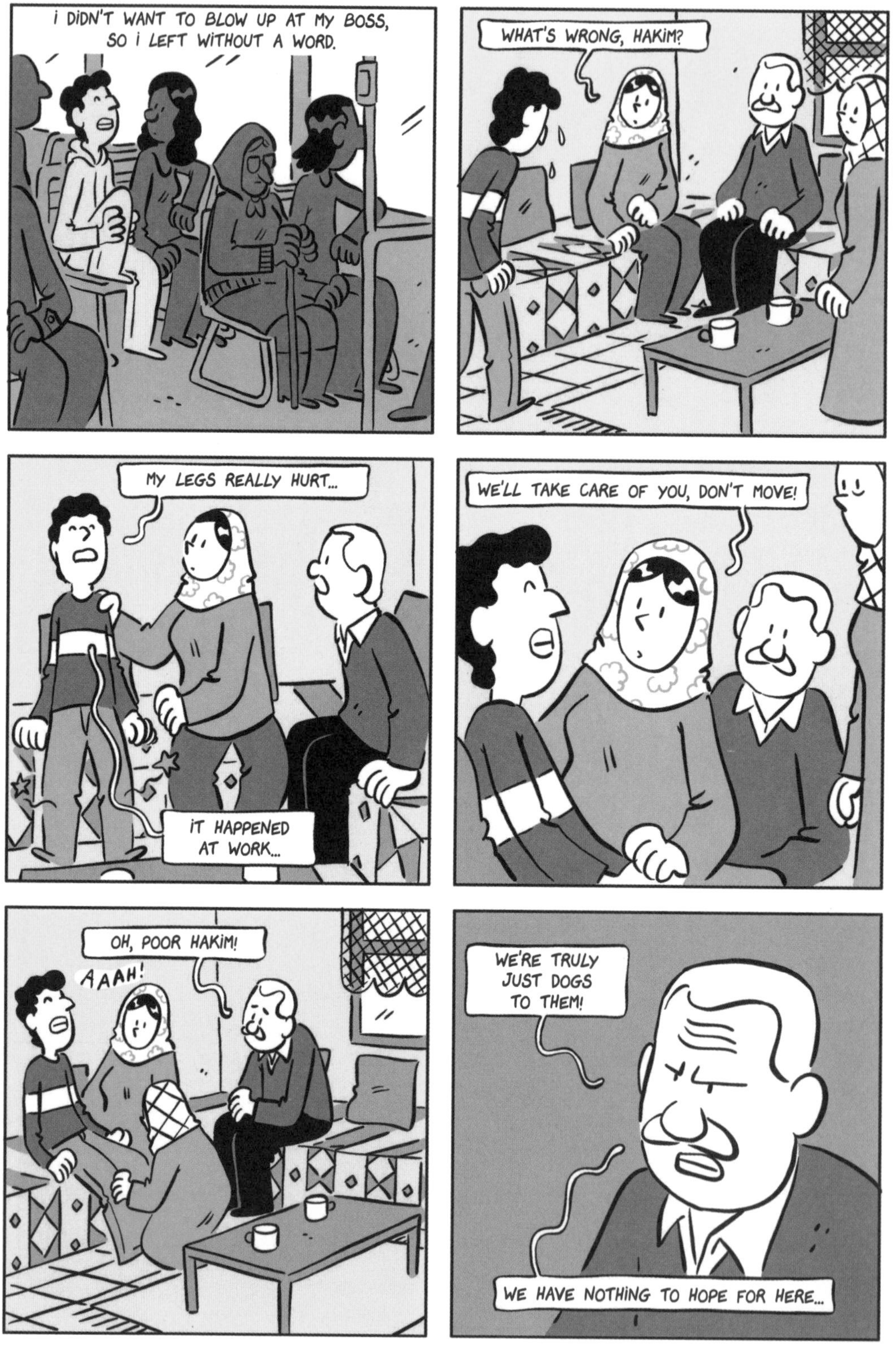
I DIDN'T WANT TO BLOW UP AT MY BOSS, SO I LEFT WITHOUT A WORD.
WHAT'S WRONG, HAKIM?
MY LEGS REALLY HURT...
IT HAPPENED AT WORK...
WE'LL TAKE CARE OF YOU, DON'T MOVE!
OH, POOR HAKIM!
AAAH!
WE'RE TRULY JUST DOGS TO THEM!
WE HAVE NOTHING TO HOPE FOR HERE...

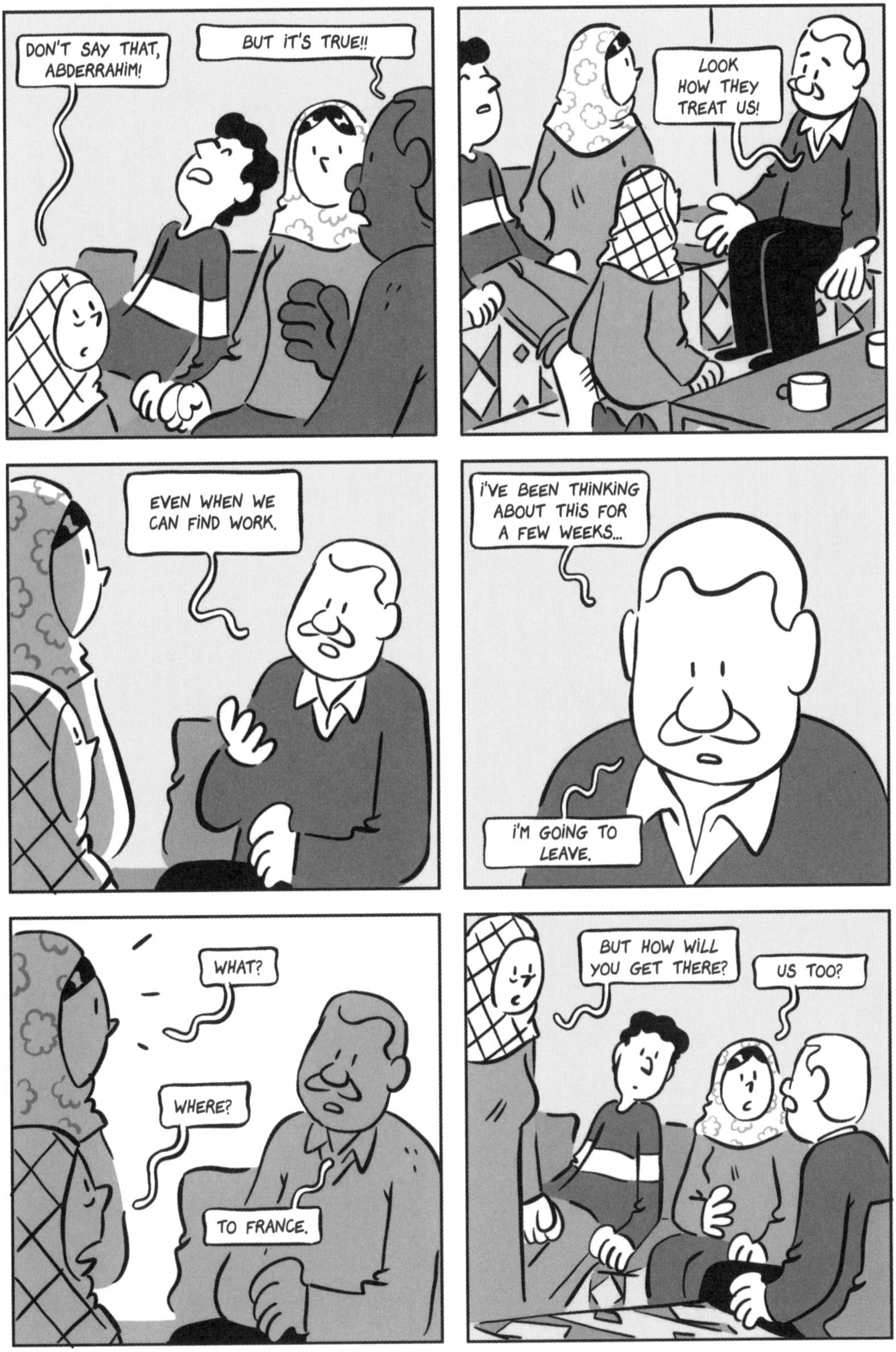
DON'T SAY THAT, ABDERRAHIM!
BUT IT'S TRUE!!
LOOK HOW THEY TREAT US!
EVEN WHEN WE CAN FIND WORK.
I'VE BEEN THINKING ABOUT THIS FOR A FEW WEEKS...
I'M GOING TO LEAVE.
WHAT?
WHERE?
TO FRANCE.
BUT HOW WILL YOU GET THERE?
US TOO?

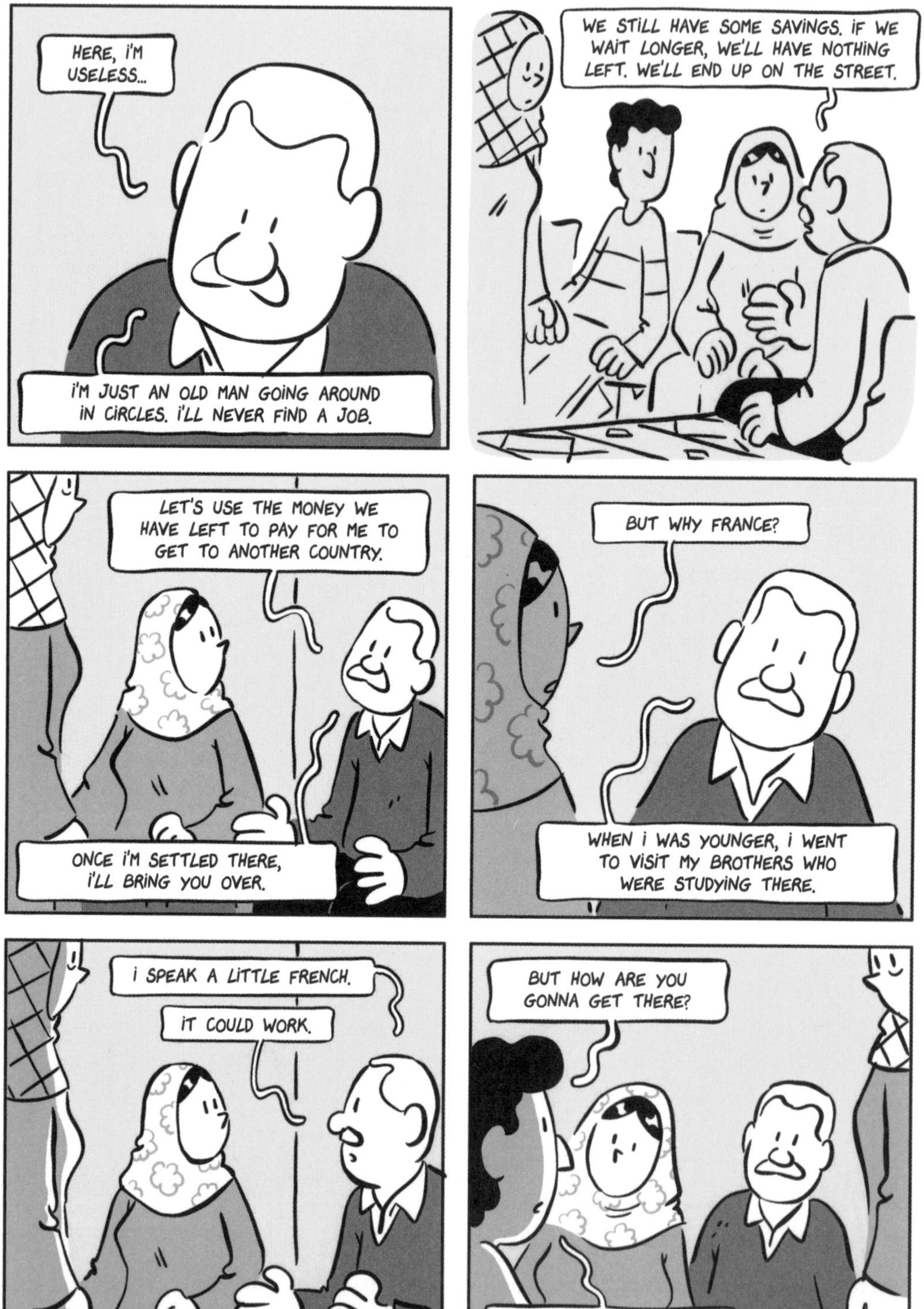
HERE, I'M USELESS...
I'M JUST AN OLD MAN GOING AROUND IN CIRCLES. I'LL NEVER FIND A JOB.
WE STILL HAVE SOME SAVINGS. IF WE WAIT LONGER, WE'LL HAVE NOTHING LEFT. WE'LL END UP ON THE STREET.
LET'S USE THE MONEY WE HAVE LEFT TO PAY FOR ME TO GET TO ANOTHER COUNTRY.
ONCE I'M SETTLED THERE, I'LL BRING YOU OVER.
BUT WHY FRANCE?
WHEN I WAS YOUNGER, I WENT TO VISIT MY BROTHERS WHO WERE STUDYING THERE.
I SPEAK A LITTLE FRENCH.
IT COULD WORK.
BUT HOW ARE YOU GONNA GET THERE?
GOING OVER THE SEA? AND ACROSS EUROPE?

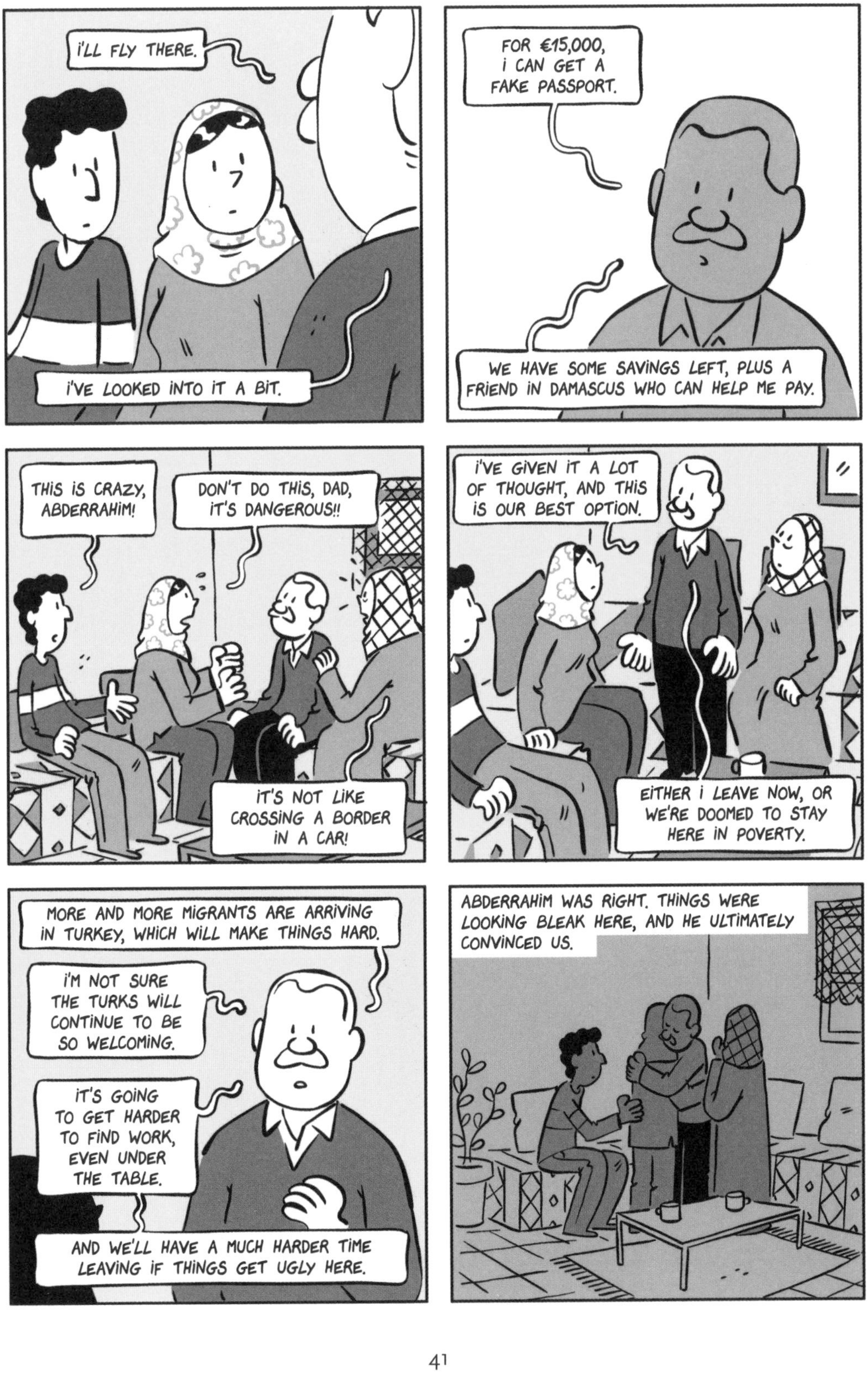
I'LL FLY THERE.
I'VE LOOKED INTO IT A BIT.
FOR €15,000, I CAN GET A FAKE PASSPORT.
WE HAVE SOME SAVINGS LEFT, PLUS A FRIEND IN DAMASCUS WHO CAN HELP ME PAY.
THIS IS CRAZY, ABDERRAHIM!
DON'T DO THIS, DAD, IT'S DANGEROUS!!
IT'S NOT LIKE CROSSING A BORDER IN A CAR!
I'VE GIVEN IT A LOT OF THOUGHT, AND THIS IS OUR BEST OPTION.
EITHER I LEAVE NOW, OR WE'RE DOOMED TO STAY HERE IN POVERTY.
MORE AND MORE MIGRANTS ARE ARRIVING IN TURKEY, WHICH WILL MAKE THINGS HARD.
I'M NOT SURE THE TURKS WILL CONTINUE TO BE SO WELCOMING.
IT'S GOING TO GET HARDER TO FIND WORK, EVEN UNDER THE TABLE.
AND WE'LL HAVE A MUCH HARDER TIME LEAVING IF THINGS GET UGLY HERE.
ABDERRAHIM WAS RIGHT. THINGS WERE LOOKING BLEAK HERE, AND HE ULTIMATELY CONVINCED US.

PREPARATIONS FOR ABDERRAHIM'S JOURNEY TOOK ABOUT A MONTH.

AND ONE DAY...

KNOCK!

KNOCK!

AH!

IT'S YOU!

WELL?

HERE ARE YOUR DOCUMENTS AND TICKETS.

YOU LEAVE NEXT WEEK.

BERNARD DUGREZ.

IS HE A REAL PERSON?

I CAN'T TELL YOU ANYTHING.

IS THERE A CHANCE I'LL BE CAUGHT?

YES, IT COULD HAPPEN.

AT CUSTOMS, ACT CASUAL WHEN YOU GIVE THEM YOUR PASSPORT, AND DON'T SAY A WORD.

YOUR SKIN IS REALLY QUITE LIGHT.

YOU COULD EASILY PASS FOR FRENCH.

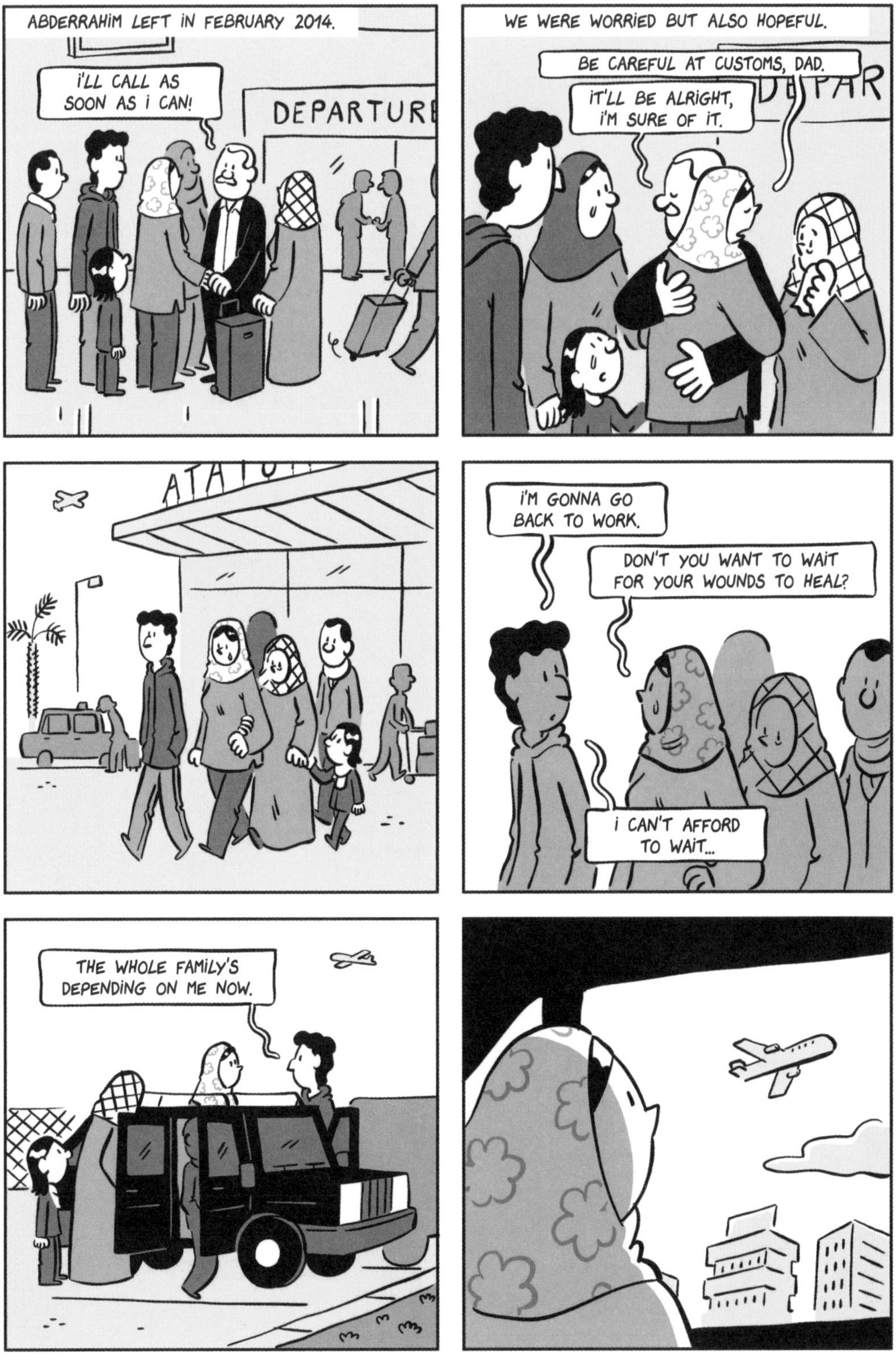
ABDERRAHIM LEFT IN FEBRUARY 2014.
I'LL CALL AS SOON AS I CAN!
DEPARTURE
WE WERE WORRIED BUT ALSO HOPEFUL.
BE CAREFUL AT CUSTOMS, DAD.
IT'LL BE ALRIGHT, I'M SURE OF IT.
DEPAR
ATAT
I'M GONNA GO BACK TO WORK.
DON'T YOU WANT TO WAIT FOR YOUR WOUNDS TO HEAL?
I CAN'T AFFORD TO WAIT...
THE WHOLE FAMILY'S DEPENDING ON ME NOW.

CLANG!
CLANG!
?
EXCUSE ME!
TATATATATATA
TATATATATA

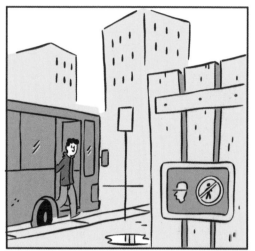

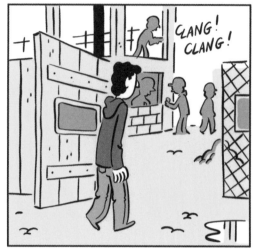

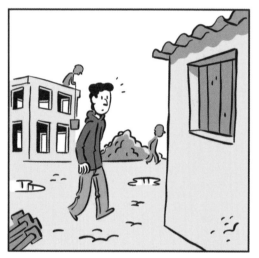

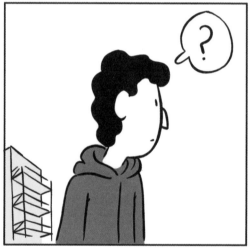

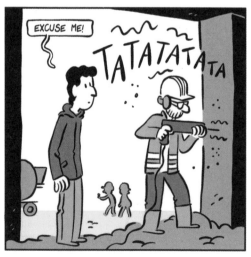

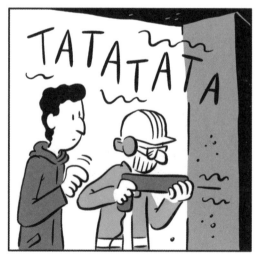

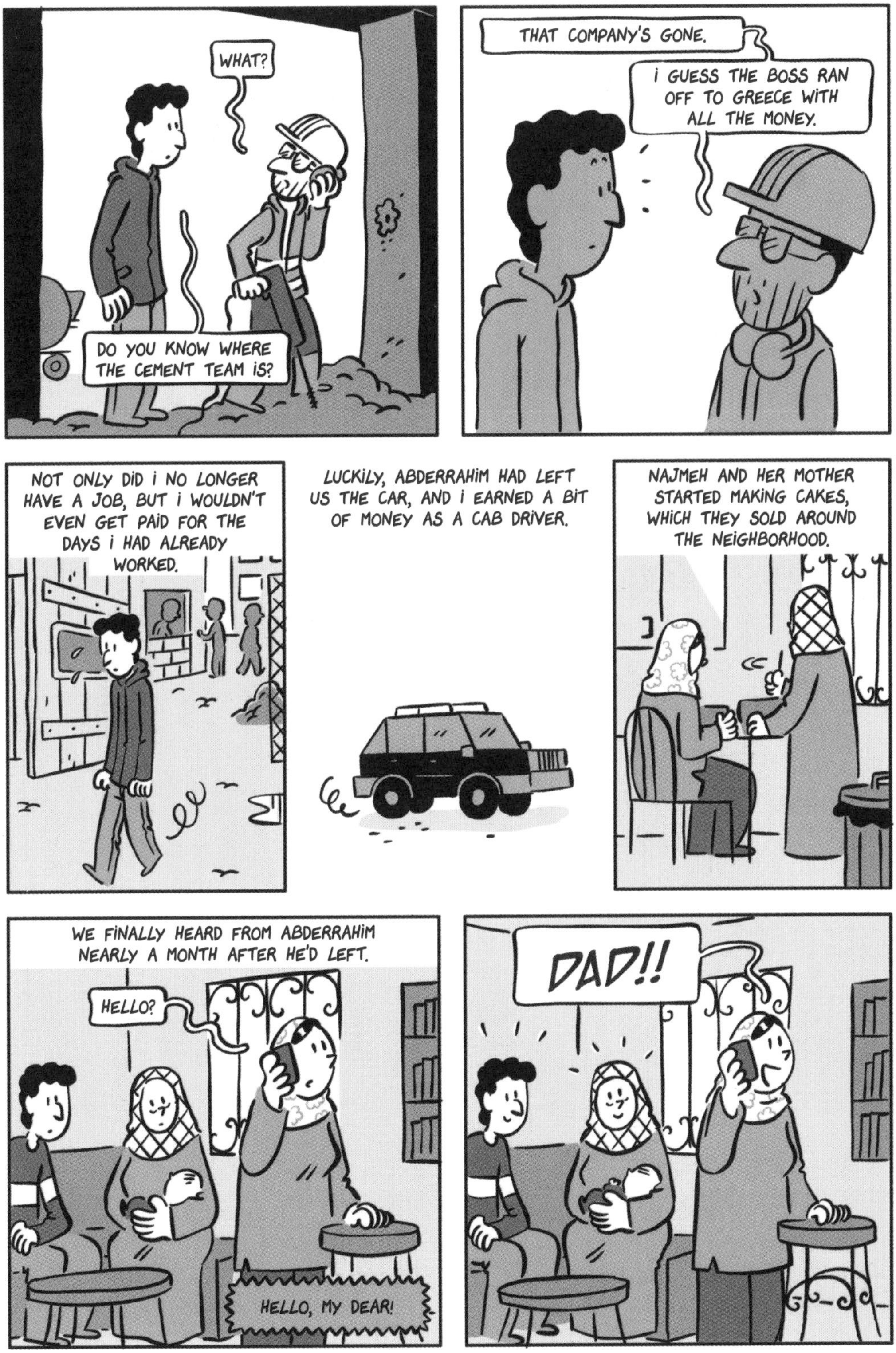
WHAT?
DO YOU KNOW WHERE THE CEMENT TEAM IS?
THAT COMPANY'S GONE.
I GUESS THE BOSS RAN OFF TO GREECE WITH ALL THE MONEY.
NOT ONLY DID I NO LONGER HAVE A JOB, BUT I WOULDN'T EVEN GET PAID FOR THE DAYS I HAD ALREADY WORKED.
LUCKILY, ABDERRAHIM HAD LEFT US THE CAR, AND I EARNED A BIT OF MONEY AS A CAB DRIVER.
NAJMEH AND HER MOTHER STARTED MAKING CAKES, WHICH THEY SOLD AROUND THE NEIGHBORHOOD.
WE FINALLY HEARD FROM ABDERRAHIM NEARLY A MONTH AFTER HE'D LEFT.
HELLO?
HELLO, MY DEAR!
DAD!!

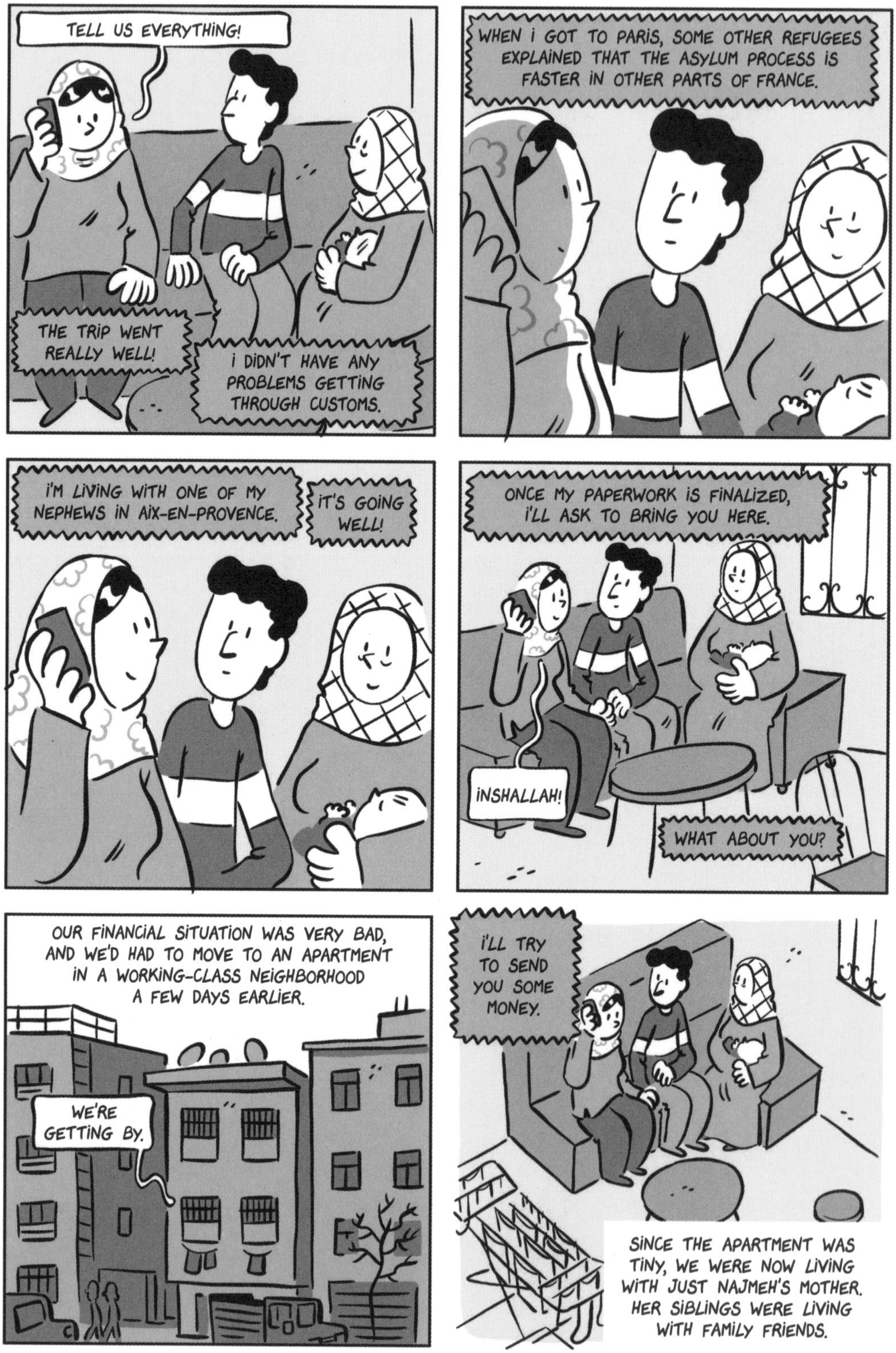

TELL US EVERYTHING!
THE TRIP WENT REALLY WELL!
I DIDN'T HAVE ANY PROBLEMS GETTING THROUGH CUSTOMS.
WHEN I GOT TO PARIS, SOME OTHER REFUGEES EXPLAINED THAT THE ASYLUM PROCESS IS FASTER IN OTHER PARTS OF FRANCE.
I'M LIVING WITH ONE OF MY NEPHEWS IN AIX-EN-PROVENCE.
IT'S GOING WELL!
ONCE MY PAPERWORK IS FINALIZED, I'LL ASK TO BRING YOU HERE.
INSHALLAH!
WHAT ABOUT YOU?
OUR FINANCIAL SITUATION WAS VERY BAD, AND WE'D HAD TO MOVE TO AN APARTMENT IN A WORKING-CLASS NEIGHBORHOOD A FEW DAYS EARLIER.
WE'RE GETTING BY.
I'LL TRY TO SEND YOU SOME MONEY.
SINCE THE APARTMENT WAS TINY, WE WERE NOW LIVING WITH JUST NAJMEH'S MOTHER. HER SIBLINGS WERE LIVING WITH FAMILY FRIENDS.

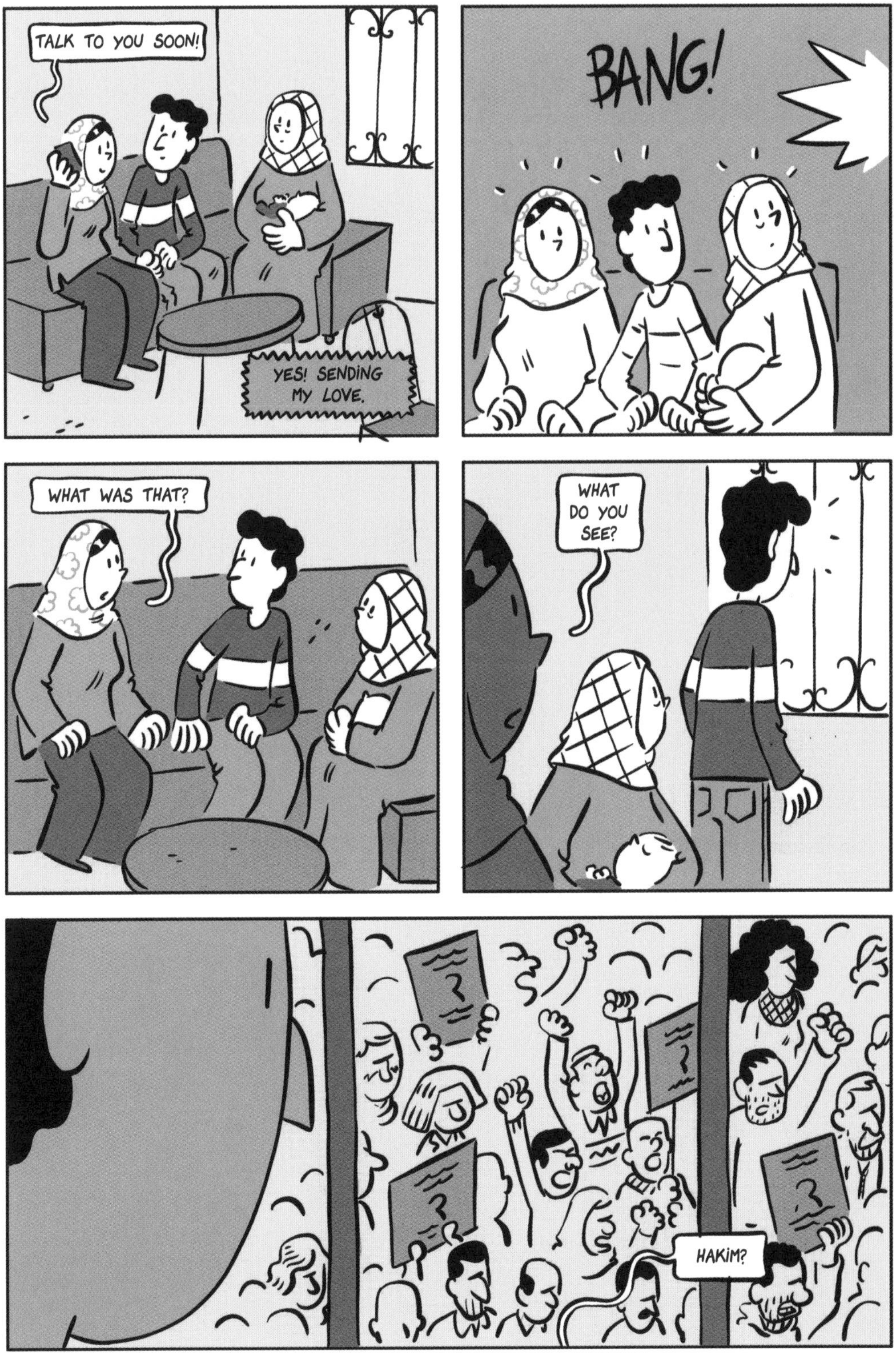
TALK TO YOU SOON!
YES! SENDING MY LOVE.
BANG!
WHAT WAS THAT?
WHAT DO YOU SEE?
HAKIM?

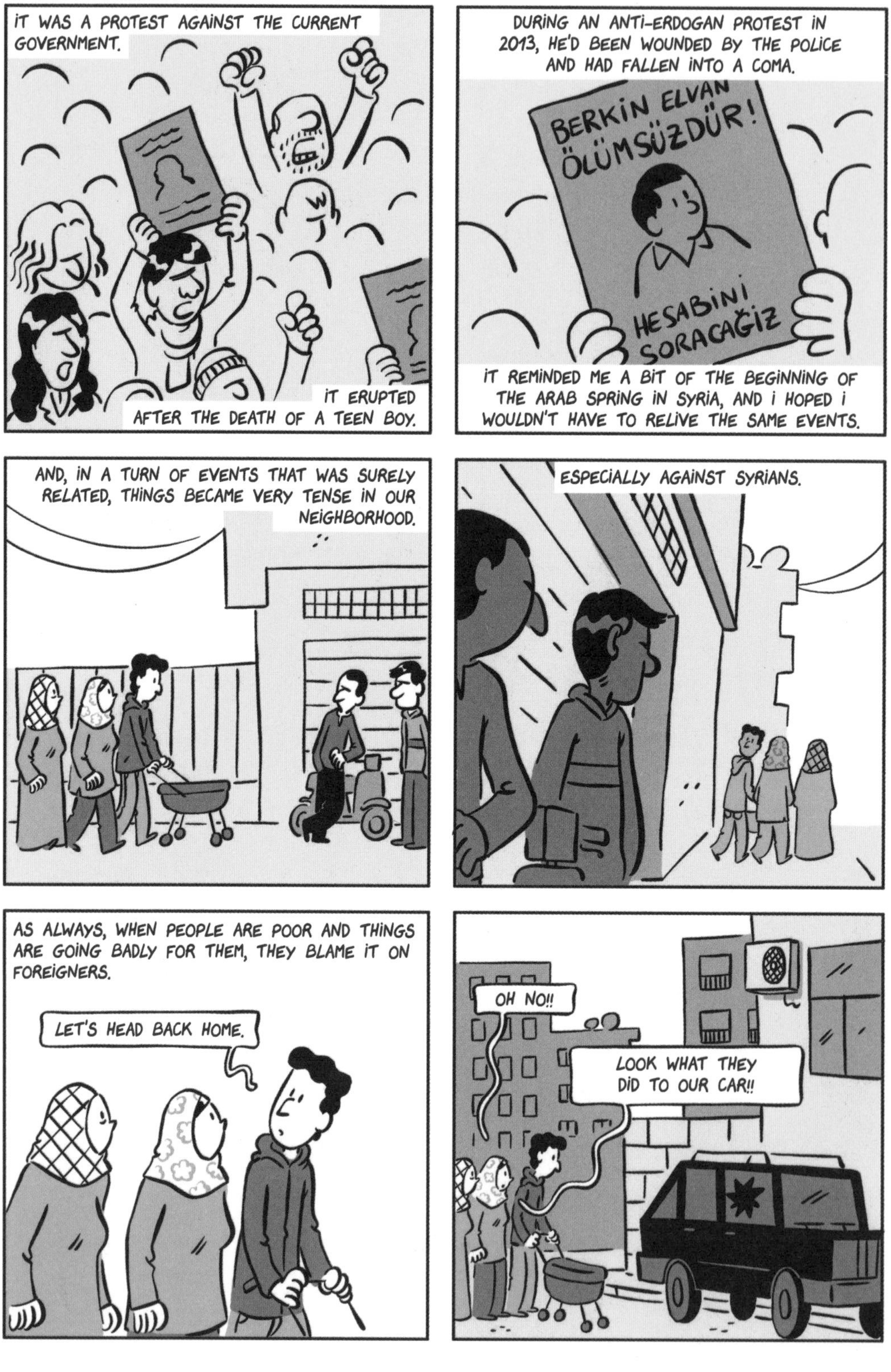
IT WAS A PROTEST AGAINST THE CURRENT GOVERNMENT.
IT ERUPTED AFTER THE DEATH OF A TEEN BOY.
DURING AN ANTI-ERDOGAN PROTEST IN 2013, HE'D BEEN WOUNDED BY THE POLICE AND HAD FALLEN INTO A COMA.
BERKIN ELVAN ÖLÜMSÜZDÜR!
HESABINI SORACAĞIZ
IT REMINDED ME A BIT OF THE BEGINNING OF THE ARAB SPRING IN SYRIA, AND I HOPED I WOULDN'T HAVE TO RELIVE THE SAME EVENTS.
AND, IN A TURN OF EVENTS THAT WAS SURELY RELATED, THINGS BECAME VERY TENSE IN OUR NEIGHBORHOOD.
ESPECIALLY AGAINST SYRIANS.
AS ALWAYS, WHEN PEOPLE ARE POOR AND THINGS ARE GOING BADLY FOR THEM, THEY BLAME IT ON FOREIGNERS.
LET'S HEAD BACK HOME.
OH NO!!
LOOK WHAT THEY DID TO OUR CAR!!

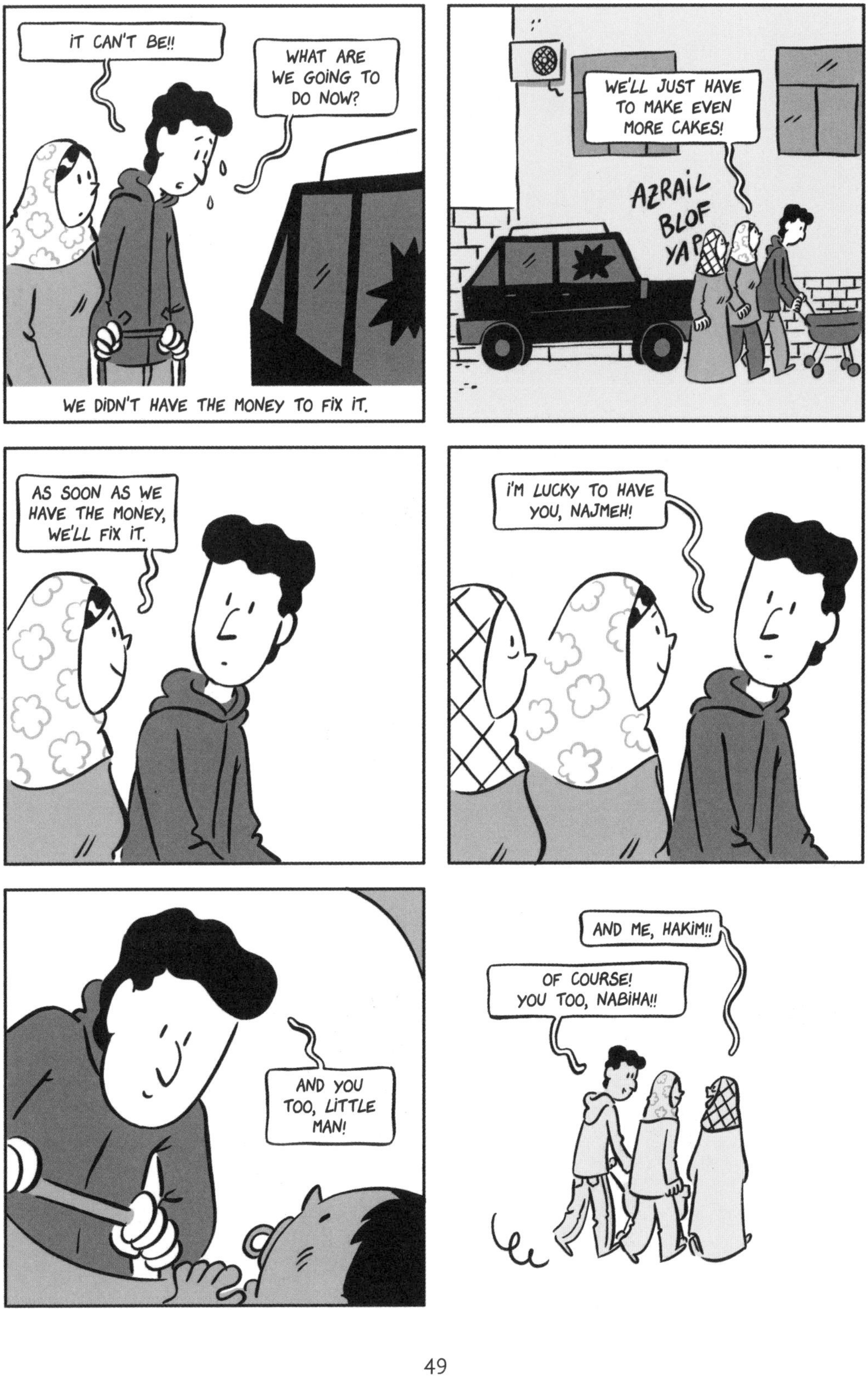
IT CAN'T BE!!
WHAT ARE WE GOING TO DO NOW?
WE DIDN'T HAVE THE MONEY TO FIX IT.
WE'LL JUST HAVE TO MAKE EVEN MORE CAKES!
AZRAIL BLOF YAP
AS SOON AS WE HAVE THE MONEY, WE'LL FIX IT.
I'M LUCKY TO HAVE YOU, NAJMEH!
AND YOU TOO, LITTLE MAN!
AND ME, HAKIM!!
OF COURSE! YOU TOO, NABIHA!!

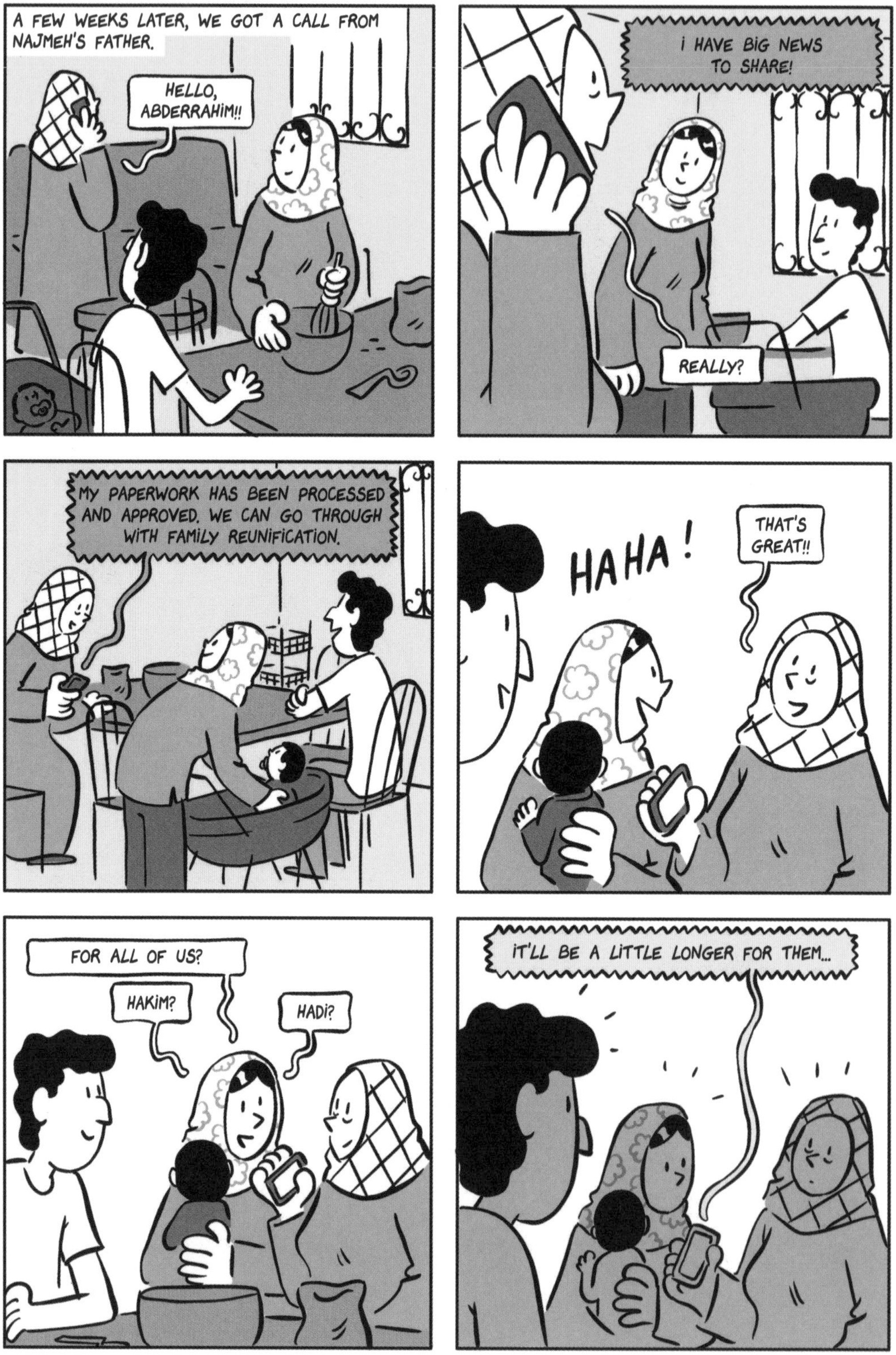
A FEW WEEKS LATER, WE GOT A CALL FROM NAJMEH'S FATHER.
HELLO, ABDERRAHIM!!
I HAVE BIG NEWS TO SHARE!
REALLY?
MY PAPERWORK HAS BEEN PROCESSED AND APPROVED. WE CAN GO THROUGH WITH FAMILY REUNIFICATION.
HAHA!
THAT'S GREAT!!
FOR ALL OF US?
HAKIM?
HADI?
IT'LL BE A LITTLE LONGER FOR THEM...

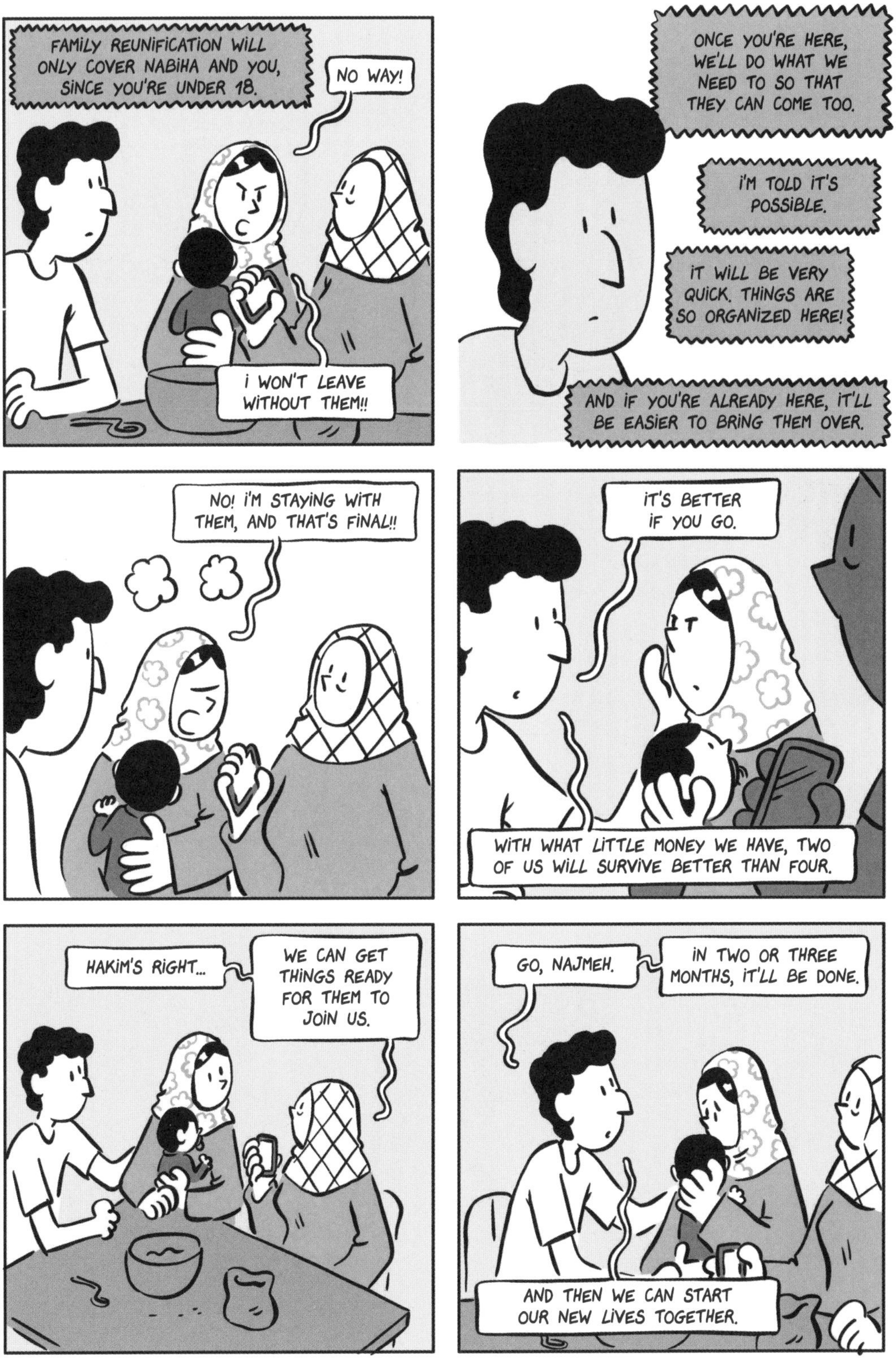
FAMILY REUNIFICATION WILL ONLY COVER NABIHA AND YOU, SINCE YOU'RE UNDER 18.
NO WAY!
I WON'T LEAVE WITHOUT THEM!!
ONCE YOU'RE HERE, WE'LL DO WHAT WE NEED TO SO THAT THEY CAN COME TOO.
I'M TOLD IT'S POSSIBLE.
IT WILL BE VERY QUICK. THINGS ARE SO ORGANIZED HERE!
AND IF YOU'RE ALREADY HERE, IT'LL BE EASIER TO BRING THEM OVER.
NO! I'M STAYING WITH THEM, AND THAT'S FINAL!!
IT'S BETTER IF YOU GO.
WITH WHAT LITTLE MONEY WE HAVE, TWO OF US WILL SURVIVE BETTER THAN FOUR.
HAKIM'S RIGHT...
WE CAN GET THINGS READY FOR THEM TO JOIN US.
GO, NAJMEH.
IN TWO OR THREE MONTHS, IT'LL BE DONE.
AND THEN WE CAN START OUR NEW LIVES TOGETHER.

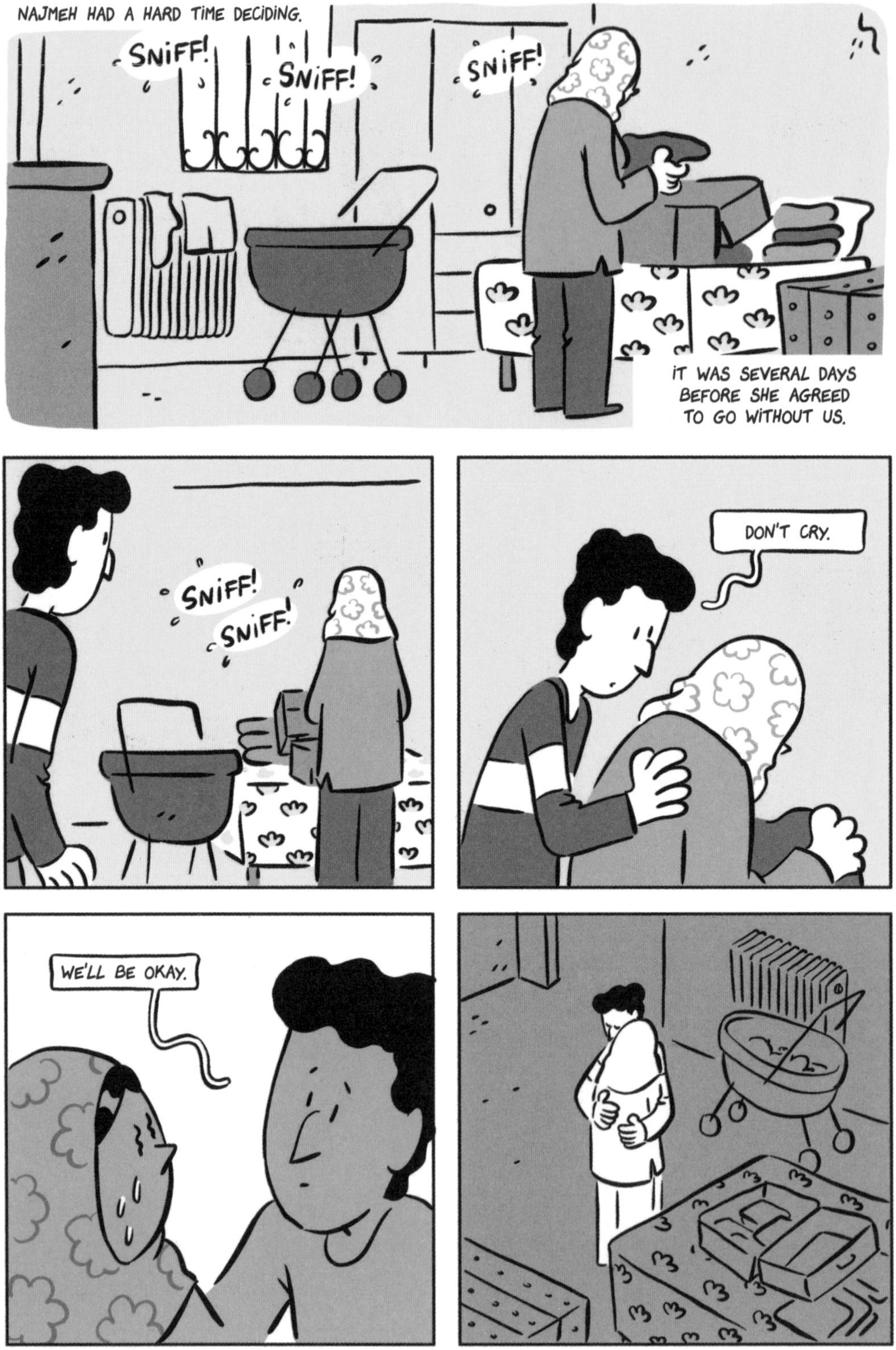
NAJMEH HAD A HARD TIME DECIDING.
SNIFF!
SNIFF!
SNIFF!
IT WAS SEVERAL DAYS BEFORE SHE AGREED TO GO WITHOUT US.
SNIFF!
SNIFF!
DON'T CRY.
WE'LL BE OKAY.

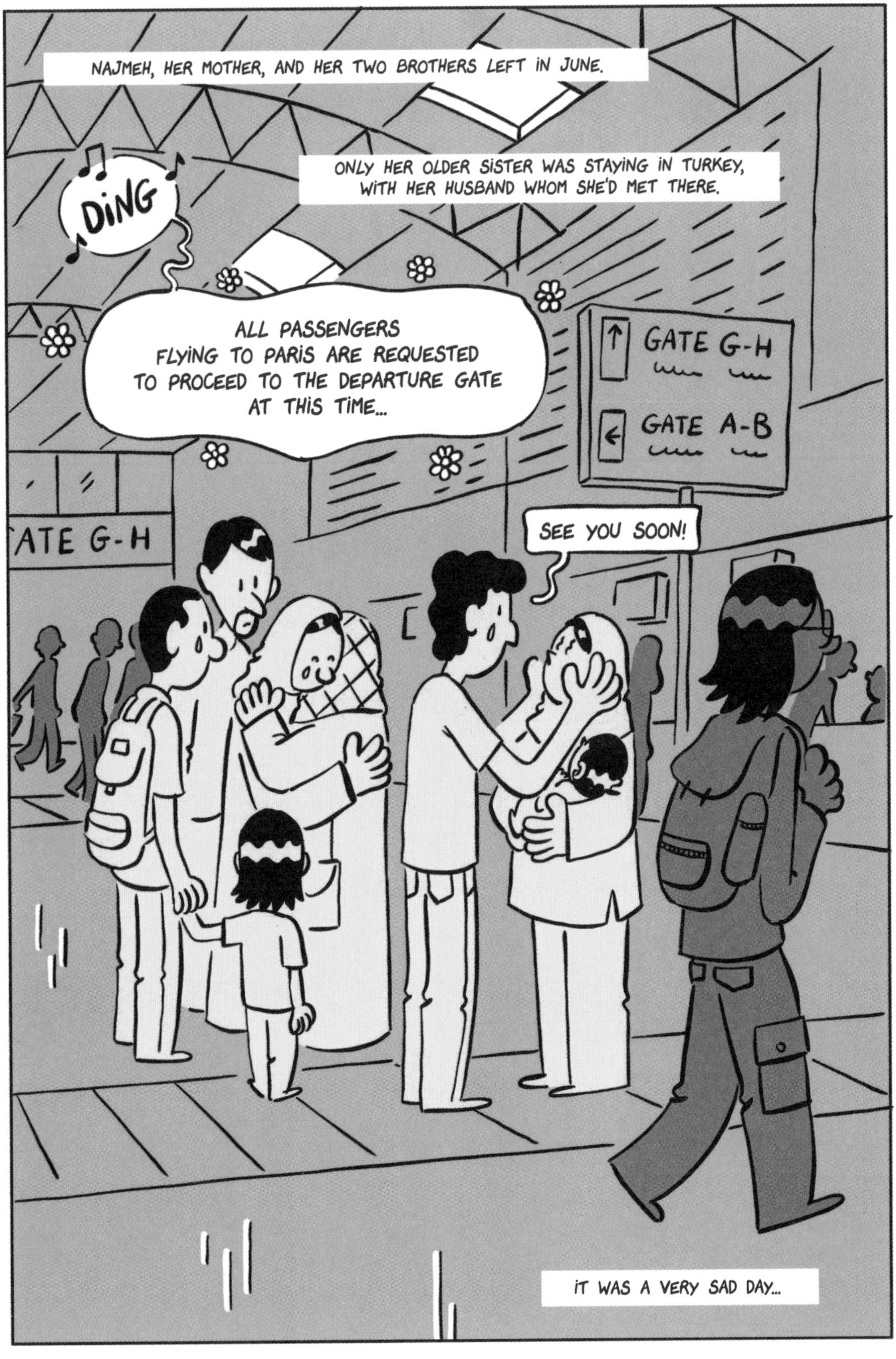
NAJMEH, HER MOTHER, AND HER TWO BROTHERS LEFT IN JUNE.
ONLY HER OLDER SISTER WAS STAYING IN TURKEY, WITH HER HUSBAND WHOM SHE'D MET THERE.
DING
ALL PASSENGERS FLYING TO PARIS ARE REQUESTED TO PROCEED TO THE DEPARTURE GATE AT THIS TIME...
GATE G-H
GATE A-B
ATE G-H
SEE YOU SOON!
IT WAS A VERY SAD DAY...

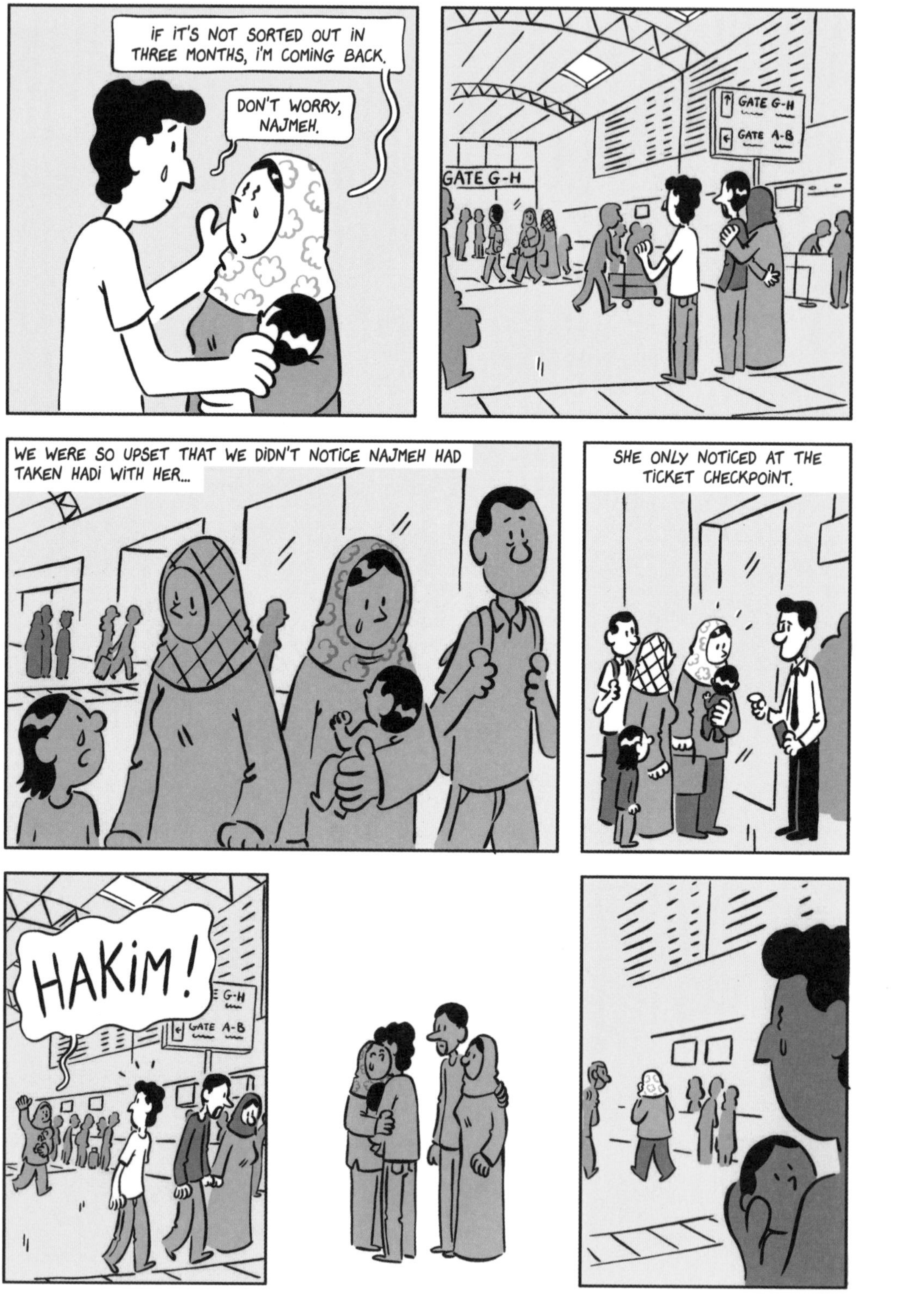

IF IT'S NOT SORTED OUT IN THREE MONTHS, I'M COMING BACK.
DON'T WORRY, NAJMEH.
GATE G-H
GATE A-B
GATE G-H
WE WERE SO UPSET THAT WE DIDN'T NOTICE NAJMEH HAD TAKEN HADI WITH HER...
SHE ONLY NOTICED AT THE TICKET CHECKPOINT.
HAKIM!
GATE A-B

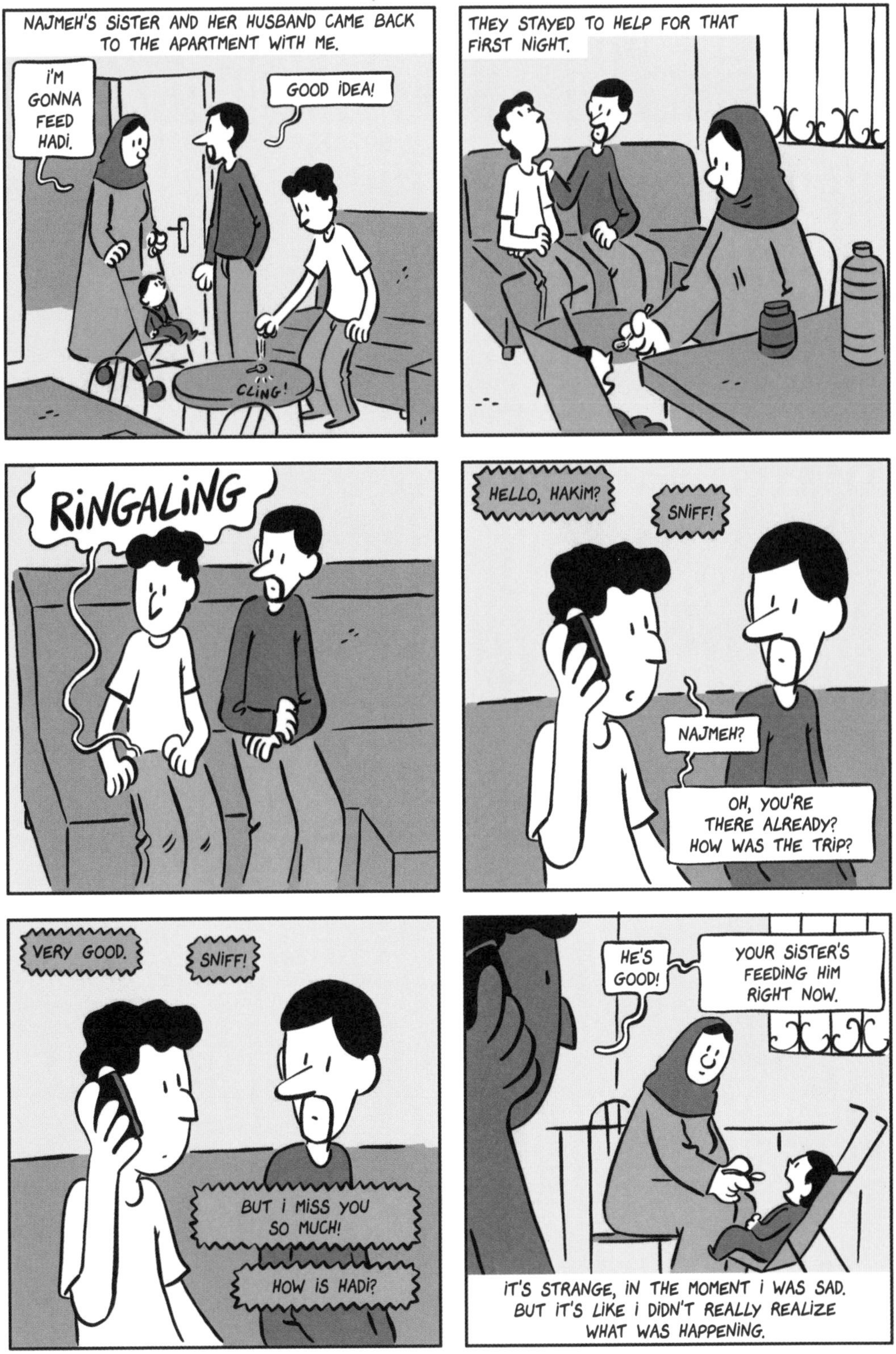
NAJMEH'S SISTER AND HER HUSBAND CAME BACK TO THE APARTMENT WITH ME.
I'M GONNA FEED HADI.
GOOD IDEA!
CLING!
THEY STAYED TO HELP FOR THAT FIRST NIGHT.
RINGALING
HELLO, HAKIM?
SNIFF!
NAJMEH?
OH, YOU'RE THERE ALREADY? HOW WAS THE TRIP?
VERY GOOD.
SNIFF!
BUT I MISS YOU SO MUCH!
HOW IS HADI?
HE'S GOOD!
YOUR SISTER'S FEEDING HIM RIGHT NOW.
IT'S STRANGE, IN THE MOMENT I WAS SAD. BUT IT'S LIKE I DIDN'T REALLY REALIZE WHAT WAS HAPPENING.

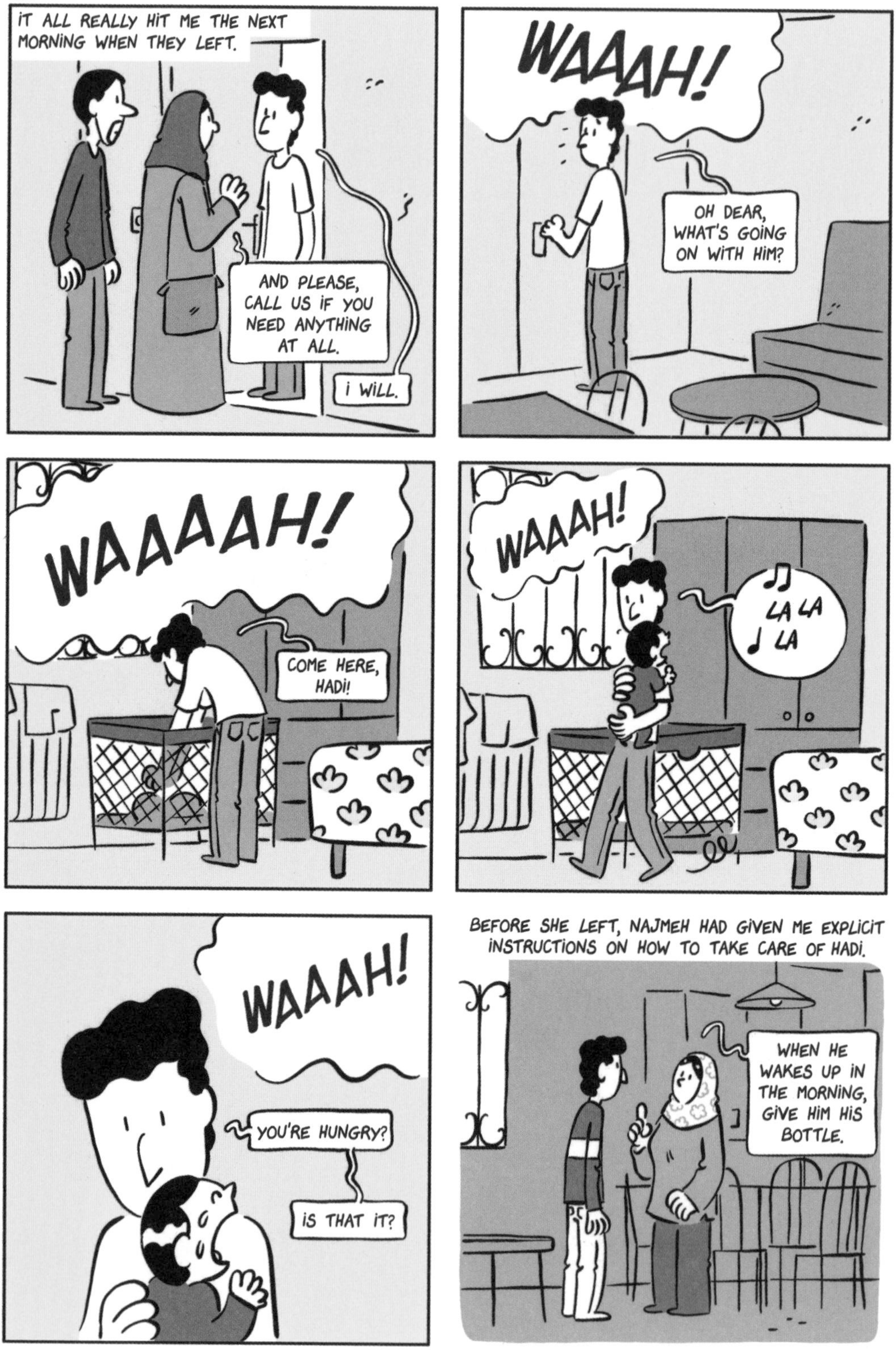
IT ALL REALLY HIT ME THE NEXT MORNING WHEN THEY LEFT.
AND PLEASE, CALL US IF YOU NEED ANYTHING AT ALL.
I WILL.
WAAAH!
OH DEAR, WHAT'S GOING ON WITH HIM?
WAAAAH!
COME HERE, HADI!
WAAAH!
LA LA LA
WAAAH!
YOU'RE HUNGRY?
IS THAT IT?
BEFORE SHE LEFT, NAJMEH HAD GIVEN ME EXPLICIT INSTRUCTIONS ON HOW TO TAKE CARE OF HADI.
WHEN HE WAKES UP IN THE MORNING, GIVE HIM HIS BOTTLE.

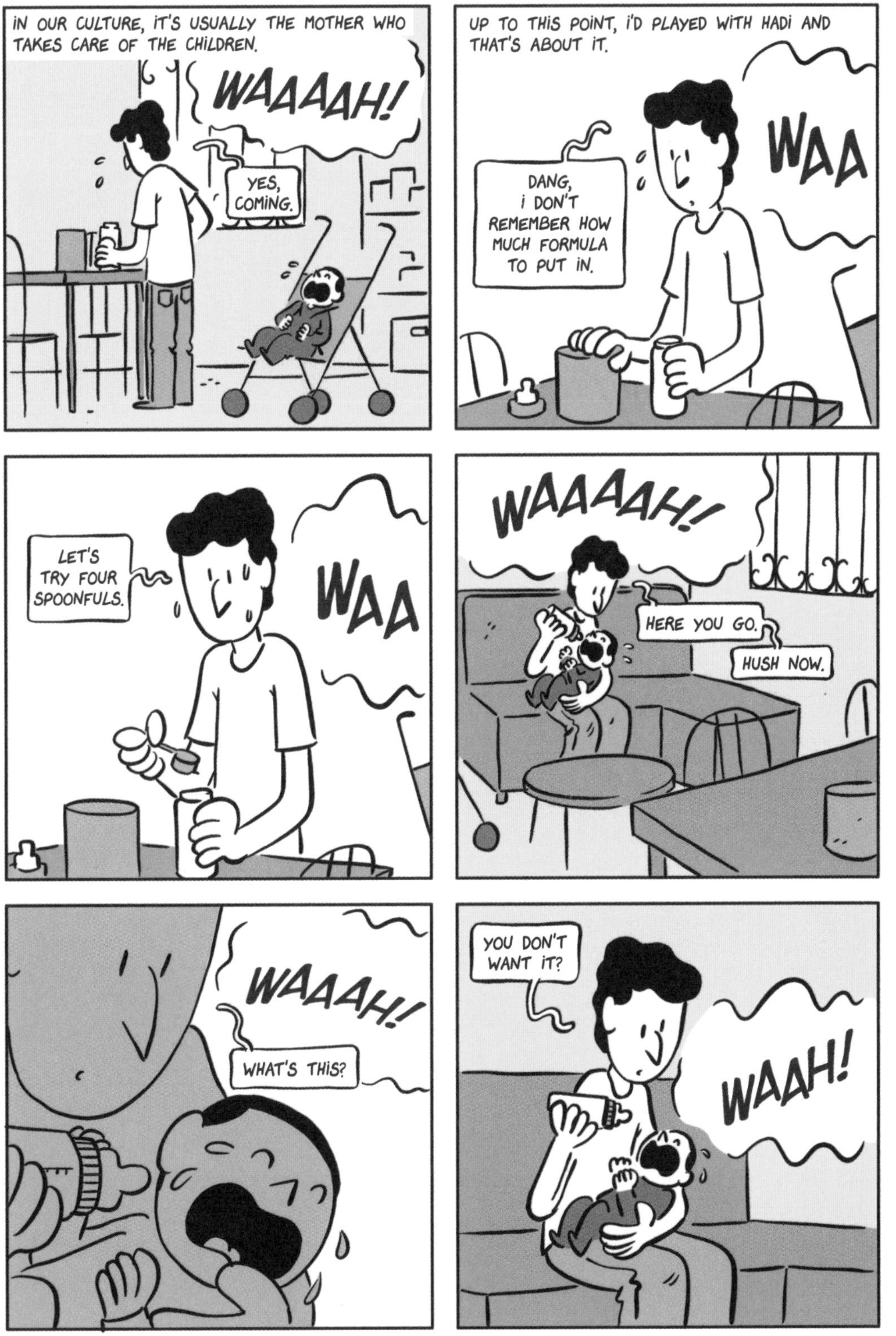
IN OUR CULTURE, IT'S USUALLY THE MOTHER WHO TAKES CARE OF THE CHILDREN.
WAAAAH!
YES, COMING.
UP TO THIS POINT, I'D PLAYED WITH HADI AND THAT'S ABOUT IT.
DANG, I DON'T REMEMBER HOW MUCH FORMULA TO PUT IN.
WAA
LET'S TRY FOUR SPOONFULS.
WAA
WAAAAH!
HERE YOU GO.
HUSH NOW.
WAAAH!
WHAT'S THIS?
YOU DON'T WANT IT?
WAAH!

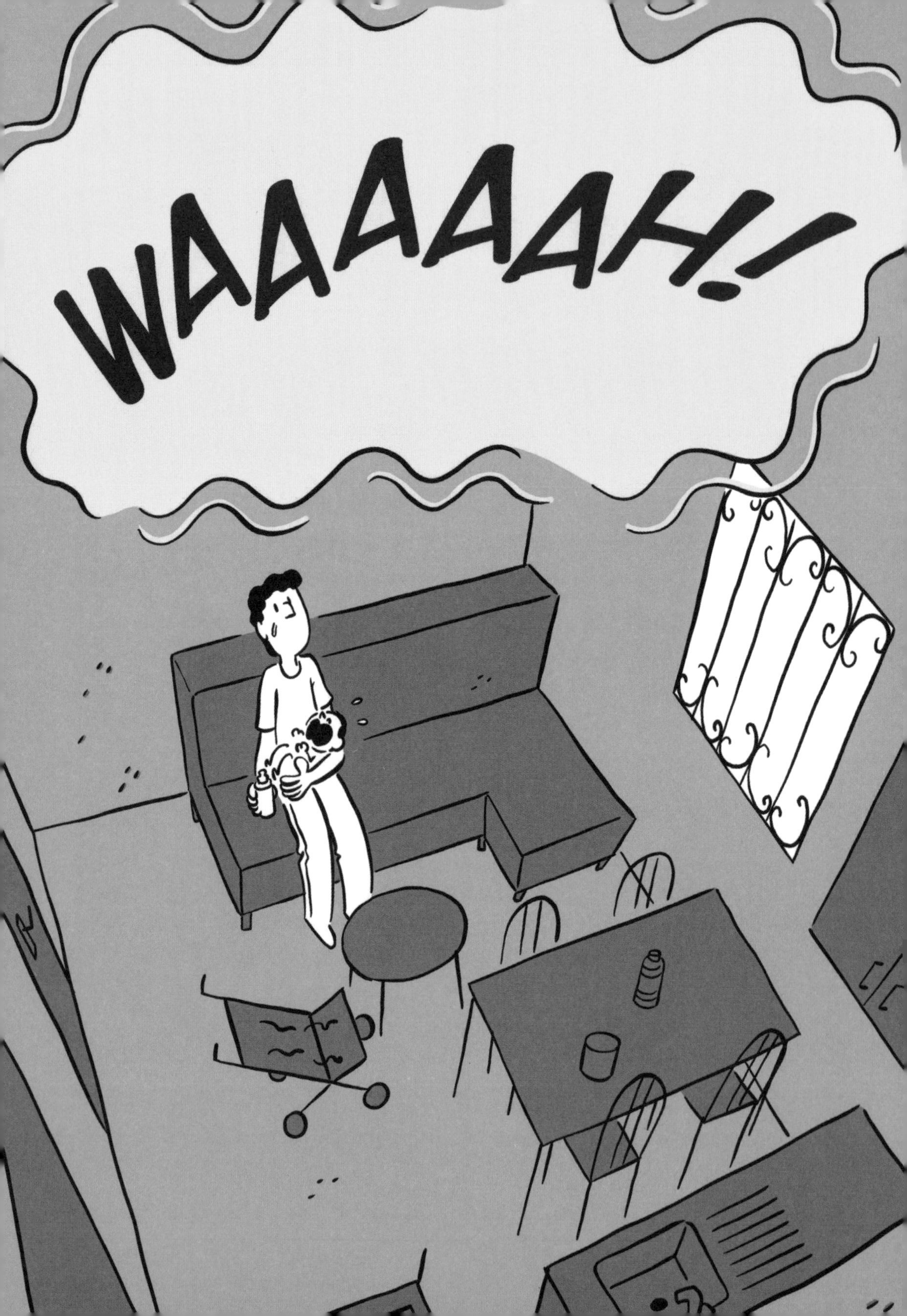
WAAAAAH!

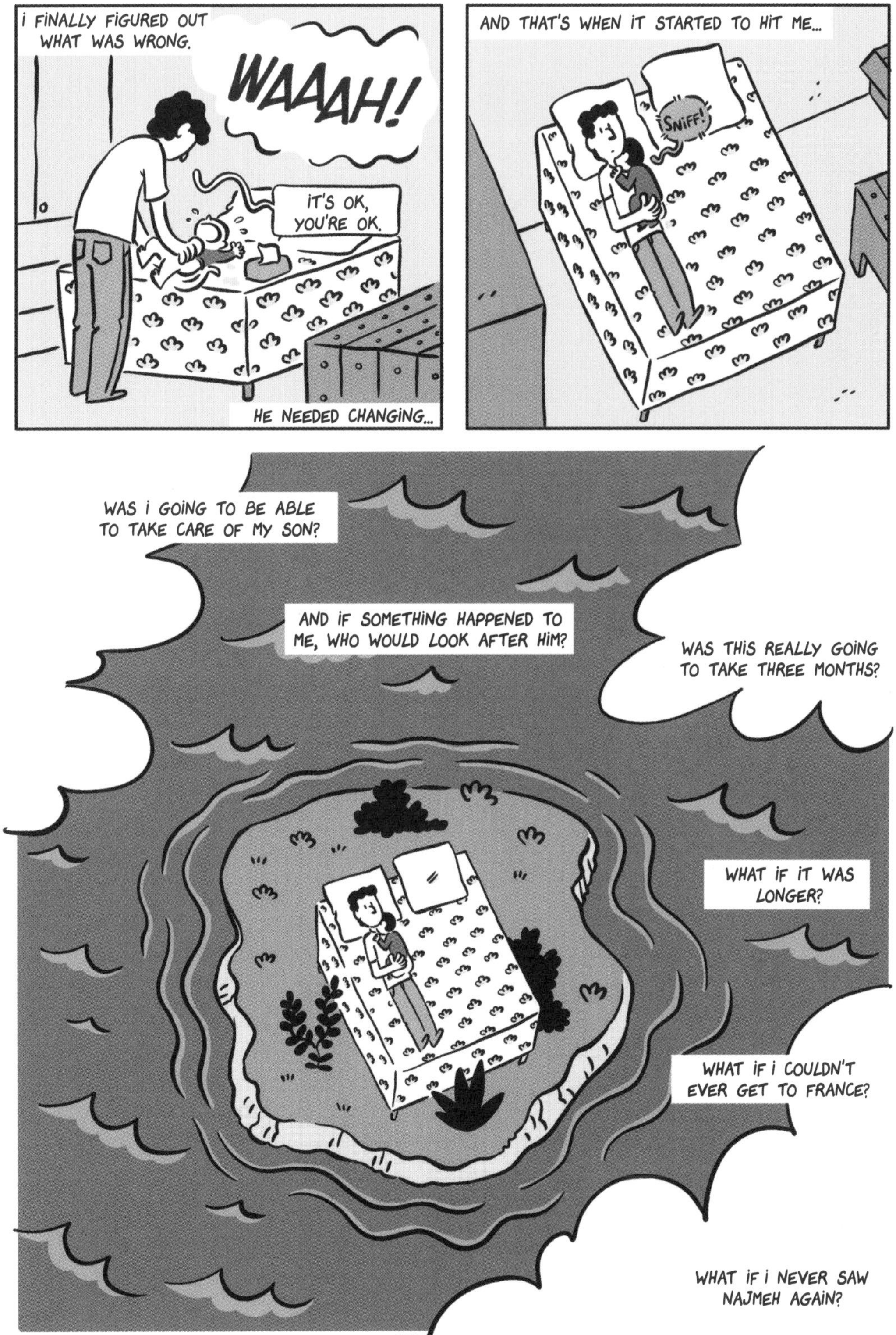
I FINALLY FIGURED OUT WHAT WAS WRONG.
WAAAH!
IT'S OK, YOU'RE OK.
HE NEEDED CHANGING...
AND THAT'S WHEN IT STARTED TO HIT ME...
SNIFF!
WAS I GOING TO BE ABLE TO TAKE CARE OF MY SON?
AND IF SOMETHING HAPPENED TO ME, WHO WOULD LOOK AFTER HIM?
WAS THIS REALLY GOING TO TAKE THREE MONTHS?
WHAT IF IT WAS LONGER?
WHAT IF I COULDN'T EVER GET TO FRANCE?
WHAT IF I NEVER SAW NAJMEH AGAIN?

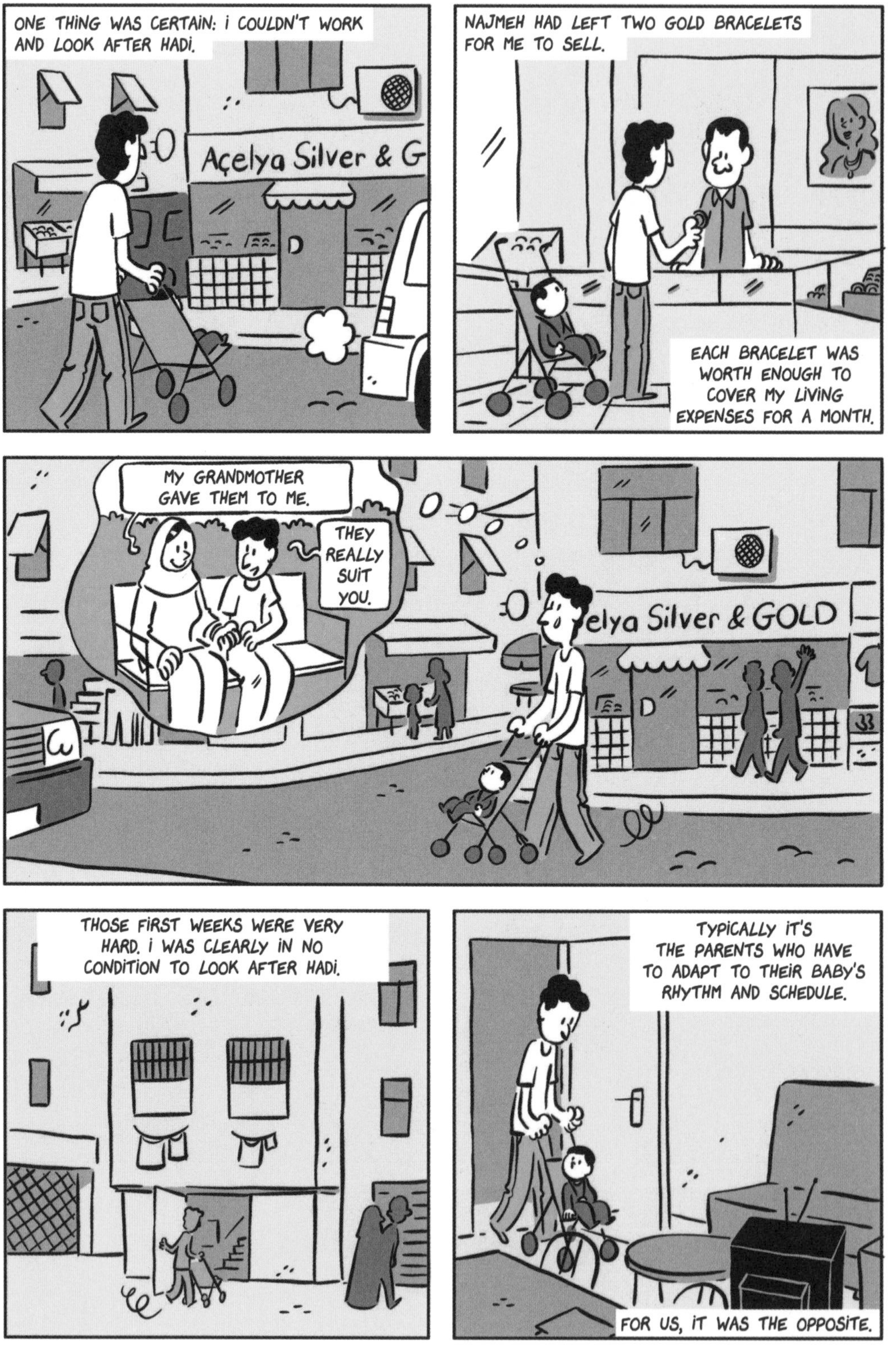
ONE THING WAS CERTAIN: I COULDN'T WORK AND LOOK AFTER HADI.
Açelya Silver & G
NAJMEH HAD LEFT TWO GOLD BRACELETS FOR ME TO SELL.
EACH BRACELET WAS WORTH ENOUGH TO COVER MY LIVING EXPENSES FOR A MONTH.
MY GRANDMOTHER GAVE THEM TO ME.
THEY REALLY SUIT YOU.
elya Silver & GOLD
THOSE FIRST WEEKS WERE VERY HARD. I WAS CLEARLY IN NO CONDITION TO LOOK AFTER HADI.
TYPICALLY IT'S THE PARENTS WHO HAVE TO ADAPT TO THEIR BABY'S RHYTHM AND SCHEDULE.
FOR US, IT WAS THE OPPOSITE.

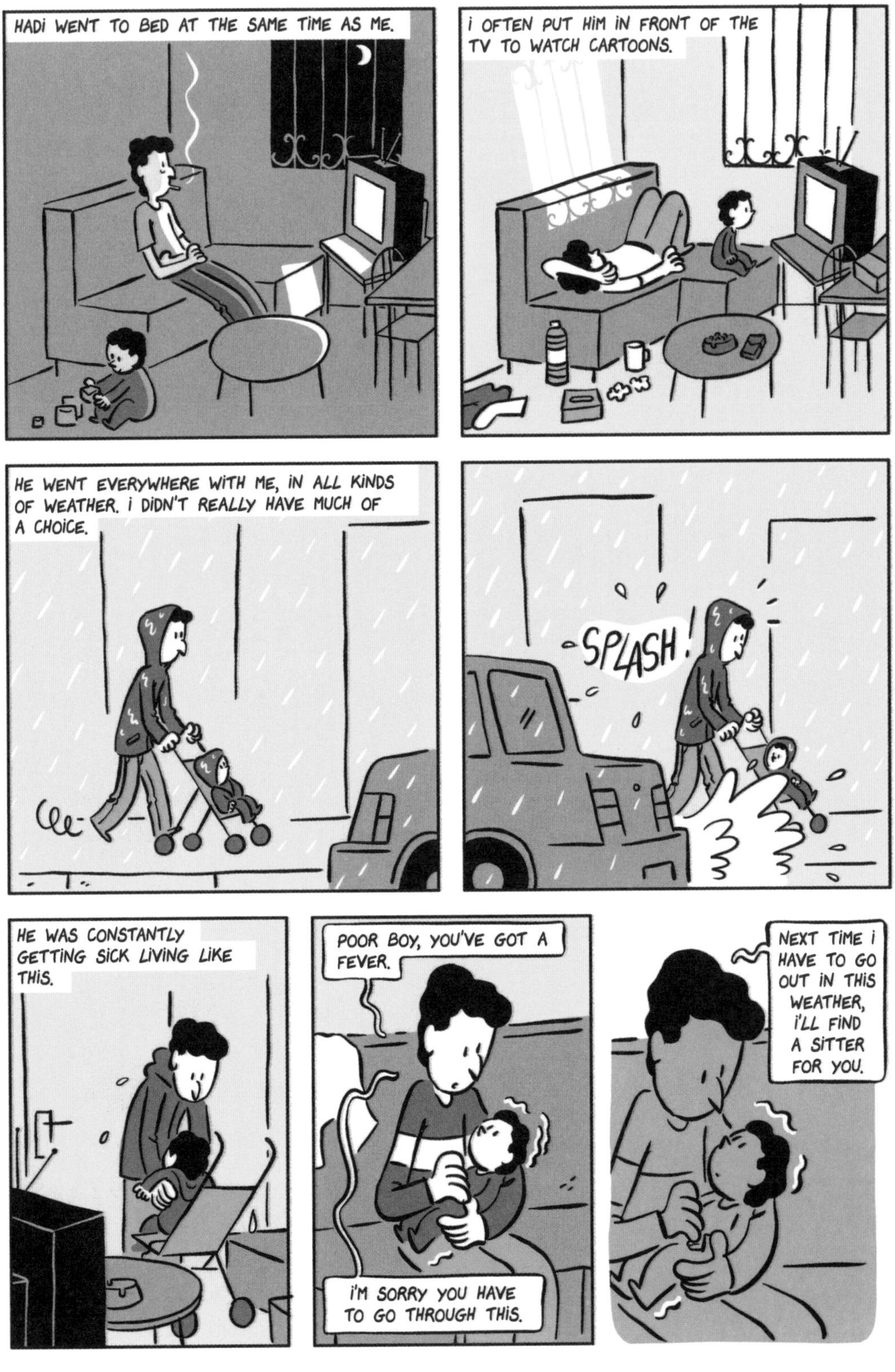
HADi WENT TO BED AT THE SAME TiME AS ME.
i OFTEN PUT HiM iN FRONT OF THE TV TO WATCH CARTOONS.
HE WENT EVERYWHERE WiTH ME, iN ALL KiNDS OF WEATHER. i DiDN'T REALLY HAVE MUCH OF A CHOiCE.
SPLASH!
HE WAS CONSTANTLY GETTiNG SiCK LiViNG LiKE THiS.
POOR BOY, YOU'VE GOT A FEVER.
i'M SORRY YOU HAVE TO GO THROUGH THiS.
NEXT TiME i HAVE TO GO OUT iN THiS WEATHER, i'LL FiND A SiTTER FOR YOU.

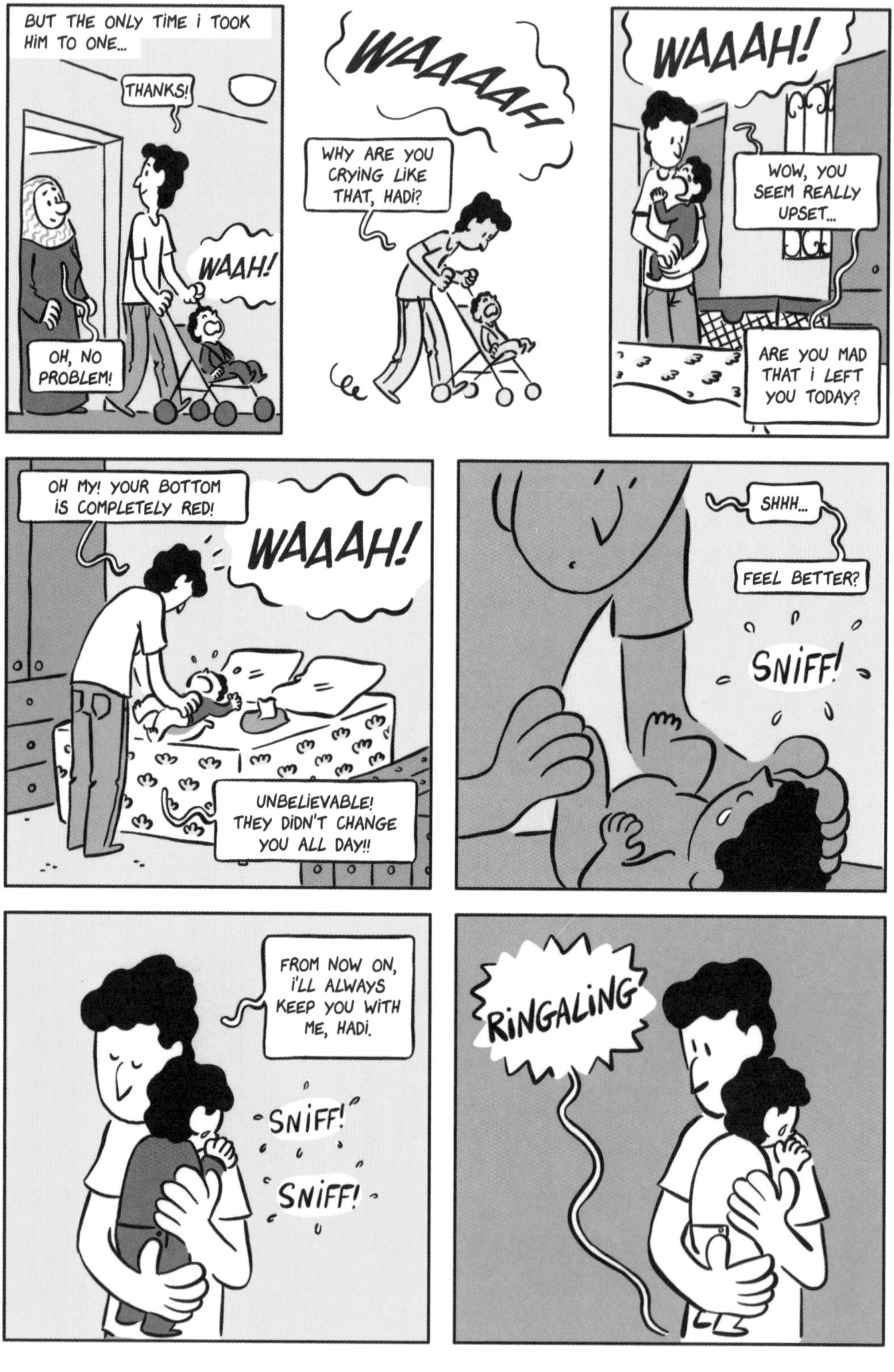
BUT THE ONLY TIME I TOOK HIM TO ONE...
THANKS!
WAAH!
OH, NO PROBLEM!
WAAAAAH
WHY ARE YOU CRYING LIKE THAT, HADI?
WAAAH!
WOW, YOU SEEM REALLY UPSET...
ARE YOU MAD THAT I LEFT YOU TODAY?
OH MY! YOUR BOTTOM IS COMPLETELY RED!
WAAAH!
UNBELIEVABLE! THEY DIDN'T CHANGE YOU ALL DAY!!
SHHH...
FEEL BETTER?
SNIFF!
FROM NOW ON, I'LL ALWAYS KEEP YOU WITH ME, HADI.
SNIFF!
SNIFF!
RINGALING

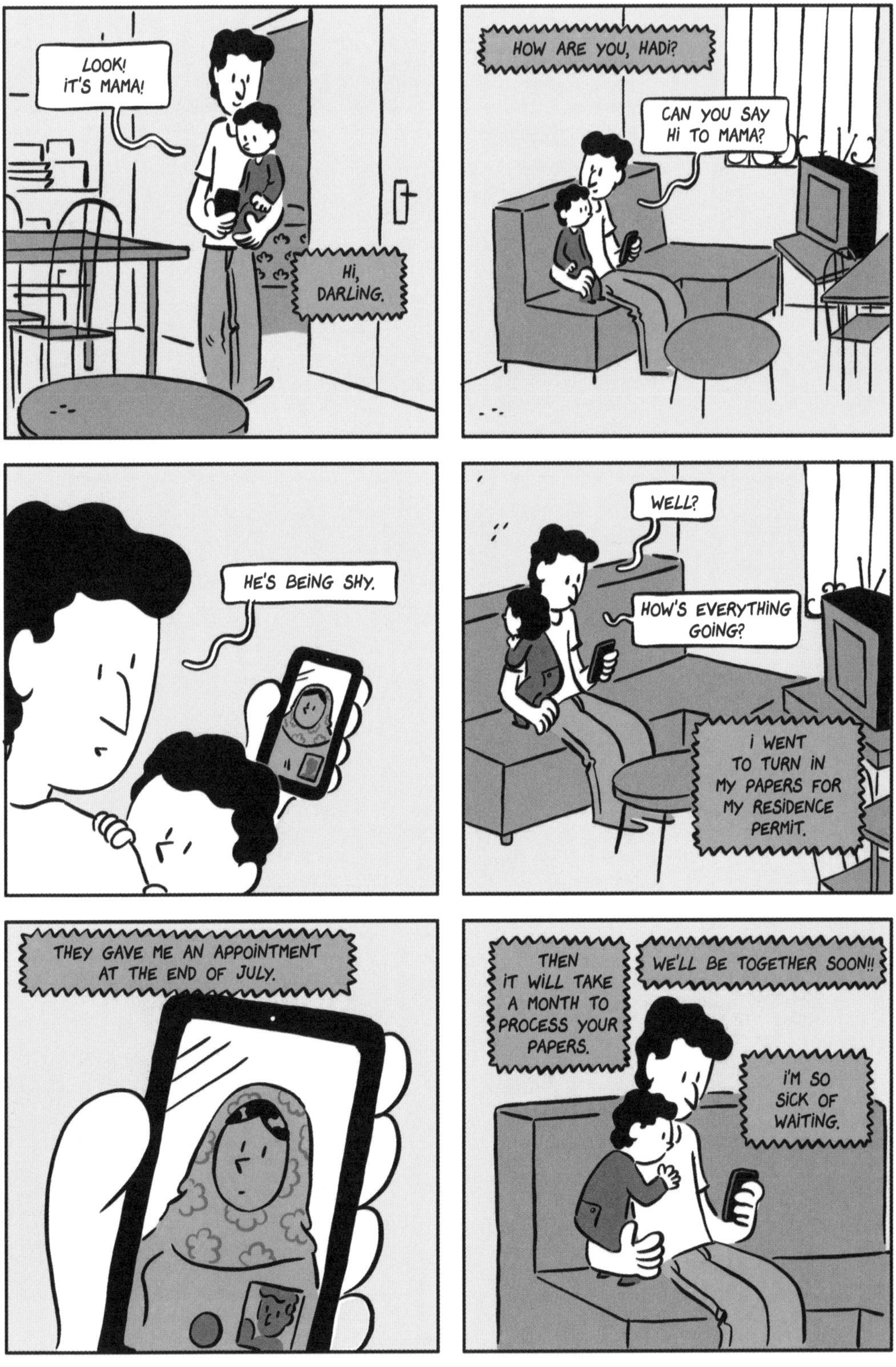
LOOK! iT'S MAMA!
Hi, DARLING.
HOW ARE YOU, HADi?
CAN YOU SAY Hi TO MAMA?
HE'S BEiNG SHY.
WELL?
HOW'S EVERYTHiNG GOiNG?
i WENT TO TURN iN MY PAPERS FOR MY RESiDENCE PERMiT.
THEY GAVE ME AN APPOiNTMENT AT THE END OF JULY.
THEN iT WiLL TAKE A MONTH TO PROCESS YOUR PAPERS.
WE'LL BE TOGETHER SOON!!
i'M SO SiCK OF WAiTiNG.

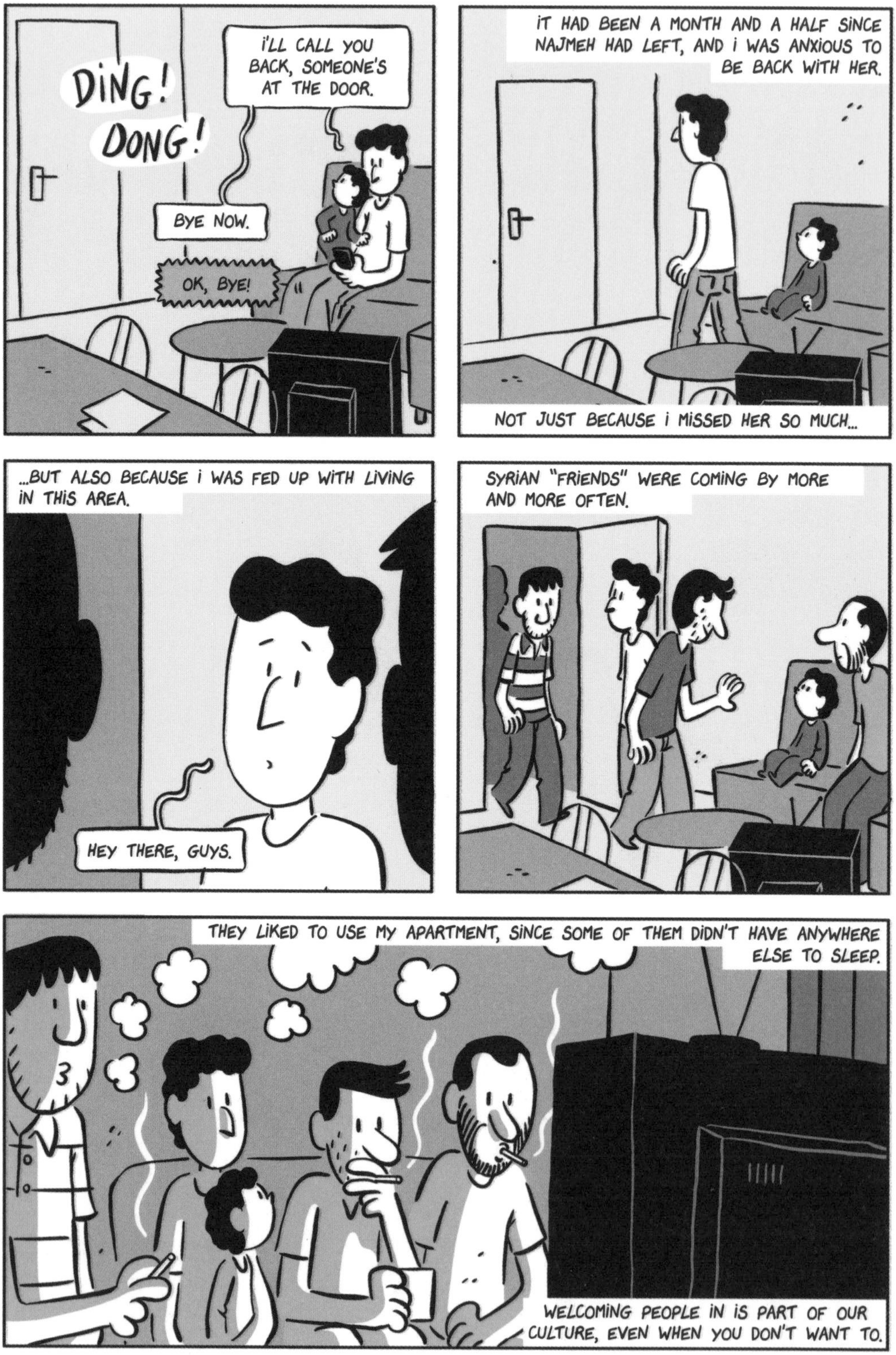
DING! DONG!
I'LL CALL YOU BACK, SOMEONE'S AT THE DOOR.
BYE NOW.
OK, BYE!
IT HAD BEEN A MONTH AND A HALF SINCE NAJMEH HAD LEFT, AND I WAS ANXIOUS TO BE BACK WITH HER.
NOT JUST BECAUSE I MISSED HER SO MUCH...
...BUT ALSO BECAUSE I WAS FED UP WITH LIVING IN THIS AREA.
HEY THERE, GUYS.
SYRIAN "FRIENDS" WERE COMING BY MORE AND MORE OFTEN.
THEY LIKED TO USE MY APARTMENT, SINCE SOME OF THEM DIDN'T HAVE ANYWHERE ELSE TO SLEEP.
WELCOMING PEOPLE IN IS PART OF OUR CULTURE, EVEN WHEN YOU DON'T WANT TO.

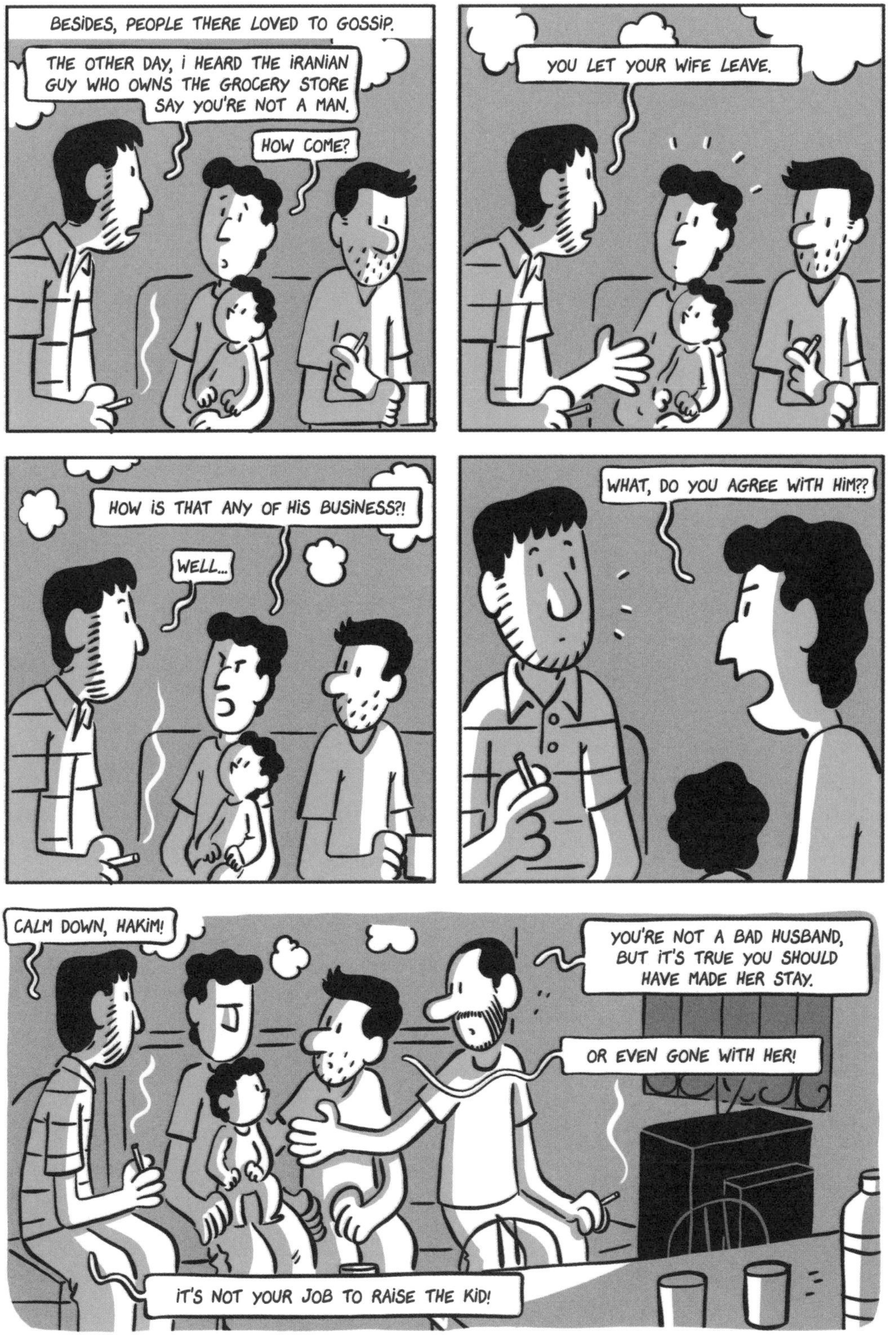
BESIDES, PEOPLE THERE LOVED TO GOSSIP.
THE OTHER DAY, I HEARD THE IRANIAN GUY WHO OWNS THE GROCERY STORE SAY YOU'RE NOT A MAN.
HOW COME?
YOU LET YOUR WIFE LEAVE.
HOW IS THAT ANY OF HIS BUSINESS?!
WELL...
WHAT, DO YOU AGREE WITH HIM??
CALM DOWN, HAKIM!
YOU'RE NOT A BAD HUSBAND, BUT IT'S TRUE YOU SHOULD HAVE MADE HER STAY.
OR EVEN GONE WITH HER!
IT'S NOT YOUR JOB TO RAISE THE KID!

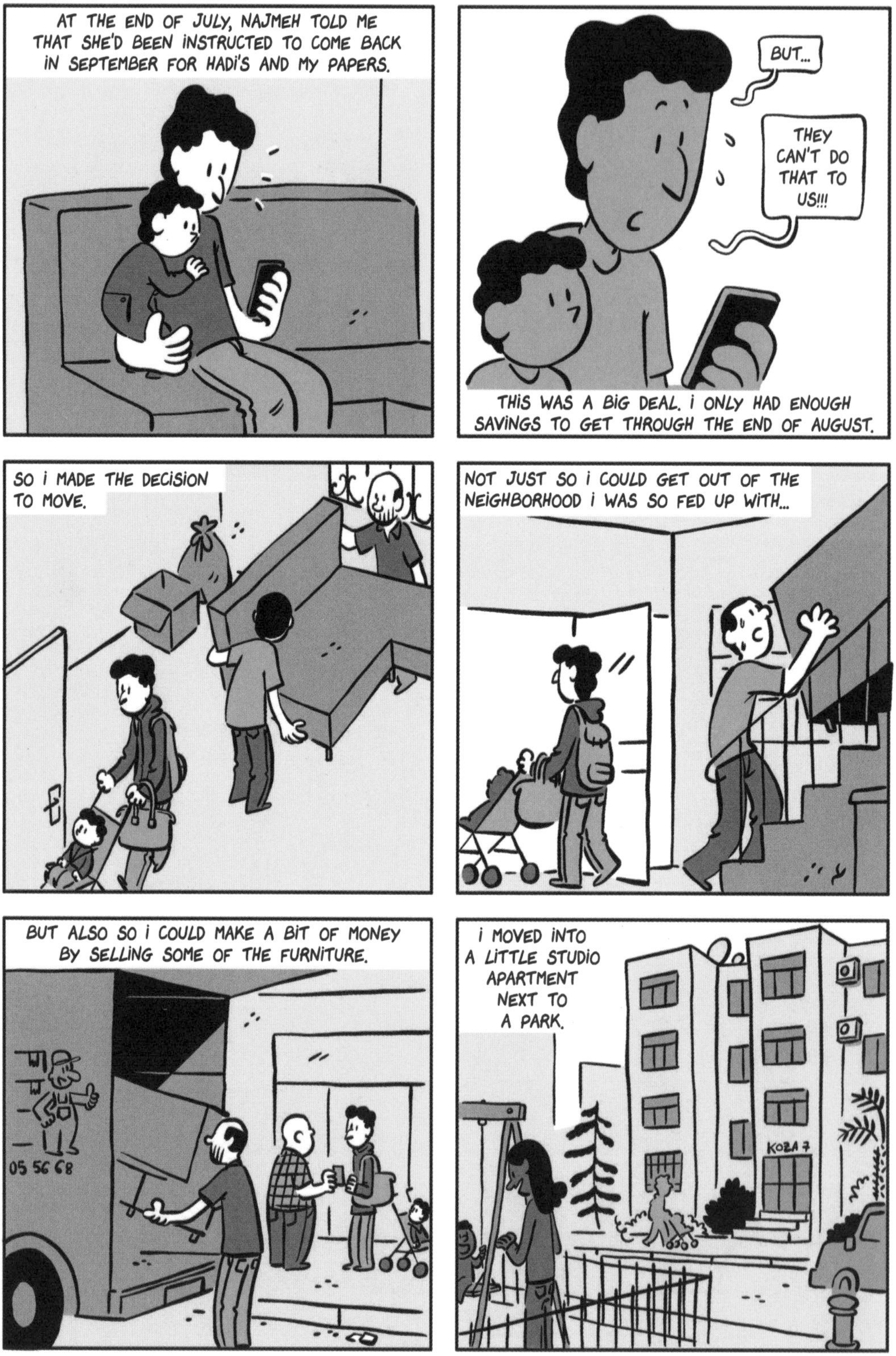
AT THE END OF JULY, NAJMEH TOLD ME THAT SHE'D BEEN INSTRUCTED TO COME BACK IN SEPTEMBER FOR HADI'S AND MY PAPERS.
BUT...
THEY CAN'T DO THAT TO US!!!
THIS WAS A BIG DEAL. I ONLY HAD ENOUGH SAVINGS TO GET THROUGH THE END OF AUGUST.
SO I MADE THE DECISION TO MOVE.
NOT JUST SO I COULD GET OUT OF THE NEIGHBORHOOD I WAS SO FED UP WITH...
BUT ALSO SO I COULD MAKE A BIT OF MONEY BY SELLING SOME OF THE FURNITURE.
05 56 68
I MOVED INTO A LITTLE STUDIO APARTMENT NEXT TO A PARK.
KOZA 7

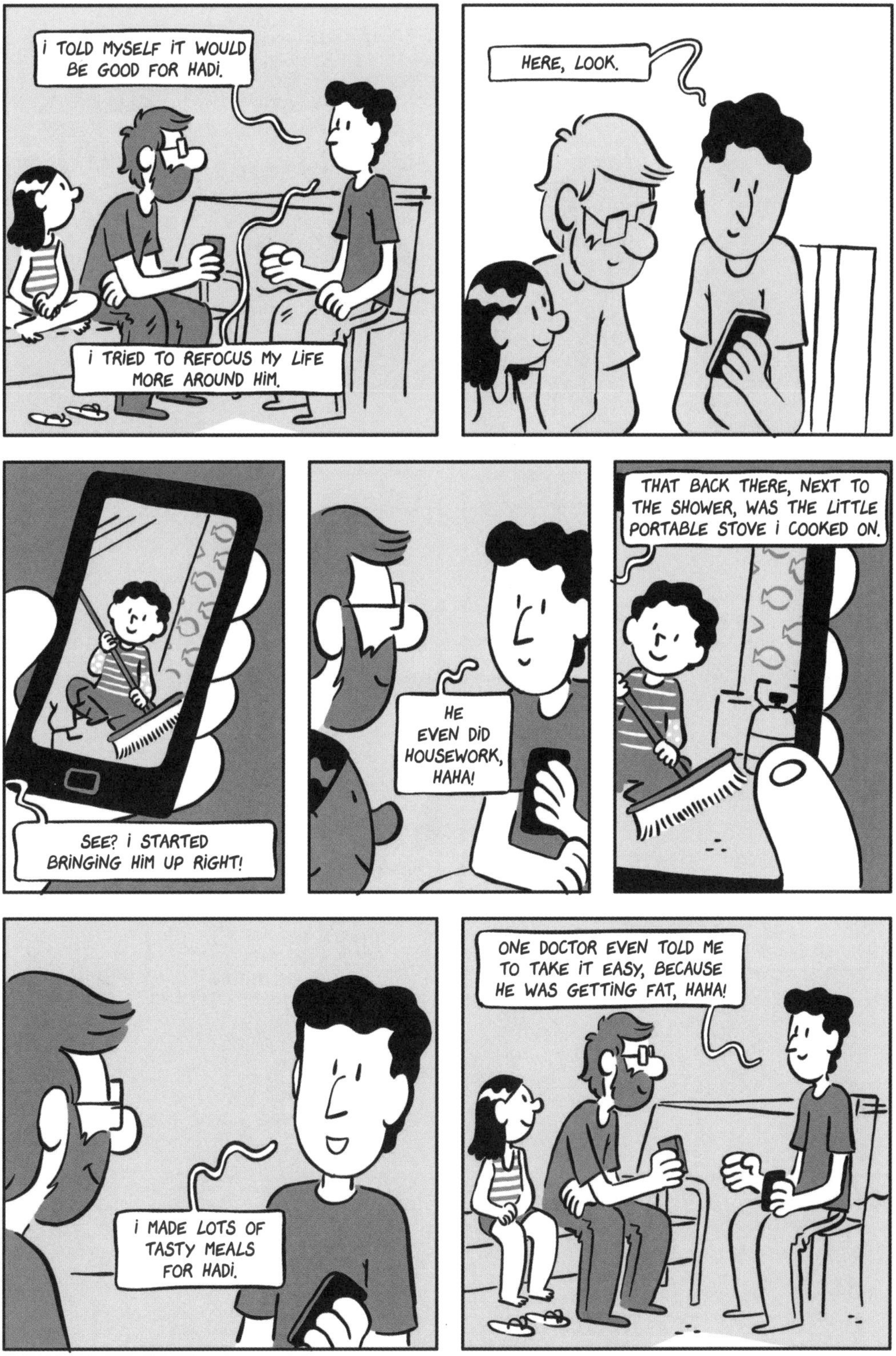
I TOLD MYSELF IT WOULD BE GOOD FOR HADI.
I TRIED TO REFOCUS MY LIFE MORE AROUND HIM.
HERE, LOOK.
SEE? I STARTED BRINGING HIM UP RIGHT!
HE EVEN DID HOUSEWORK, HAHA!
THAT BACK THERE, NEXT TO THE SHOWER, WAS THE LITTLE PORTABLE STOVE I COOKED ON.
I MADE LOTS OF TASTY MEALS FOR HADI.
ONE DOCTOR EVEN TOLD ME TO TAKE IT EASY, BECAUSE HE WAS GETTING FAT, HAHA!

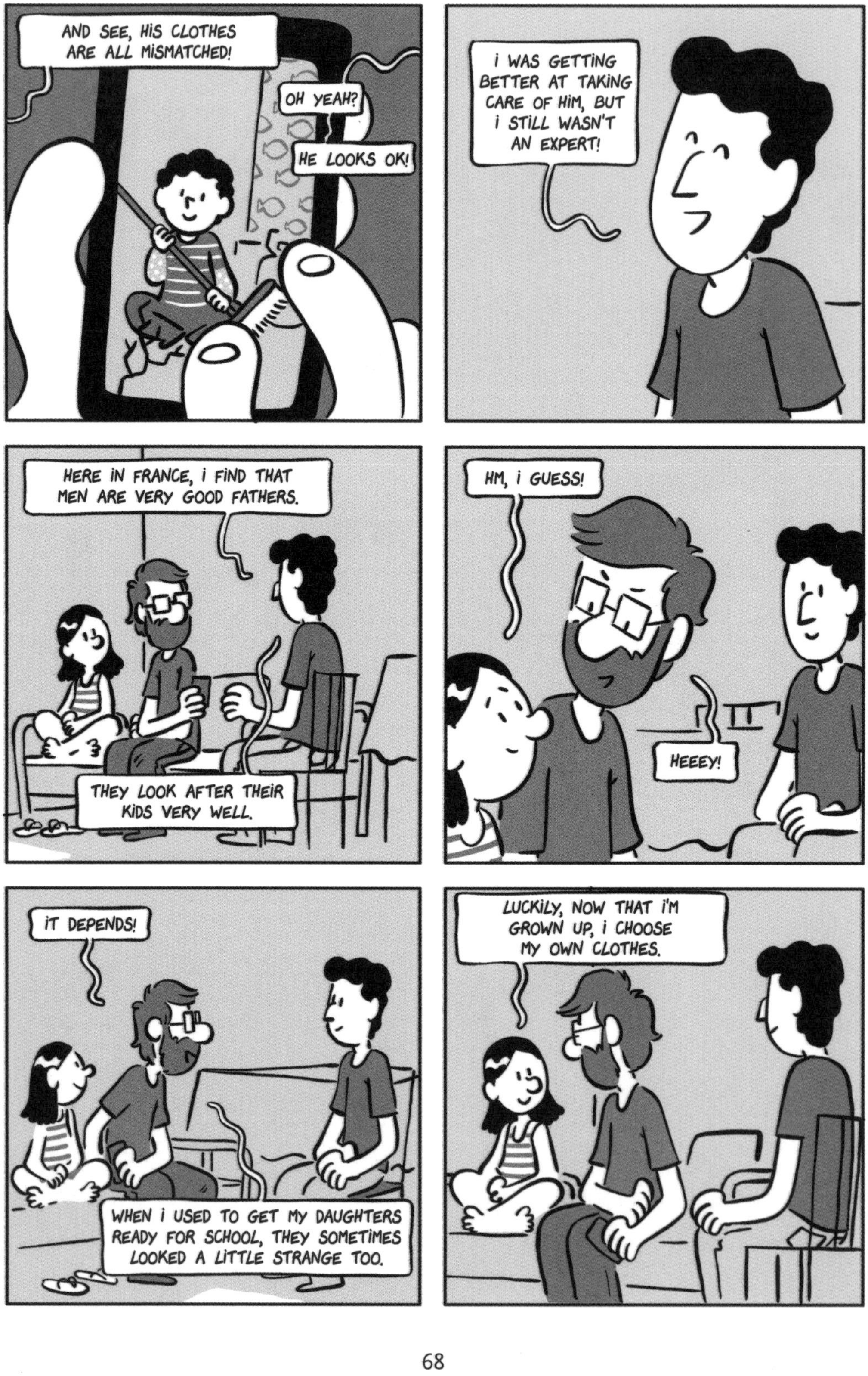
AND SEE, HIS CLOTHES ARE ALL MISMATCHED!
OH YEAH?
HE LOOKS OK!
I WAS GETTING BETTER AT TAKING CARE OF HIM, BUT I STILL WASN'T AN EXPERT!
HERE IN FRANCE, I FIND THAT MEN ARE VERY GOOD FATHERS.
THEY LOOK AFTER THEIR KIDS VERY WELL.
HM, I GUESS!
HEEEY!
IT DEPENDS!
WHEN I USED TO GET MY DAUGHTERS READY FOR SCHOOL, THEY SOMETIMES LOOKED A LITTLE STRANGE TOO.
LUCKILY, NOW THAT I'M GROWN UP, I CHOOSE MY OWN CLOTHES.

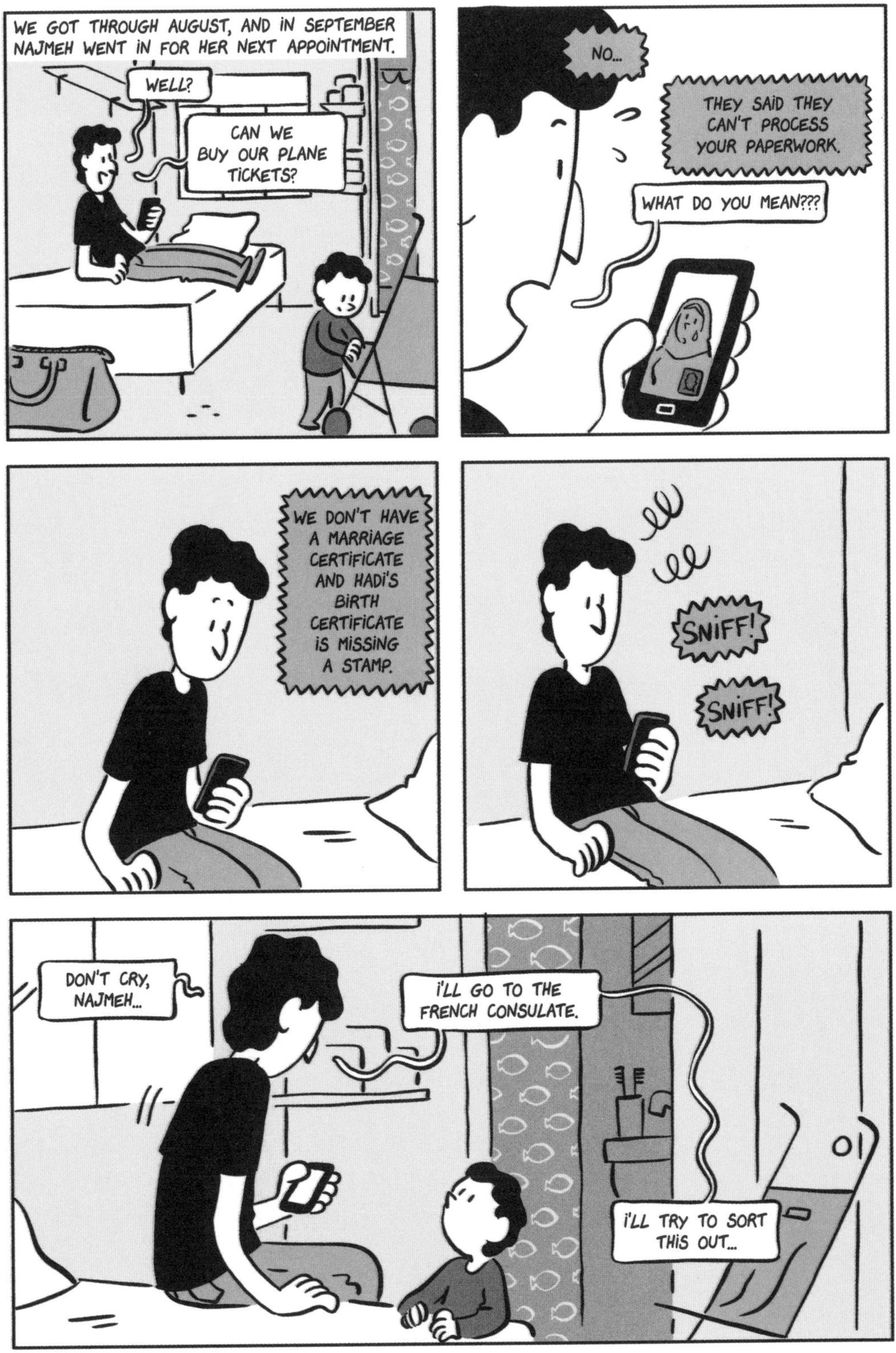
WE GOT THROUGH AUGUST, AND IN SEPTEMBER NAJMEH WENT IN FOR HER NEXT APPOINTMENT.
WELL?
CAN WE BUY OUR PLANE TICKETS?
NO...
THEY SAID THEY CAN'T PROCESS YOUR PAPERWORK.
WHAT DO YOU MEAN???
WE DON'T HAVE A MARRIAGE CERTIFICATE AND HADI'S BIRTH CERTIFICATE IS MISSING A STAMP.
SNIFF!
SNIFF!
DON'T CRY, NAJMEH...
I'LL GO TO THE FRENCH CONSULATE.
I'LL TRY TO SORT THIS OUT...

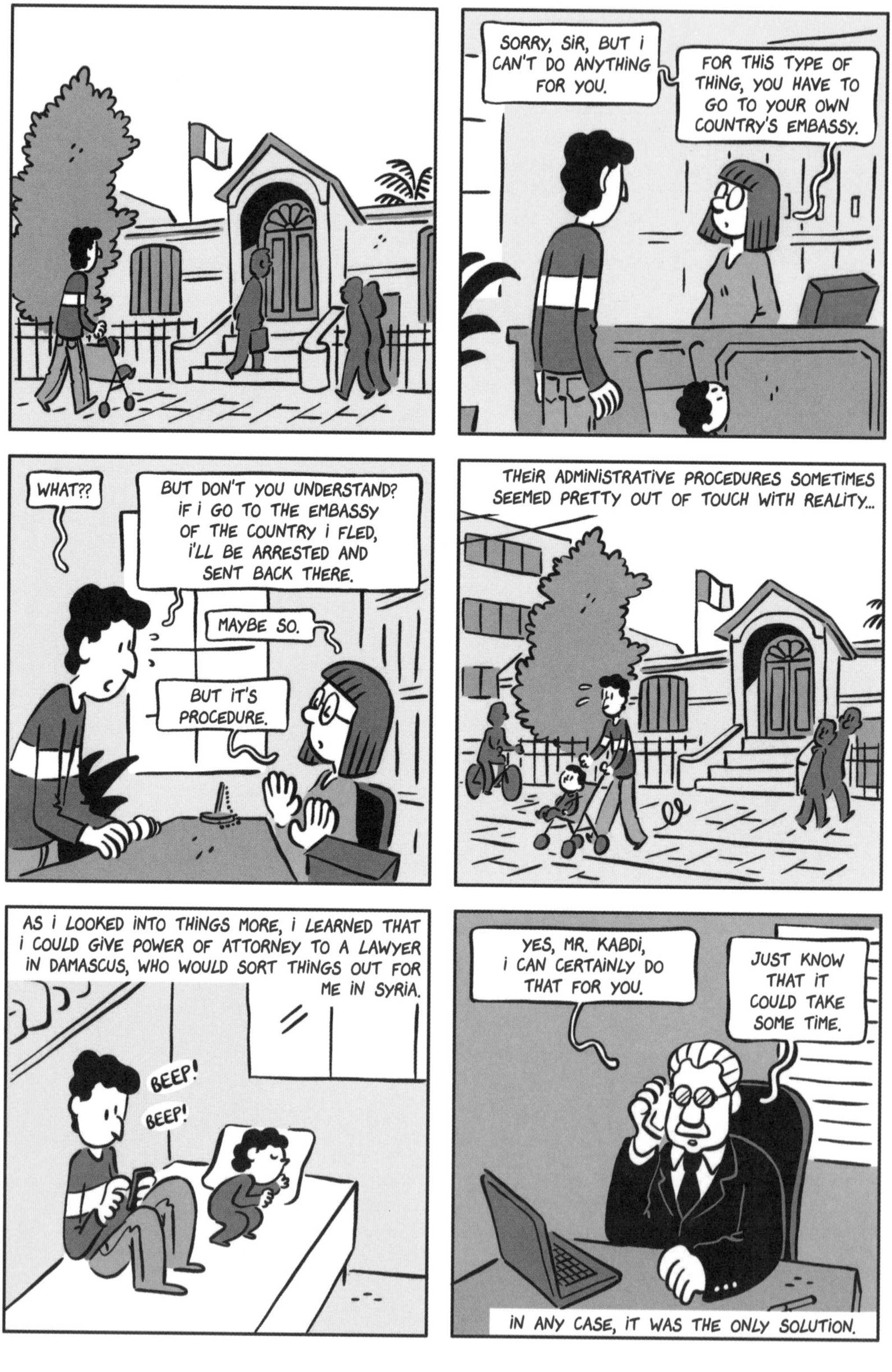
SORRY, SIR, BUT I CAN'T DO ANYTHING FOR YOU.
FOR THIS TYPE OF THING, YOU HAVE TO GO TO YOUR OWN COUNTRY'S EMBASSY.
WHAT??
BUT DON'T YOU UNDERSTAND? IF I GO TO THE EMBASSY OF THE COUNTRY I FLED, I'LL BE ARRESTED AND SENT BACK THERE.
MAYBE SO.
BUT IT'S PROCEDURE.
THEIR ADMINISTRATIVE PROCEDURES SOMETIMES SEEMED PRETTY OUT OF TOUCH WITH REALITY...
AS I LOOKED INTO THINGS MORE, I LEARNED THAT I COULD GIVE POWER OF ATTORNEY TO A LAWYER IN DAMASCUS, WHO WOULD SORT THINGS OUT FOR ME IN SYRIA.
BEEP!
BEEP!
YES, MR. KABDI, I CAN CERTAINLY DO THAT FOR YOU.
JUST KNOW THAT IT COULD TAKE SOME TIME.
IN ANY CASE, IT WAS THE ONLY SOLUTION.

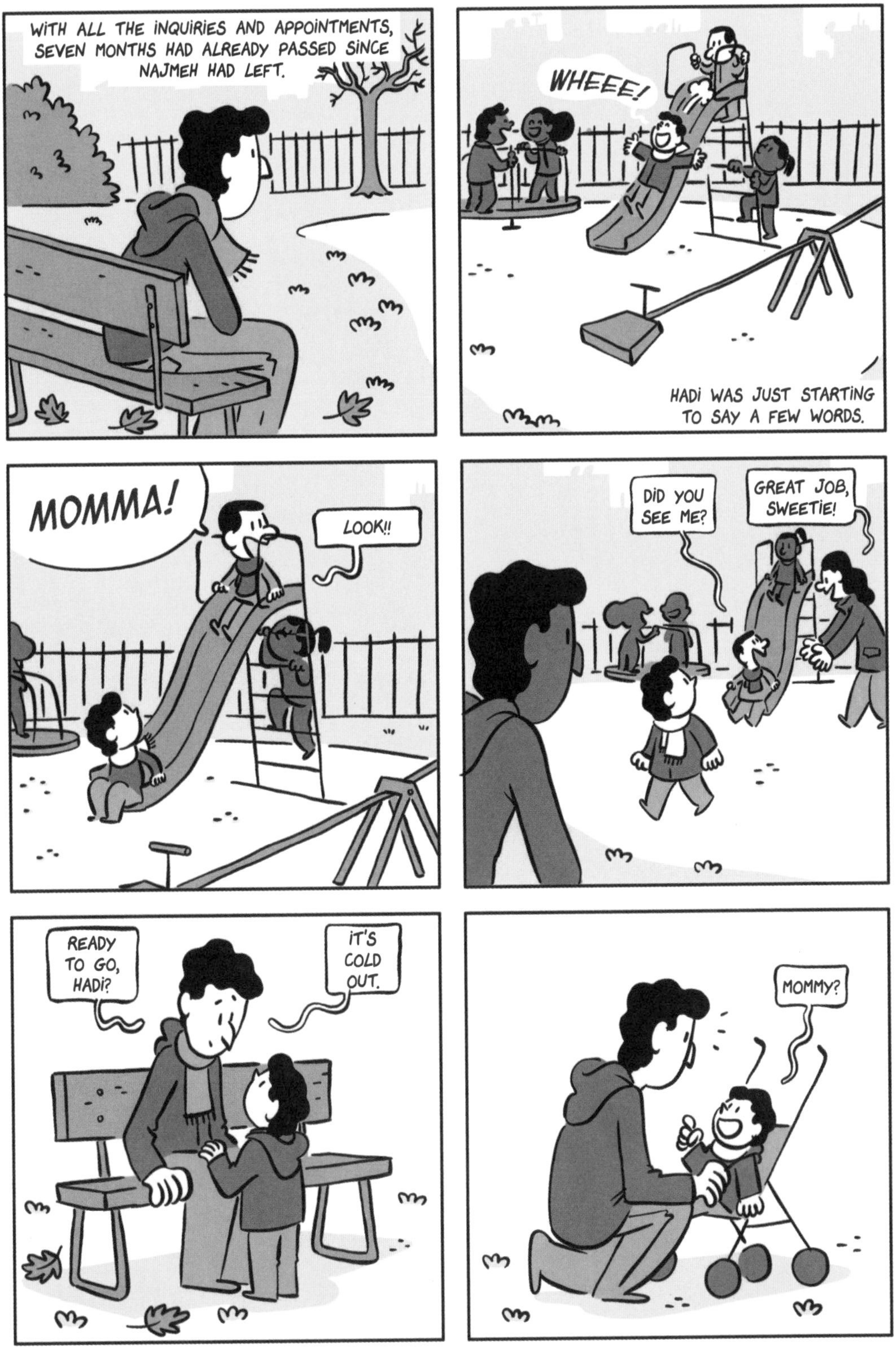
WITH ALL THE INQUIRIES AND APPOINTMENTS, SEVEN MONTHS HAD ALREADY PASSED SINCE NAJMEH HAD LEFT.
WHEEE!
HADI WAS JUST STARTING TO SAY A FEW WORDS.
MOMMA!
LOOK!!
DID YOU SEE ME?
GREAT JOB, SWEETIE!
READY TO GO, HADI?
IT'S COLD OUT.
MOMMY?

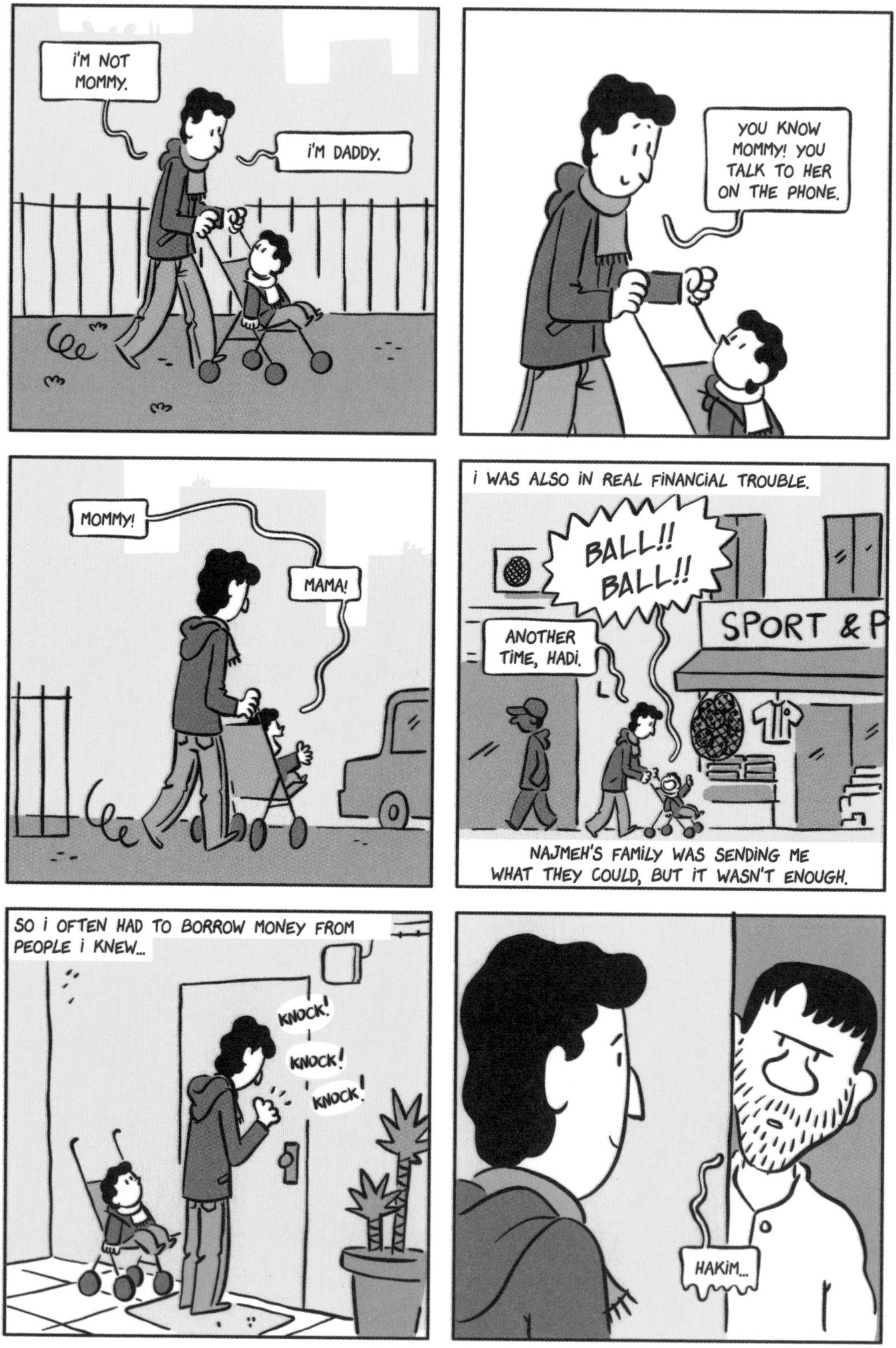
I'M NOT MOMMY.
I'M DADDY.
YOU KNOW MOMMY! YOU TALK TO HER ON THE PHONE.
MOMMY!
MAMA!
I WAS ALSO IN REAL FINANCIAL TROUBLE.
BALL!! BALL!!
ANOTHER TIME, HADI.
SPORT & P
NAJMEH'S FAMILY WAS SENDING ME WHAT THEY COULD, BUT IT WASN'T ENOUGH.
SO I OFTEN HAD TO BORROW MONEY FROM PEOPLE I KNEW...
KNOCK!
KNOCK!
KNOCK!
HAKIM...

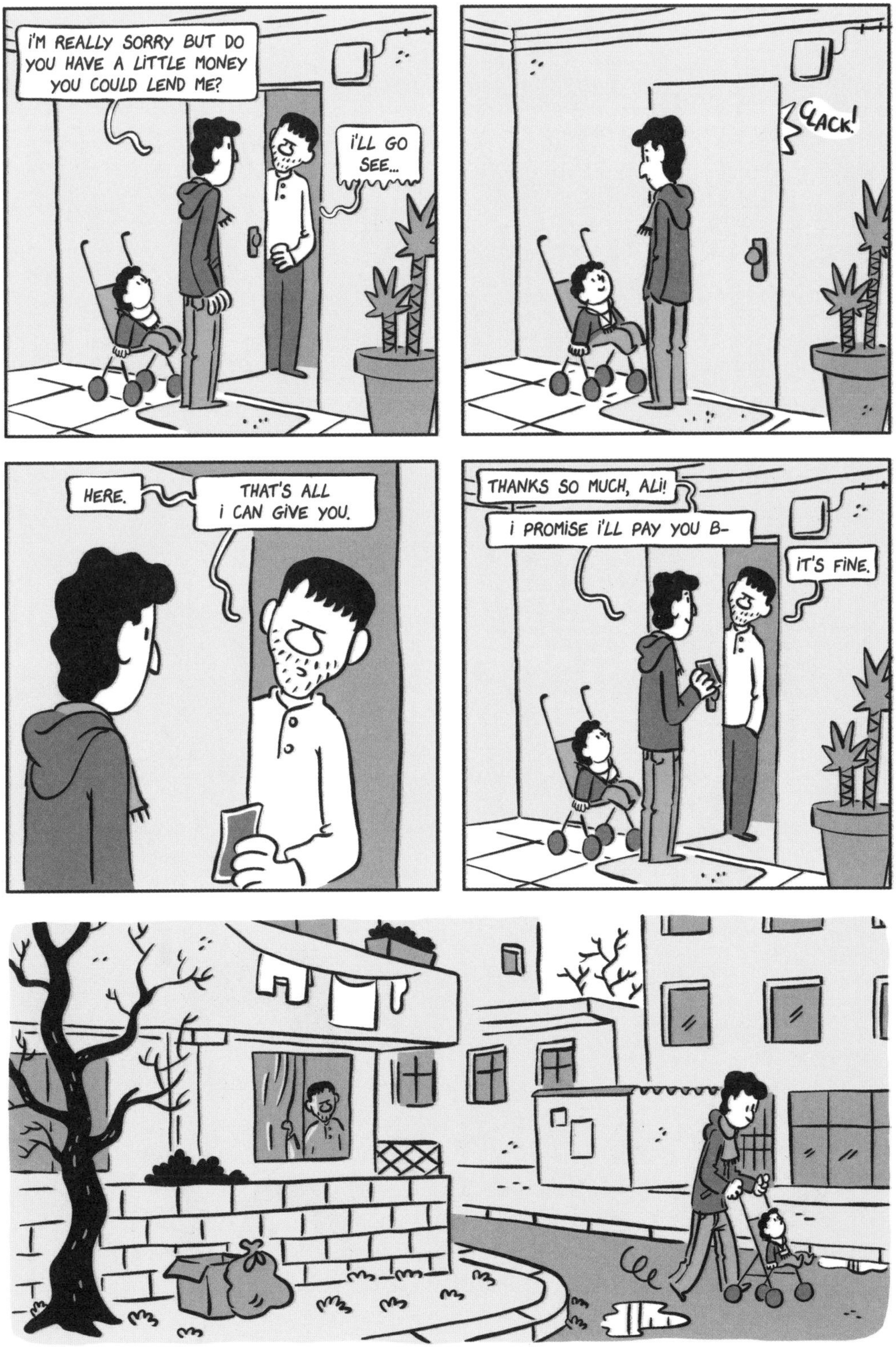
I'M REALLY SORRY BUT DO YOU HAVE A LITTLE MONEY YOU COULD LEND ME?
I'LL GO SEE...
CLACK!
HERE.
THAT'S ALL I CAN GIVE YOU.
THANKS SO MUCH, ALI!
I PROMISE I'LL PAY YOU B-
IT'S FINE.

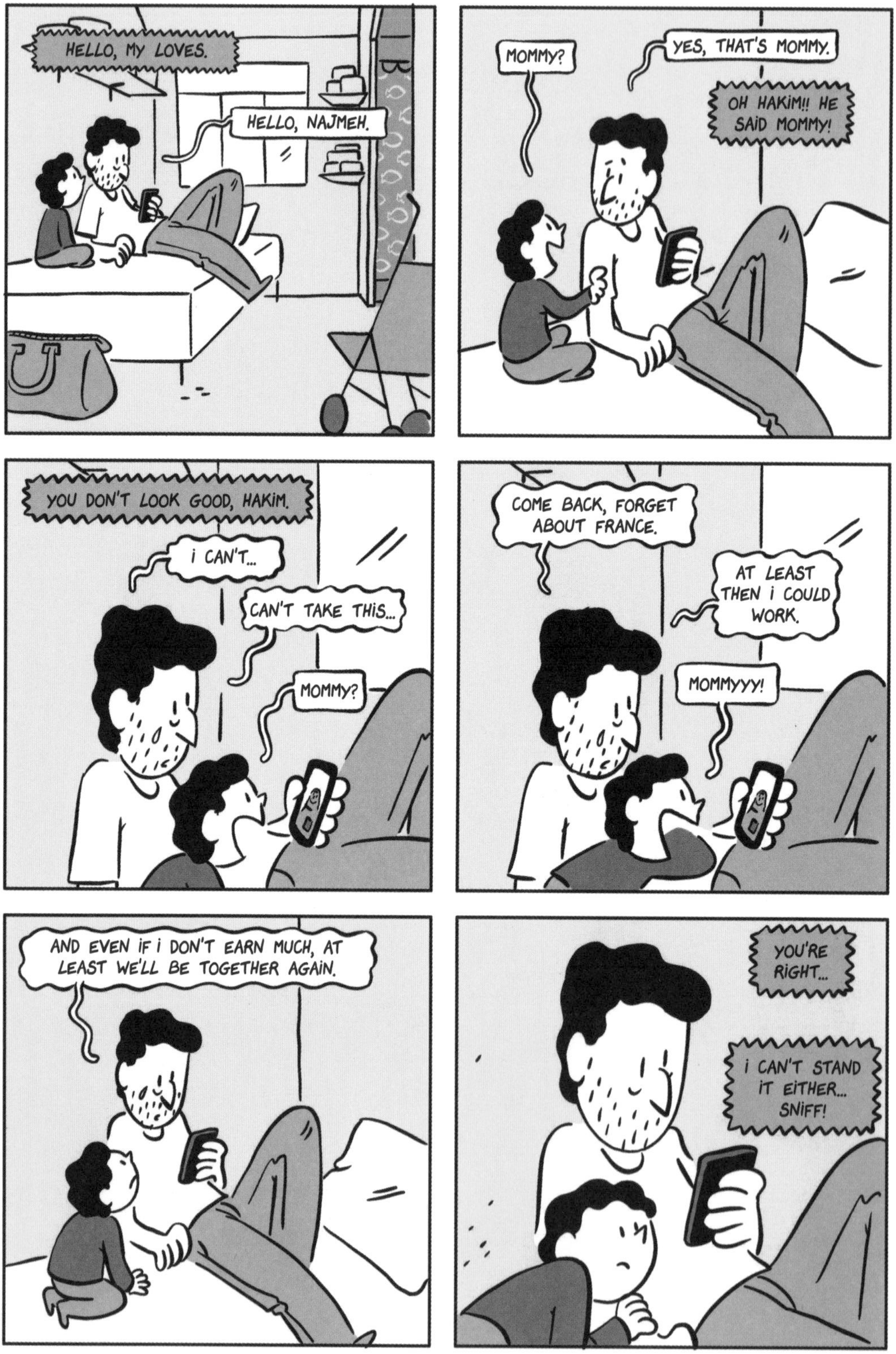
HELLO, MY LOVES.
HELLO, NAJMEH.
MOMMY?
YES, THAT'S MOMMY.
OH HAKIM!! HE SAID MOMMY!
YOU DON'T LOOK GOOD, HAKIM.
I CAN'T...
CAN'T TAKE THIS...
MOMMY?
COME BACK, FORGET ABOUT FRANCE.
AT LEAST THEN I COULD WORK.
MOMMYYY!
AND EVEN IF I DON'T EARN MUCH, AT LEAST WE'LL BE TOGETHER AGAIN.
YOU'RE RIGHT...
I CAN'T STAND IT EITHER... SNIFF!

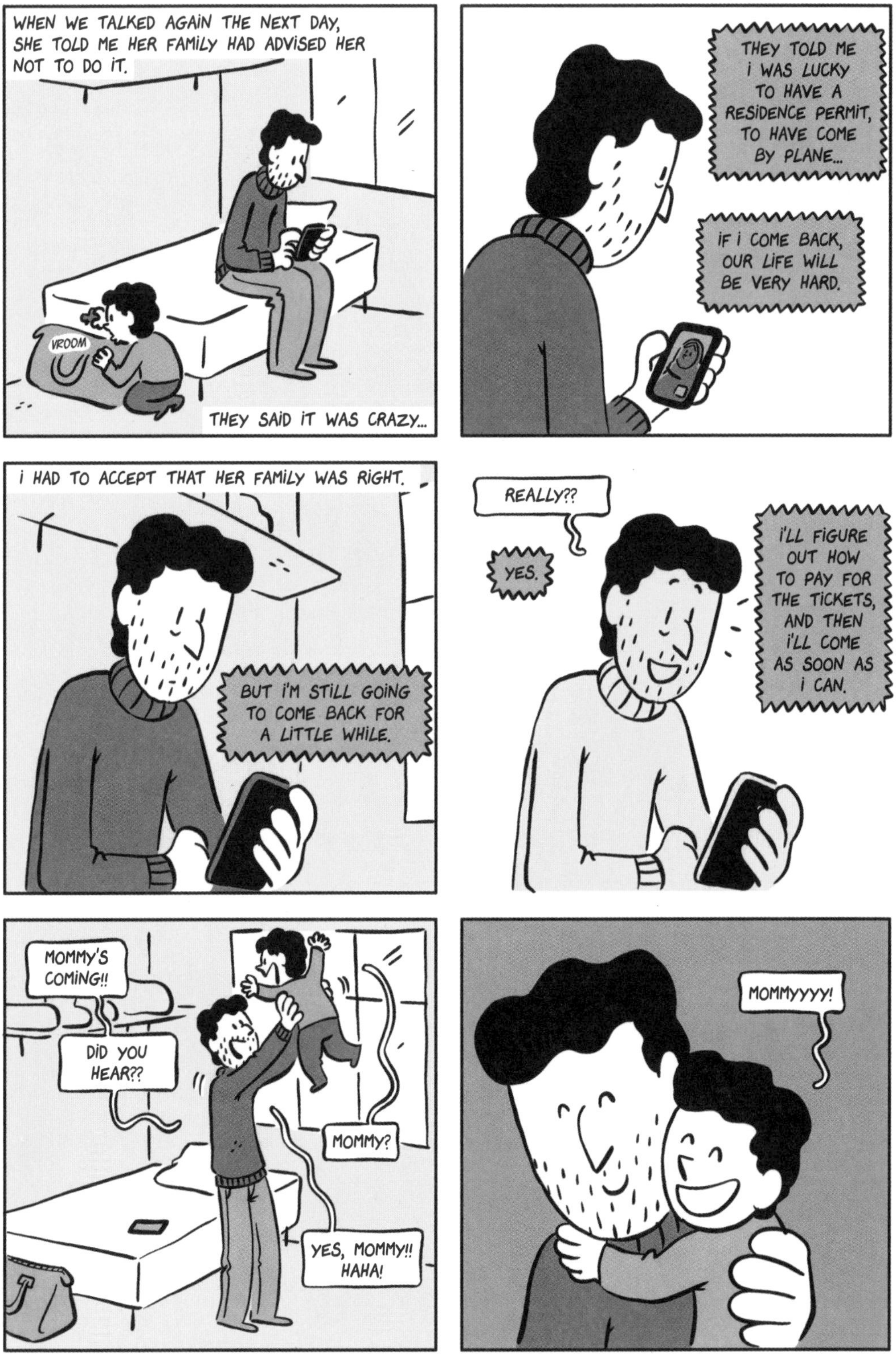

WHEN WE TALKED AGAIN THE NEXT DAY, SHE TOLD ME HER FAMILY HAD ADVISED HER NOT TO DO IT.
VROOM
THEY SAID IT WAS CRAZY...
THEY TOLD ME I WAS LUCKY TO HAVE A RESIDENCE PERMIT, TO HAVE COME BY PLANE...
IF I COME BACK, OUR LIFE WILL BE VERY HARD.
I HAD TO ACCEPT THAT HER FAMILY WAS RIGHT.
BUT I'M STILL GOING TO COME BACK FOR A LITTLE WHILE.
REALLY??
YES.
I'LL FIGURE OUT HOW TO PAY FOR THE TICKETS, AND THEN I'LL COME AS SOON AS I CAN.
MOMMY'S COMING!!
DID YOU HEAR??
MOMMY?
YES, MOMMY!! HAHA!
MOMMYYYY!

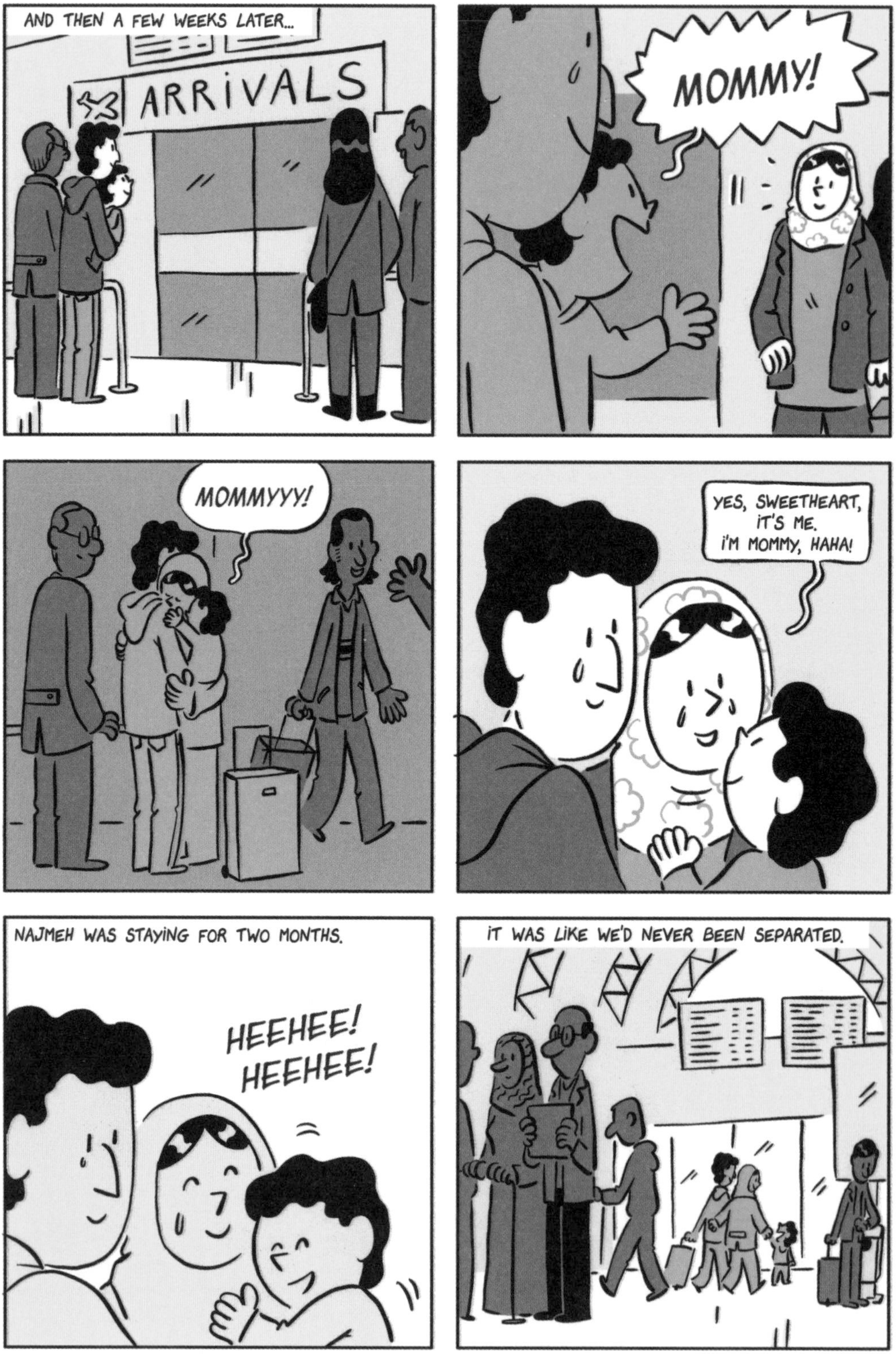
AND THEN A FEW WEEKS LATER...
ARRIVALS
MOMMY!
MOMMYYY!
YES, SWEETHEART, IT'S ME. I'M MOMMY, HAHA!
NAJMEH WAS STAYING FOR TWO MONTHS.
HEEHEE! HEEHEE!
IT WAS LIKE WE'D NEVER BEEN SEPARATED.

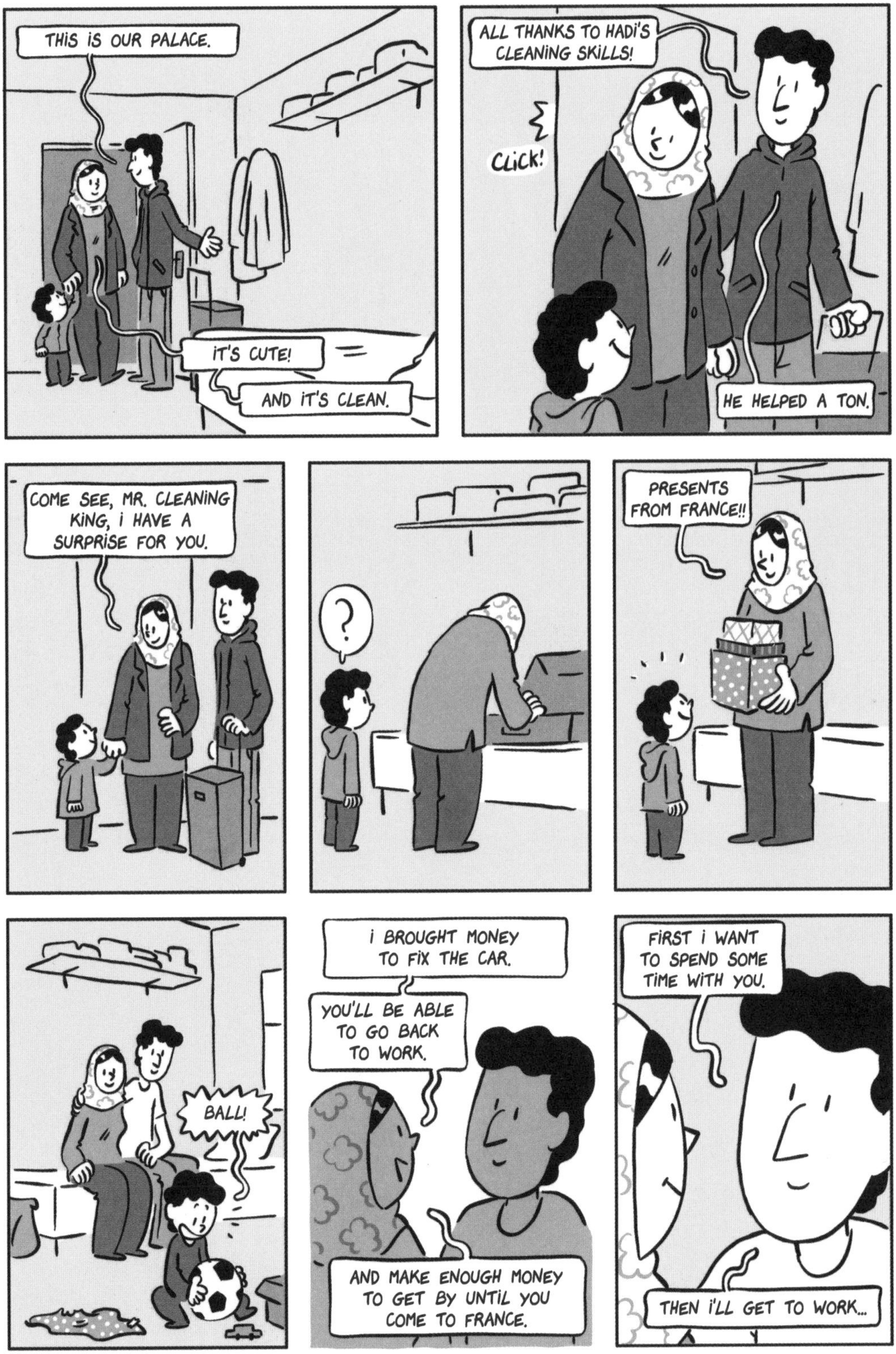
THIS IS OUR PALACE.
IT'S CUTE!
AND IT'S CLEAN.
ALL THANKS TO HADI'S CLEANING SKILLS!
CLICK!
HE HELPED A TON.
COME SEE, MR. CLEANING KING, I HAVE A SURPRISE FOR YOU.
?
PRESENTS FROM FRANCE!!
BALL!
I BROUGHT MONEY TO FIX THE CAR.
YOU'LL BE ABLE TO GO BACK TO WORK.
AND MAKE ENOUGH MONEY TO GET BY UNTIL YOU COME TO FRANCE.
FIRST I WANT TO SPEND SOME TIME WITH YOU.
THEN I'LL GET TO WORK...

KOZA 7

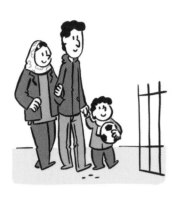

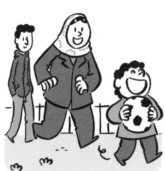

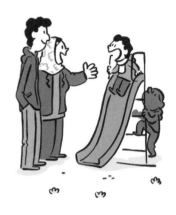

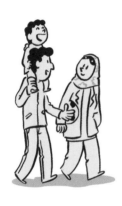

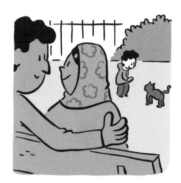

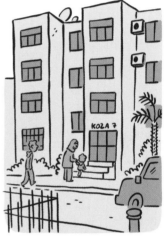

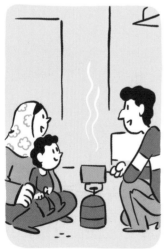

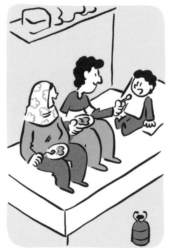

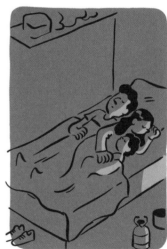

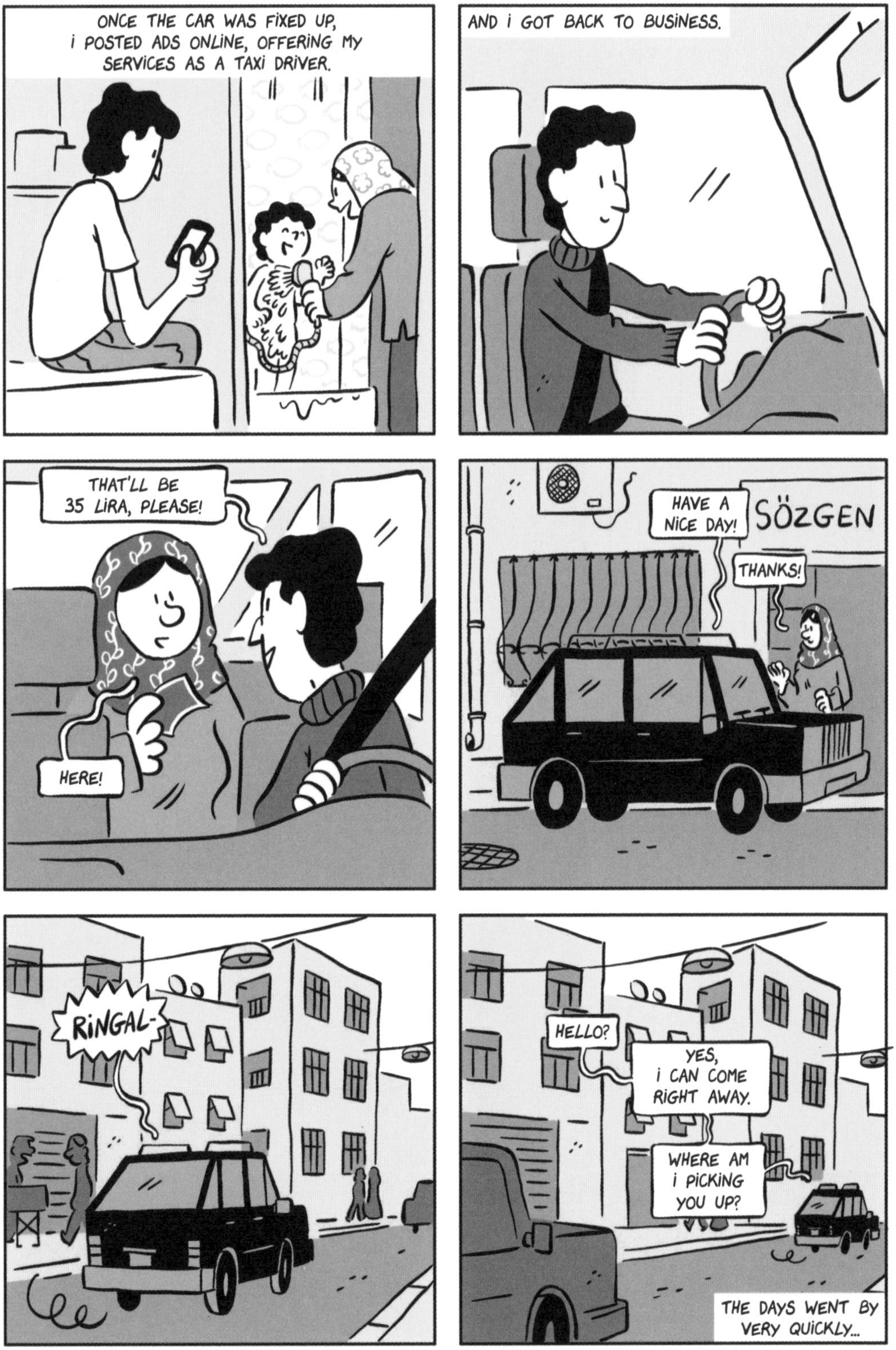

ONCE THE CAR WAS FIXED UP, I POSTED ADS ONLINE, OFFERING MY SERVICES AS A TAXI DRIVER.
AND I GOT BACK TO BUSINESS.
THAT'LL BE 35 LIRA, PLEASE!
HERE!
HAVE A NICE DAY!
SÖZGEN
THANKS!
RINGAL-
HELLO?
YES, I CAN COME RIGHT AWAY.
WHERE AM I PICKING YOU UP?
THE DAYS WENT BY VERY QUICKLY...

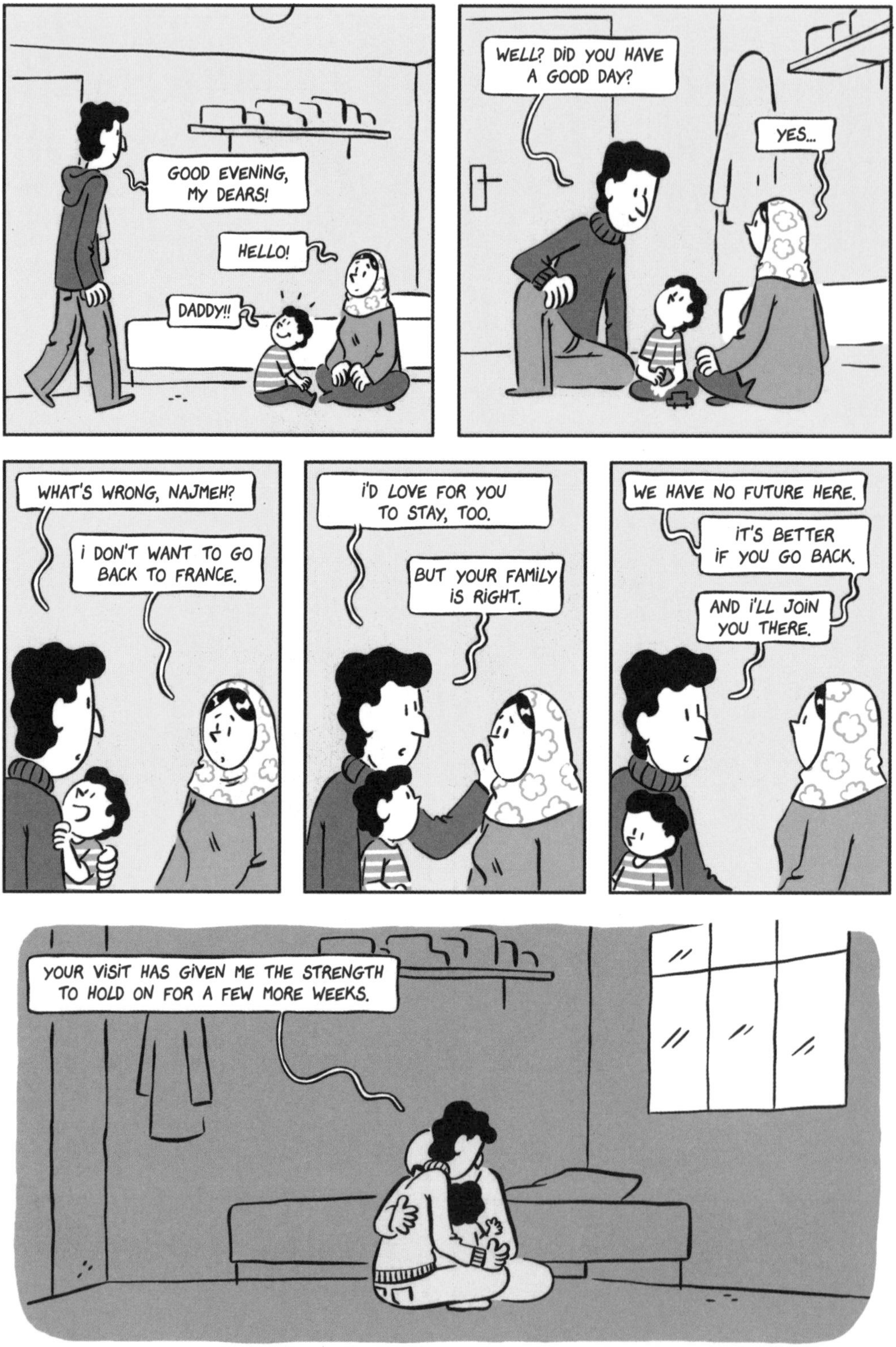
GOOD EVENING, MY DEARS!
HELLO!
DADDY!!
WELL? DID YOU HAVE A GOOD DAY?
YES...
WHAT'S WRONG, NAJMEH?
I DON'T WANT TO GO BACK TO FRANCE.
I'D LOVE FOR YOU TO STAY, TOO.
BUT YOUR FAMILY IS RIGHT.
WE HAVE NO FUTURE HERE.
IT'S BETTER IF YOU GO BACK.
AND I'LL JOIN YOU THERE.
YOUR VISIT HAS GIVEN ME THE STRENGTH TO HOLD ON FOR A FEW MORE WEEKS.

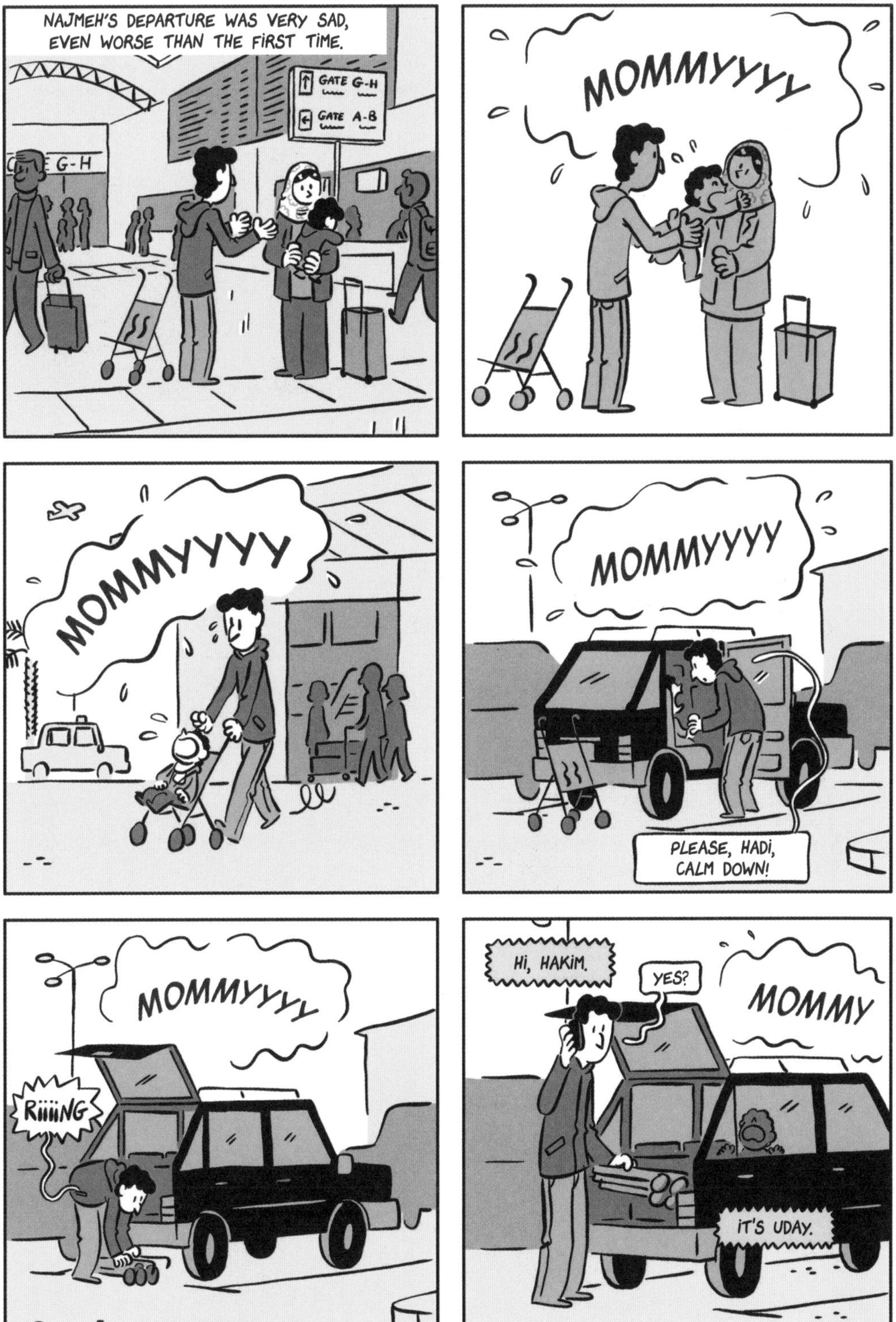
NAJMEH'S DEPARTURE WAS VERY SAD, EVEN WORSE THAN THE FIRST TIME.
GATE G-H
GATE A-B
G-H
MOMMYYYY
MOMMYYYY
MOMMYYYY
PLEASE, HADI, CALM DOWN!
MOMMYYYY
RiiiiNG
HI, HAKIM.
YES?
MOMMY
IT'S UDAY.

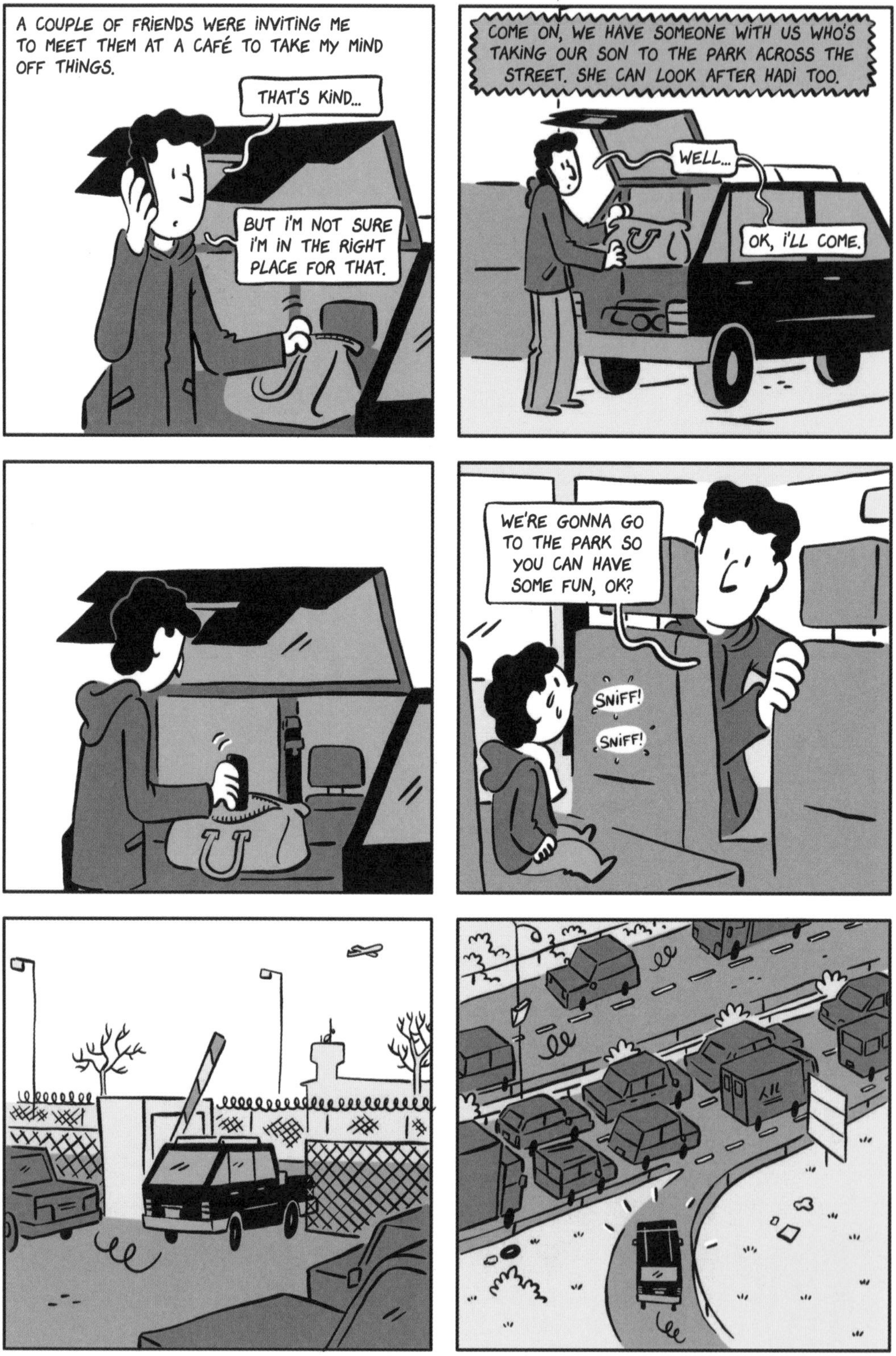
A COUPLE OF FRIENDS WERE INVITING ME TO MEET THEM AT A CAFÉ TO TAKE MY MIND OFF THINGS.
THAT'S KIND...
BUT I'M NOT SURE I'M IN THE RIGHT PLACE FOR THAT.
COME ON, WE HAVE SOMEONE WITH US WHO'S TAKING OUR SON TO THE PARK ACROSS THE STREET. SHE CAN LOOK AFTER HADI TOO.
WELL...
OK, I'LL COME.
WE'RE GONNA GO TO THE PARK SO YOU CAN HAVE SOME FUN, OK?
SNIFF!
SNIFF!

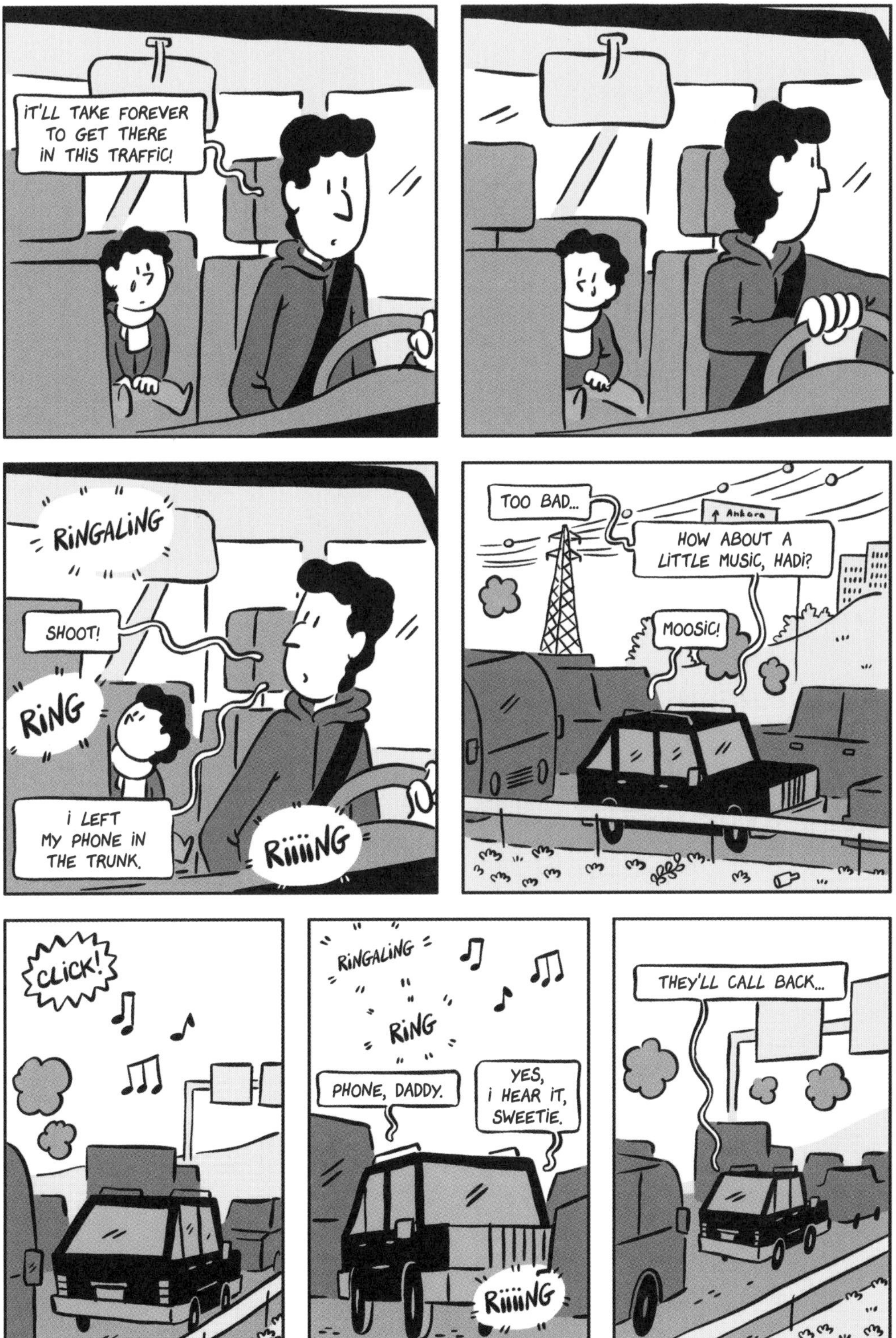
IT'LL TAKE FOREVER TO GET THERE IN THIS TRAFFIC!
RINGALING
SHOOT!
RING
I LEFT MY PHONE IN THE TRUNK.
RIIIING
TOO BAD...
HOW ABOUT A LITTLE MUSIC, HADI?
MOOSIC!
CLICK!
RINGALING
RING
PHONE, DADDY.
YES, I HEAR IT, SWEETIE.
RIIIING
THEY'LL CALL BACK...

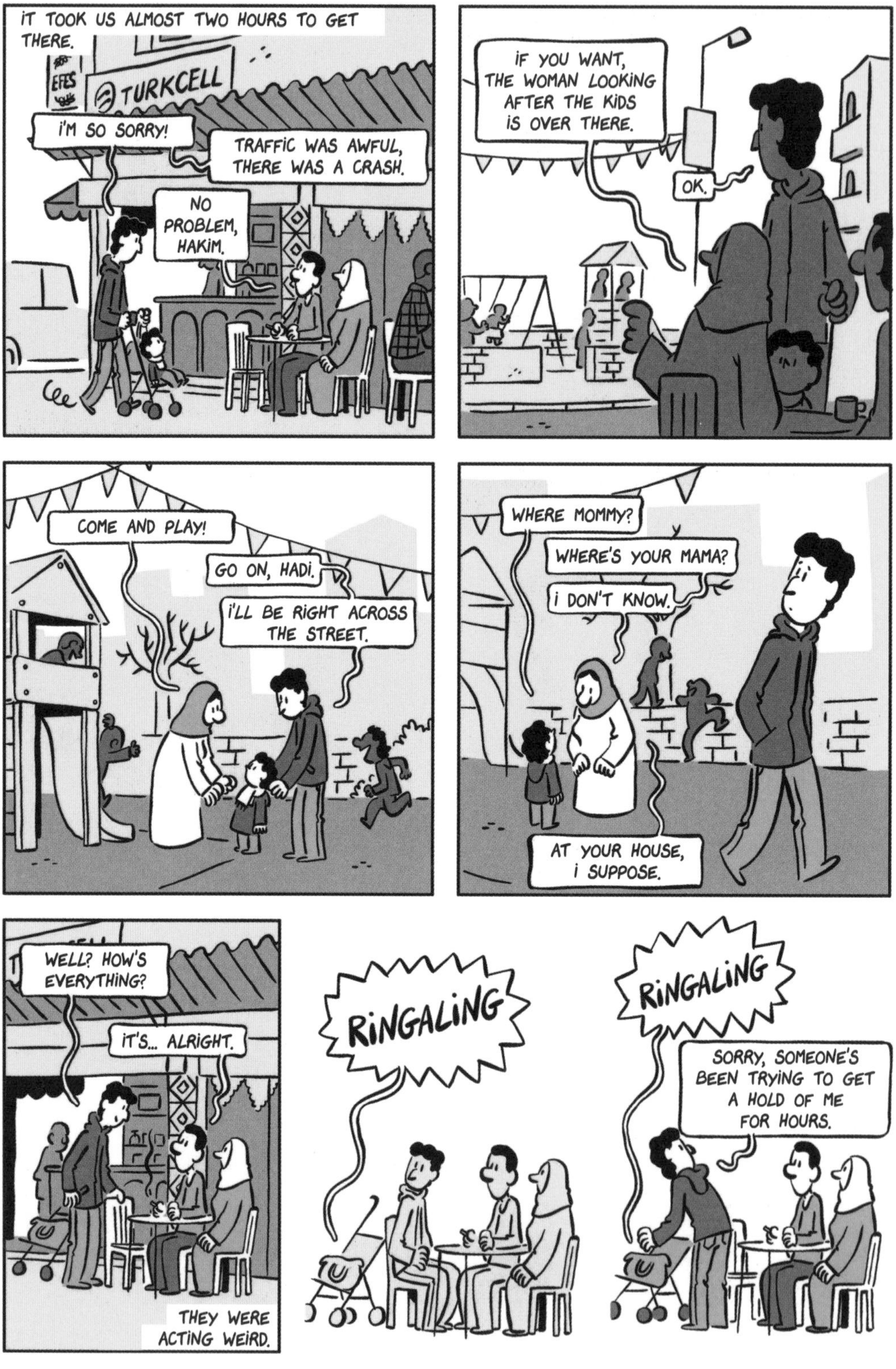
IT TOOK US ALMOST TWO HOURS TO GET THERE.
EFES
TURKCELL
I'M SO SORRY!
TRAFFIC WAS AWFUL, THERE WAS A CRASH.
NO PROBLEM, HAKIM.
IF YOU WANT, THE WOMAN LOOKING AFTER THE KIDS IS OVER THERE.
OK.
COME AND PLAY!
GO ON, HADI.
I'LL BE RIGHT ACROSS THE STREET.
WHERE MOMMY?
WHERE'S YOUR MAMA?
I DON'T KNOW.
AT YOUR HOUSE, I SUPPOSE.
WELL? HOW'S EVERYTHING?
IT'S... ALRIGHT.
THEY WERE ACTING WEIRD.
RINGALING
RINGALING
SORRY, SOMEONE'S BEEN TRYING TO GET A HOLD OF ME FOR HOURS.

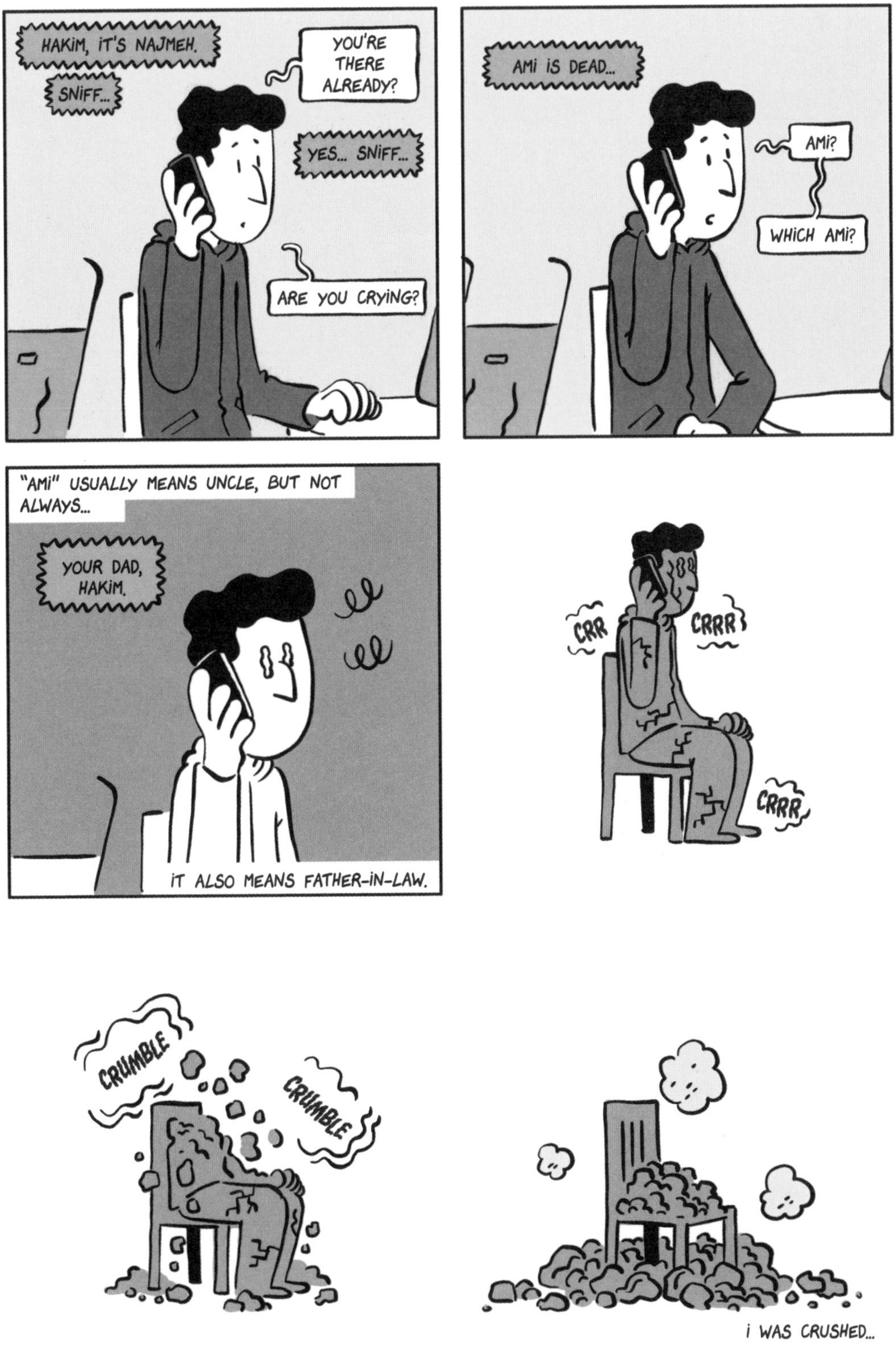
HAKIM, IT'S NAJMEH.
SNIFF...
YOU'RE THERE ALREADY?
YES... SNIFF...
ARE YOU CRYING?
AMI IS DEAD...
AMI?
WHICH AMI?
"AMI" USUALLY MEANS UNCLE, BUT NOT ALWAYS...
YOUR DAD, HAKIM.
IT ALSO MEANS FATHER-IN-LAW.
CRR
CRRR
CRRR
CRUMBLE
CRUMBLE
I WAS CRUSHED...

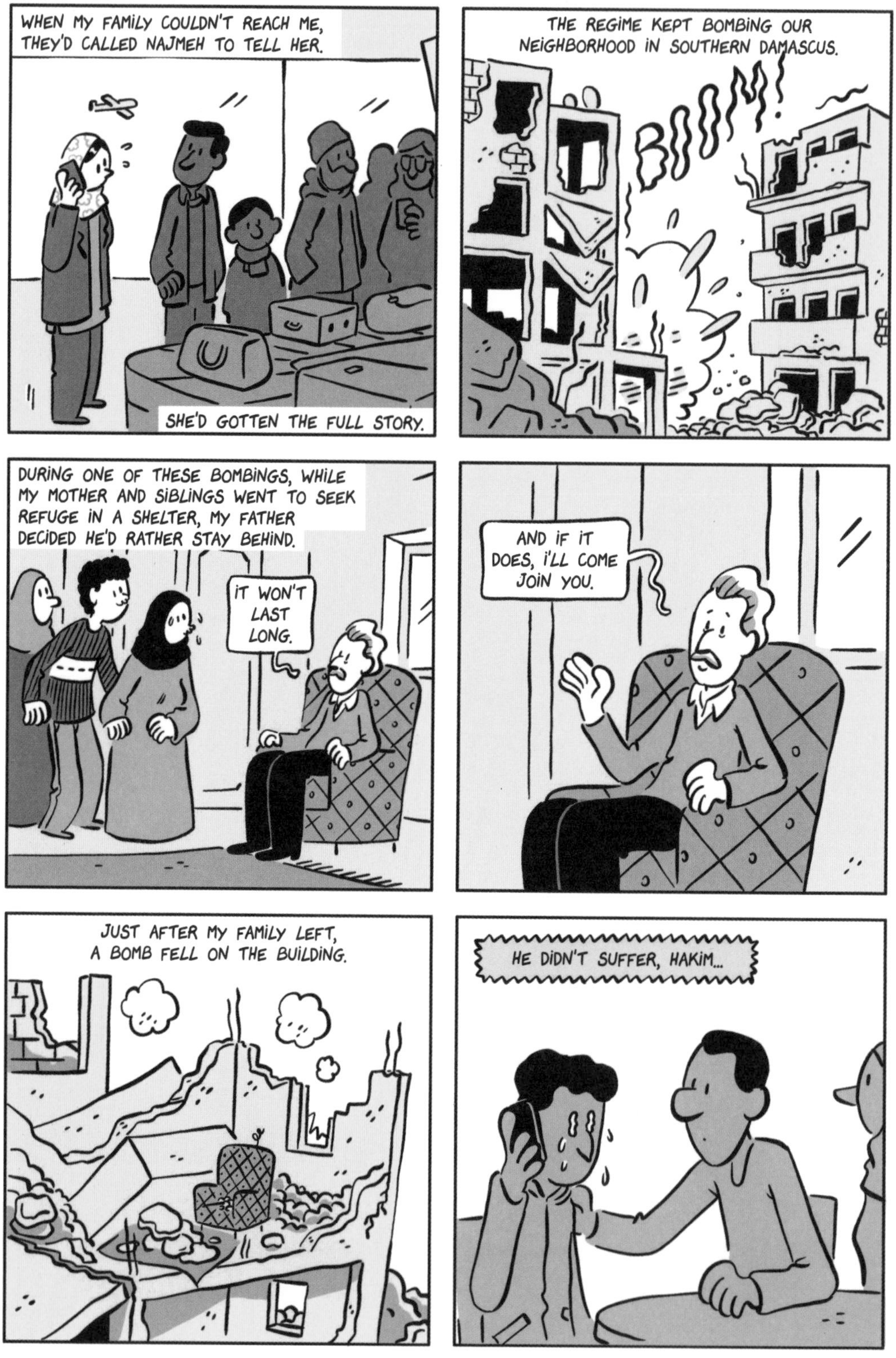
WHEN MY FAMILY COULDN'T REACH ME, THEY'D CALLED NAJMEH TO TELL HER.
SHE'D GOTTEN THE FULL STORY.
THE REGIME KEPT BOMBING OUR NEIGHBORHOOD IN SOUTHERN DAMASCUS.
BOOM!
DURING ONE OF THESE BOMBINGS, WHILE MY MOTHER AND SIBLINGS WENT TO SEEK REFUGE IN A SHELTER, MY FATHER DECIDED HE'D RATHER STAY BEHIND.
IT WON'T LAST LONG.
AND IF IT DOES, I'LL COME JOIN YOU.
JUST AFTER MY FAMILY LEFT, A BOMB FELL ON THE BUILDING.
HE DIDN'T SUFFER, HAKIM...

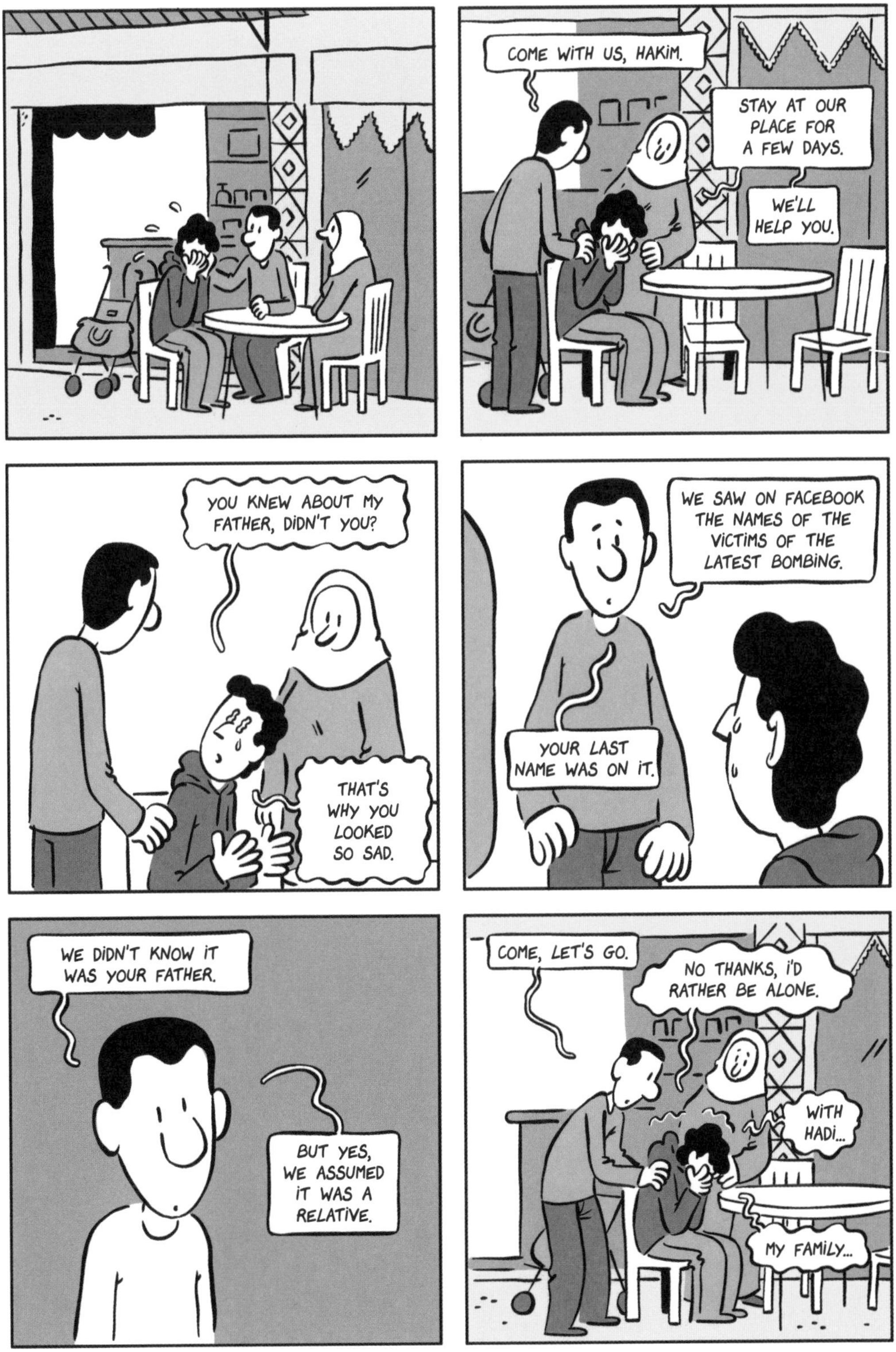
COME WITH US, HAKIM.
STAY AT OUR PLACE FOR A FEW DAYS.
WE'LL HELP YOU.
YOU KNEW ABOUT MY FATHER, DIDN'T YOU?
THAT'S WHY YOU LOOKED SO SAD.
WE SAW ON FACEBOOK THE NAMES OF THE VICTIMS OF THE LATEST BOMBING.
YOUR LAST NAME WAS ON IT.
WE DIDN'T KNOW IT WAS YOUR FATHER.
BUT YES, WE ASSUMED IT WAS A RELATIVE.
COME, LET'S GO.
NO THANKS, I'D RATHER BE ALONE.
WITH HADI...
MY FAMILY...

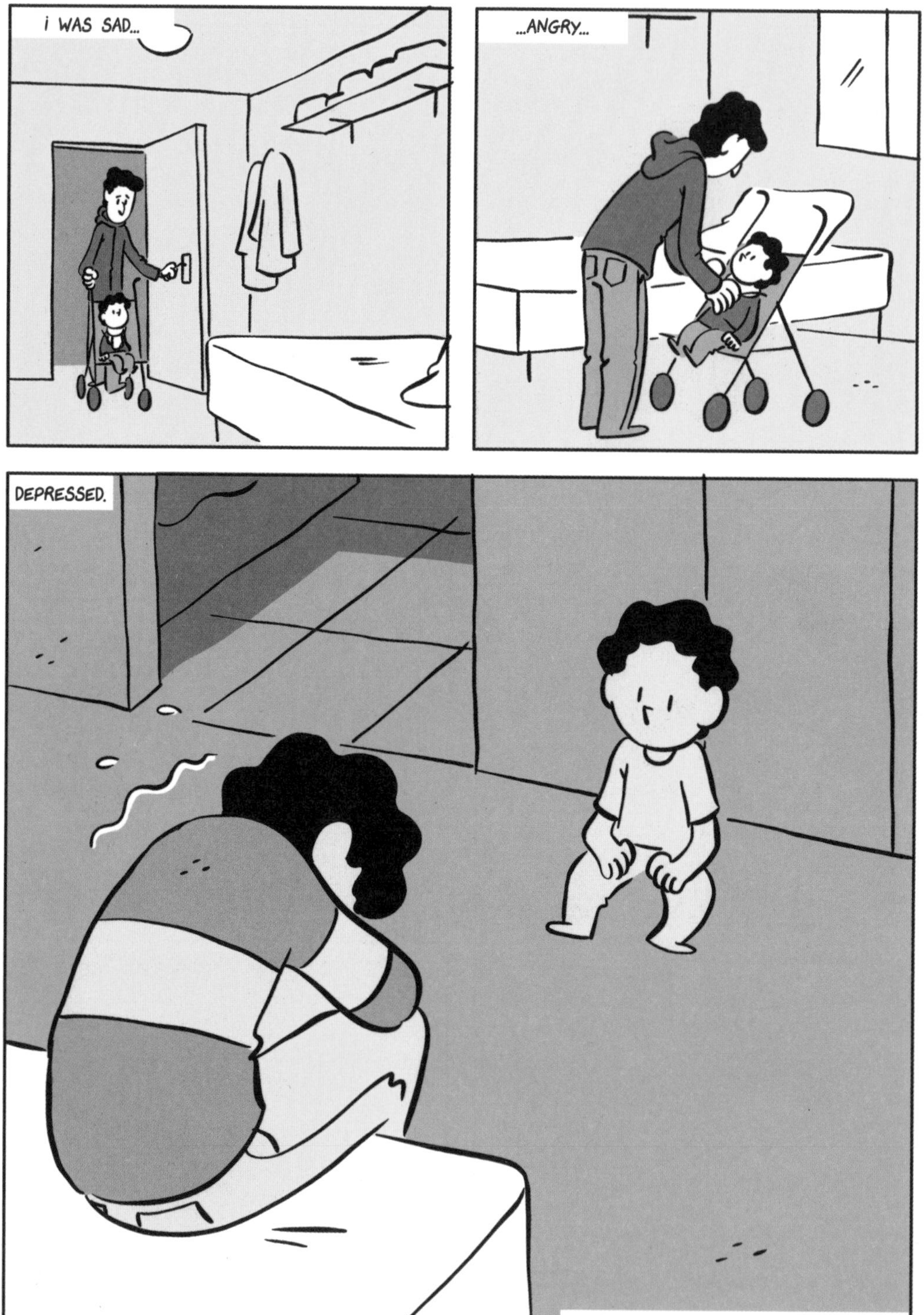
i WAS SAD...
...ANGRY...
DEPRESSED.
THiS WAS UNDOUBTEDLY ONE OF THE WORST PERiODS OF MY LiFE, AND THERE WAS STiLL MORE TO COME...

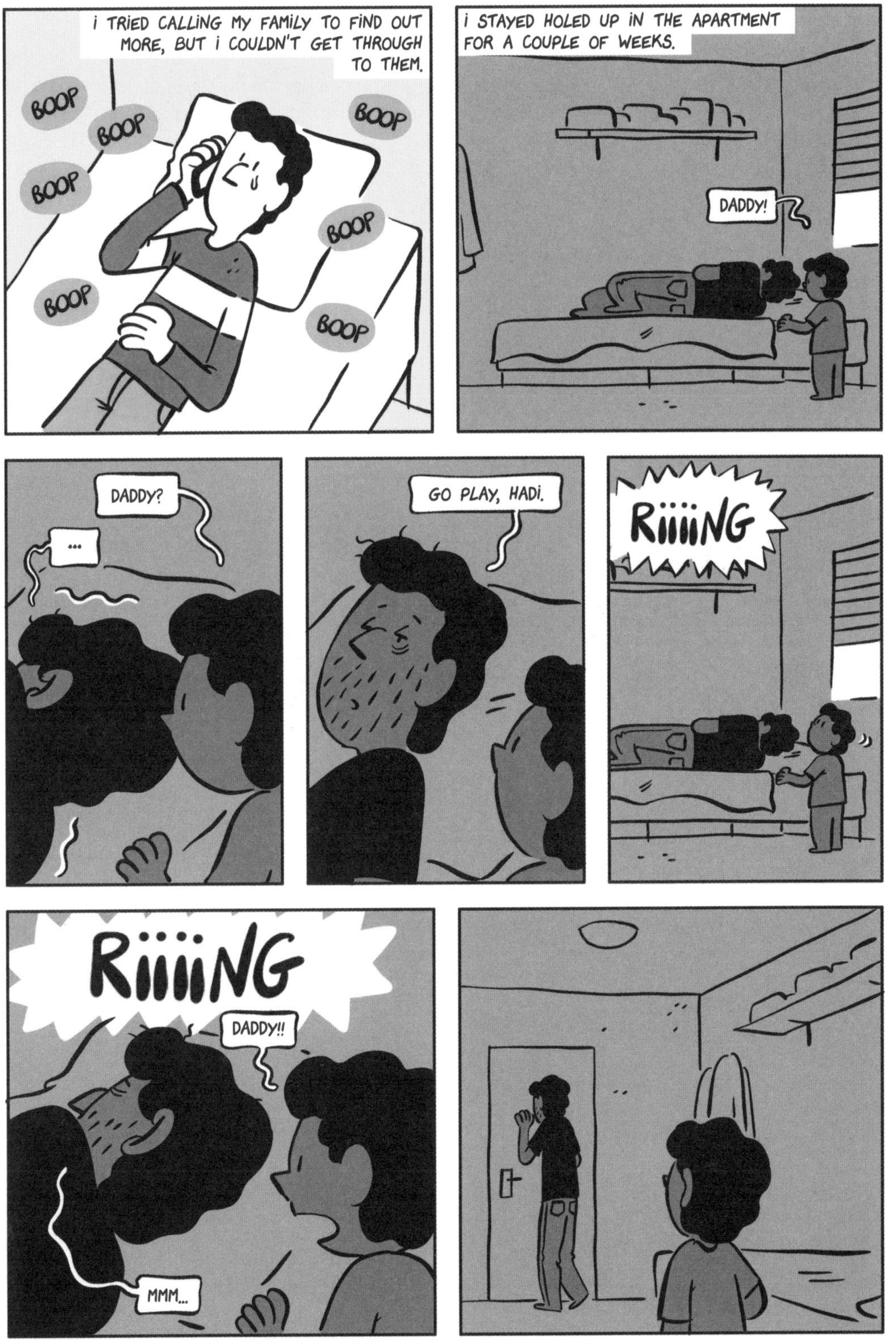

I TRIED CALLING MY FAMILY TO FIND OUT MORE, BUT I COULDN'T GET THROUGH TO THEM.
BOOP
BOOP
BOOP
BOOP
BOOP
BOOP
BOOP
I STAYED HOLED UP IN THE APARTMENT FOR A COUPLE OF WEEKS.
DADDY!
DADDY?
...
GO PLAY, HADI.
RIIIING
RIIIING
DADDY!!
MMM...

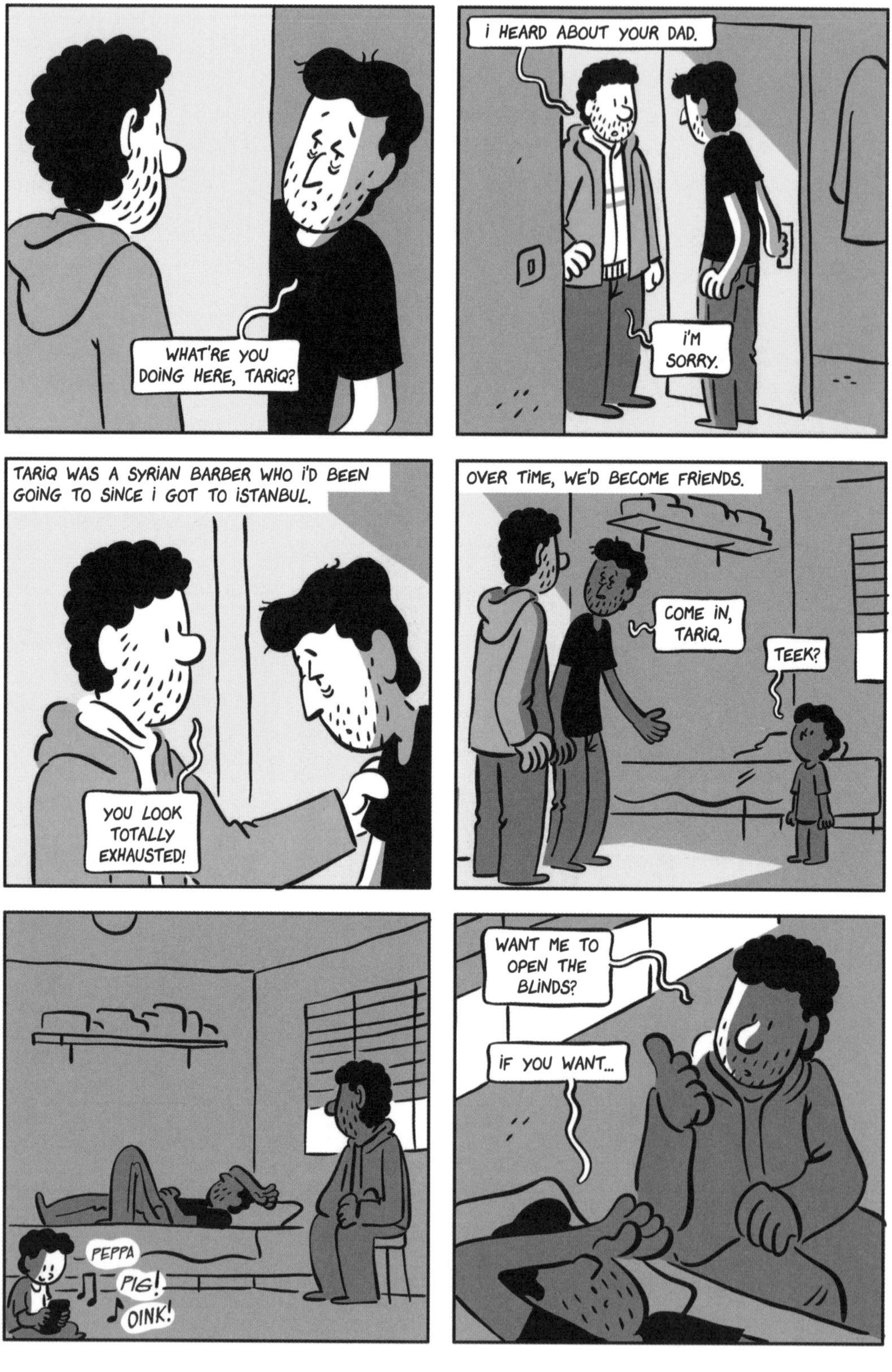
WHAT'RE YOU DOING HERE, TARIQ?
I HEARD ABOUT YOUR DAD.
I'M SORRY.
TARIQ WAS A SYRIAN BARBER WHO I'D BEEN GOING TO SINCE I GOT TO ISTANBUL.
YOU LOOK TOTALLY EXHAUSTED!
OVER TIME, WE'D BECOME FRIENDS.
COME IN, TARIQ.
TEEK?
PEPPA
PIG!
OINK!
WANT ME TO OPEN THE BLINDS?
IF YOU WANT...

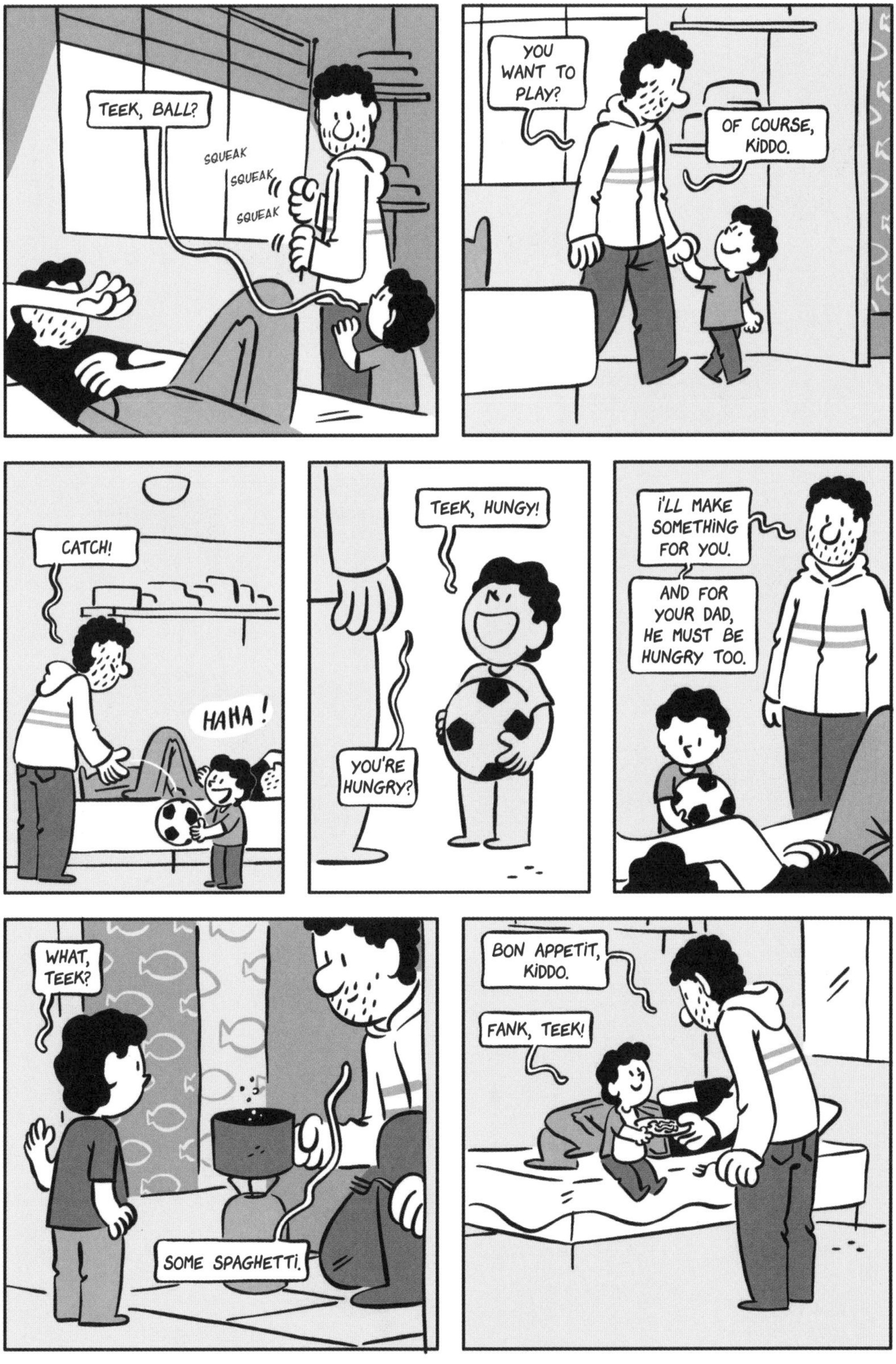
TEEK, BALL?
SQUEAK
SQUEAK
SQUEAK
YOU WANT TO PLAY?
OF COURSE, KIDDO.
CATCH!
HAHA!
TEEK, HUNGY!
YOU'RE HUNGRY?
I'LL MAKE SOMETHING FOR YOU.
AND FOR YOUR DAD, HE MUST BE HUNGRY TOO.
WHAT, TEEK?
SOME SPAGHETTI.
BON APPETIT, KIDDO.
FANK, TEEK!

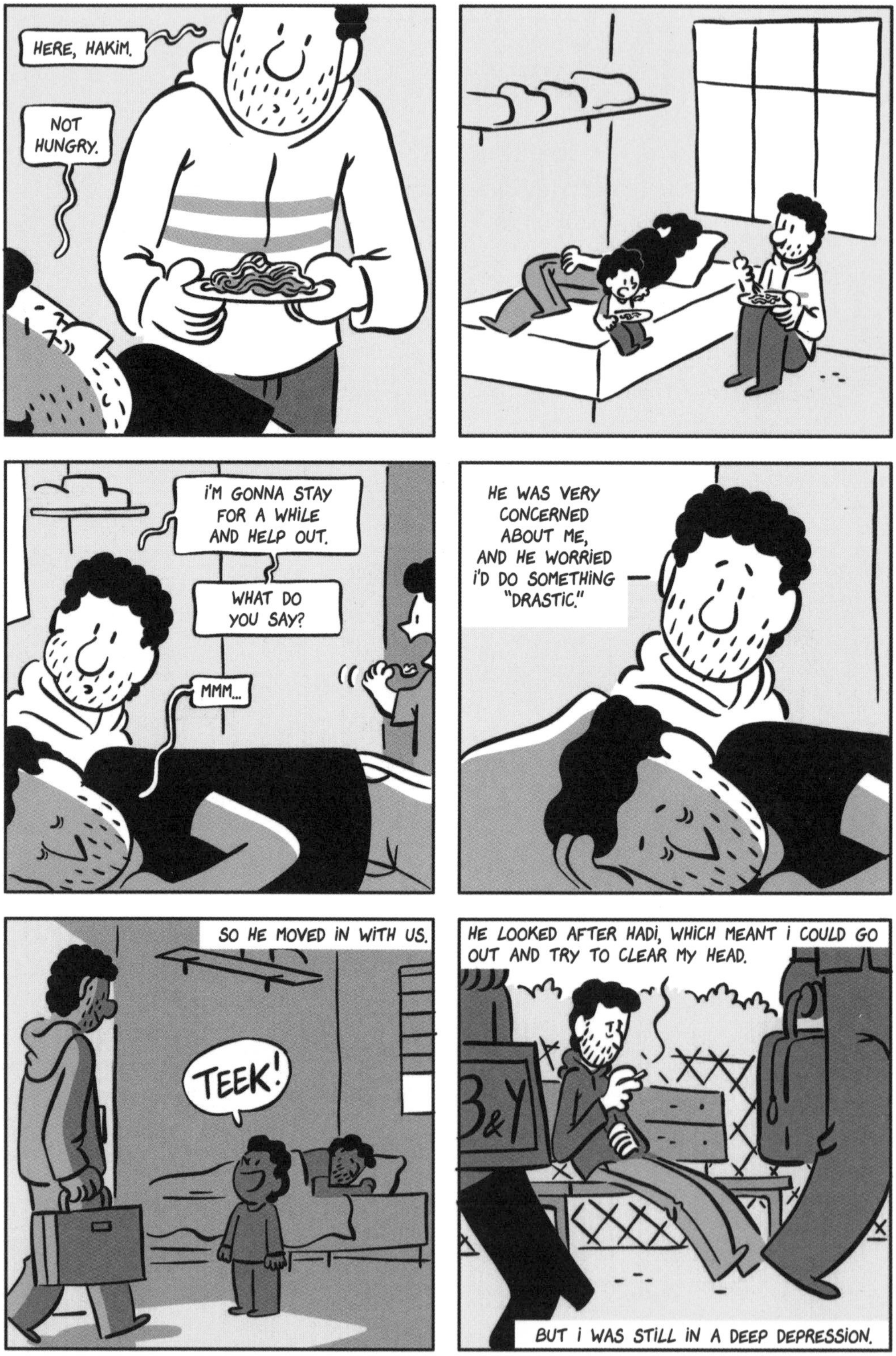
HERE, HAKIM.
NOT HUNGRY.
I'M GONNA STAY FOR A WHILE AND HELP OUT.
WHAT DO YOU SAY?
MMM...
HE WAS VERY CONCERNED ABOUT ME, AND HE WORRIED I'D DO SOMETHING "DRASTIC."
SO HE MOVED IN WITH US.
TEEK!
HE LOOKED AFTER HADI, WHICH MEANT I COULD GO OUT AND TRY TO CLEAR MY HEAD.
B&Y
BUT I WAS STILL IN A DEEP DEPRESSION.

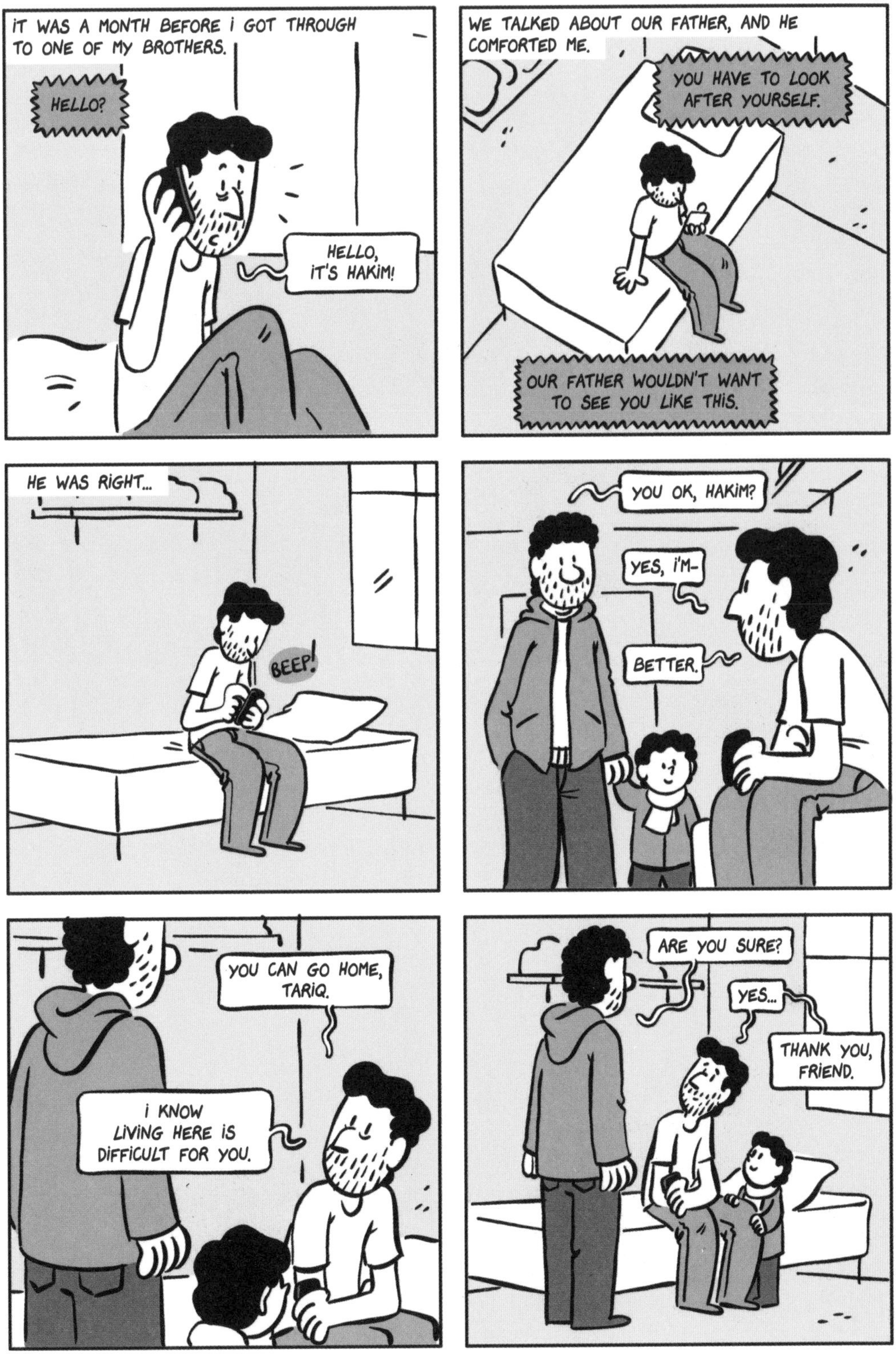
IT WAS A MONTH BEFORE I GOT THROUGH TO ONE OF MY BROTHERS.
HELLO?
HELLO, IT'S HAKIM!
WE TALKED ABOUT OUR FATHER, AND HE COMFORTED ME.
YOU HAVE TO LOOK AFTER YOURSELF.
OUR FATHER WOULDN'T WANT TO SEE YOU LIKE THIS.
HE WAS RIGHT...
BEEP!
YOU OK, HAKIM?
YES, I'M-
BETTER.
YOU CAN GO HOME, TARIQ.
I KNOW LIVING HERE IS DIFFICULT FOR YOU.
ARE YOU SURE?
YES...
THANK YOU, FRIEND.

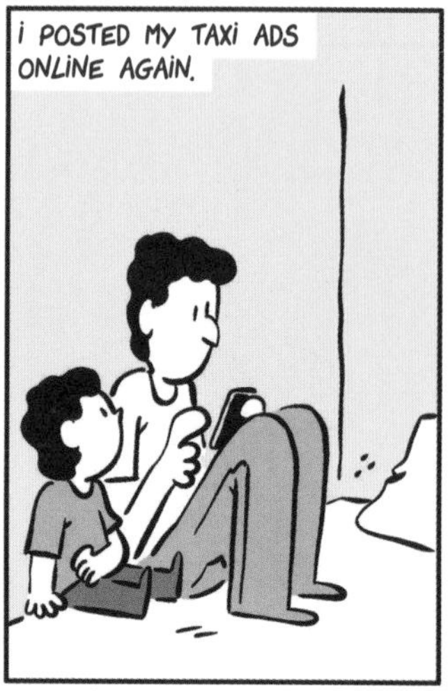
i POSTED MY TAXi ADS ONLiNE AGAiN.

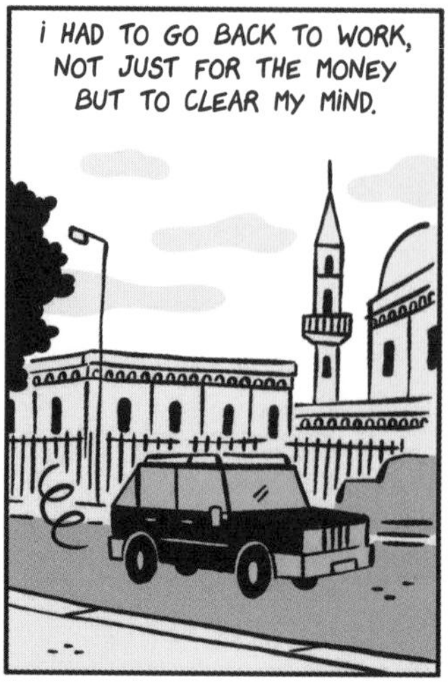
i HAD TO GO BACK TO WORK, NOT JUST FOR THE MONEY BUT TO CLEAR MY MiND.

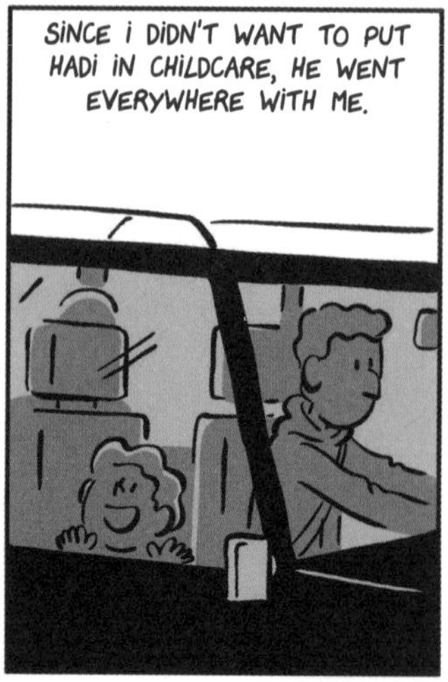
SiNCE i DiDN'T WANT TO PUT HADi iN CHiLDCARE, HE WENT EVERYWHERE WiTH ME.

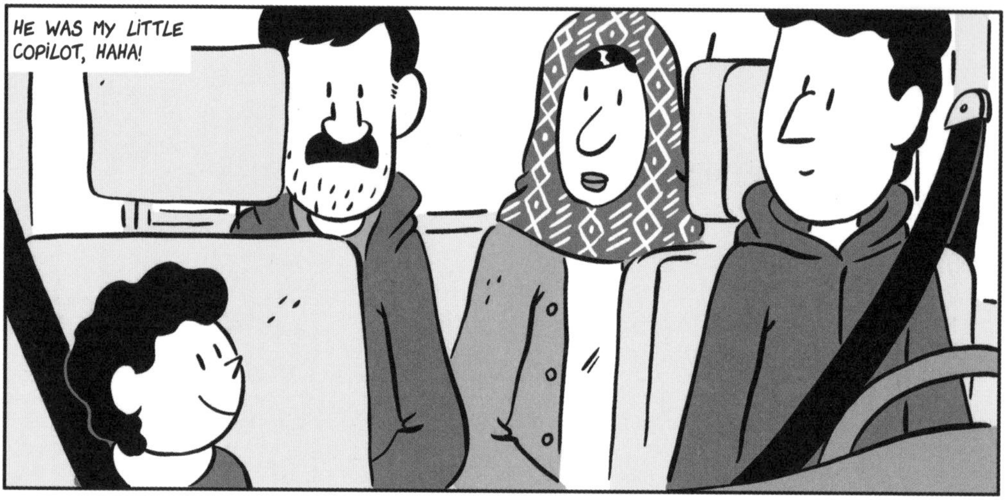
HE WAS MY LiTTLE COPiLOT, HAHA!

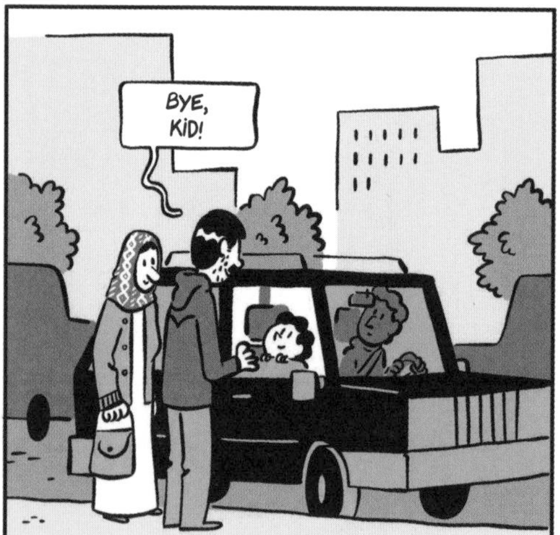
BYE, KiD!

MY CUSTOMERS WERE REFUGEES, LiKE ME. THEY WERE UNDERSTANDiNG.

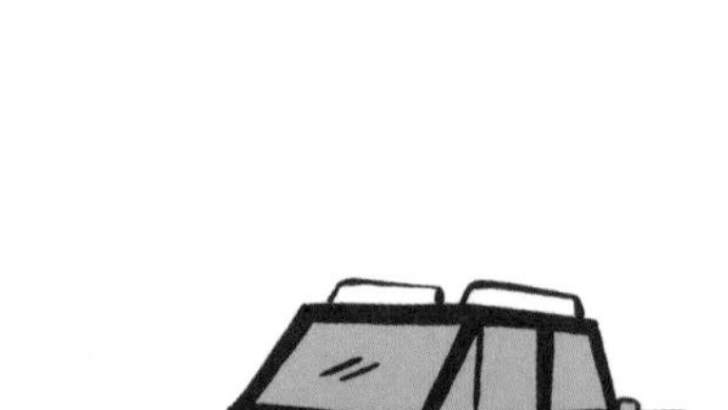

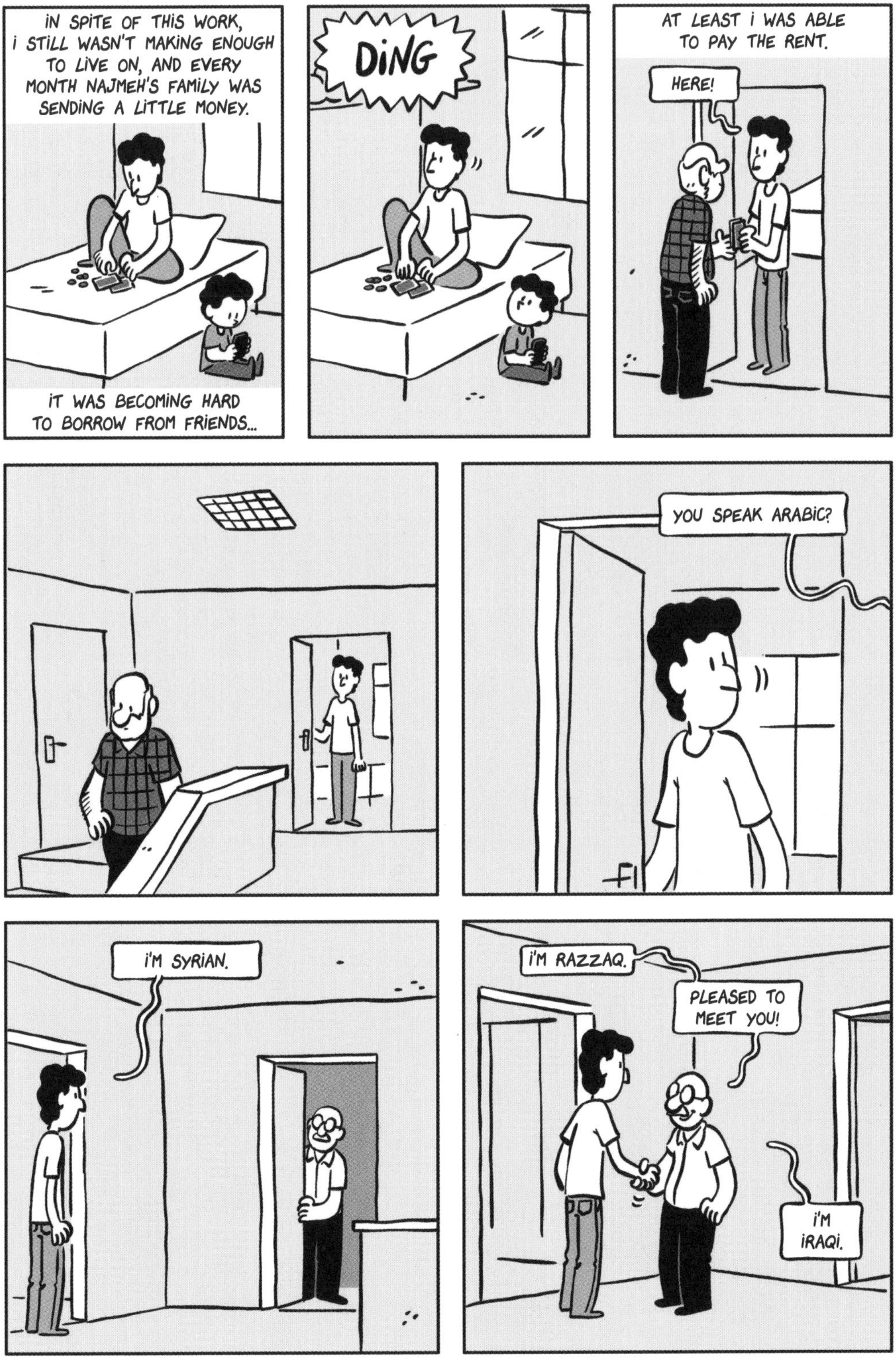
IN SPITE OF THIS WORK, I STILL WASN'T MAKING ENOUGH TO LIVE ON, AND EVERY MONTH NAJMEH'S FAMILY WAS SENDING A LITTLE MONEY.
IT WAS BECOMING HARD TO BORROW FROM FRIENDS...
DING
AT LEAST I WAS ABLE TO PAY THE RENT.
HERE!
YOU SPEAK ARABIC?
I'M SYRIAN.
I'M RAZZAQ.
PLEASED TO MEET YOU!
I'M IRAQI.

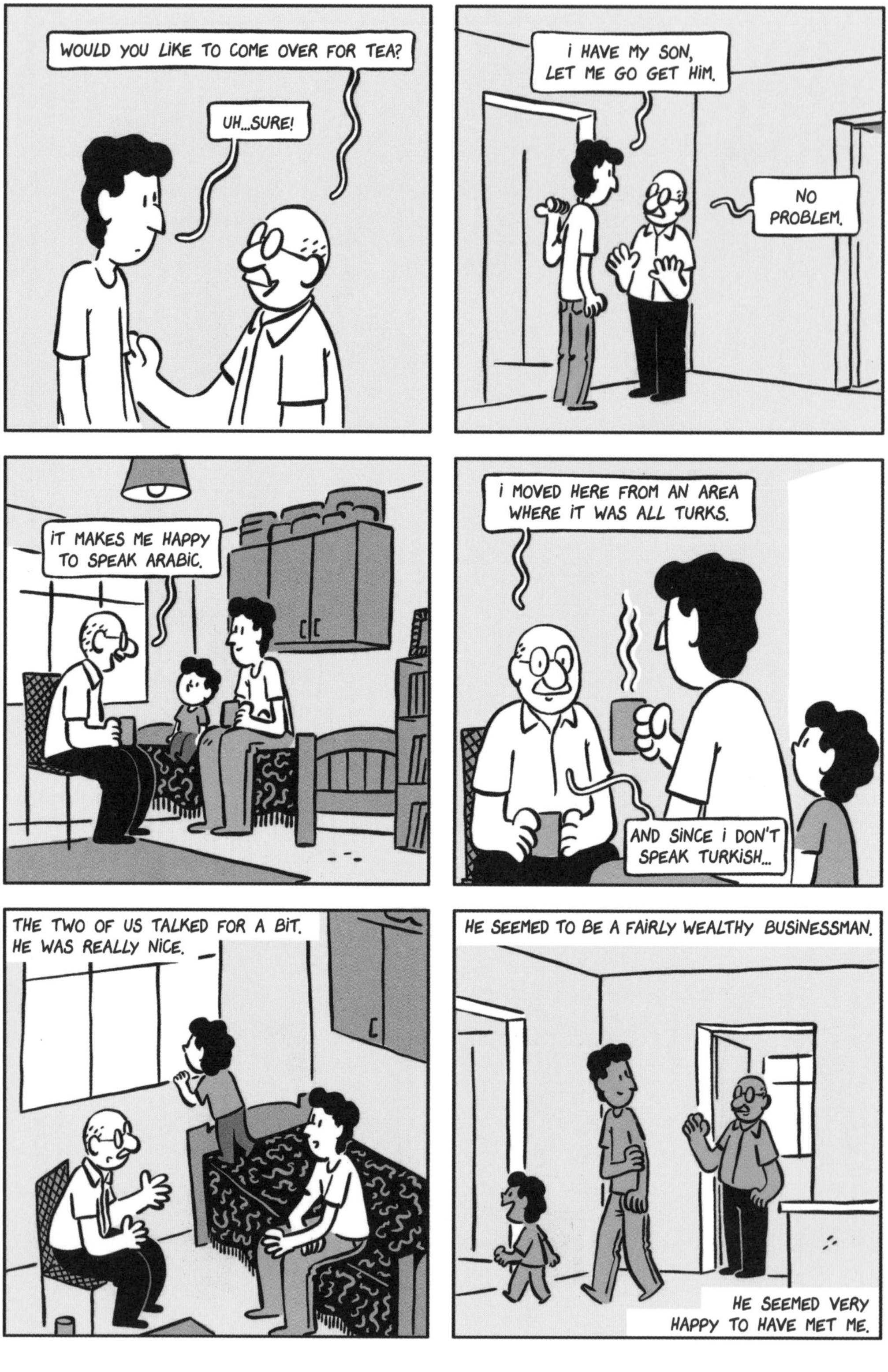
WOULD YOU LIKE TO COME OVER FOR TEA?
UH...SURE!
I HAVE MY SON, LET ME GO GET HIM.
NO PROBLEM.
IT MAKES ME HAPPY TO SPEAK ARABIC.
I MOVED HERE FROM AN AREA WHERE IT WAS ALL TURKS.
AND SINCE I DON'T SPEAK TURKISH...
THE TWO OF US TALKED FOR A BIT. HE WAS REALLY NICE.
HE SEEMED TO BE A FAIRLY WEALTHY BUSINESSMAN.
HE SEEMED VERY HAPPY TO HAVE MET ME.

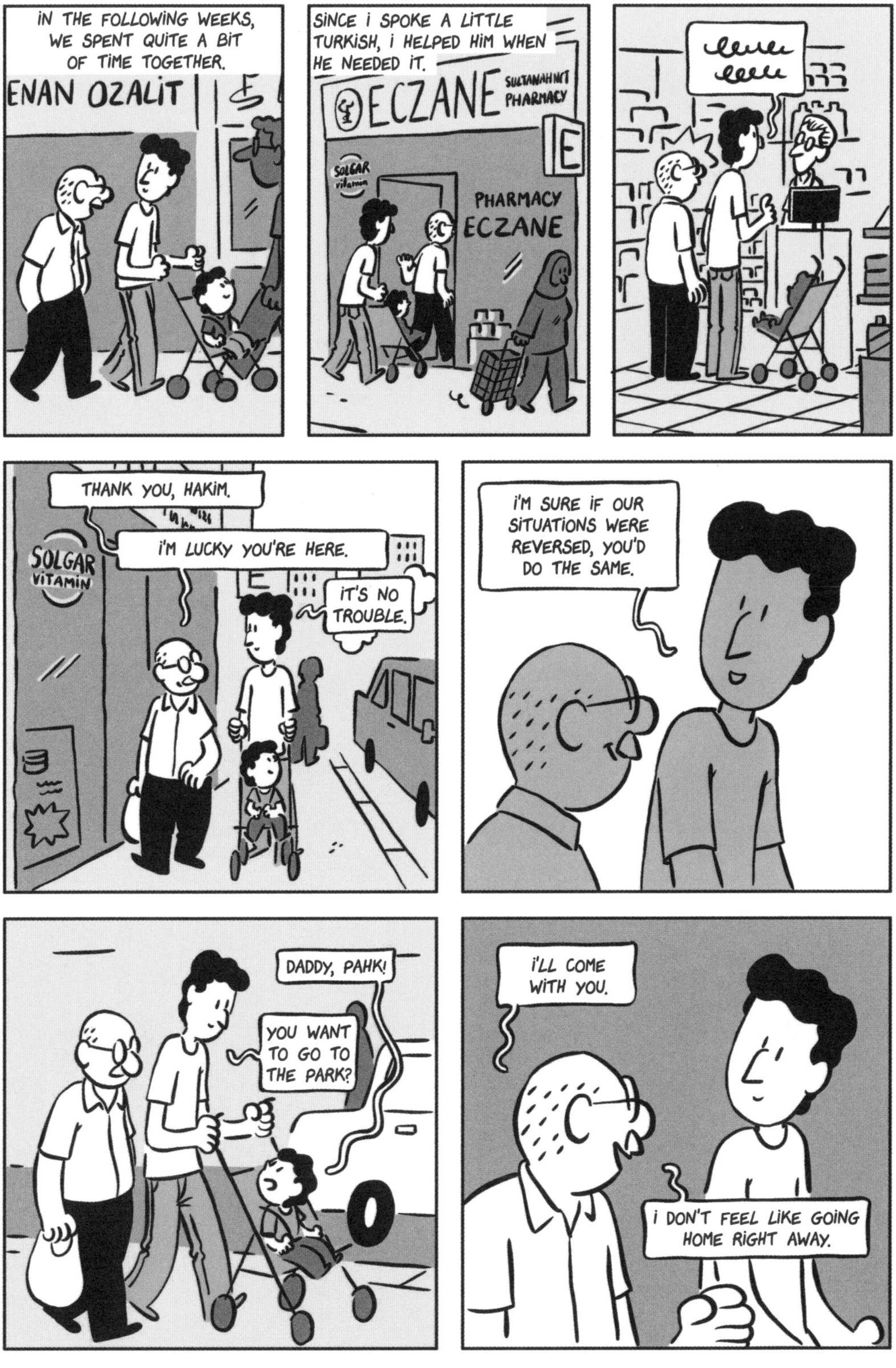
IN THE FOLLOWING WEEKS, WE SPENT QUITE A BIT OF TIME TOGETHER.
ENAN OZALIT
SINCE I SPOKE A LITTLE TURKISH, I HELPED HIM WHEN HE NEEDED IT.
ECZANE
SULTANAHMET PHARMACY
SOLGAR vitamin
E
PHARMACY
ECZANE
THANK YOU, HAKIM.
I'M LUCKY YOU'RE HERE.
SOLGAR VITAMIN
IT'S NO TROUBLE.
I'M SURE IF OUR SITUATIONS WERE REVERSED, YOU'D DO THE SAME.
DADDY, PAHK!
YOU WANT TO GO TO THE PARK?
I'LL COME WITH YOU.
I DON'T FEEL LIKE GOING HOME RIGHT AWAY.

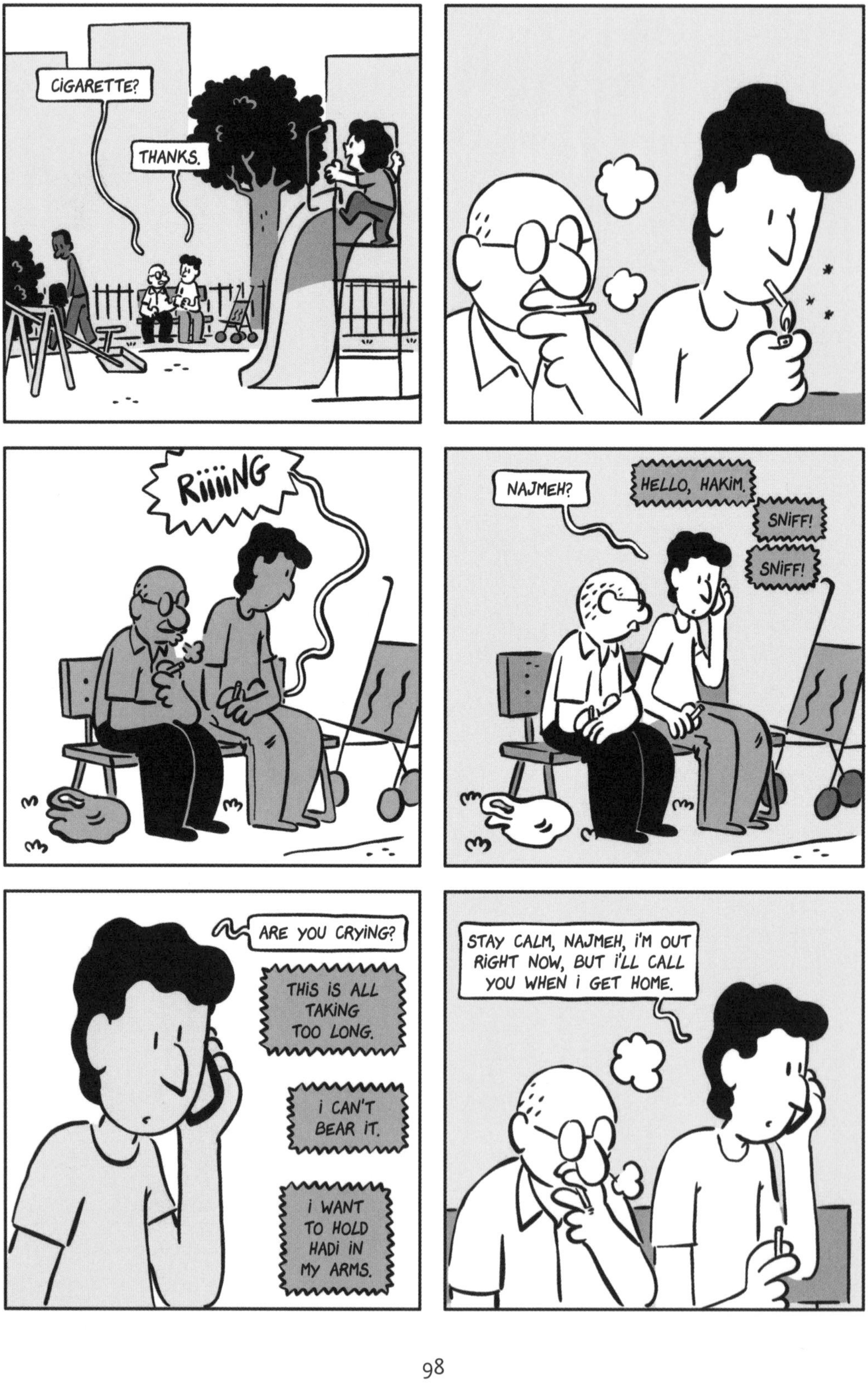
CIGARETTE?
THANKS.
RIiiiNG
NAJMEH?
HELLO, HAKIM.
SNIFF!
SNIFF!
ARE YOU CRYING?
THIS IS ALL TAKING TOO LONG.
I CAN'T BEAR IT.
I WANT TO HOLD HADI IN MY ARMS.
STAY CALM, NAJMEH, I'M OUT RIGHT NOW, BUT I'LL CALL YOU WHEN I GET HOME.

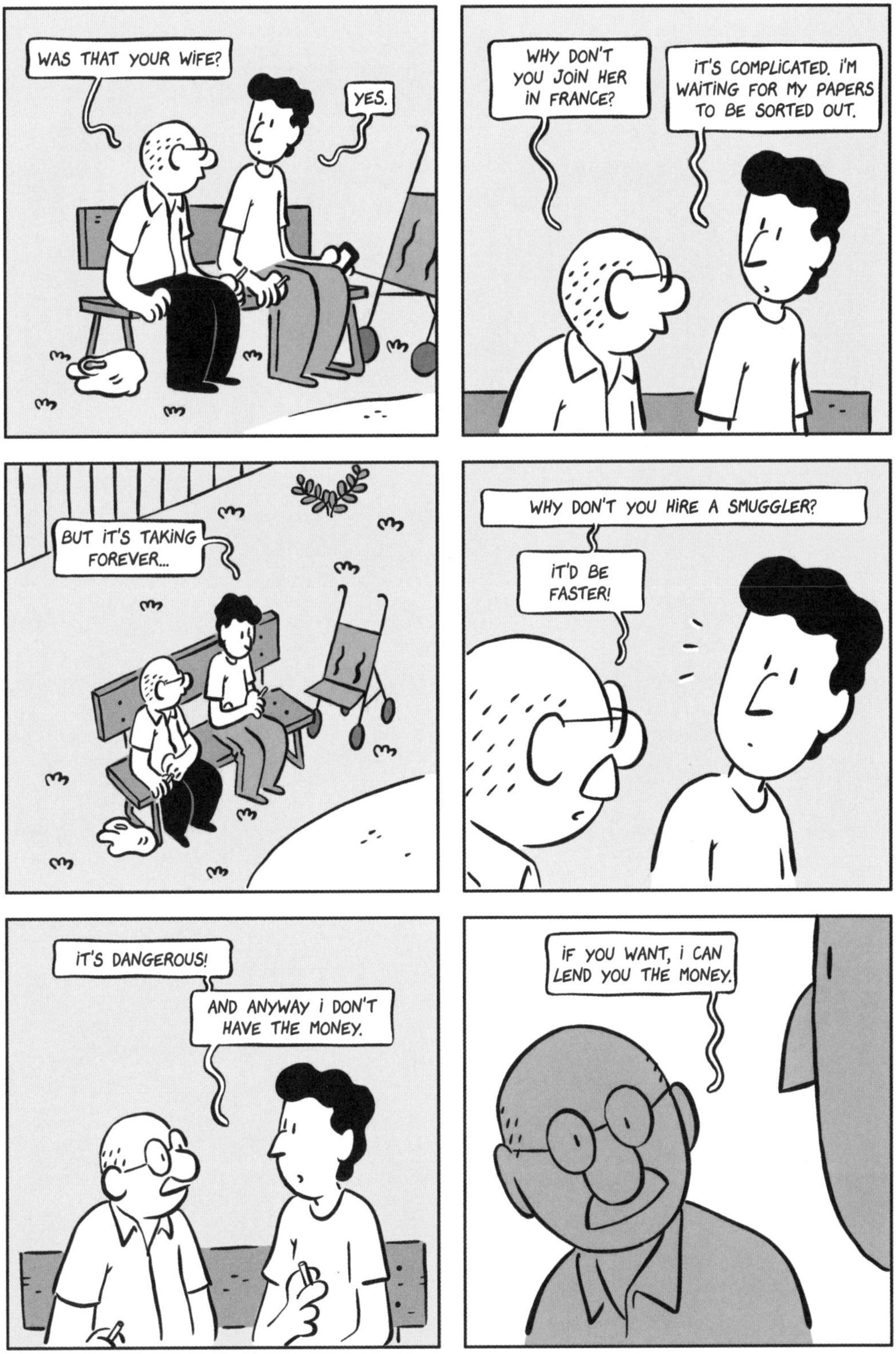
WAS THAT YOUR WIFE?
YES.
WHY DON'T YOU JOIN HER IN FRANCE?
IT'S COMPLICATED. I'M WAITING FOR MY PAPERS TO BE SORTED OUT.
BUT IT'S TAKING FOREVER...
WHY DON'T YOU HIRE A SMUGGLER?
IT'D BE FASTER!
IT'S DANGEROUS!
AND ANYWAY I DON'T HAVE THE MONEY.
IF YOU WANT, I CAN LEND YOU THE MONEY.

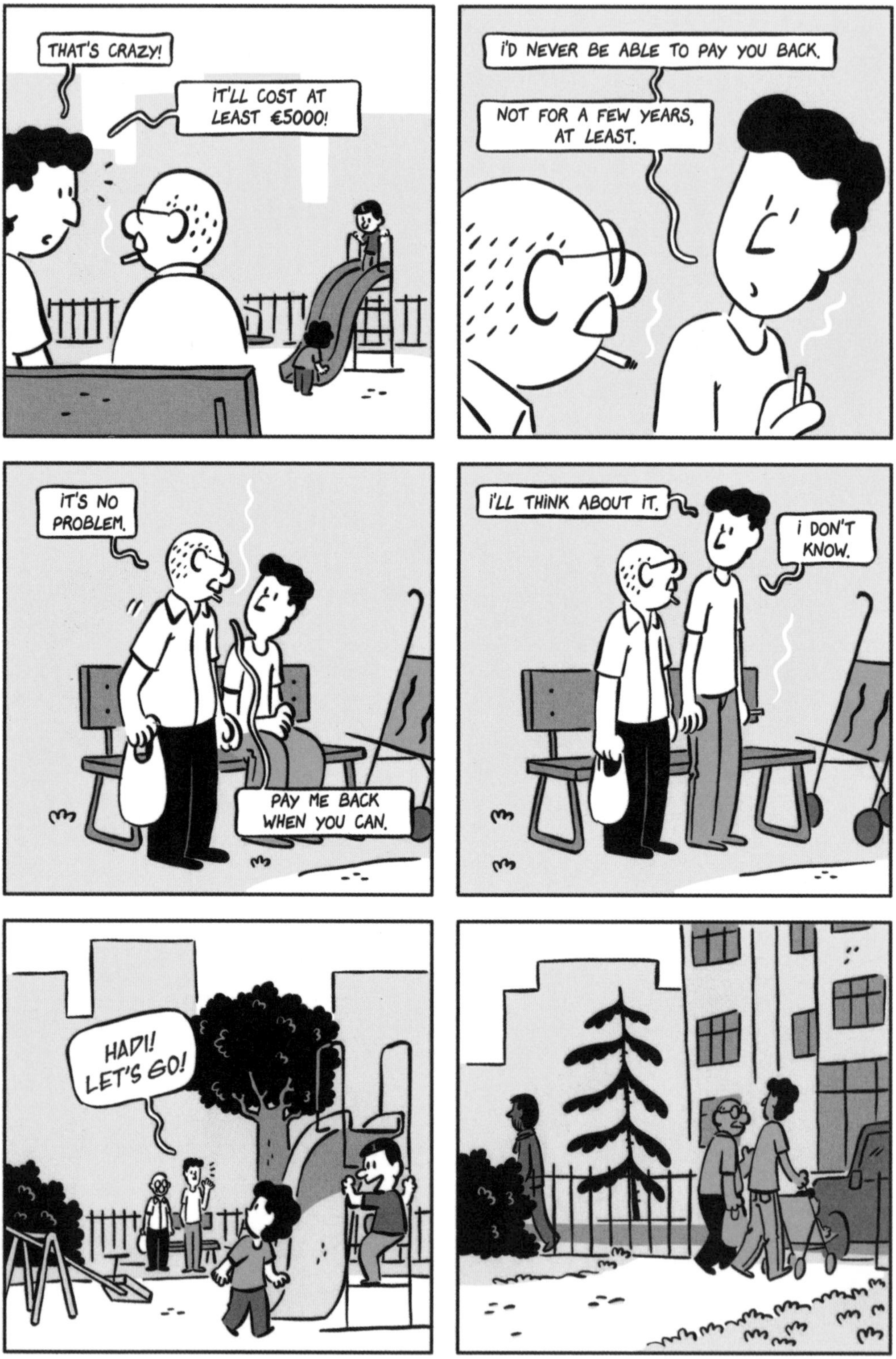
THAT'S CRAZY!
IT'LL COST AT LEAST €5000!
I'D NEVER BE ABLE TO PAY YOU BACK.
NOT FOR A FEW YEARS, AT LEAST.
IT'S NO PROBLEM.
PAY ME BACK WHEN YOU CAN.
I'LL THINK ABOUT IT.
I DON'T KNOW.
HADI! LET'S GO!

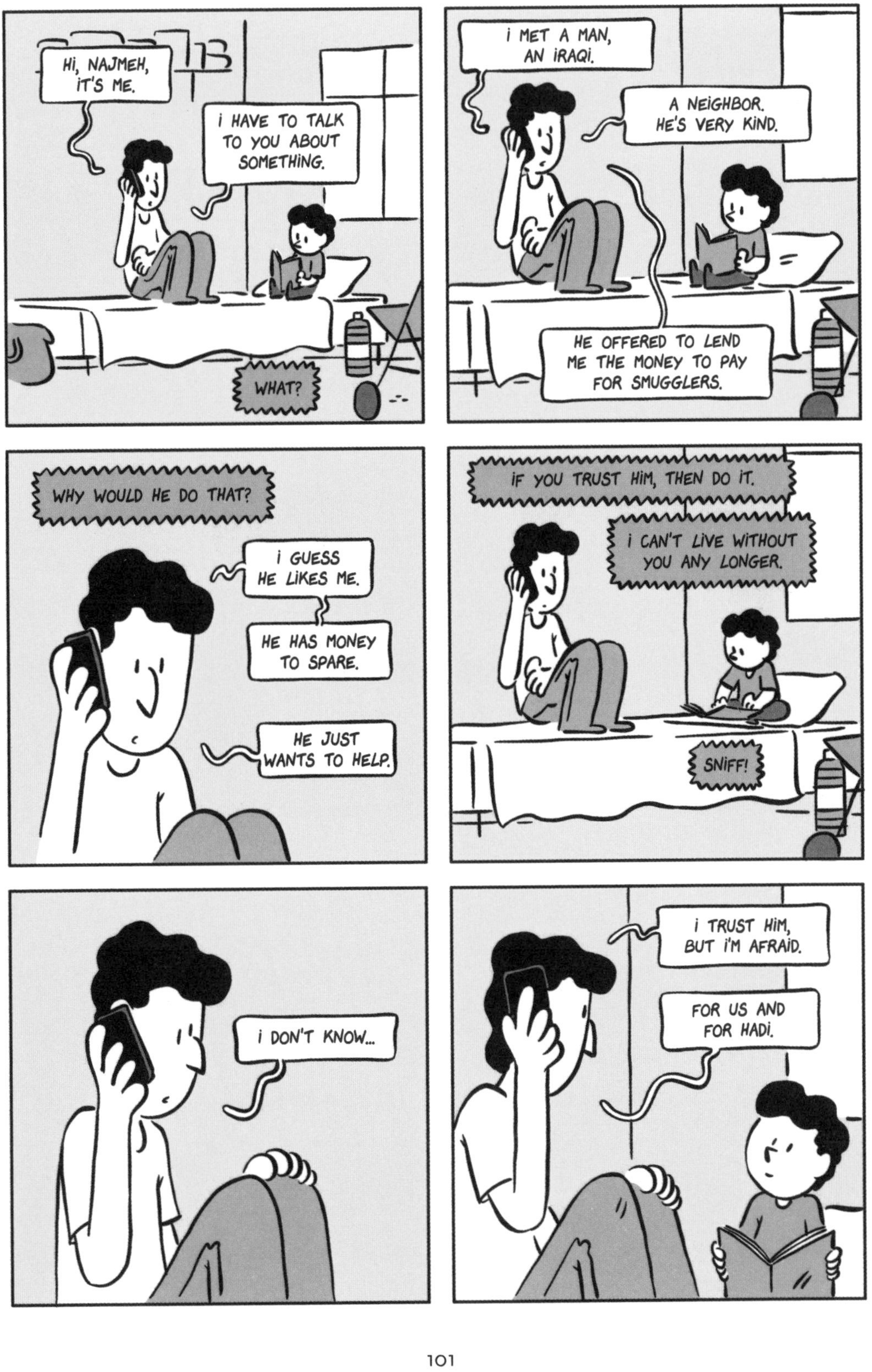
HI, NAJMEH, IT'S ME.
I HAVE TO TALK TO YOU ABOUT SOMETHING.
WHAT?
I MET A MAN, AN IRAQI.
A NEIGHBOR. HE'S VERY KIND.
HE OFFERED TO LEND ME THE MONEY TO PAY FOR SMUGGLERS.
WHY WOULD HE DO THAT?
I GUESS HE LIKES ME.
HE HAS MONEY TO SPARE.
HE JUST WANTS TO HELP.
IF YOU TRUST HIM, THEN DO IT.
I CAN'T LIVE WITHOUT YOU ANY LONGER.
SNIFF!
I DON'T KNOW...
I TRUST HIM, BUT I'M AFRAID.
FOR US AND FOR HADI.

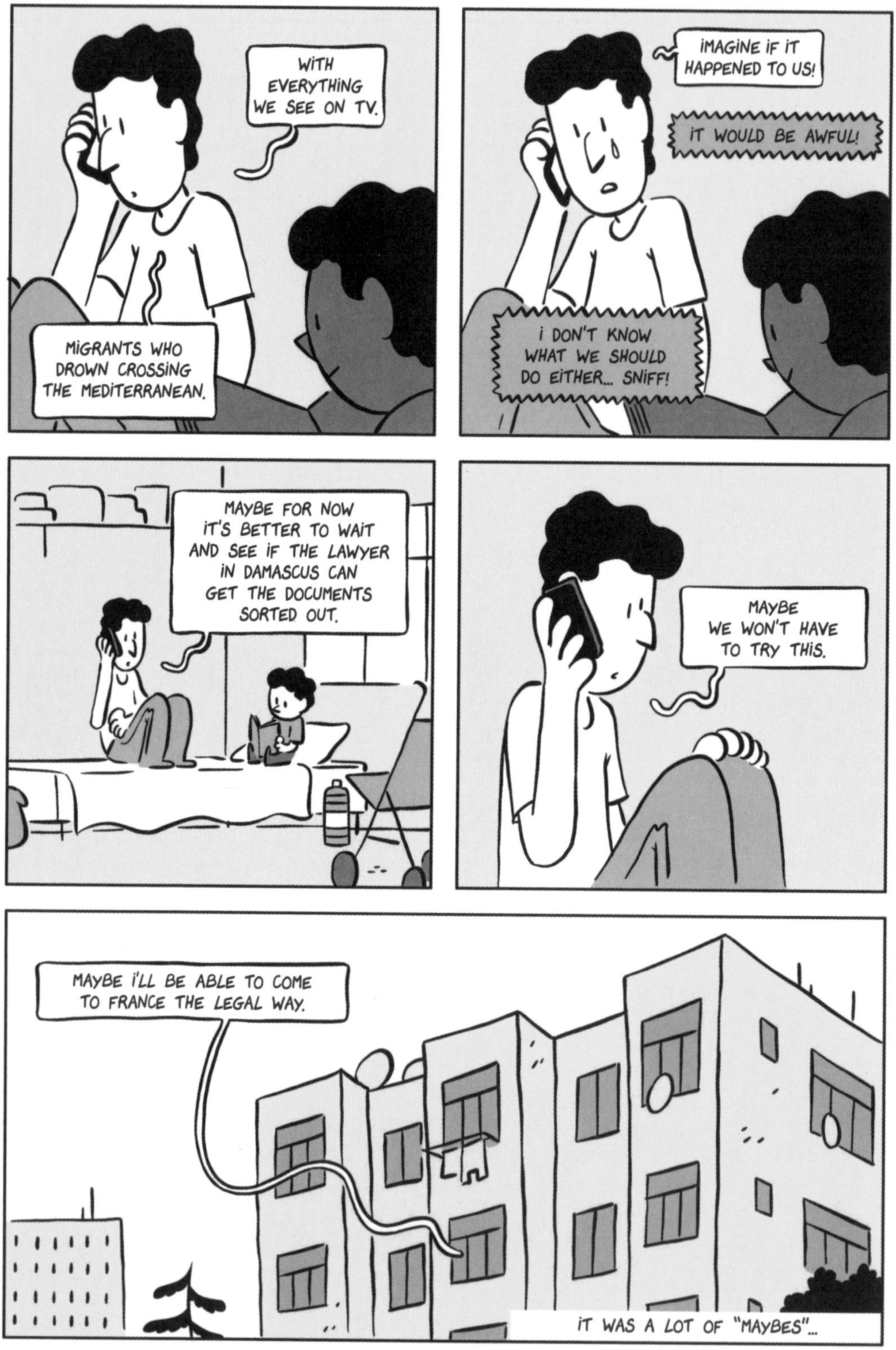
WITH EVERYTHING WE SEE ON TV.
MIGRANTS WHO DROWN CROSSING THE MEDITERRANEAN.
IMAGINE IF IT HAPPENED TO US!
IT WOULD BE AWFUL!
I DON'T KNOW WHAT WE SHOULD DO EITHER... SNIFF!
MAYBE FOR NOW IT'S BETTER TO WAIT AND SEE IF THE LAWYER IN DAMASCUS CAN GET THE DOCUMENTS SORTED OUT.
MAYBE WE WON'T HAVE TO TRY THIS.
MAYBE I'LL BE ABLE TO COME TO FRANCE THE LEGAL WAY.
IT WAS A LOT OF "MAYBES"...

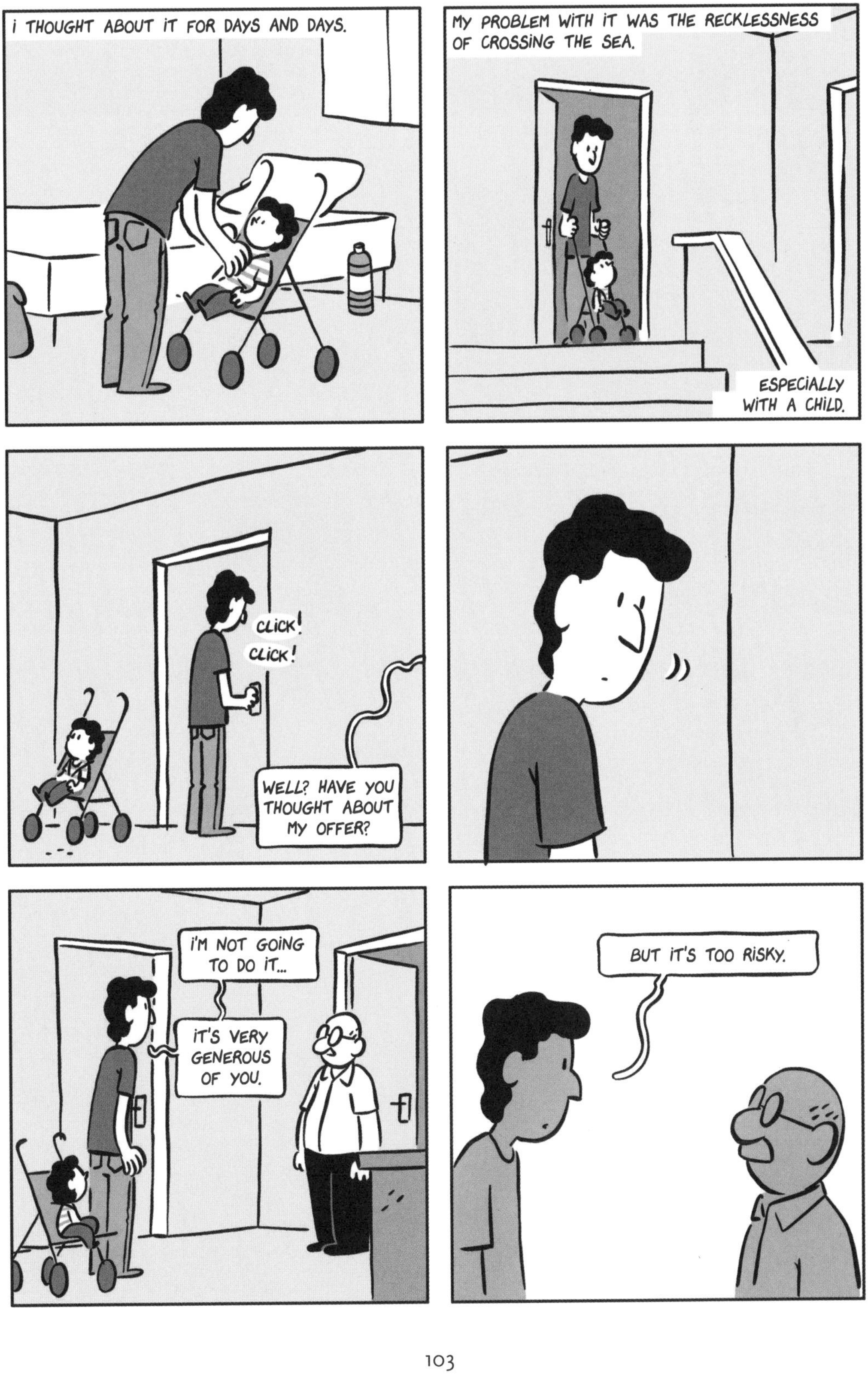
I THOUGHT ABOUT IT FOR DAYS AND DAYS.
MY PROBLEM WITH IT WAS THE RECKLESSNESS OF CROSSING THE SEA.
ESPECIALLY WITH A CHILD.
CLICK!
CLICK!
WELL? HAVE YOU THOUGHT ABOUT MY OFFER?
I'M NOT GOING TO DO IT...
IT'S VERY GENEROUS OF YOU.
BUT IT'S TOO RISKY.

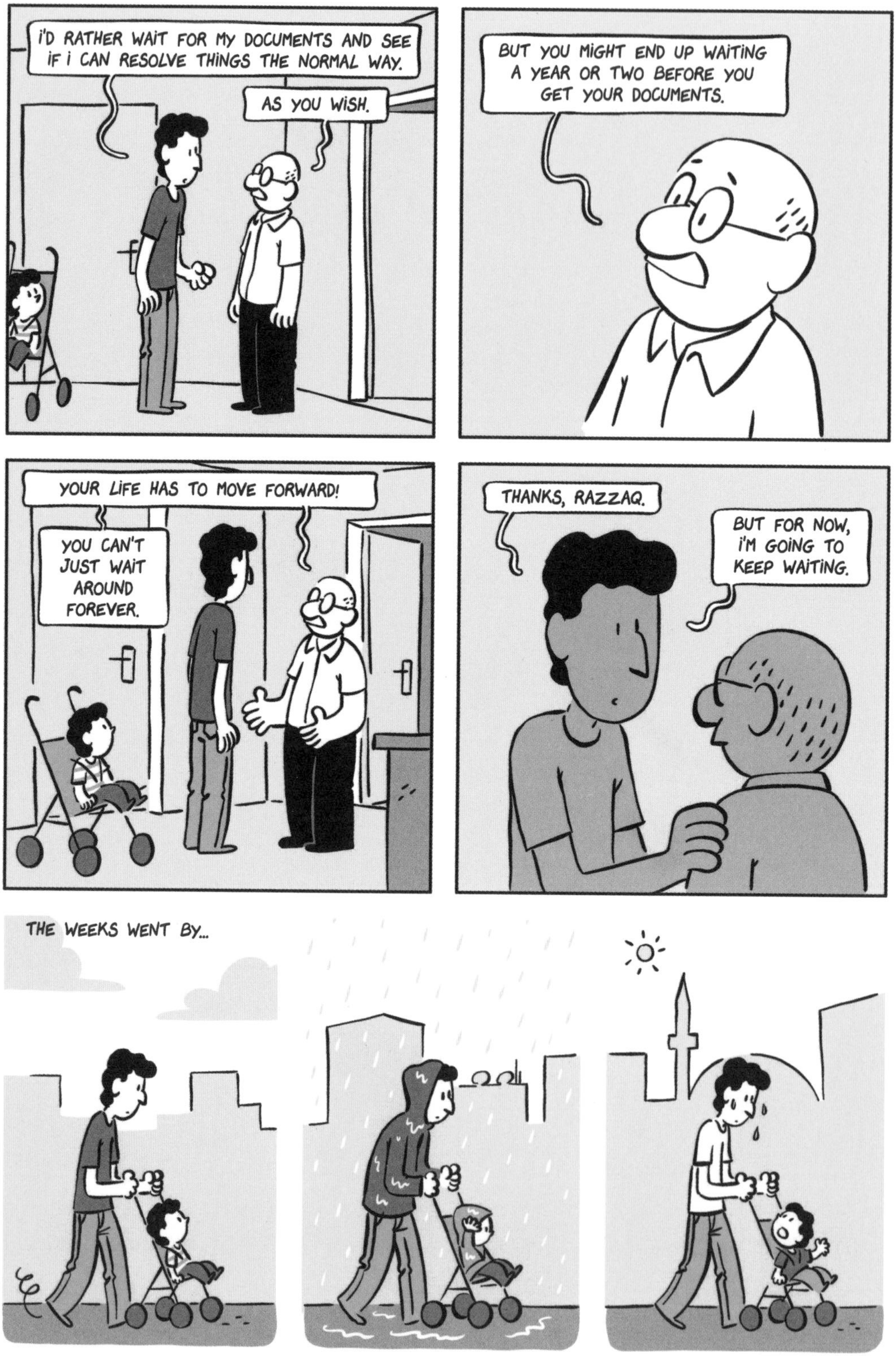
I'D RATHER WAIT FOR MY DOCUMENTS AND SEE IF I CAN RESOLVE THINGS THE NORMAL WAY.
AS YOU WISH.
BUT YOU MIGHT END UP WAITING A YEAR OR TWO BEFORE YOU GET YOUR DOCUMENTS.
YOUR LIFE HAS TO MOVE FORWARD!
YOU CAN'T JUST WAIT AROUND FOREVER.
THANKS, RAZZAQ.
BUT FOR NOW, I'M GOING TO KEEP WAITING.
THE WEEKS WENT BY...

AND ONE DAY...

CLICK!
CLICK!

RiiiPP

HADi!!

DADDY GOT THE DOCUMENTS!

WE CAN GO BE WITH MAMA!

MAMA?

HAHA!
HAHA!

HELLO, MA'AM!

I'VE BROUGHT THE DOCUMENTS FOR MY APPLICATION FOR A RESIDENCE PERMIT.

HMM...

SO YOU GOT MARRIED THIS YEAR?

NO, IN 2013.

THEN WHY DOES YOUR MARRIAGE CERTIFICATE SAY 2015?

W...WHAT?

THIS IS A MISTAKE!

OUR LAWYER IN SYRIA MESSED UP!

I PROMISE YOU, IT'S TRUE!!

THEY THOUGHT I WAS FALSIFYING DOCUMENTS AND THEY CLOSED MY FILE.

NAJMEH AND I WERE DISTRAUGHT.

IT SEEMED TO US THAT I'D NEVER MANAGE TO GET OUT OF TURKEY.

A FEW DAYS LATER, I GOT A CALL.

HELLO, HAKIM. IT'S FUAD.*

HI, FUAD, IT'S BEEN A WHILE.

*A COUSIN IN AMMAN, SEE BOOK 1

YOUR MOM TOLD ME YOU'RE LIVING IN ISTANBUL NOW.

YES.

HOW ABOUT YOU? STILL IN AMMAN?

YES, BUT NOT FOR MUCH LONGER, INSHALLAH.

I'M GOING TO EUROPE.

REALLY?

BUT HOW?

THAT'S WHY I'M CALLING...

SINCE YOU LIVE IN TURKEY, YOU MUST KNOW HOW TO FIND A SMUGGLER?

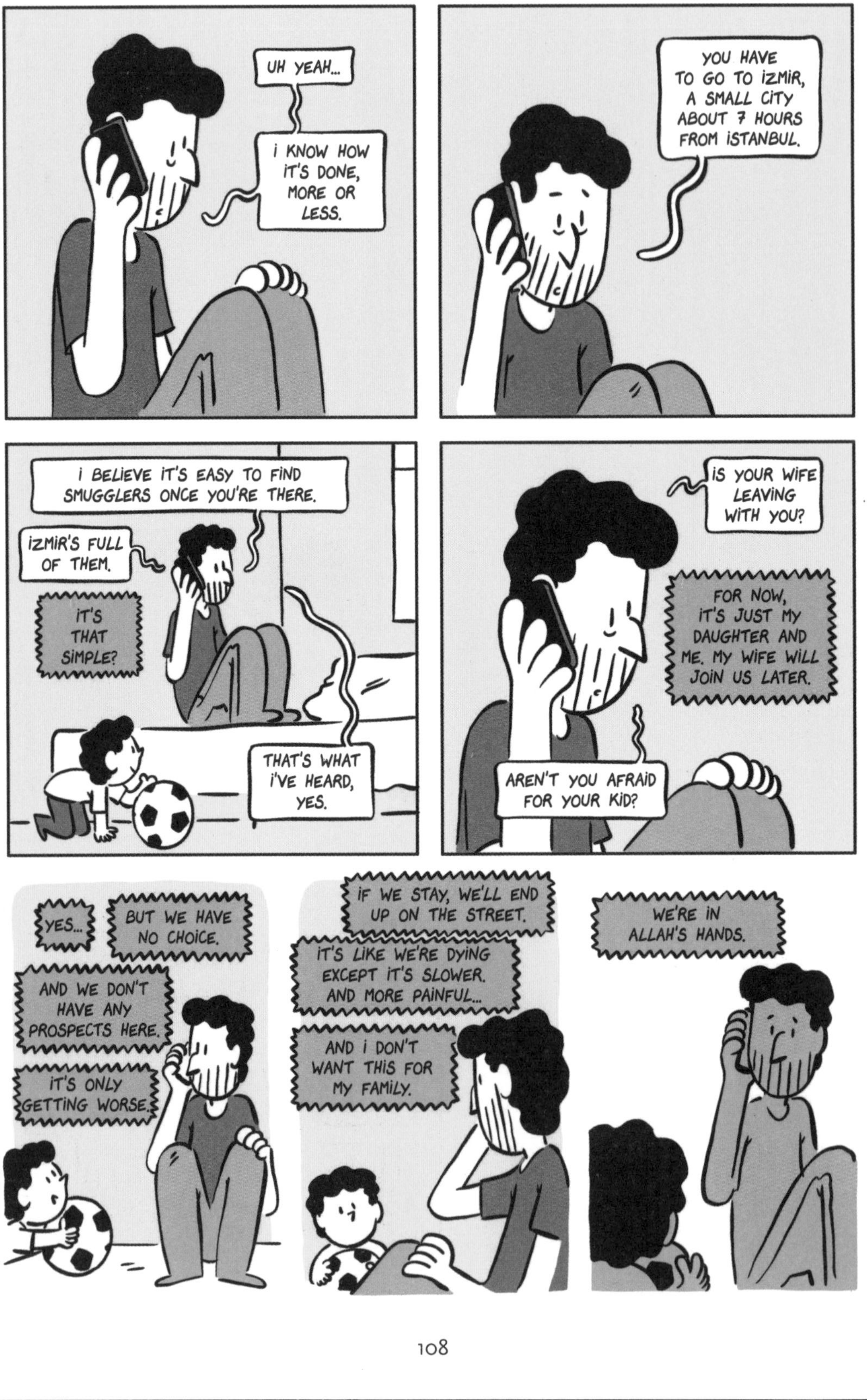
UH YEAH...
i KNOW HOW iT'S DONE, MORE OR LESS.
YOU HAVE TO GO TO iZMiR, A SMALL CiTY ABOUT 7 HOURS FROM iSTANBUL.
i BELiEVE iT'S EASY TO FiND SMUGGLERS ONCE YOU'RE THERE.
iZMiR'S FULL OF THEM.
iT'S THAT SiMPLE?
THAT'S WHAT i'VE HEARD, YES.
iS YOUR WiFE LEAViNG WiTH YOU?
FOR NOW, iT'S JUST MY DAUGHTER AND ME. MY WiFE WiLL JOiN US LATER.
AREN'T YOU AFRAiD FOR YOUR KiD?
YES...
BUT WE HAVE NO CHOiCE.
AND WE DON'T HAVE ANY PROSPECTS HERE.
iT'S ONLY GETTiNG WORSE.
iF WE STAY, WE'LL END UP ON THE STREET.
iT'S LiKE WE'RE DYiNG EXCEPT iT'S SLOWER. AND MORE PAiNFUL...
AND i DON'T WANT THiS FOR MY FAMiLY.
WE'RE iN ALLAH'S HANDS.

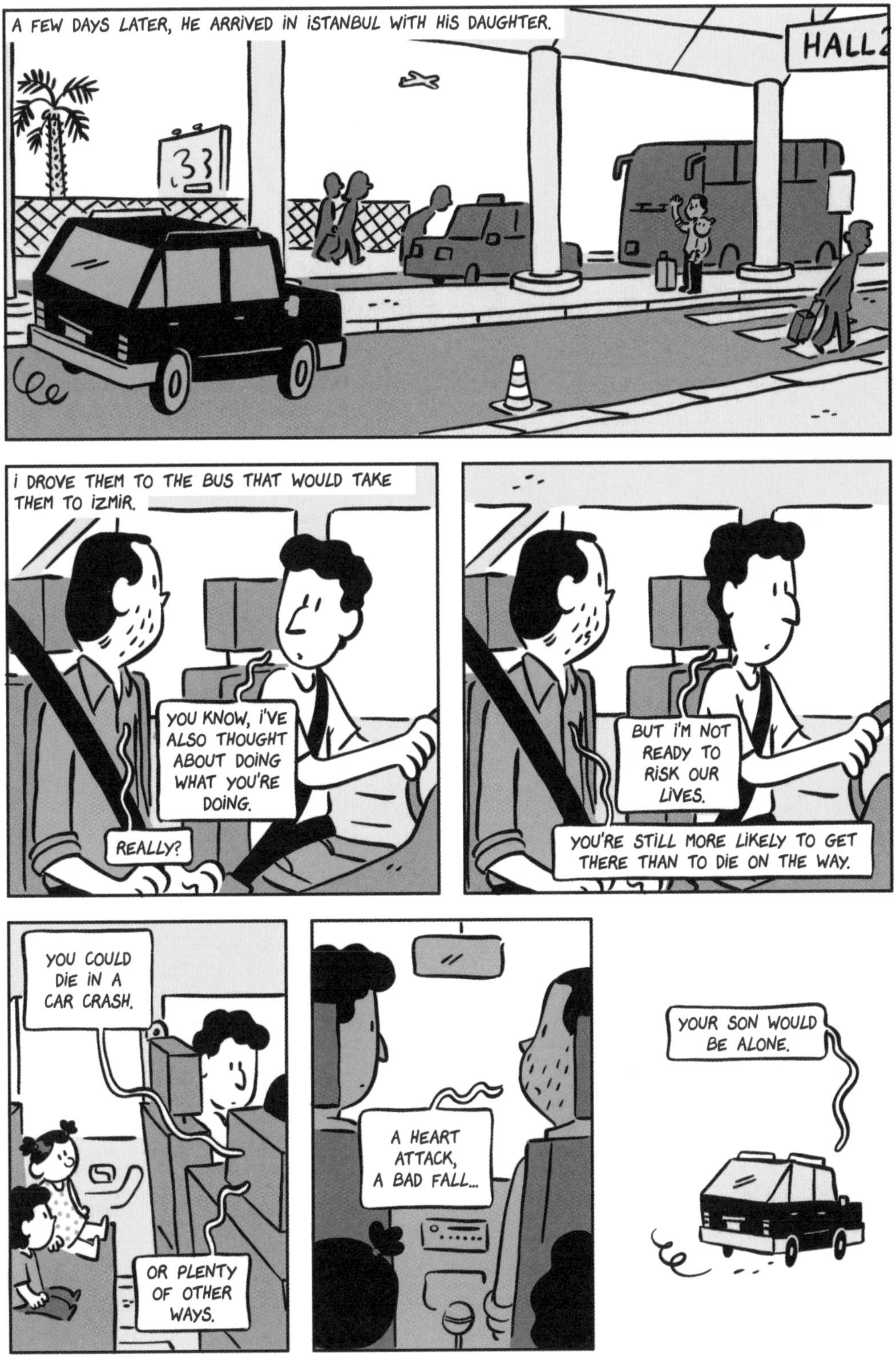
A FEW DAYS LATER, HE ARRIVED IN ISTANBUL WITH HIS DAUGHTER.
HALL
I DROVE THEM TO THE BUS THAT WOULD TAKE THEM TO IZMIR.
YOU KNOW, I'VE ALSO THOUGHT ABOUT DOING WHAT YOU'RE DOING.
REALLY?
BUT I'M NOT READY TO RISK OUR LIVES.
YOU'RE STILL MORE LIKELY TO GET THERE THAN TO DIE ON THE WAY.
YOU COULD DIE IN A CAR CRASH.
OR PLENTY OF OTHER WAYS.
A HEART ATTACK, A BAD FALL...
YOUR SON WOULD BE ALONE.

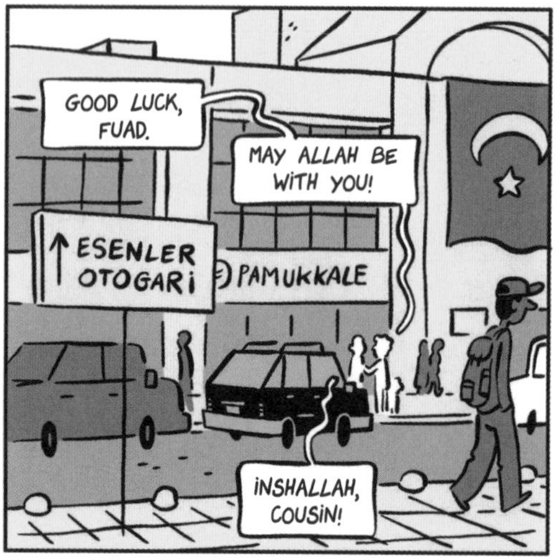
GOOD LUCK, FUAD.
MAY ALLAH BE WITH YOU!
ESENLER OTOGARİ
PAMUKKALE
İNSHALLAH, COUSİN!

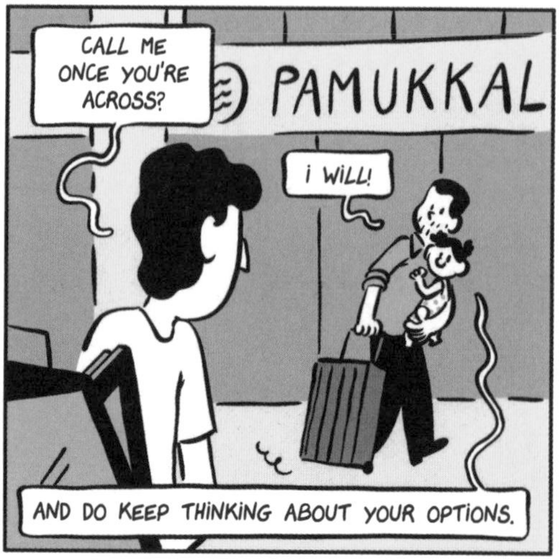
CALL ME ONCE YOU'RE ACROSS?
PAMUKKAL
İ WİLL!
AND DO KEEP THİNKİNG ABOUT YOUR OPTİONS.

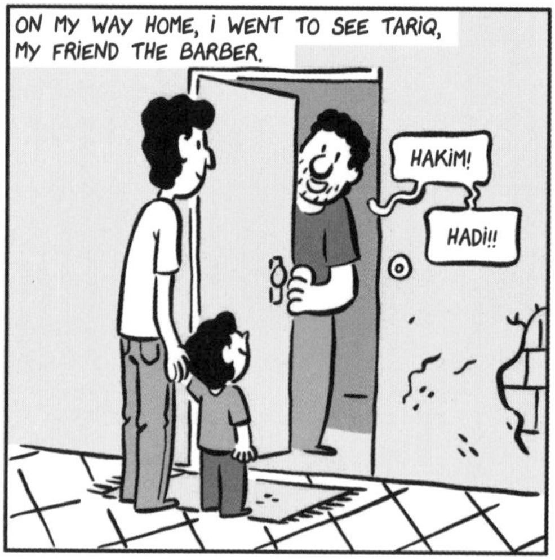
ON MY WAY HOME, İ WENT TO SEE TARİQ, MY FRIEND THE BARBER.
HAKİM!
HADİ!!

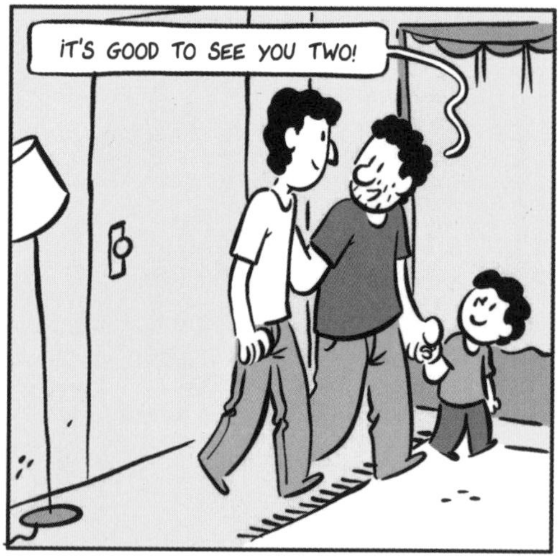
İT'S GOOD TO SEE YOU TWO!

HE LİVED İN A CRAMPED LİTTLE APARTMENT WİTH SİX OTHER SYRİANS.

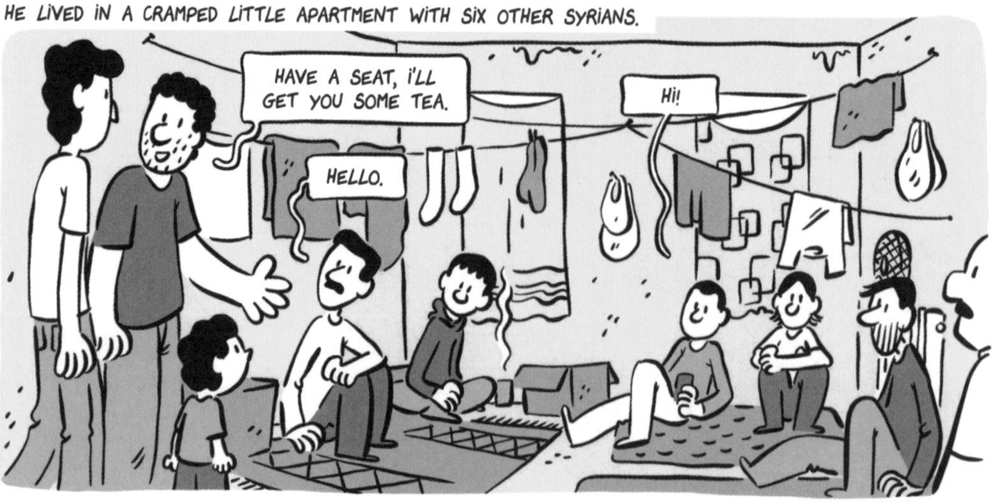
HAVE A SEAT, İ'LL GET YOU SOME TEA.
HELLO.
Hİ!

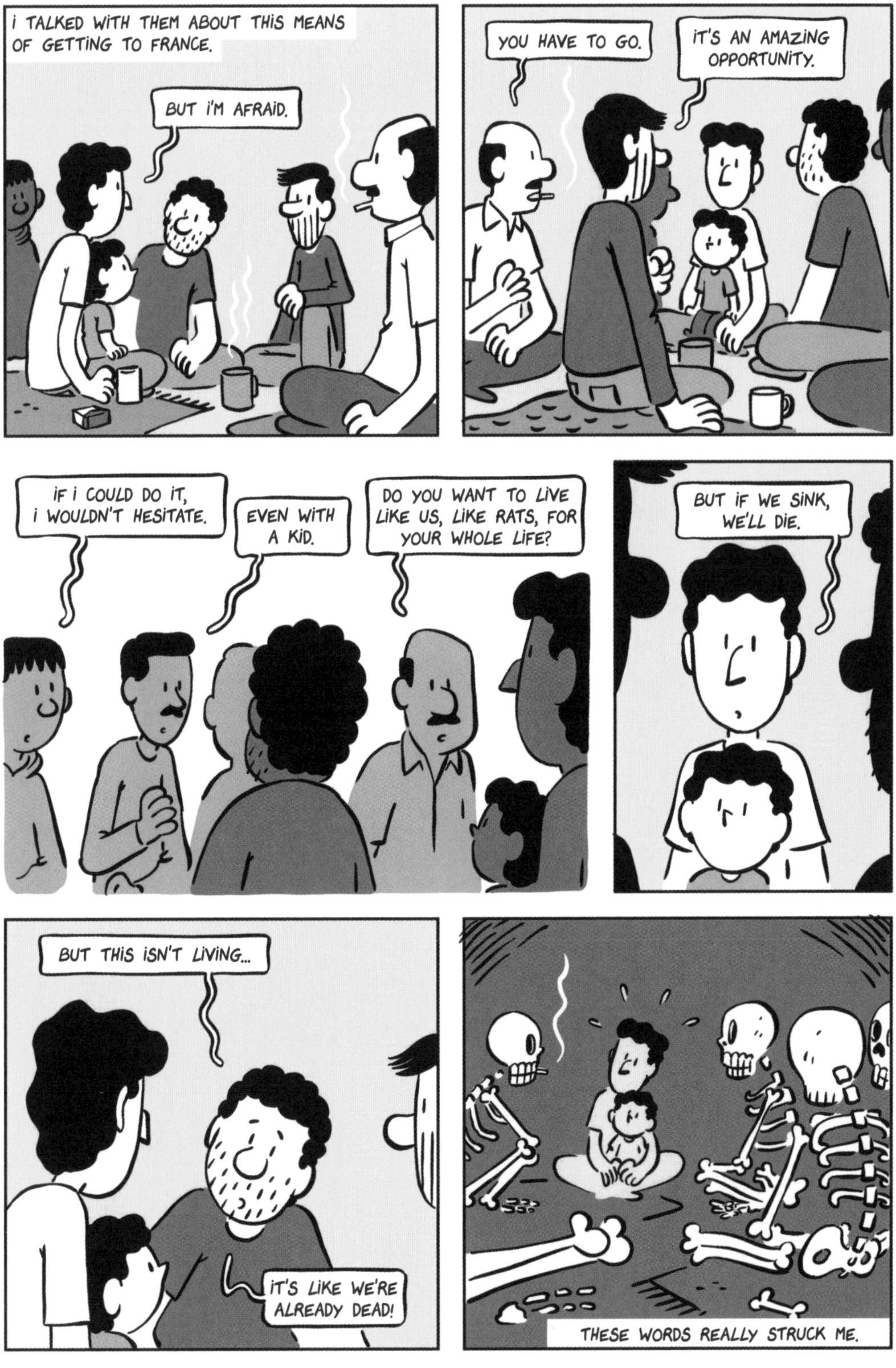
I TALKED WITH THEM ABOUT THIS MEANS OF GETTING TO FRANCE.
BUT I'M AFRAID.
YOU HAVE TO GO.
IT'S AN AMAZING OPPORTUNITY.
IF I COULD DO IT, I WOULDN'T HESITATE.
EVEN WITH A KID.
DO YOU WANT TO LIVE LIKE US, LIKE RATS, FOR YOUR WHOLE LIFE?
BUT IF WE SINK, WE'LL DIE.
BUT THIS ISN'T LIVING...
IT'S LIKE WE'RE ALREADY DEAD!
THESE WORDS REALLY STRUCK ME.

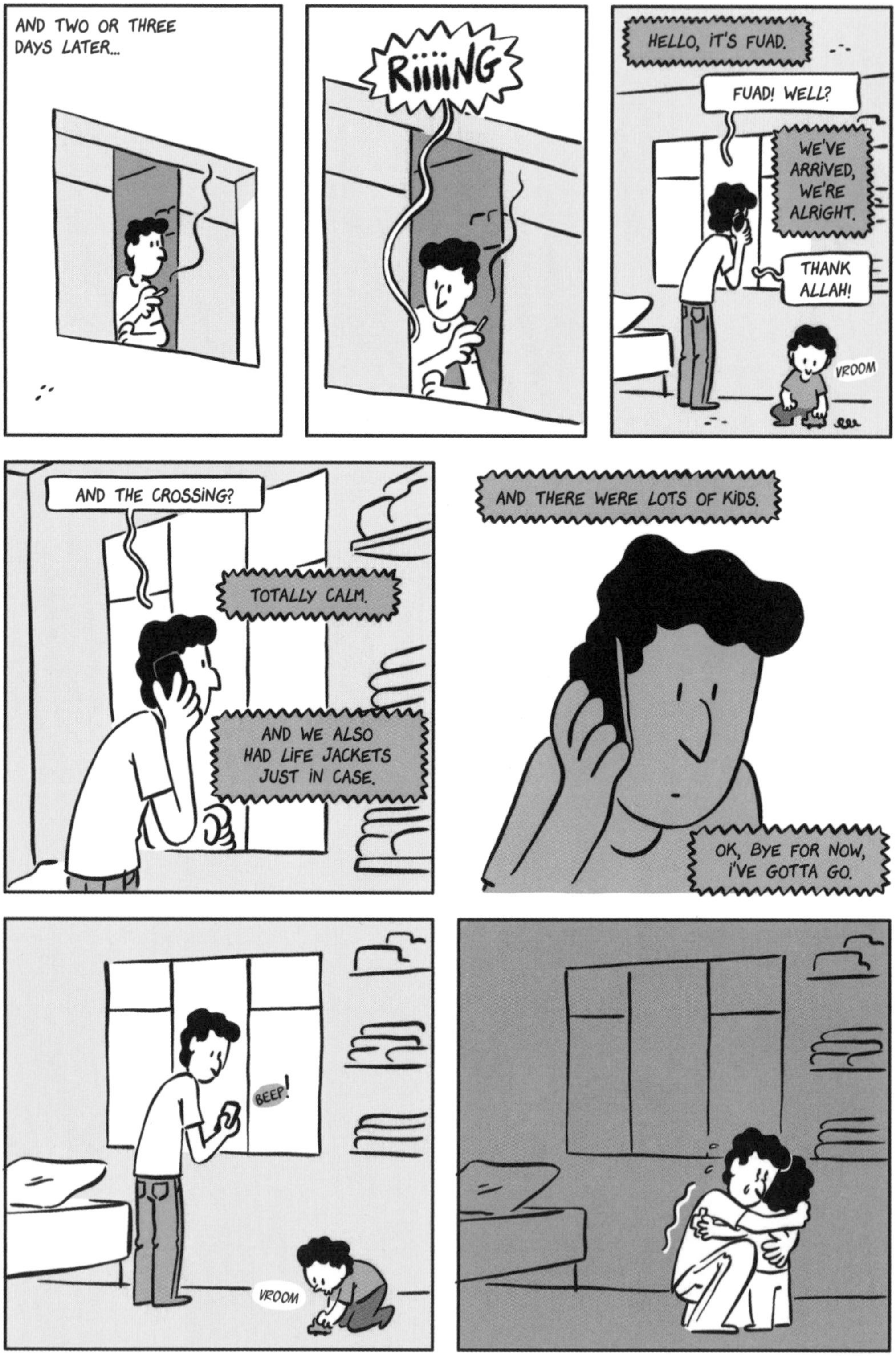
AND TWO OR THREE DAYS LATER...
RIIIING
HELLO, IT'S FUAD.
FUAD! WELL?
WE'VE ARRIVED, WE'RE ALRIGHT.
THANK ALLAH!
VROOM
AND THE CROSSING?
TOTALLY CALM.
AND WE ALSO HAD LIFE JACKETS JUST IN CASE.
AND THERE WERE LOTS OF KIDS.
OK, BYE FOR NOW, I'VE GOTTA GO.
BEEP!
VROOM

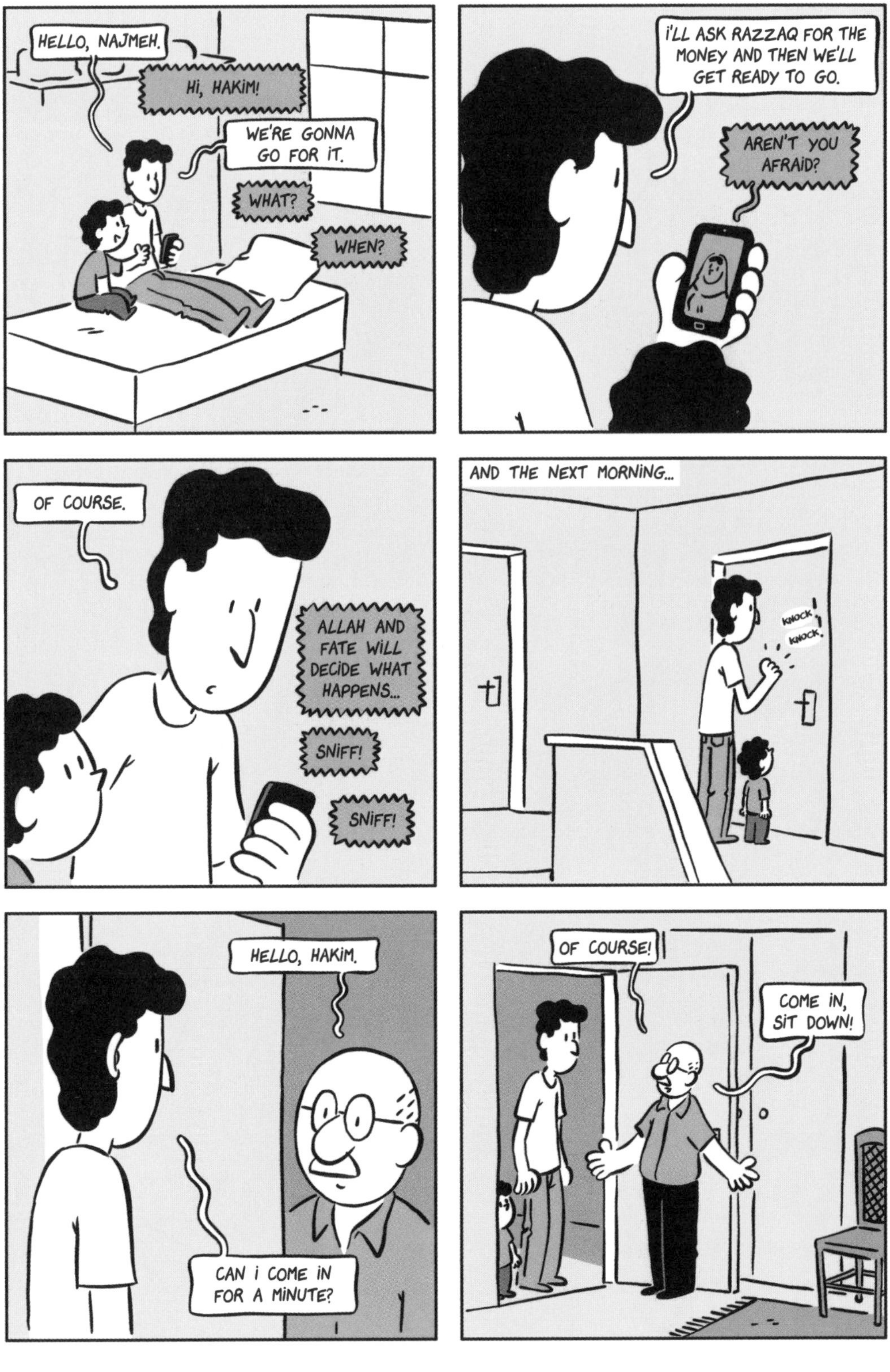
HELLO, NAJMEH.
Hi, HAKiM!
WE'RE GONNA GO FOR iT.
WHAT?
WHEN?
i'LL ASK RAZZAQ FOR THE MONEY AND THEN WE'LL GET READY TO GO.
AREN'T YOU AFRAiD?
OF COURSE.
ALLAH AND FATE WiLL DECiDE WHAT HAPPENS...
SNiFF!
SNiFF!
AND THE NEXT MORNiNG...
KNOCK
KNOCK
HELLO, HAKiM.
CAN i COME iN FOR A MiNUTE?
OF COURSE!
COME iN, SiT DOWN!

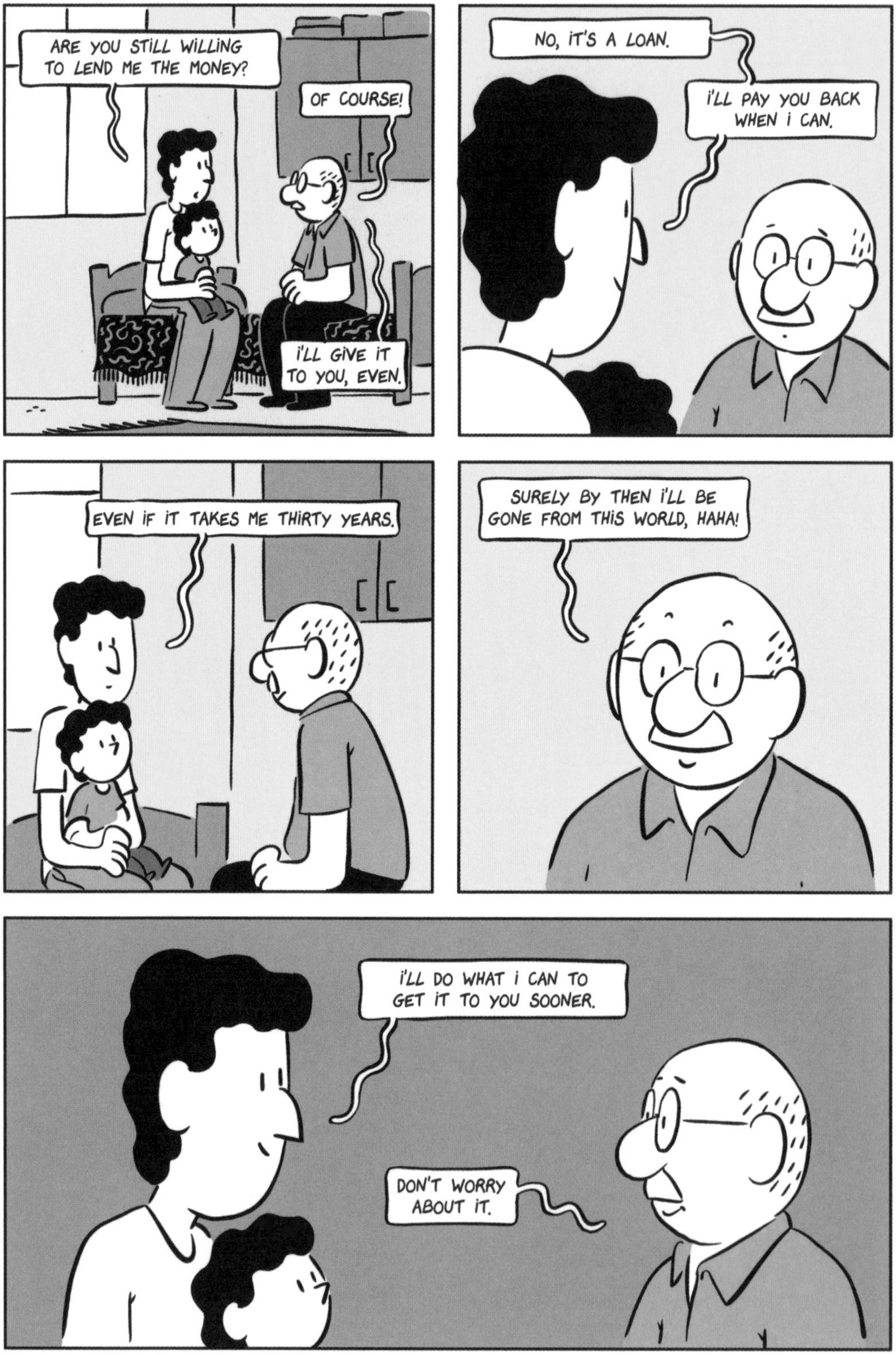
ARE YOU STILL WILLING TO LEND ME THE MONEY?
OF COURSE!
I'LL GIVE IT TO YOU, EVEN.
NO, IT'S A LOAN.
I'LL PAY YOU BACK WHEN I CAN.
EVEN IF IT TAKES ME THIRTY YEARS.
SURELY BY THEN I'LL BE GONE FROM THIS WORLD, HAHA!
I'LL DO WHAT I CAN TO GET IT TO YOU SOONER.
DON'T WORRY ABOUT IT.

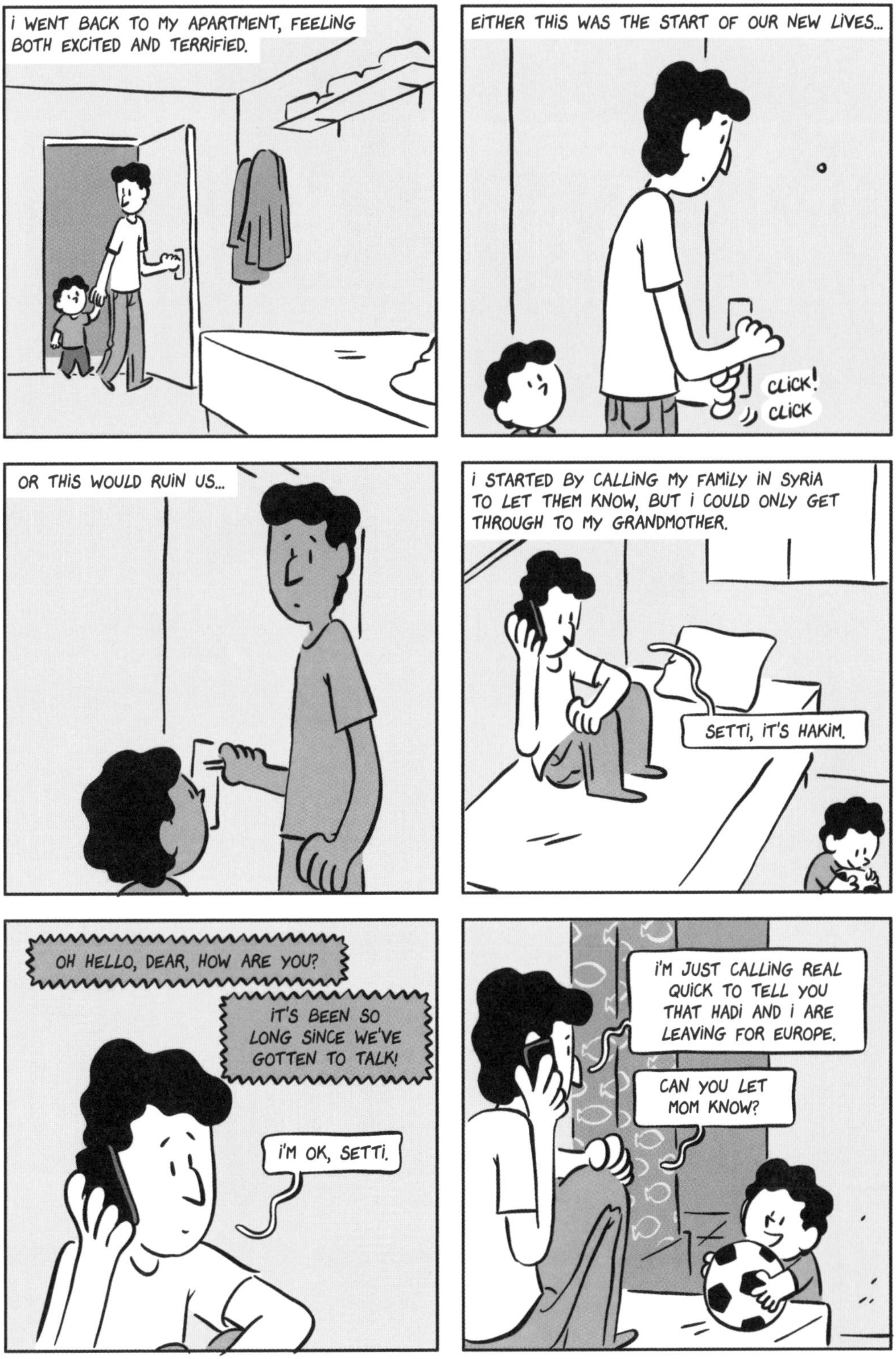
i WENT BACK TO MY APARTMENT, FEELING BOTH EXCITED AND TERRIFIED.
EITHER THIS WAS THE START OF OUR NEW LIVES...
CLICK!
CLICK
OR THIS WOULD RUIN US...
i STARTED BY CALLING MY FAMILY IN SYRIA TO LET THEM KNOW, BUT i COULD ONLY GET THROUGH TO MY GRANDMOTHER.
SETTi, iT'S HAKiM.
OH HELLO, DEAR, HOW ARE YOU?
iT'S BEEN SO LONG SiNCE WE'VE GOTTEN TO TALK!
i'M OK, SETTi.
i'M JUST CALLiNG REAL QUiCK TO TELL YOU THAT HADi AND i ARE LEAViNG FOR EUROPE.
CAN YOU LET MOM KNOW?

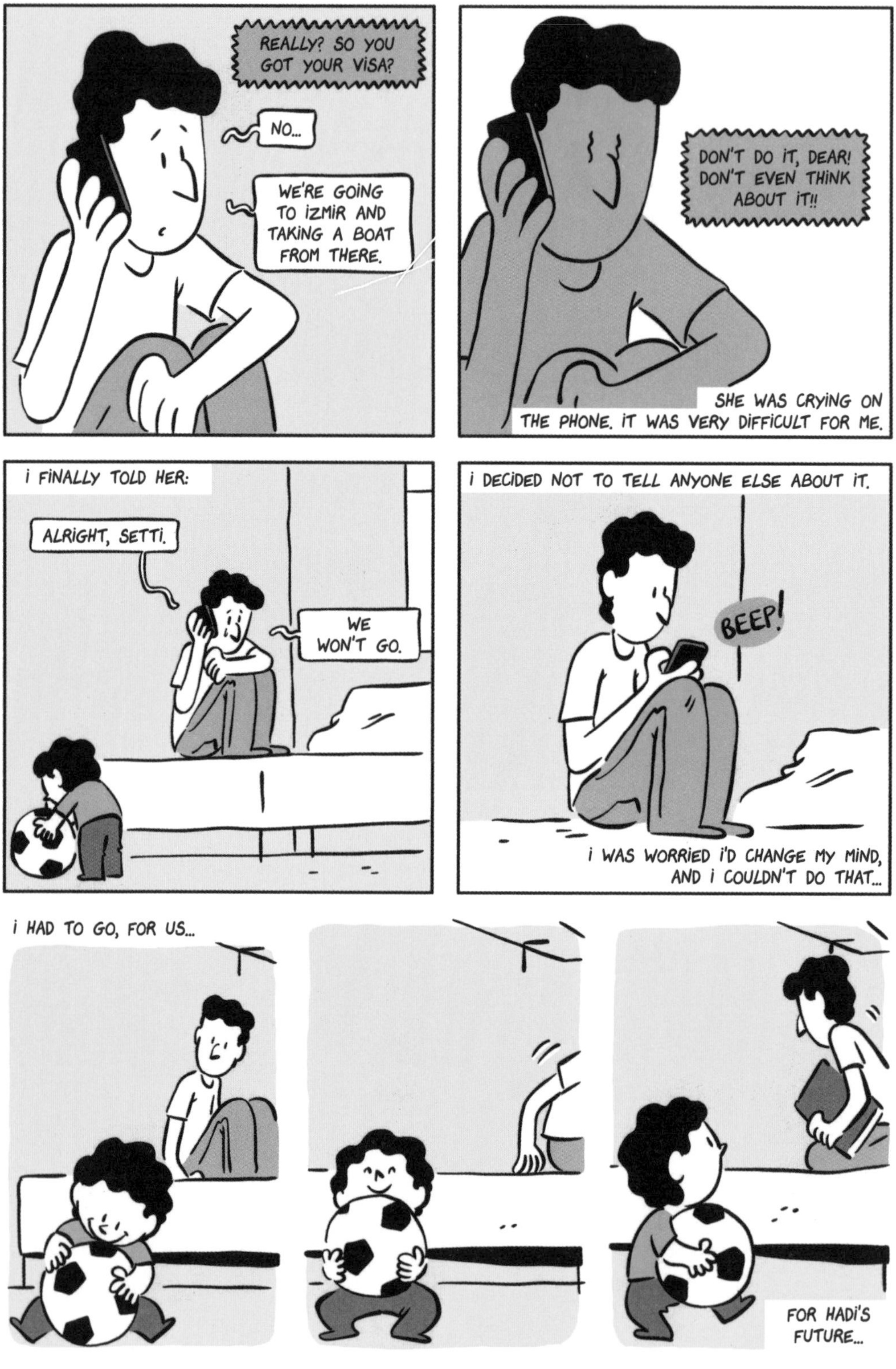
REALLY? SO YOU GOT YOUR VISA?
NO...
WE'RE GOING TO IZMIR AND TAKING A BOAT FROM THERE.
DON'T DO IT, DEAR! DON'T EVEN THINK ABOUT IT!!
SHE WAS CRYING ON THE PHONE. IT WAS VERY DIFFICULT FOR ME.
I FINALLY TOLD HER:
ALRIGHT, SETTI.
WE WON'T GO.
I DECIDED NOT TO TELL ANYONE ELSE ABOUT IT.
BEEP!
I WAS WORRIED I'D CHANGE MY MIND, AND I COULDN'T DO THAT...
I HAD TO GO, FOR US...
FOR HADI'S FUTURE...

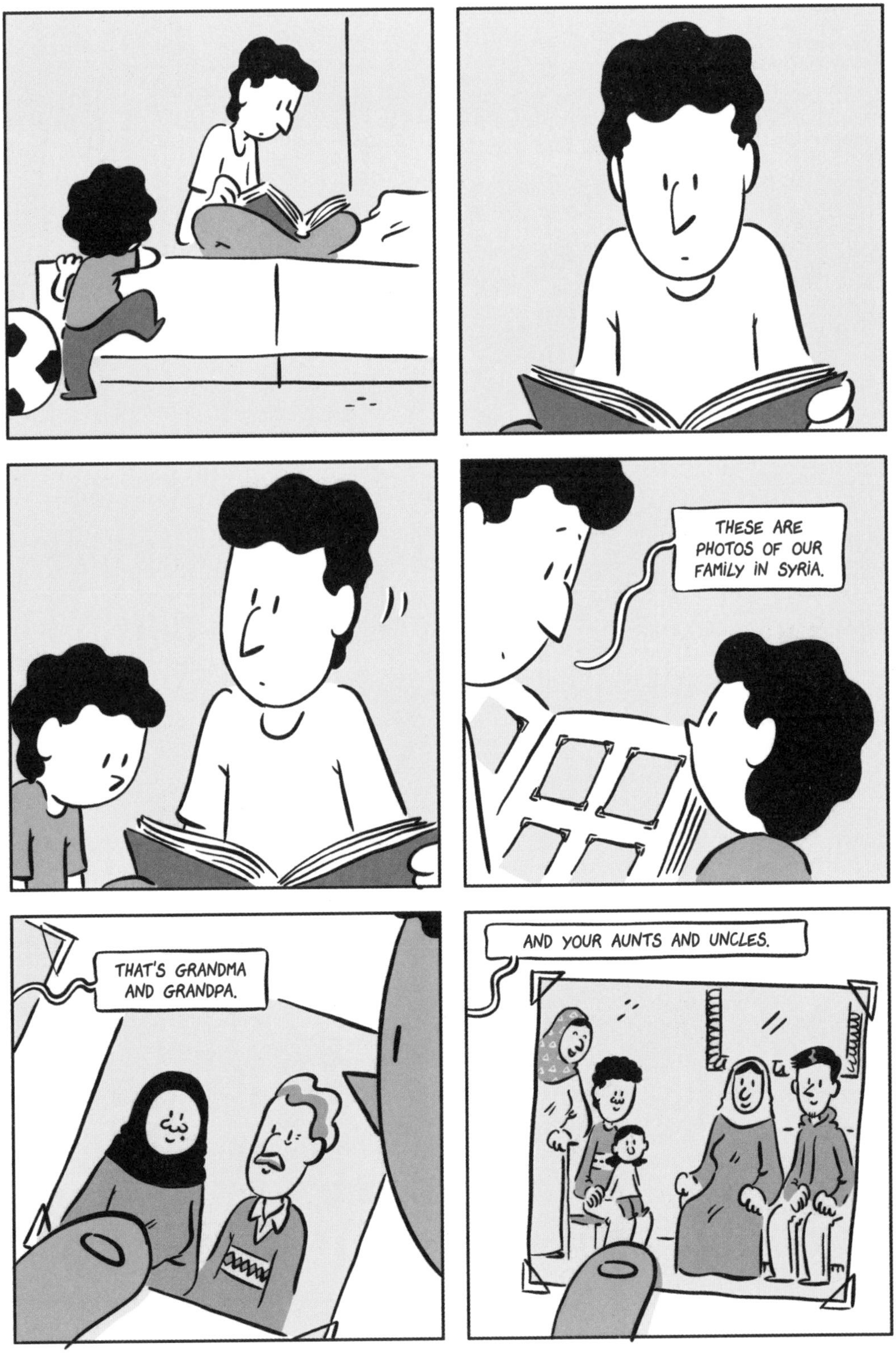
THESE ARE PHOTOS OF OUR FAMILY IN SYRIA.
THAT'S GRANDMA AND GRANDPA.
AND YOUR AUNTS AND UNCLES.

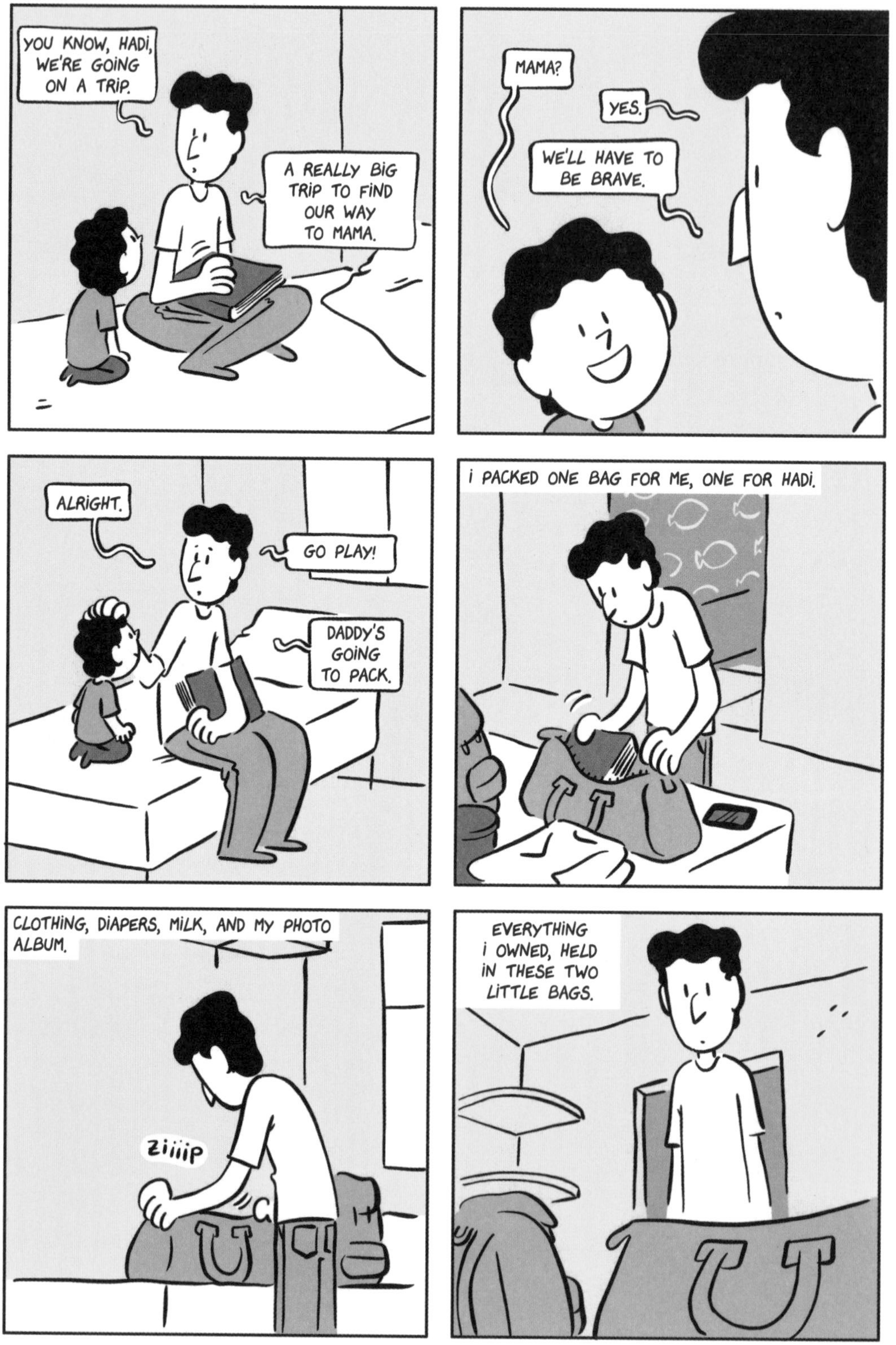
YOU KNOW, HADI, WE'RE GOING ON A TRIP.
A REALLY BIG TRIP TO FIND OUR WAY TO MAMA.
MAMA?
YES.
WE'LL HAVE TO BE BRAVE.
ALRIGHT.
GO PLAY!
DADDY'S GOING TO PACK.
I PACKED ONE BAG FOR ME, ONE FOR HADI.
CLOTHING, DIAPERS, MILK, AND MY PHOTO ALBUM.
ZIIIIP
EVERYTHING I OWNED, HELD IN THESE TWO LITTLE BAGS.

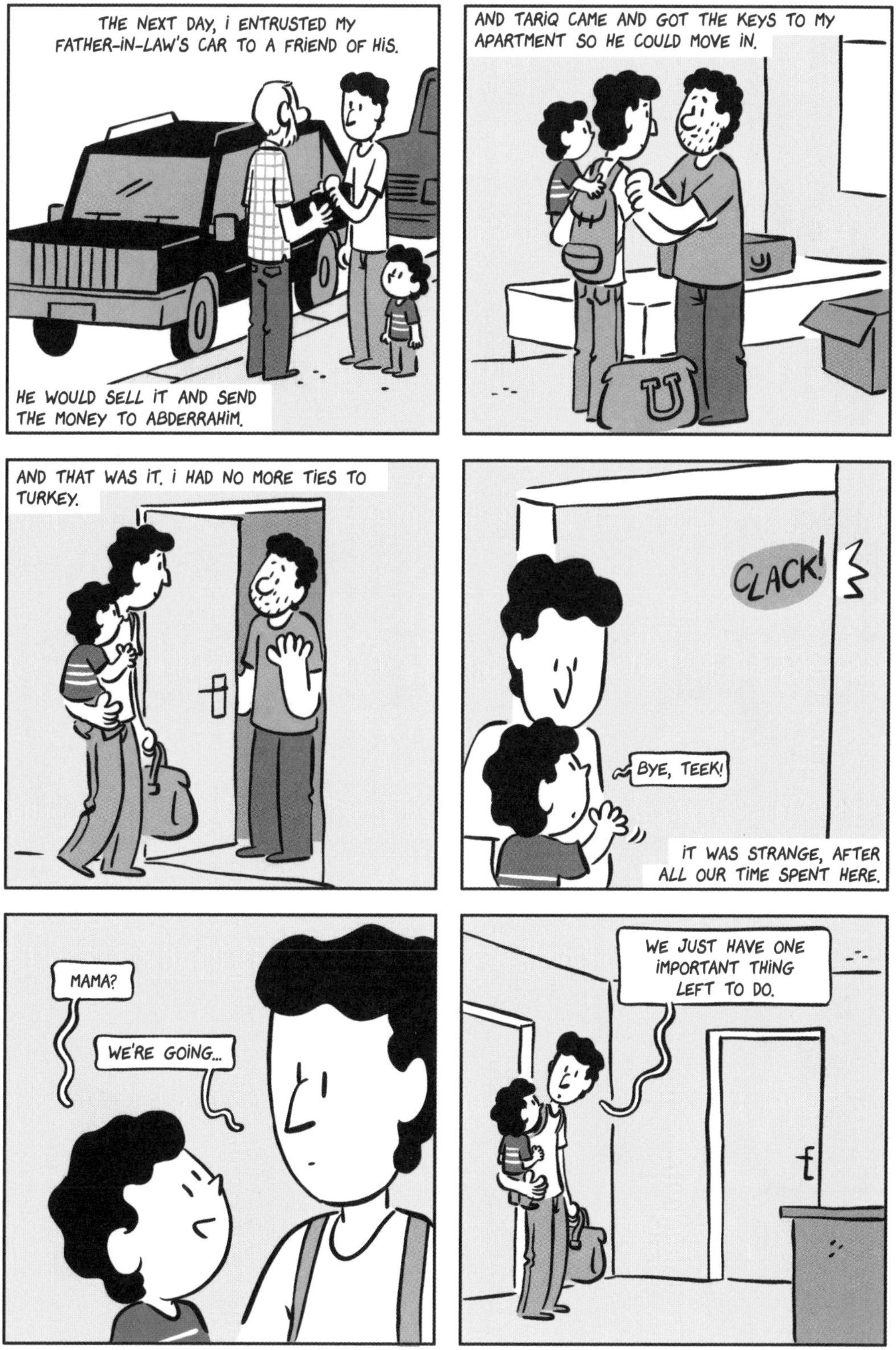
THE NEXT DAY, I ENTRUSTED MY FATHER-IN-LAW'S CAR TO A FRIEND OF HIS.
HE WOULD SELL IT AND SEND THE MONEY TO ABDERRAHIM.
AND TARIQ CAME AND GOT THE KEYS TO MY APARTMENT SO HE COULD MOVE IN.
AND THAT WAS IT. I HAD NO MORE TIES TO TURKEY.
CLACK!
BYE, TEEK!
IT WAS STRANGE, AFTER ALL OUR TIME SPENT HERE.
MAMA?
WE'RE GOING...
WE JUST HAVE ONE IMPORTANT THING LEFT TO DO.

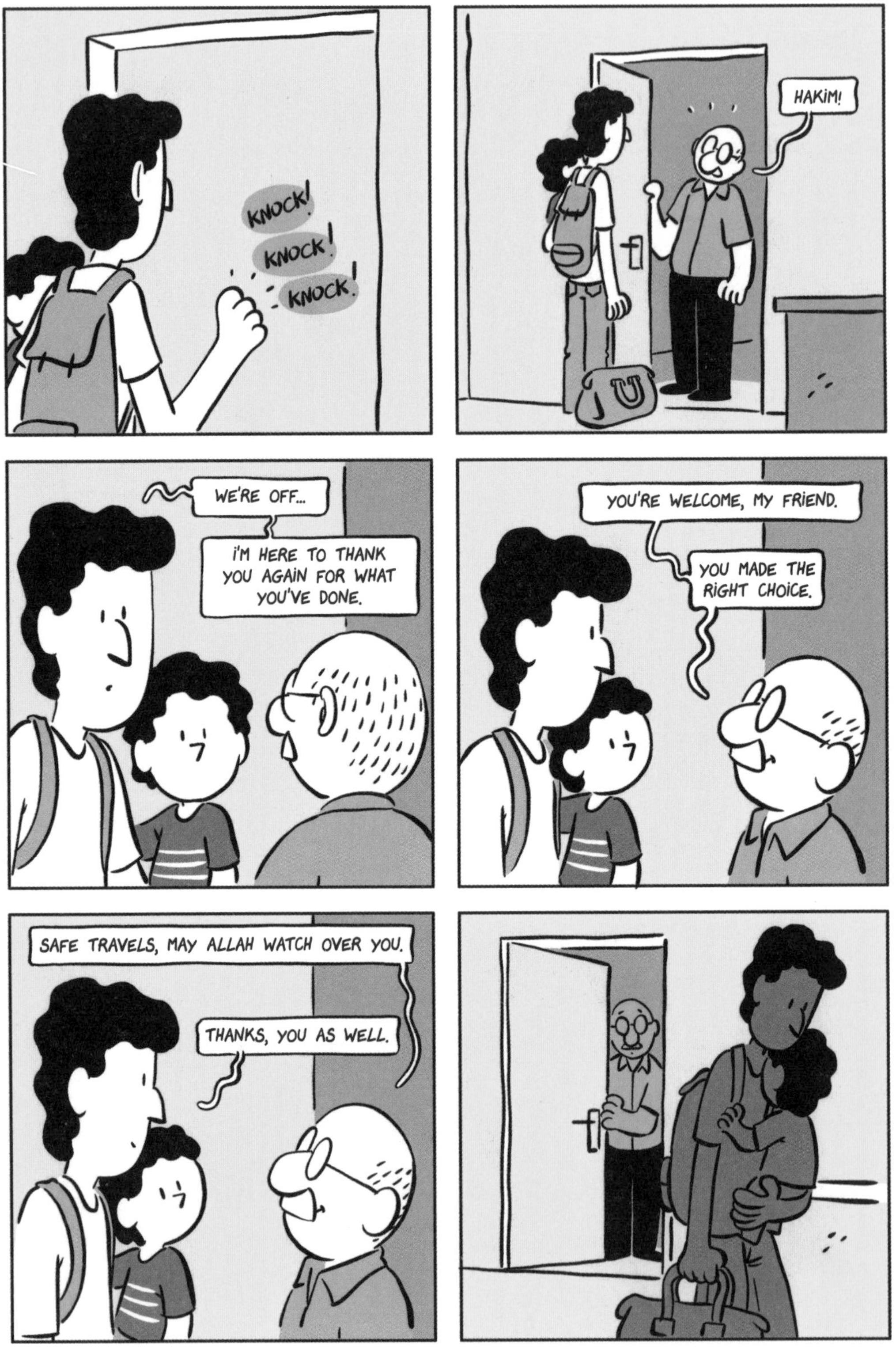
KNOCK!
KNOCK!
KNOCK!
HAKIM!
WE'RE OFF...
I'M HERE TO THANK YOU AGAIN FOR WHAT YOU'VE DONE.
YOU'RE WELCOME, MY FRIEND.
YOU MADE THE RIGHT CHOICE.
SAFE TRAVELS, MAY ALLAH WATCH OVER YOU.
THANKS, YOU AS WELL.

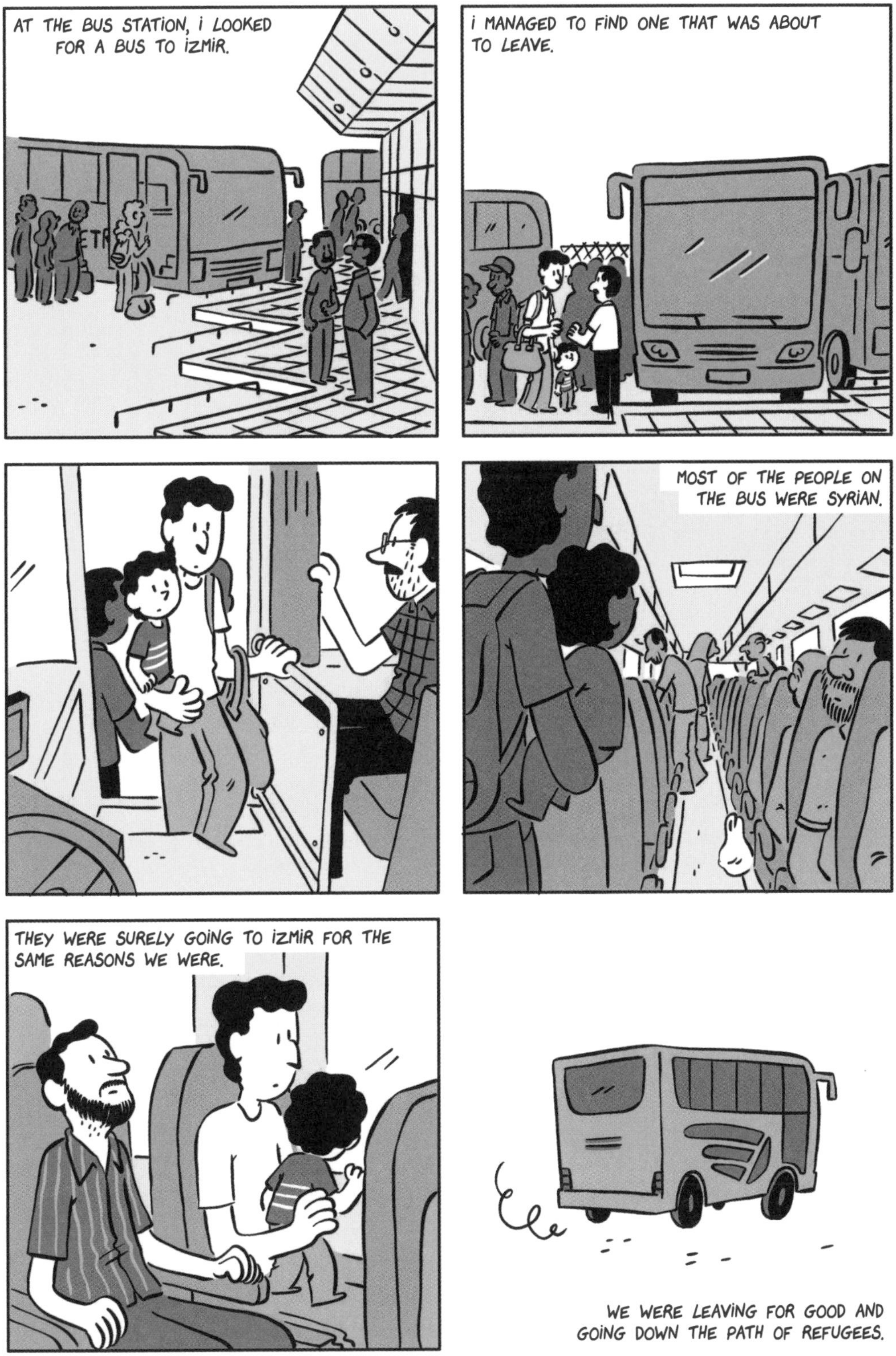
AT THE BUS STATION, I LOOKED FOR A BUS TO İZMIR.
I MANAGED TO FIND ONE THAT WAS ABOUT TO LEAVE.
MOST OF THE PEOPLE ON THE BUS WERE SYRIAN.
THEY WERE SURELY GOING TO İZMIR FOR THE SAME REASONS WE WERE.
WE WERE LEAVING FOR GOOD AND GOING DOWN THE PATH OF REFUGEES.

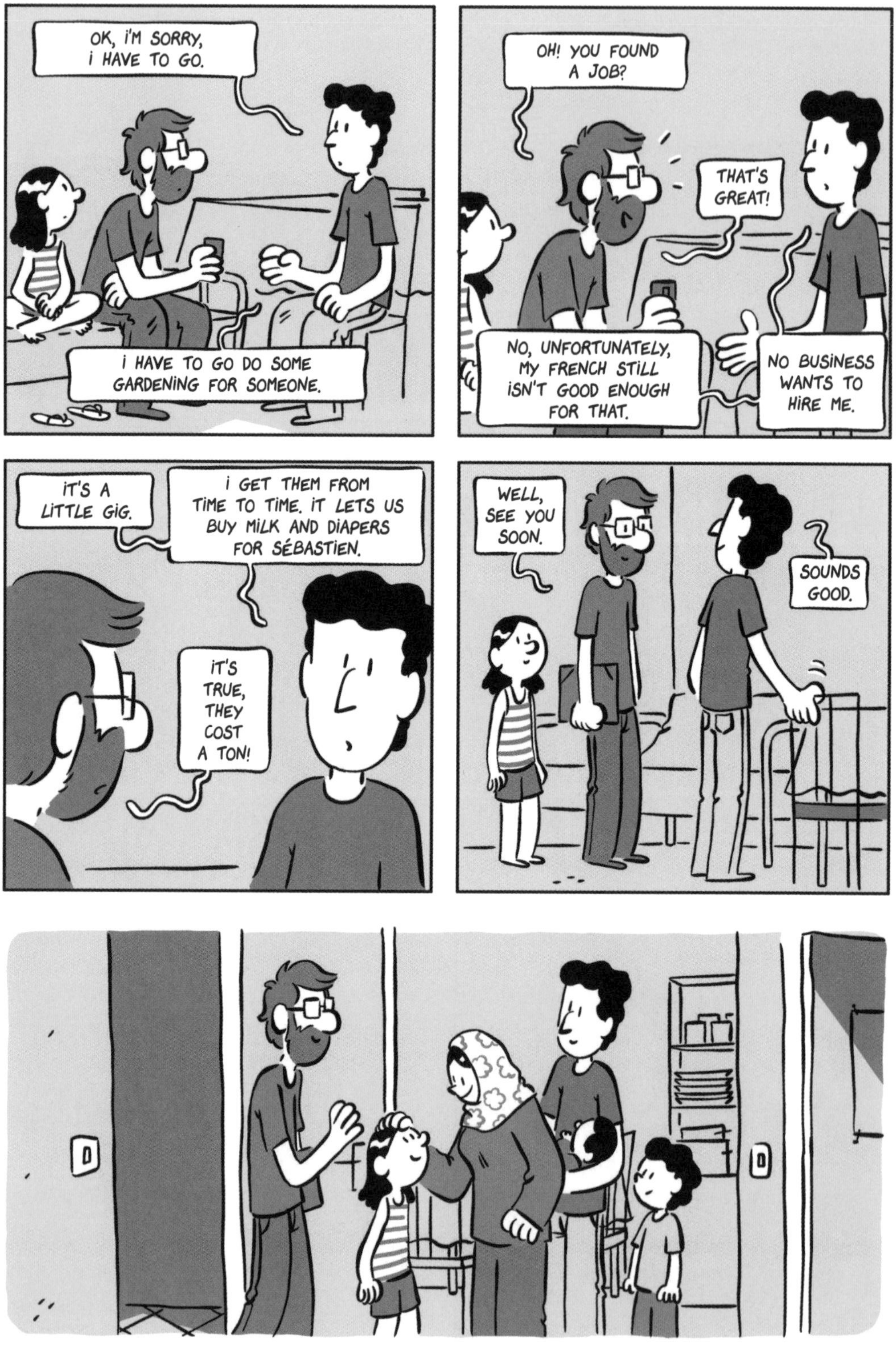
OK, i'M SORRY, i HAVE TO GO.
i HAVE TO GO DO SOME GARDENiNG FOR SOMEONE.
OH! YOU FOUND A JOB?
THAT'S GREAT!
NO, UNFORTUNATELY, MY FRENCH STiLL iSN'T GOOD ENOUGH FOR THAT.
NO BUSiNESS WANTS TO HiRE ME.
iT'S A LiTTLE GiG.
i GET THEM FROM TiME TO TiME. iT LETS US BUY MiLK AND DiAPERS FOR SÉBASTiEN.
iT'S TRUE, THEY COST A TON!
WELL, SEE YOU SOON.
SOUNDS GOOD.

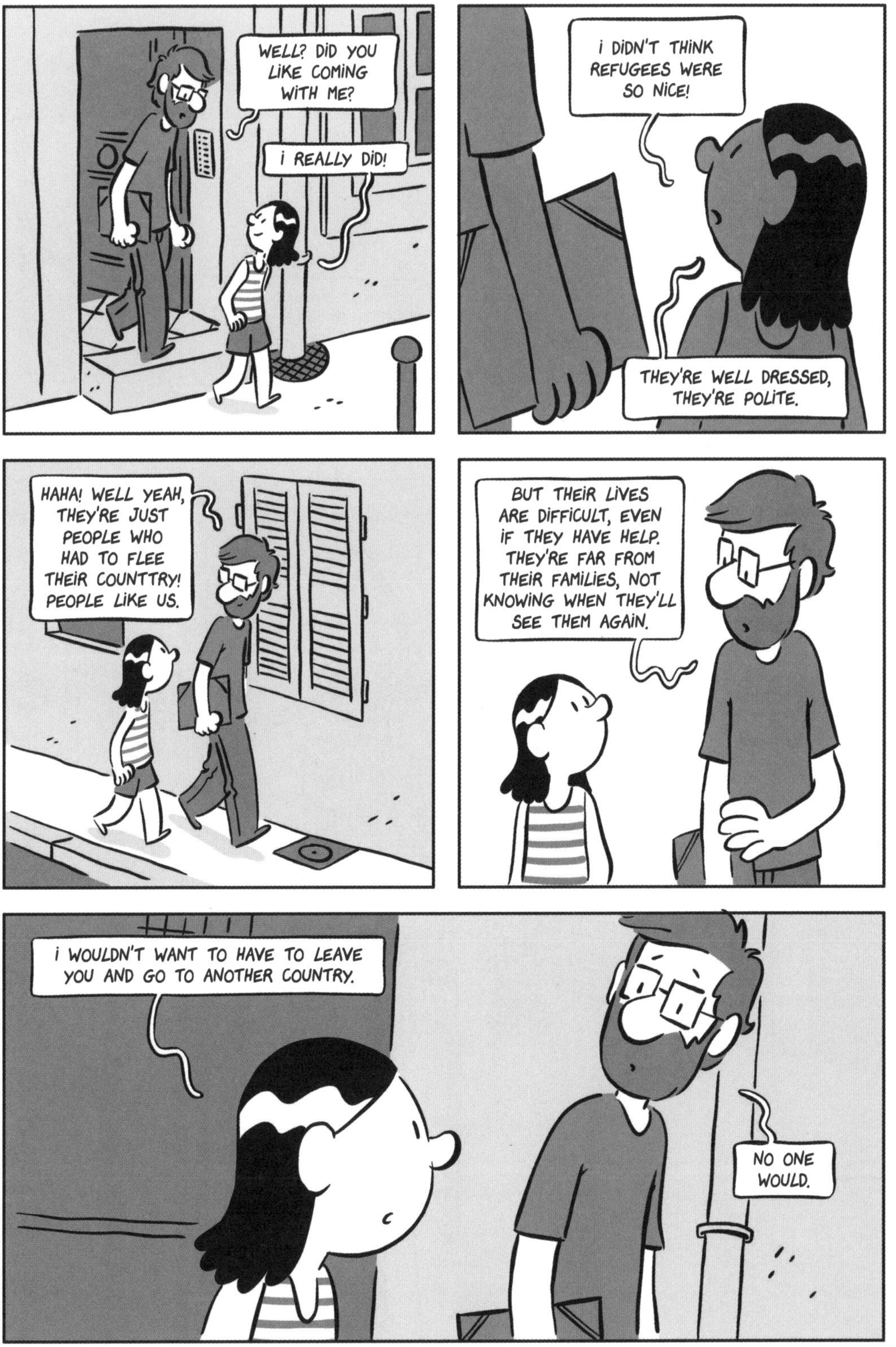
WELL? DID YOU LIKE COMING WITH ME?
I REALLY DID!
I DIDN'T THINK REFUGEES WERE SO NICE!
THEY'RE WELL DRESSED, THEY'RE POLITE.
HAHA! WELL YEAH, THEY'RE JUST PEOPLE WHO HAD TO FLEE THEIR COUNTTRY! PEOPLE LIKE US.
BUT THEIR LIVES ARE DIFFICULT, EVEN IF THEY HAVE HELP. THEY'RE FAR FROM THEIR FAMILIES, NOT KNOWING WHEN THEY'LL SEE THEM AGAIN.
I WOULDN'T WANT TO HAVE TO LEAVE YOU AND GO TO ANOTHER COUNTRY.
NO ONE WOULD.

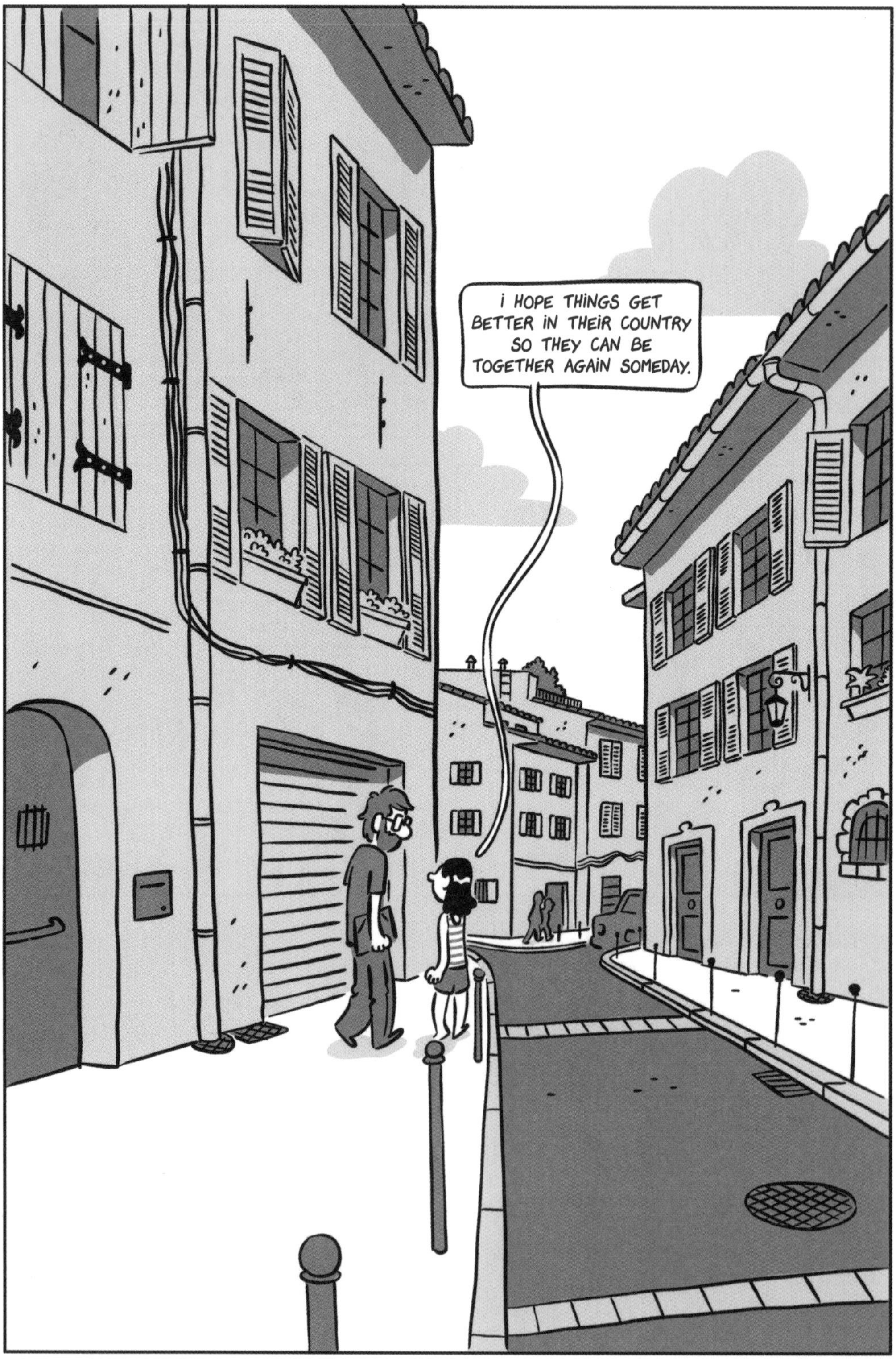
I HOPE THINGS GET BETTER IN THEIR COUNTRY SO THEY CAN BE TOGETHER AGAIN SOMEDAY.

Chapter 10:
Izmir
(August 2015)

"MAY ALLAH PROTECT US!"

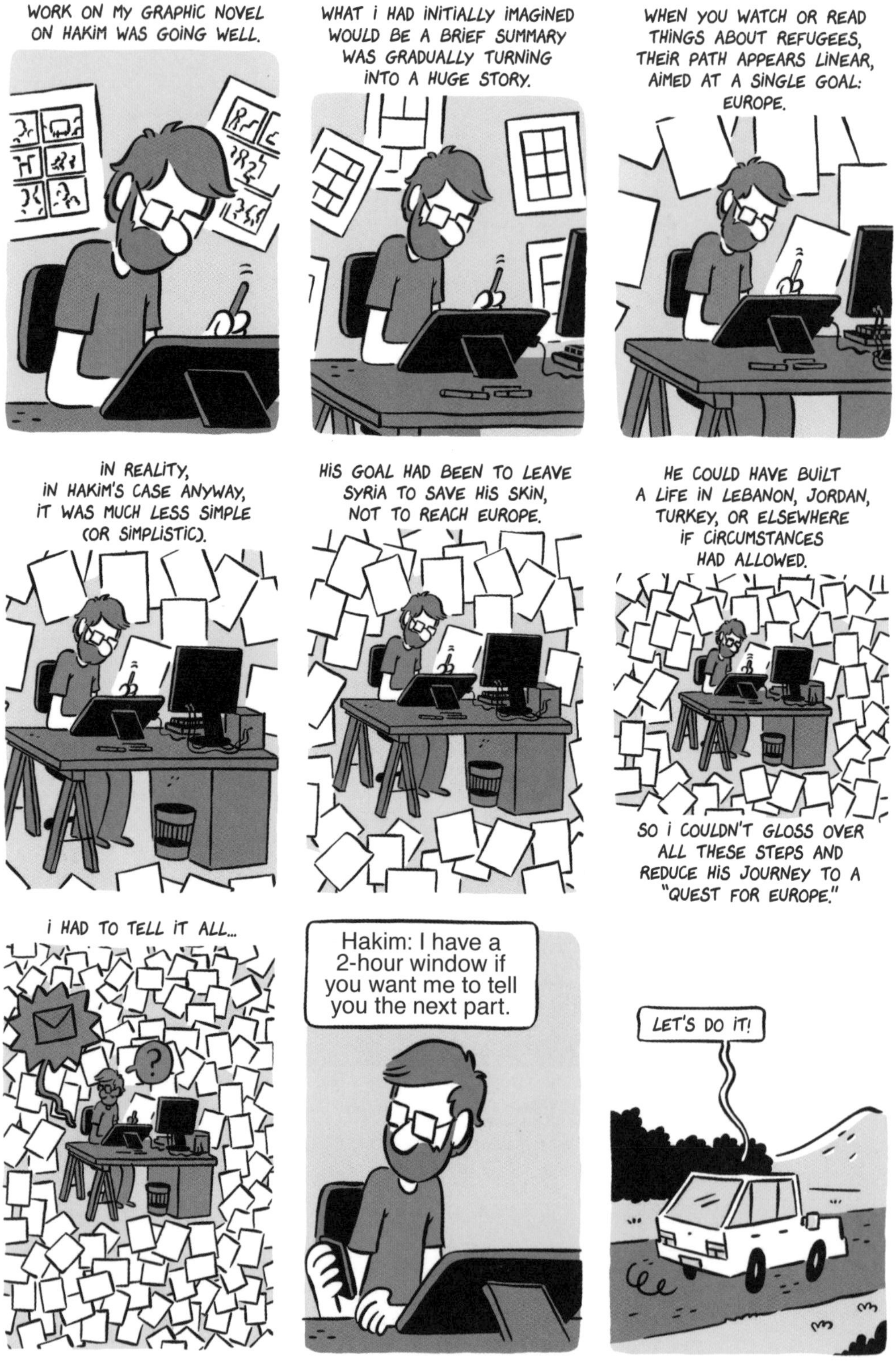
WORK ON MY GRAPHIC NOVEL ON HAKIM WAS GOING WELL.
WHAT I HAD INITIALLY IMAGINED WOULD BE A BRIEF SUMMARY WAS GRADUALLY TURNING INTO A HUGE STORY.
WHEN YOU WATCH OR READ THINGS ABOUT REFUGEES, THEIR PATH APPEARS LINEAR, AIMED AT A SINGLE GOAL: EUROPE.
IN REALITY, IN HAKIM'S CASE ANYWAY, IT WAS MUCH LESS SIMPLE (OR SIMPLISTIC).
HIS GOAL HAD BEEN TO LEAVE SYRIA TO SAVE HIS SKIN, NOT TO REACH EUROPE.
HE COULD HAVE BUILT A LIFE IN LEBANON, JORDAN, TURKEY, OR ELSEWHERE IF CIRCUMSTANCES HAD ALLOWED.
SO I COULDN'T GLOSS OVER ALL THESE STEPS AND REDUCE HIS JOURNEY TO A "QUEST FOR EUROPE."
I HAD TO TELL IT ALL...
?
Hakim: I have a 2-hour window if you want me to tell you the next part.
LET'S DO IT!

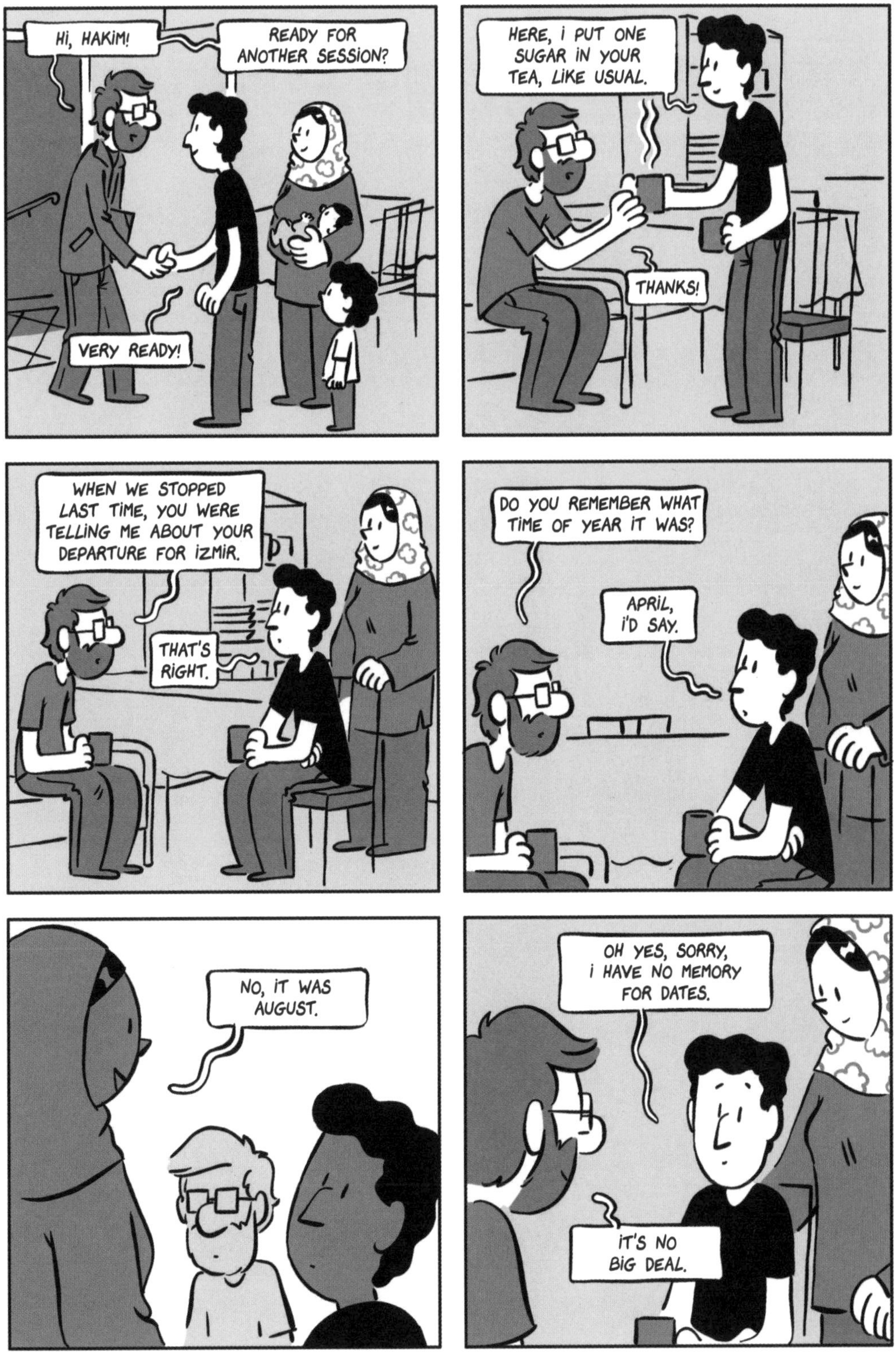
HI, HAKIM!
READY FOR ANOTHER SESSION?
VERY READY!
HERE, I PUT ONE SUGAR IN YOUR TEA, LIKE USUAL.
THANKS!
WHEN WE STOPPED LAST TIME, YOU WERE TELLING ME ABOUT YOUR DEPARTURE FOR IZMIR.
THAT'S RIGHT.
DO YOU REMEMBER WHAT TIME OF YEAR IT WAS?
APRIL, I'D SAY.
NO, IT WAS AUGUST.
OH YES, SORRY, I HAVE NO MEMORY FOR DATES.
IT'S NO BIG DEAL.

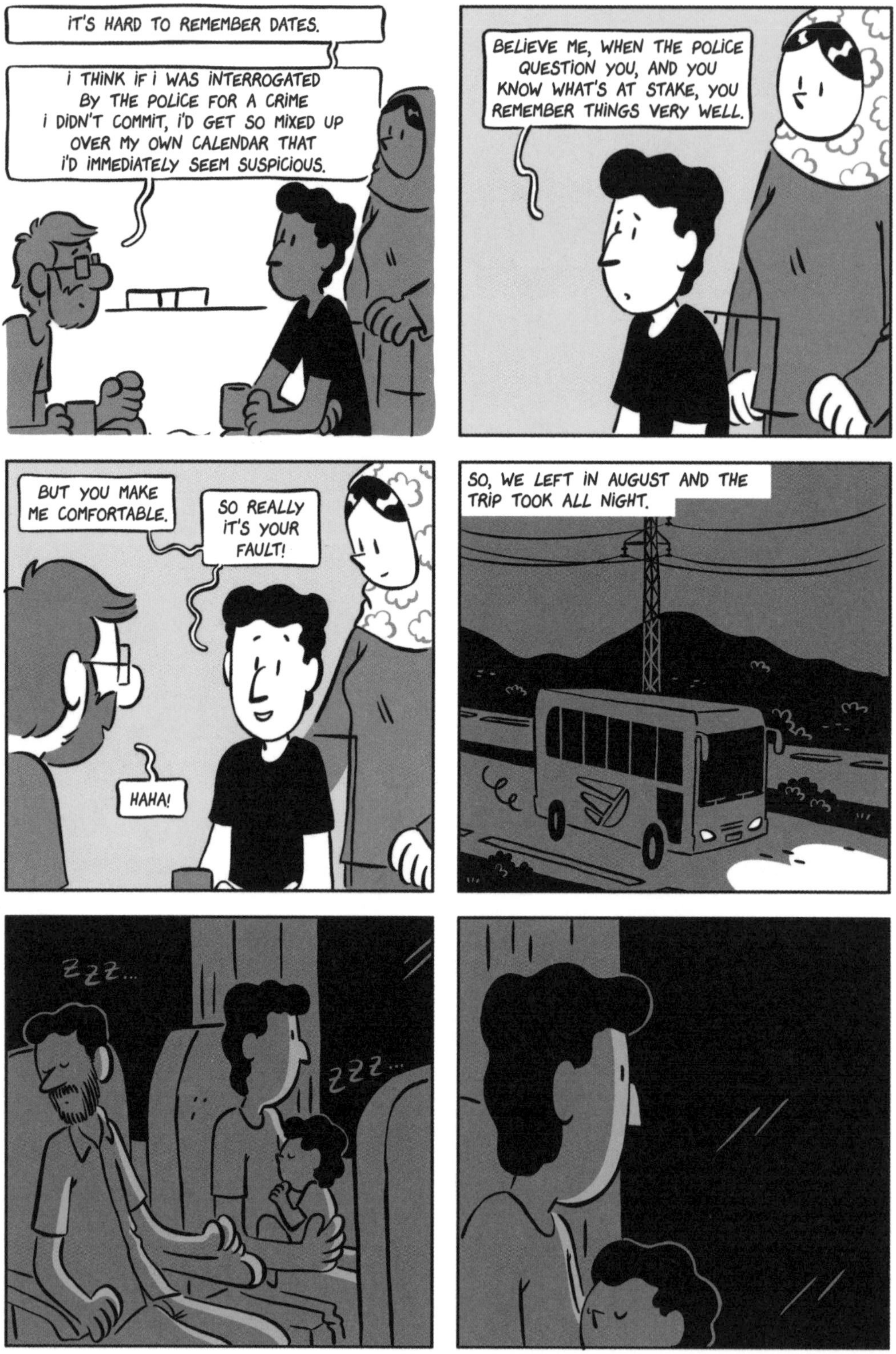
IT'S HARD TO REMEMBER DATES.
I THINK IF I WAS INTERROGATED BY THE POLICE FOR A CRIME I DIDN'T COMMIT, I'D GET SO MIXED UP OVER MY OWN CALENDAR THAT I'D IMMEDIATELY SEEM SUSPICIOUS.
BELIEVE ME, WHEN THE POLICE QUESTION YOU, AND YOU KNOW WHAT'S AT STAKE, YOU REMEMBER THINGS VERY WELL.
BUT YOU MAKE ME COMFORTABLE.
SO REALLY IT'S YOUR FAULT!
HAHA!
SO, WE LEFT IN AUGUST AND THE TRIP TOOK ALL NIGHT.
ZZZ...
ZZZ...

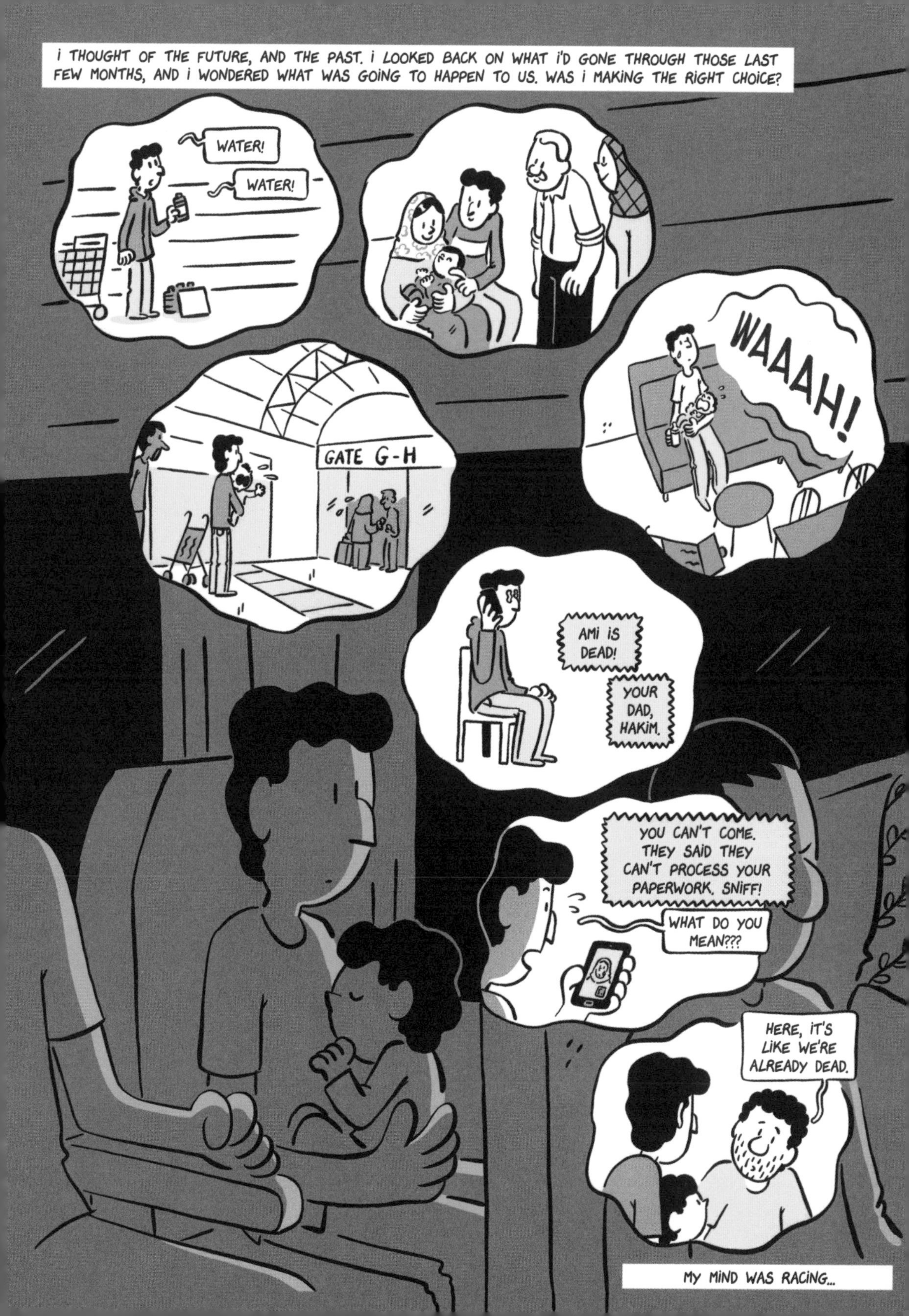
I THOUGHT OF THE FUTURE, AND THE PAST. I LOOKED BACK ON WHAT I'D GONE THROUGH THOSE LAST FEW MONTHS, AND I WONDERED WHAT WAS GOING TO HAPPEN TO US. WAS I MAKING THE RIGHT CHOICE?
WATER!
WATER!
GATE G-H
WAAAH!
AMI IS DEAD!
YOUR DAD, HAKIM.
YOU CAN'T COME. THEY SAID THEY CAN'T PROCESS YOUR PAPERWORK. SNIFF!
WHAT DO YOU MEAN???
HERE, IT'S LIKE WE'RE ALREADY DEAD.
MY MIND WAS RACING...

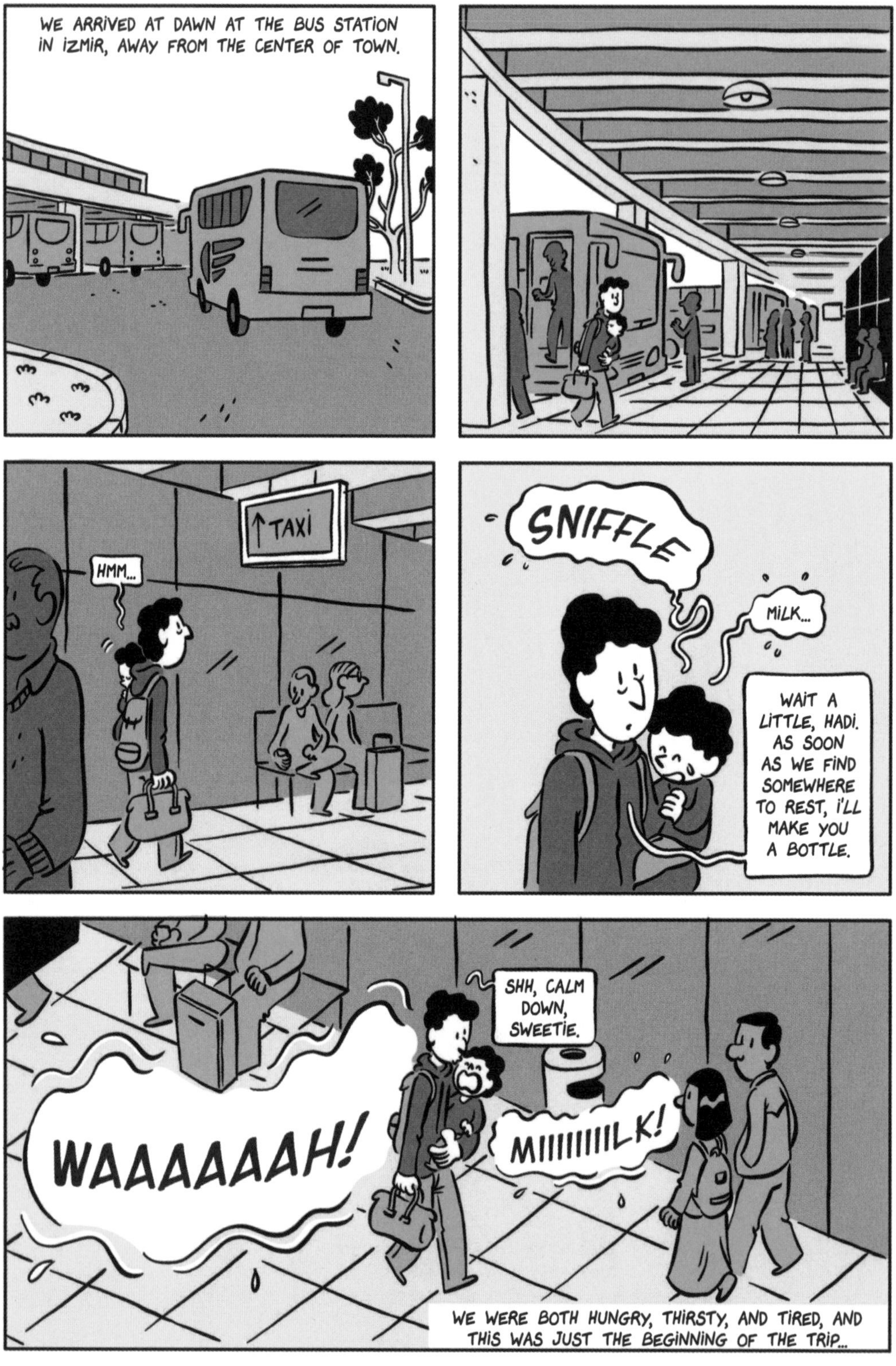
WE ARRIVED AT DAWN AT THE BUS STATION IN IZMIR, AWAY FROM THE CENTER OF TOWN.
↑TAXI
HMM...
SNIFFLE
MILK...
WAIT A LITTLE, HADI. AS SOON AS WE FIND SOMEWHERE TO REST, I'LL MAKE YOU A BOTTLE.
SHH, CALM DOWN, SWEETIE.
WAAAAAAH!
MIIIIIIIILK!
WE WERE BOTH HUNGRY, THIRSTY, AND TIRED, AND THIS WAS JUST THE BEGINNING OF THE TRIP...

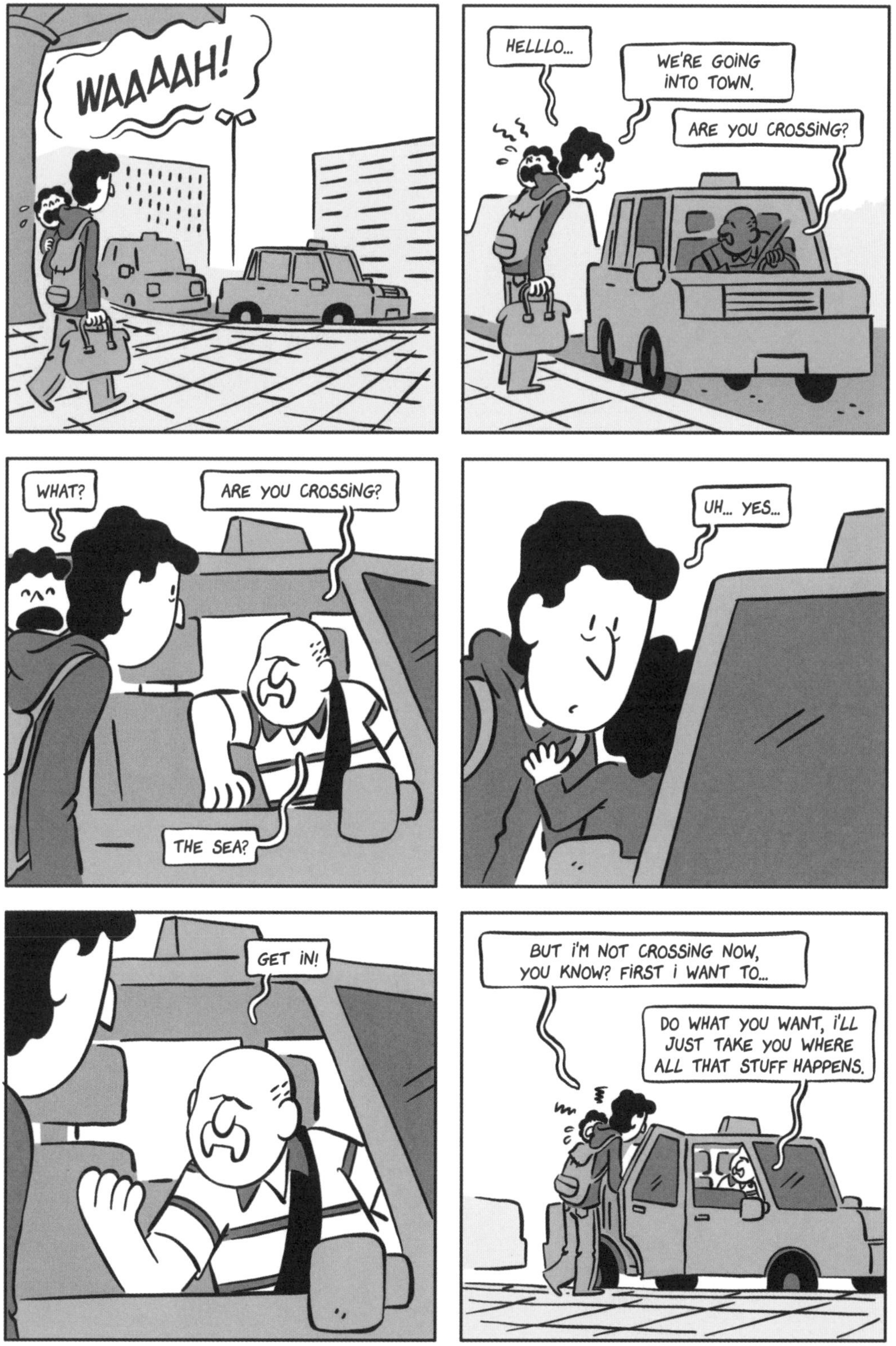
WAAAAH!
HELLLO...
WE'RE GOING INTO TOWN.
ARE YOU CROSSING?
WHAT?
ARE YOU CROSSING?
THE SEA?
UH... YES...
GET IN!
BUT I'M NOT CROSSING NOW, YOU KNOW? FIRST I WANT TO...
DO WHAT YOU WANT, I'LL JUST TAKE YOU WHERE ALL THAT STUFF HAPPENS.

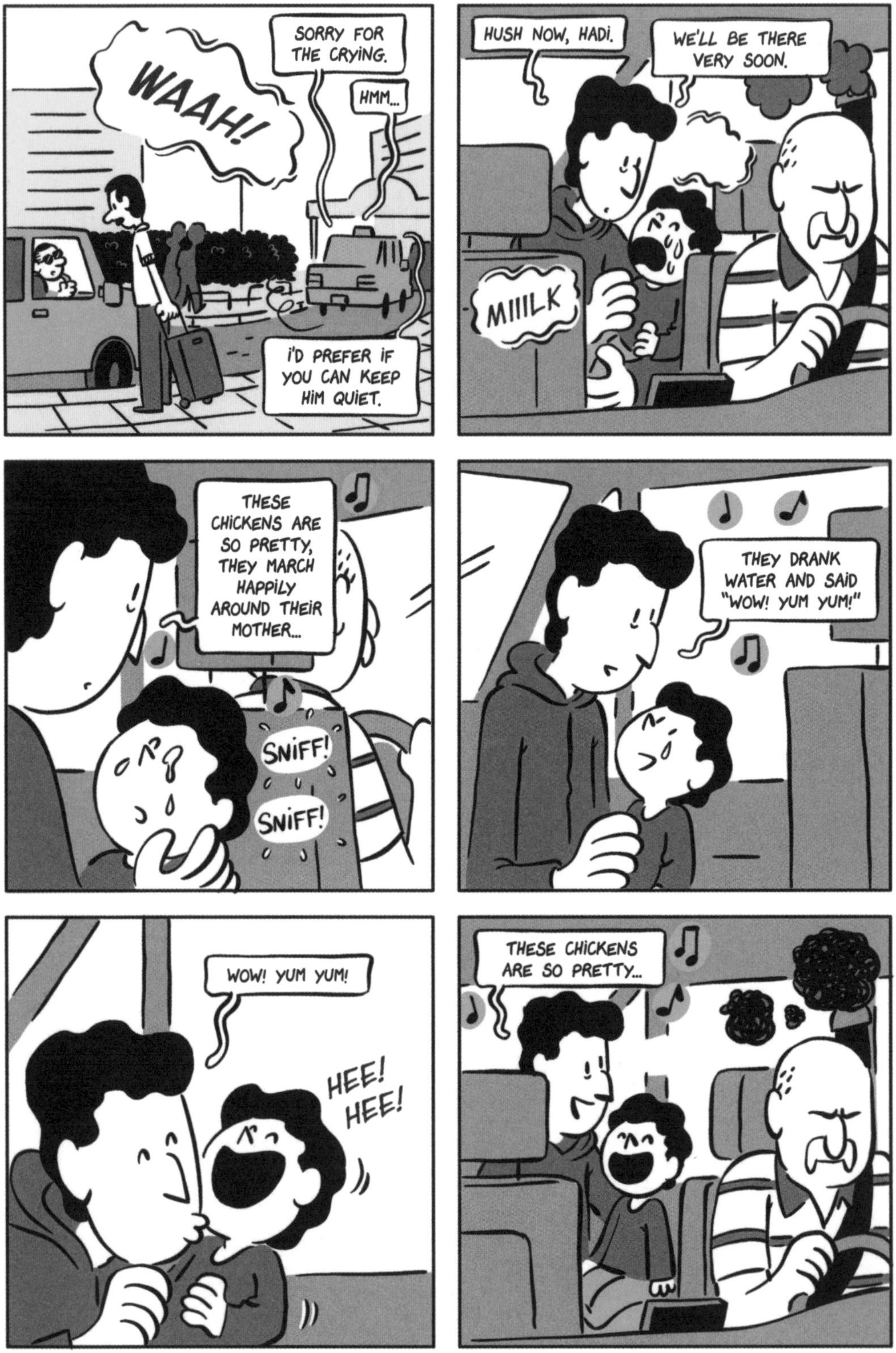
WAAH!
SORRY FOR THE CRYING.
HMM...
I'D PREFER IF YOU CAN KEEP HIM QUIET.
HUSH NOW, HADI.
WE'LL BE THERE VERY SOON.
MIIIILK
THESE CHICKENS ARE SO PRETTY, THEY MARCH HAPPILY AROUND THEIR MOTHER...
SNIFF!
SNIFF!
THEY DRANK WATER AND SAID "WOW! YUM YUM!"
WOW! YUM YUM!
HEE! HEE!
THESE CHICKENS ARE SO PRETTY...

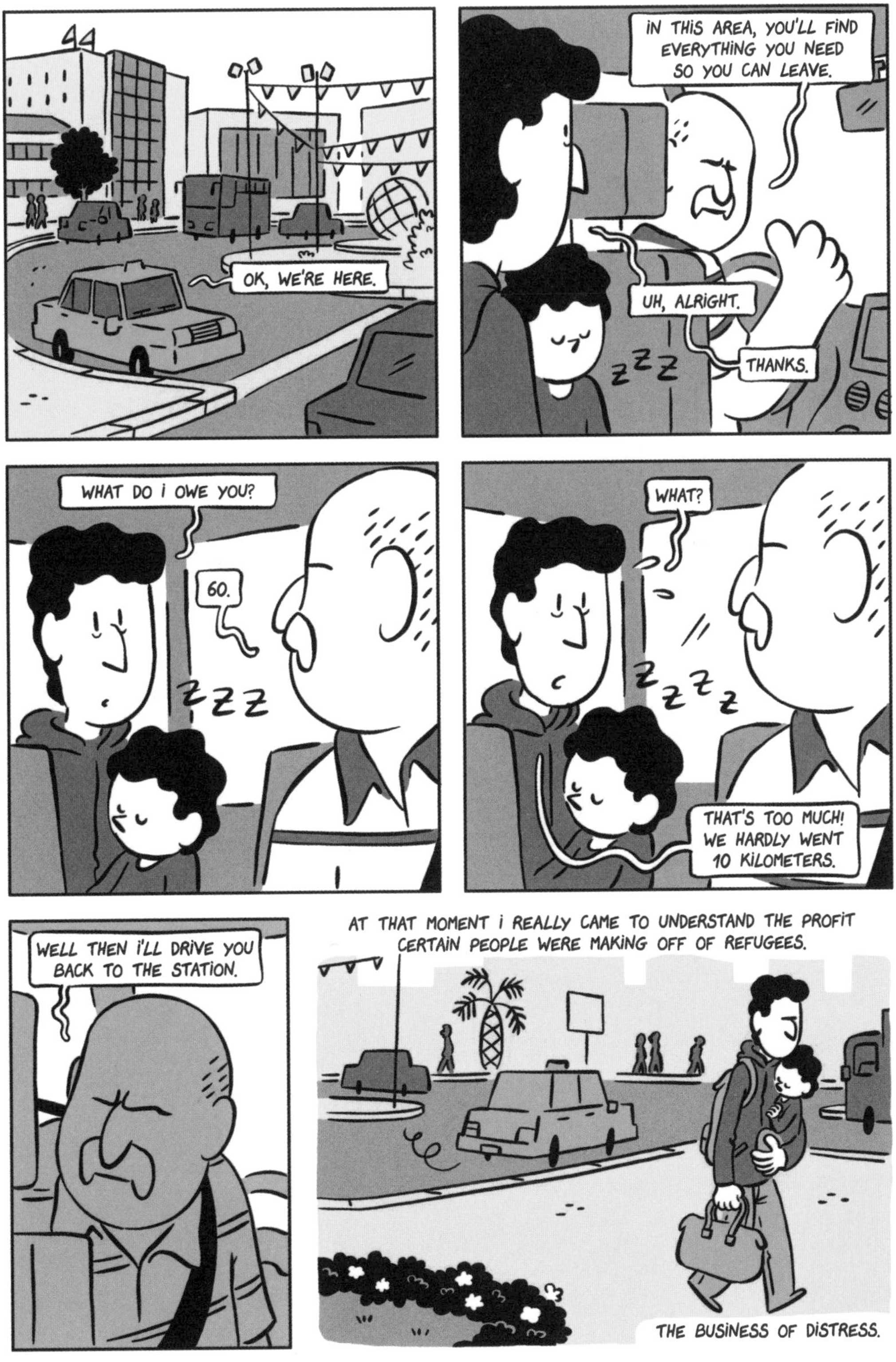
OK, WE'RE HERE.
IN THIS AREA, YOU'LL FIND EVERYTHING YOU NEED SO YOU CAN LEAVE.
UH, ALRIGHT.
THANKS.
ZZZ
WHAT DO I OWE YOU?
60.
ZZZ
WHAT?
ZZZZZ
THAT'S TOO MUCH! WE HARDLY WENT 10 KILOMETERS.
WELL THEN I'LL DRIVE YOU BACK TO THE STATION.
AT THAT MOMENT I REALLY CAME TO UNDERSTAND THE PROFIT CERTAIN PEOPLE WERE MAKING OFF OF REFUGEES.
THE BUSINESS OF DISTRESS.

THIS BUSINESS WAS EASY TO SEE WHERE THE TAXI DRIVER HAD DROPPED ME OFF:

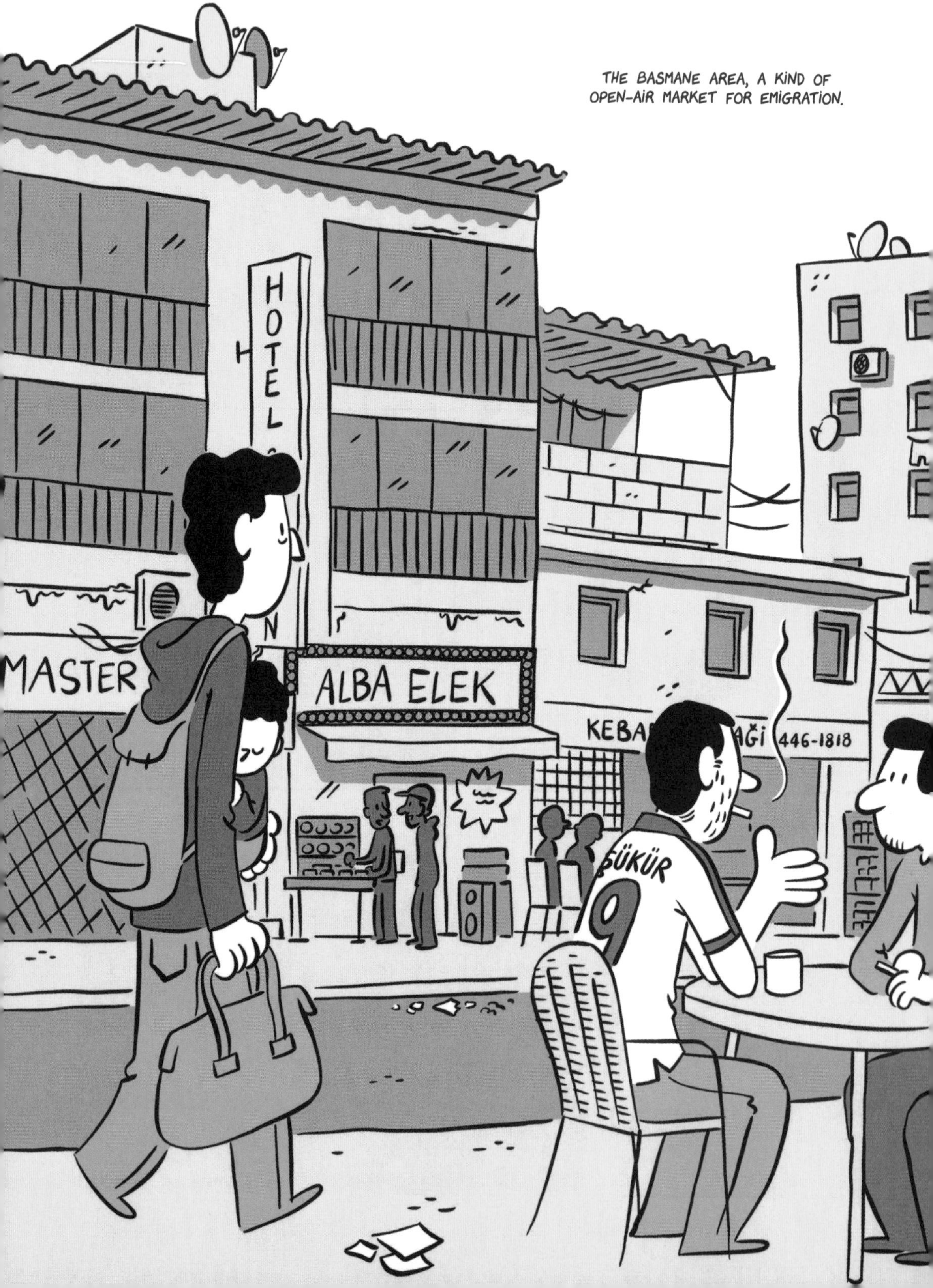

THE BASMANE AREA, A KIND OF OPEN-AIR MARKET FOR EMIGRATION.
HOTEL
MASTER
ALBA ELEK

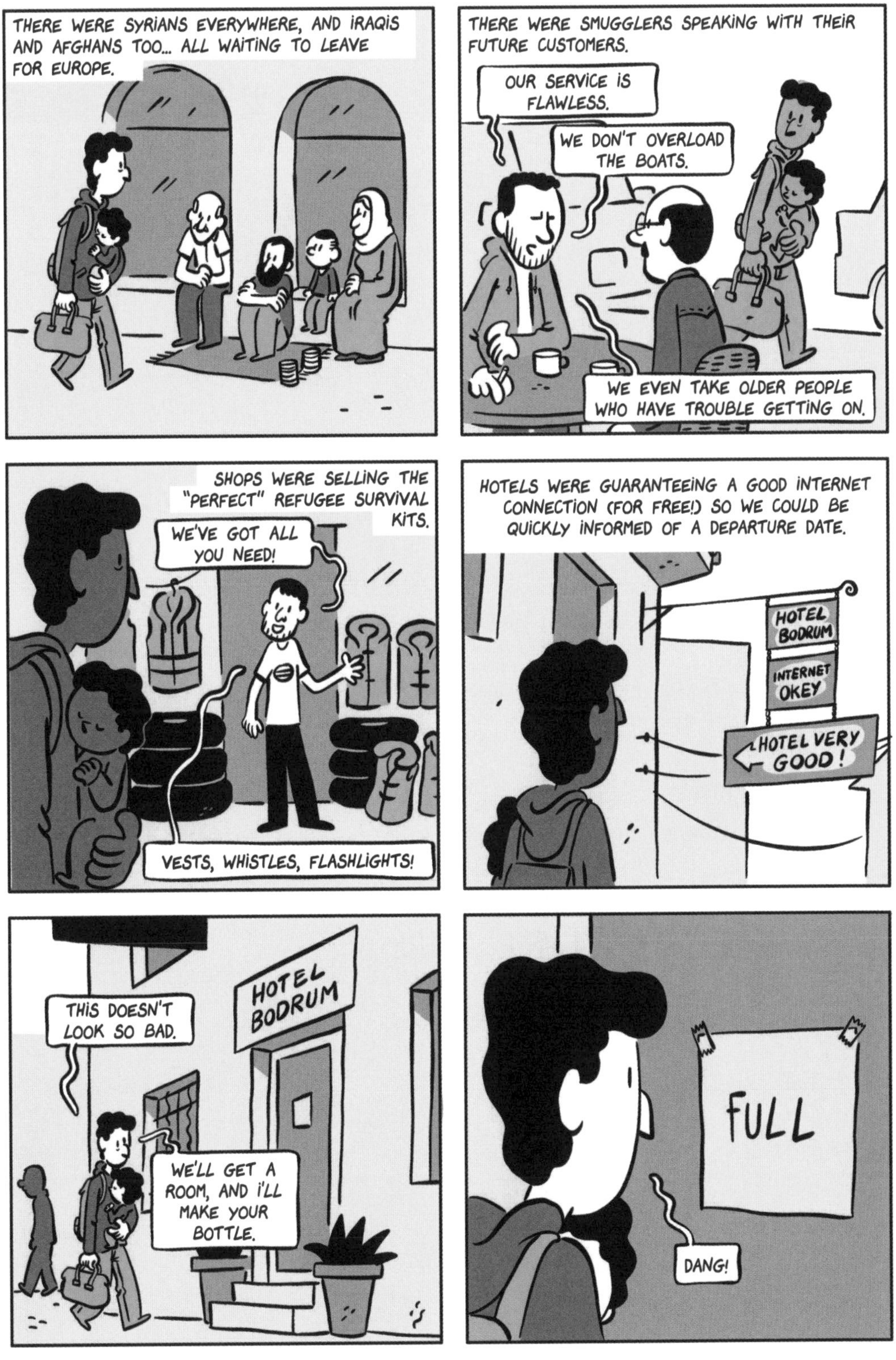
THERE WERE SYRIANS EVERYWHERE, AND IRAQIS AND AFGHANS TOO... ALL WAITING TO LEAVE FOR EUROPE.
THERE WERE SMUGGLERS SPEAKING WITH THEIR FUTURE CUSTOMERS.
OUR SERVICE IS FLAWLESS.
WE DON'T OVERLOAD THE BOATS.
WE EVEN TAKE OLDER PEOPLE WHO HAVE TROUBLE GETTING ON.
SHOPS WERE SELLING THE "PERFECT" REFUGEE SURVIVAL KITS.
WE'VE GOT ALL YOU NEED!
VESTS, WHISTLES, FLASHLIGHTS!
HOTELS WERE GUARANTEEING A GOOD INTERNET CONNECTION (FOR FREE!) SO WE COULD BE QUICKLY INFORMED OF A DEPARTURE DATE.
HOTEL BODRUM
INTERNET OKEY
HOTEL VERY GOOD!
THIS DOESN'T LOOK SO BAD.
HOTEL BODRUM
WE'LL GET A ROOM, AND I'LL MAKE YOUR BOTTLE.
FULL
DANG!

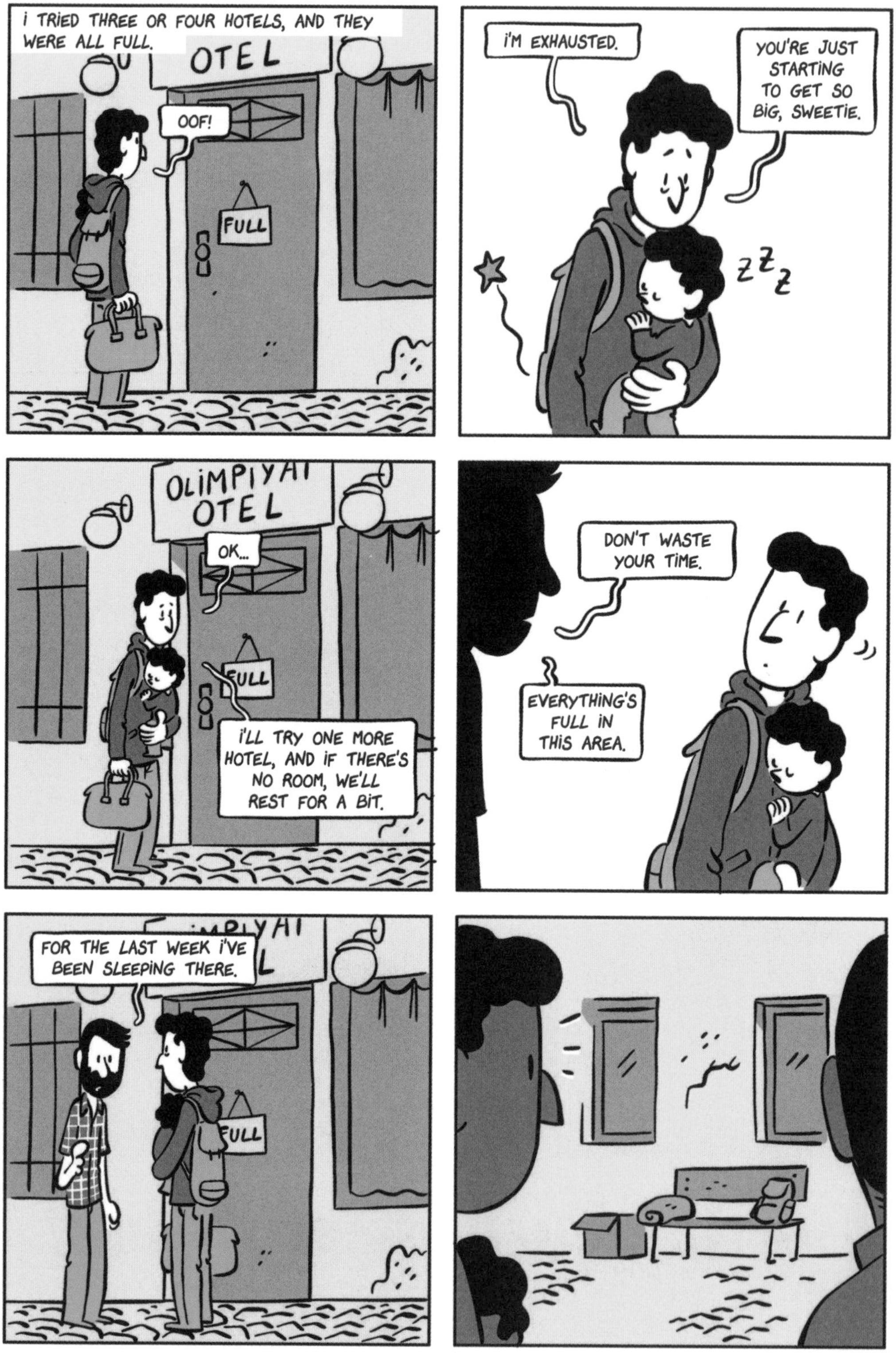
I TRIED THREE OR FOUR HOTELS, AND THEY WERE ALL FULL.
OTEL
OOF!
FULL
I'M EXHAUSTED.
YOU'RE JUST STARTING TO GET SO BIG, SWEETIE.
ZZZ
OLIMPIYAT OTEL
OK...
FULL
I'LL TRY ONE MORE HOTEL, AND IF THERE'S NO ROOM, WE'LL REST FOR A BIT.
DON'T WASTE YOUR TIME.
EVERYTHING'S FULL IN THIS AREA.
FOR THE LAST WEEK I'VE BEEN SLEEPING THERE.
FULL

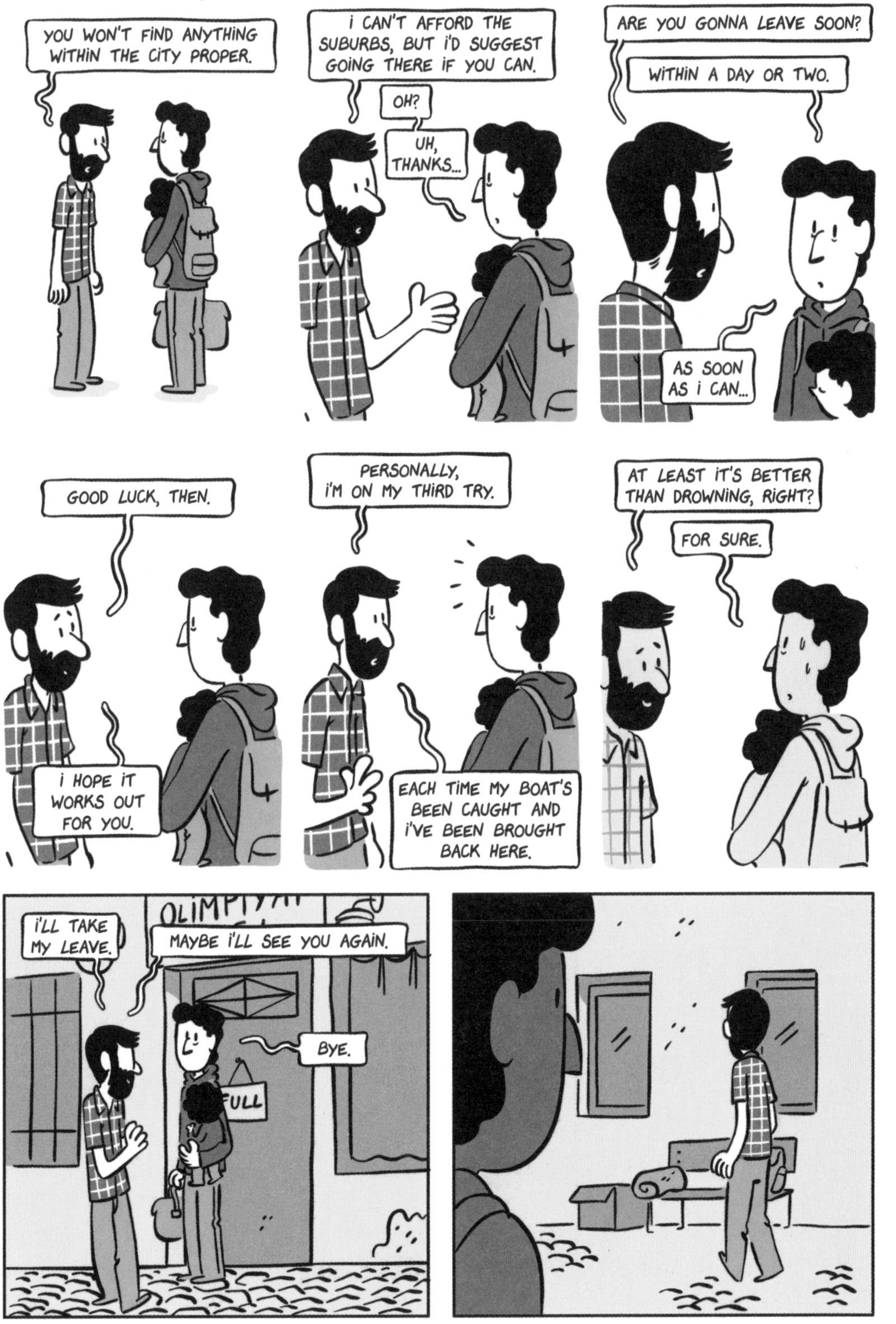
YOU WON'T FIND ANYTHING WITHIN THE CITY PROPER.
I CAN'T AFFORD THE SUBURBS, BUT I'D SUGGEST GOING THERE IF YOU CAN.
OH?
UH, THANKS...
ARE YOU GONNA LEAVE SOON?
WITHIN A DAY OR TWO.
AS SOON AS I CAN...
GOOD LUCK, THEN.
I HOPE IT WORKS OUT FOR YOU.
PERSONALLY, I'M ON MY THIRD TRY.
EACH TIME MY BOAT'S BEEN CAUGHT AND I'VE BEEN BROUGHT BACK HERE.
AT LEAST IT'S BETTER THAN DROWNING, RIGHT?
FOR SURE.
I'LL TAKE MY LEAVE.
MAYBE I'LL SEE YOU AGAIN.
BYE.
FULL

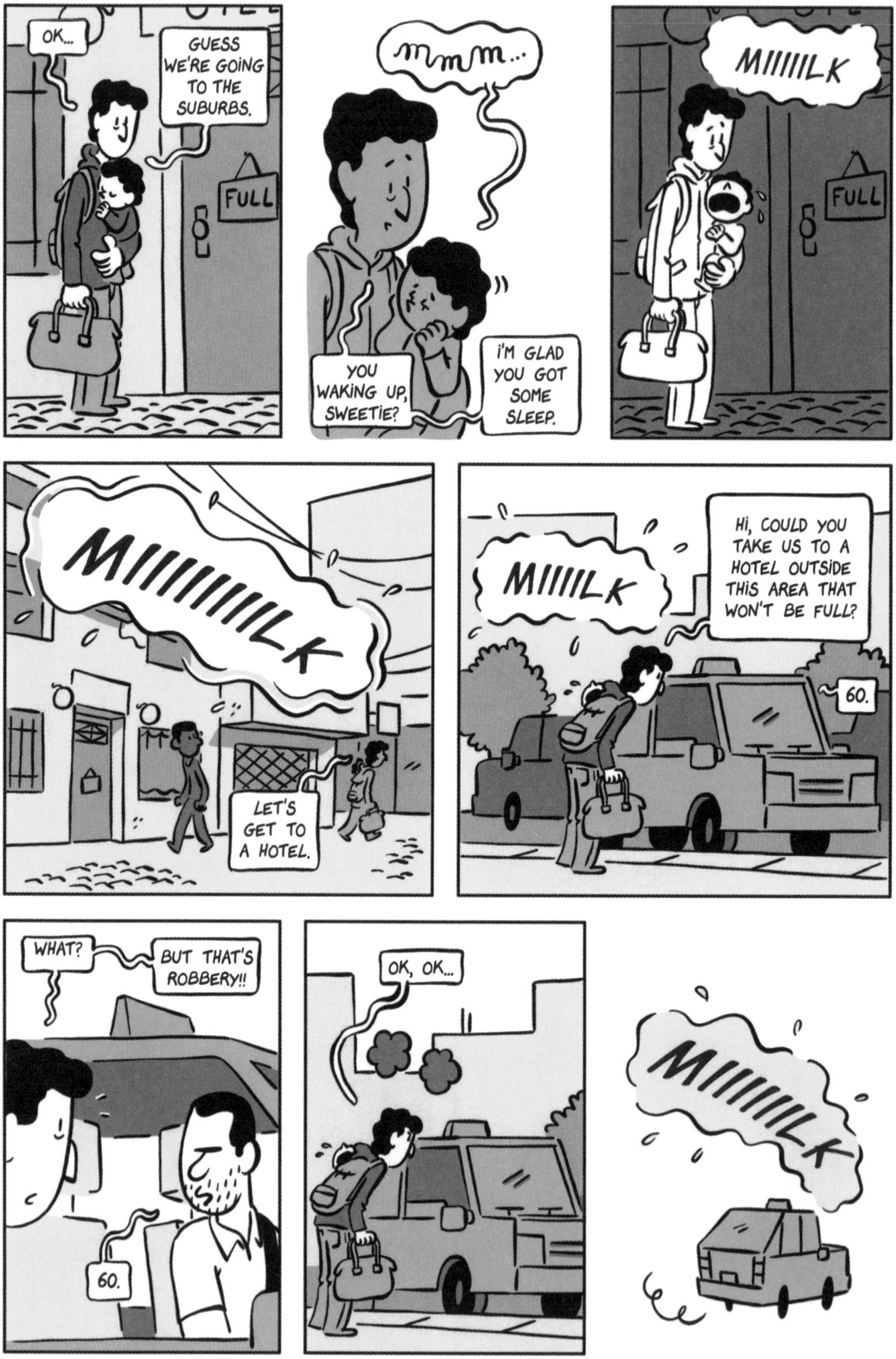
OK...
GUESS WE'RE GOING TO THE SUBURBS.
mmm...
YOU WAKING UP, SWEETIE?
I'M GLAD YOU GOT SOME SLEEP.
MIIIIILK
MIIIIIIIIILK
LET'S GET TO A HOTEL.
MIIIILK
HI, COULD YOU TAKE US TO A HOTEL OUTSIDE THIS AREA THAT WON'T BE FULL?
60.
WHAT?
BUT THAT'S ROBBERY!!
60.
OK, OK...
MIIIIIILK

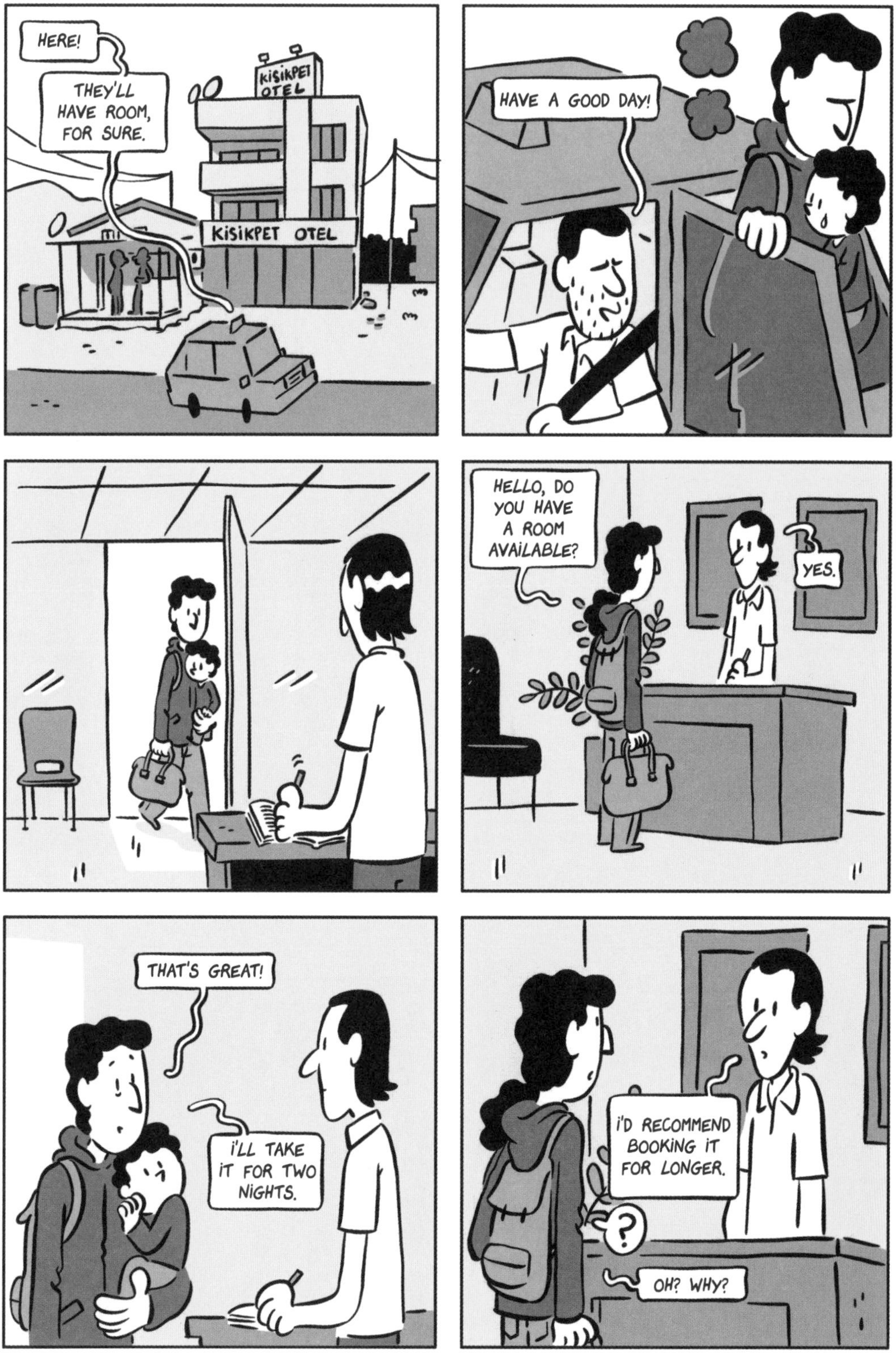
HERE!
THEY'LL HAVE ROOM, FOR SURE.
KISIKPET OTEL
KISIKPET OTEL
HAVE A GOOD DAY!
HELLO, DO YOU HAVE A ROOM AVAILABLE?
YES.
THAT'S GREAT!
I'LL TAKE IT FOR TWO NIGHTS.
I'D RECOMMEND BOOKING IT FOR LONGER.
?
OH? WHY?

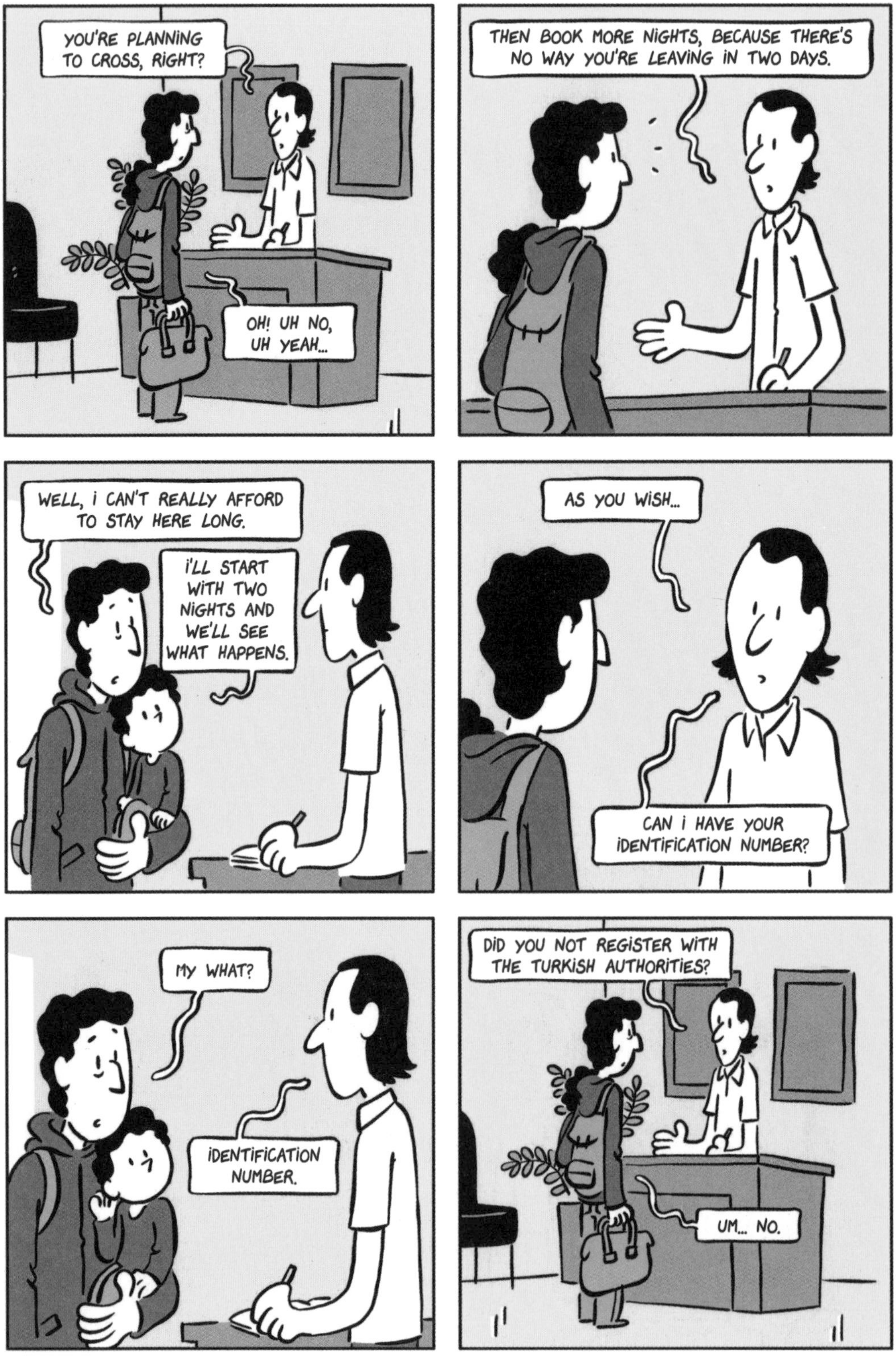
YOU'RE PLANNING TO CROSS, RIGHT?
OH! UH NO, UH YEAH...
THEN BOOK MORE NIGHTS, BECAUSE THERE'S NO WAY YOU'RE LEAVING IN TWO DAYS.
WELL, I CAN'T REALLY AFFORD TO STAY HERE LONG.
I'LL START WITH TWO NIGHTS AND WE'LL SEE WHAT HAPPENS.
AS YOU WISH...
CAN I HAVE YOUR IDENTIFICATION NUMBER?
MY WHAT?
IDENTIFICATION NUMBER.
DID YOU NOT REGISTER WITH THE TURKISH AUTHORITIES?
UM... NO.

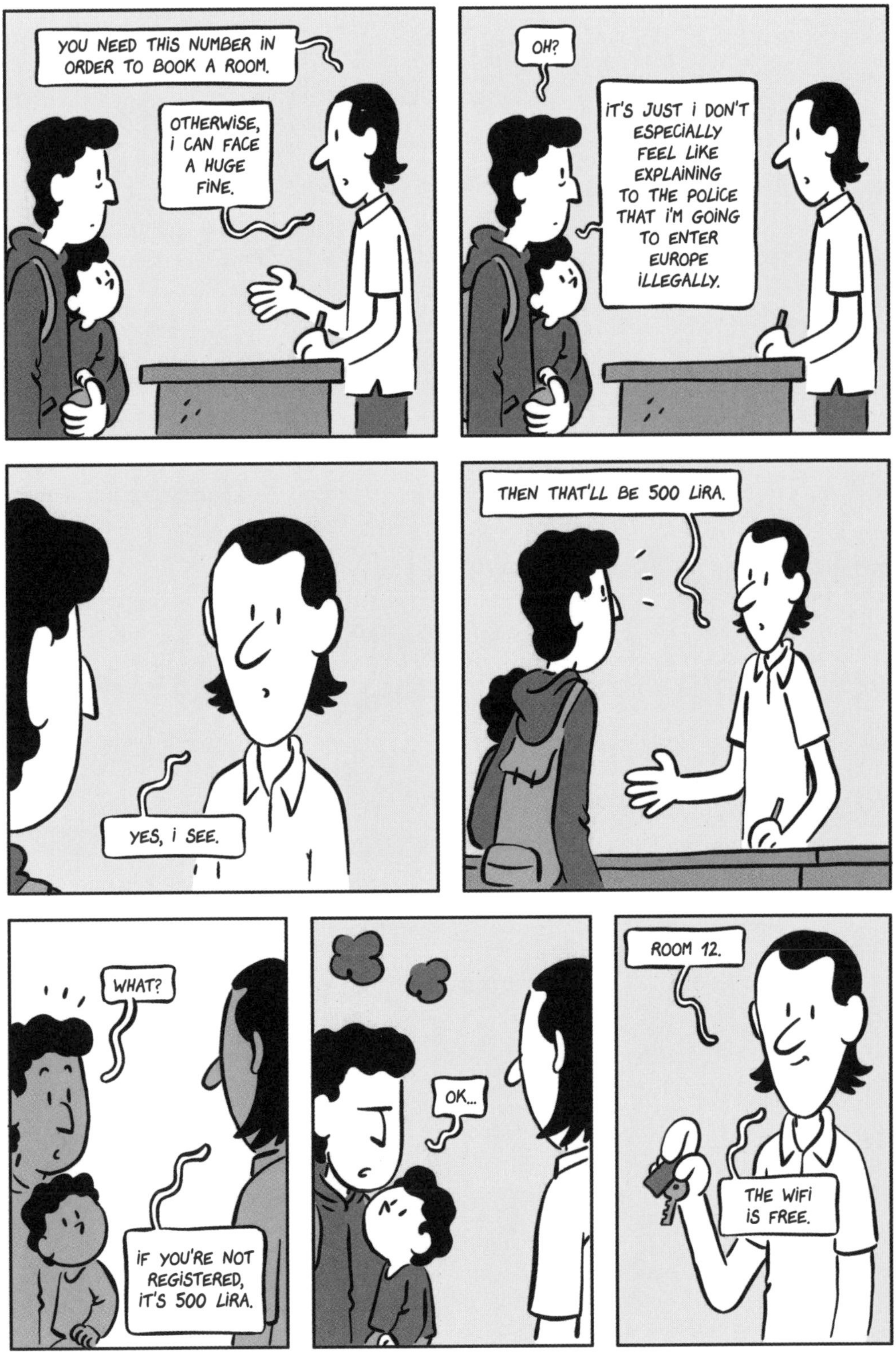
YOU NEED THIS NUMBER IN ORDER TO BOOK A ROOM.
OTHERWISE, i CAN FACE A HUGE FiNE.
OH?
iT'S JUST i DON'T ESPECiALLY FEEL LiKE EXPLAiNiNG TO THE POLiCE THAT i'M GOiNG TO ENTER EUROPE iLLEGALLY.
YES, i SEE.
THEN THAT'LL BE 500 LiRA.
WHAT?
iF YOU'RE NOT REGiSTERED, iT'S 500 LiRA.
OK...
ROOM 12.
THE WiFi iS FREE.

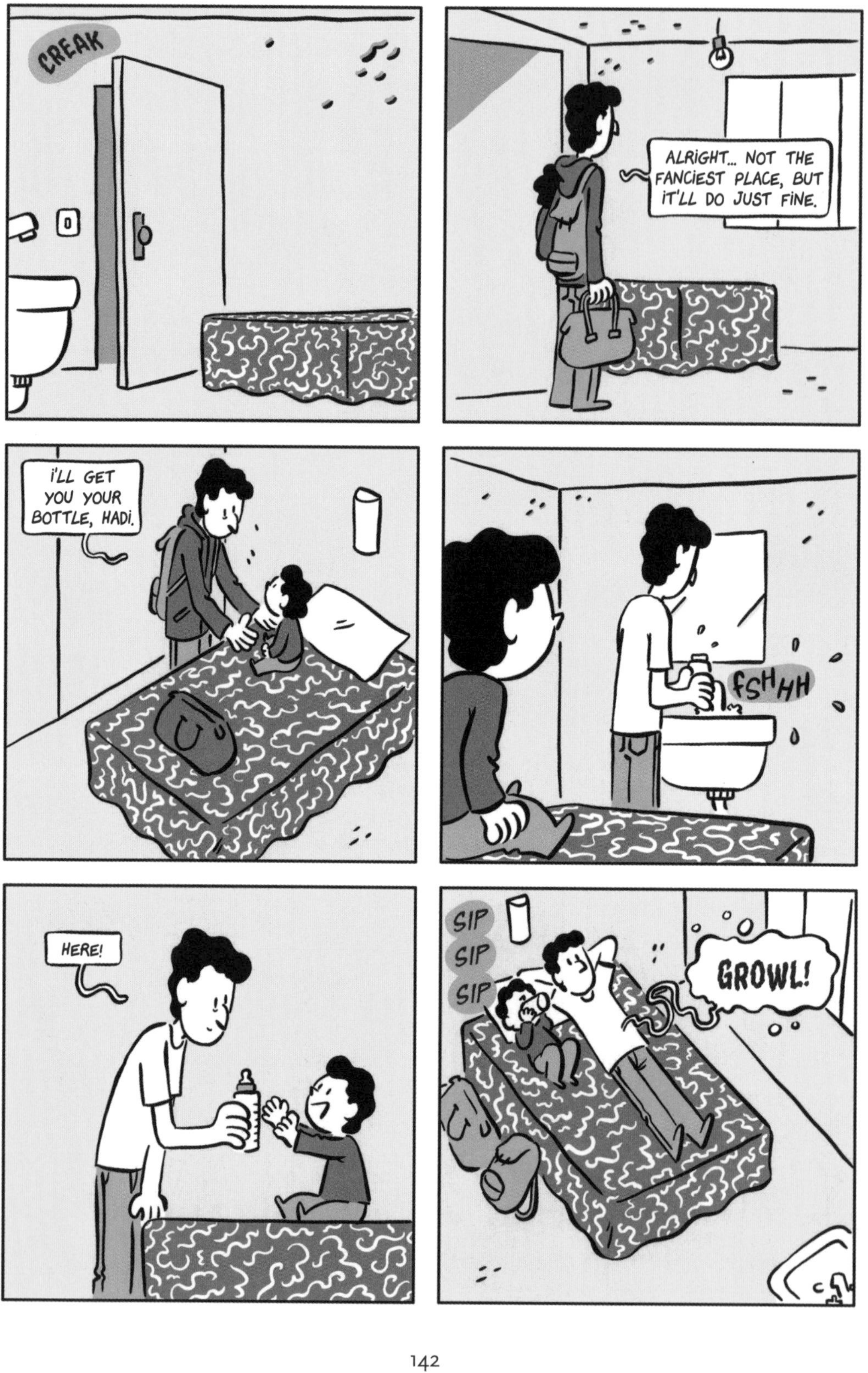
CREAK
ALRIGHT... NOT THE FANCIEST PLACE, BUT IT'LL DO JUST FINE.
I'LL GET YOU YOUR BOTTLE, HADI.
FSHHH
HERE!
SIP
SIP
SIP
GROWL!

THE NEXT MORNING, i TOOK A TAXI BACK TO BASMANE.

THANKS!

i HAD TO FIND A SMUGGLER, BUT i DIDN'T REALLY KNOW HOW TO GO ABOUT IT.

iT CERTAINLY SEEMED LIKE THEY ALL SPOKE ARABIC (MOST OF THEM WERE SYRIAN).

BUT i DIDN'T KNOW WHETHER i COULD SPEAK TO THEM OPENLY, OR WHETHER THERE WERE CODES TO USE OR THINGS i SHOULDN'T SAY.

WHEN i REALIZED THEY WERE CARRYING ON IN FULL VIEW OF THE POLICE, i MADE UP MY MIND TO APPROACH THEM.

iT WAS A LITTLE LIKE CHECKING OUT DIFFERENT TRAVEL AGENCIES AT A TRAVEL EXPO.

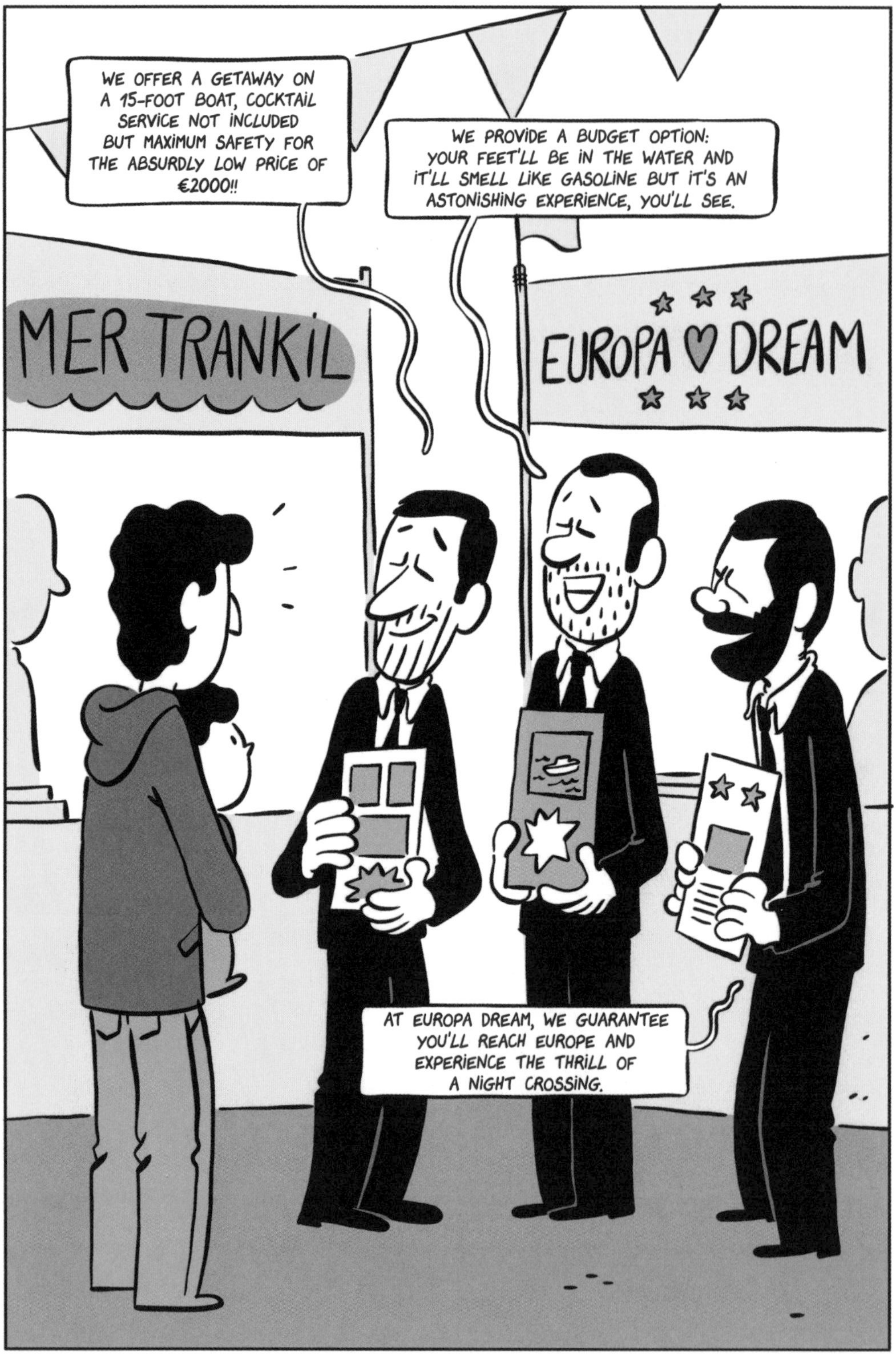
WE OFFER A GETAWAY ON A 15-FOOT BOAT, COCKTAIL SERVICE NOT INCLUDED BUT MAXIMUM SAFETY FOR THE ABSURDLY LOW PRICE OF €2000!!
WE PROVIDE A BUDGET OPTION: YOUR FEET'LL BE IN THE WATER AND IT'LL SMELL LIKE GASOLINE BUT IT'S AN ASTONISHING EXPERIENCE, YOU'LL SEE.
MER TRANKIL
EUROPA DREAM
AT EUROPA DREAM, WE GUARANTEE YOU'LL REACH EUROPE AND EXPERIENCE THE THRILL OF A NIGHT CROSSING.

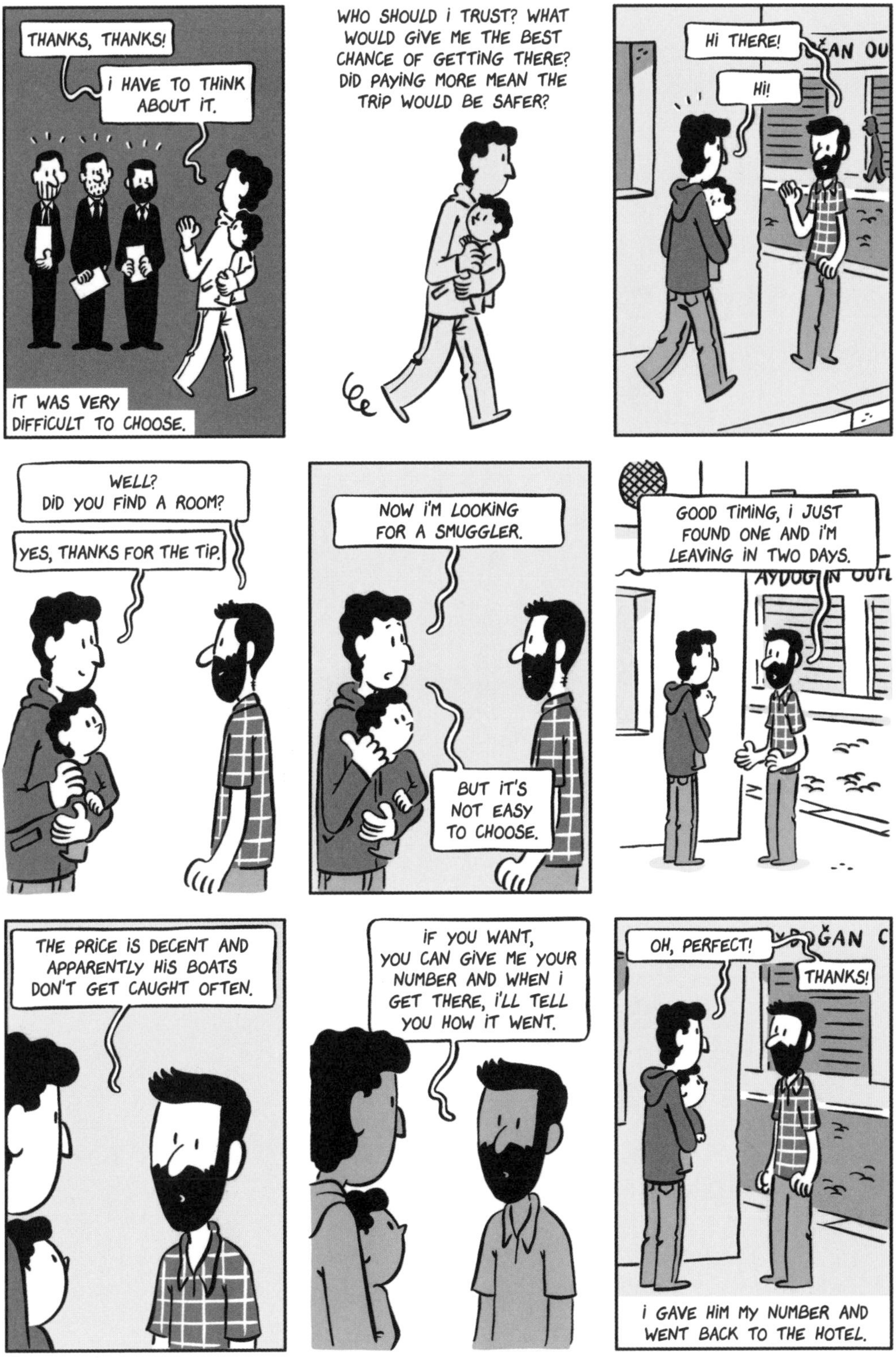
THANKS, THANKS!
I HAVE TO THINK ABOUT IT.
IT WAS VERY DIFFICULT TO CHOOSE.
WHO SHOULD I TRUST? WHAT WOULD GIVE ME THE BEST CHANCE OF GETTING THERE? DID PAYING MORE MEAN THE TRIP WOULD BE SAFER?
HI THERE!
HI!
WELL? DID YOU FIND A ROOM?
YES, THANKS FOR THE TIP.
NOW I'M LOOKING FOR A SMUGGLER.
BUT IT'S NOT EASY TO CHOOSE.
GOOD TIMING, I JUST FOUND ONE AND I'M LEAVING IN TWO DAYS.
THE PRICE IS DECENT AND APPARENTLY HIS BOATS DON'T GET CAUGHT OFTEN.
IF YOU WANT, YOU CAN GIVE ME YOUR NUMBER AND WHEN I GET THERE, I'LL TELL YOU HOW IT WENT.
OH, PERFECT!
THANKS!
I GAVE HIM MY NUMBER AND WENT BACK TO THE HOTEL.

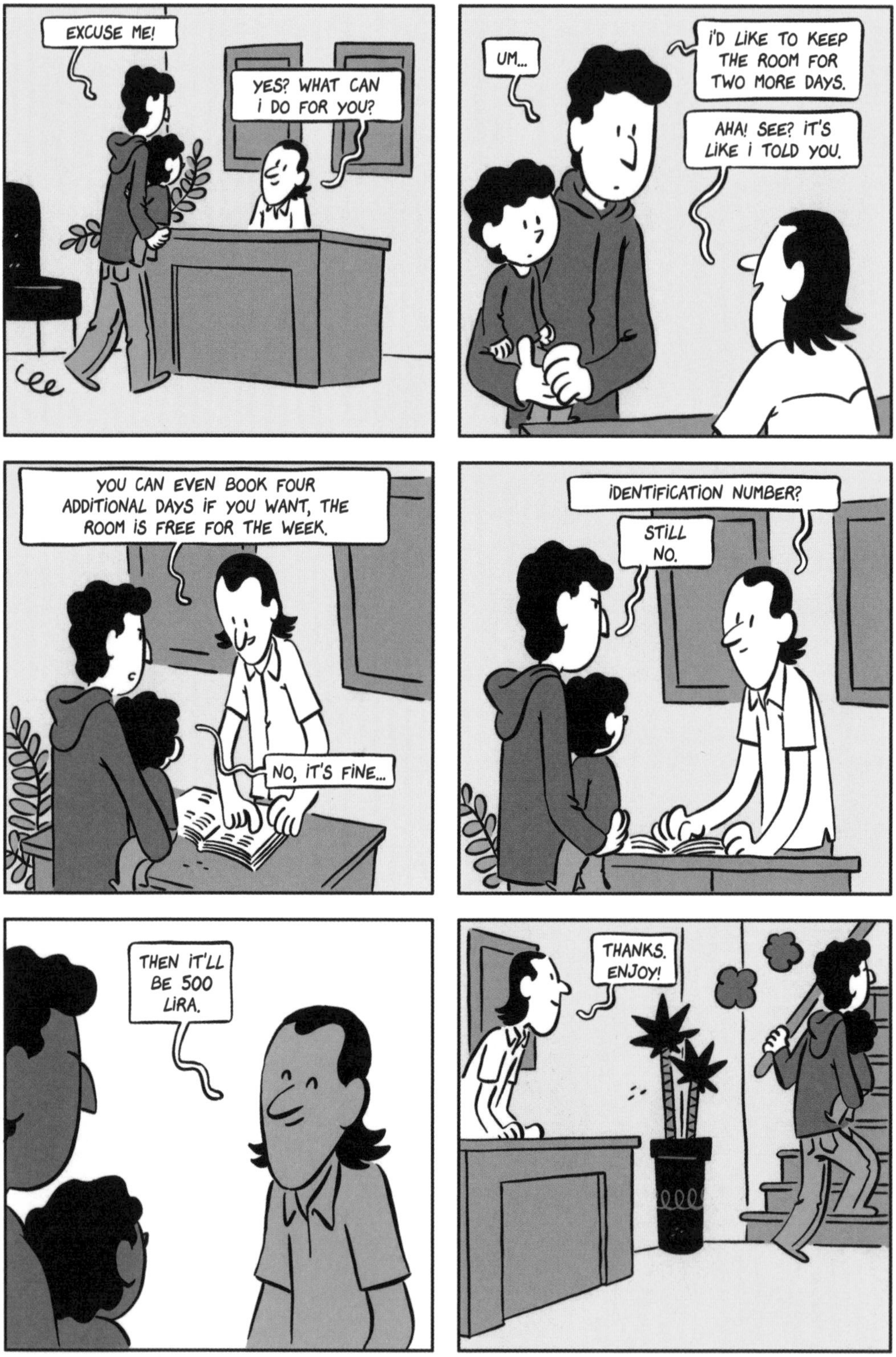
EXCUSE ME!
YES? WHAT CAN i DO FOR YOU?
UM...
i'D LiKE TO KEEP THE ROOM FOR TWO MORE DAYS.
AHA! SEE? iT'S LiKE i TOLD YOU.
YOU CAN EVEN BOOK FOUR ADDiTiONAL DAYS iF YOU WANT, THE ROOM iS FREE FOR THE WEEK.
NO, iT'S FiNE...
iDENTiFiCATiON NUMBER?
STiLL NO.
THEN iT'LL BE 500 LiRA.
THANKS. ENJOY!

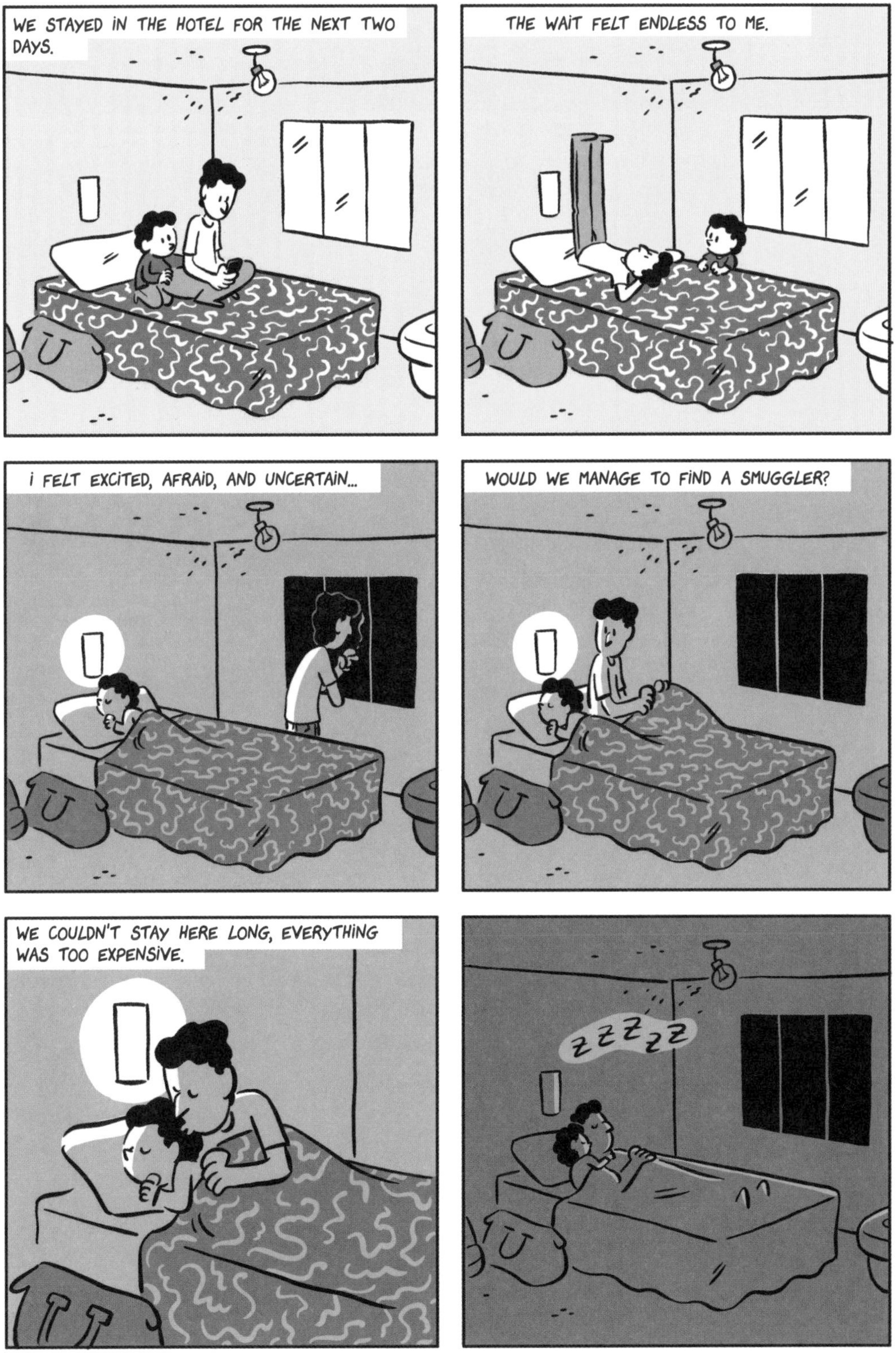
WE STAYED IN THE HOTEL FOR THE NEXT TWO DAYS.
THE WAIT FELT ENDLESS TO ME.
I FELT EXCITED, AFRAID, AND UNCERTAIN...
WOULD WE MANAGE TO FIND A SMUGGLER?
WE COULDN'T STAY HERE LONG, EVERYTHING WAS TOO EXPENSIVE.
ZZZZZ

AT THE END OF THE SECOND DAY OF WAITING, I GOT A TEXT.

THANKS, HADI!

Safely arrived in Greece. All good to go, here's the number.

IT MUST HAVE BEEN ABOUT 6 PM. I CALLED RIGHT AWAY.

HELLO?

YES, HI, A FRIEND OF MINE WHO "TRAVELED" WITH YOU GAVE ME YOUR NUMBER.

I'M ALSO LOOKING TO GET TO GREECE.

. . .

MAMA?

MEET ME AT THE CAFÉ BEHIND THE TRAIN STATION IN 20 MINUTES.

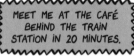

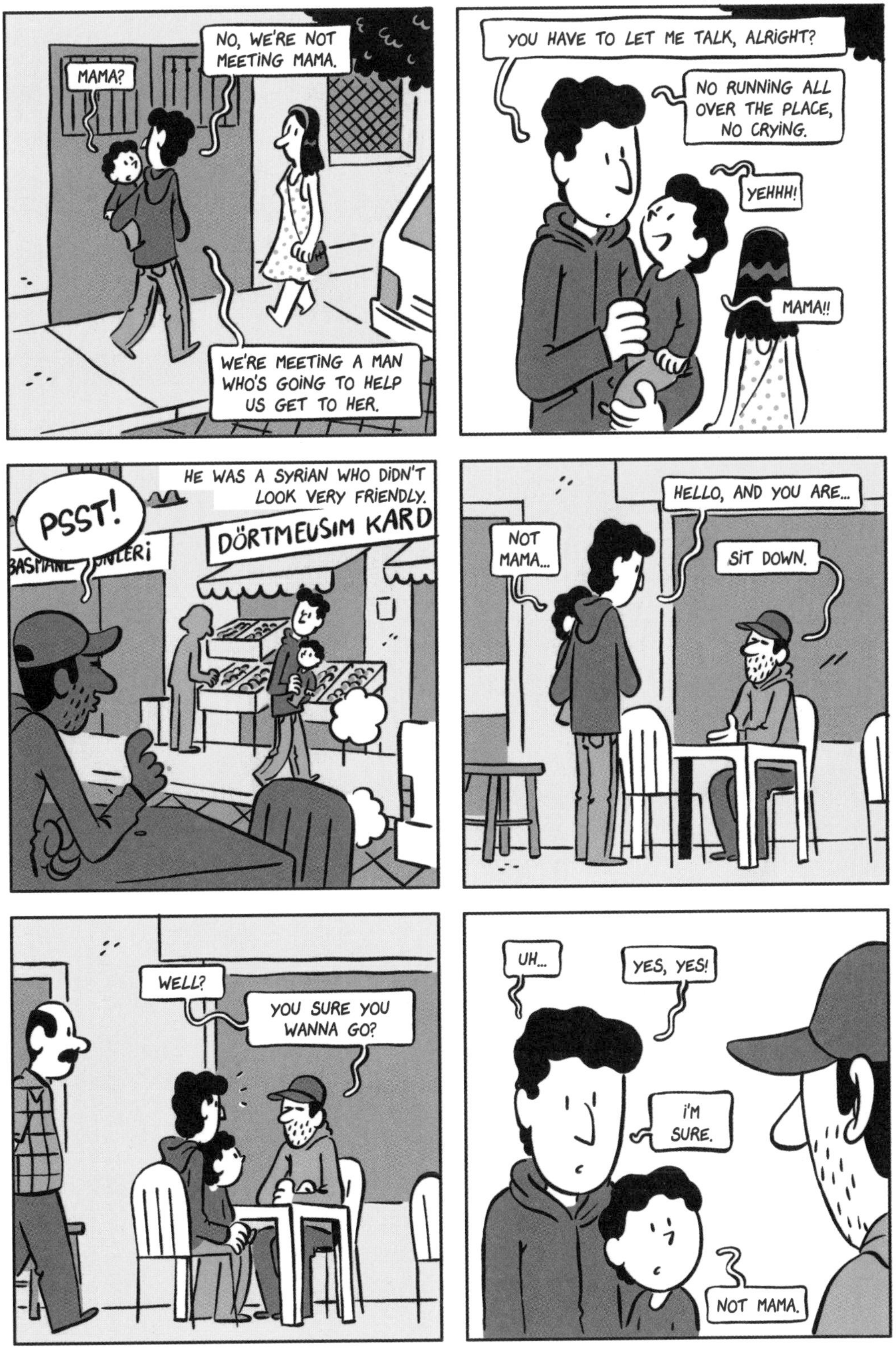
MAMA?
NO, WE'RE NOT MEETING MAMA.
WE'RE MEETING A MAN WHO'S GOING TO HELP US GET TO HER.
YOU HAVE TO LET ME TALK, ALRIGHT?
NO RUNNING ALL OVER THE PLACE, NO CRYING.
YEHHH!
MAMA!!
HE WAS A SYRIAN WHO DIDN'T LOOK VERY FRIENDLY.
PSST!
DÖRTMEUSIM KARD
HELLO, AND YOU ARE...
NOT MAMA...
SIT DOWN.
WELL?
YOU SURE YOU WANNA GO?
UH...
YES, YES!
I'M SURE.
NOT MAMA.

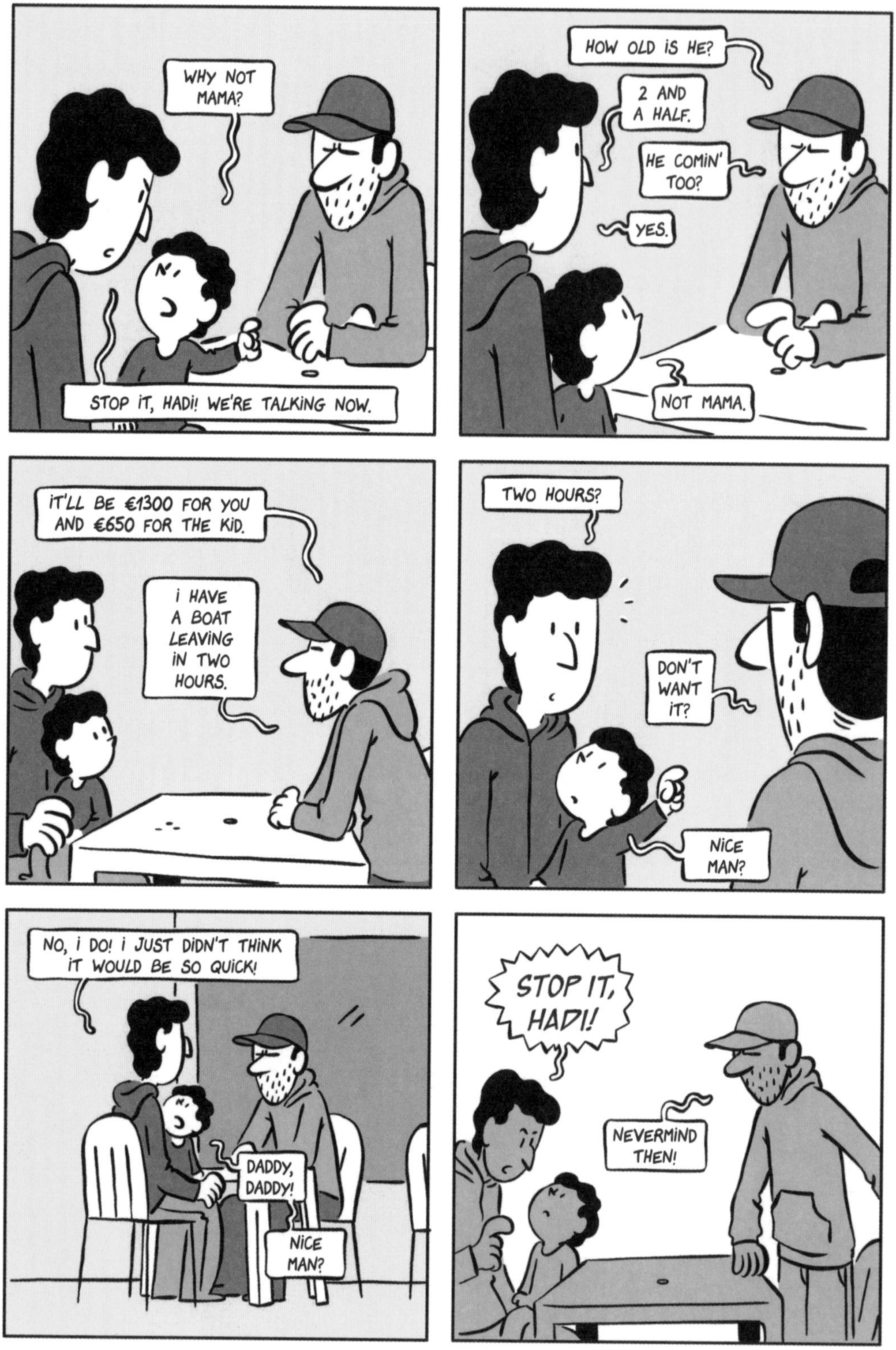
WHY NOT MAMA?
STOP IT, HADI! WE'RE TALKING NOW.
HOW OLD IS HE?
2 AND A HALF.
HE COMIN' TOO?
YES.
NOT MAMA.
IT'LL BE €1300 FOR YOU AND €650 FOR THE KID.
I HAVE A BOAT LEAVING IN TWO HOURS.
TWO HOURS?
DON'T WANT IT?
NICE MAN?
NO, I DO! I JUST DIDN'T THINK IT WOULD BE SO QUICK!
DADDY, DADDY!
NICE MAN?
STOP IT, HADI!
NEVERMIND THEN!

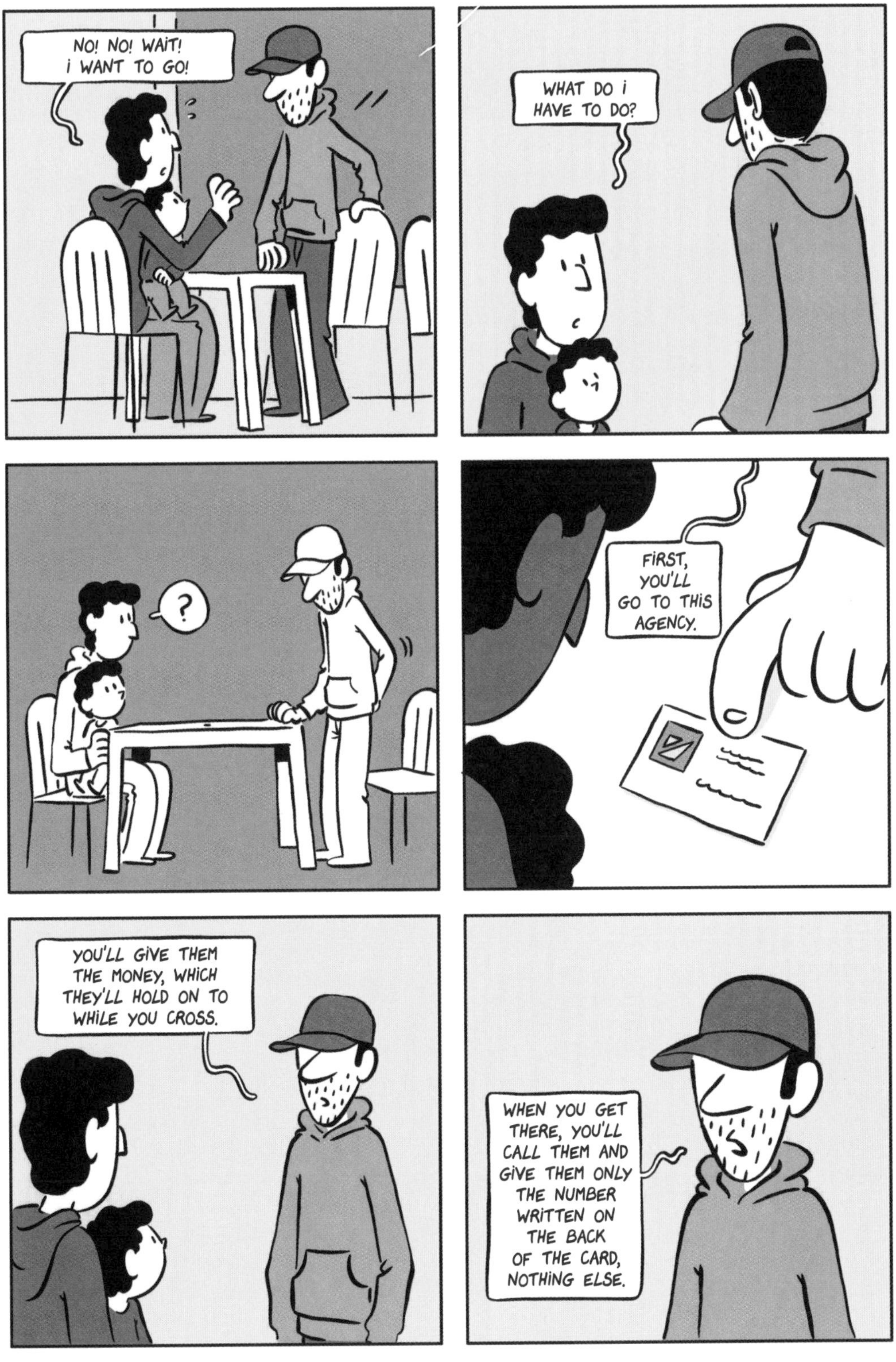
NO! NO! WAIT! I WANT TO GO!
WHAT DO I HAVE TO DO?
?
FIRST, YOU'LL GO TO THIS AGENCY.
YOU'LL GIVE THEM THE MONEY, WHICH THEY'LL HOLD ON TO WHILE YOU CROSS.
WHEN YOU GET THERE, YOU'LL CALL THEM AND GIVE THEM ONLY THE NUMBER WRITTEN ON THE BACK OF THE CARD, NOTHING ELSE.

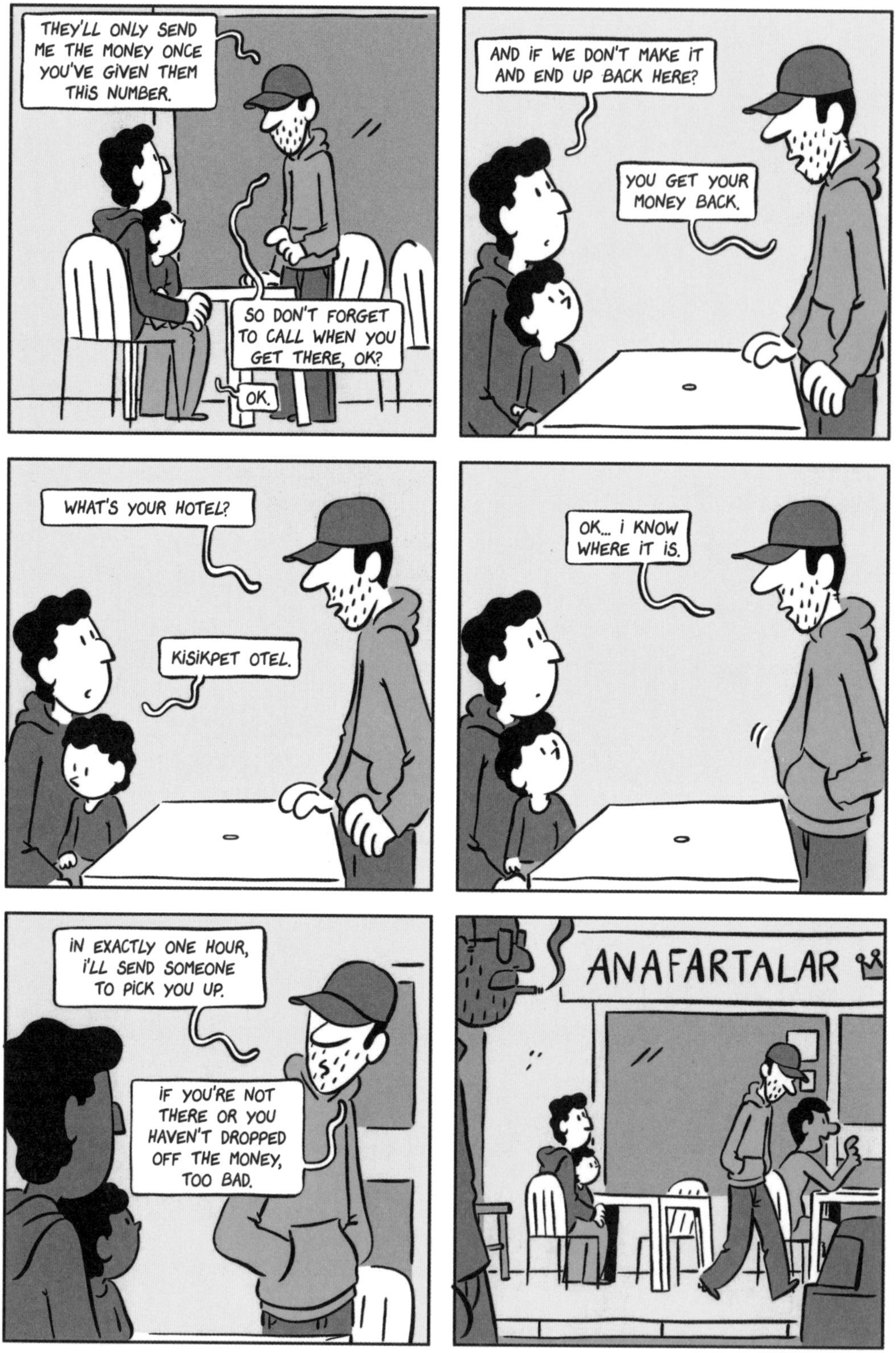
THEY'LL ONLY SEND ME THE MONEY ONCE YOU'VE GIVEN THEM THIS NUMBER.
SO DON'T FORGET TO CALL WHEN YOU GET THERE, OK?
OK.
AND IF WE DON'T MAKE IT AND END UP BACK HERE?
YOU GET YOUR MONEY BACK.
WHAT'S YOUR HOTEL?
KISIKPET OTEL.
OK... I KNOW WHERE IT IS.
IN EXACTLY ONE HOUR, I'LL SEND SOMEONE TO PICK YOU UP.
IF YOU'RE NOT THERE OR YOU HAVEN'T DROPPED OFF THE MONEY, TOO BAD.
ANAFARTALAR

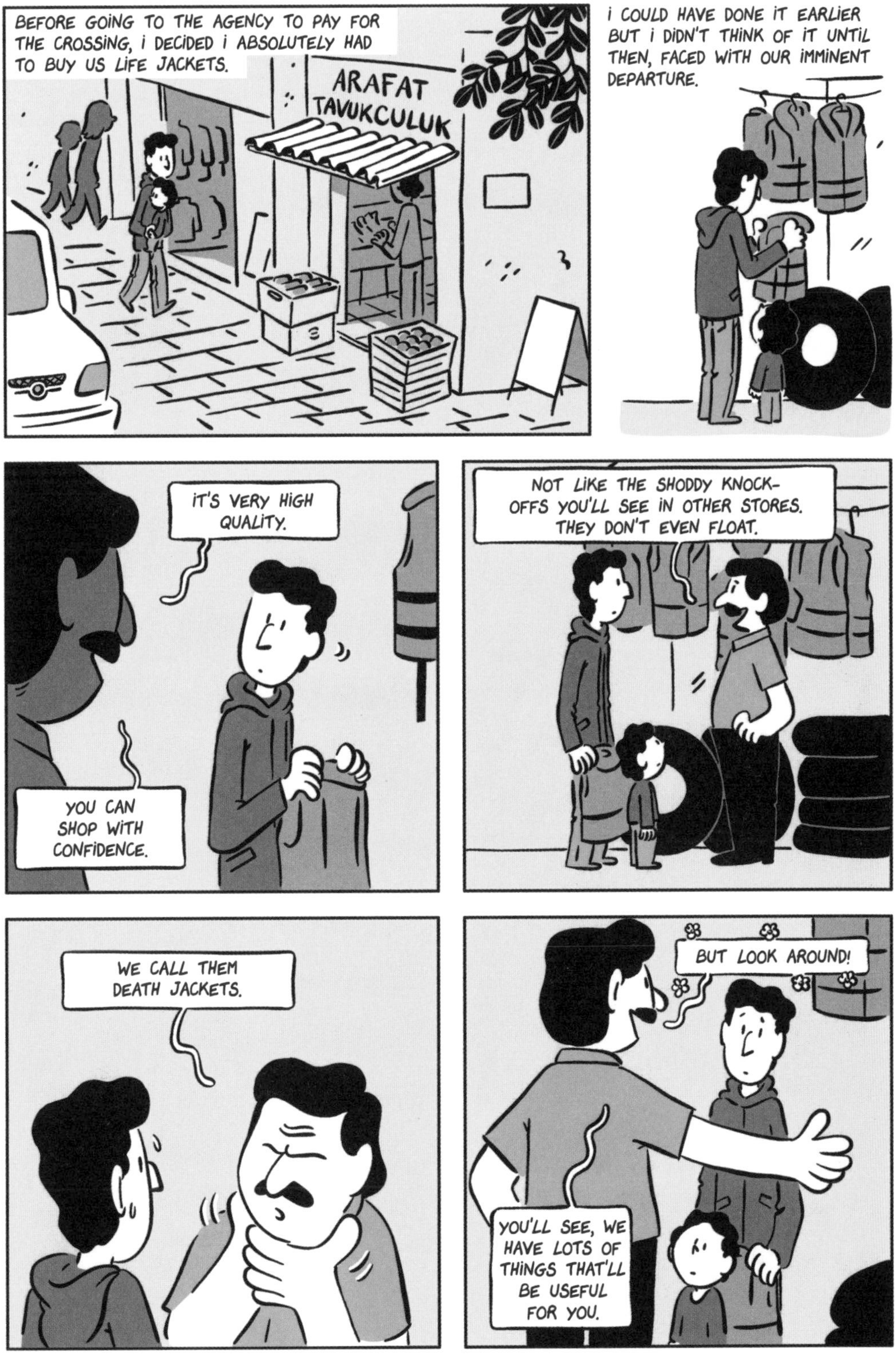
BEFORE GOING TO THE AGENCY TO PAY FOR THE CROSSING, I DECIDED I ABSOLUTELY HAD TO BUY US LIFE JACKETS.
ARAFAT TAVUKCULUK
I COULD HAVE DONE IT EARLIER BUT I DIDN'T THINK OF IT UNTIL THEN, FACED WITH OUR IMMINENT DEPARTURE.
IT'S VERY HIGH QUALITY.
YOU CAN SHOP WITH CONFIDENCE.
NOT LIKE THE SHODDY KNOCK-OFFS YOU'LL SEE IN OTHER STORES. THEY DON'T EVEN FLOAT.
WE CALL THEM DEATH JACKETS.
BUT LOOK AROUND!
YOU'LL SEE, WE HAVE LOTS OF THINGS THAT'LL BE USEFUL FOR YOU.

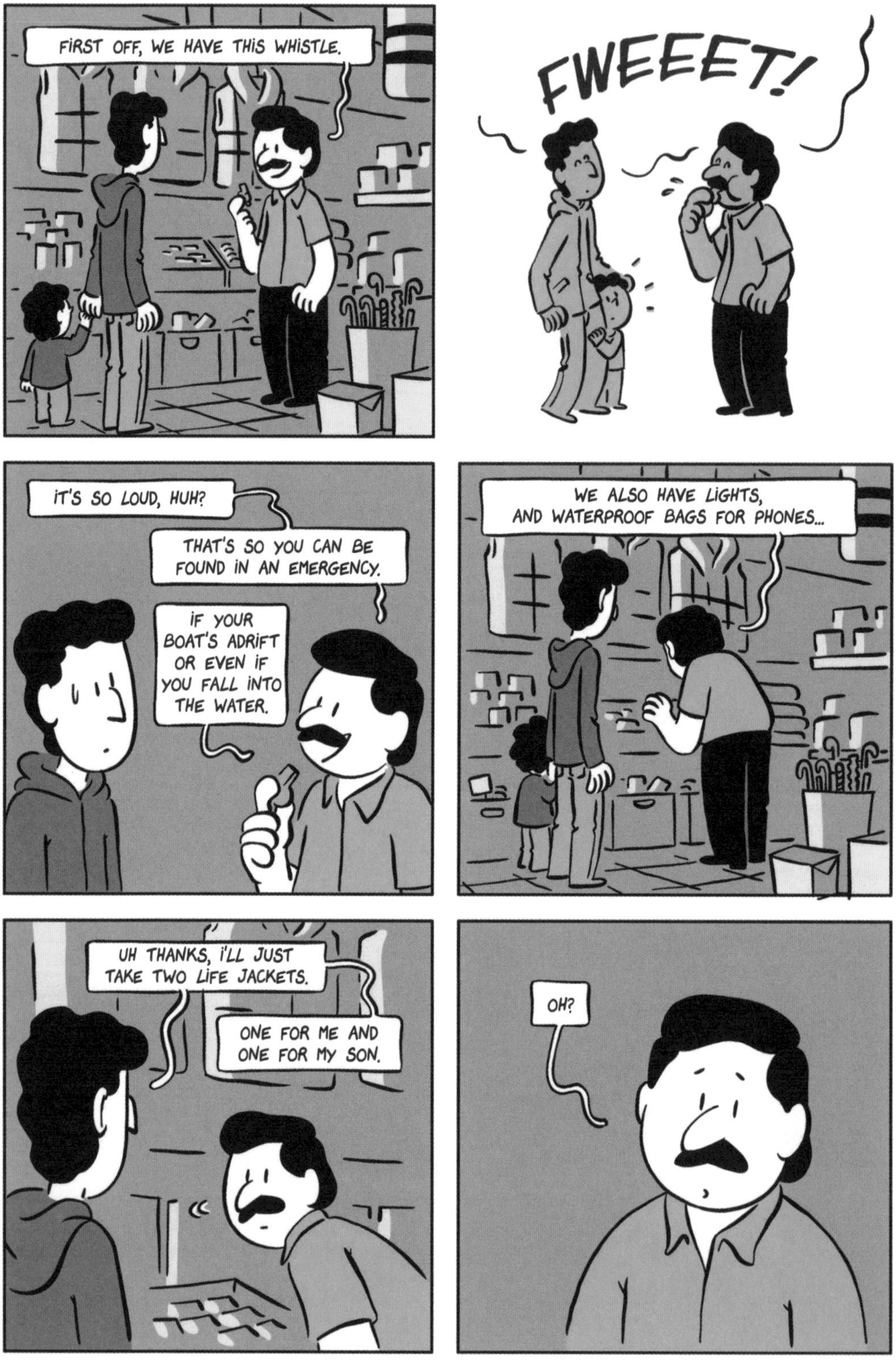
FIRST OFF, WE HAVE THIS WHISTLE.
FWEEET!
IT'S SO LOUD, HUH?
THAT'S SO YOU CAN BE FOUND IN AN EMERGENCY.
IF YOUR BOAT'S ADRIFT OR EVEN IF YOU FALL INTO THE WATER.
WE ALSO HAVE LIGHTS, AND WATERPROOF BAGS FOR PHONES...
UH THANKS, I'LL JUST TAKE TWO LIFE JACKETS.
ONE FOR ME AND ONE FOR MY SON.
OH?

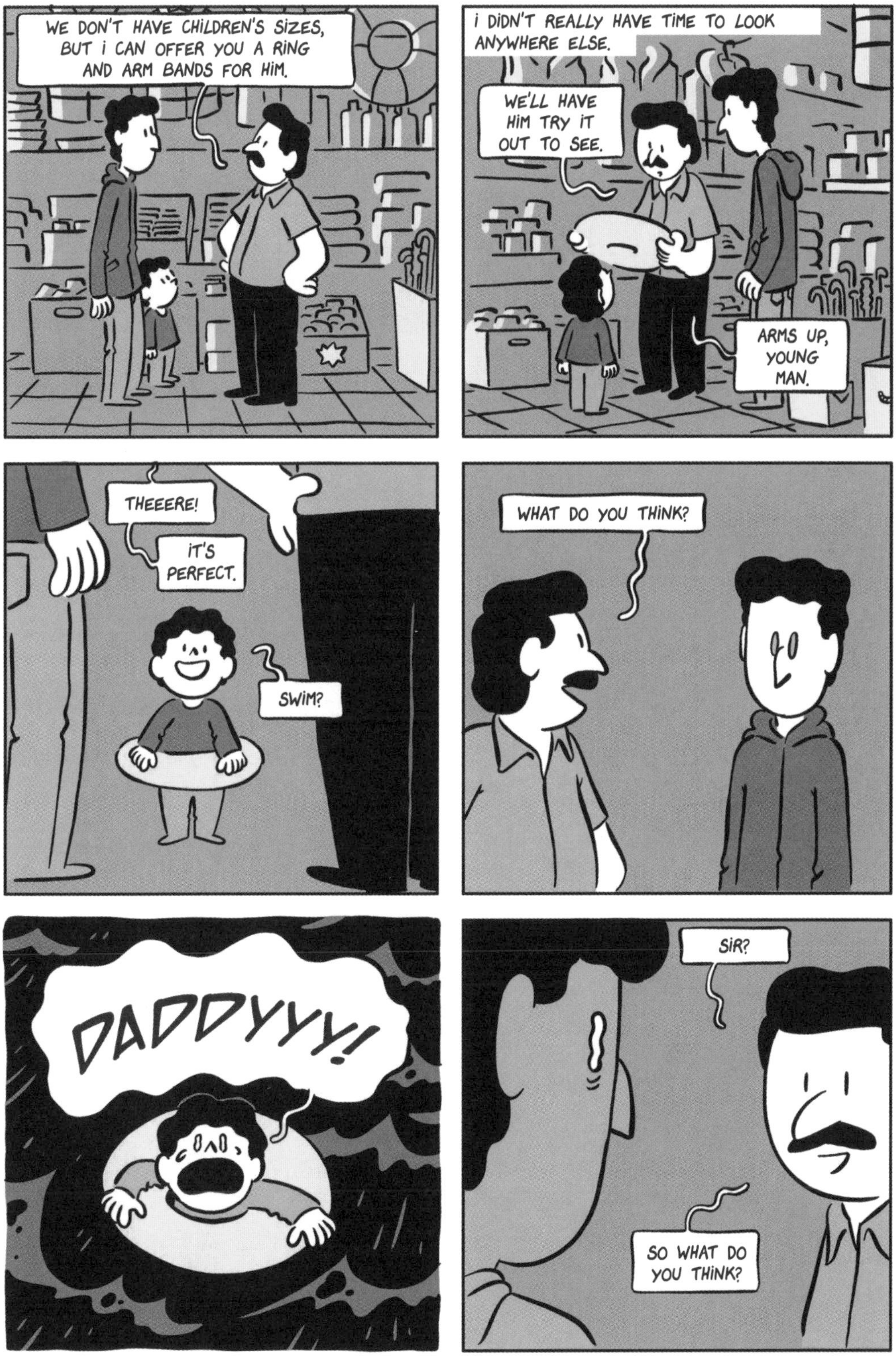
WE DON'T HAVE CHILDREN'S SIZES, BUT I CAN OFFER YOU A RING AND ARM BANDS FOR HIM.
I DIDN'T REALLY HAVE TIME TO LOOK ANYWHERE ELSE.
WE'LL HAVE HIM TRY IT OUT TO SEE.
ARMS UP, YOUNG MAN.
THEEERE!
IT'S PERFECT.
SWIM?
WHAT DO YOU THINK?
DADDYYY!
SIR?
SO WHAT DO YOU THINK?

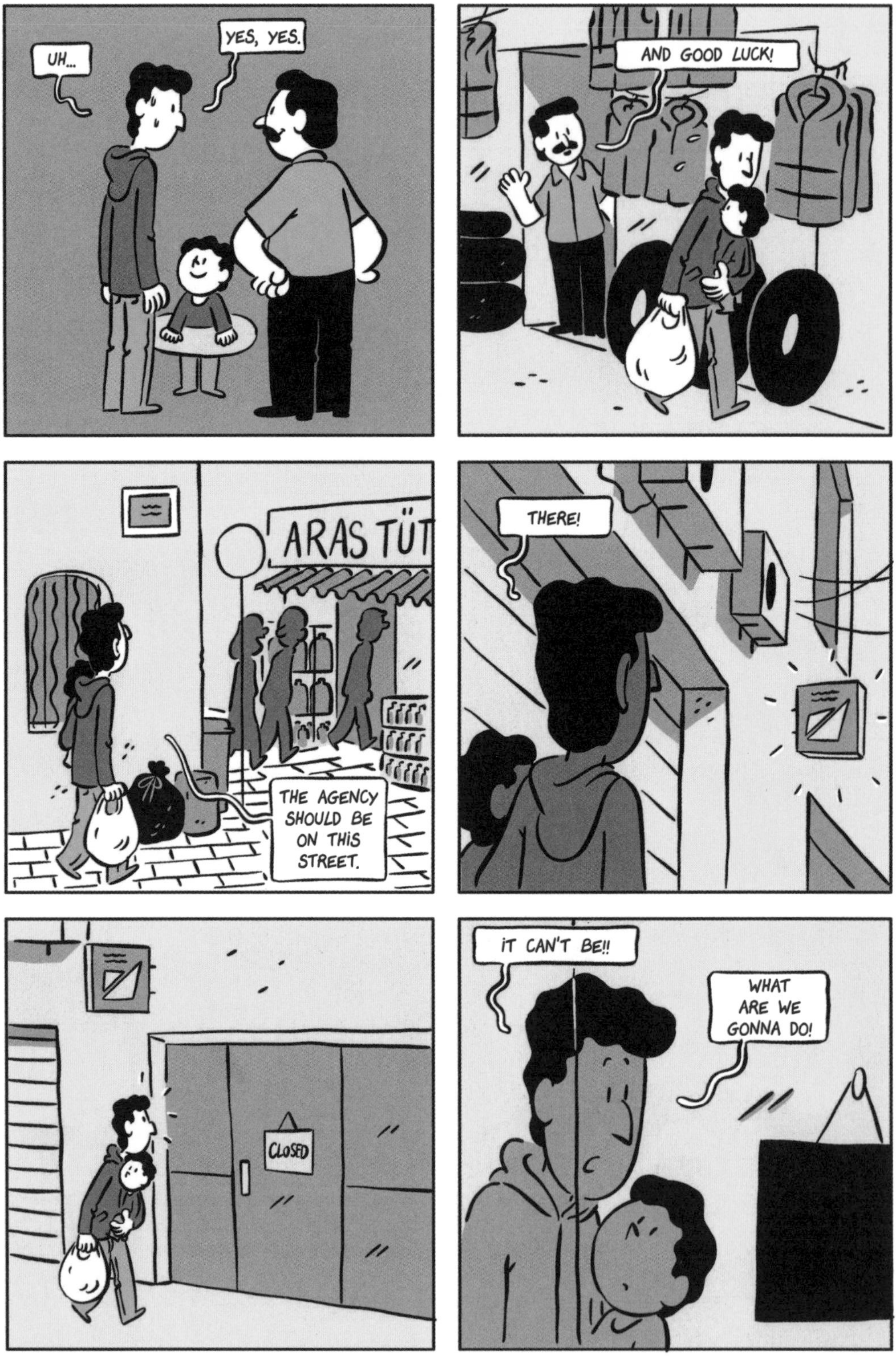
UH...
YES, YES.
AND GOOD LUCK!
ARAS TÜT
THE AGENCY SHOULD BE ON THIS STREET.
THERE!
CLOSED
IT CAN'T BE!!
WHAT ARE WE GONNA DO!

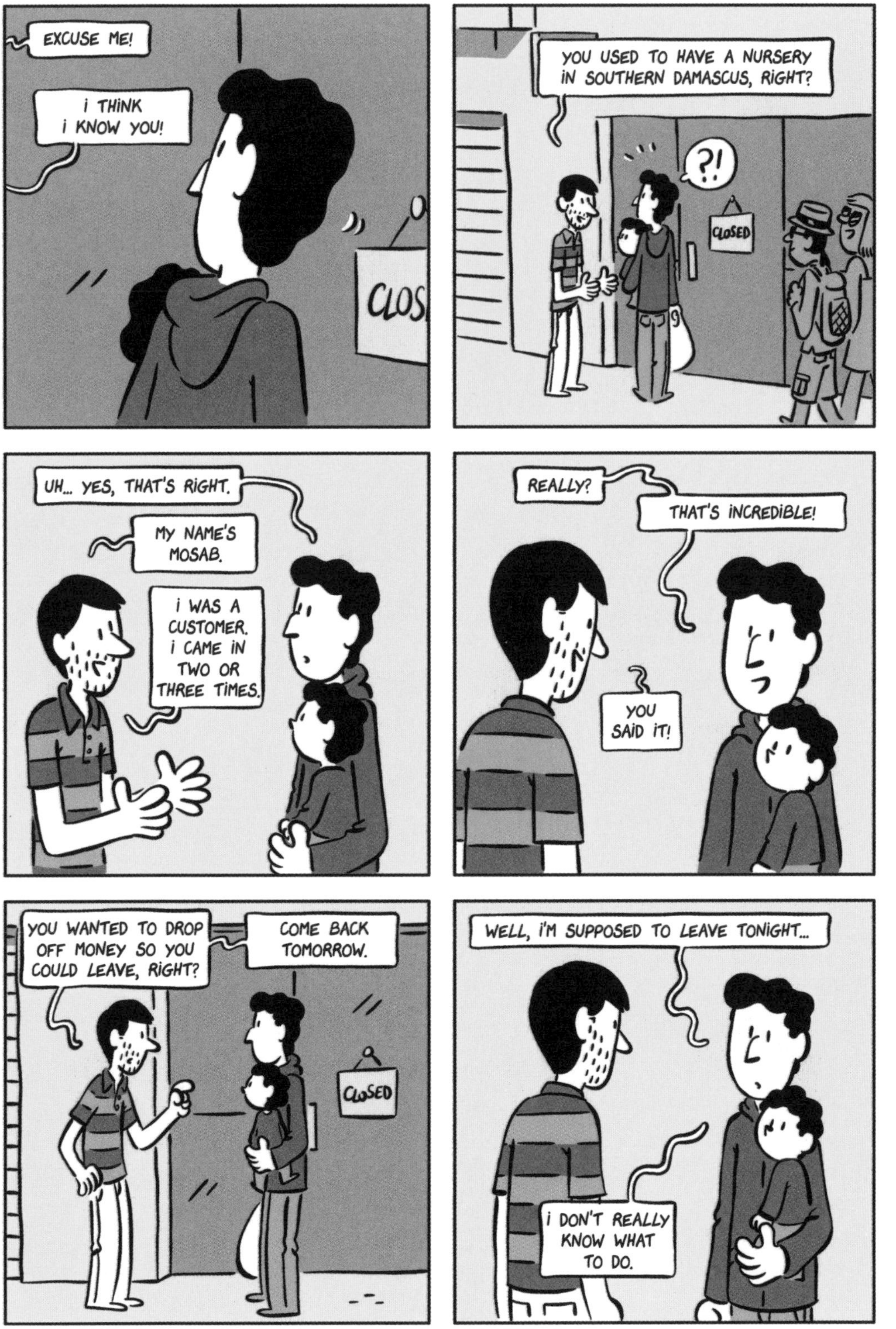
EXCUSE ME!
i THiNK i KNOW YOU!
CLOS
YOU USED TO HAVE A NURSERY iN SOUTHERN DAMASCUS, RiGHT?
?!
CLOSED
UH... YES, THAT'S RiGHT.
MY NAME'S MOSAB.
i WAS A CUSTOMER. i CAME iN TWO OR THREE TiMES.
REALLY?
THAT'S iNCREDiBLE!
YOU SAiD iT!
YOU WANTED TO DROP OFF MONEY SO YOU COULD LEAVE, RiGHT?
COME BACK TOMORROW.
CLOSED
WELL, i'M SUPPOSED TO LEAVE TONiGHT...
i DON'T REALLY KNOW WHAT TO DO.

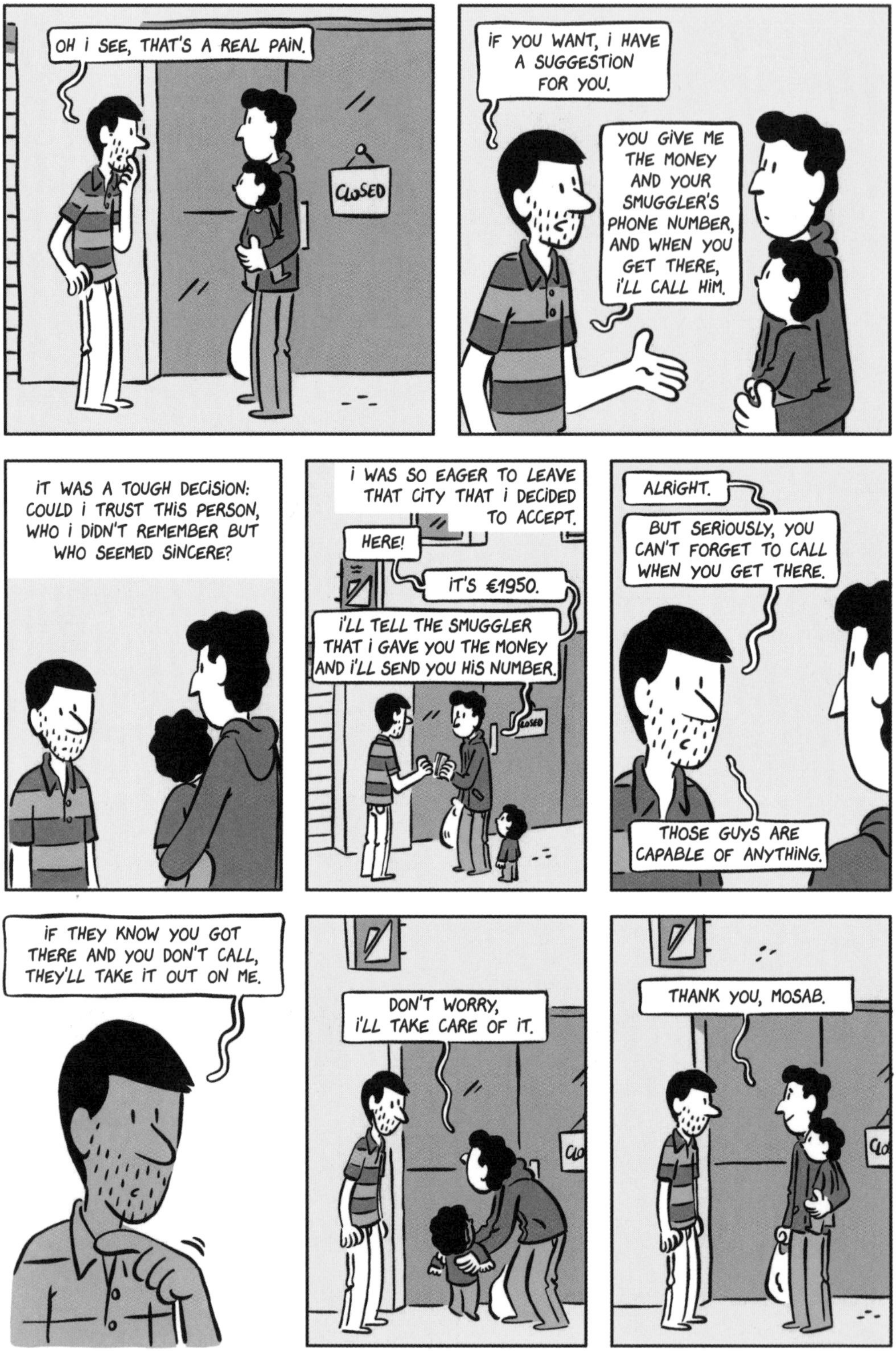
OH I SEE, THAT'S A REAL PAIN.
CLOSED
IF YOU WANT, I HAVE A SUGGESTION FOR YOU.
YOU GIVE ME THE MONEY AND YOUR SMUGGLER'S PHONE NUMBER, AND WHEN YOU GET THERE, I'LL CALL HIM.
IT WAS A TOUGH DECISION: COULD I TRUST THIS PERSON, WHO I DIDN'T REMEMBER BUT WHO SEEMED SINCERE?
I WAS SO EAGER TO LEAVE THAT CITY THAT I DECIDED TO ACCEPT.
HERE!
IT'S €1950.
I'LL TELL THE SMUGGLER THAT I GAVE YOU THE MONEY AND I'LL SEND YOU HIS NUMBER.
CLOSED
ALRIGHT.
BUT SERIOUSLY, YOU CAN'T FORGET TO CALL WHEN YOU GET THERE.
THOSE GUYS ARE CAPABLE OF ANYTHING.
IF THEY KNOW YOU GOT THERE AND YOU DON'T CALL, THEY'LL TAKE IT OUT ON ME.
DON'T WORRY, I'LL TAKE CARE OF IT.
THANK YOU, MOSAB.

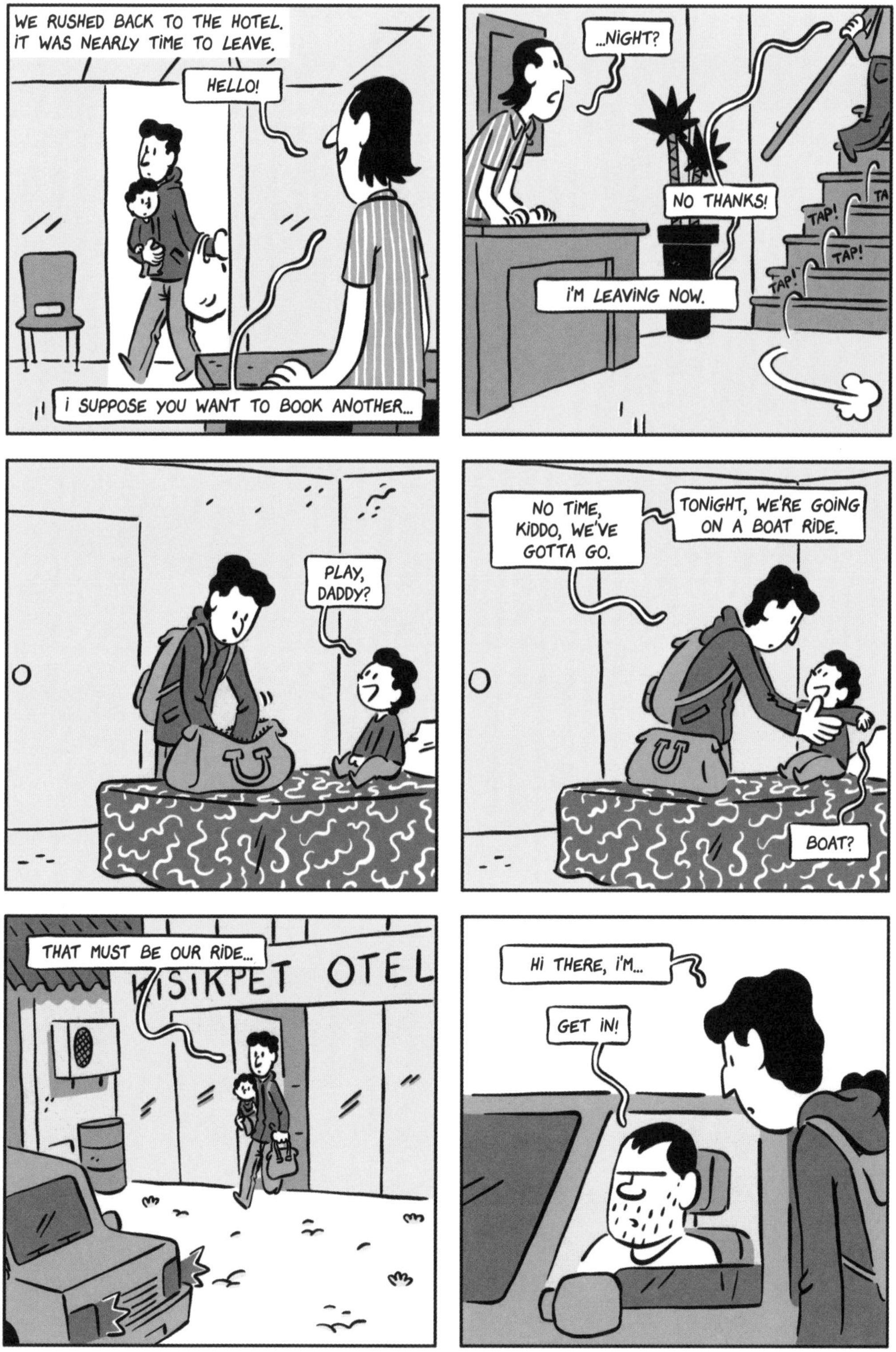
WE RUSHED BACK TO THE HOTEL. IT WAS NEARLY TIME TO LEAVE.
HELLO!
I SUPPOSE YOU WANT TO BOOK ANOTHER...
...NIGHT?
NO THANKS!
I'M LEAVING NOW.
TAP!
TAP!
TAP!
TA
PLAY, DADDY?
NO TIME, KIDDO, WE'VE GOTTA GO.
TONIGHT, WE'RE GOING ON A BOAT RIDE.
BOAT?
THAT MUST BE OUR RIDE...
KISIKPET OTEL
HI THERE, I'M...
GET IN!

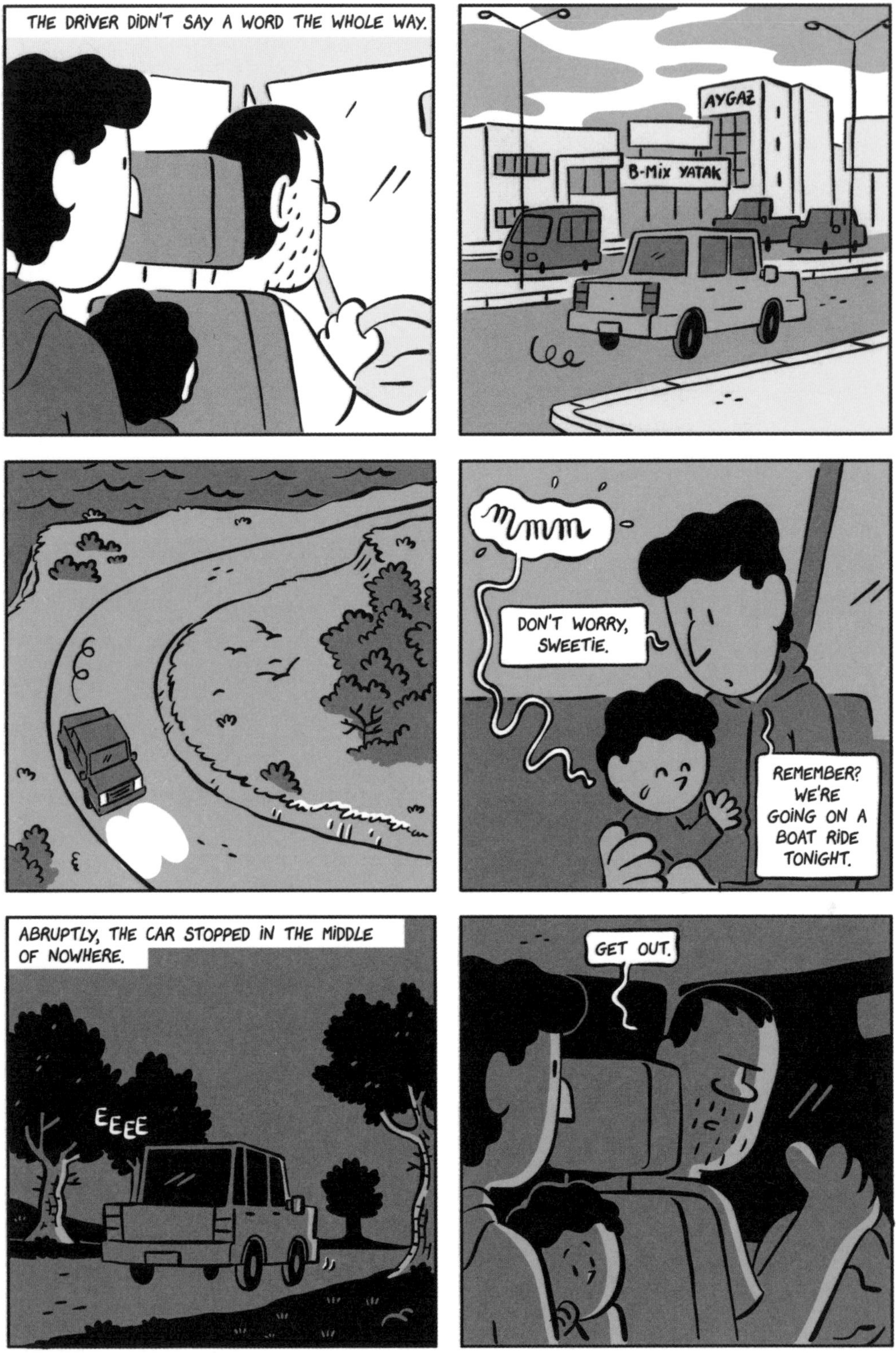
THE DRIVER DIDN'T SAY A WORD THE WHOLE WAY.
AYGAZ
B-MIX YATAK
MMM
DON'T WORRY, SWEETIE.
REMEMBER? WE'RE GOING ON A BOAT RIDE TONIGHT.
ABRUPTLY, THE CAR STOPPED IN THE MIDDLE OF NOWHERE.
EEEE
GET OUT.

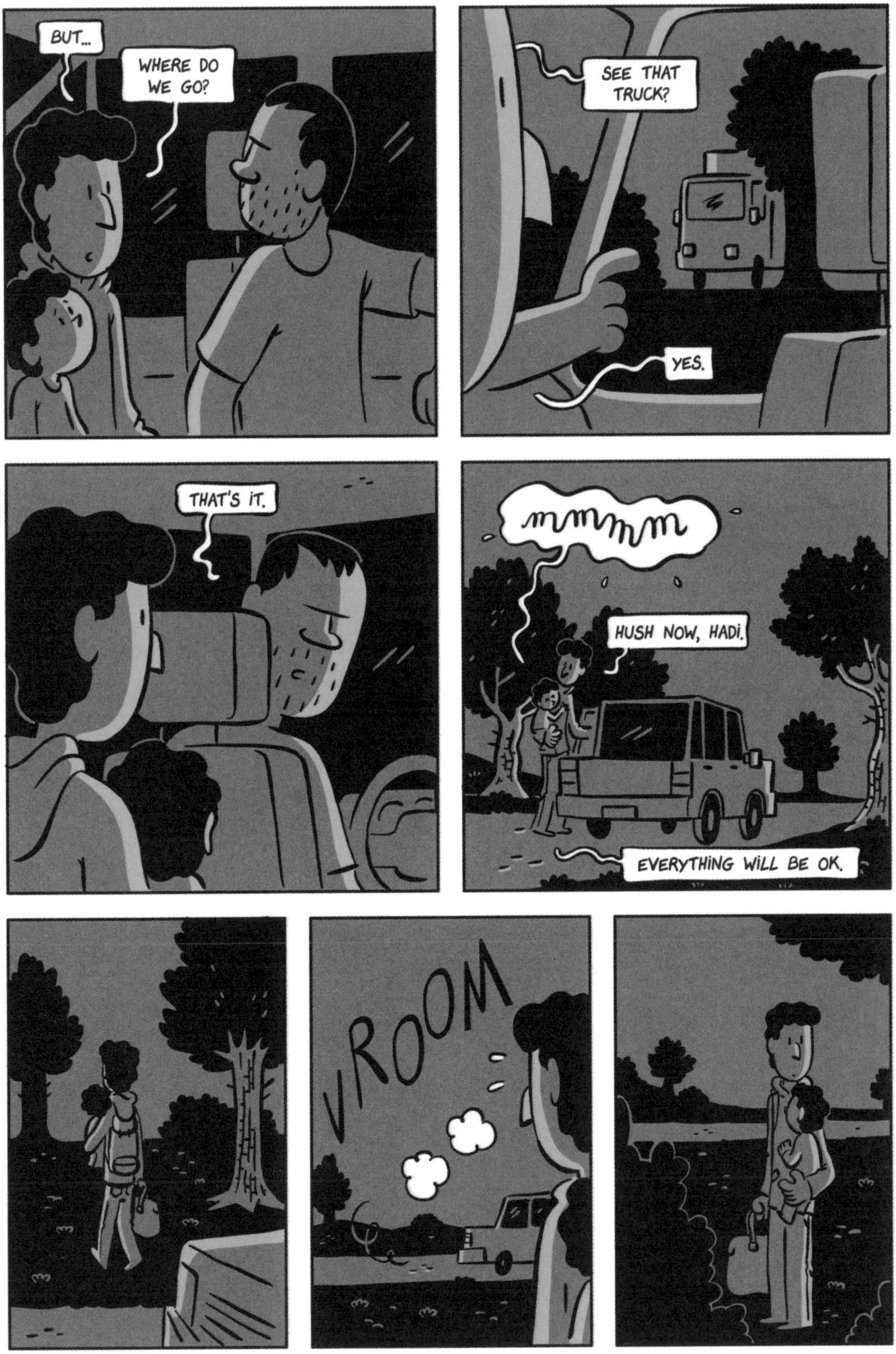
BUT...
WHERE DO WE GO?
SEE THAT TRUCK?
YES.
THAT'S IT.
mmmm
HUSH NOW, HADI.
EVERYTHING WILL BE OK.
VROOM

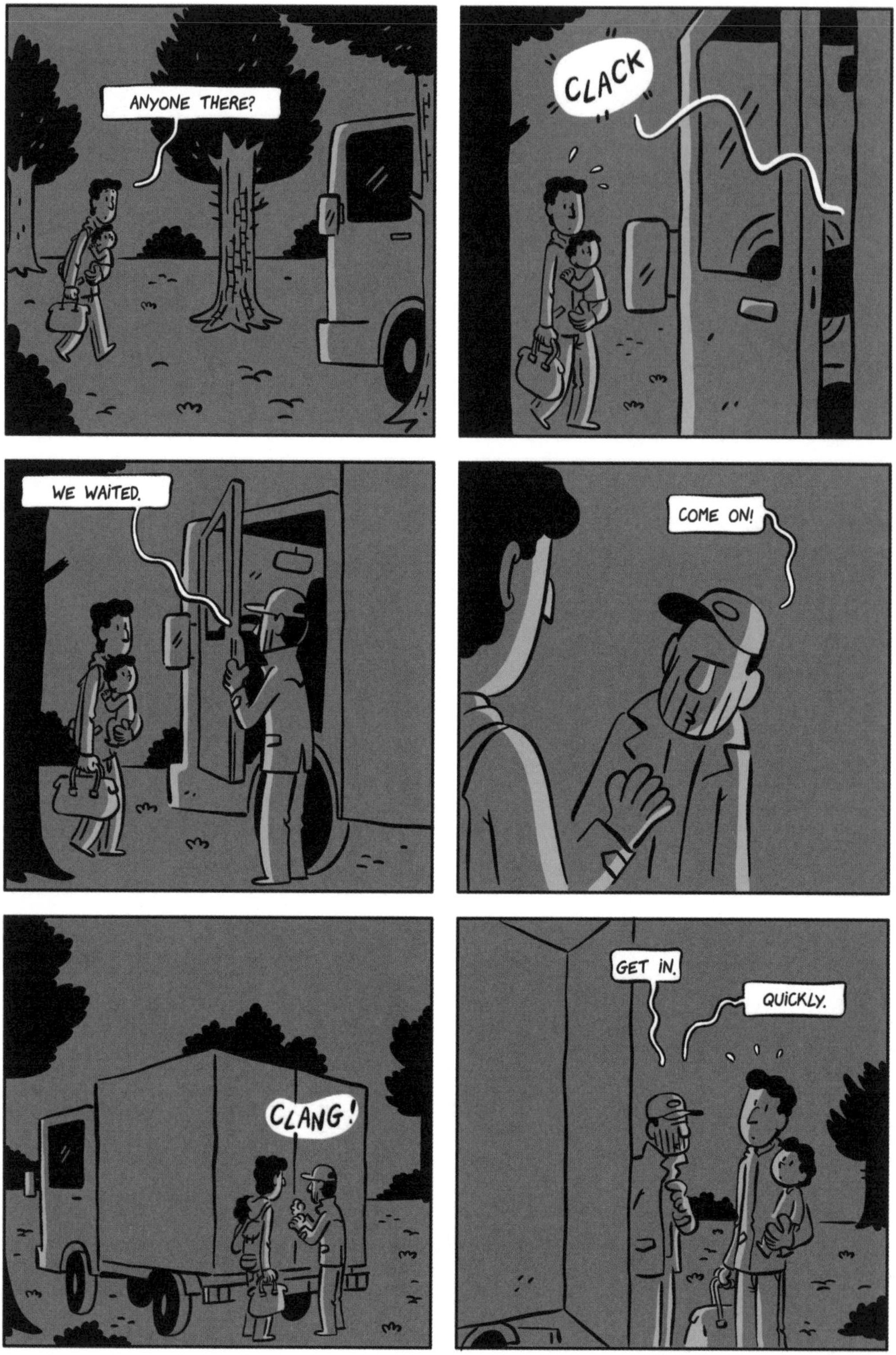
ANYONE THERE?
CLACK
WE WAITED.
COME ON!
CLANG!
GET IN.
QUICKLY.

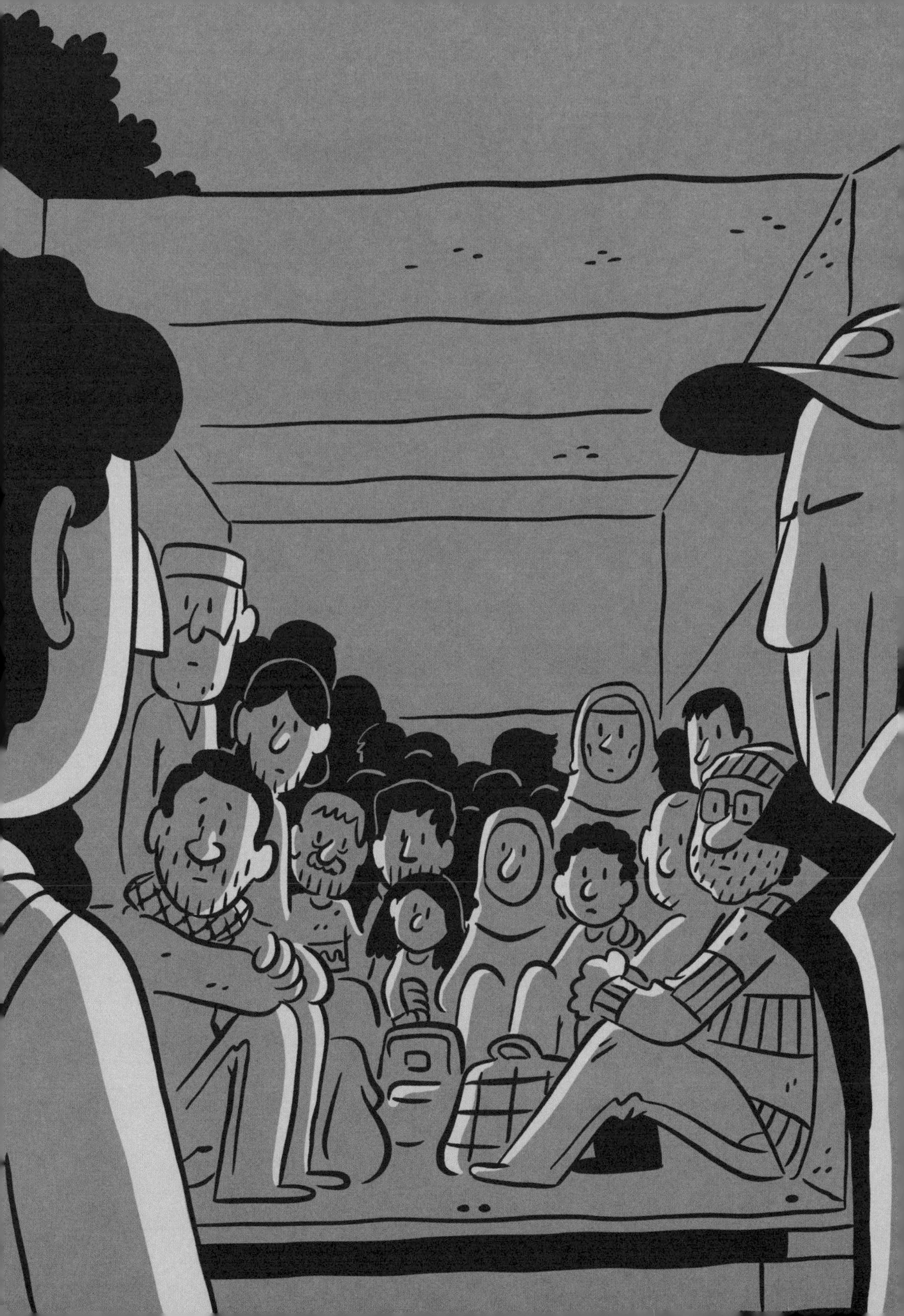

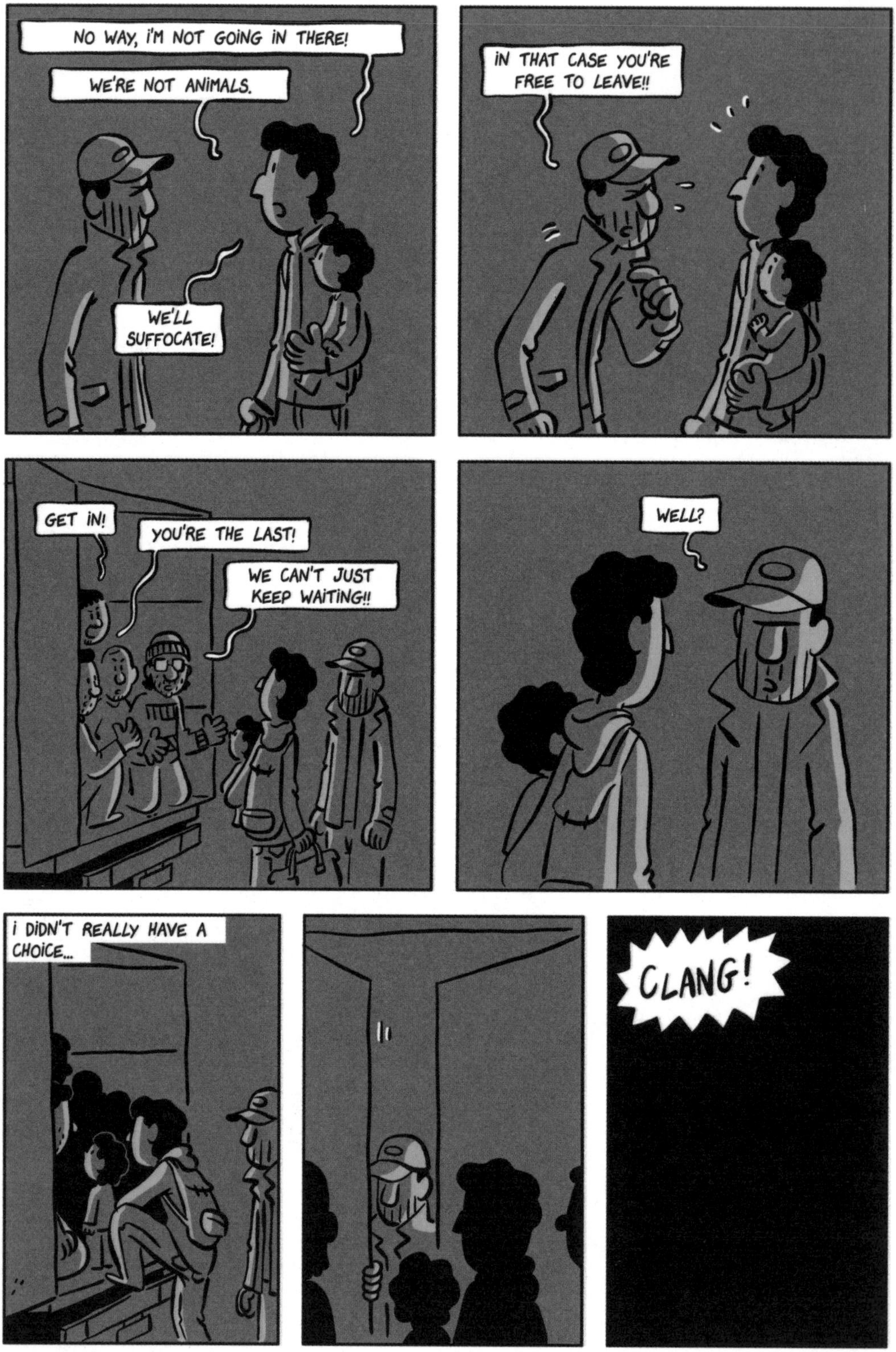
NO WAY, I'M NOT GOING IN THERE!
WE'RE NOT ANIMALS.
WE'LL SUFFOCATE!
IN THAT CASE YOU'RE FREE TO LEAVE!!
GET IN!
YOU'RE THE LAST!
WE CAN'T JUST KEEP WAITING!!
WELL?
I DIDN'T REALLY HAVE A CHOICE...
CLANG!

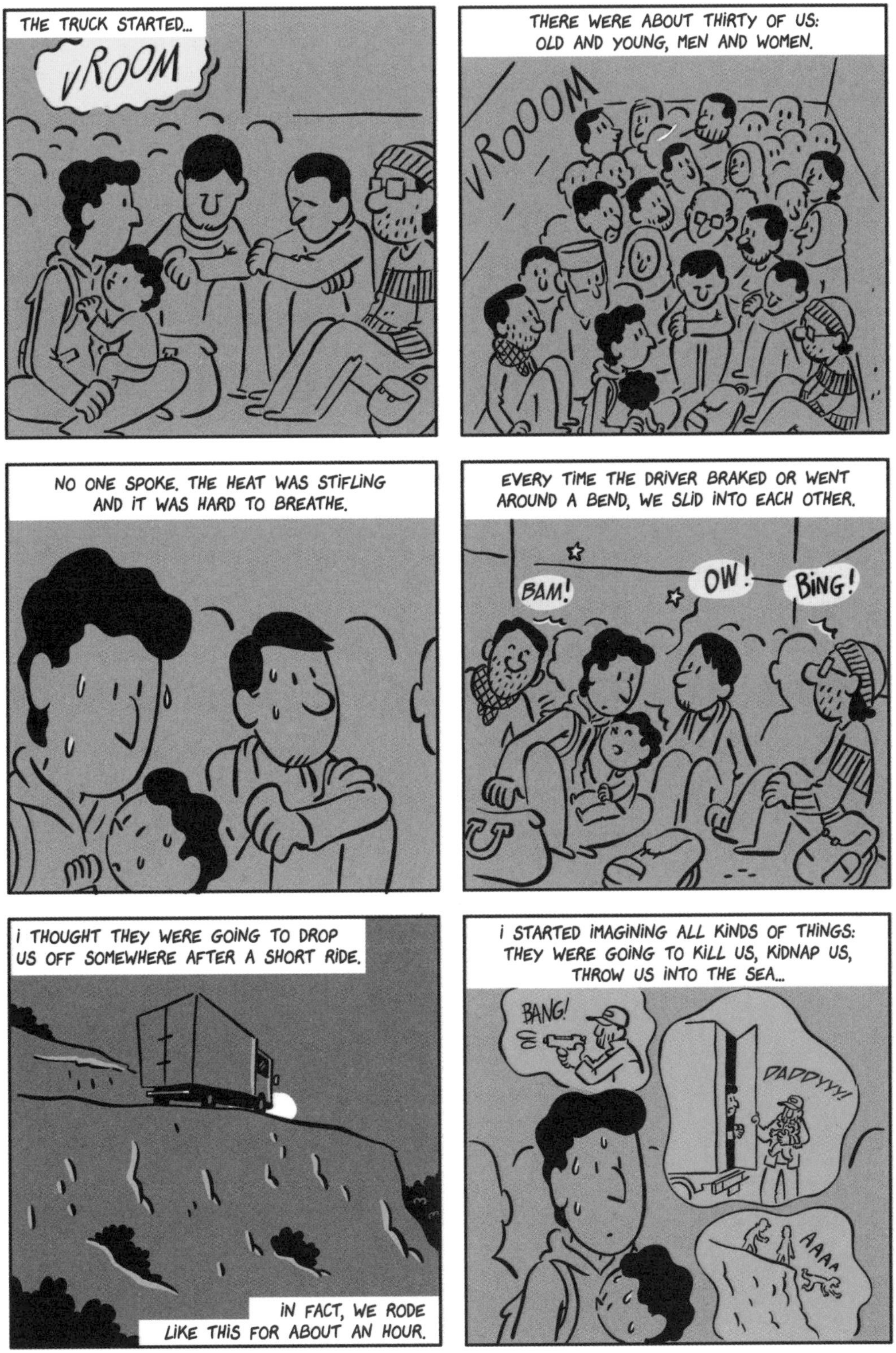
THE TRUCK STARTED...
VROOM
THERE WERE ABOUT THIRTY OF US: OLD AND YOUNG, MEN AND WOMEN.
VROOOM
NO ONE SPOKE. THE HEAT WAS STIFLING AND IT WAS HARD TO BREATHE.
EVERY TIME THE DRIVER BRAKED OR WENT AROUND A BEND, WE SLID INTO EACH OTHER.
BAM!
OW!
BING!
I THOUGHT THEY WERE GOING TO DROP US OFF SOMEWHERE AFTER A SHORT RIDE.
IN FACT, WE RODE LIKE THIS FOR ABOUT AN HOUR.
I STARTED IMAGINING ALL KINDS OF THINGS: THEY WERE GOING TO KILL US, KIDNAP US, THROW US INTO THE SEA...
BANG!
DADDYYY!
AAAA

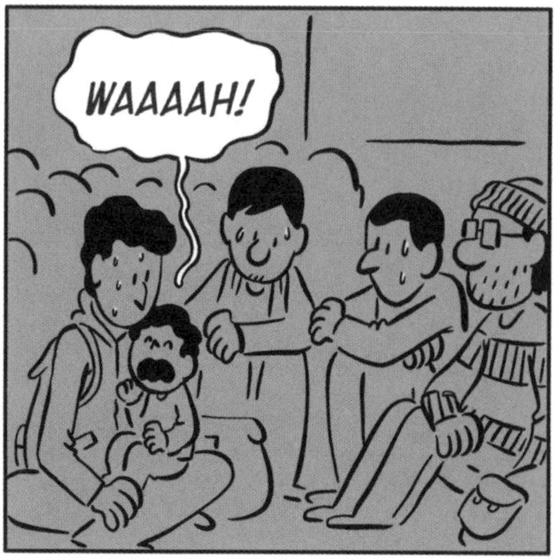
WAAAAH!

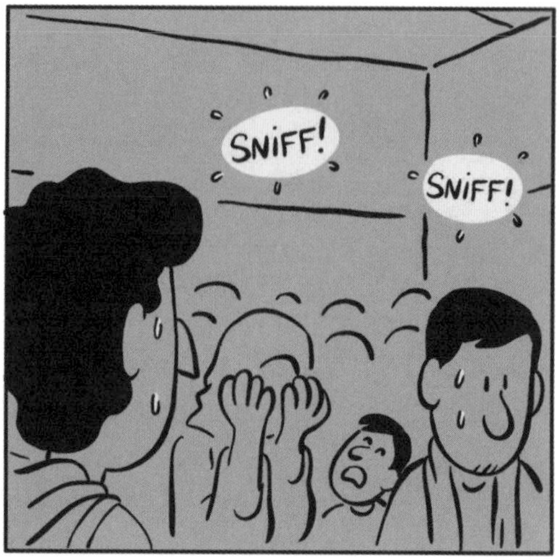
SNIFF!
SNIFF!

TO TAKE MY MIND OFF THINGS, I STARTED RECITING NIZAR QABBANI'S* POEMS TO MYSELF.

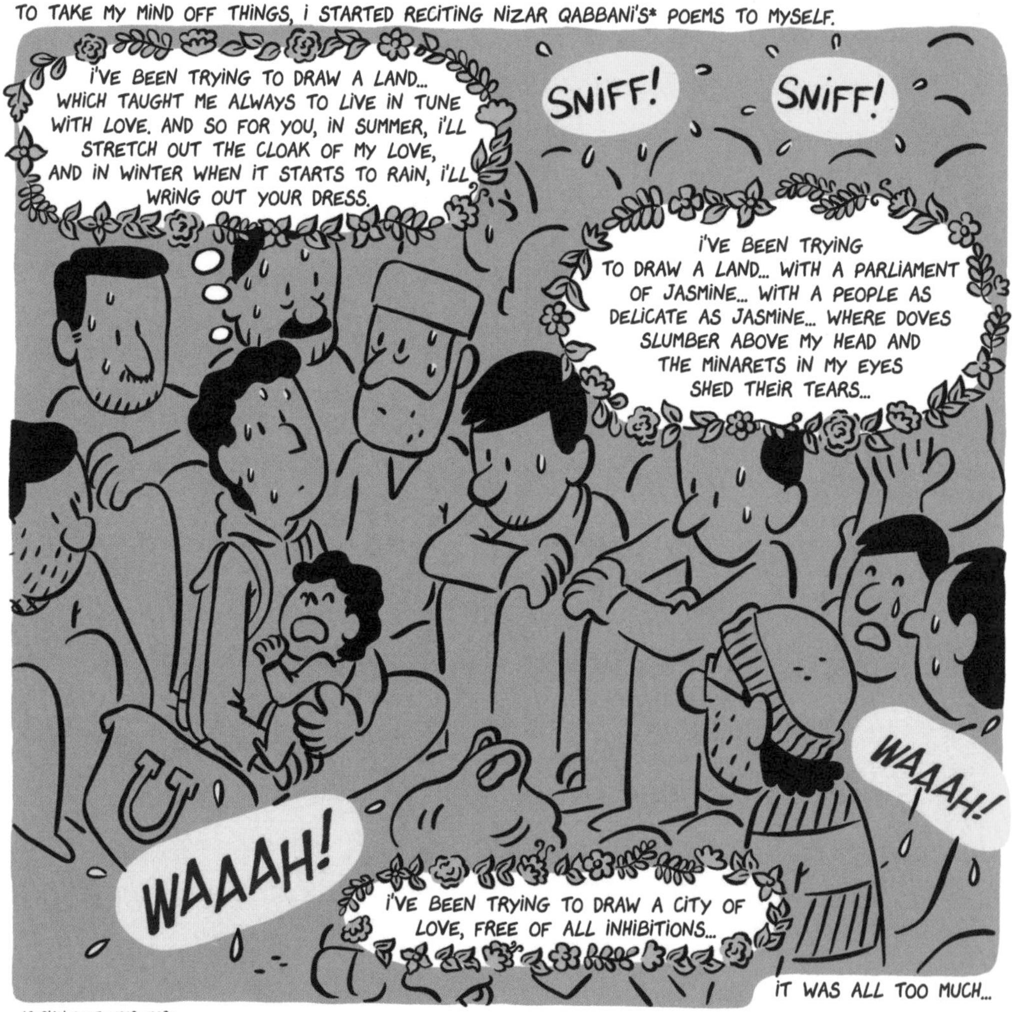
I'VE BEEN TRYING TO DRAW A LAND... WHICH TAUGHT ME ALWAYS TO LIVE IN TUNE WITH LOVE. AND SO FOR YOU, IN SUMMER, I'LL STRETCH OUT THE CLOAK OF MY LOVE, AND IN WINTER WHEN IT STARTS TO RAIN, I'LL WRING OUT YOUR DRESS.
SNIFF!
SNIFF!
I'VE BEEN TRYING TO DRAW A LAND... WITH A PARLIAMENT OF JASMINE... WITH A PEOPLE AS DELICATE AS JASMINE... WHERE DOVES SLUMBER ABOVE MY HEAD AND THE MINARETS IN MY EYES SHED THEIR TEARS...
WAAAH!
WAAAH!
I'VE BEEN TRYING TO DRAW A CITY OF LOVE, FREE OF ALL INHIBITIONS...

IT WAS ALL TOO MUCH...

*SYRIAN POET (1923–1998).

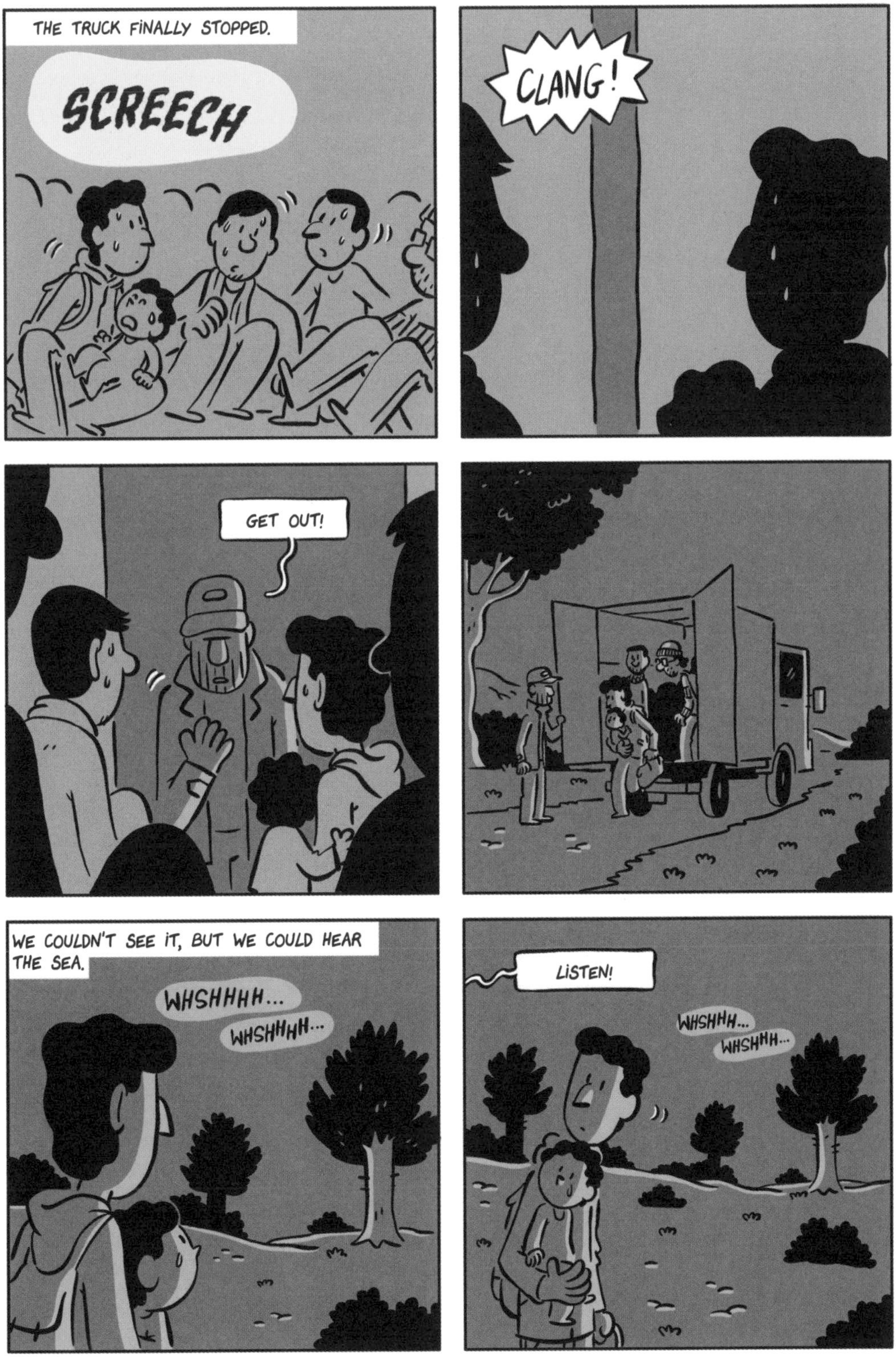
THE TRUCK FINALLY STOPPED.
SCREECH
CLANG!
GET OUT!
WE COULDN'T SEE IT, BUT WE COULD HEAR THE SEA.
WHSHHHH...
WHSHHHH...
LISTEN!
WHSHHH...
WHSHHH...

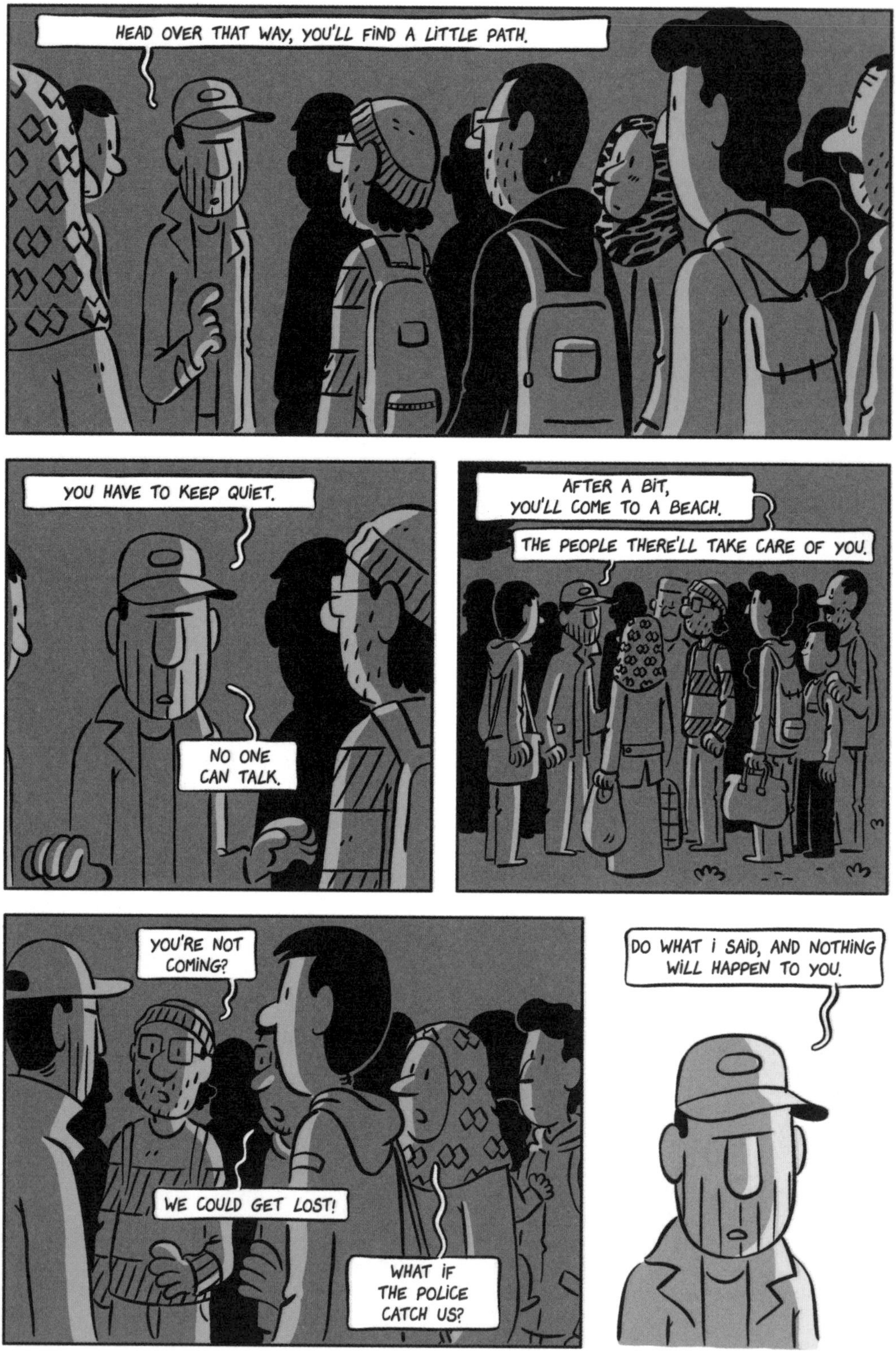
HEAD OVER THAT WAY, YOU'LL FIND A LITTLE PATH.
YOU HAVE TO KEEP QUIET.
NO ONE CAN TALK.
AFTER A BIT, YOU'LL COME TO A BEACH.
THE PEOPLE THERE'LL TAKE CARE OF YOU.
YOU'RE NOT COMING?
WE COULD GET LOST!
WHAT IF THE POLICE CATCH US?
DO WHAT I SAID, AND NOTHING WILL HAPPEN TO YOU.

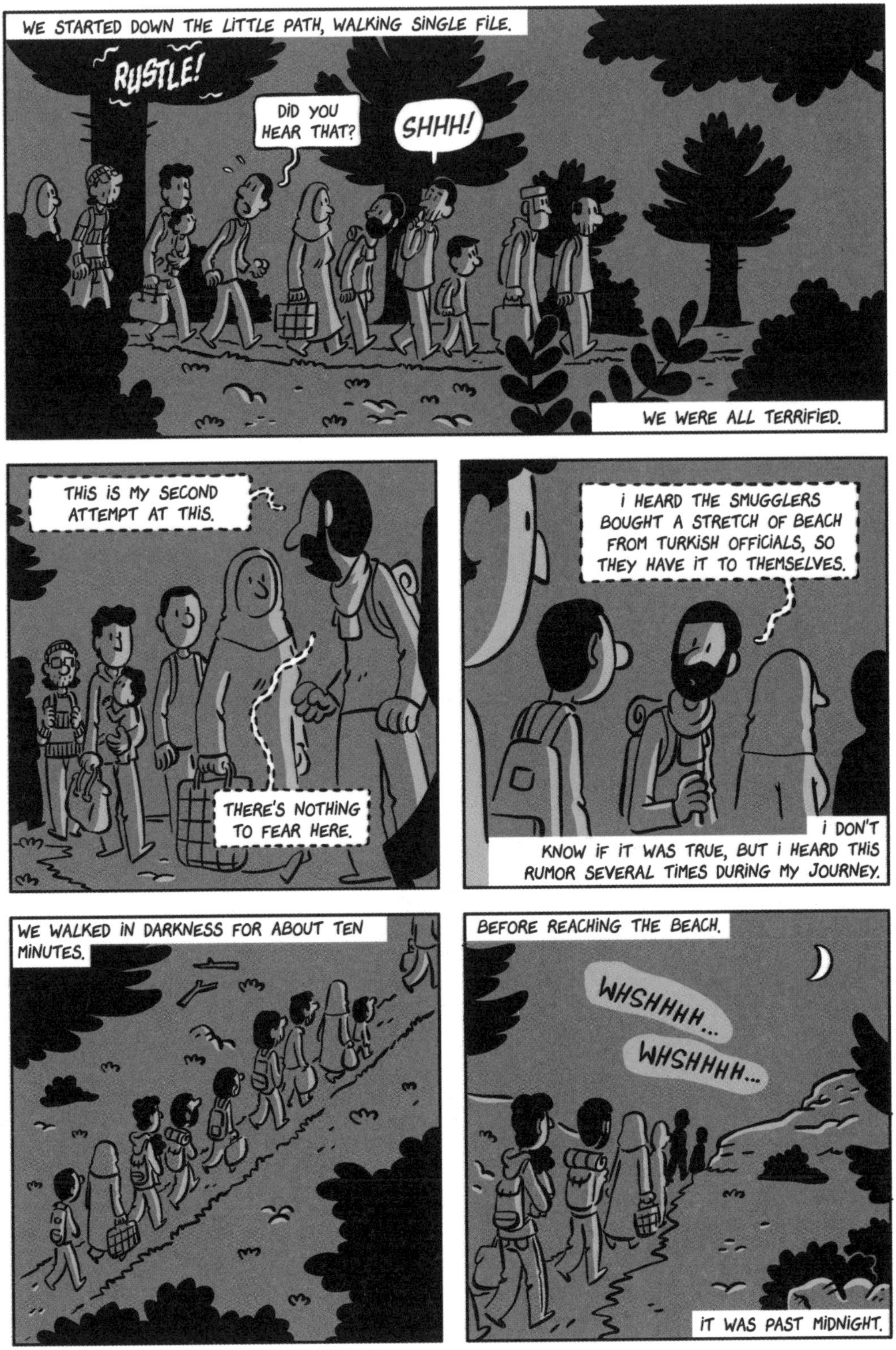
WE STARTED DOWN THE LITTLE PATH, WALKING SINGLE FILE.
RUSTLE!
DID YOU HEAR THAT?
SHHH!
WE WERE ALL TERRIFIED.
THIS IS MY SECOND ATTEMPT AT THIS.
THERE'S NOTHING TO FEAR HERE.
I HEARD THE SMUGGLERS BOUGHT A STRETCH OF BEACH FROM TURKISH OFFICIALS, SO THEY HAVE IT TO THEMSELVES.
I DON'T KNOW IF IT WAS TRUE, BUT I HEARD THIS RUMOR SEVERAL TIMES DURING MY JOURNEY.
WE WALKED IN DARKNESS FOR ABOUT TEN MINUTES.
BEFORE REACHING THE BEACH.
WHSHHHH...
WHSHHHH...
IT WAS PAST MIDNIGHT.

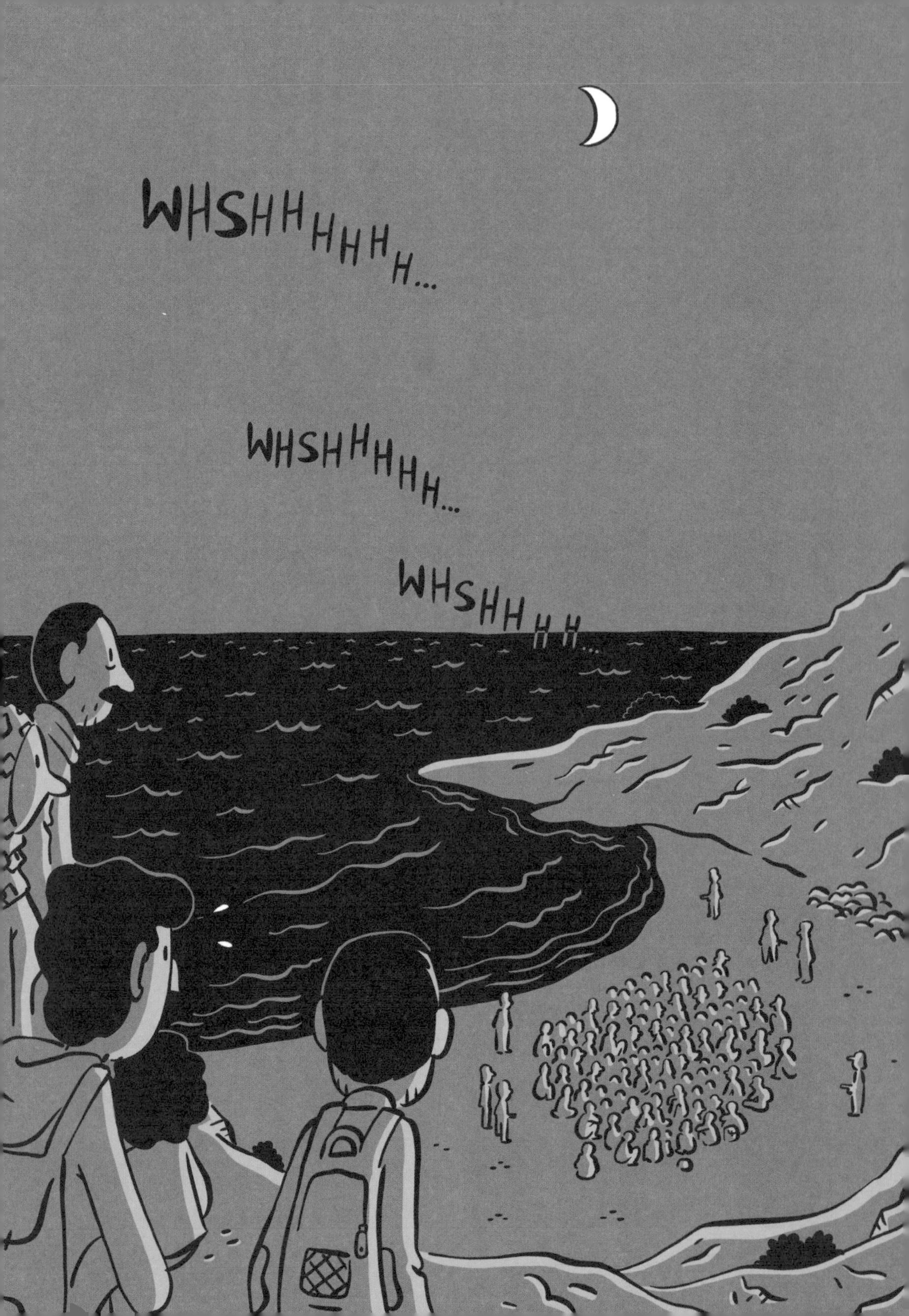
WHSHHHHHH...
WHSHHHHHH...
WHSHHHHH...

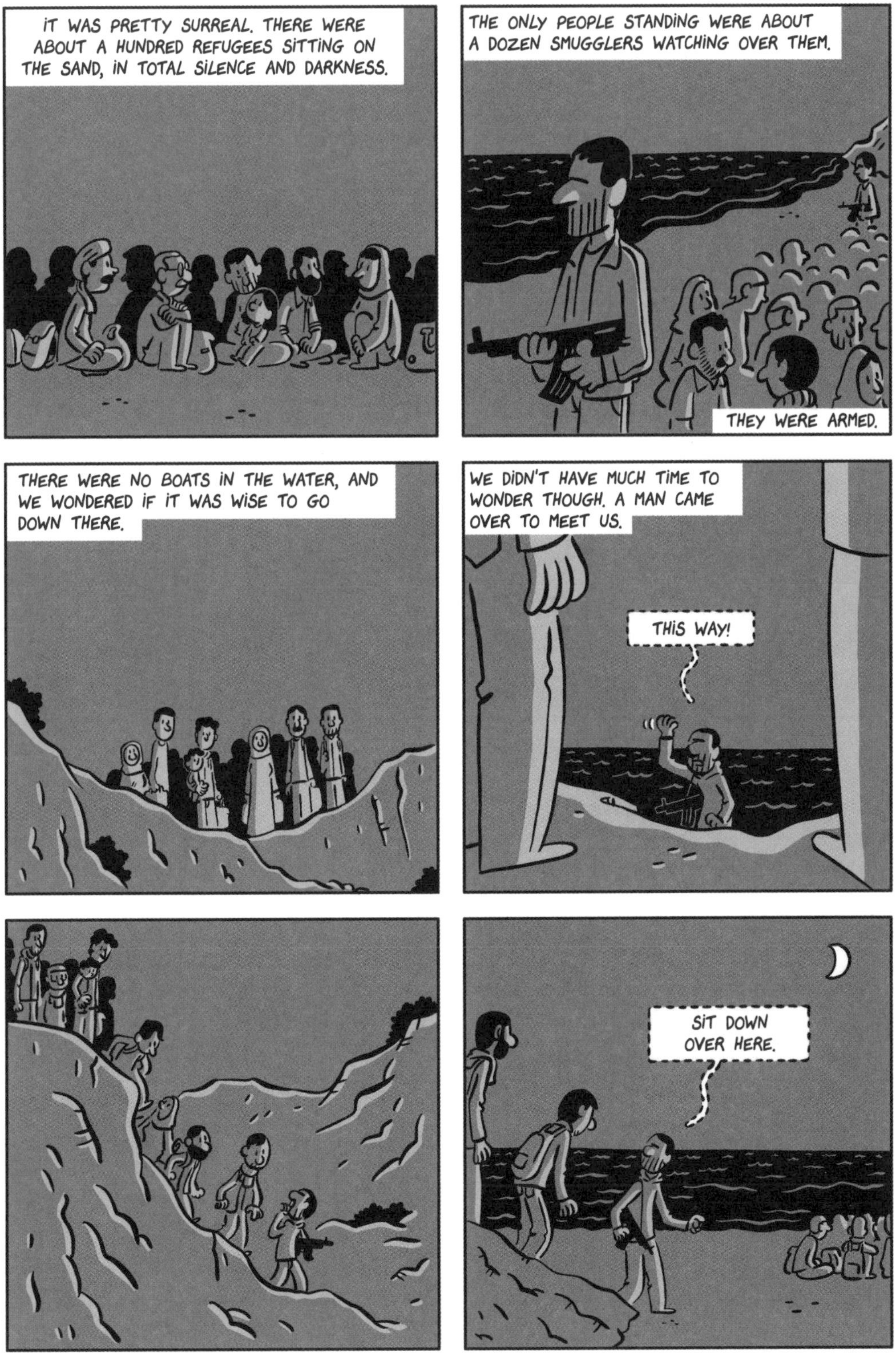
IT WAS PRETTY SURREAL. THERE WERE ABOUT A HUNDRED REFUGEES SITTING ON THE SAND, IN TOTAL SILENCE AND DARKNESS.
THE ONLY PEOPLE STANDING WERE ABOUT A DOZEN SMUGGLERS WATCHING OVER THEM.
THEY WERE ARMED.
THERE WERE NO BOATS IN THE WATER, AND WE WONDERED IF IT WAS WISE TO GO DOWN THERE.
WE DIDN'T HAVE MUCH TIME TO WONDER THOUGH. A MAN CAME OVER TO MEET US.
THIS WAY!
SIT DOWN OVER HERE.

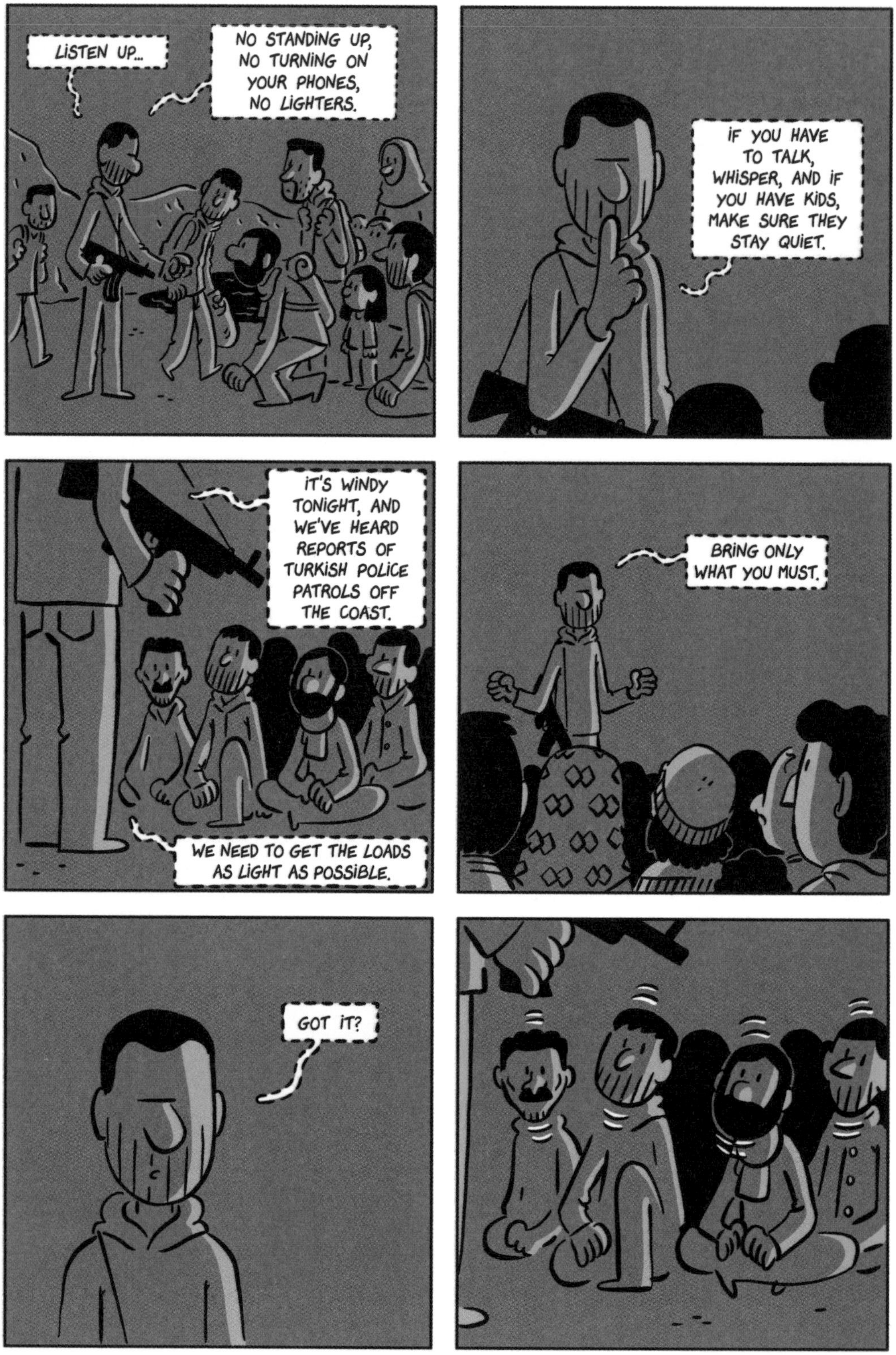
LISTEN UP...
NO STANDING UP, NO TURNING ON YOUR PHONES, NO LIGHTERS.
IF YOU HAVE TO TALK, WHISPER, AND IF YOU HAVE KIDS, MAKE SURE THEY STAY QUIET.
IT'S WINDY TONIGHT, AND WE'VE HEARD REPORTS OF TURKISH POLICE PATROLS OFF THE COAST.
WE NEED TO GET THE LOADS AS LIGHT AS POSSIBLE.
BRING ONLY WHAT YOU MUST.
GOT IT?

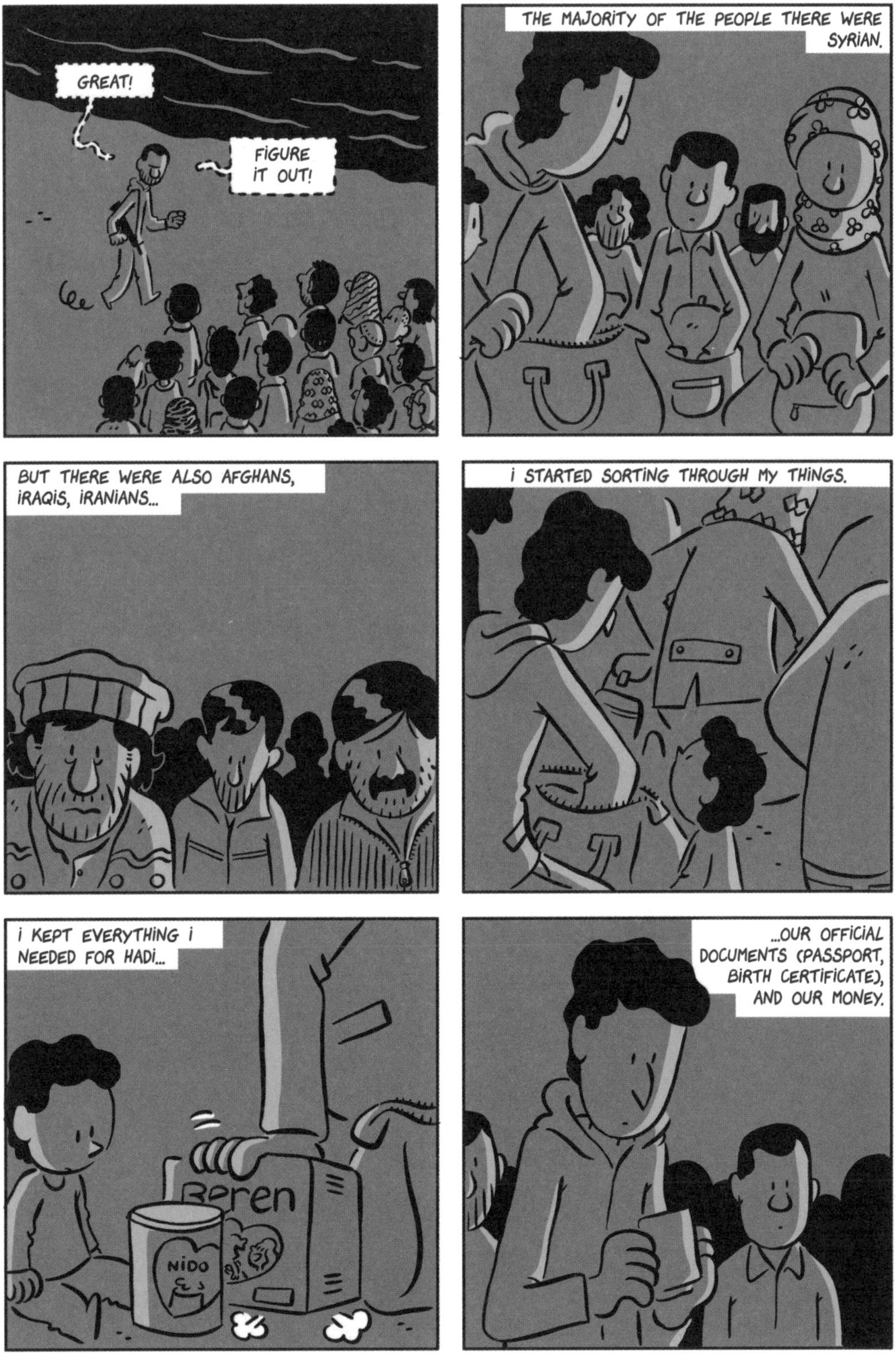
GREAT!
FIGURE IT OUT!
THE MAJORITY OF THE PEOPLE THERE WERE SYRIAN.
BUT THERE WERE ALSO AFGHANS, IRAQIS, IRANIANS...
I STARTED SORTING THROUGH MY THINGS.
I KEPT EVERYTHING I NEEDED FOR HADI...
NIDO
...OUR OFFICIAL DOCUMENTS (PASSPORT, BIRTH CERTIFICATE), AND OUR MONEY.

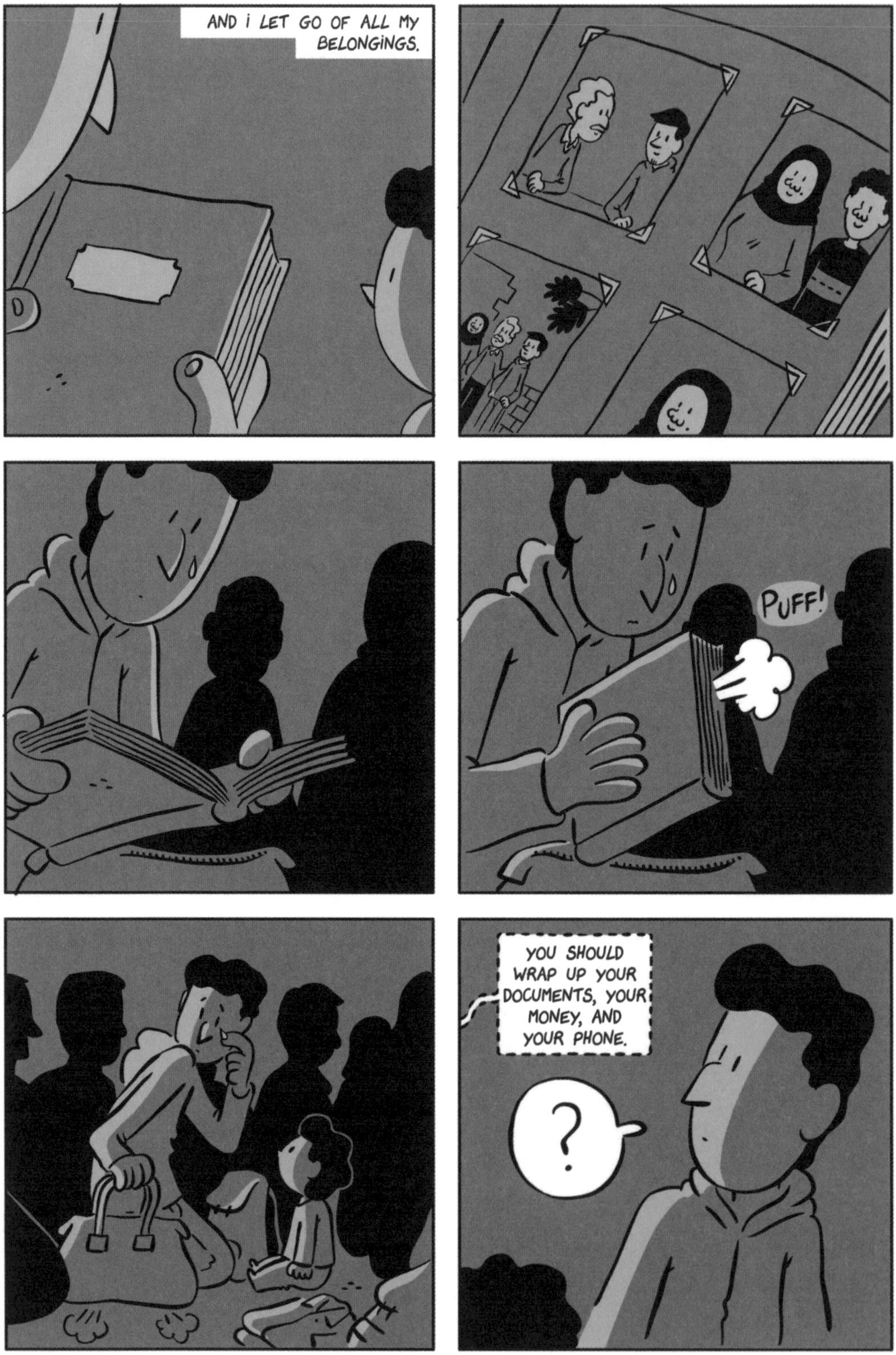
AND I LET GO OF ALL MY BELONGINGS.
PUFF!
YOU SHOULD WRAP UP YOUR DOCUMENTS, YOUR MONEY, AND YOUR PHONE.
?

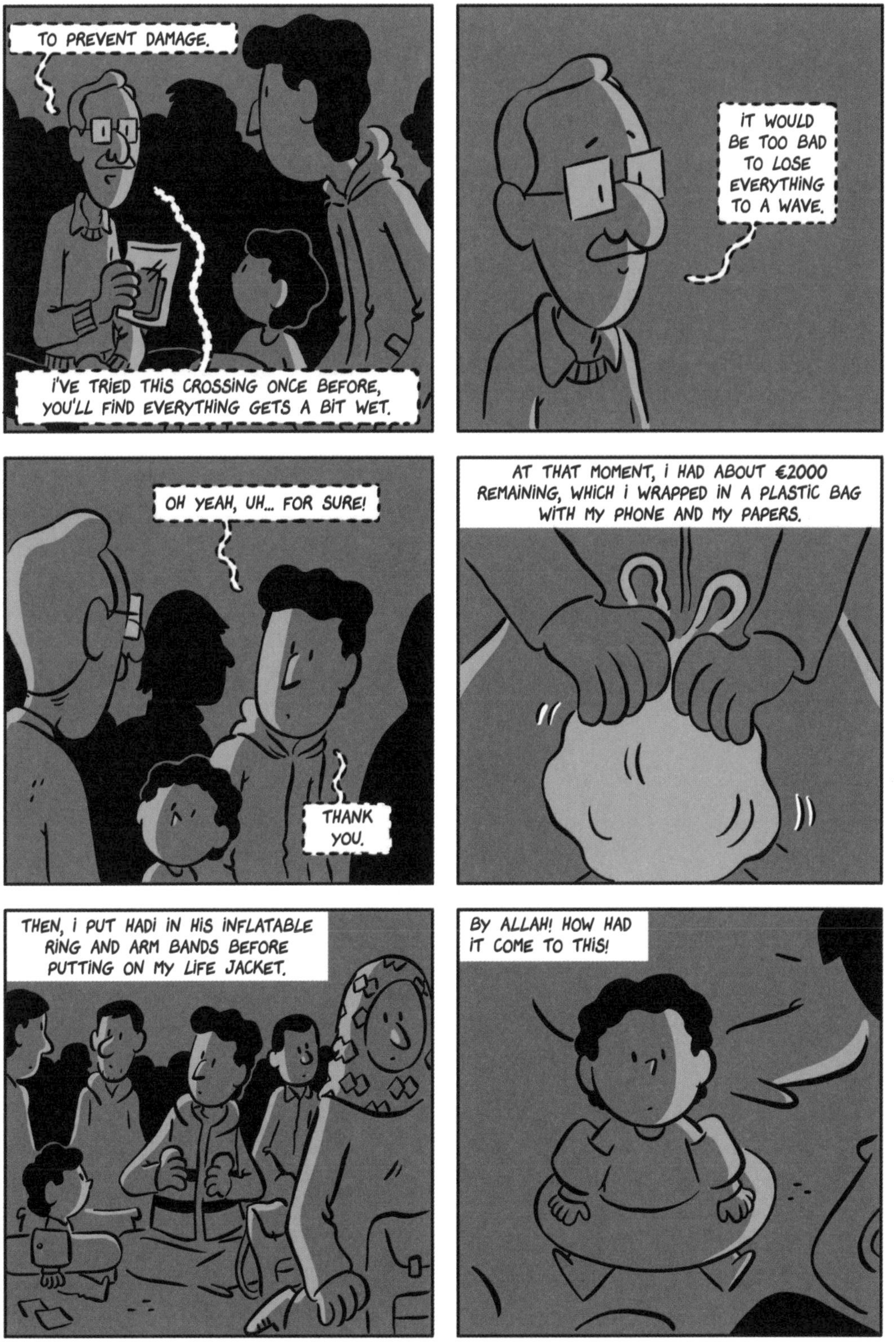
TO PREVENT DAMAGE.
I'VE TRIED THIS CROSSING ONCE BEFORE, YOU'LL FIND EVERYTHING GETS A BIT WET.
IT WOULD BE TOO BAD TO LOSE EVERYTHING TO A WAVE.
OH YEAH, UH... FOR SURE!
THANK YOU.
AT THAT MOMENT, I HAD ABOUT €2000 REMAINING, WHICH I WRAPPED IN A PLASTIC BAG WITH MY PHONE AND MY PAPERS.
THEN, I PUT HADI IN HIS INFLATABLE RING AND ARM BANDS BEFORE PUTTING ON MY LIFE JACKET.
BY ALLAH! HOW HAD IT COME TO THIS!

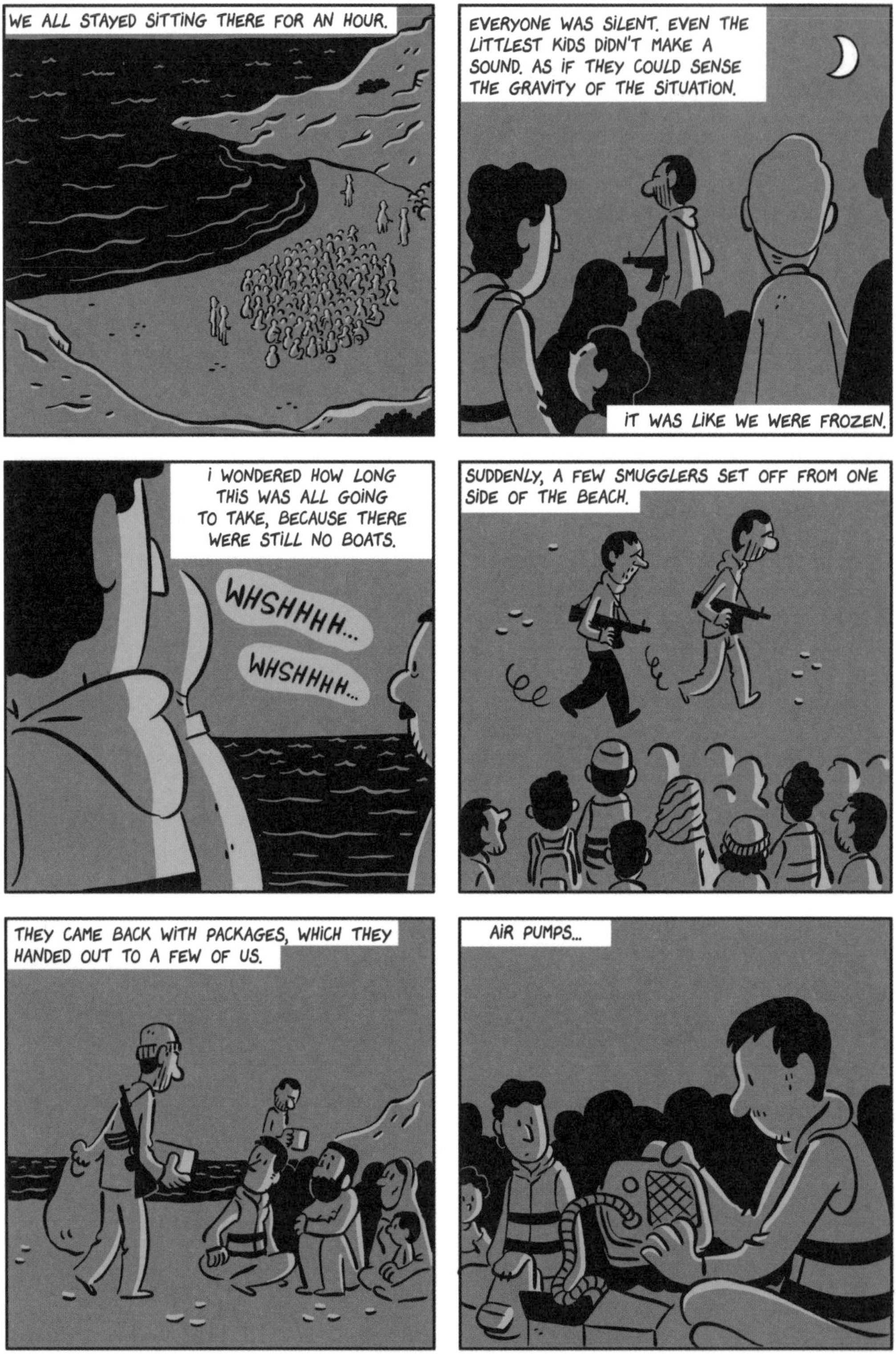
WE ALL STAYED SITTING THERE FOR AN HOUR.
EVERYONE WAS SILENT. EVEN THE LITTLEST KIDS DIDN'T MAKE A SOUND. AS IF THEY COULD SENSE THE GRAVITY OF THE SITUATION.
IT WAS LIKE WE WERE FROZEN.
I WONDERED HOW LONG THIS WAS ALL GOING TO TAKE, BECAUSE THERE WERE STILL NO BOATS.
WHSHHHH...
WHSHHHH...
SUDDENLY, A FEW SMUGGLERS SET OFF FROM ONE SIDE OF THE BEACH.
THEY CAME BACK WITH PACKAGES, WHICH THEY HANDED OUT TO A FEW OF US.
AIR PUMPS...

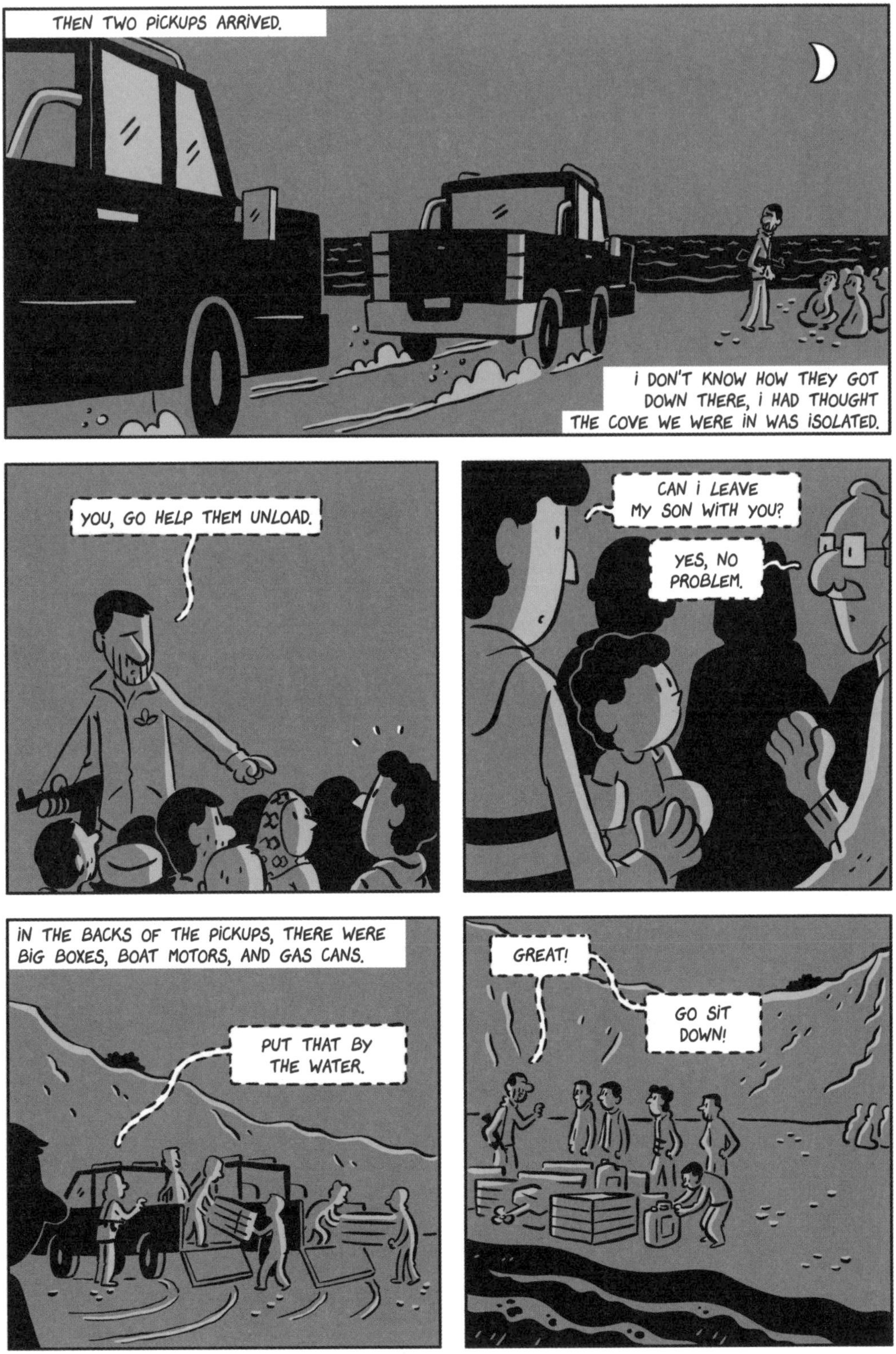
THEN TWO PICKUPS ARRIVED.
I DON'T KNOW HOW THEY GOT DOWN THERE, I HAD THOUGHT THE COVE WE WERE IN WAS ISOLATED.
YOU, GO HELP THEM UNLOAD.
CAN I LEAVE MY SON WITH YOU?
YES, NO PROBLEM.
IN THE BACKS OF THE PICKUPS, THERE WERE BIG BOXES, BOAT MOTORS, AND GAS CANS.
PUT THAT BY THE WATER.
GREAT!
GO SIT DOWN!

THEN THEY CALLED OVER THE YOUNG GUYS WHO HAD THE AIR PUMPS.

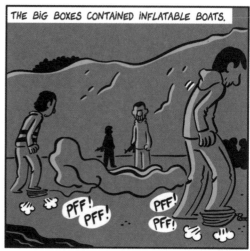

THE BIG BOXES CONTAINED INFLATABLE BOATS.

PFF! PFF! PFF! PFF!

THANKS!

NOT A PROBLEM!

HE WAS VERY GOOD.

WHERE'S HIS MOM?

SHE'S NOT HERE.

I'D GOTTEN IN THE HABIT OF NOT SAYING MUCH ABOUT MYSELF.

I'M SYRIAN, LIKE YOU.

I'M FROM IDLIB.*

*A CITY IN NORTHERN SYRIA.

I'M FROM DAMASCUS.

GREETINGS, BROTHER.

HE WAS MY FATHER'S AGE, BUT IN SYRIA IT'S COMMON TO CALL SOMEONE "BROTHER" LIKE THIS.

I'M HERE WITH MY WIFE AND MY TWO SONS.

HELLO!

HELLO.

THE BOATS WERE FINALLY INFLATED AFTER ABOUT AN HOUR AND A HALF.

ONE SMUGGLER SIGNALED TO A FIRST GROUP OF ABOUT FIFTY PEOPLE TO GET UP.

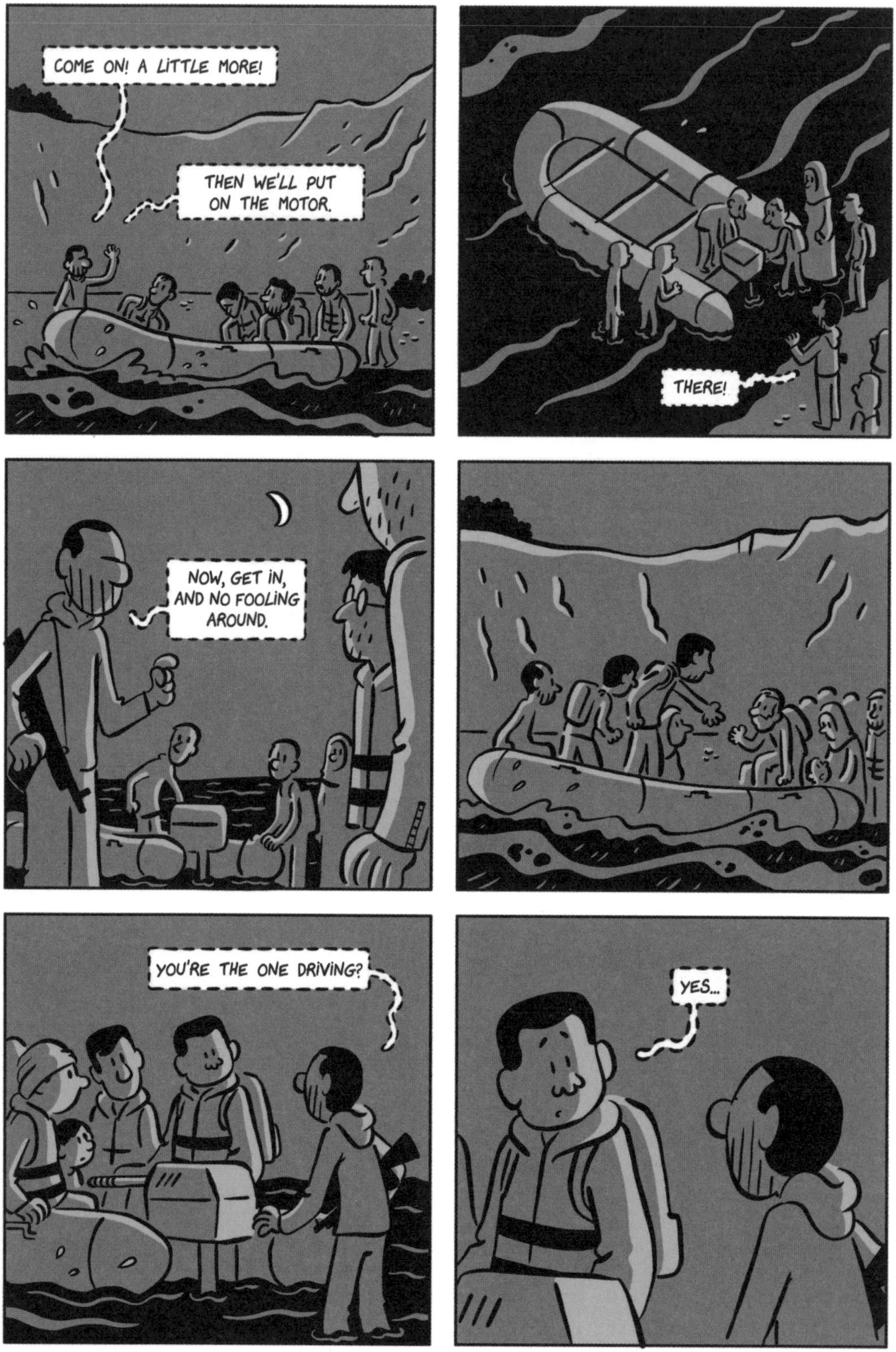
COME ON! A LITTLE MORE!
THEN WE'LL PUT ON THE MOTOR.
THERE!
NOW, GET IN, AND NO FOOLING AROUND.
YOU'RE THE ONE DRIVING?
YES...

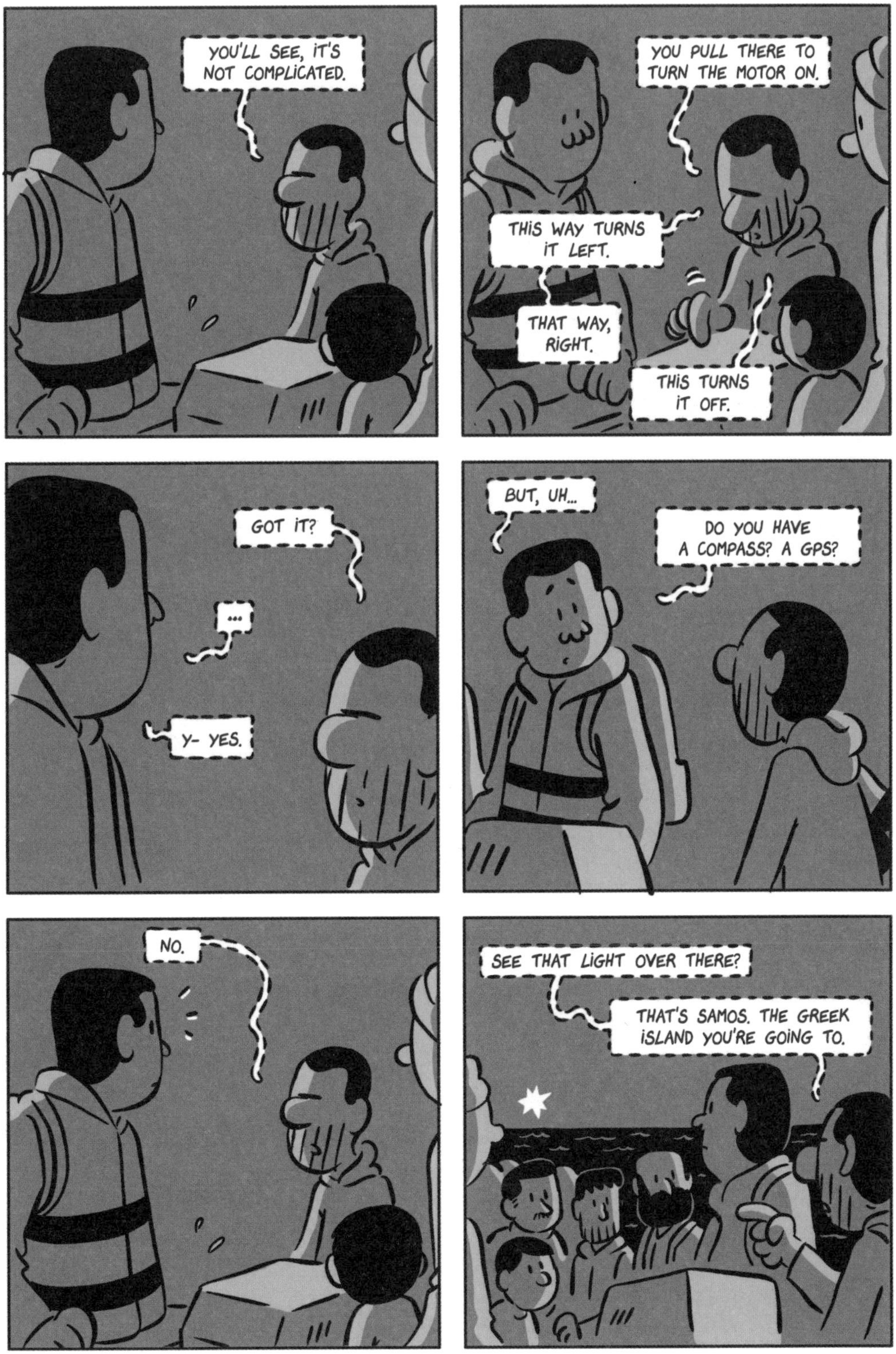
YOU'LL SEE, IT'S NOT COMPLICATED.
YOU PULL THERE TO TURN THE MOTOR ON.
THIS WAY TURNS IT LEFT.
THAT WAY, RIGHT.
THIS TURNS IT OFF.
GOT IT?
...
Y- YES.
BUT, UH...
DO YOU HAVE A COMPASS? A GPS?
NO.
SEE THAT LIGHT OVER THERE?
THAT'S SAMOS. THE GREEK ISLAND YOU'RE GOING TO.

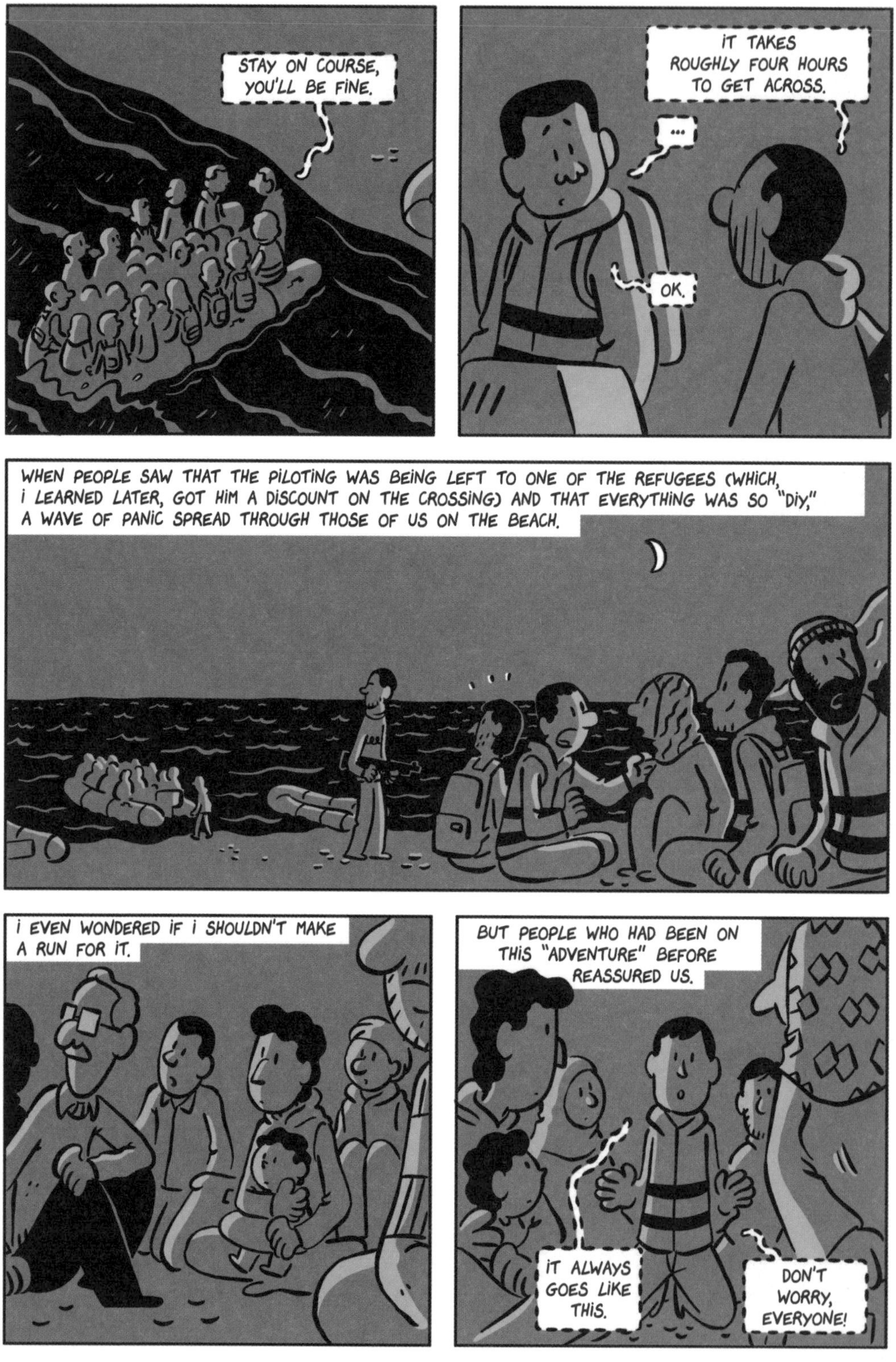
STAY ON COURSE, YOU'LL BE FINE.
IT TAKES ROUGHLY FOUR HOURS TO GET ACROSS.
...
OK.
WHEN PEOPLE SAW THAT THE PILOTING WAS BEING LEFT TO ONE OF THE REFUGEES (WHICH, I LEARNED LATER, GOT HIM A DISCOUNT ON THE CROSSING) AND THAT EVERYTHING WAS SO "DIY," A WAVE OF PANIC SPREAD THROUGH THOSE OF US ON THE BEACH.
I EVEN WONDERED IF I SHOULDN'T MAKE A RUN FOR IT.
BUT PEOPLE WHO HAD BEEN ON THIS "ADVENTURE" BEFORE REASSURED US.
IT ALWAYS GOES LIKE THIS.
DON'T WORRY, EVERYONE!

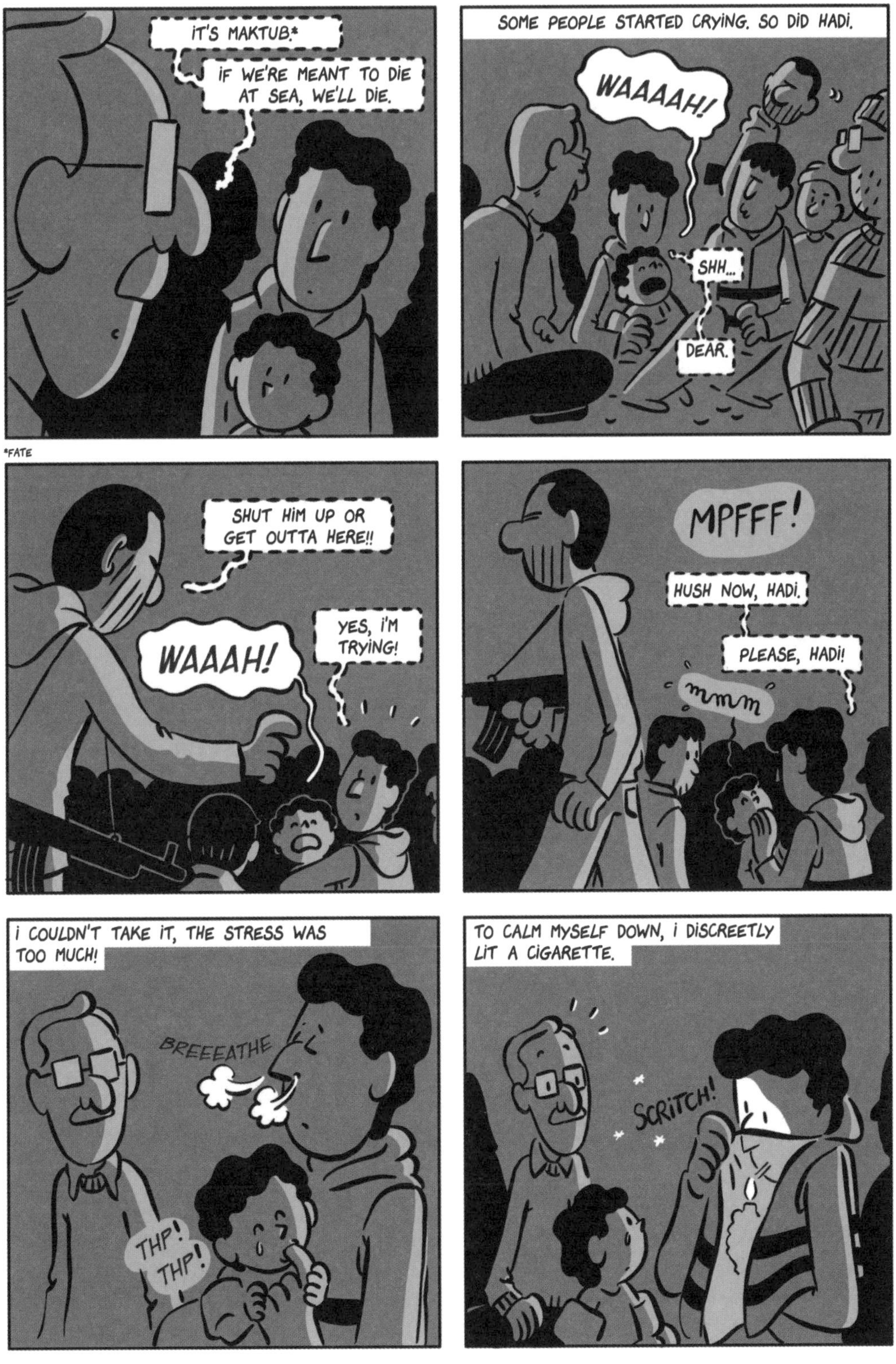
IT'S MAKTUB.*
IF WE'RE MEANT TO DIE AT SEA, WE'LL DIE.
SOME PEOPLE STARTED CRYING. SO DID HADI.
WAAAAH!
SHH...
DEAR.
SHUT HIM UP OR GET OUTTA HERE!!
WAAAH!
YES, I'M TRYING!
MPFFF!
HUSH NOW, HADI.
PLEASE, HADI!
mmm
I COULDN'T TAKE IT, THE STRESS WAS TOO MUCH!
BREEEATHE
THP! THP!
TO CALM MYSELF DOWN, I DISCREETLY LIT A CIGARETTE.
SCRITCH!

*FATE

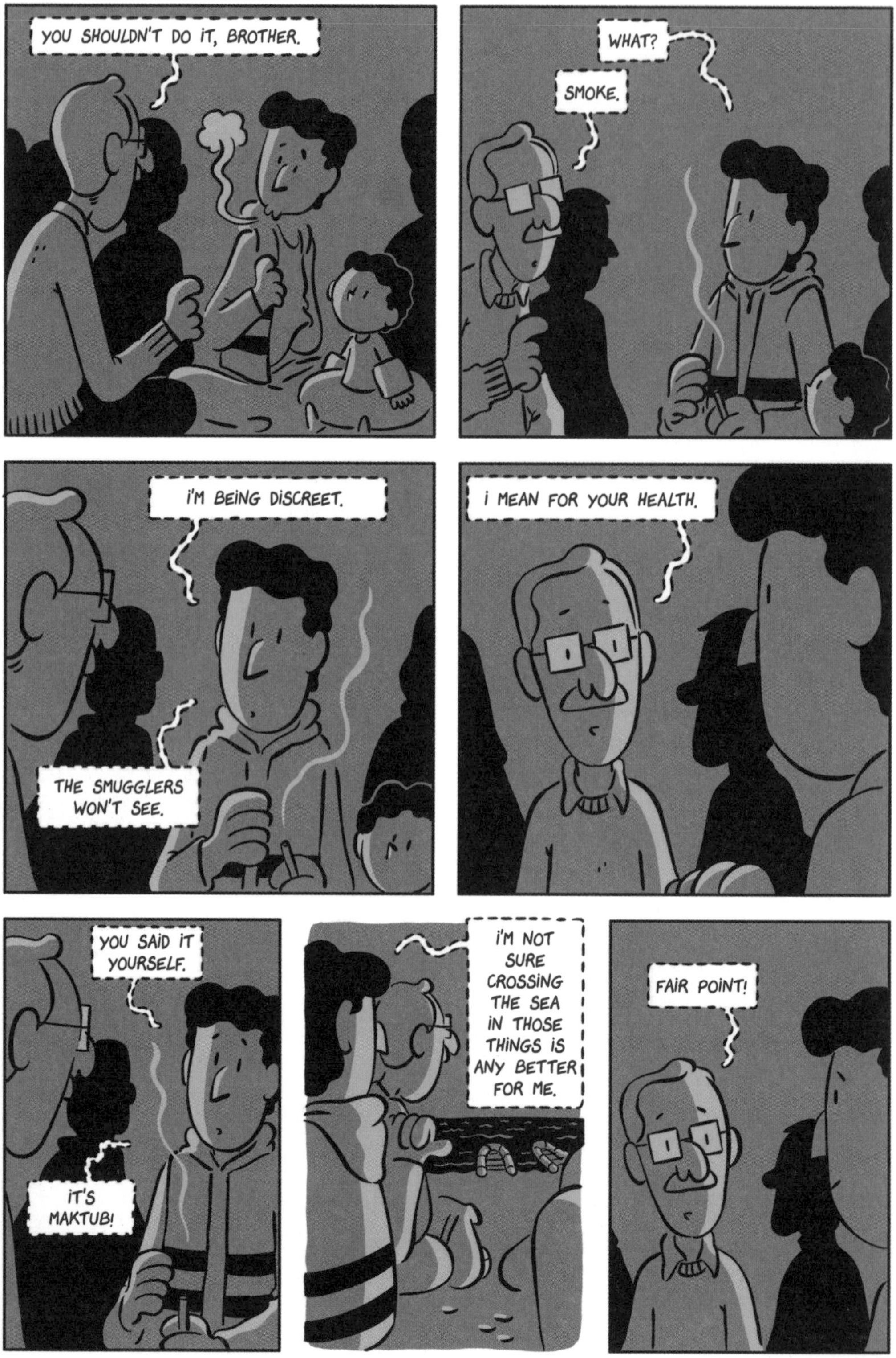
YOU SHOULDN'T DO IT, BROTHER.
WHAT?
SMOKE.
I'M BEING DISCREET.
THE SMUGGLERS WON'T SEE.
I MEAN FOR YOUR HEALTH.
YOU SAID IT YOURSELF.
IT'S MAKTUB!
I'M NOT SURE CROSSING THE SEA IN THOSE THINGS IS ANY BETTER FOR ME.
FAIR POINT!

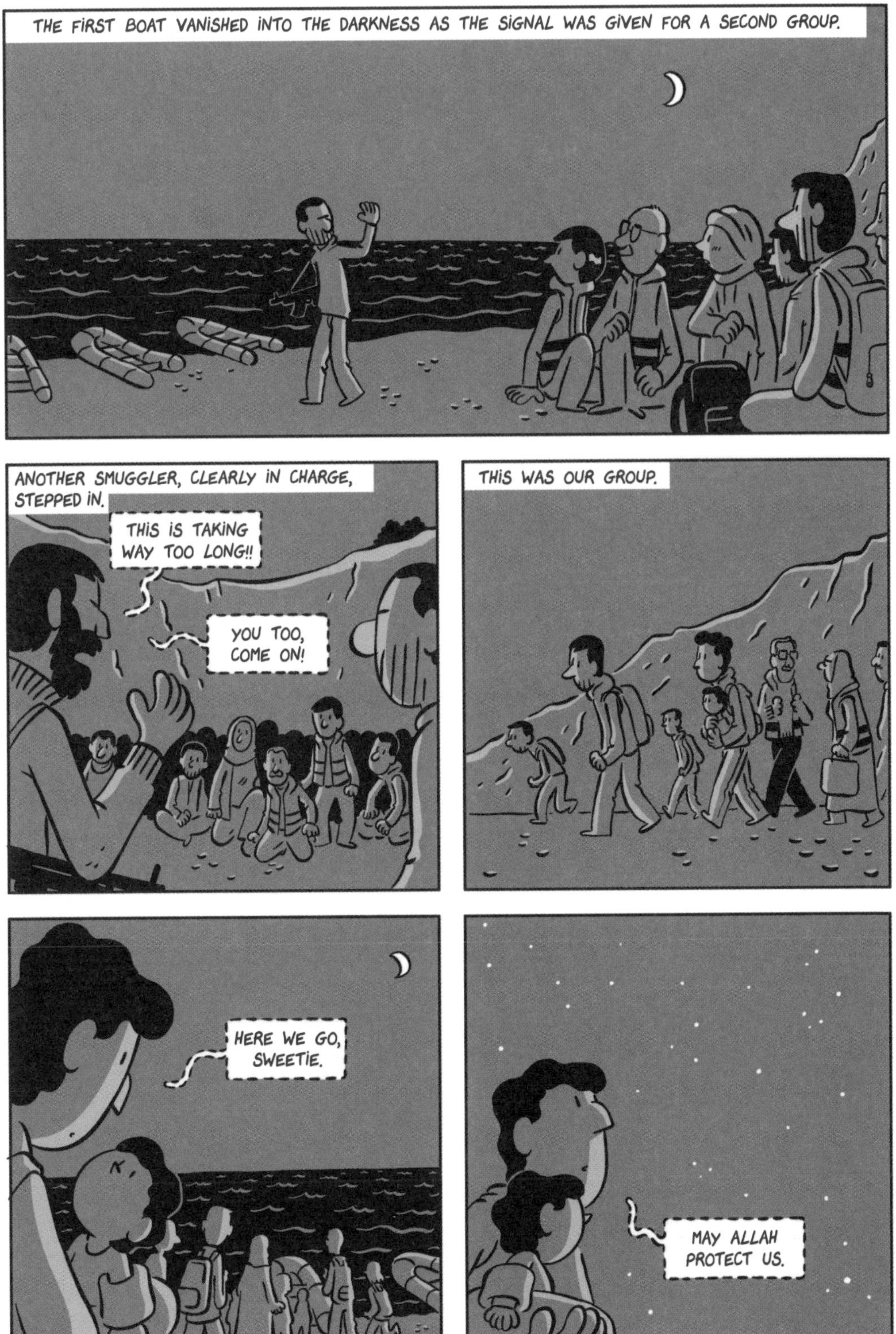
THE FIRST BOAT VANISHED INTO THE DARKNESS AS THE SIGNAL WAS GIVEN FOR A SECOND GROUP.
ANOTHER SMUGGLER, CLEARLY IN CHARGE, STEPPED IN.
THIS IS TAKING WAY TOO LONG!!
YOU TOO, COME ON!
THIS WAS OUR GROUP.
HERE WE GO, SWEETIE.
MAY ALLAH PROTECT US.

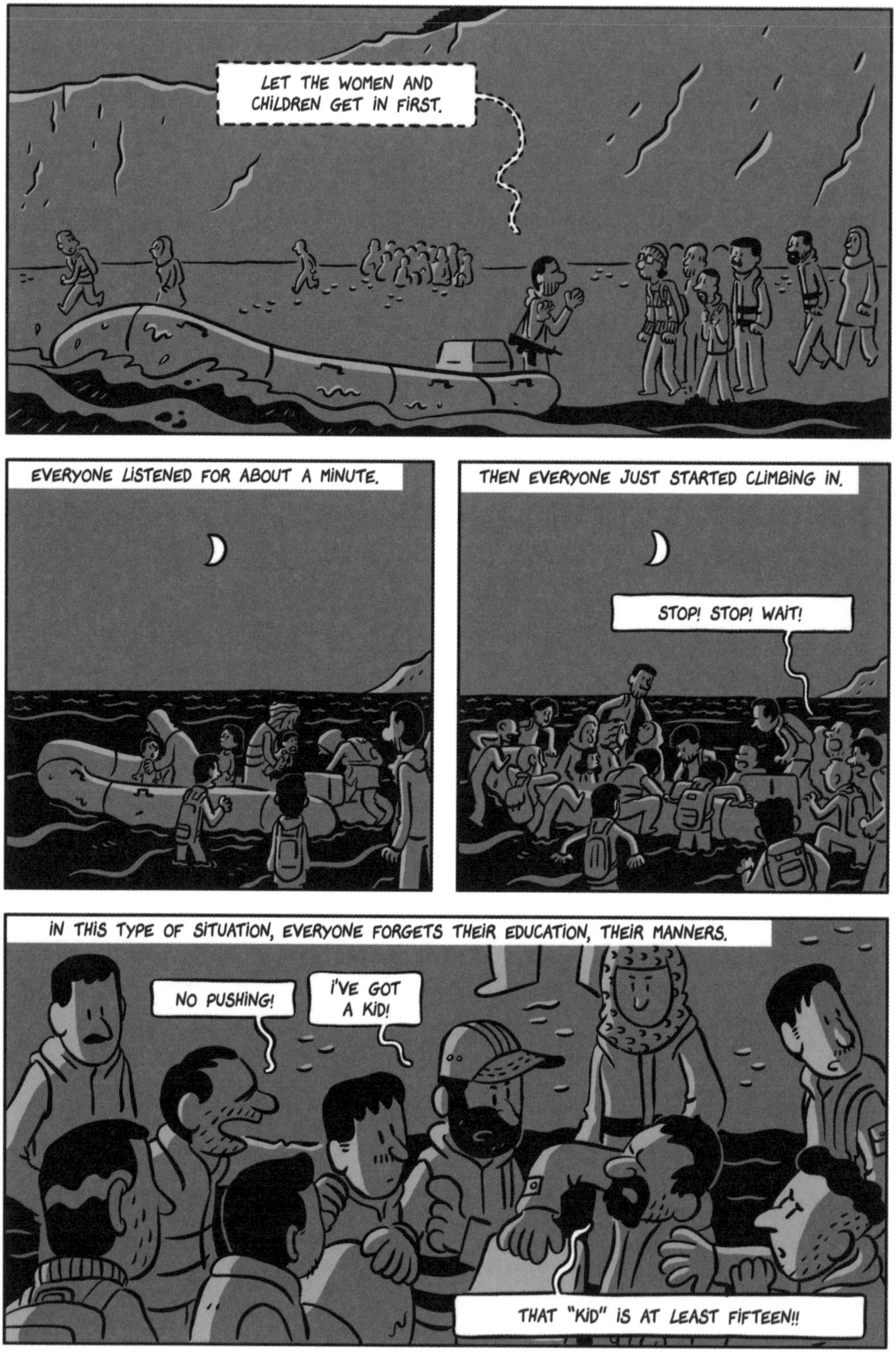
LET THE WOMEN AND CHILDREN GET IN FIRST.
EVERYONE LISTENED FOR ABOUT A MINUTE.
THEN EVERYONE JUST STARTED CLIMBING IN.
STOP! STOP! WAIT!
IN THIS TYPE OF SITUATION, EVERYONE FORGETS THEIR EDUCATION, THEIR MANNERS.
NO PUSHING!
I'VE GOT A KID!
THAT "KID" IS AT LEAST FIFTEEN!!

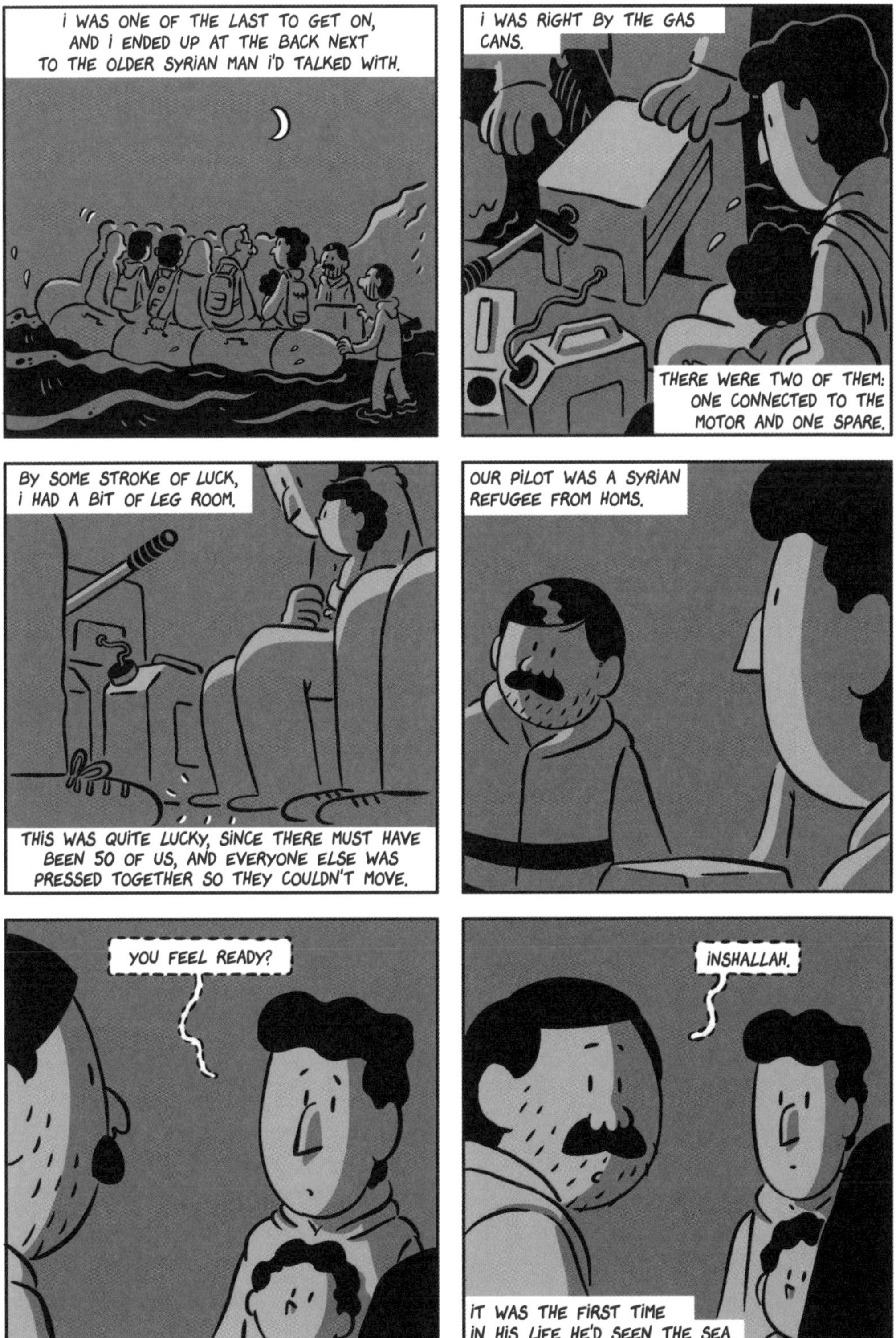
i WAS ONE OF THE LAST TO GET ON, AND i ENDED UP AT THE BACK NEXT TO THE OLDER SYRiAN MAN i'D TALKED WiTH.
i WAS RiGHT BY THE GAS CANS.
THERE WERE TWO OF THEM: ONE CONNECTED TO THE MOTOR AND ONE SPARE.
BY SOME STROKE OF LUCK, i HAD A BiT OF LEG ROOM.
THiS WAS QUiTE LUCKY, SiNCE THERE MUST HAVE BEEN 50 OF US, AND EVERYONE ELSE WAS PRESSED TOGETHER SO THEY COULDN'T MOVE.
OUR PiLOT WAS A SYRiAN REFUGEE FROM HOMS.
YOU FEEL READY?
iNSHALLAH.
iT WAS THE FiRST TiME iN HiS LiFE HE'D SEEN THE SEA.

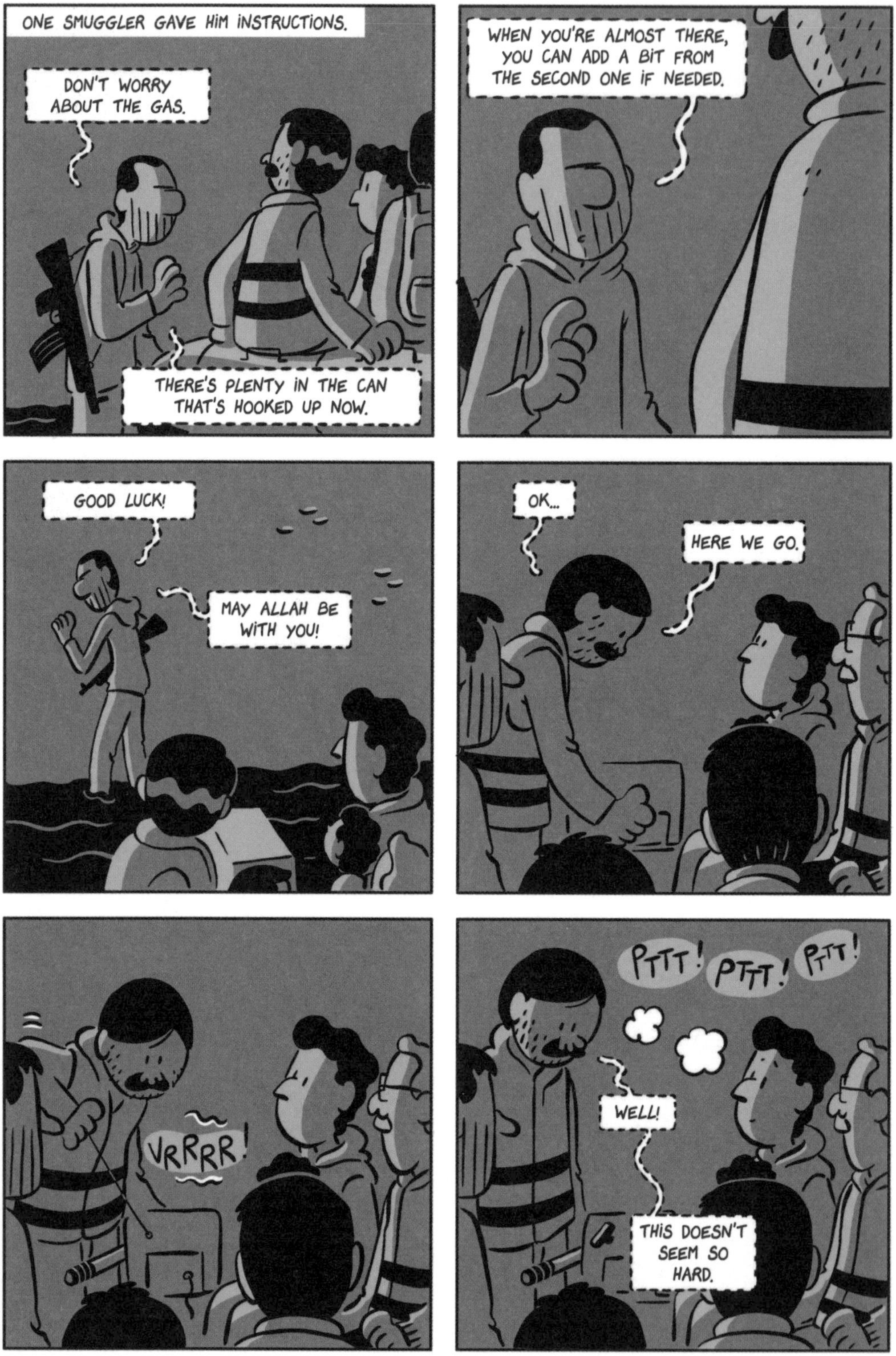
ONE SMUGGLER GAVE HIM INSTRUCTIONS.
DON'T WORRY ABOUT THE GAS.
THERE'S PLENTY IN THE CAN THAT'S HOOKED UP NOW.
WHEN YOU'RE ALMOST THERE, YOU CAN ADD A BIT FROM THE SECOND ONE IF NEEDED.
GOOD LUCK!
MAY ALLAH BE WITH YOU!
OK...
HERE WE GO.
VRRRR!
PTTT! PTTT! PTTT!
WELL!
THIS DOESN'T SEEM SO HARD.

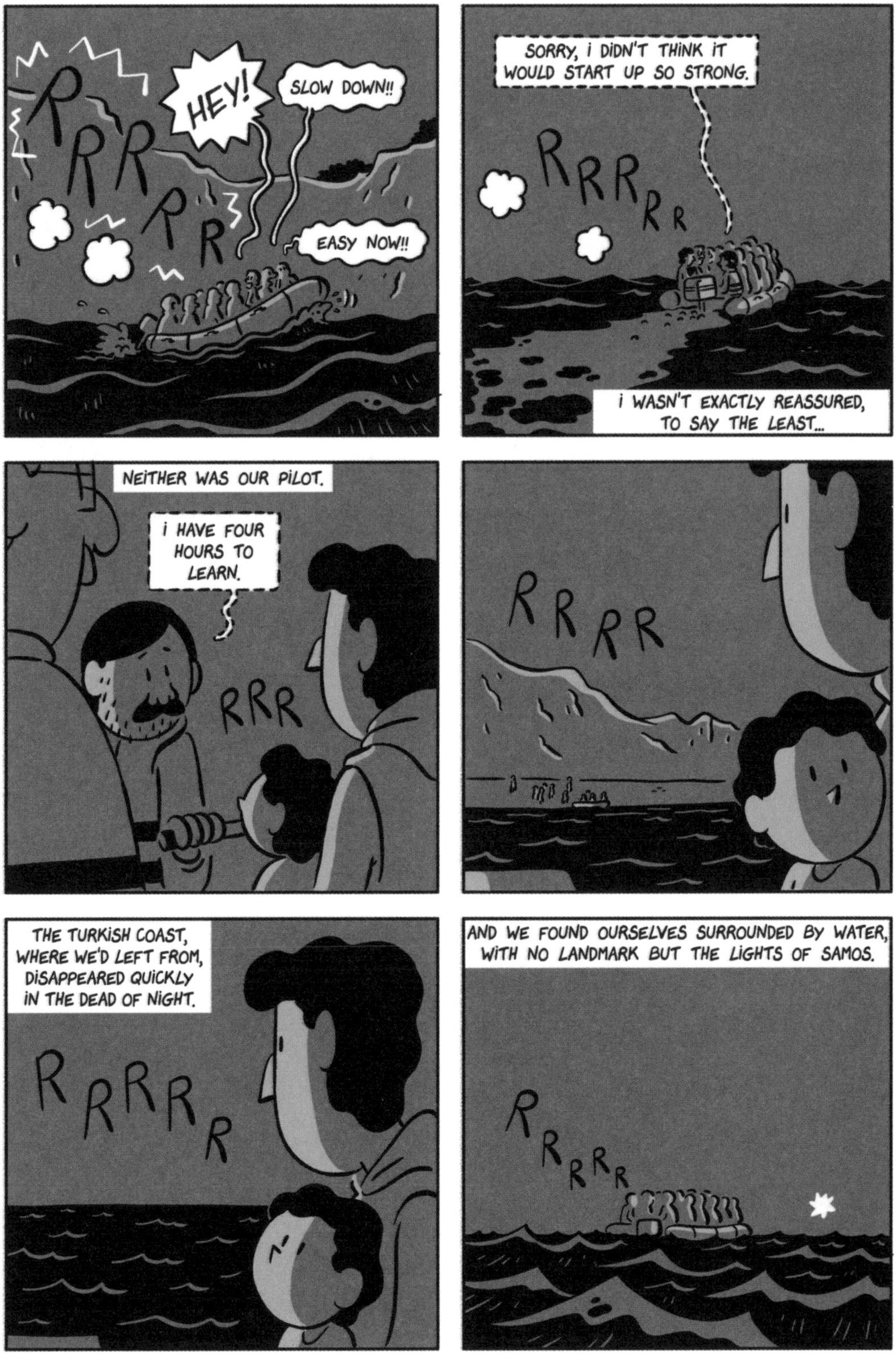
RRRRR
HEY!
SLOW DOWN!!
EASY NOW!!
SORRY, I DIDN'T THINK IT WOULD START UP SO STRONG.
RRRRR
I WASN'T EXACTLY REASSURED, TO SAY THE LEAST...
NEITHER WAS OUR PILOT.
I HAVE FOUR HOURS TO LEARN.
RRR
RRRR
THE TURKISH COAST, WHERE WE'D LEFT FROM, DISAPPEARED QUICKLY IN THE DEAD OF NIGHT.
RRRRR
AND WE FOUND OURSELVES SURROUNDED BY WATER, WITH NO LANDMARK BUT THE LIGHTS OF SAMOS.
RRRRR

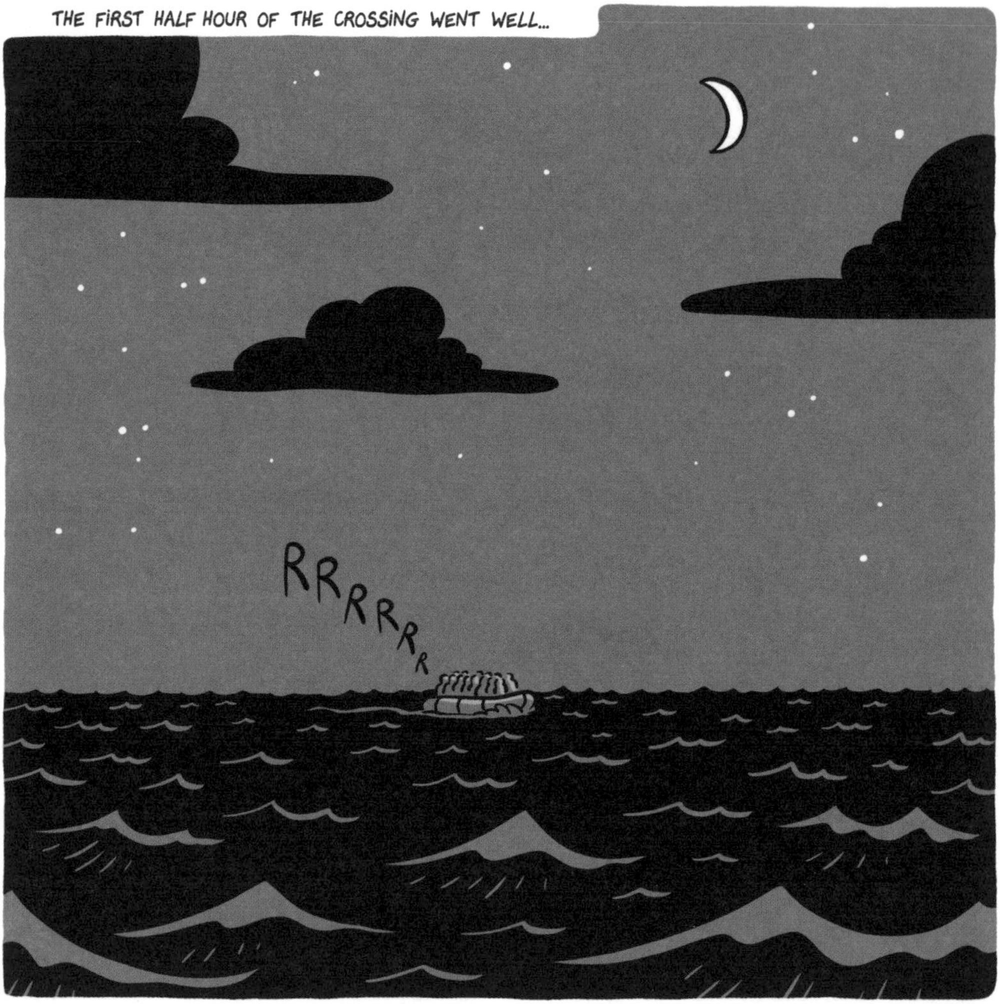
THE FIRST HALF HOUR OF THE CROSSING WENT WELL...
RRRRRR

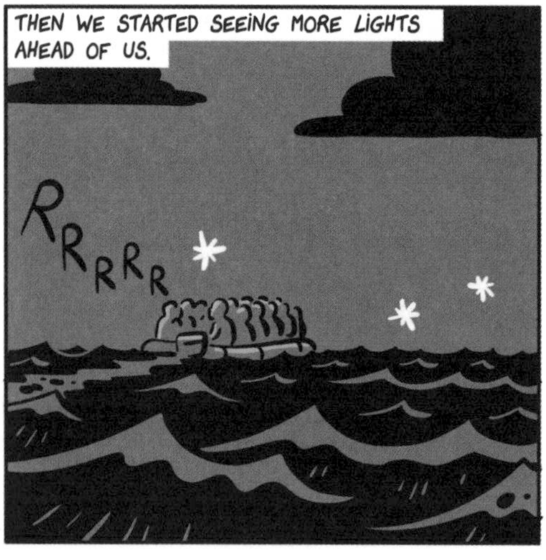
THEN WE STARTED SEEING MORE LIGHTS AHEAD OF US.
RRRRR

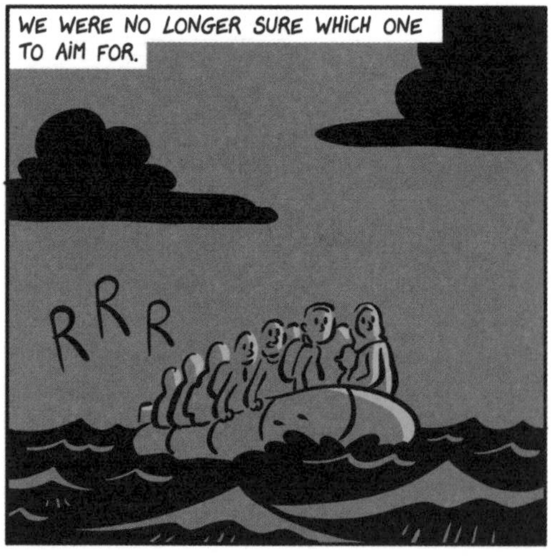
WE WERE NO LONGER SURE WHICH ONE TO AIM FOR.
RRR

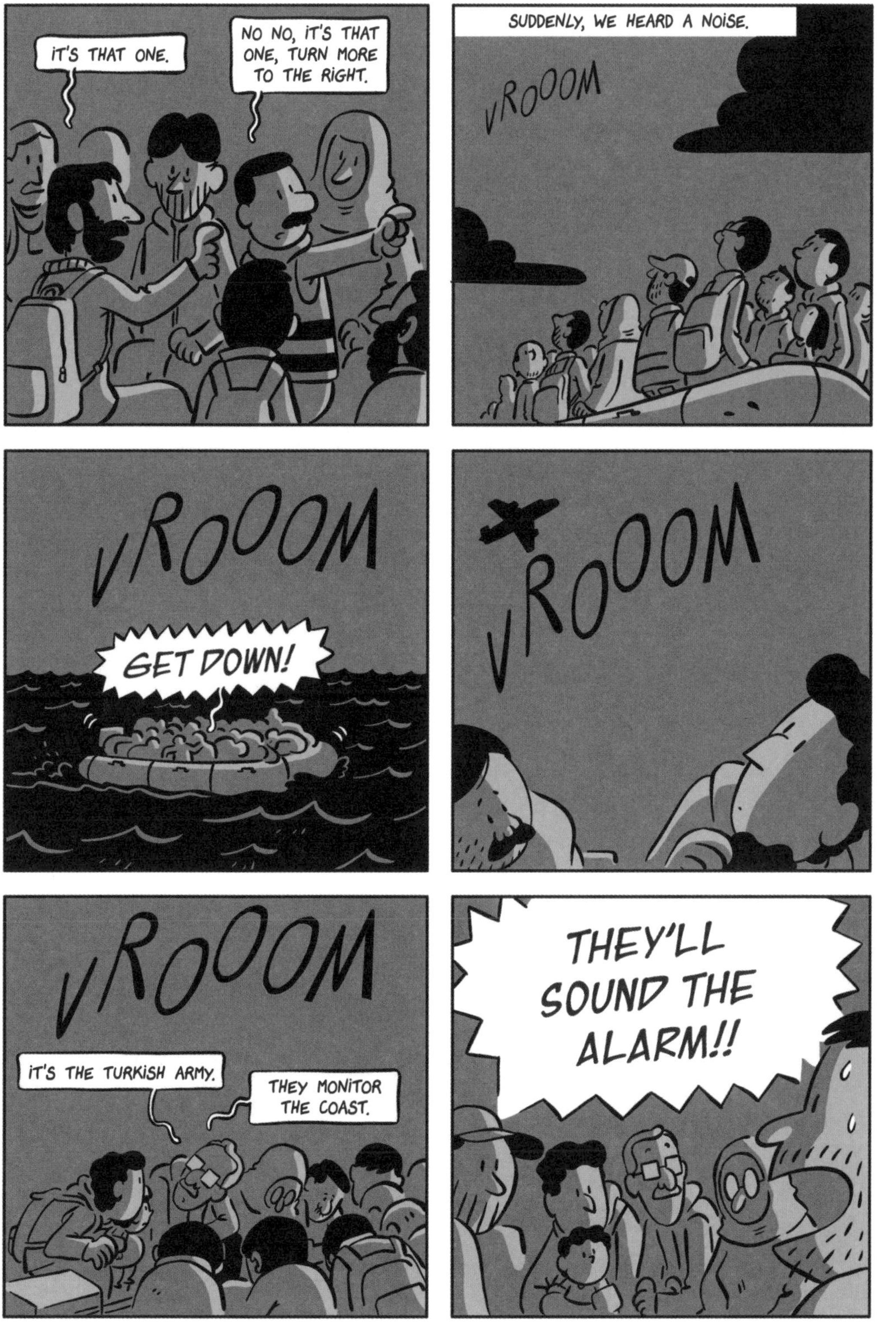
IT'S THAT ONE.
NO NO, IT'S THAT ONE, TURN MORE TO THE RIGHT.
SUDDENLY, WE HEARD A NOISE.
VROOOM
VROOOM
GET DOWN!
VROOOM
VROOOM
IT'S THE TURKISH ARMY.
THEY MONITOR THE COAST.
THEY'LL SOUND THE ALARM!!

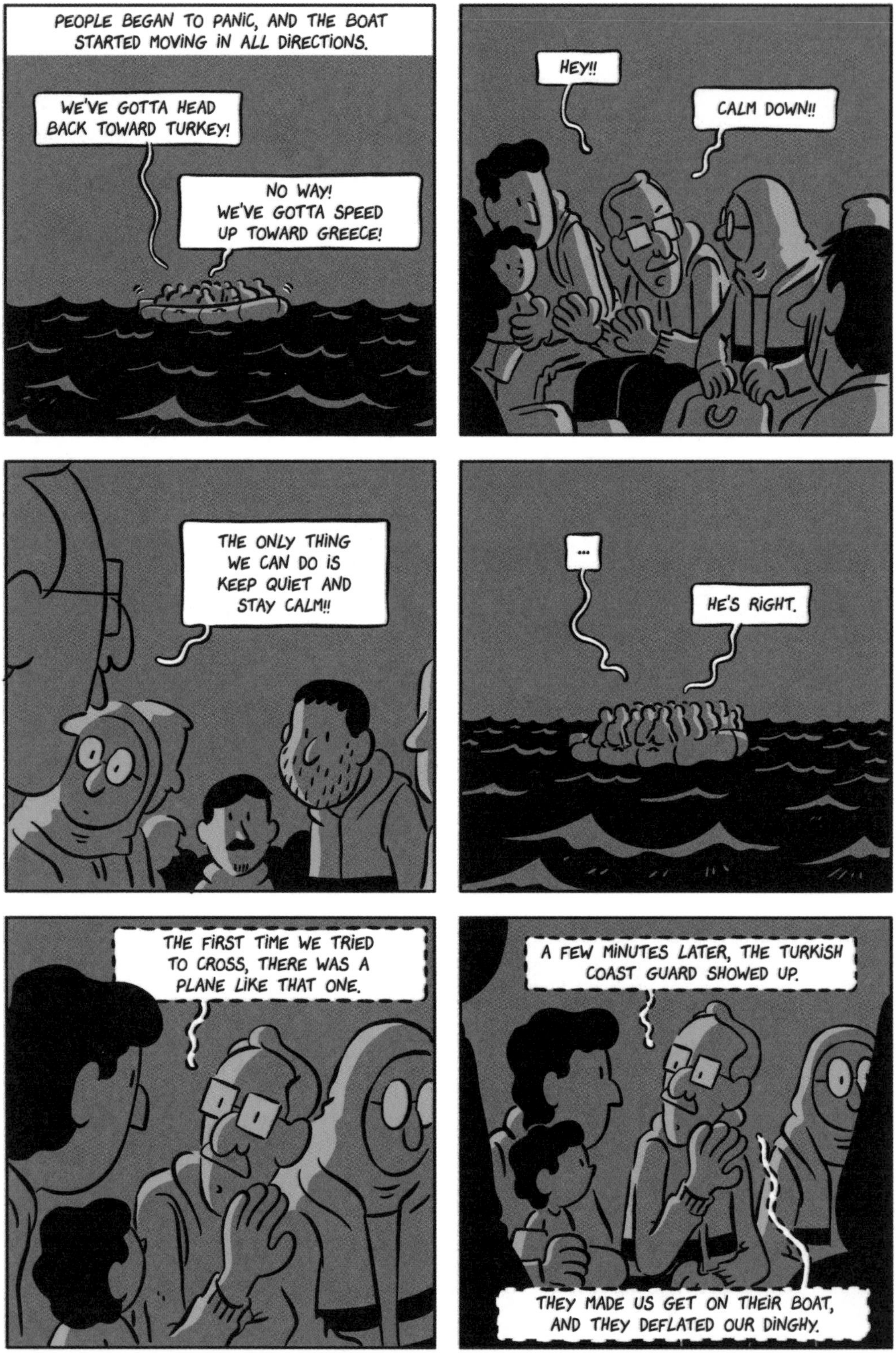
PEOPLE BEGAN TO PANIC, AND THE BOAT STARTED MOVING IN ALL DIRECTIONS.
WE'VE GOTTA HEAD BACK TOWARD TURKEY!
NO WAY! WE'VE GOTTA SPEED UP TOWARD GREECE!
HEY!!
CALM DOWN!!
THE ONLY THING WE CAN DO IS KEEP QUIET AND STAY CALM!!
...
HE'S RIGHT.
THE FIRST TIME WE TRIED TO CROSS, THERE WAS A PLANE LIKE THAT ONE.
A FEW MINUTES LATER, THE TURKISH COAST GUARD SHOWED UP.
THEY MADE US GET ON THEIR BOAT, AND THEY DEFLATED OUR DINGHY.

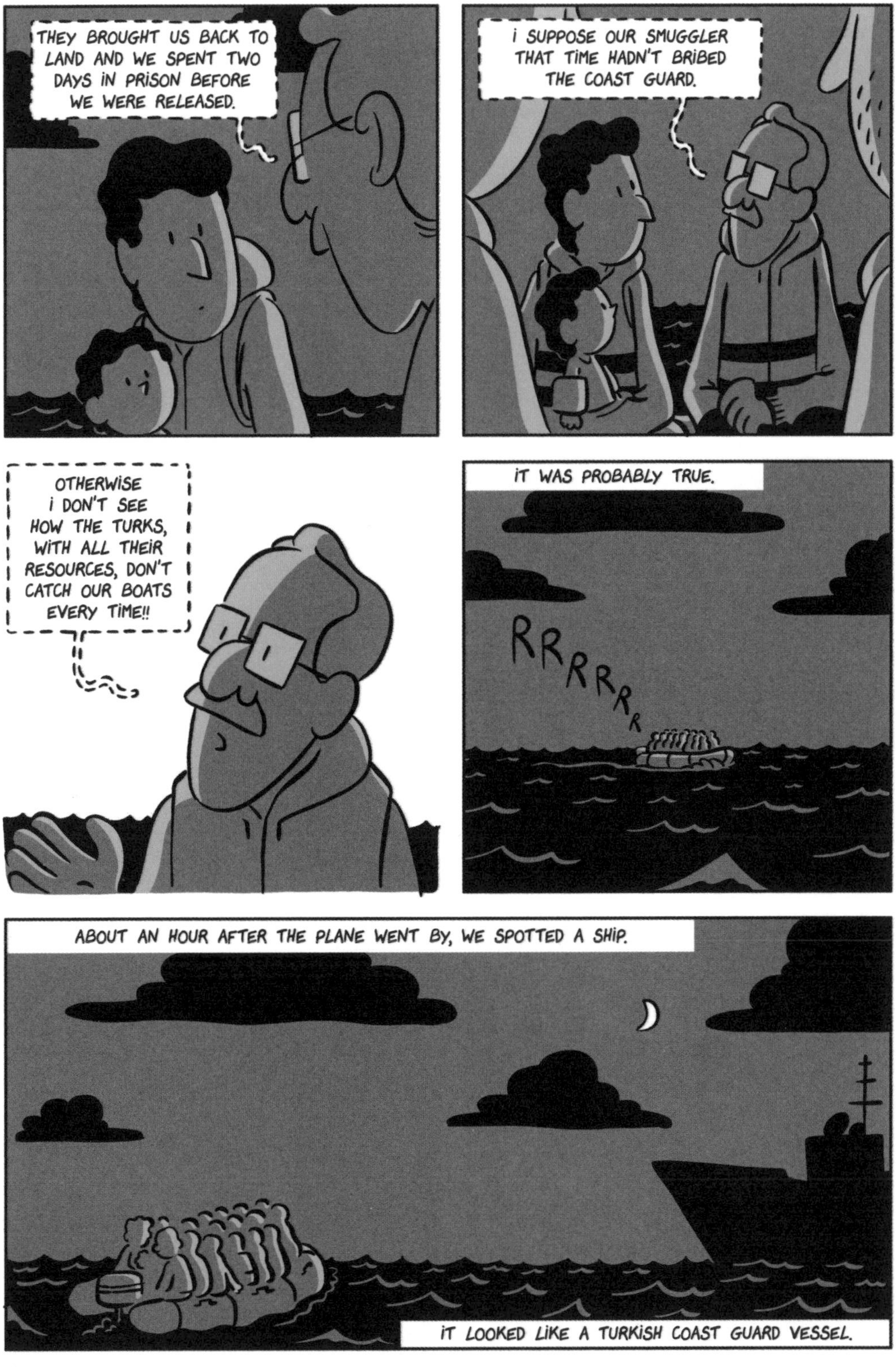
THEY BROUGHT US BACK TO LAND AND WE SPENT TWO DAYS IN PRISON BEFORE WE WERE RELEASED.
I SUPPOSE OUR SMUGGLER THAT TIME HADN'T BRIBED THE COAST GUARD.
OTHERWISE I DON'T SEE HOW THE TURKS, WITH ALL THEIR RESOURCES, DON'T CATCH OUR BOATS EVERY TIME!!
IT WAS PROBABLY TRUE.
RRRRRR
ABOUT AN HOUR AFTER THE PLANE WENT BY, WE SPOTTED A SHIP.
IT LOOKED LIKE A TURKISH COAST GUARD VESSEL.

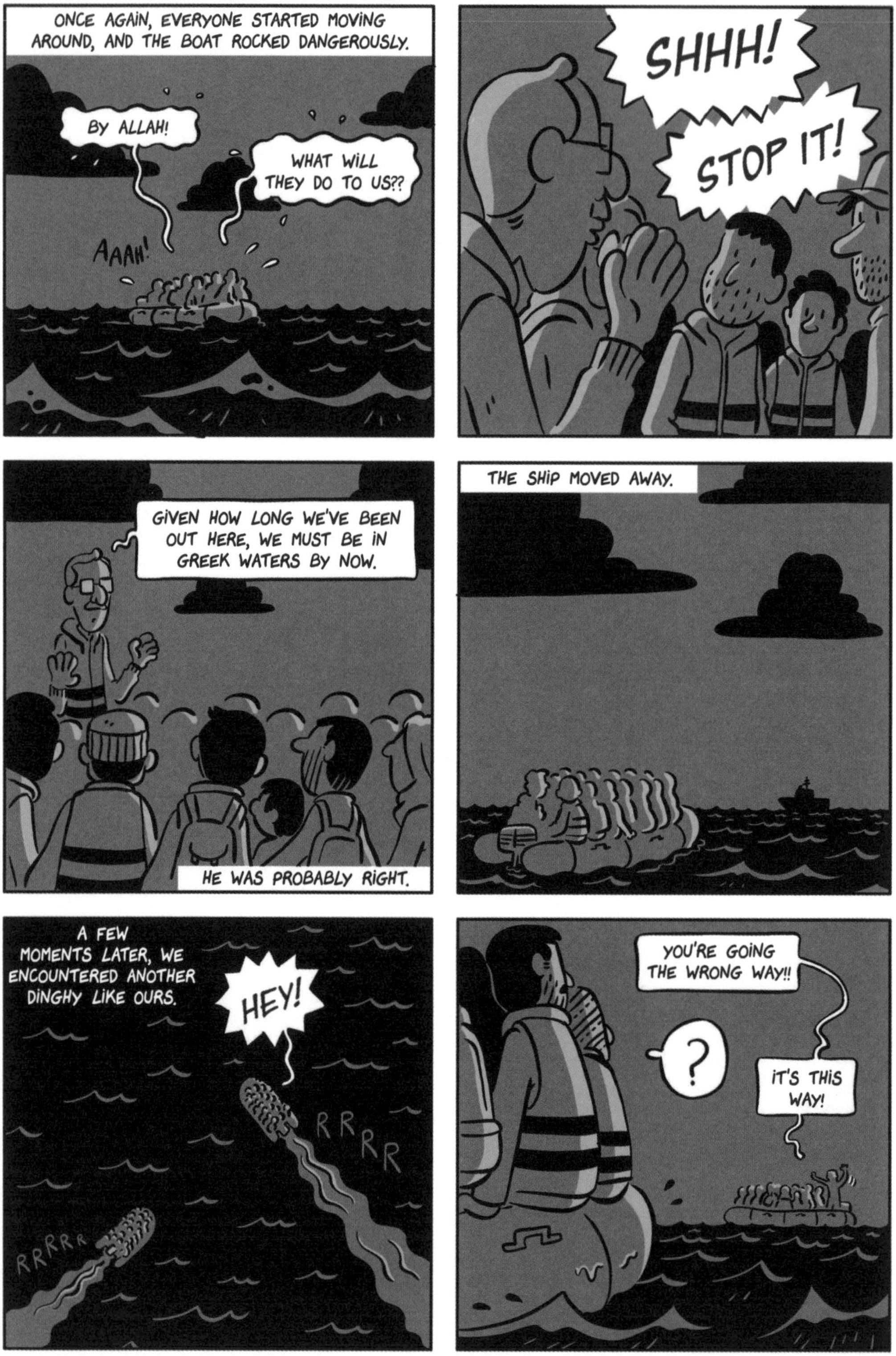
ONCE AGAIN, EVERYONE STARTED MOVING AROUND, AND THE BOAT ROCKED DANGEROUSLY.
BY ALLAH!
WHAT WILL THEY DO TO US??
AAAH!
SHHH!
STOP IT!
GIVEN HOW LONG WE'VE BEEN OUT HERE, WE MUST BE IN GREEK WATERS BY NOW.
HE WAS PROBABLY RIGHT.
THE SHIP MOVED AWAY.
A FEW MOMENTS LATER, WE ENCOUNTERED ANOTHER DINGHY LIKE OURS.
HEY!
RRRR
RRRRR
YOU'RE GOING THE WRONG WAY!!
?
IT'S THIS WAY!

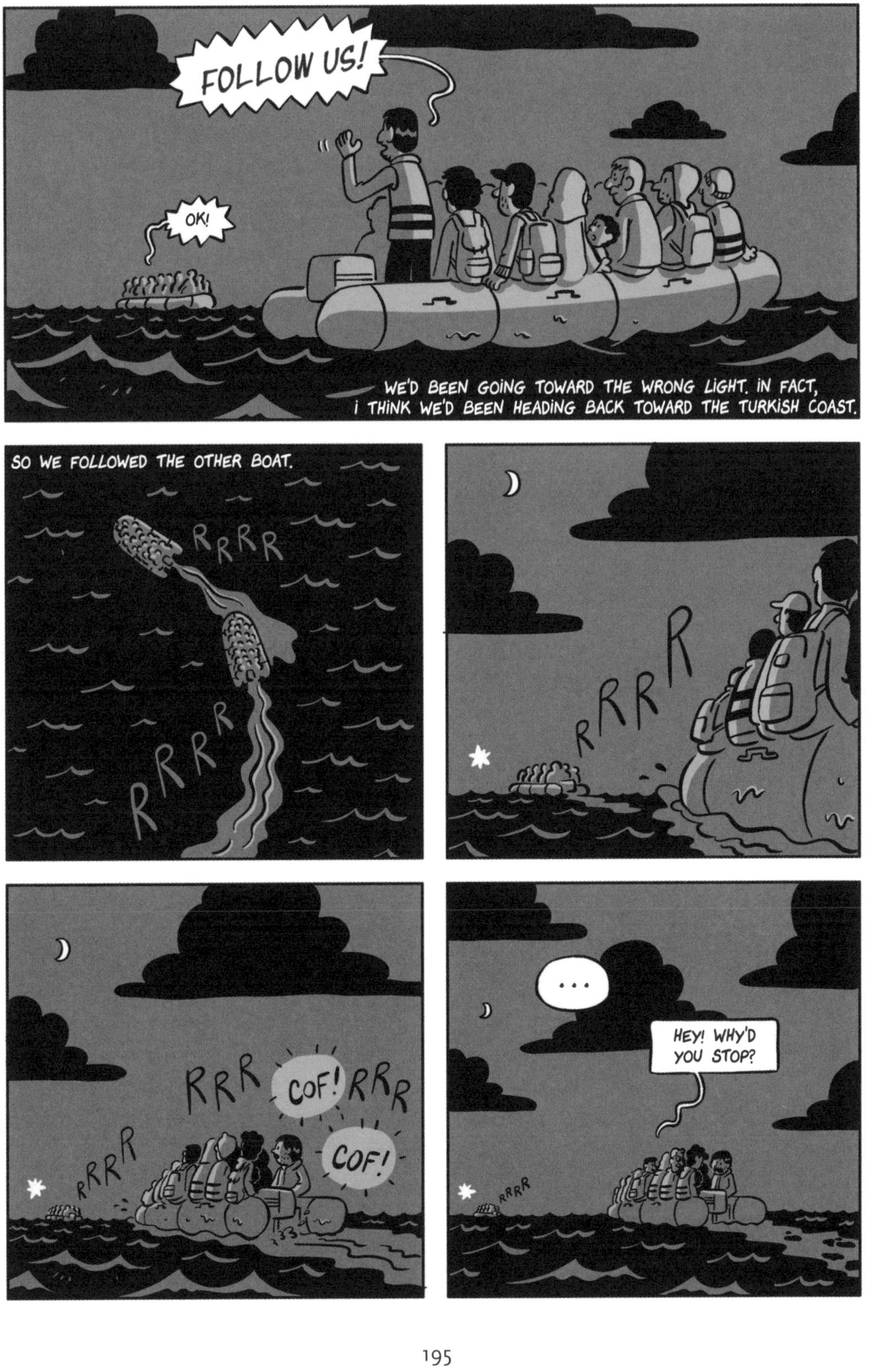
FOLLOW US!
OK!
WE'D BEEN GOING TOWARD THE WRONG LIGHT. IN FACT, I THINK WE'D BEEN HEADING BACK TOWARD THE TURKISH COAST.
SO WE FOLLOWED THE OTHER BOAT.
RRRR
RRRR
RRRR
RRR
COF!
RRR
COF!
RRRR
...
HEY! WHY'D YOU STOP?
RRRR

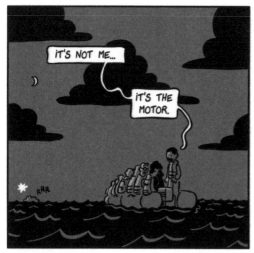

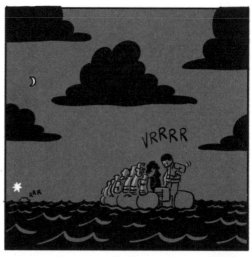

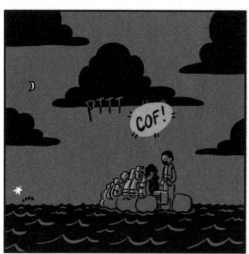

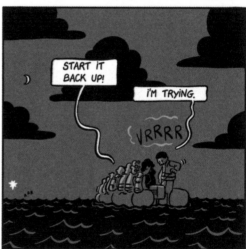

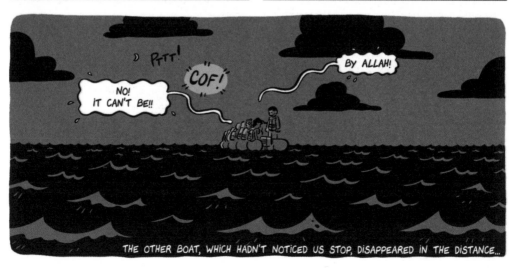

IT'S NOT ME...
IT'S THE MOTOR.
VRRRR
PTTT
COF!
START IT BACK UP!
I'M TRYING.
VRRRR
PTTT!
COF!
NO! IT CAN'T BE!!
BY ALLAH!
THE OTHER BOAT, WHICH HADN'T NOTICED US STOP, DISAPPEARED IN THE DISTANCE...

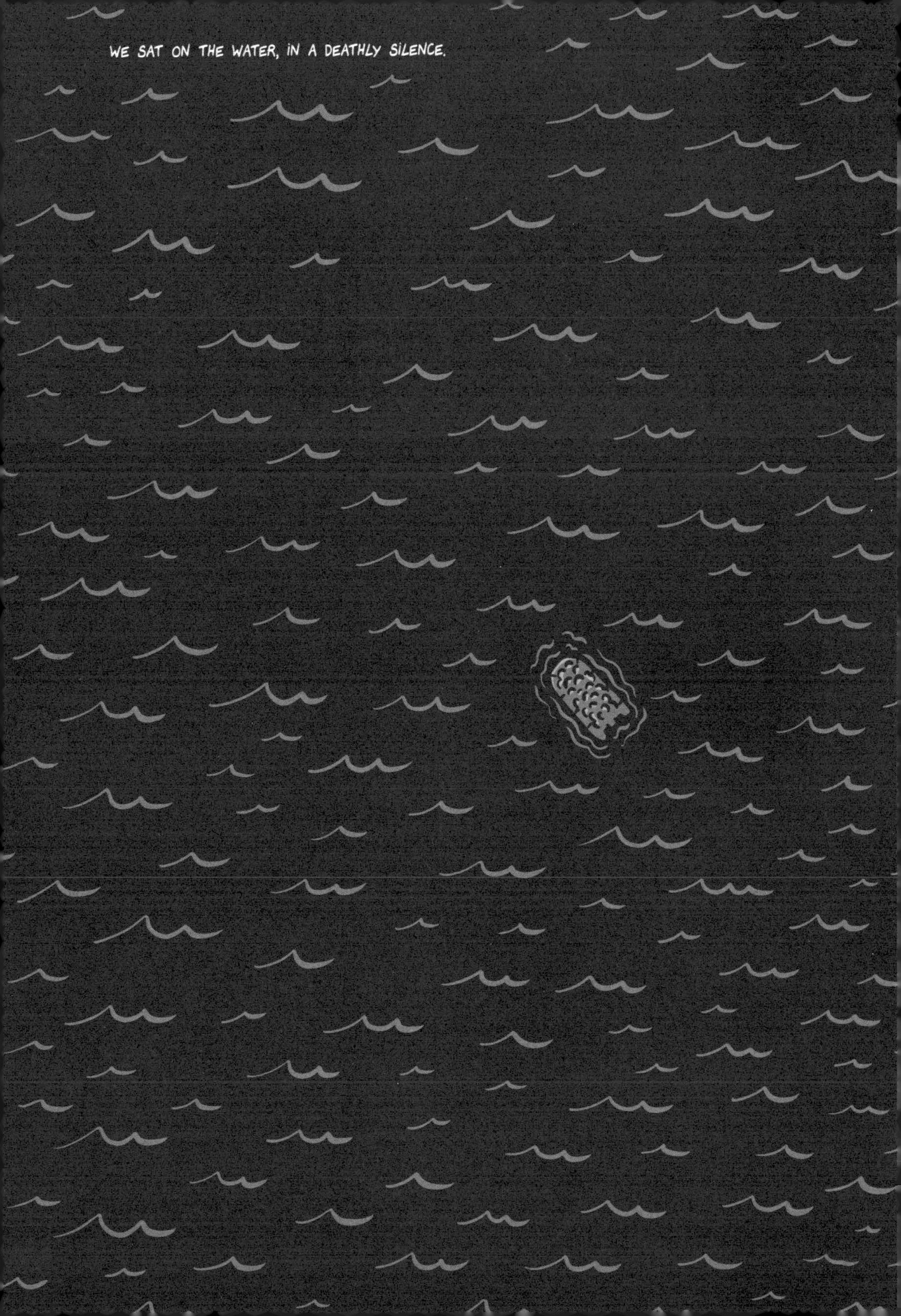
WE SAT ON THE WATER, IN A DEATHLY SILENCE.

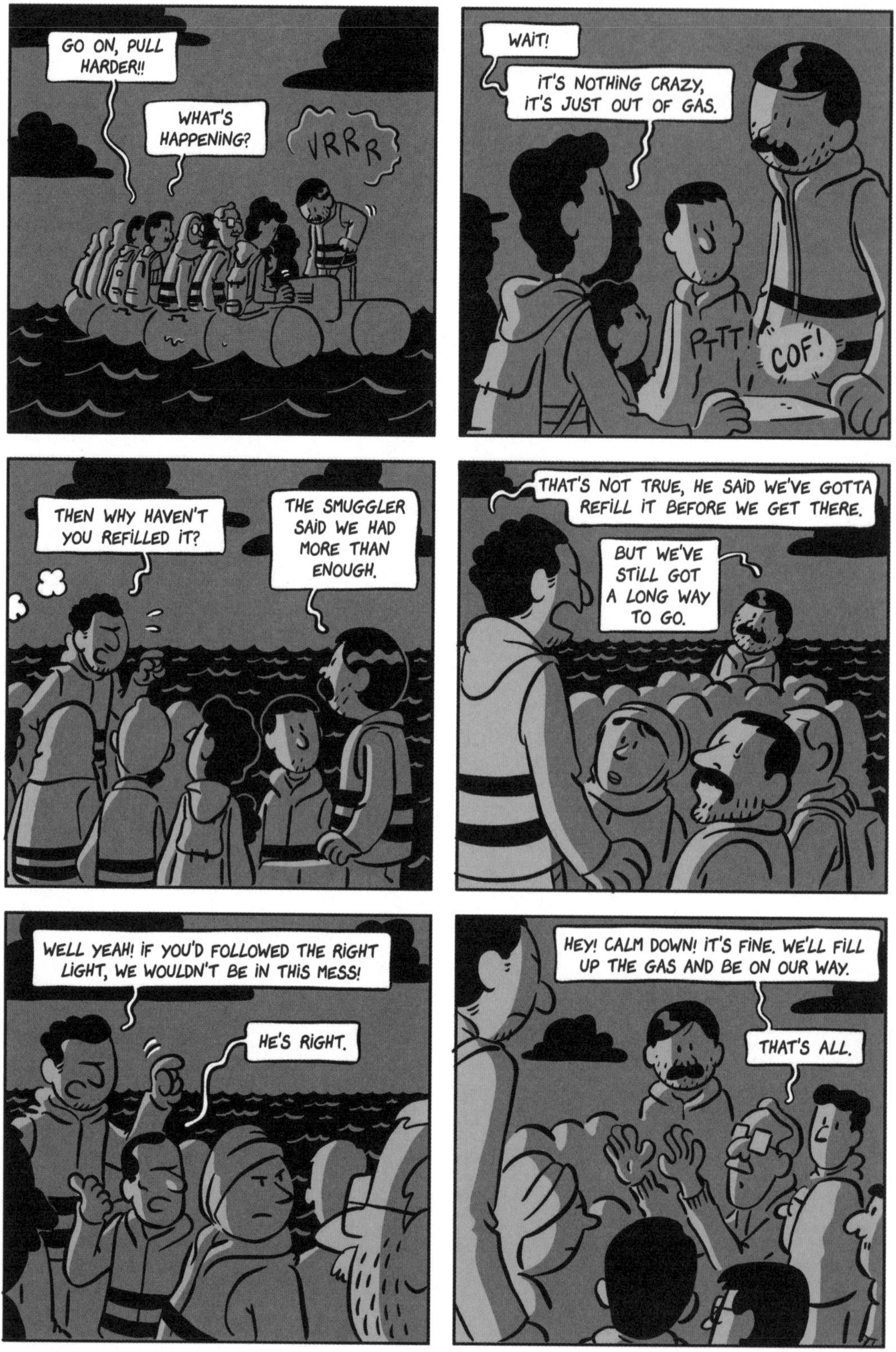
GO ON, PULL HARDER!!
WHAT'S HAPPENING?
VRRR
WAIT!
IT'S NOTHING CRAZY, IT'S JUST OUT OF GAS.
PTTT!
COF!
THEN WHY HAVEN'T YOU REFILLED IT?
THE SMUGGLER SAID WE HAD MORE THAN ENOUGH.
THAT'S NOT TRUE, HE SAID WE'VE GOTTA REFILL IT BEFORE WE GET THERE.
BUT WE'VE STILL GOT A LONG WAY TO GO.
WELL YEAH! IF YOU'D FOLLOWED THE RIGHT LIGHT, WE WOULDN'T BE IN THIS MESS!
HE'S RIGHT.
HEY! CALM DOWN! IT'S FINE. WE'LL FILL UP THE GAS AND BE ON OUR WAY.
THAT'S ALL.

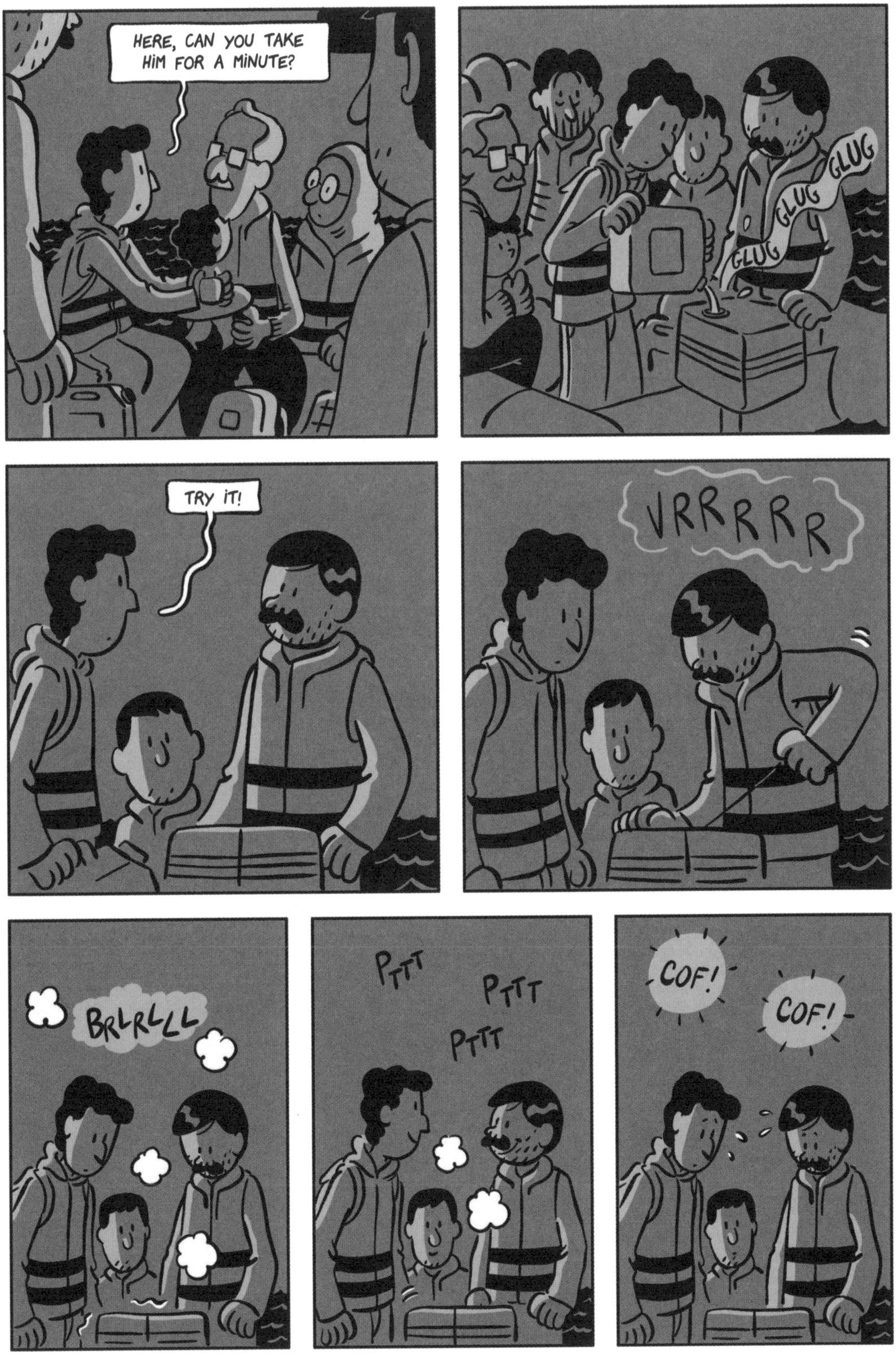
HERE, CAN YOU TAKE HIM FOR A MINUTE?
GLUG GLUG GLUG
TRY IT!
VRRRRRR
BRLRLLL
PTTT PTTT PTTT
COF! COF!

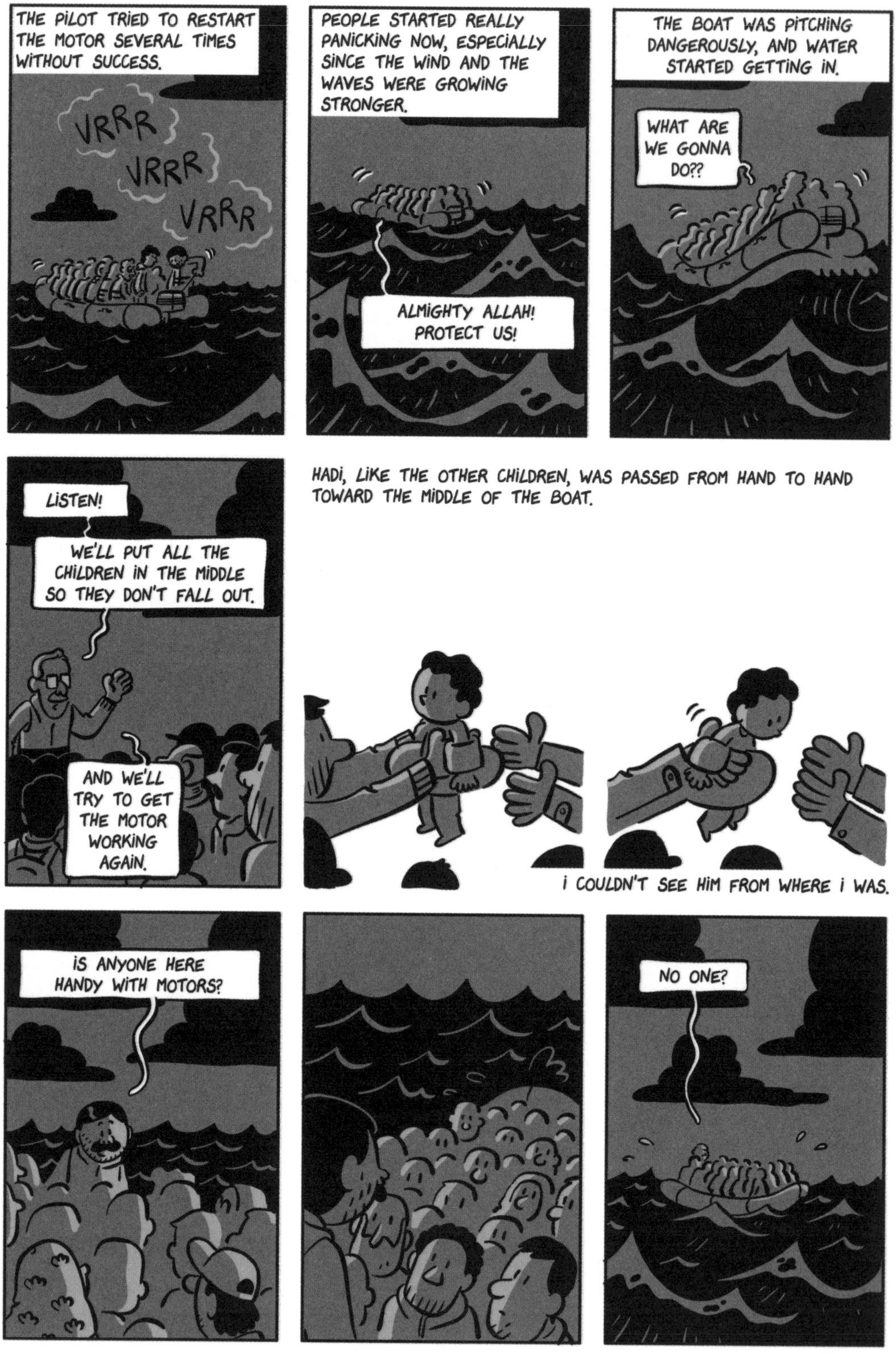
THE PILOT TRIED TO RESTART THE MOTOR SEVERAL TIMES WITHOUT SUCCESS.
VRRR
VRRR
VRRR
PEOPLE STARTED REALLY PANICKING NOW, ESPECIALLY SINCE THE WIND AND THE WAVES WERE GROWING STRONGER.
ALMIGHTY ALLAH! PROTECT US!
THE BOAT WAS PITCHING DANGEROUSLY, AND WATER STARTED GETTING IN.
WHAT ARE WE GONNA DO??
LISTEN!
WE'LL PUT ALL THE CHILDREN IN THE MIDDLE SO THEY DON'T FALL OUT.
AND WE'LL TRY TO GET THE MOTOR WORKING AGAIN.
HADI, LIKE THE OTHER CHILDREN, WAS PASSED FROM HAND TO HAND TOWARD THE MIDDLE OF THE BOAT.
I COULDN'T SEE HIM FROM WHERE I WAS.
IS ANYONE HERE HANDY WITH MOTORS?
NO ONE?

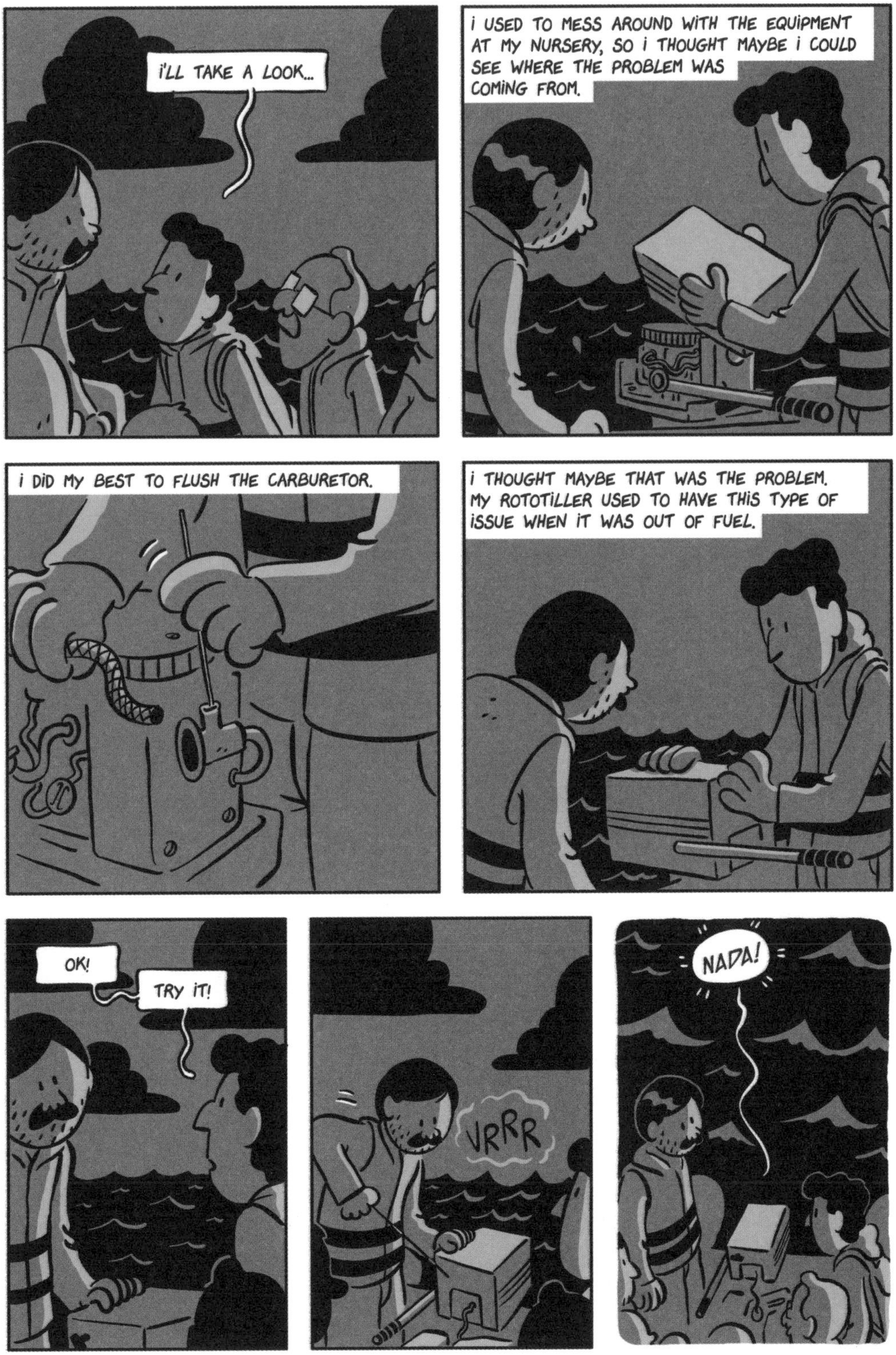
I'LL TAKE A LOOK...
I USED TO MESS AROUND WITH THE EQUIPMENT AT MY NURSERY, SO I THOUGHT MAYBE I COULD SEE WHERE THE PROBLEM WAS COMING FROM.
I DID MY BEST TO FLUSH THE CARBURETOR.
I THOUGHT MAYBE THAT WAS THE PROBLEM. MY ROTOTILLER USED TO HAVE THIS TYPE OF ISSUE WHEN IT WAS OUT OF FUEL.
OK!
TRY IT!
VRRR
NADA!

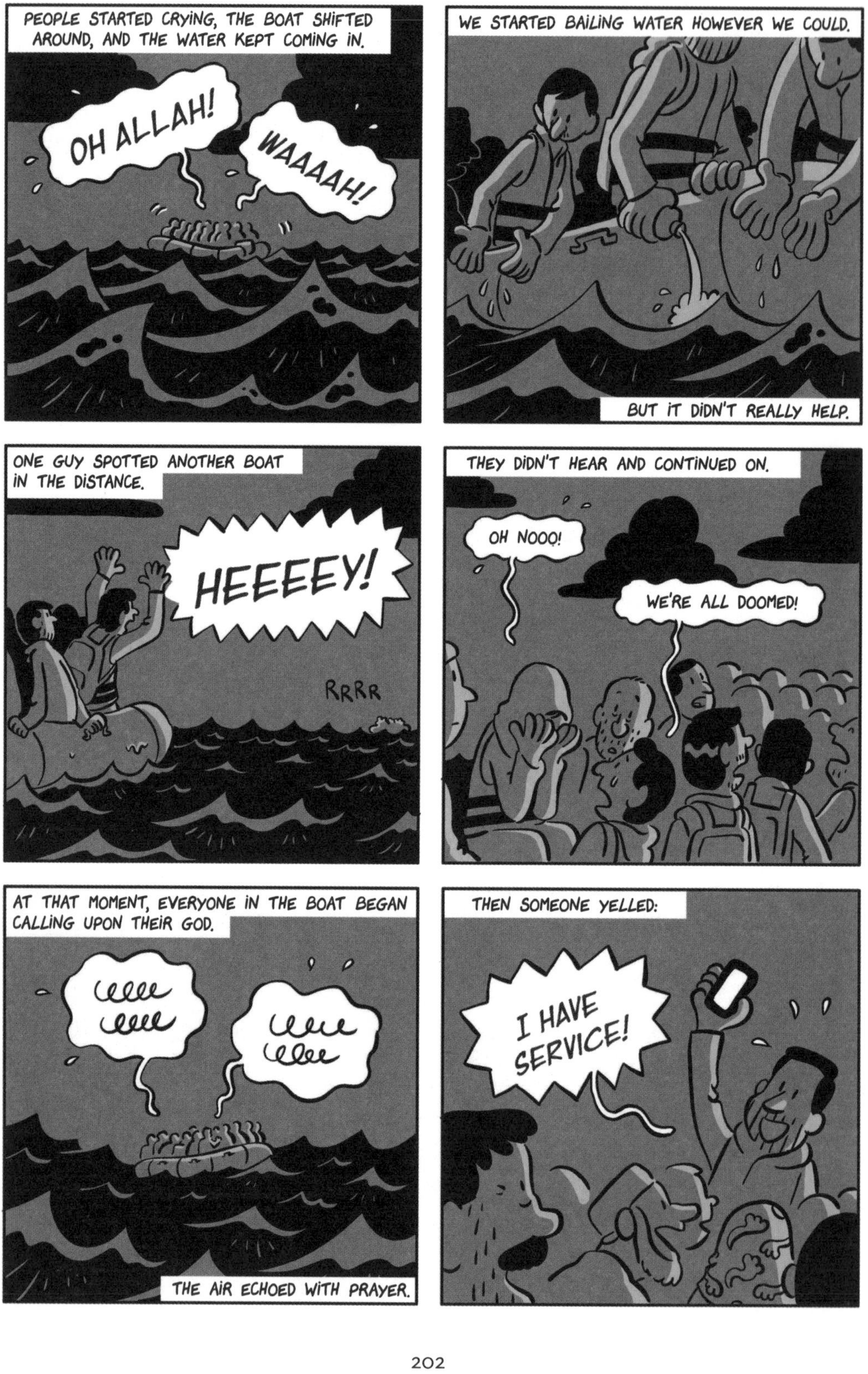
PEOPLE STARTED CRYING, THE BOAT SHIFTED AROUND, AND THE WATER KEPT COMING IN.
OH ALLAH!
WAAAAH!
WE STARTED BAILING WATER HOWEVER WE COULD.
BUT IT DIDN'T REALLY HELP.
ONE GUY SPOTTED ANOTHER BOAT IN THE DISTANCE.
HEEEEY!
RRRR
THEY DIDN'T HEAR AND CONTINUED ON.
OH NOOO!
WE'RE ALL DOOMED!
AT THAT MOMENT, EVERYONE IN THE BOAT BEGAN CALLING UPON THEIR GOD.
THE AIR ECHOED WITH PRAYER.
THEN SOMEONE YELLED:
I HAVE SERVICE!

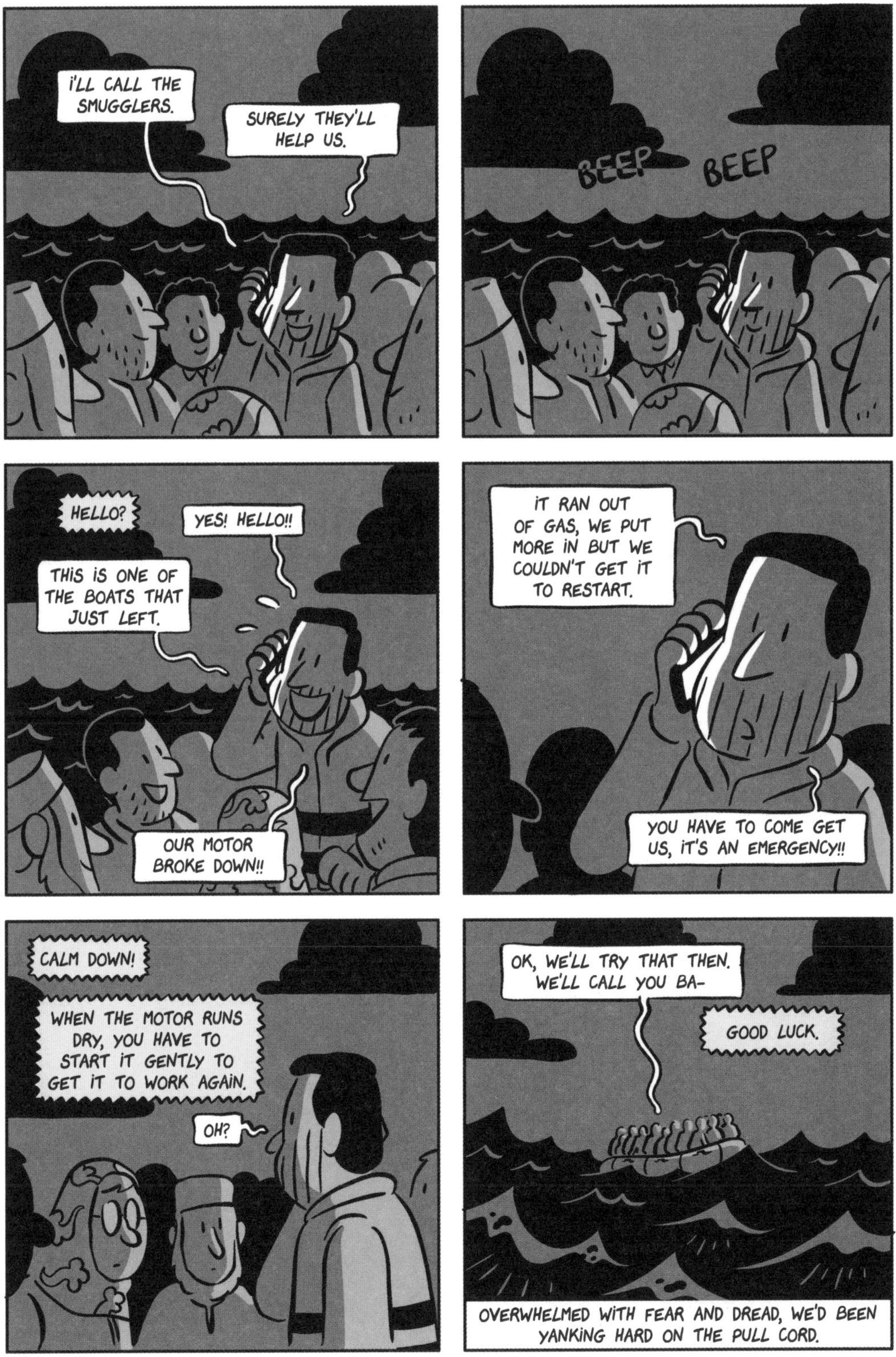
I'LL CALL THE SMUGGLERS.
SURELY THEY'LL HELP US.
BEEP
BEEP
HELLO?
YES! HELLO!!
THIS IS ONE OF THE BOATS THAT JUST LEFT.
OUR MOTOR BROKE DOWN!!
IT RAN OUT OF GAS, WE PUT MORE IN BUT WE COULDN'T GET IT TO RESTART.
YOU HAVE TO COME GET US, IT'S AN EMERGENCY!!
CALM DOWN!
WHEN THE MOTOR RUNS DRY, YOU HAVE TO START IT GENTLY TO GET IT TO WORK AGAIN.
OH?
OK, WE'LL TRY THAT THEN. WE'LL CALL YOU BA-
GOOD LUCK.
OVERWHELMED WITH FEAR AND DREAD, WE'D BEEN YANKING HARD ON THE PULL CORD.

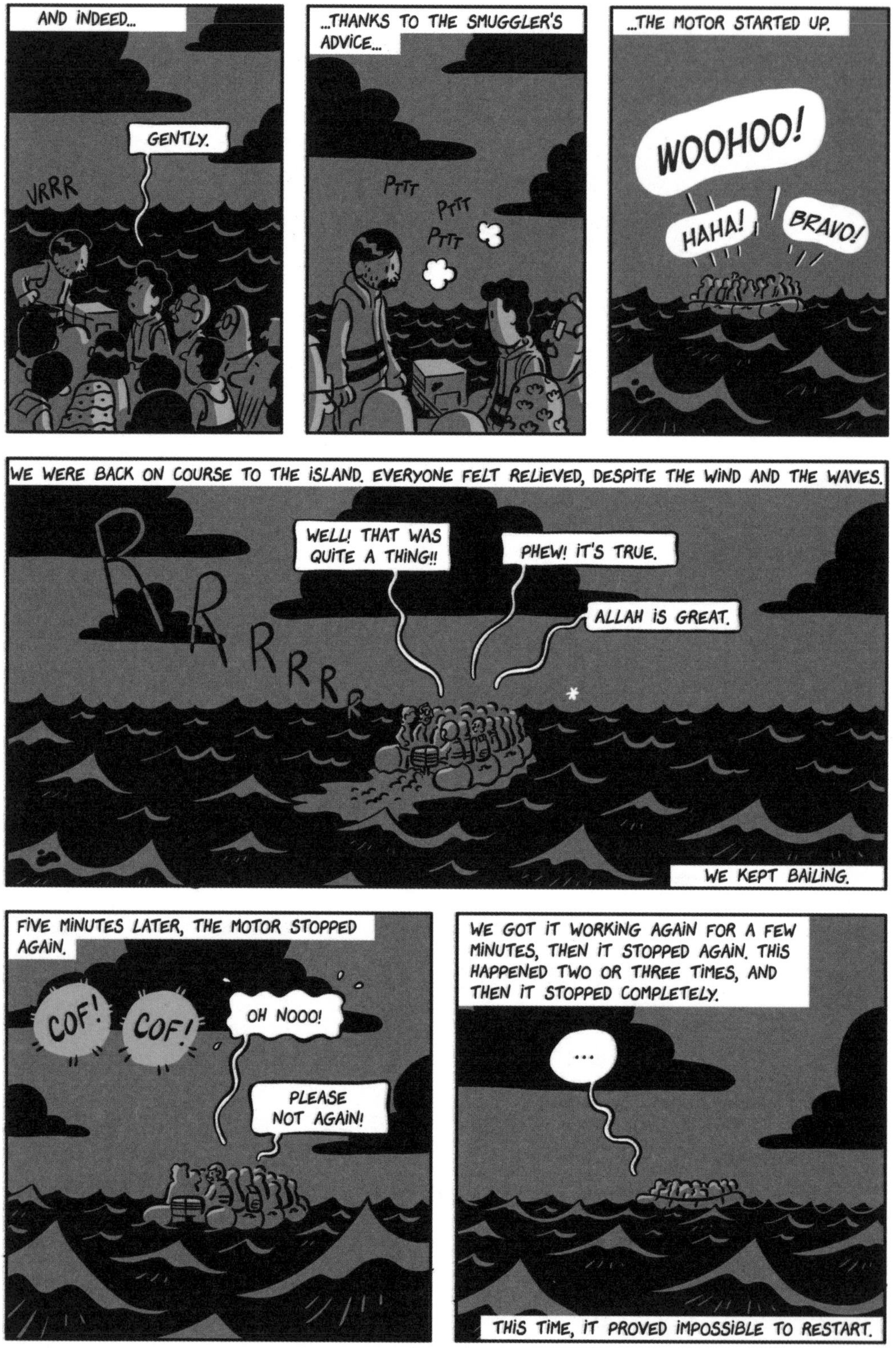
AND INDEED...
GENTLY.
VRRR
...THANKS TO THE SMUGGLER'S ADVICE...
PTTT
PTTT
PTTT
...THE MOTOR STARTED UP.
WOOHOO!
HAHA!
BRAVO!
WE WERE BACK ON COURSE TO THE ISLAND. EVERYONE FELT RELIEVED, DESPITE THE WIND AND THE WAVES.
RRRRRRR
WELL! THAT WAS QUITE A THING!!
PHEW! IT'S TRUE.
ALLAH IS GREAT.
WE KEPT BAILING.
FIVE MINUTES LATER, THE MOTOR STOPPED AGAIN.
COF!
COF!
OH NOOO!
PLEASE NOT AGAIN!
WE GOT IT WORKING AGAIN FOR A FEW MINUTES, THEN IT STOPPED AGAIN. THIS HAPPENED TWO OR THREE TIMES, AND THEN IT STOPPED COMPLETELY.
...
THIS TIME, IT PROVED IMPOSSIBLE TO RESTART.

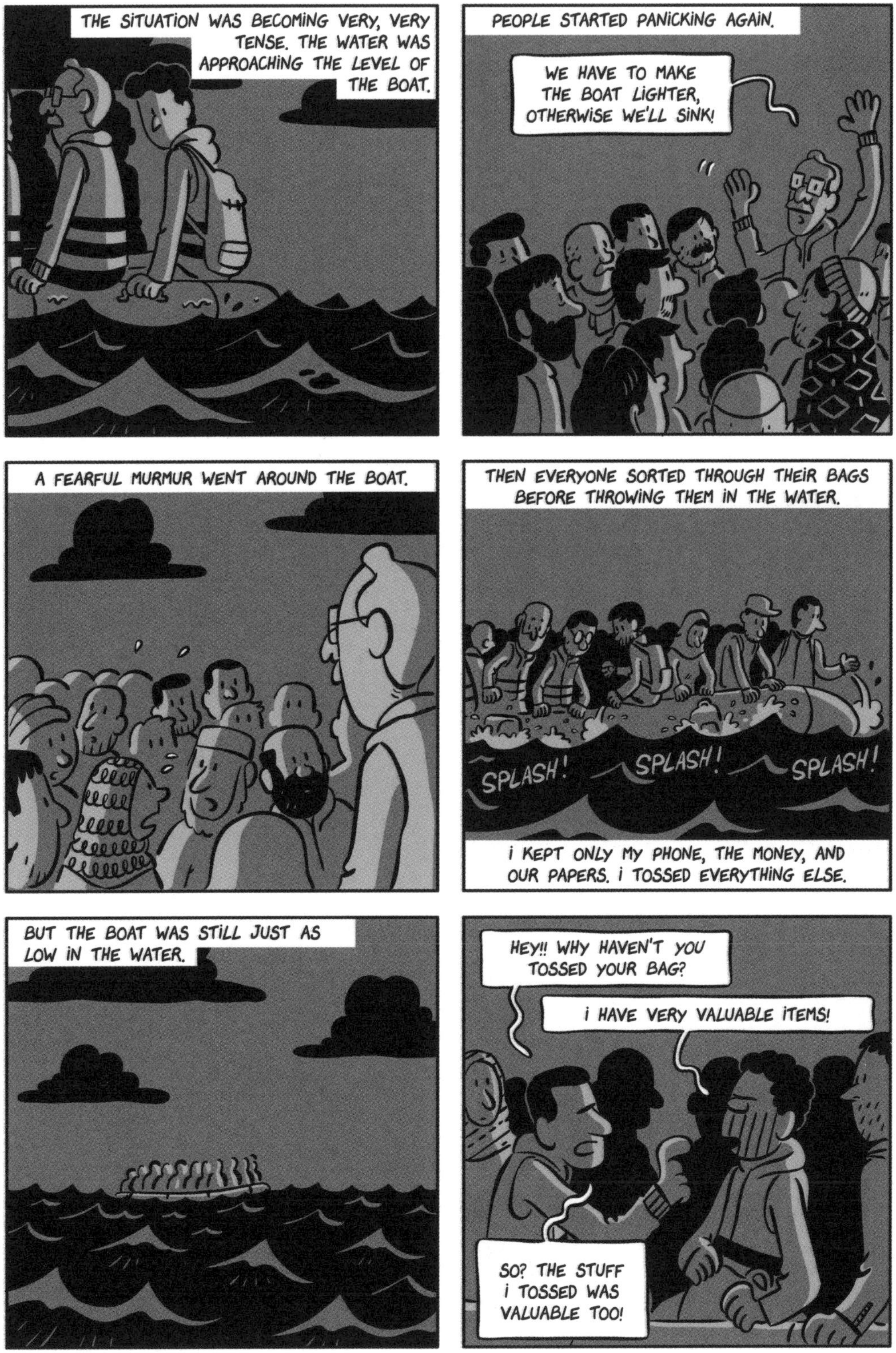
THE SITUATION WAS BECOMING VERY, VERY TENSE. THE WATER WAS APPROACHING THE LEVEL OF THE BOAT.
PEOPLE STARTED PANICKING AGAIN.
WE HAVE TO MAKE THE BOAT LIGHTER, OTHERWISE WE'LL SINK!
A FEARFUL MURMUR WENT AROUND THE BOAT.
THEN EVERYONE SORTED THROUGH THEIR BAGS BEFORE THROWING THEM IN THE WATER.
SPLASH!
SPLASH!
SPLASH!
I KEPT ONLY MY PHONE, THE MONEY, AND OUR PAPERS. I TOSSED EVERYTHING ELSE.
BUT THE BOAT WAS STILL JUST AS LOW IN THE WATER.
HEY!! WHY HAVEN'T YOU TOSSED YOUR BAG?
I HAVE VERY VALUABLE ITEMS!
SO? THE STUFF I TOSSED WAS VALUABLE TOO!

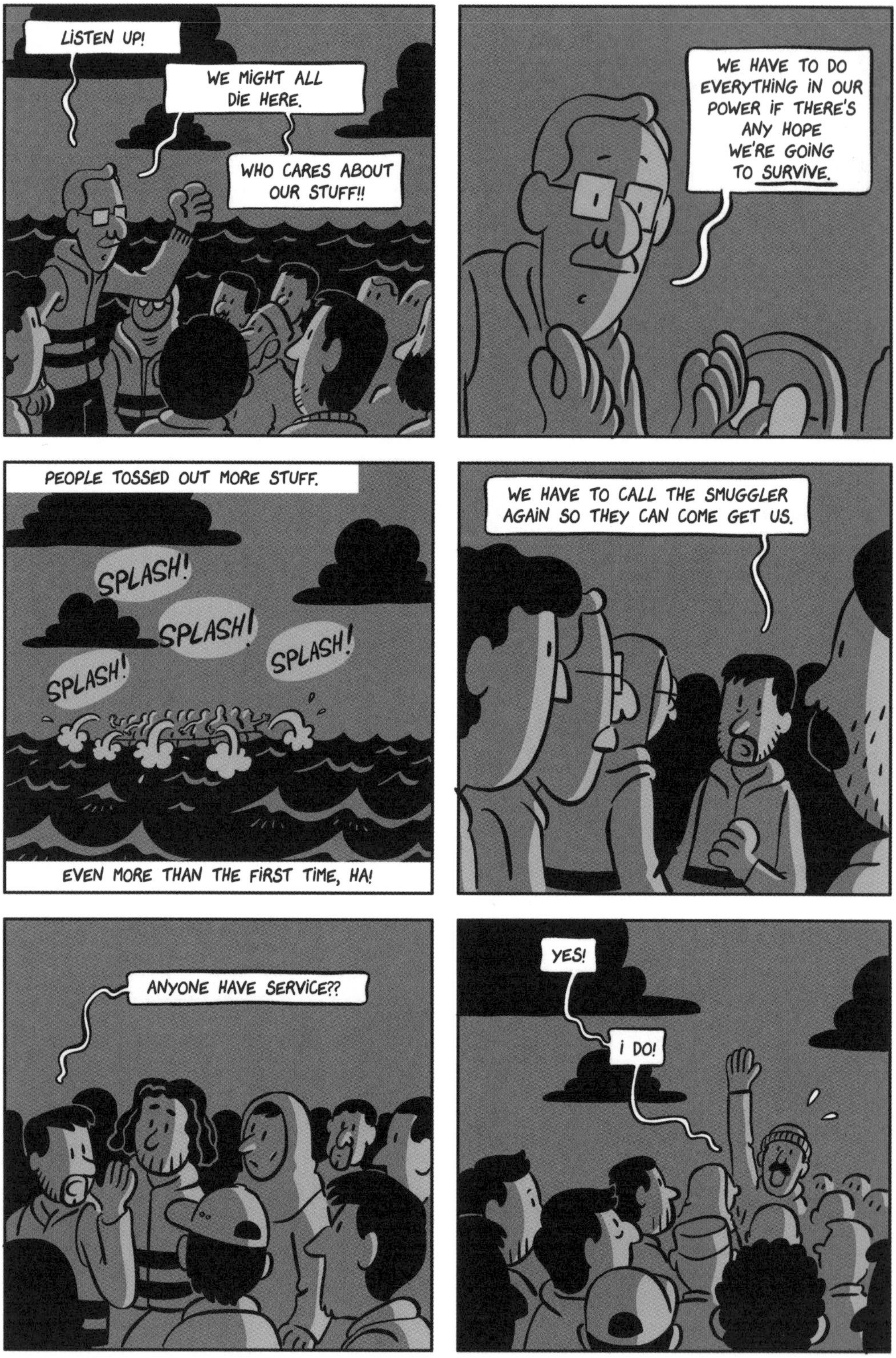
LISTEN UP!
WE MIGHT ALL DIE HERE.
WHO CARES ABOUT OUR STUFF!!
WE HAVE TO DO EVERYTHING IN OUR POWER IF THERE'S ANY HOPE WE'RE GOING TO SURVIVE.
PEOPLE TOSSED OUT MORE STUFF.
SPLASH!
SPLASH!
SPLASH!
SPLASH!
EVEN MORE THAN THE FIRST TIME, HA!
WE HAVE TO CALL THE SMUGGLER AGAIN SO THEY CAN COME GET US.
ANYONE HAVE SERVICE??
YES!
I DO!

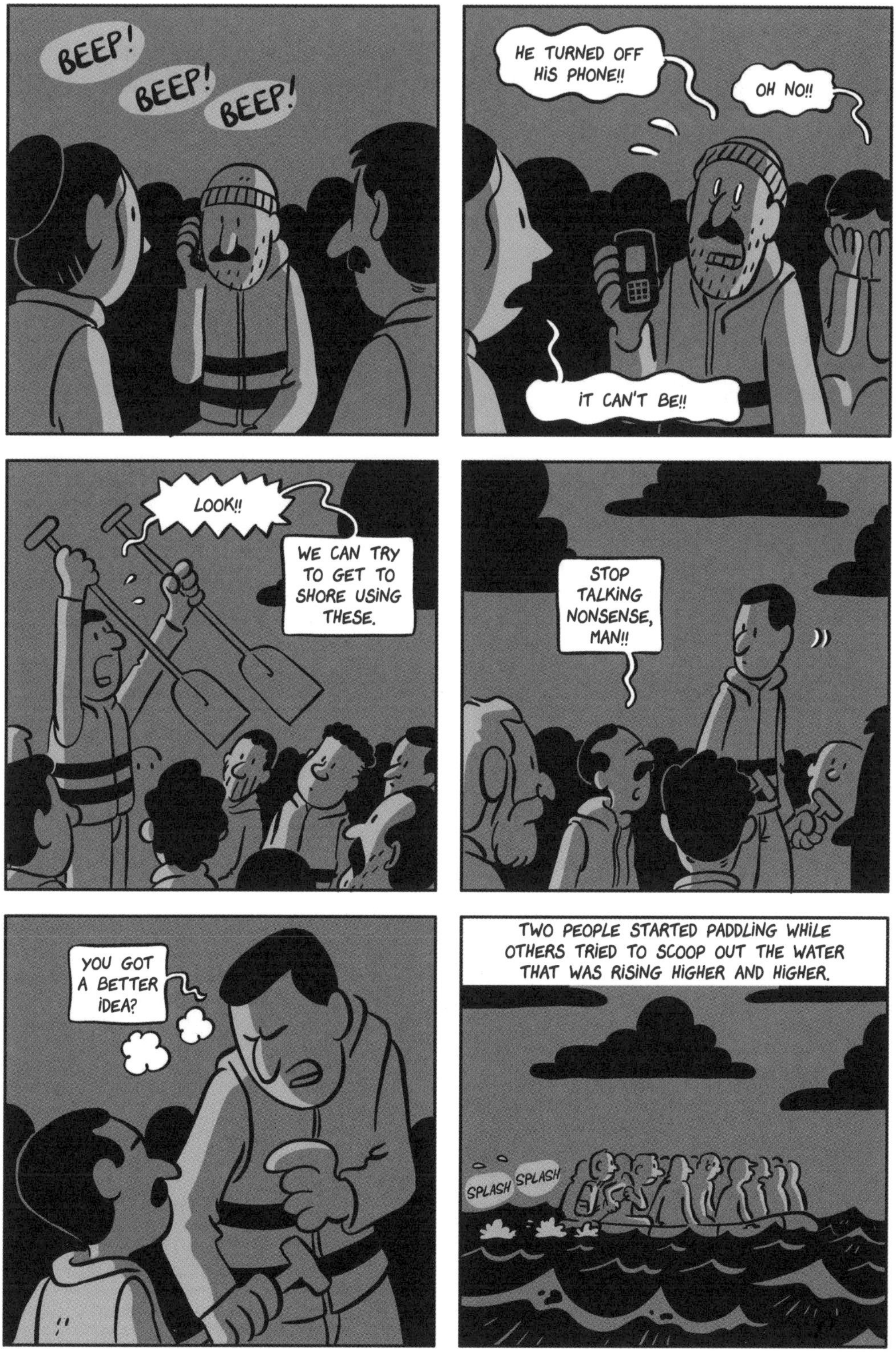
BEEP!
BEEP!
BEEP!
HE TURNED OFF HIS PHONE!!
OH NO!!
IT CAN'T BE!!
LOOK!!
WE CAN TRY TO GET TO SHORE USING THESE.
STOP TALKING NONSENSE, MAN!!
YOU GOT A BETTER IDEA?
TWO PEOPLE STARTED PADDLING WHILE OTHERS TRIED TO SCOOP OUT THE WATER THAT WAS RISING HIGHER AND HIGHER.
SPLASH
SPLASH

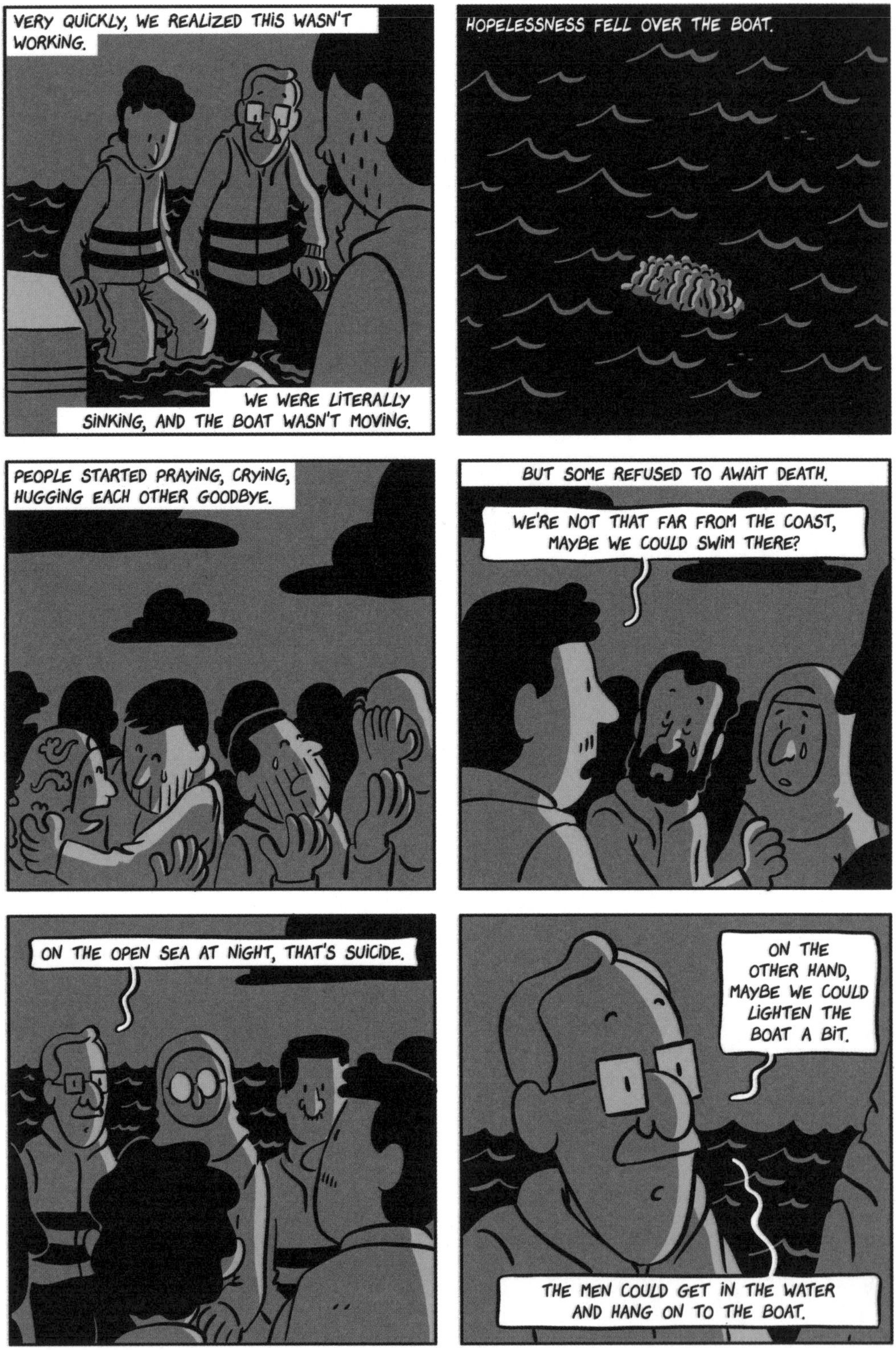
VERY QUICKLY, WE REALIZED THIS WASN'T WORKING.
WE WERE LITERALLY SINKING, AND THE BOAT WASN'T MOVING.
HOPELESSNESS FELL OVER THE BOAT.
PEOPLE STARTED PRAYING, CRYING, HUGGING EACH OTHER GOODBYE.
BUT SOME REFUSED TO AWAIT DEATH.
WE'RE NOT THAT FAR FROM THE COAST, MAYBE WE COULD SWIM THERE?
ON THE OPEN SEA AT NIGHT, THAT'S SUICIDE.
ON THE OTHER HAND, MAYBE WE COULD LIGHTEN THE BOAT A BIT.
THE MEN COULD GET IN THE WATER AND HANG ON TO THE BOAT.

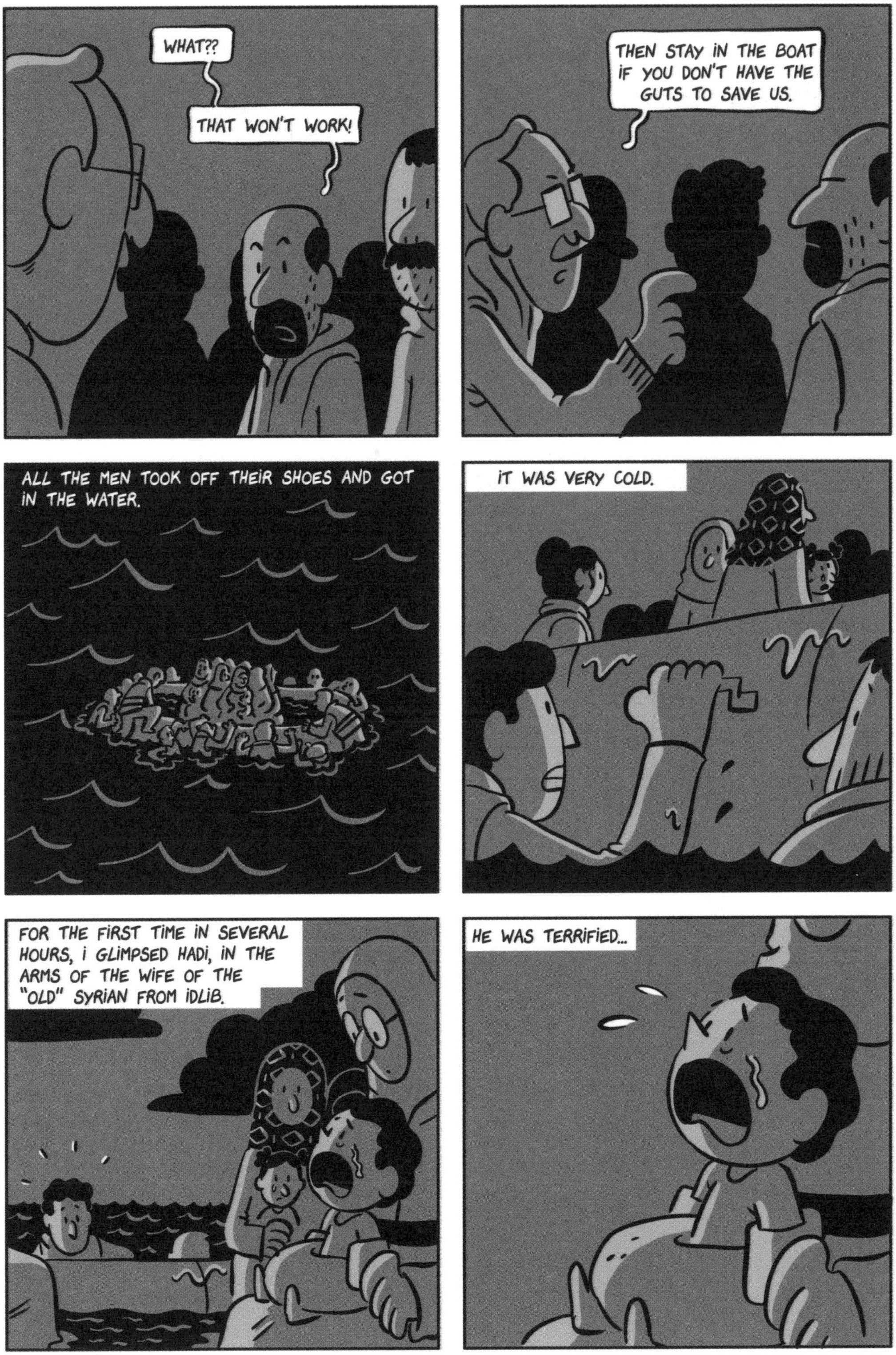
WHAT??
THAT WON'T WORK!
THEN STAY IN THE BOAT IF YOU DON'T HAVE THE GUTS TO SAVE US.
ALL THE MEN TOOK OFF THEIR SHOES AND GOT IN THE WATER.
IT WAS VERY COLD.
FOR THE FIRST TIME IN SEVERAL HOURS, I GLIMPSED HADI, IN THE ARMS OF THE WIFE OF THE "OLD" SYRIAN FROM IDLIB.
HE WAS TERRIFIED...

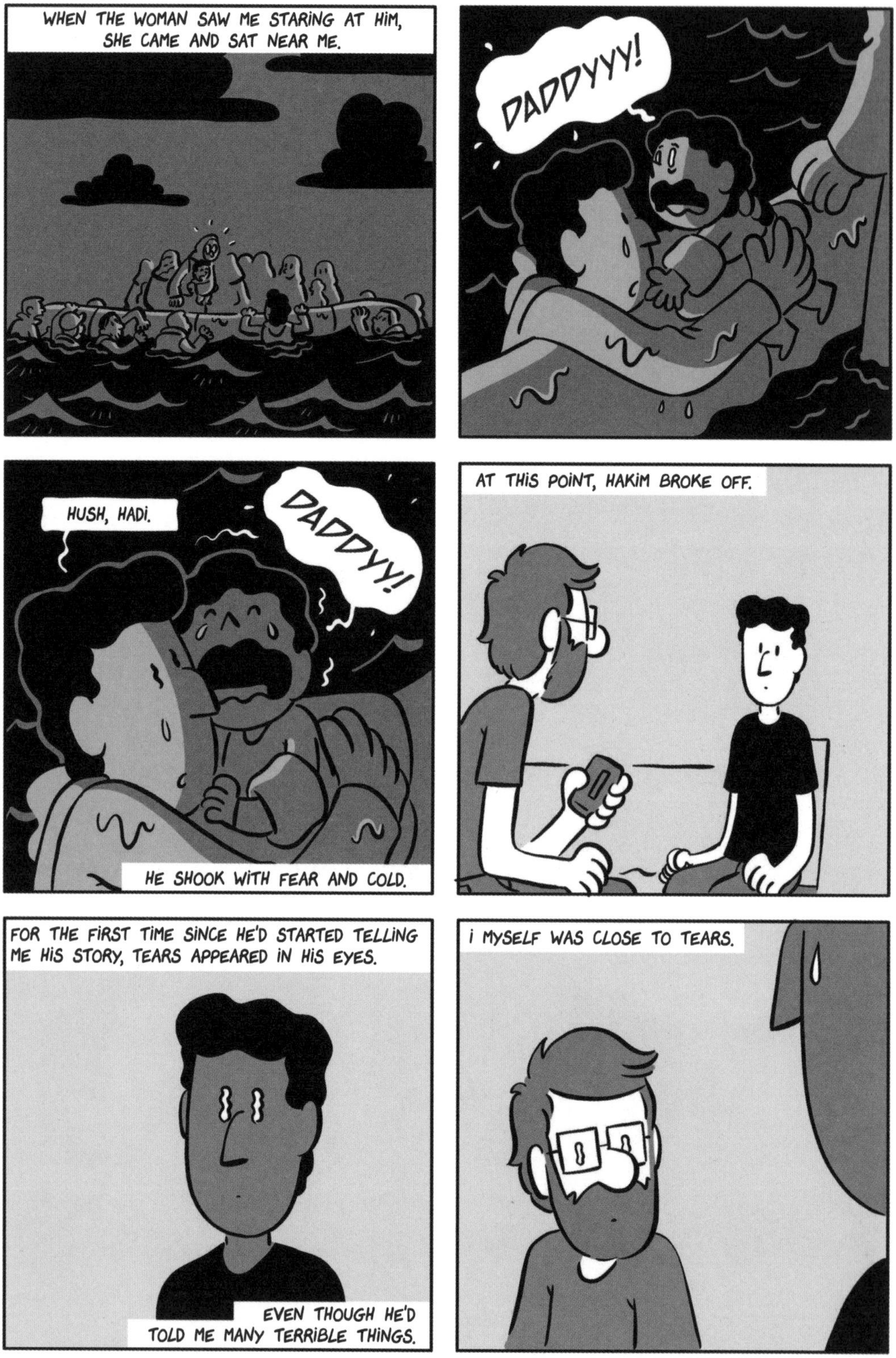
WHEN THE WOMAN SAW ME STARING AT HIM, SHE CAME AND SAT NEAR ME.
DADDYYY!
HUSH, HADI.
DADDYY!
HE SHOOK WITH FEAR AND COLD.
AT THIS POINT, HAKIM BROKE OFF.
FOR THE FIRST TIME SINCE HE'D STARTED TELLING ME HIS STORY, TEARS APPEARED IN HIS EYES.
EVEN THOUGH HE'D TOLD ME MANY TERRIBLE THINGS.
I MYSELF WAS CLOSE TO TEARS.

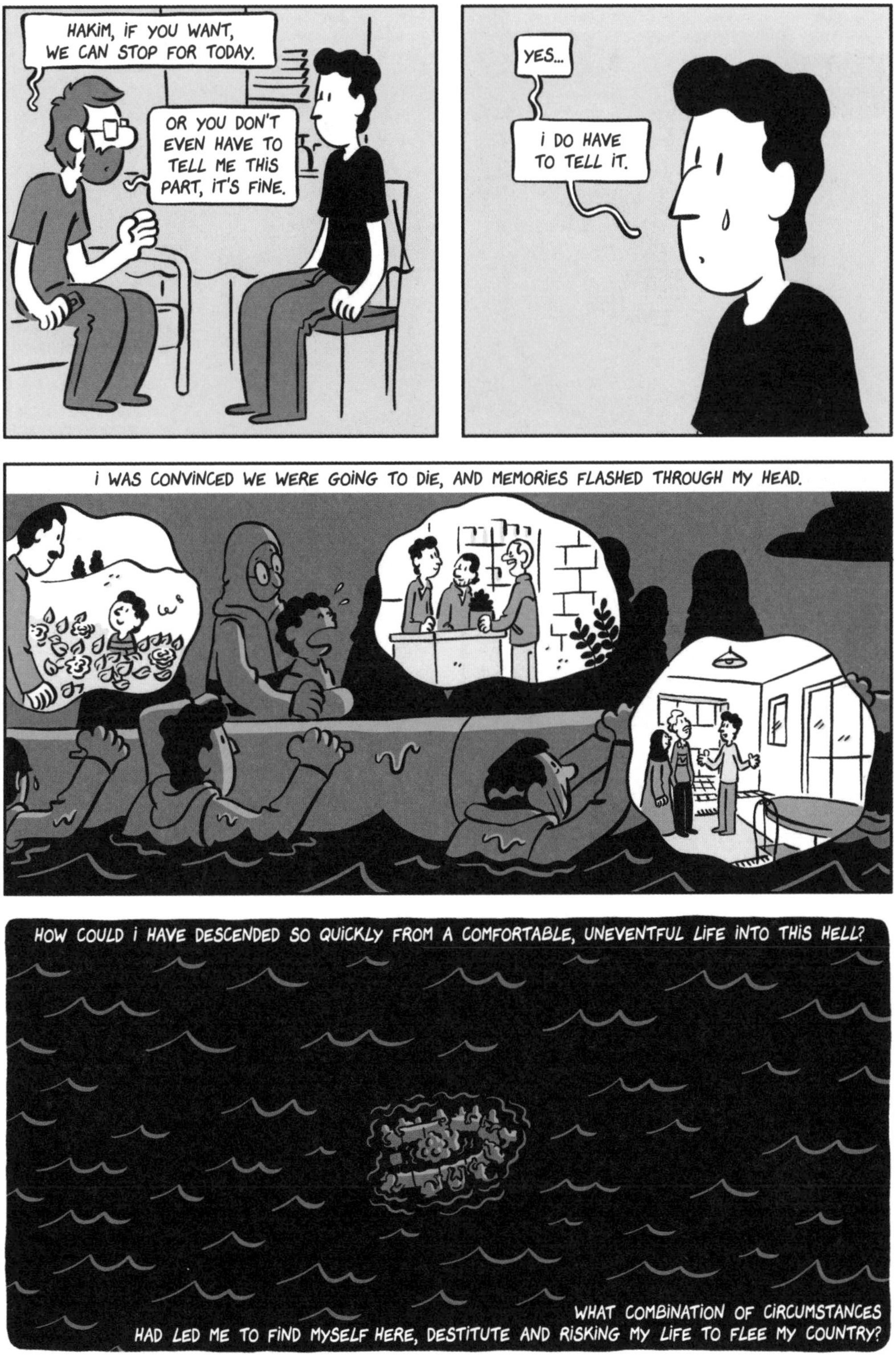

HAKIM, IF YOU WANT, WE CAN STOP FOR TODAY.
OR YOU DON'T EVEN HAVE TO TELL ME THIS PART, IT'S FINE.
YES...
I DO HAVE TO TELL IT.
I WAS CONVINCED WE WERE GOING TO DIE, AND MEMORIES FLASHED THROUGH MY HEAD.
HOW COULD I HAVE DESCENDED SO QUICKLY FROM A COMFORTABLE, UNEVENTFUL LIFE INTO THIS HELL?
WHAT COMBINATION OF CIRCUMSTANCES HAD LED ME TO FIND MYSELF HERE, DESTITUTE AND RISKING MY LIFE TO FLEE MY COUNTRY?

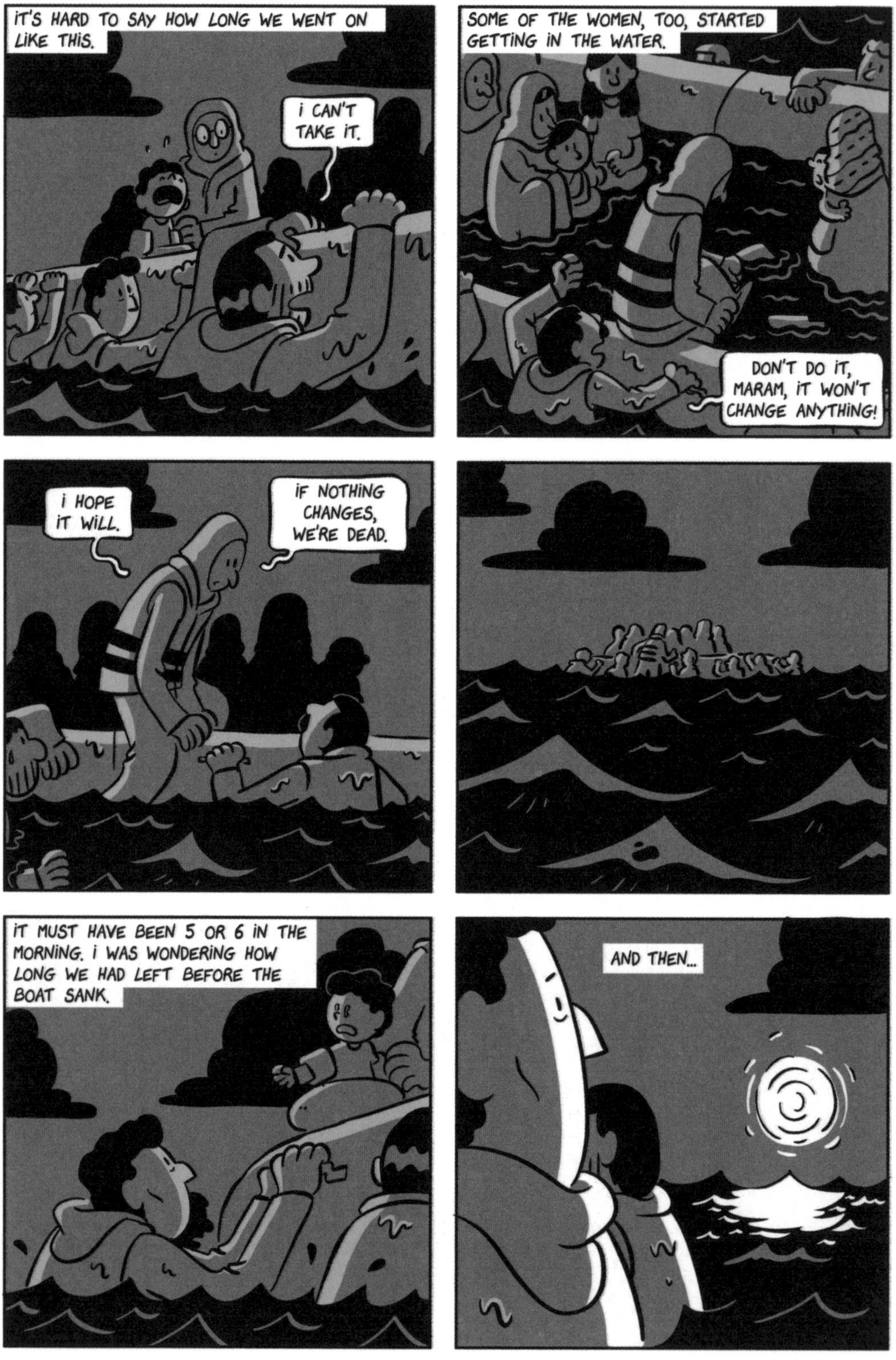
IT'S HARD TO SAY HOW LONG WE WENT ON LIKE THIS.
I CAN'T TAKE IT.
SOME OF THE WOMEN, TOO, STARTED GETTING IN THE WATER.
DON'T DO IT, MARAM, IT WON'T CHANGE ANYTHING!
I HOPE IT WILL.
IF NOTHING CHANGES, WE'RE DEAD.
IT MUST HAVE BEEN 5 OR 6 IN THE MORNING. I WAS WONDERING HOW LONG WE HAD LEFT BEFORE THE BOAT SANK.
AND THEN...

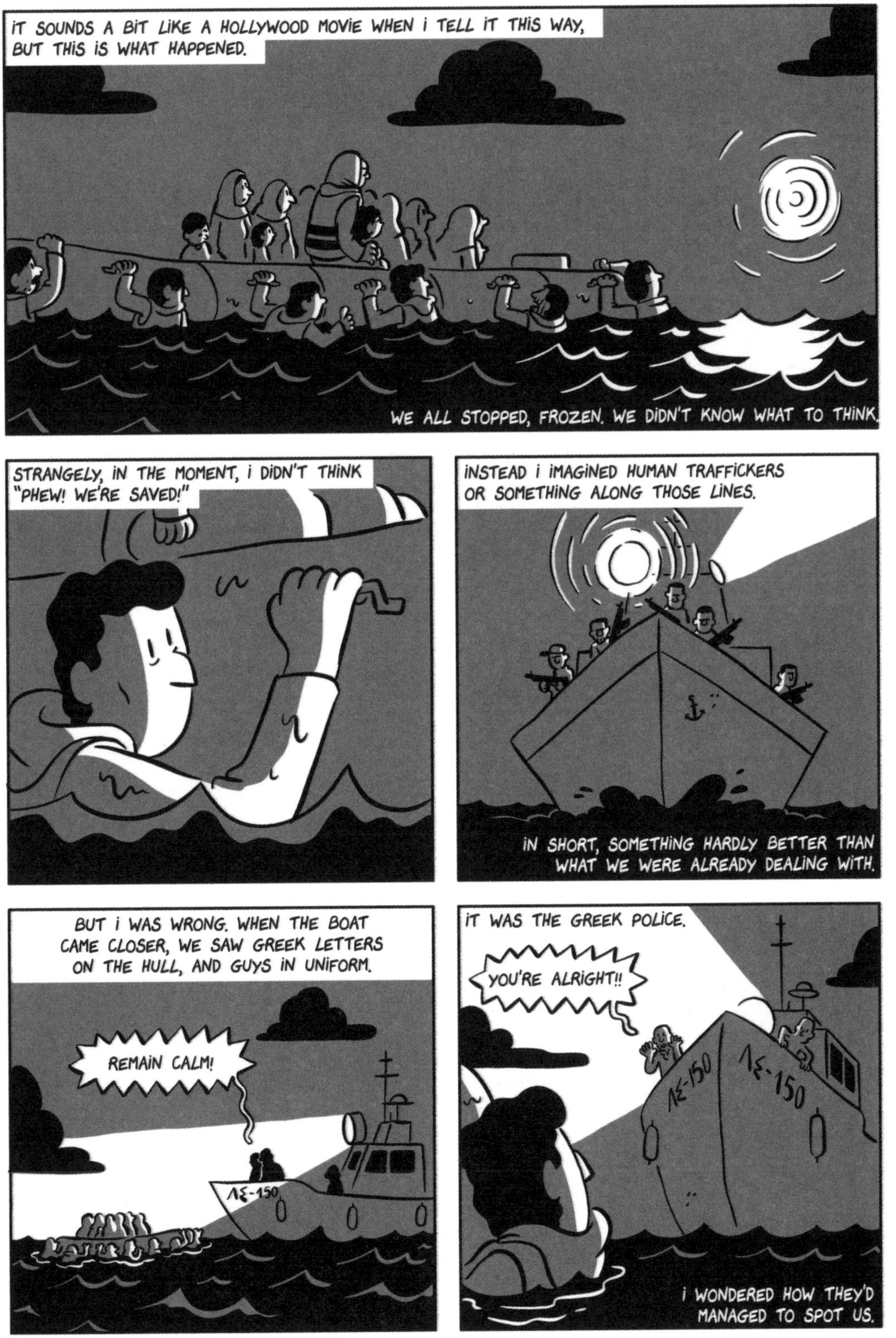
IT SOUNDS A BIT LIKE A HOLLYWOOD MOVIE WHEN I TELL IT THIS WAY, BUT THIS IS WHAT HAPPENED.
WE ALL STOPPED, FROZEN. WE DIDN'T KNOW WHAT TO THINK.
STRANGELY, IN THE MOMENT, I DIDN'T THINK "PHEW! WE'RE SAVED!"
INSTEAD I IMAGINED HUMAN TRAFFICKERS OR SOMETHING ALONG THOSE LINES.
IN SHORT, SOMETHING HARDLY BETTER THAN WHAT WE WERE ALREADY DEALING WITH.
BUT I WAS WRONG. WHEN THE BOAT CAME CLOSER, WE SAW GREEK LETTERS ON THE HULL, AND GUYS IN UNIFORM.
REMAIN CALM!
ΛΣ-150
IT WAS THE GREEK POLICE.
YOU'RE ALRIGHT!!
ΛΣ-150
ΛΣ-150
I WONDERED HOW THEY'D MANAGED TO SPOT US.

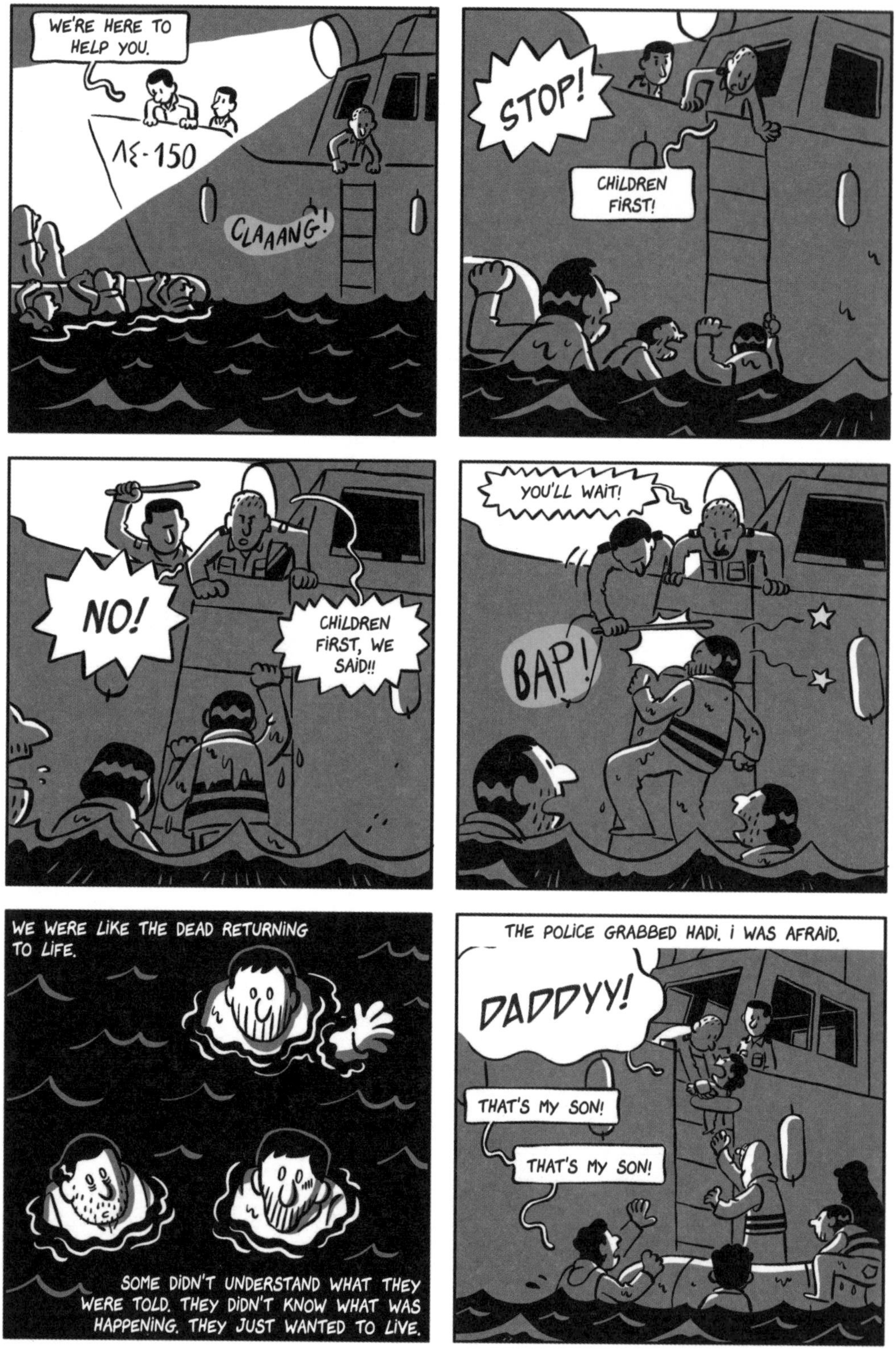
WE'RE HERE TO HELP YOU.
ΛΣ-150
CLAAANG!
STOP!
CHILDREN FIRST!
NO!
CHILDREN FIRST, WE SAID!!
YOU'LL WAIT!
BAP!
WE WERE LIKE THE DEAD RETURNING TO LIFE.
SOME DIDN'T UNDERSTAND WHAT THEY WERE TOLD. THEY DIDN'T KNOW WHAT WAS HAPPENING. THEY JUST WANTED TO LIVE.
THE POLICE GRABBED HADI. I WAS AFRAID.
DADDYY!
THAT'S MY SON!
THAT'S MY SON!

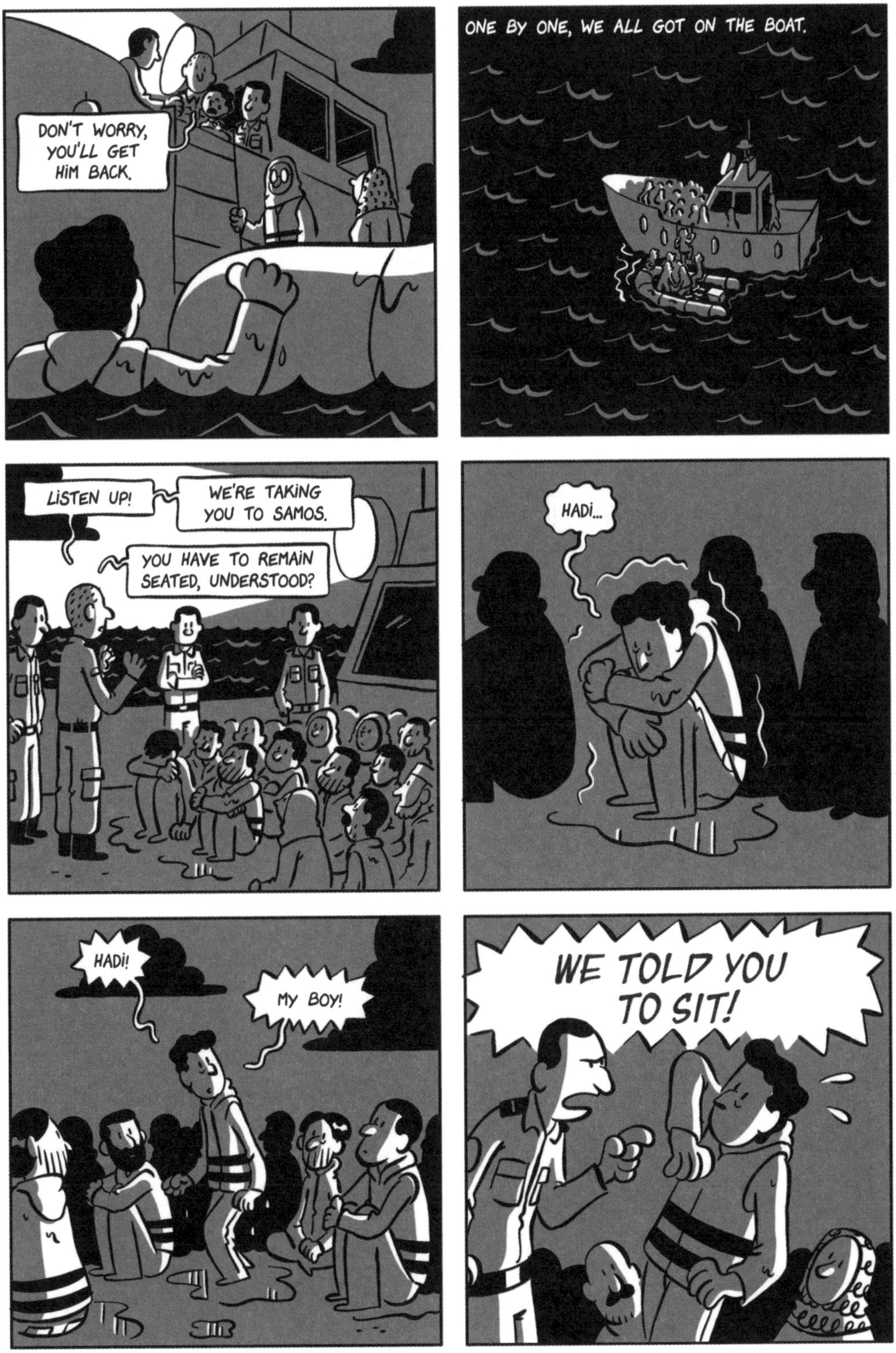
DON'T WORRY, YOU'LL GET HIM BACK.
ONE BY ONE, WE ALL GOT ON THE BOAT.
LISTEN UP!
WE'RE TAKING YOU TO SAMOS.
YOU HAVE TO REMAIN SEATED, UNDERSTOOD?
HADI...
HADI!
MY BOY!
WE TOLD YOU TO SIT!

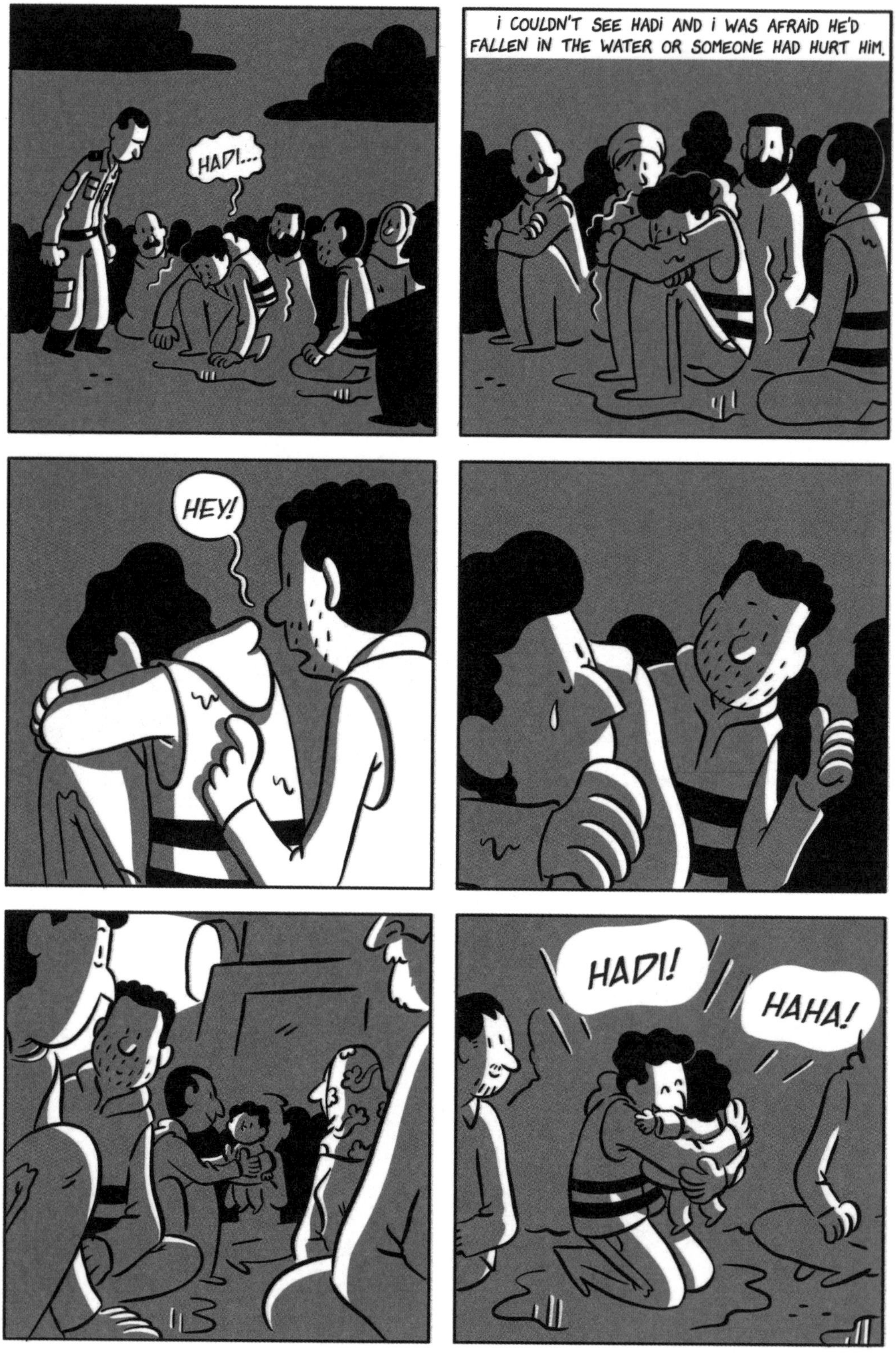
HADI...
i COULDN'T SEE HADI AND i WAS AFRAID HE'D FALLEN IN THE WATER OR SOMEONE HAD HURT HIM.
HEY!
HADI!
HAHA!

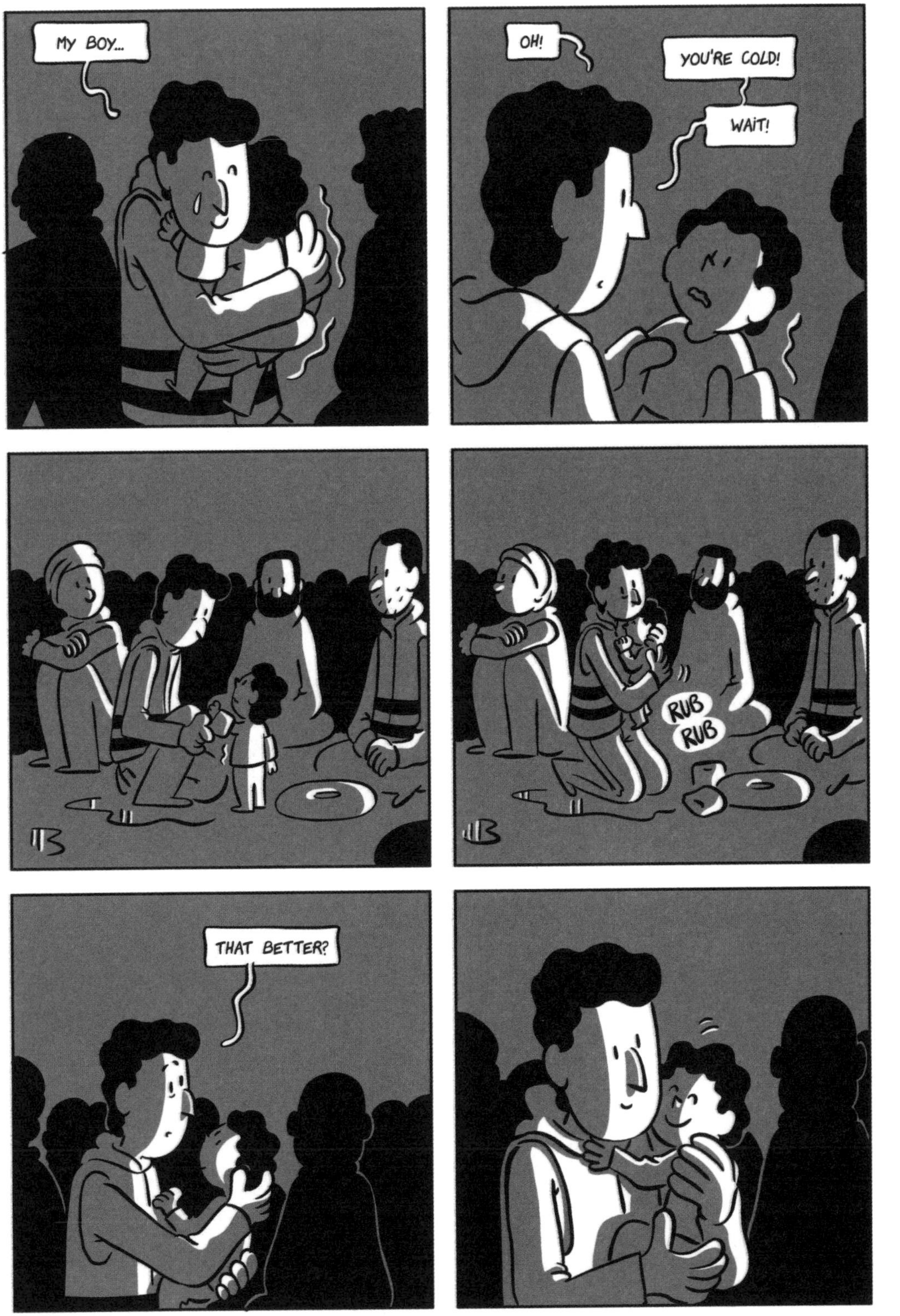
MY BOY...
OH!
YOU'RE COLD!
WAIT!
RUB
RUB
THAT BETTER?

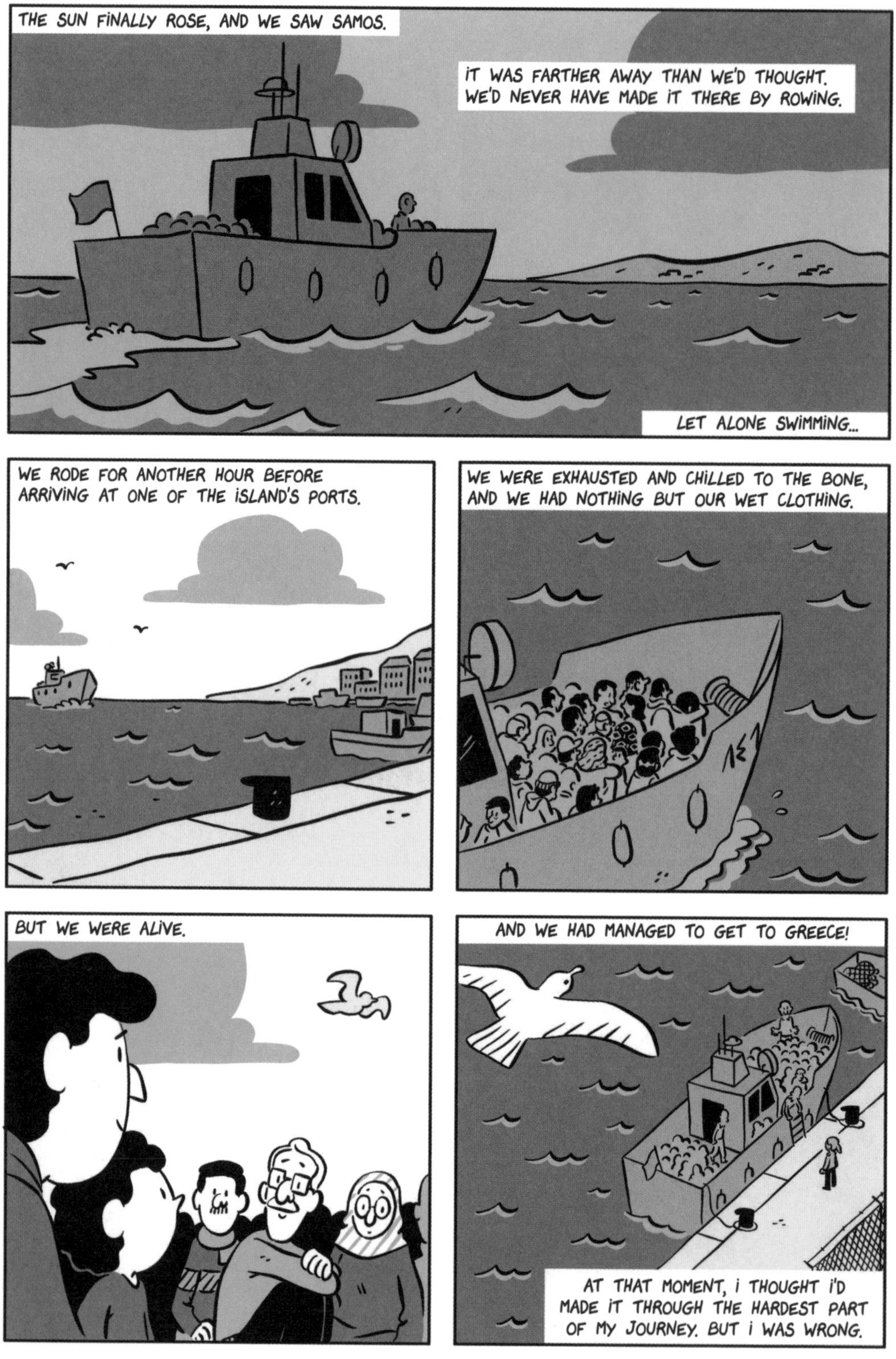
THE SUN FINALLY ROSE, AND WE SAW SAMOS.
IT WAS FARTHER AWAY THAN WE'D THOUGHT. WE'D NEVER HAVE MADE IT THERE BY ROWING.
LET ALONE SWIMMING...
WE RODE FOR ANOTHER HOUR BEFORE ARRIVING AT ONE OF THE ISLAND'S PORTS.
WE WERE EXHAUSTED AND CHILLED TO THE BONE, AND WE HAD NOTHING BUT OUR WET CLOTHING.
BUT WE WERE ALIVE.
AND WE HAD MANAGED TO GET TO GREECE!
AT THAT MOMENT, I THOUGHT I'D MADE IT THROUGH THE HARDEST PART OF MY JOURNEY. BUT I WAS WRONG.

Chapter II:
Greece
(September 2015)

"YOU TRYING TO GO NORTH?"

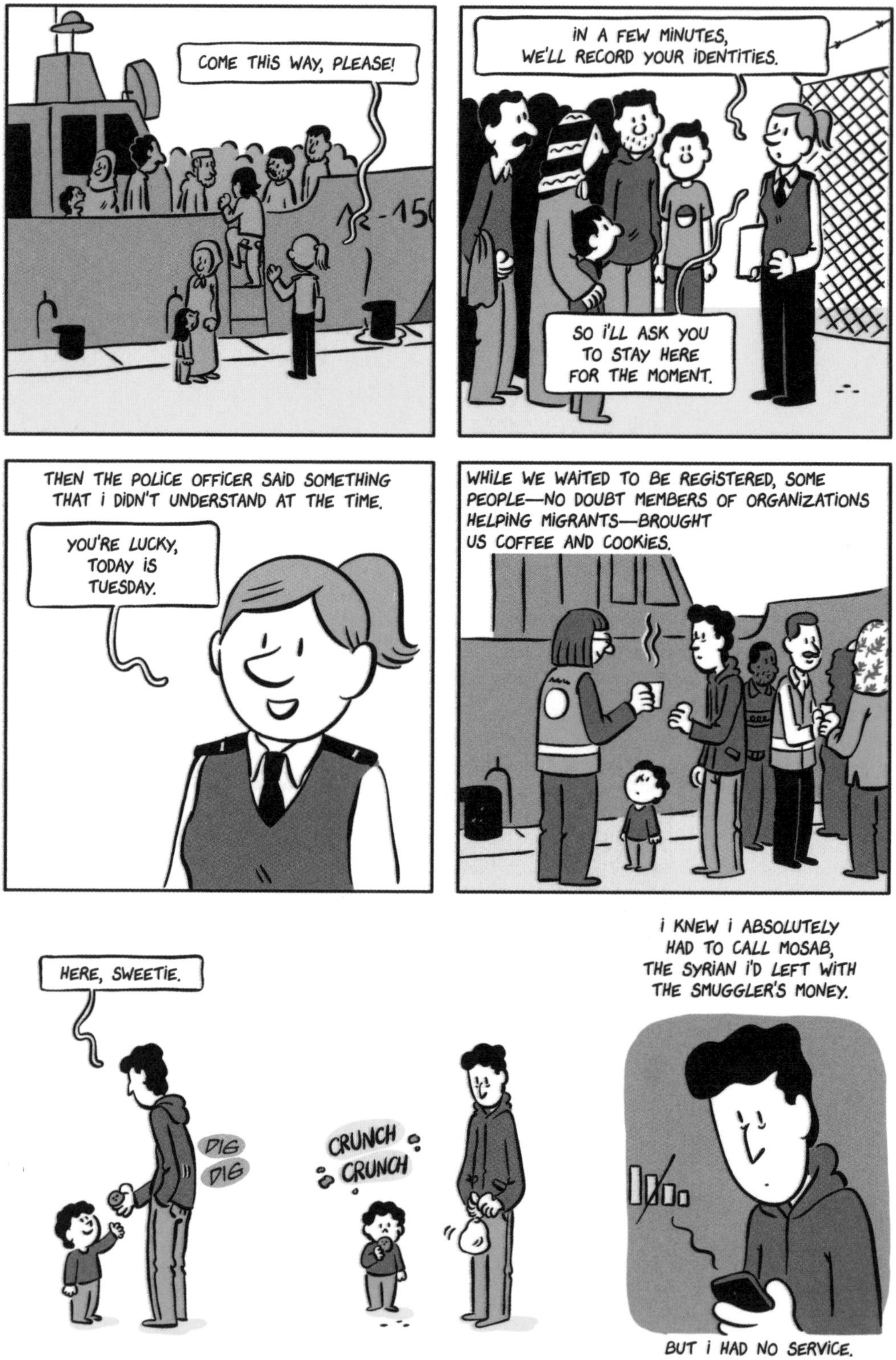
COME THIS WAY, PLEASE!
IN A FEW MINUTES, WE'LL RECORD YOUR IDENTITIES.
SO I'LL ASK YOU TO STAY HERE FOR THE MOMENT.
THEN THE POLICE OFFICER SAID SOMETHING THAT I DIDN'T UNDERSTAND AT THE TIME.
YOU'RE LUCKY, TODAY IS TUESDAY.
WHILE WE WAITED TO BE REGISTERED, SOME PEOPLE—NO DOUBT MEMBERS OF ORGANIZATIONS HELPING MIGRANTS—BROUGHT US COFFEE AND COOKIES.
HERE, SWEETIE.
DIG
DIG
CRUNCH
CRUNCH
I KNEW I ABSOLUTELY HAD TO CALL MOSAB, THE SYRIAN I'D LEFT WITH THE SMUGGLER'S MONEY.
BUT I HAD NO SERVICE.

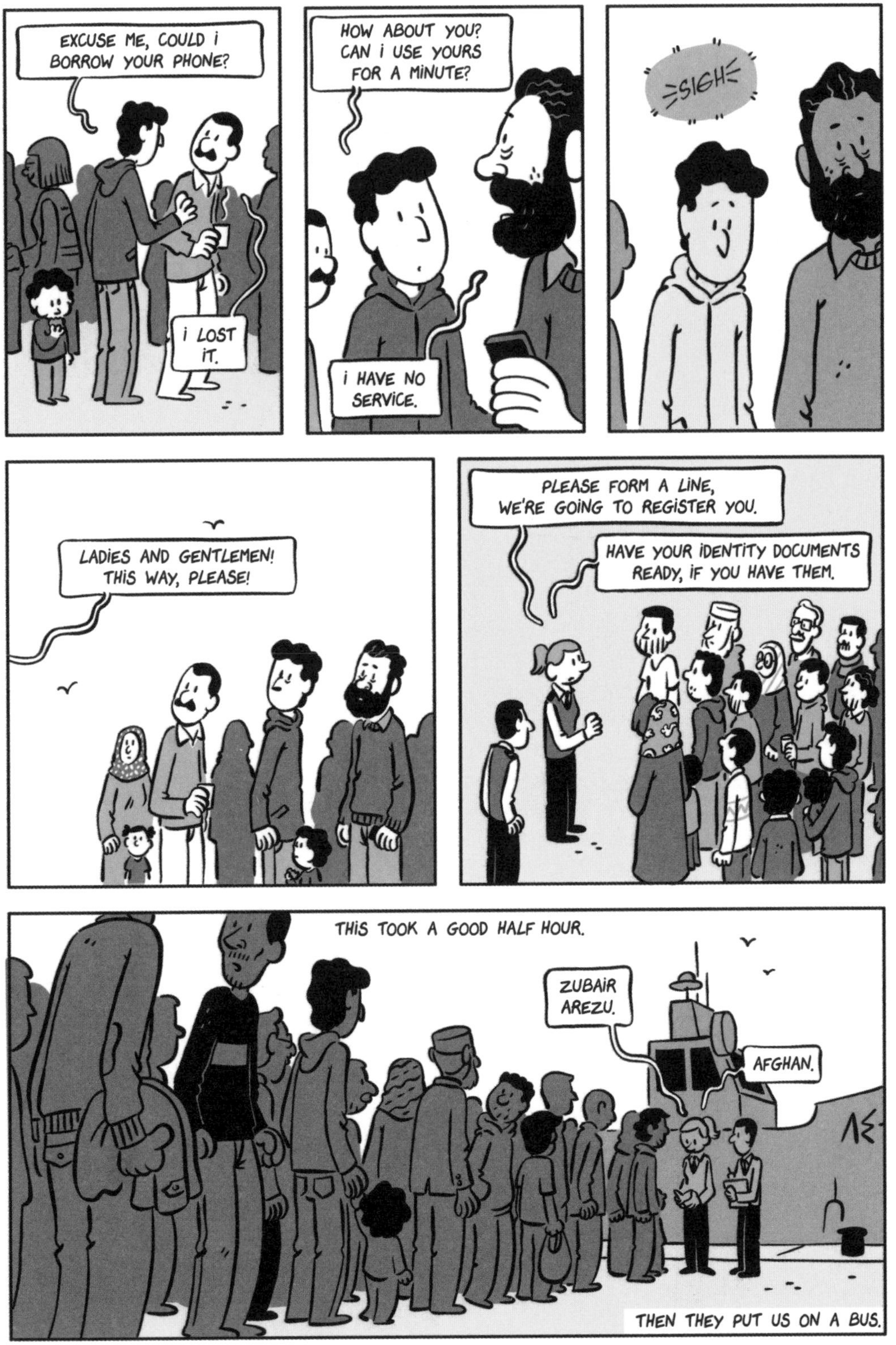
EXCUSE ME, COULD I BORROW YOUR PHONE?
I LOST IT.
HOW ABOUT YOU? CAN I USE YOURS FOR A MINUTE?
I HAVE NO SERVICE.
SIGH
LADIES AND GENTLEMEN! THIS WAY, PLEASE!
PLEASE FORM A LINE, WE'RE GOING TO REGISTER YOU.
HAVE YOUR IDENTITY DOCUMENTS READY, IF YOU HAVE THEM.
THIS TOOK A GOOD HALF HOUR.
ZUBAIR AREZU.
AFGHAN.
THEN THEY PUT US ON A BUS.

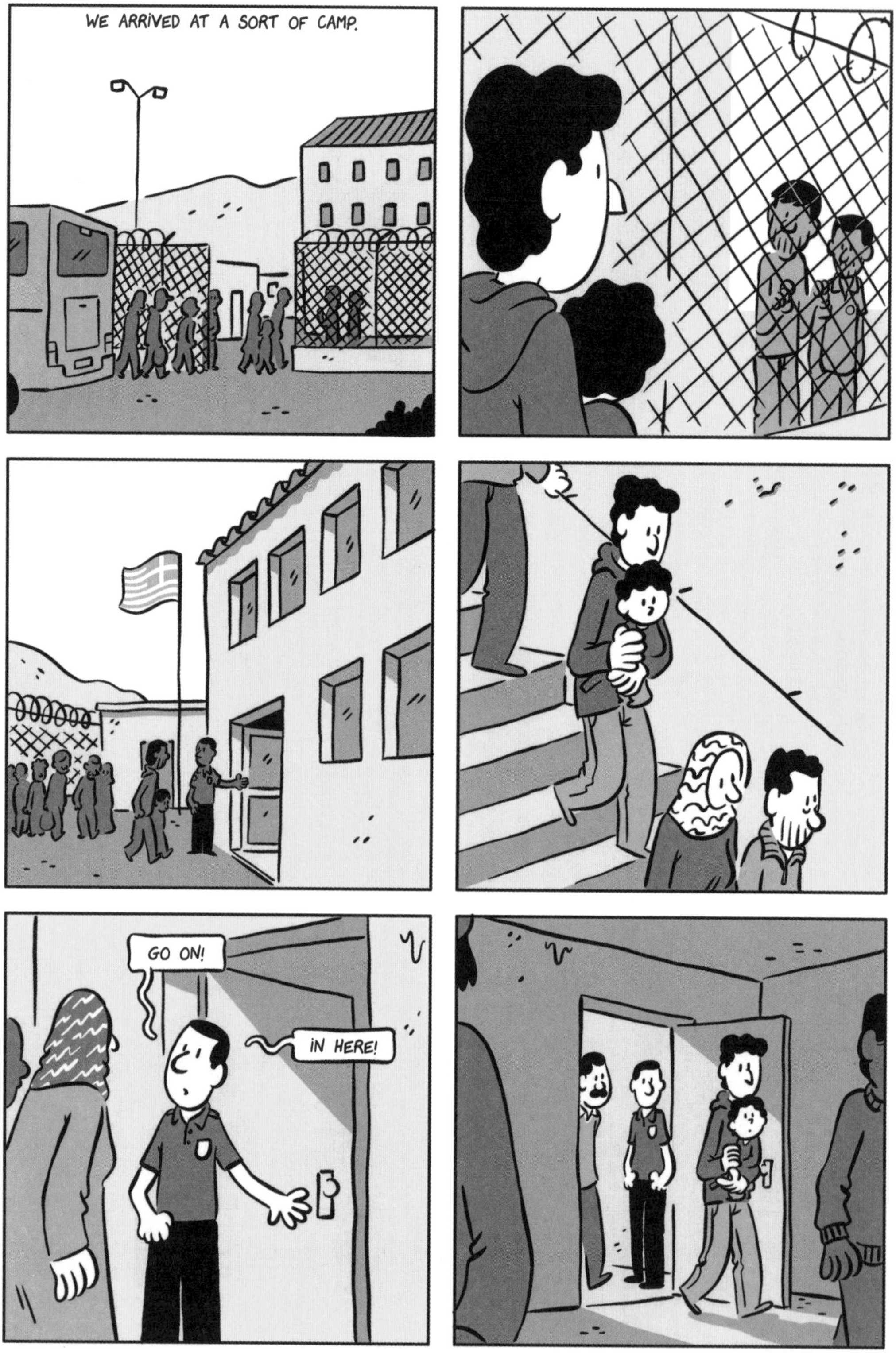
WE ARRIVED AT A SORT OF CAMP.
GO ON!
IN HERE!

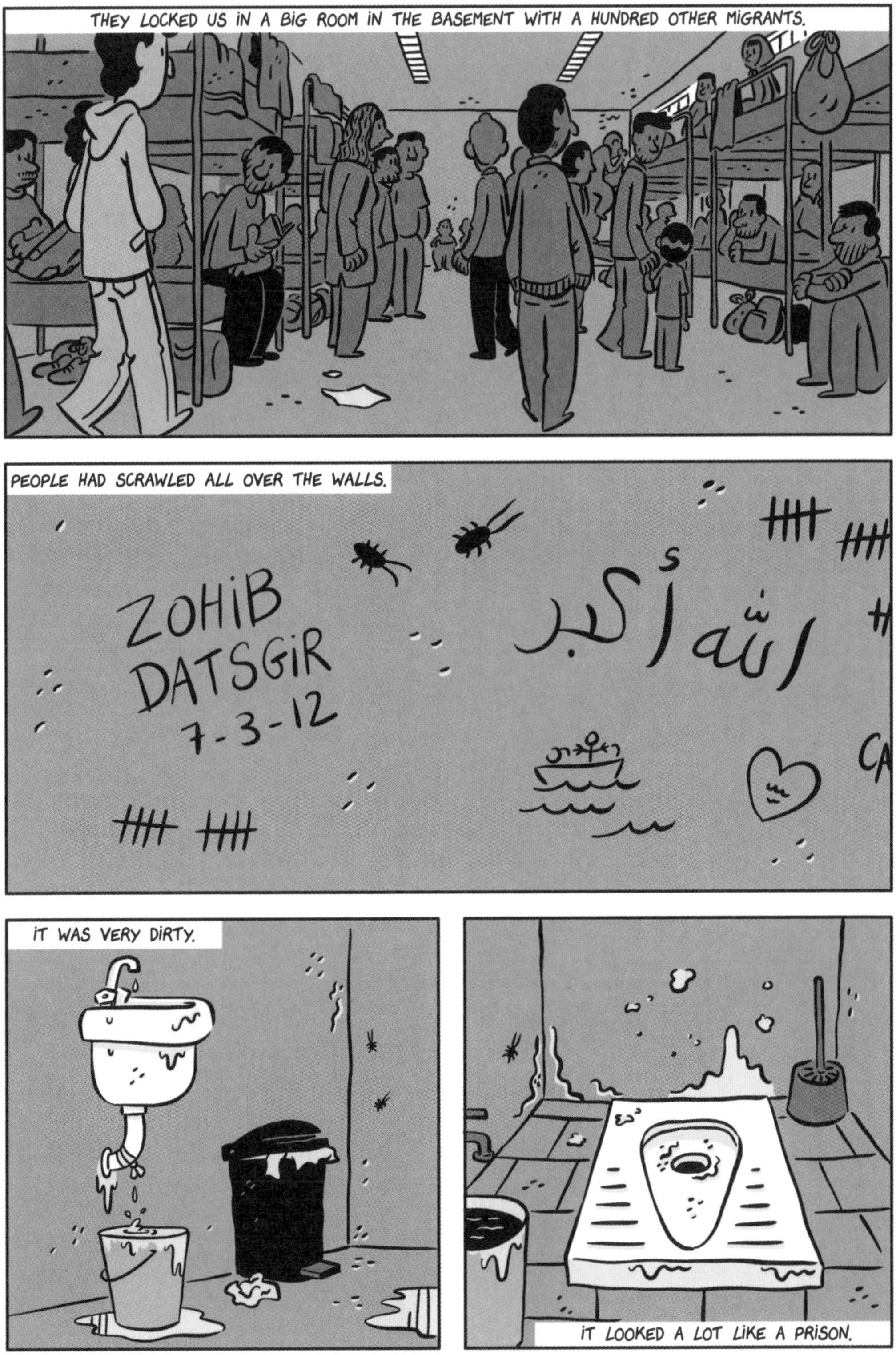
THEY LOCKED US IN A BIG ROOM IN THE BASEMENT WITH A HUNDRED OTHER MIGRANTS.
PEOPLE HAD SCRAWLED ALL OVER THE WALLS.
ZOHIB
DATSGIR
7-3-12
الله أكبر
IT WAS VERY DIRTY.
IT LOOKED A LOT LIKE A PRISON.

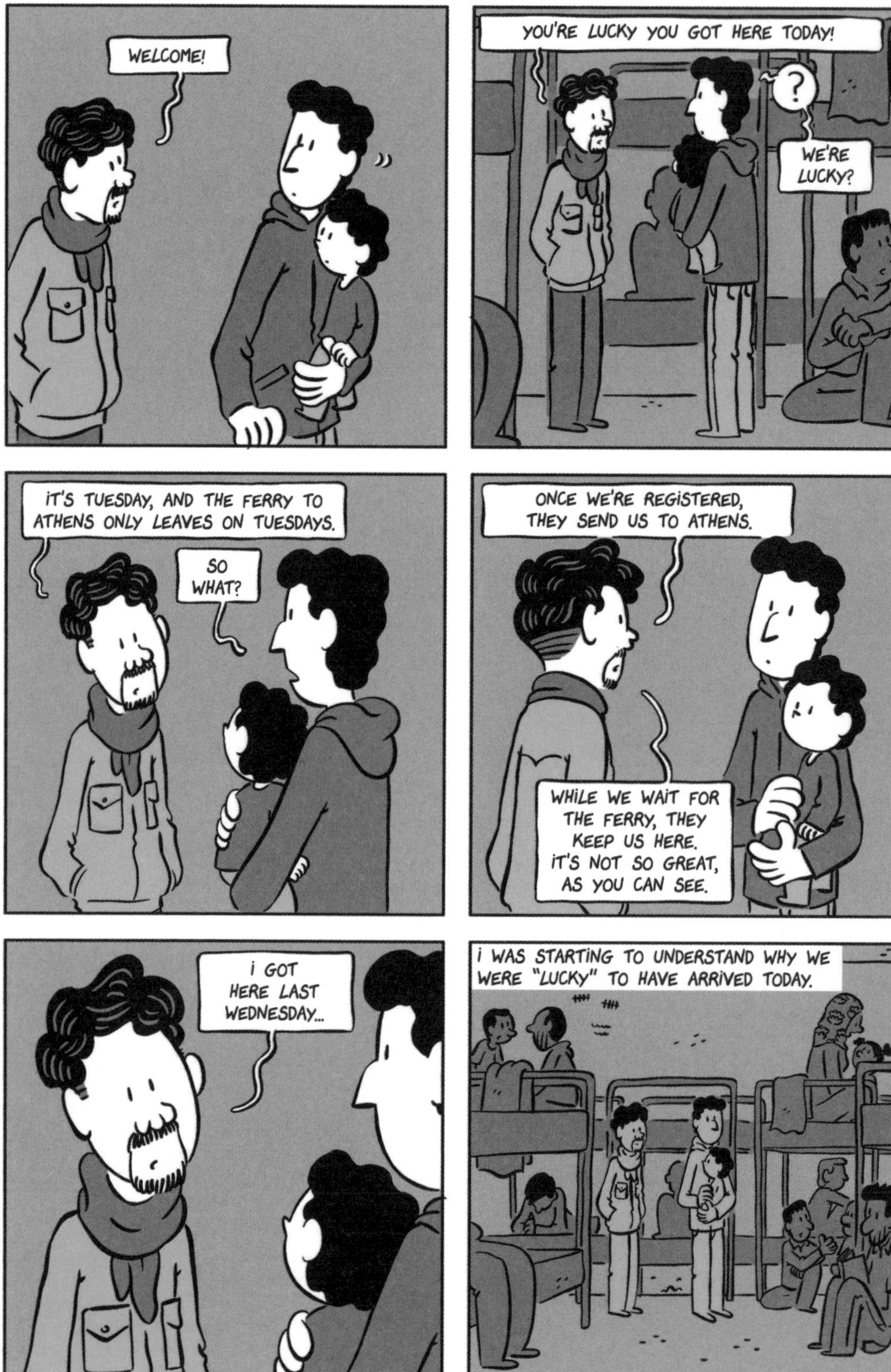
WELCOME!
YOU'RE LUCKY YOU GOT HERE TODAY!
?
WE'RE LUCKY?
IT'S TUESDAY, AND THE FERRY TO ATHENS ONLY LEAVES ON TUESDAYS.
SO WHAT?
ONCE WE'RE REGISTERED, THEY SEND US TO ATHENS.
WHILE WE WAIT FOR THE FERRY, THEY KEEP US HERE. IT'S NOT SO GREAT, AS YOU CAN SEE.
I GOT HERE LAST WEDNESDAY...
I WAS STARTING TO UNDERSTAND WHY WE WERE "LUCKY" TO HAVE ARRIVED TODAY.

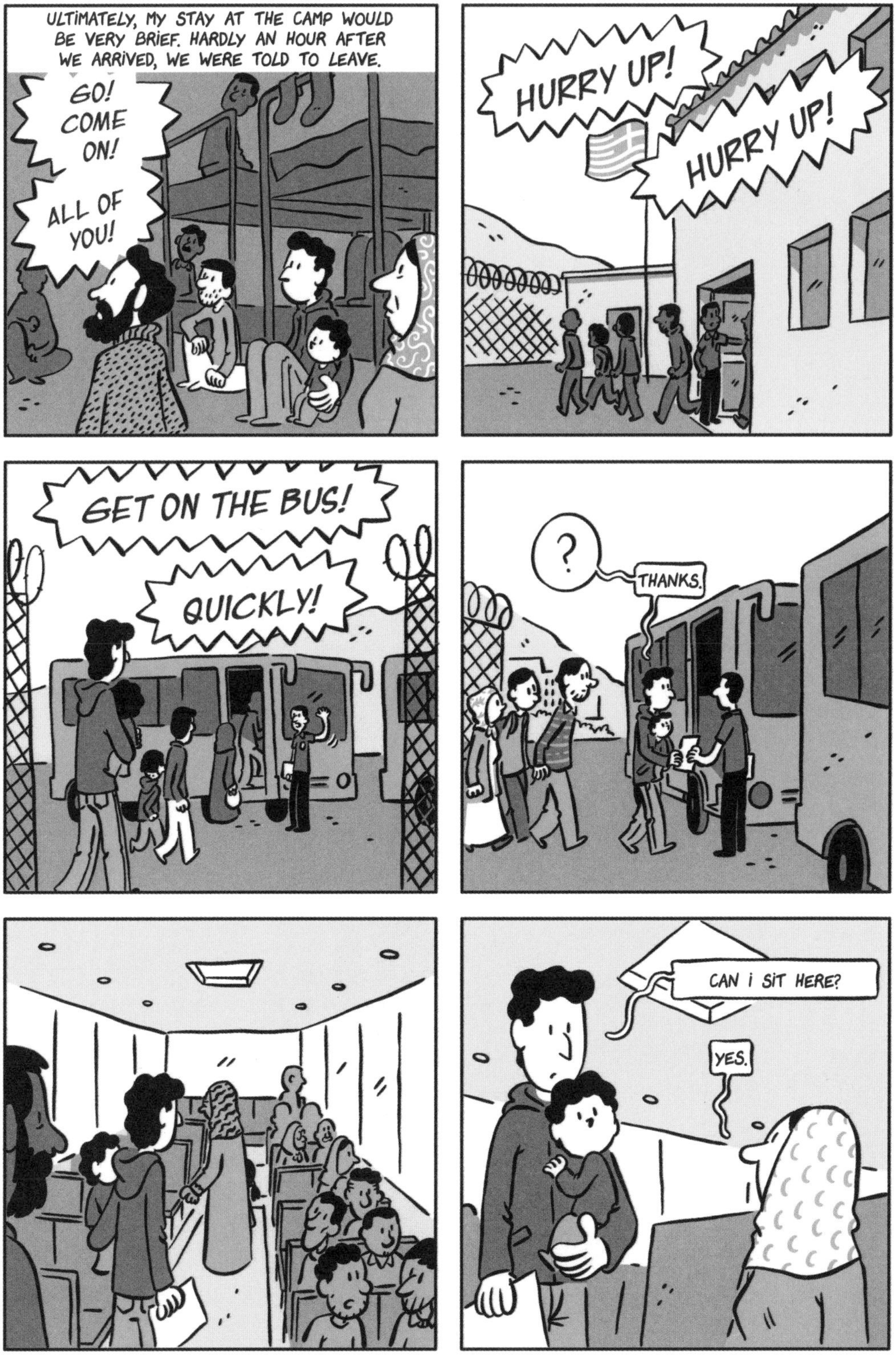
ULTIMATELY, MY STAY AT THE CAMP WOULD BE VERY BRIEF. HARDLY AN HOUR AFTER WE ARRIVED, WE WERE TOLD TO LEAVE.
GO! COME ON!
ALL OF YOU!
HURRY UP!
HURRY UP!
GET ON THE BUS!
QUICKLY!
?
THANKS.
CAN I SIT HERE?
YES.

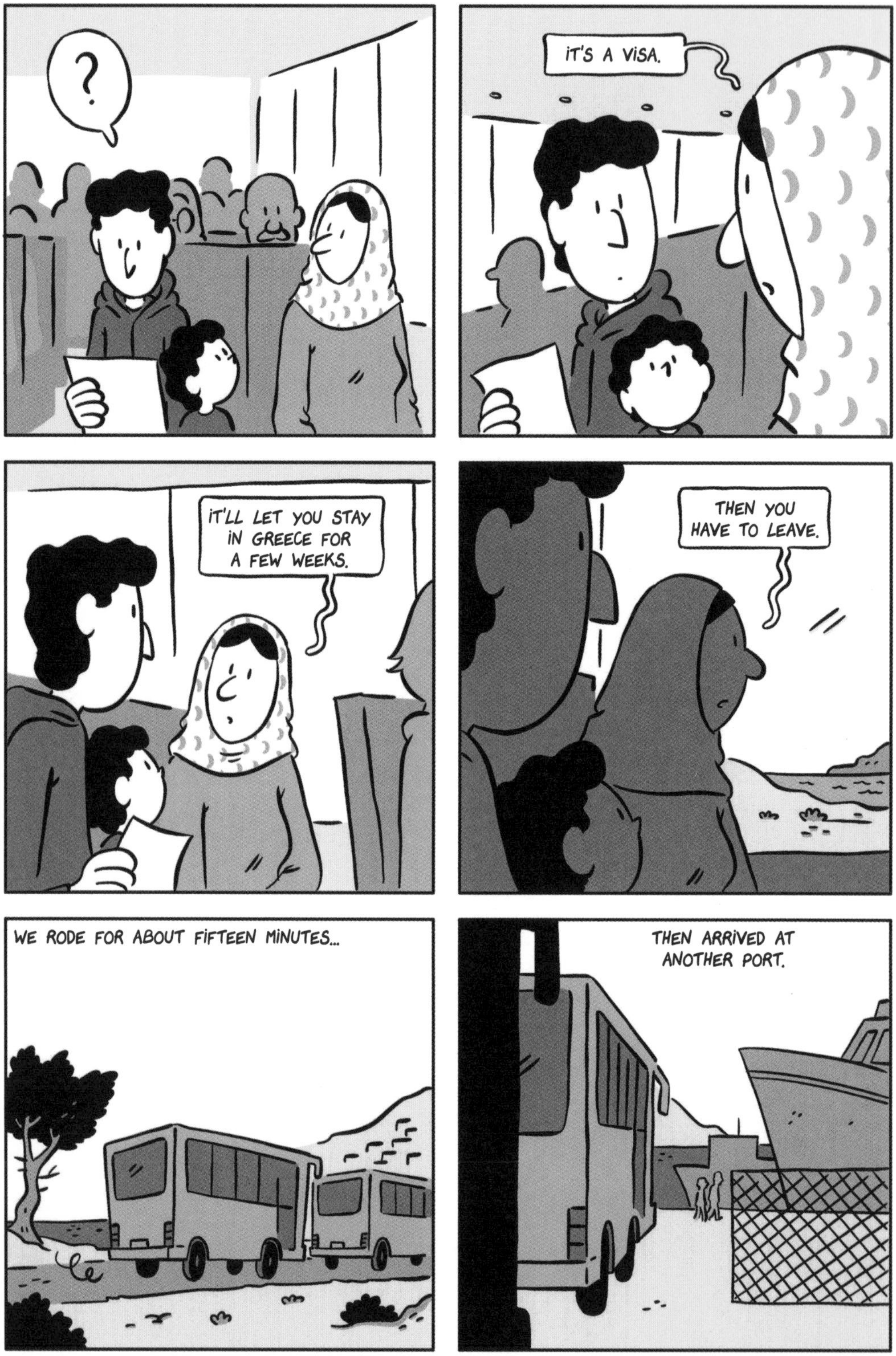
?
IT'S A VISA.
IT'LL LET YOU STAY IN GREECE FOR A FEW WEEKS.
THEN YOU HAVE TO LEAVE.
WE RODE FOR ABOUT FIFTEEN MINUTES...
THEN ARRIVED AT ANOTHER PORT.

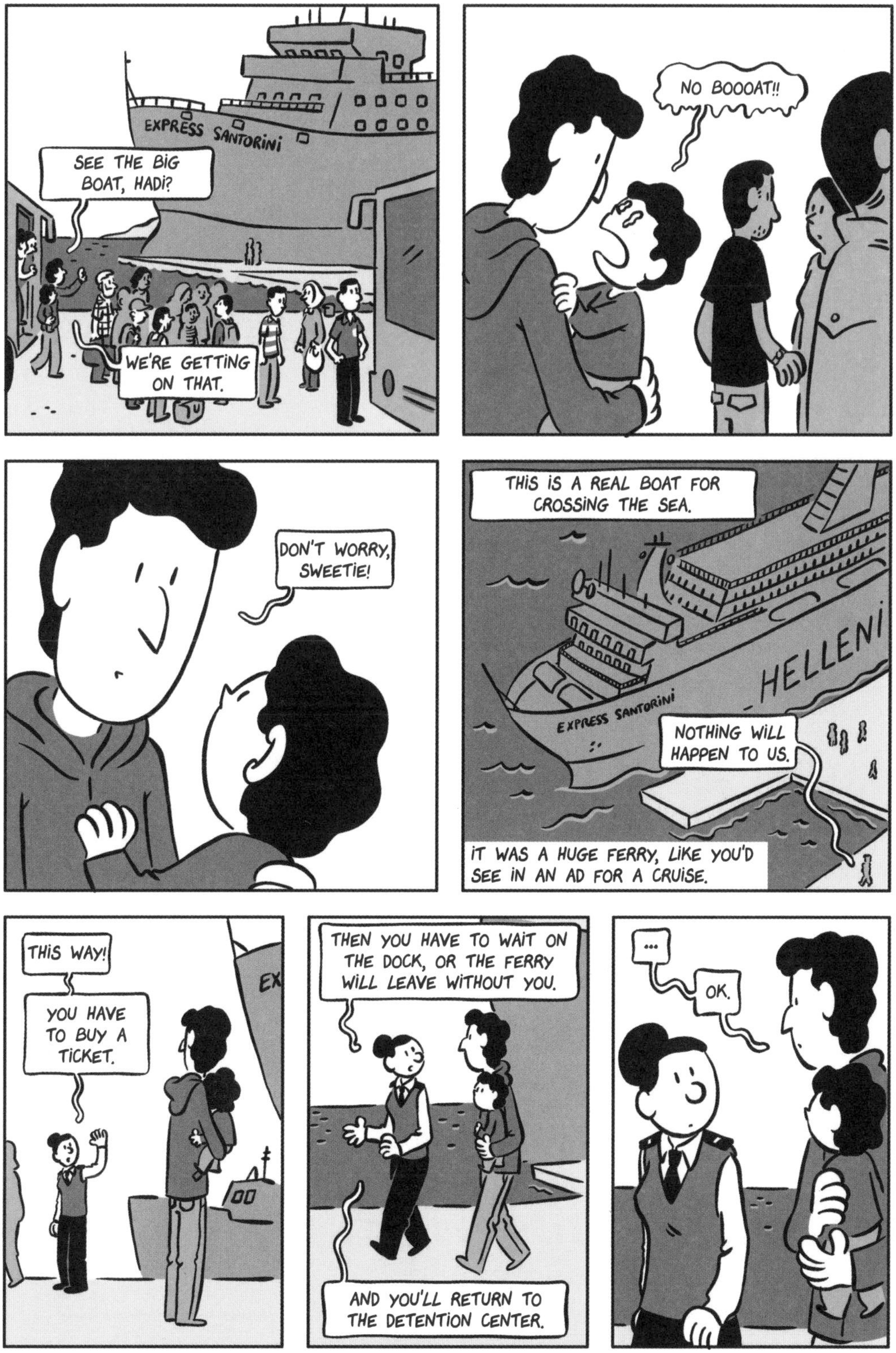
EXPRESS SANTORINI
SEE THE BIG BOAT, HADI?
WE'RE GETTING ON THAT.
NO BOOOAT!!
DON'T WORRY, SWEETIE!
THIS IS A REAL BOAT FOR CROSSING THE SEA.
HELLENI
EXPRESS SANTORINI
NOTHING WILL HAPPEN TO US.
IT WAS A HUGE FERRY, LIKE YOU'D SEE IN AN AD FOR A CRUISE.
THIS WAY!
YOU HAVE TO BUY A TICKET.
EX
THEN YOU HAVE TO WAIT ON THE DOCK, OR THE FERRY WILL LEAVE WITHOUT YOU.
AND YOU'LL RETURN TO THE DETENTION CENTER.
...
OK.

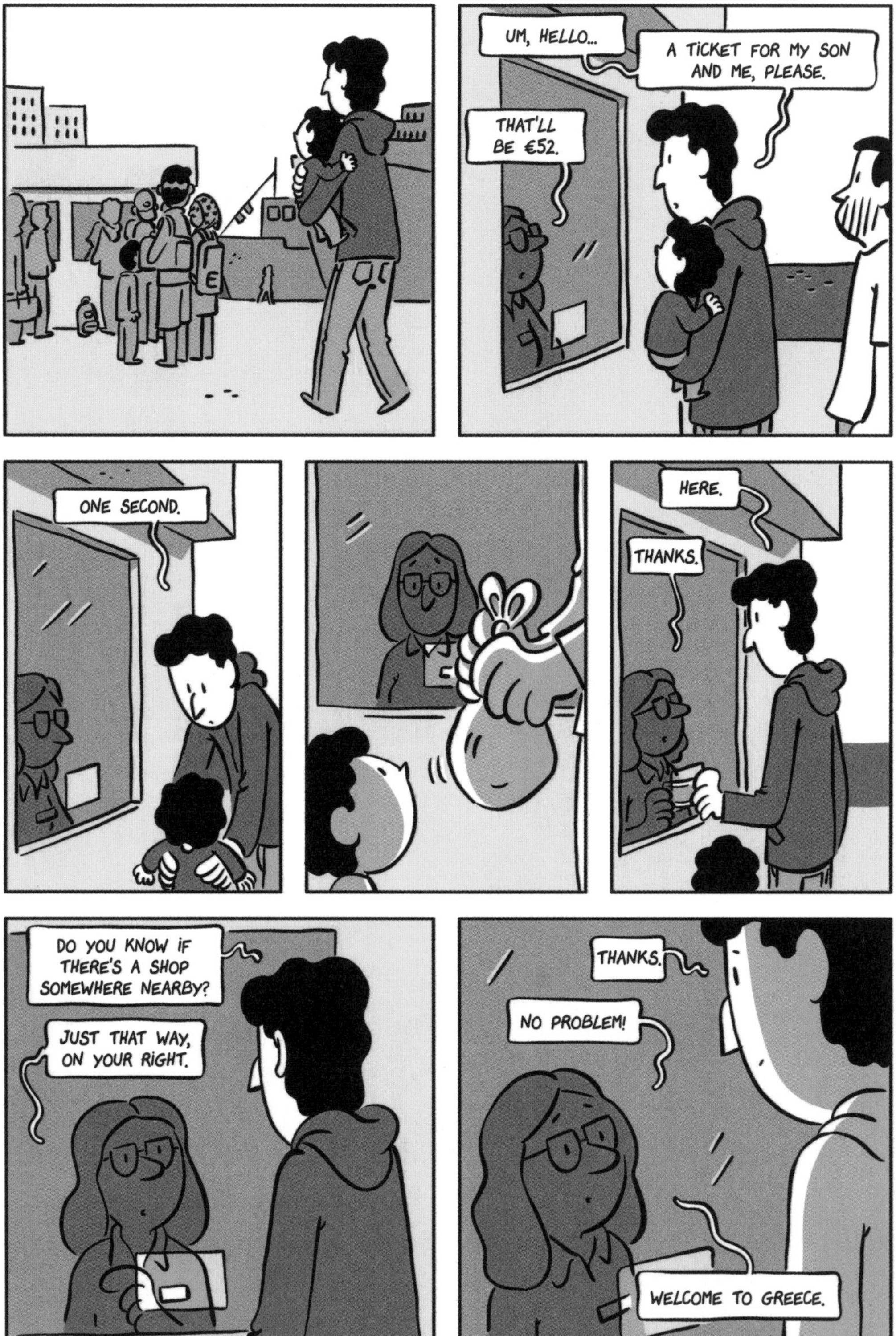
UM, HELLO...
A TICKET FOR MY SON AND ME, PLEASE.
THAT'LL BE €52.
ONE SECOND.
HERE.
THANKS.
DO YOU KNOW IF THERE'S A SHOP SOMEWHERE NEARBY?
JUST THAT WAY, ON YOUR RIGHT.
THANKS.
NO PROBLEM!
WELCOME TO GREECE.

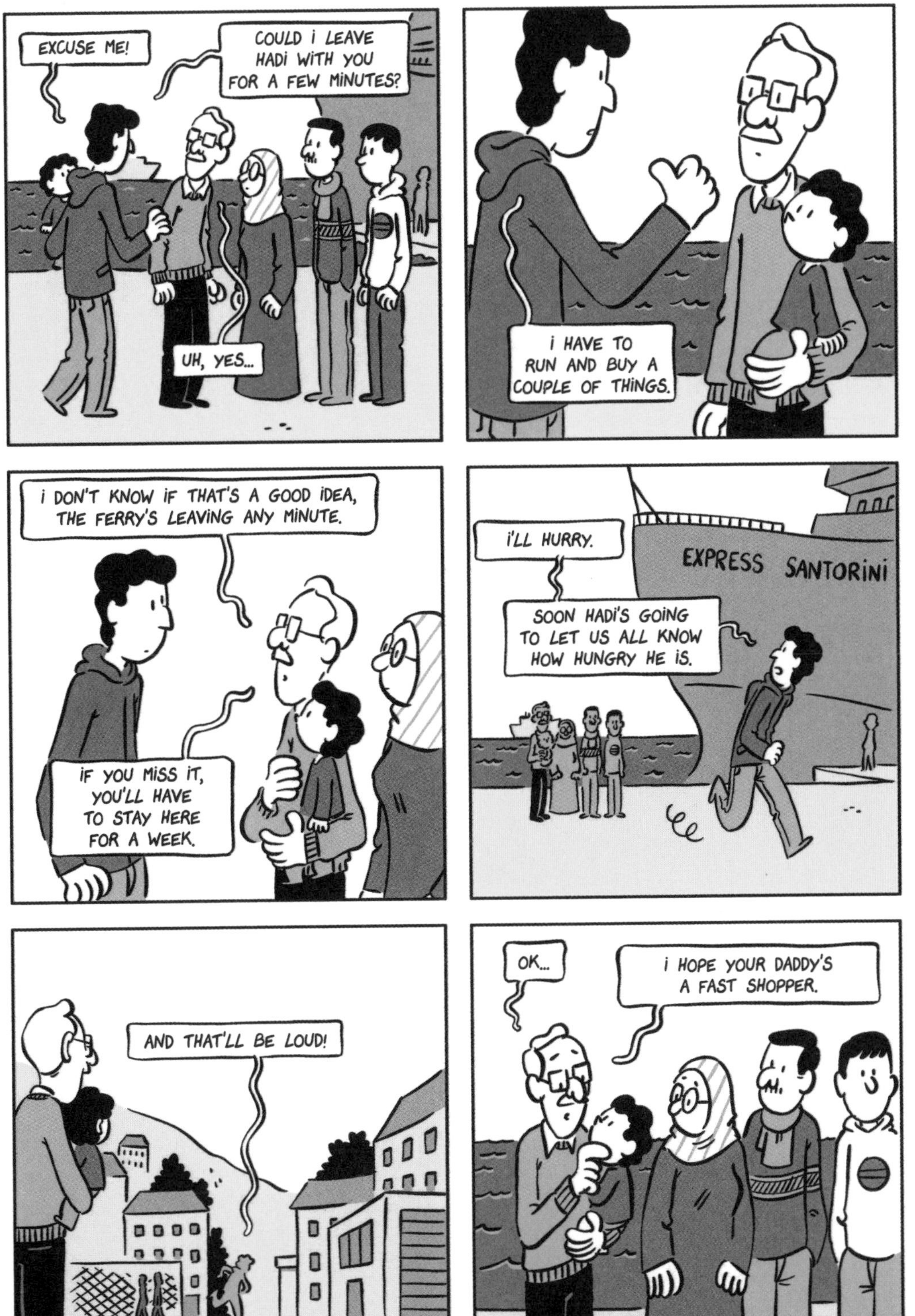
EXCUSE ME!
COULD i LEAVE HADi WiTH YOU FOR A FEW MiNUTES?
UH, YES...
i HAVE TO RUN AND BUY A COUPLE OF THiNGS.
i DON'T KNOW iF THAT'S A GOOD iDEA, THE FERRY'S LEAViNG ANY MiNUTE.
iF YOU MiSS iT, YOU'LL HAVE TO STAY HERE FOR A WEEK.
i'LL HURRY.
EXPRESS SANTORINI
SOON HADi'S GOiNG TO LET US ALL KNOW HOW HUNGRY HE iS.
AND THAT'LL BE LOUD!
OK...
i HOPE YOUR DADDY'S A FAST SHOPPER.

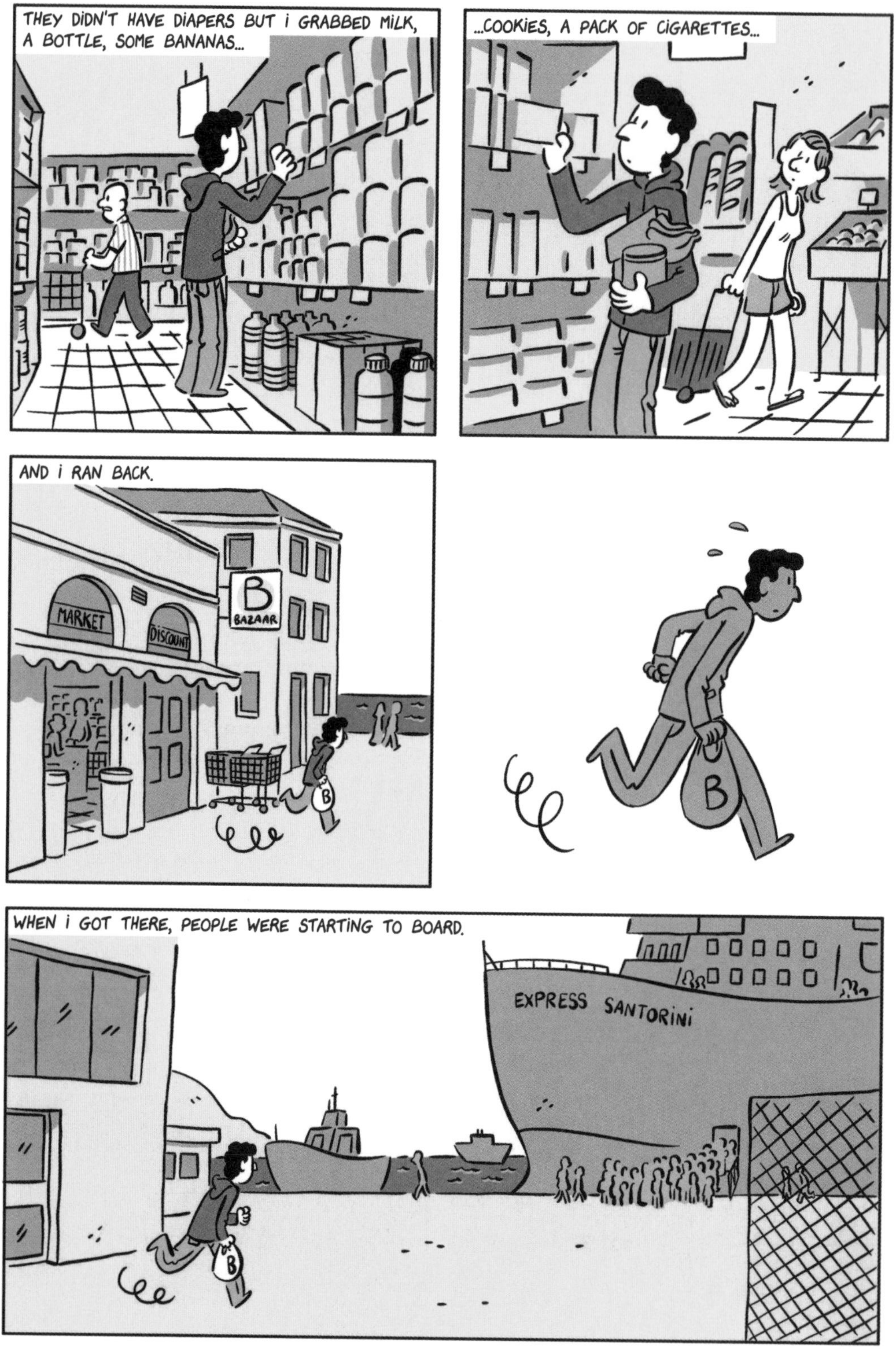
THEY DIDN'T HAVE DIAPERS BUT I GRABBED MILK, A BOTTLE, SOME BANANAS...
...COOKIES, A PACK OF CIGARETTES...
AND I RAN BACK.
MARKET
DISCOUNT
B
BAZAAR
B
B
WHEN I GOT THERE, PEOPLE WERE STARTING TO BOARD.
EXPRESS SANTORINI
B

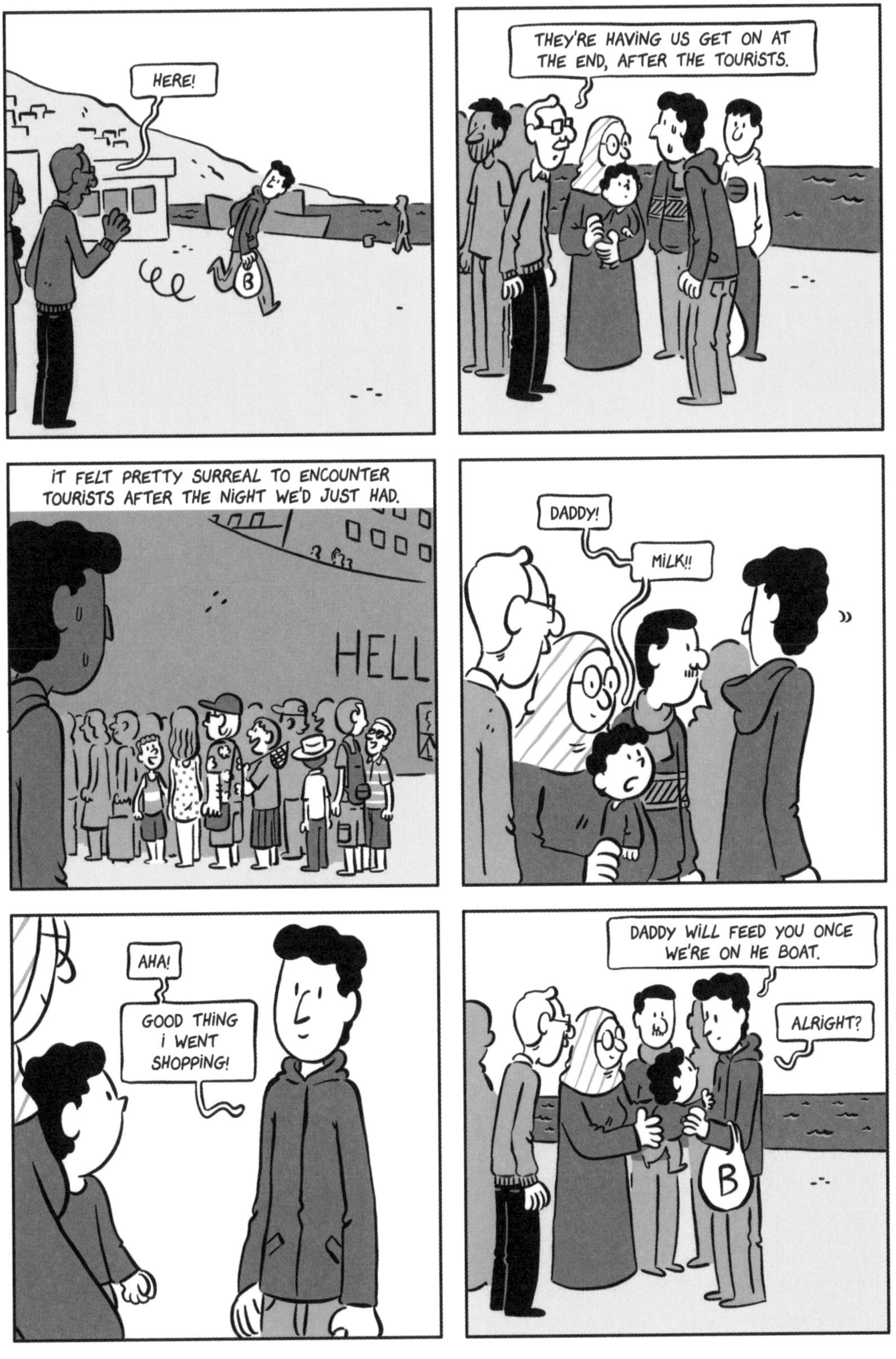
HERE!
THEY'RE HAVING US GET ON AT THE END, AFTER THE TOURISTS.
IT FELT PRETTY SURREAL TO ENCOUNTER TOURISTS AFTER THE NIGHT WE'D JUST HAD.
HELL
DADDY!
MILK!!
AHA!
GOOD THING I WENT SHOPPING!
DADDY WILL FEED YOU ONCE WE'RE ON HE BOAT.
ALRIGHT?

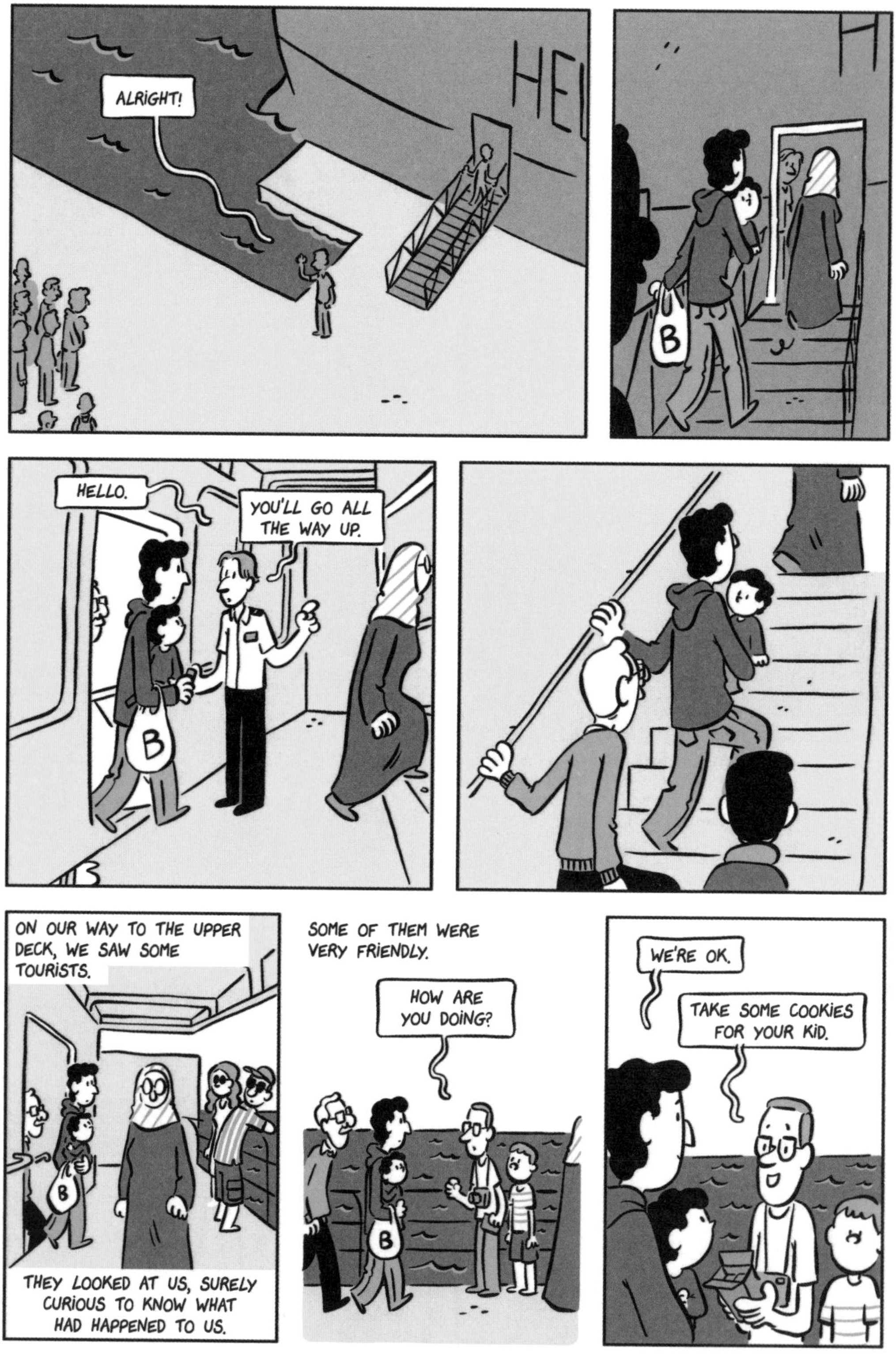
ALRIGHT!
HE
H
HELLO.
YOU'LL GO ALL THE WAY UP.
B
ON OUR WAY TO THE UPPER DECK, WE SAW SOME TOURISTS.
THEY LOOKED AT US, SURELY CURIOUS TO KNOW WHAT HAD HAPPENED TO US.
SOME OF THEM WERE VERY FRIENDLY.
HOW ARE YOU DOING?
WE'RE OK.
TAKE SOME COOKIES FOR YOUR KID.

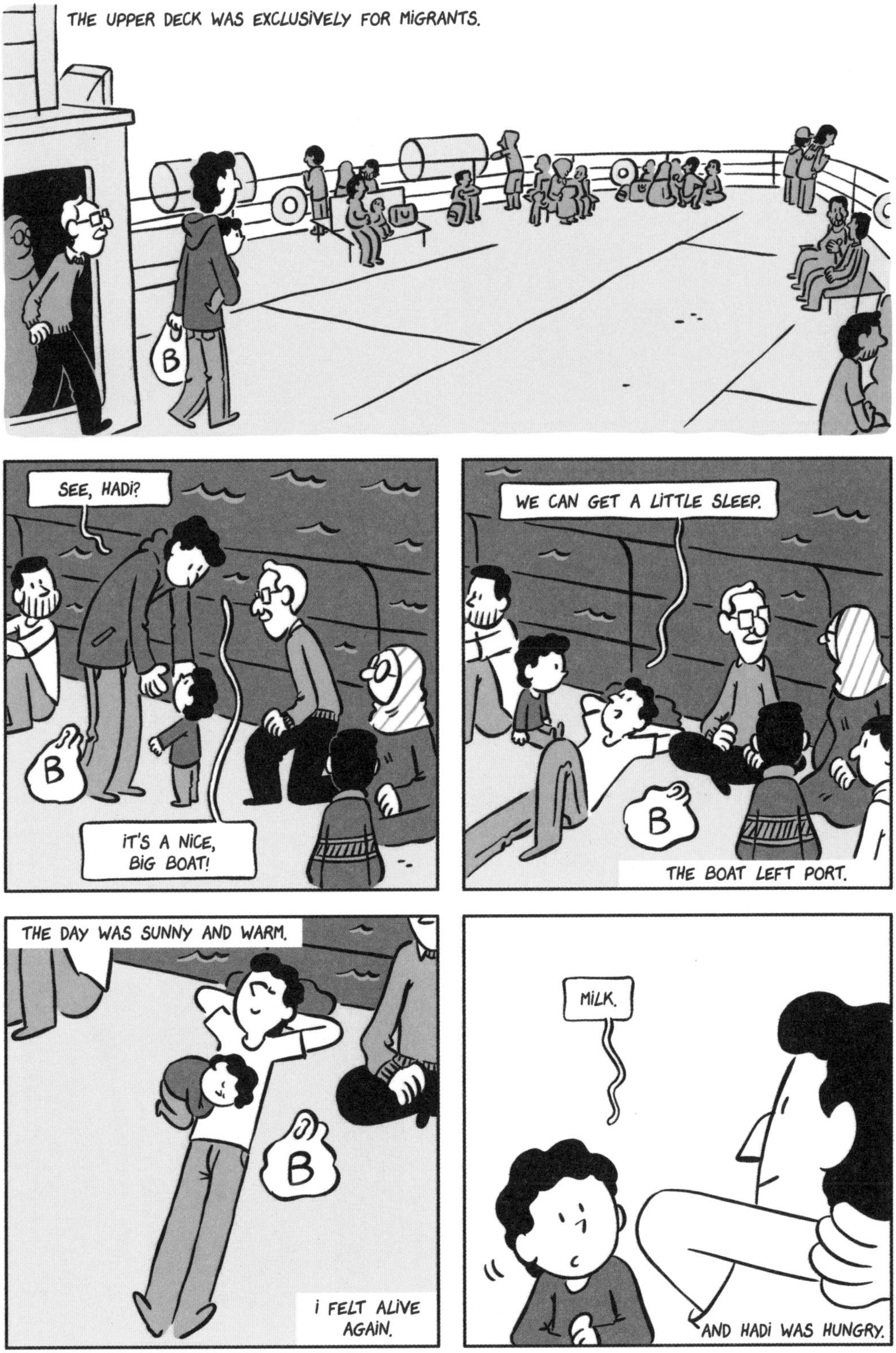
THE UPPER DECK WAS EXCLUSIVELY FOR MIGRANTS.
SEE, HADI?
IT'S A NICE, BIG BOAT!
WE CAN GET A LITTLE SLEEP.
THE BOAT LEFT PORT.
THE DAY WAS SUNNY AND WARM.
I FELT ALIVE AGAIN.
MILK.
AND HADI WAS HUNGRY.

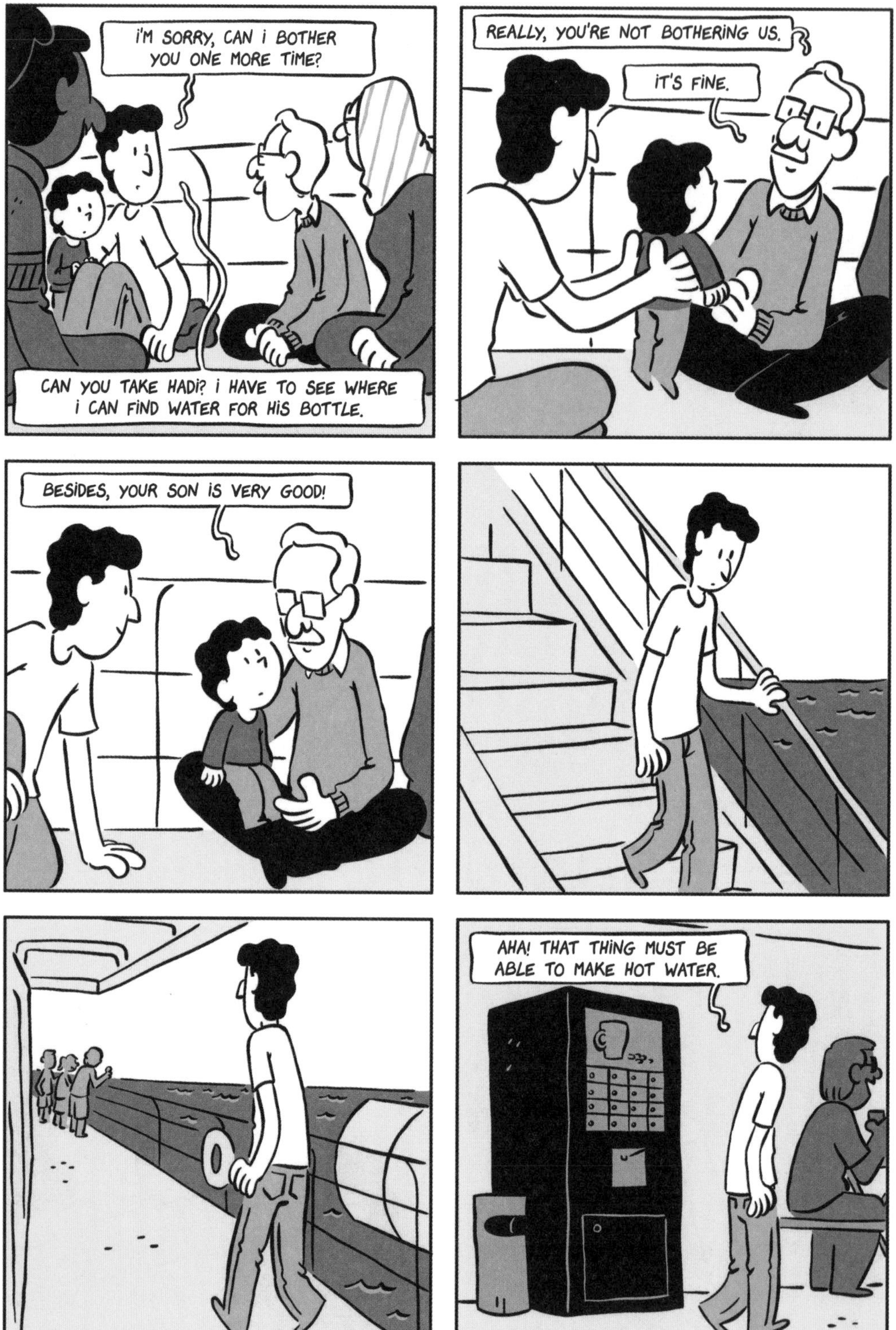
I'M SORRY, CAN I BOTHER YOU ONE MORE TIME?
CAN YOU TAKE HADI? I HAVE TO SEE WHERE I CAN FIND WATER FOR HIS BOTTLE.
REALLY, YOU'RE NOT BOTHERING US.
IT'S FINE.
BESIDES, YOUR SON IS VERY GOOD!
AHA! THAT THING MUST BE ABLE TO MAKE HOT WATER.

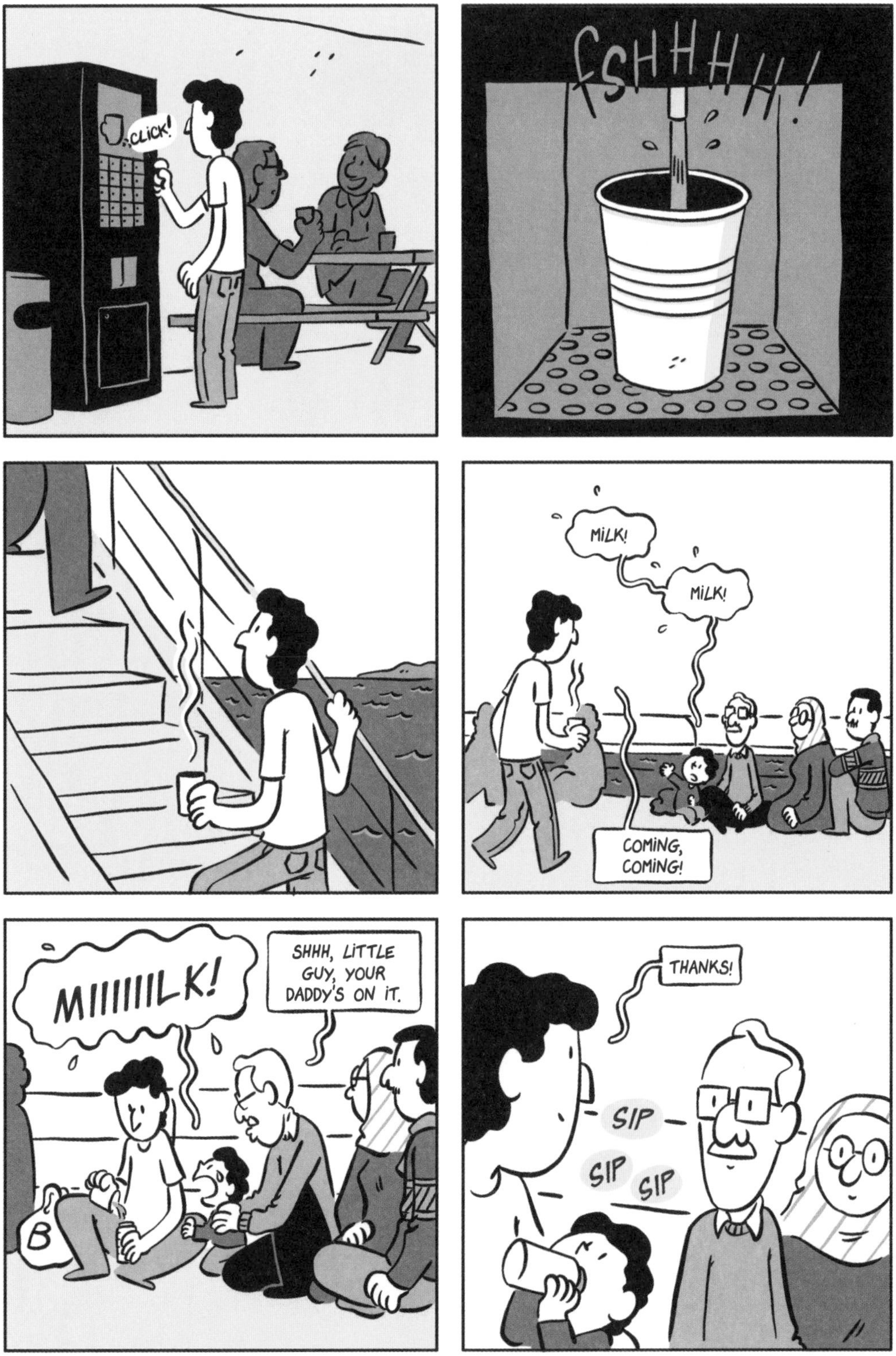
CLICK!
fSHHHHH!
MILK!
MILK!
COMING, COMING!
MIIIIIILK!
SHHH, LITTLE GUY, YOUR DADDY'S ON IT.
THANKS!
SIP
SIP
SIP

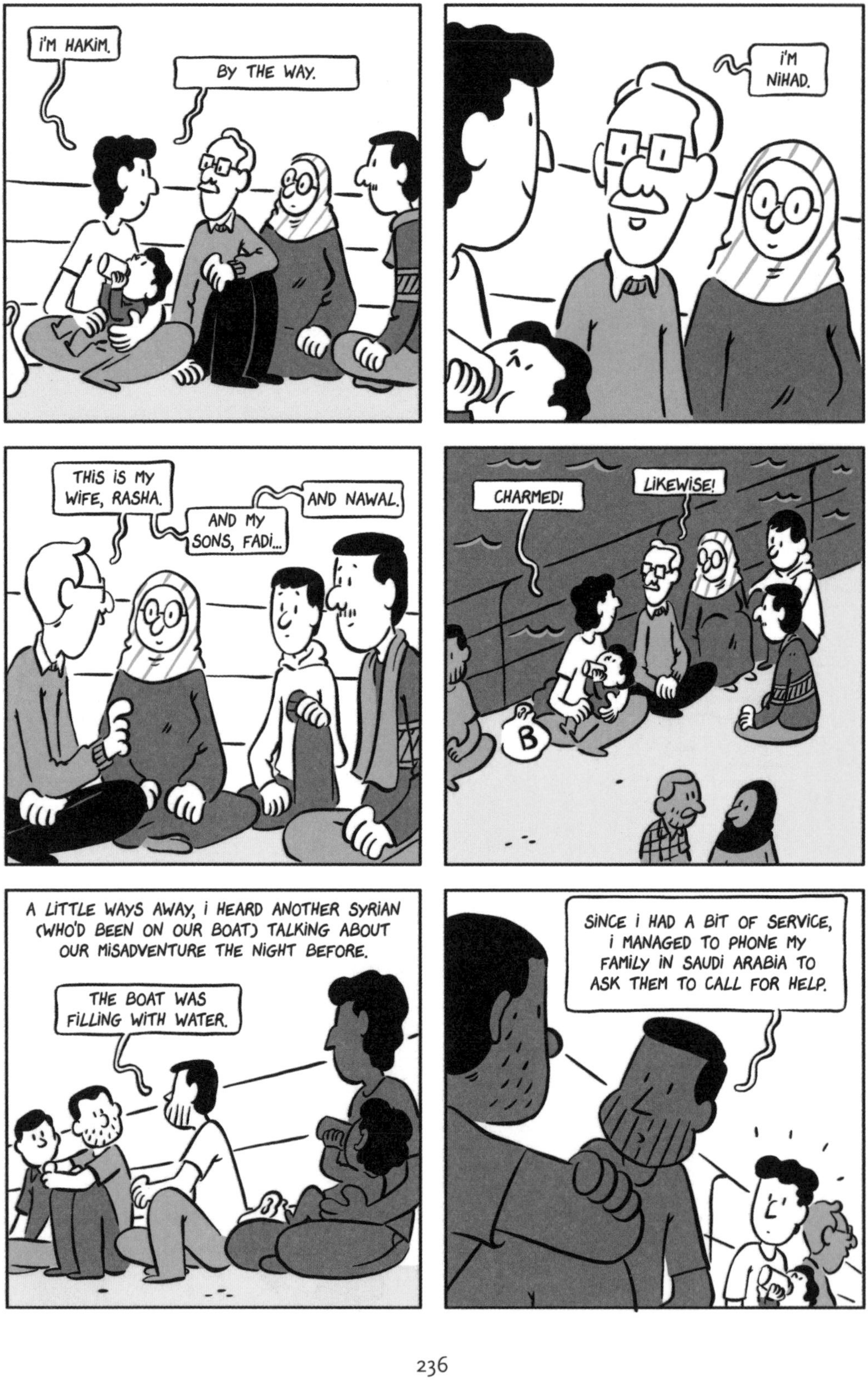
I'M HAKIM.
BY THE WAY.
I'M NIHAD.
THIS IS MY WIFE, RASHA.
AND MY SONS, FADI...
AND NAWAL.
CHARMED!
LIKEWISE!
B
A LITTLE WAYS AWAY, I HEARD ANOTHER SYRIAN (WHO'D BEEN ON OUR BOAT) TALKING ABOUT OUR MISADVENTURE THE NIGHT BEFORE.
THE BOAT WAS FILLING WITH WATER.
SINCE I HAD A BIT OF SERVICE, I MANAGED TO PHONE MY FAMILY IN SAUDI ARABIA TO ASK THEM TO CALL FOR HELP.

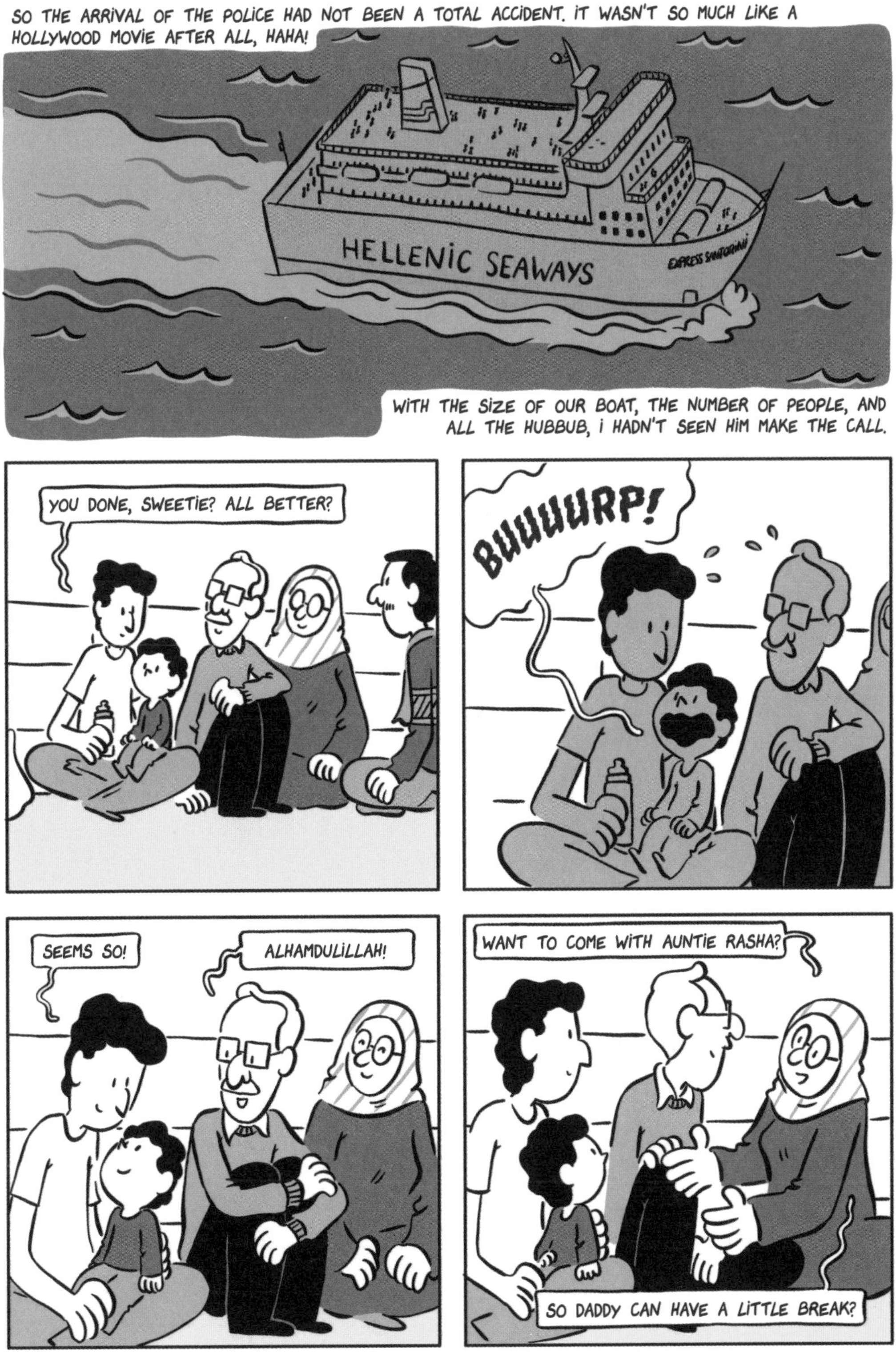
SO THE ARRIVAL OF THE POLICE HAD NOT BEEN A TOTAL ACCIDENT. IT WASN'T SO MUCH LIKE A HOLLYWOOD MOVIE AFTER ALL, HAHA!
HELLENIC SEAWAYS
EXPRESS SANTORINI
WITH THE SIZE OF OUR BOAT, THE NUMBER OF PEOPLE, AND ALL THE HUBBUB, I HADN'T SEEN HIM MAKE THE CALL.
YOU DONE, SWEETIE? ALL BETTER?
BUUUURP!
SEEMS SO!
ALHAMDULILLAH!
WANT TO COME WITH AUNTIE RASHA?
SO DADDY CAN HAVE A LITTLE BREAK?

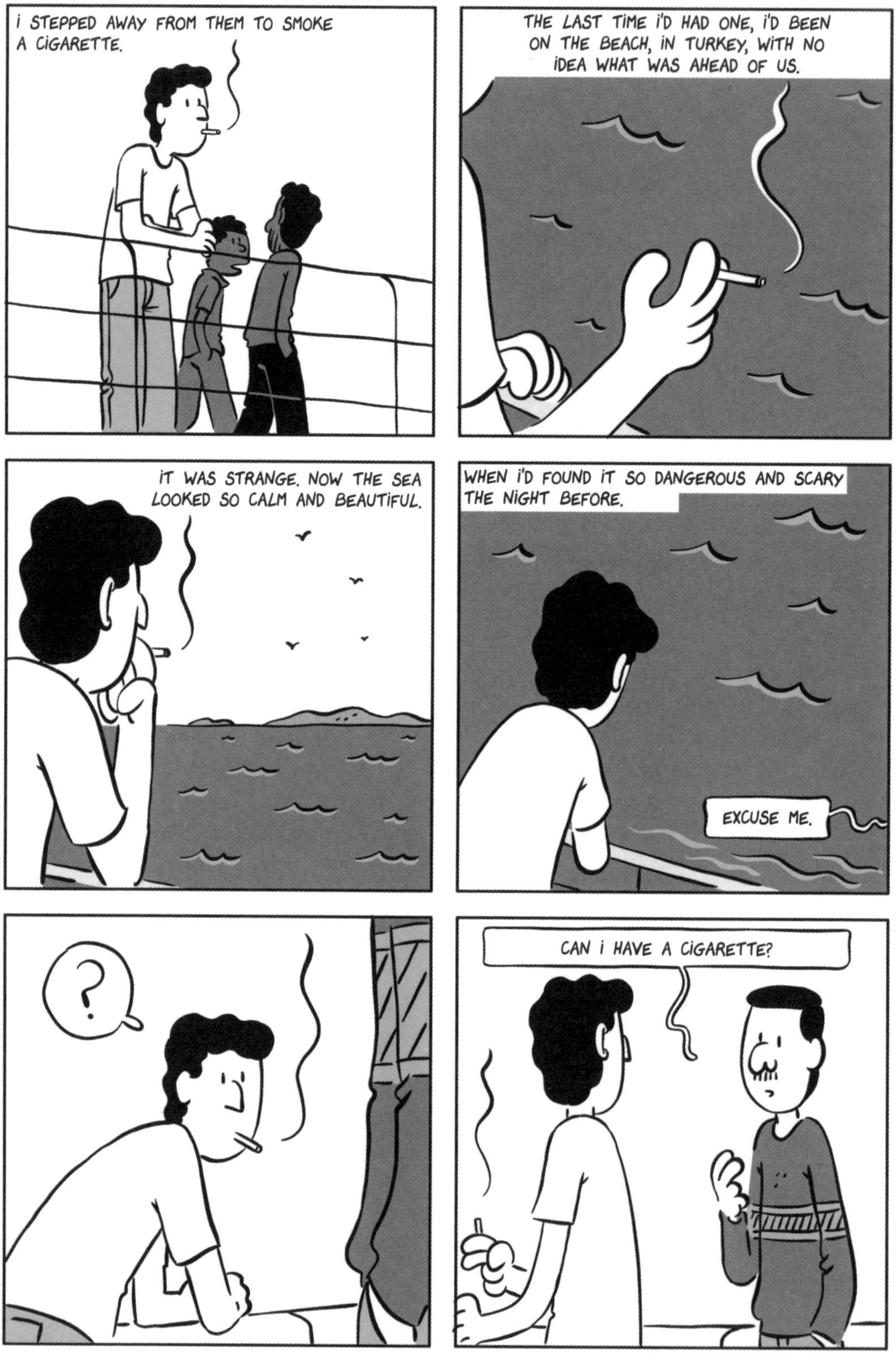
I STEPPED AWAY FROM THEM TO SMOKE A CIGARETTE.
THE LAST TIME I'D HAD ONE, I'D BEEN ON THE BEACH, IN TURKEY, WITH NO IDEA WHAT WAS AHEAD OF US.
IT WAS STRANGE. NOW THE SEA LOOKED SO CALM AND BEAUTIFUL.
WHEN I'D FOUND IT SO DANGEROUS AND SCARY THE NIGHT BEFORE.
EXCUSE ME.
?
CAN I HAVE A CIGARETTE?

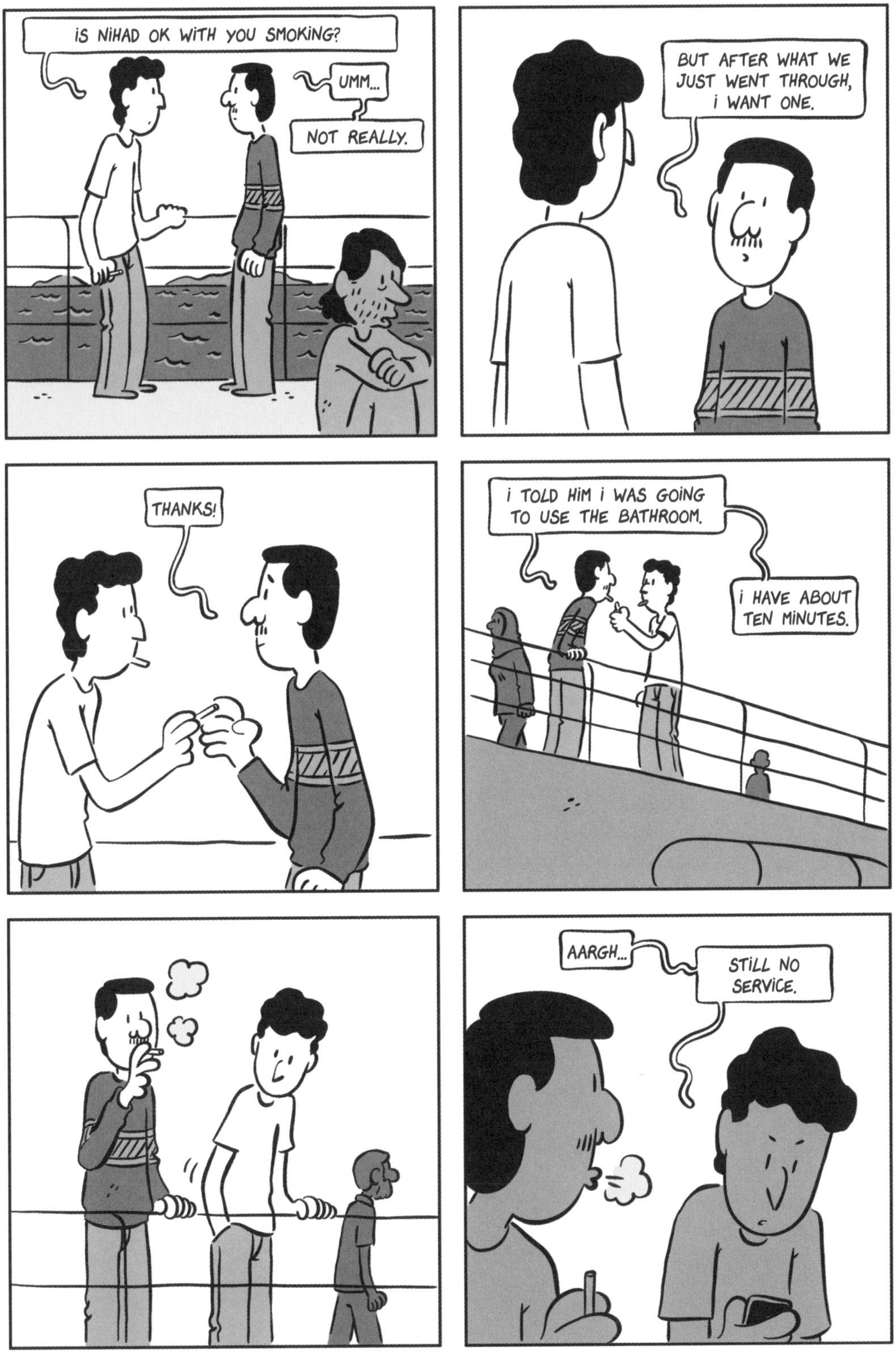
iS NiHAD OK WiTH YOU SMOKiNG?
UMM...
NOT REALLY.
BUT AFTER WHAT WE JUST WENT THROUGH, i WANT ONE.
THANKS!
i TOLD HiM i WAS GOiNG TO USE THE BATHROOM.
i HAVE ABOUT TEN MiNUTES.
AARGH...
STiLL NO SERViCE.

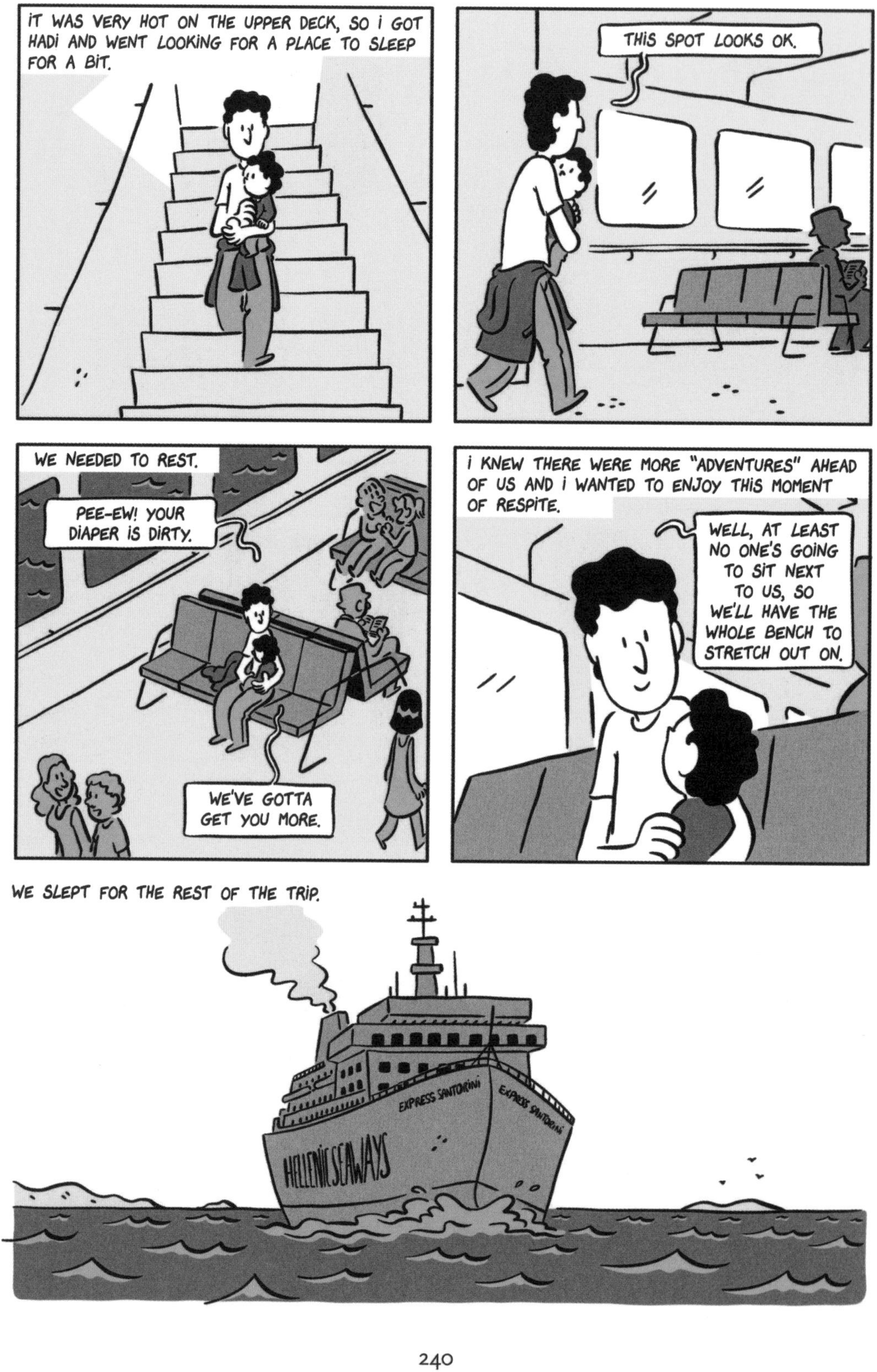
IT WAS VERY HOT ON THE UPPER DECK, SO I GOT HADI AND WENT LOOKING FOR A PLACE TO SLEEP FOR A BIT.
THIS SPOT LOOKS OK.
WE NEEDED TO REST.
PEE-EW! YOUR DIAPER IS DIRTY.
WE'VE GOTTA GET YOU MORE.
I KNEW THERE WERE MORE "ADVENTURES" AHEAD OF US AND I WANTED TO ENJOY THIS MOMENT OF RESPITE.
WELL, AT LEAST NO ONE'S GOING TO SIT NEXT TO US, SO WE'LL HAVE THE WHOLE BENCH TO STRETCH OUT ON.
WE SLEPT FOR THE REST OF THE TRIP.
EXPRESS SANTORINI
EXPRESS SANTORINI
HELLENIC SEAWAYS

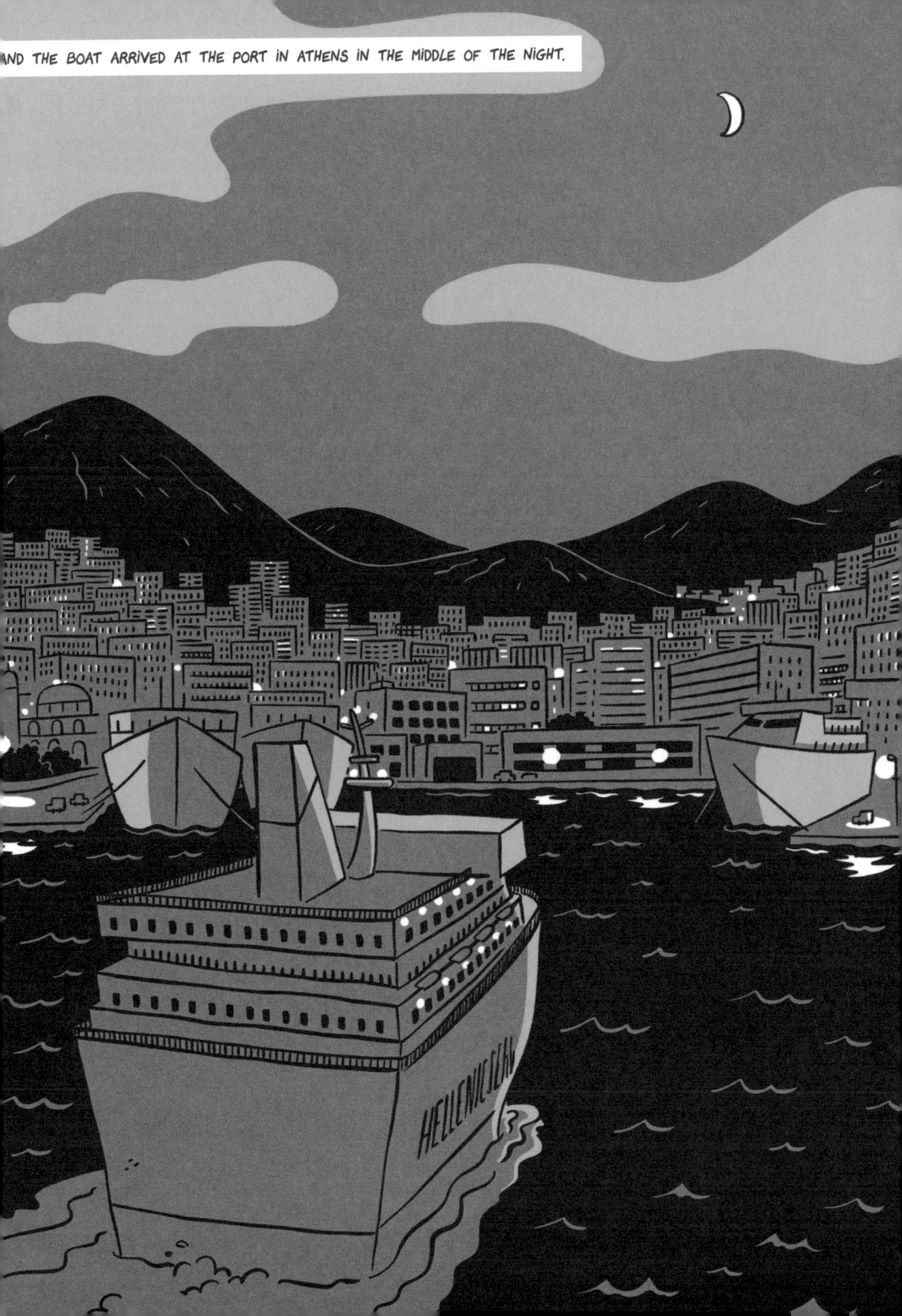
AND THE BOAT ARRIVED AT THE PORT IN ATHENS IN THE MIDDLE OF THE NIGHT.
HELLENIC SEA

AS MIGRANTS, WE WERE THE LAST TO GET OFF.

THE CITY SEEMED GIGANTIC.

THAT'S WEIRD.

THERE'S NO ONE TO SUPERVISE OUR ARRIVAL.

WHAT ARE WE SUPPOSED TO DO?

OUR FUTURES ARE IN OUR OWN HANDS NOW, MY FRIENDS.

WE HAVE VISAS, WE'RE FREE.

WELL, SORT OF...

WE'RE STILL REQUIRED TO GET OUT OF GREECE...

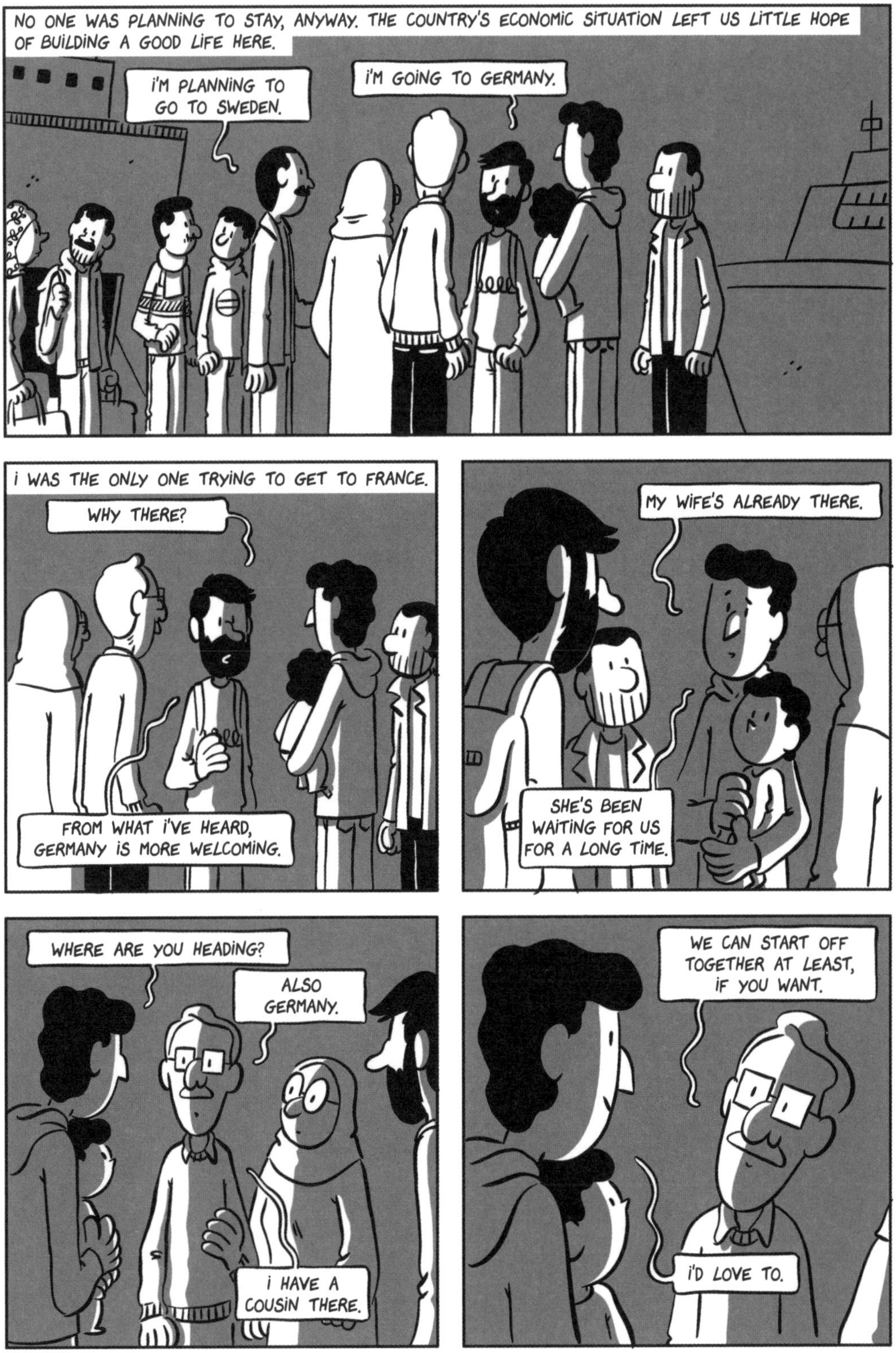
NO ONE WAS PLANNING TO STAY, ANYWAY. THE COUNTRY'S ECONOMIC SITUATION LEFT US LITTLE HOPE OF BUILDING A GOOD LIFE HERE.
I'M PLANNING TO GO TO SWEDEN.
I'M GOING TO GERMANY.
I WAS THE ONLY ONE TRYING TO GET TO FRANCE.
WHY THERE?
FROM WHAT I'VE HEARD, GERMANY IS MORE WELCOMING.
MY WIFE'S ALREADY THERE.
SHE'S BEEN WAITING FOR US FOR A LONG TIME.
WHERE ARE YOU HEADING?
ALSO GERMANY.
I HAVE A COUSIN THERE.
WE CAN START OFF TOGETHER AT LEAST, IF YOU WANT.
I'D LOVE TO.

HELLO!!
?
YOU'RE COMING FROM SAMOS, RIGHT?
IF YOU'D LIKE, WE HAVE TAXIS.
THEY CAN TAKE YOU WHERE YOU NEED TO GO TO CONTINUE YOUR "TRAVELS."
UH... SURE.
OK...
PERFECT!
FOLLOW ME!

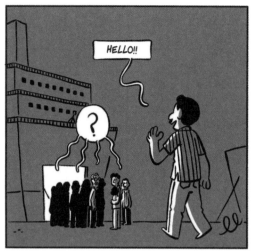

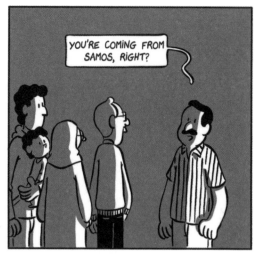

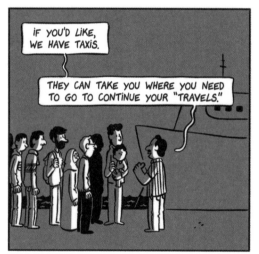

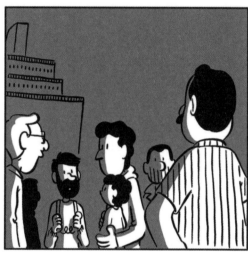

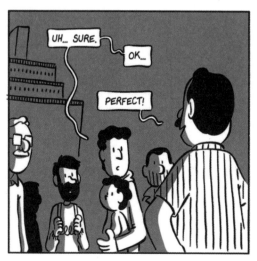

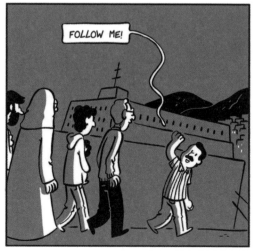

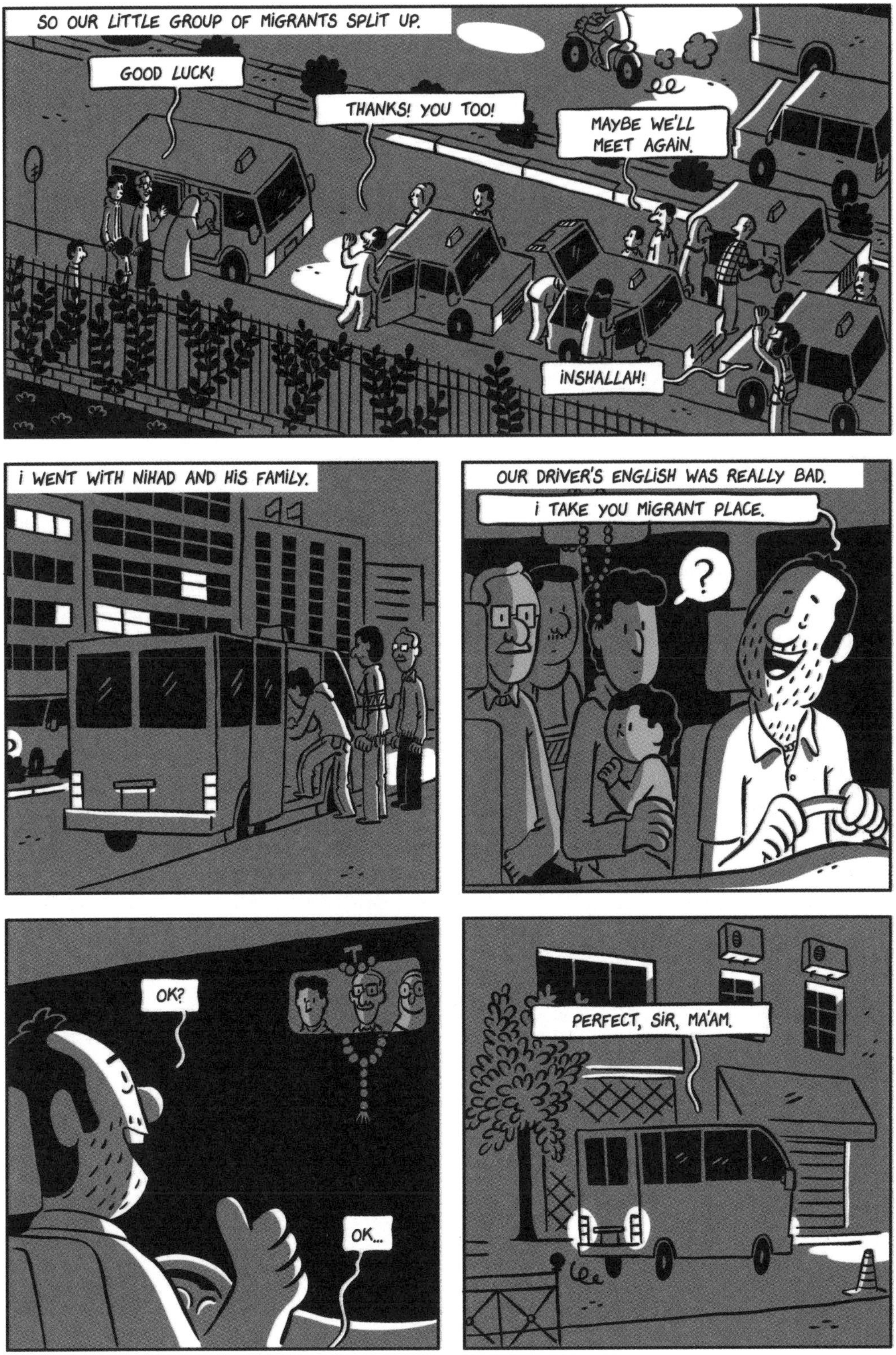
SO OUR LITTLE GROUP OF MIGRANTS SPLIT UP.
GOOD LUCK!
THANKS! YOU TOO!
MAYBE WE'LL MEET AGAIN.
INSHALLAH!
I WENT WITH NIHAD AND HIS FAMILY.
OUR DRIVER'S ENGLISH WAS REALLY BAD.
I TAKE YOU MIGRANT PLACE.
?
OK?
OK...
PERFECT, SIR, MA'AM.

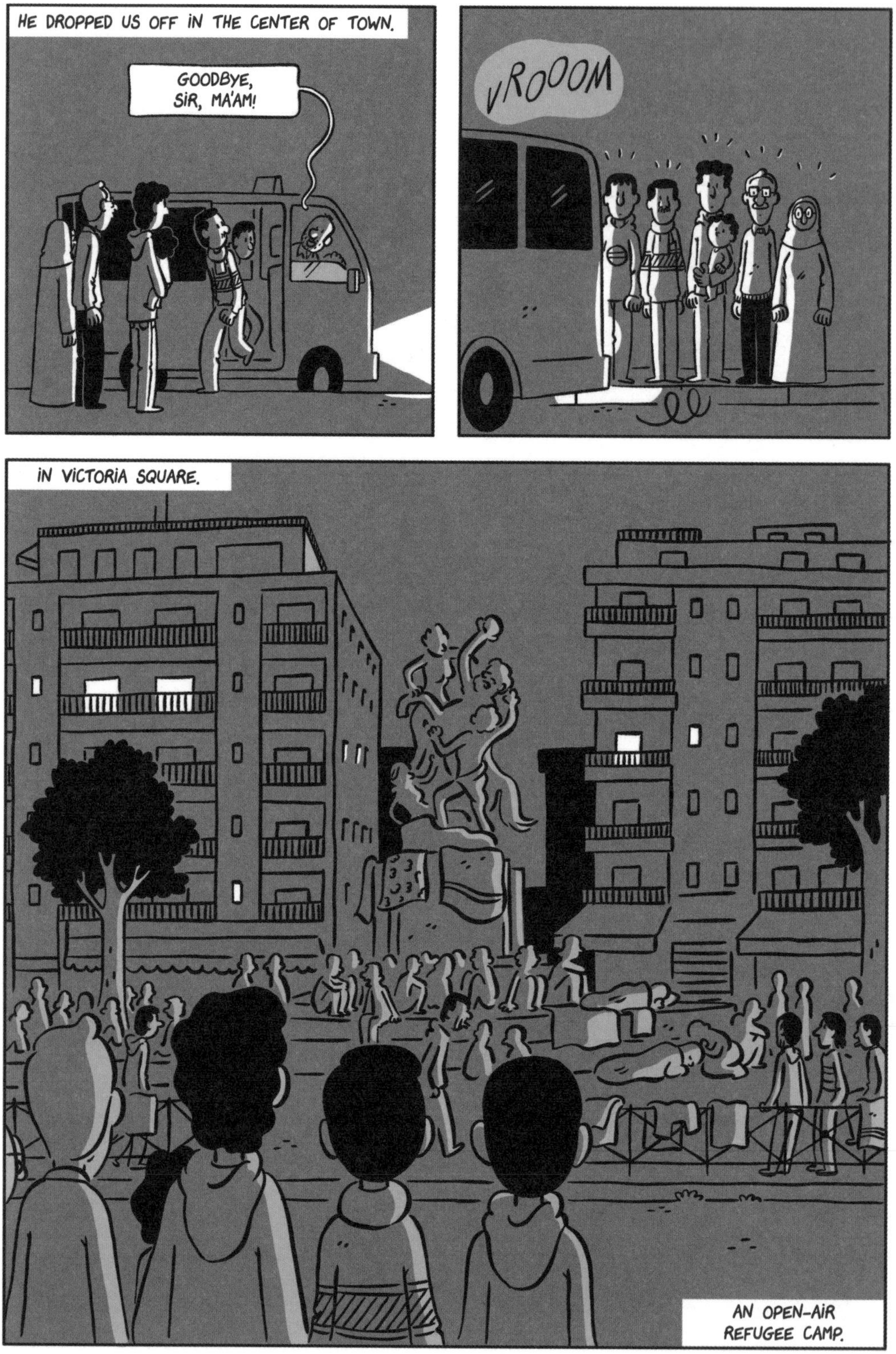
HE DROPPED US OFF IN THE CENTER OF TOWN.
GOODBYE, SIR, MA'AM!
VROOOM
IN VICTORIA SQUARE.
AN OPEN-AIR REFUGEE CAMP.

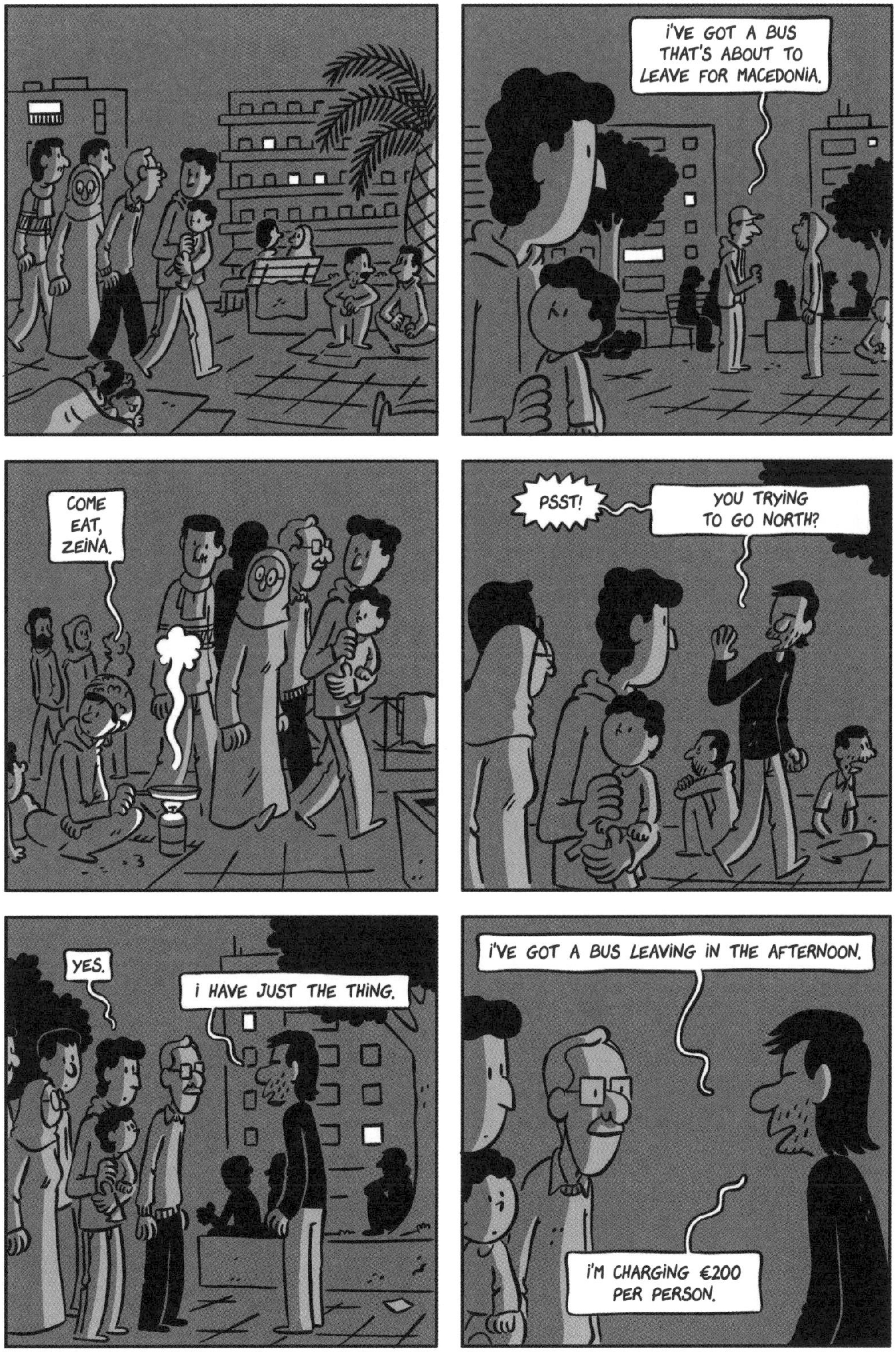
I'VE GOT A BUS THAT'S ABOUT TO LEAVE FOR MACEDONIA.
COME EAT, ZEINA.
PSST!
YOU TRYING TO GO NORTH?
YES.
I HAVE JUST THE THING.
I'VE GOT A BUS LEAVING IN THE AFTERNOON.
I'M CHARGING €200 PER PERSON.

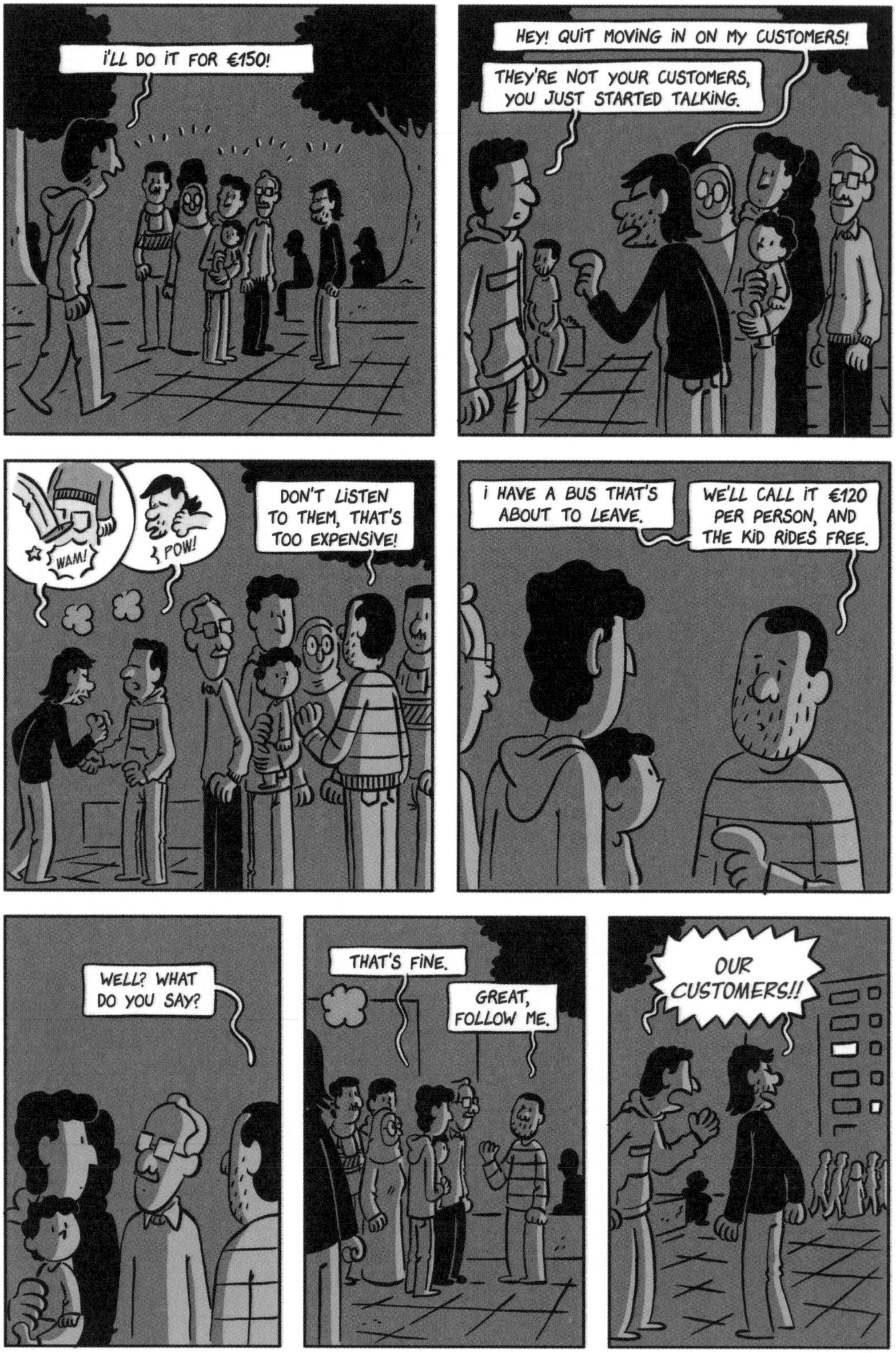
I'LL DO IT FOR €150!
HEY! QUIT MOVING IN ON MY CUSTOMERS!
THEY'RE NOT YOUR CUSTOMERS, YOU JUST STARTED TALKING.
WAM!
POW!
DON'T LISTEN TO THEM, THAT'S TOO EXPENSIVE!
I HAVE A BUS THAT'S ABOUT TO LEAVE.
WE'LL CALL IT €120 PER PERSON, AND THE KID RIDES FREE.
WELL? WHAT DO YOU SAY?
THAT'S FINE.
GREAT, FOLLOW ME.
OUR CUSTOMERS!!

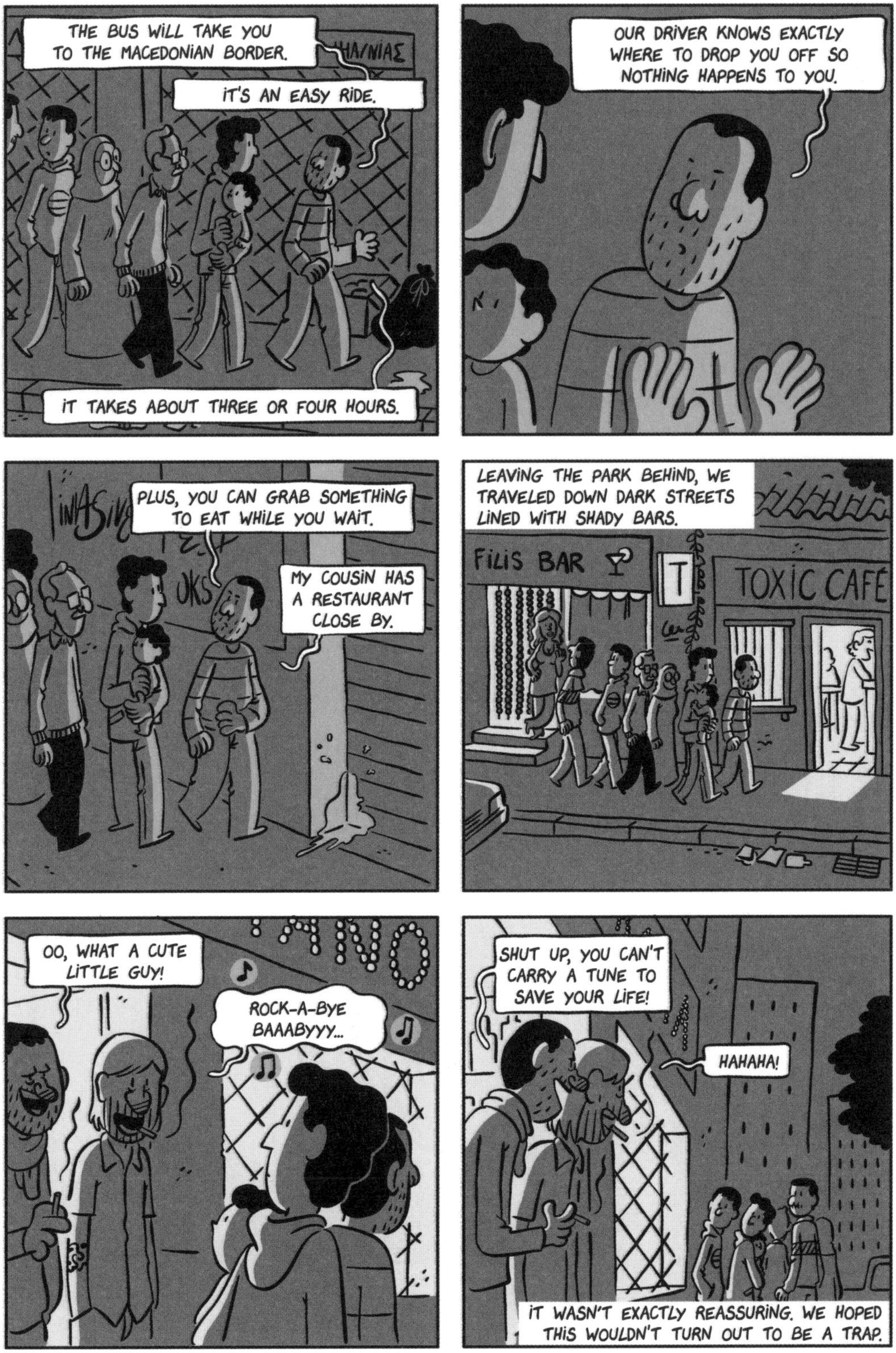
THE BUS WILL TAKE YOU TO THE MACEDONIAN BORDER.
IT'S AN EASY RIDE.
IT TAKES ABOUT THREE OR FOUR HOURS.
OUR DRIVER KNOWS EXACTLY WHERE TO DROP YOU OFF SO NOTHING HAPPENS TO YOU.
PLUS, YOU CAN GRAB SOMETHING TO EAT WHILE YOU WAIT.
MY COUSIN HAS A RESTAURANT CLOSE BY.
LEAVING THE PARK BEHIND, WE TRAVELED DOWN DARK STREETS LINED WITH SHADY BARS.
FILIS BAR
TOXIC CAFÉ
OO, WHAT A CUTE LITTLE GUY!
ROCK-A-BYE BAAABYYY...
SHUT UP, YOU CAN'T CARRY A TUNE TO SAVE YOUR LIFE!
HAHAHA!
IT WASN'T EXACTLY REASSURING. WE HOPED THIS WOULDN'T TURN OUT TO BE A TRAP.

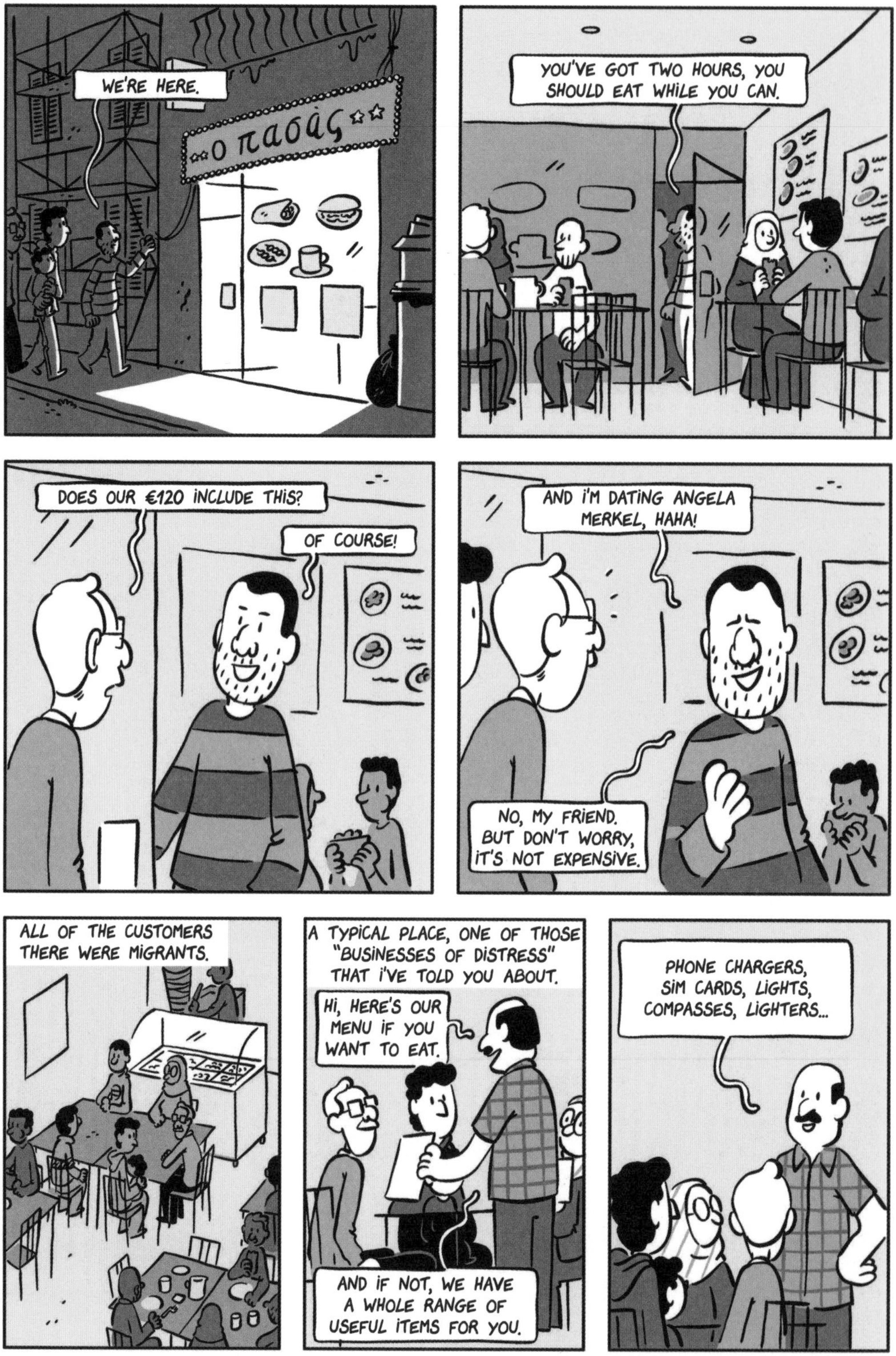
WE'RE HERE.
ο πασάς
YOU'VE GOT TWO HOURS, YOU SHOULD EAT WHILE YOU CAN.
DOES OUR €120 INCLUDE THIS?
OF COURSE!
AND I'M DATING ANGELA MERKEL, HAHA!
NO, MY FRIEND. BUT DON'T WORRY, IT'S NOT EXPENSIVE.
ALL OF THE CUSTOMERS THERE WERE MIGRANTS.
A TYPICAL PLACE, ONE OF THOSE "BUSINESSES OF DISTRESS" THAT I'VE TOLD YOU ABOUT.
HI, HERE'S OUR MENU IF YOU WANT TO EAT.
AND IF NOT, WE HAVE A WHOLE RANGE OF USEFUL ITEMS FOR YOU.
PHONE CHARGERS, SIM CARDS, LIGHTS, COMPASSES, LIGHTERS...

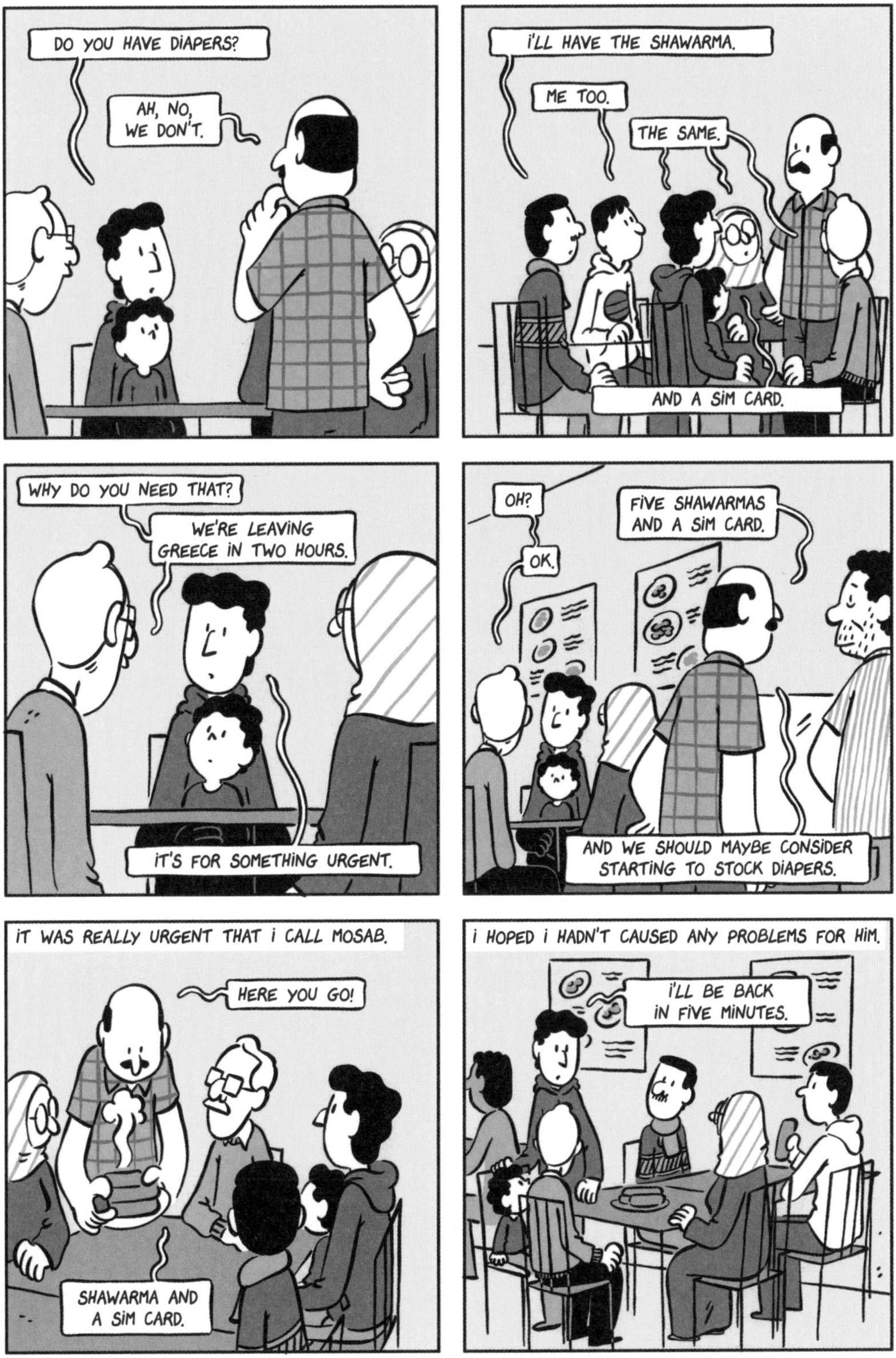
DO YOU HAVE DIAPERS?
AH, NO, WE DON'T.
I'LL HAVE THE SHAWARMA.
ME TOO.
THE SAME.
AND A SIM CARD.
WHY DO YOU NEED THAT?
WE'RE LEAVING GREECE IN TWO HOURS.
IT'S FOR SOMETHING URGENT.
OH?
OK.
FIVE SHAWARMAS AND A SIM CARD.
AND WE SHOULD MAYBE CONSIDER STARTING TO STOCK DIAPERS.
IT WAS REALLY URGENT THAT I CALL MOSAB.
HERE YOU GO!
SHAWARMA AND A SIM CARD.
I HOPED I HADN'T CAUSED ANY PROBLEMS FOR HIM.
I'LL BE BACK IN FIVE MINUTES.

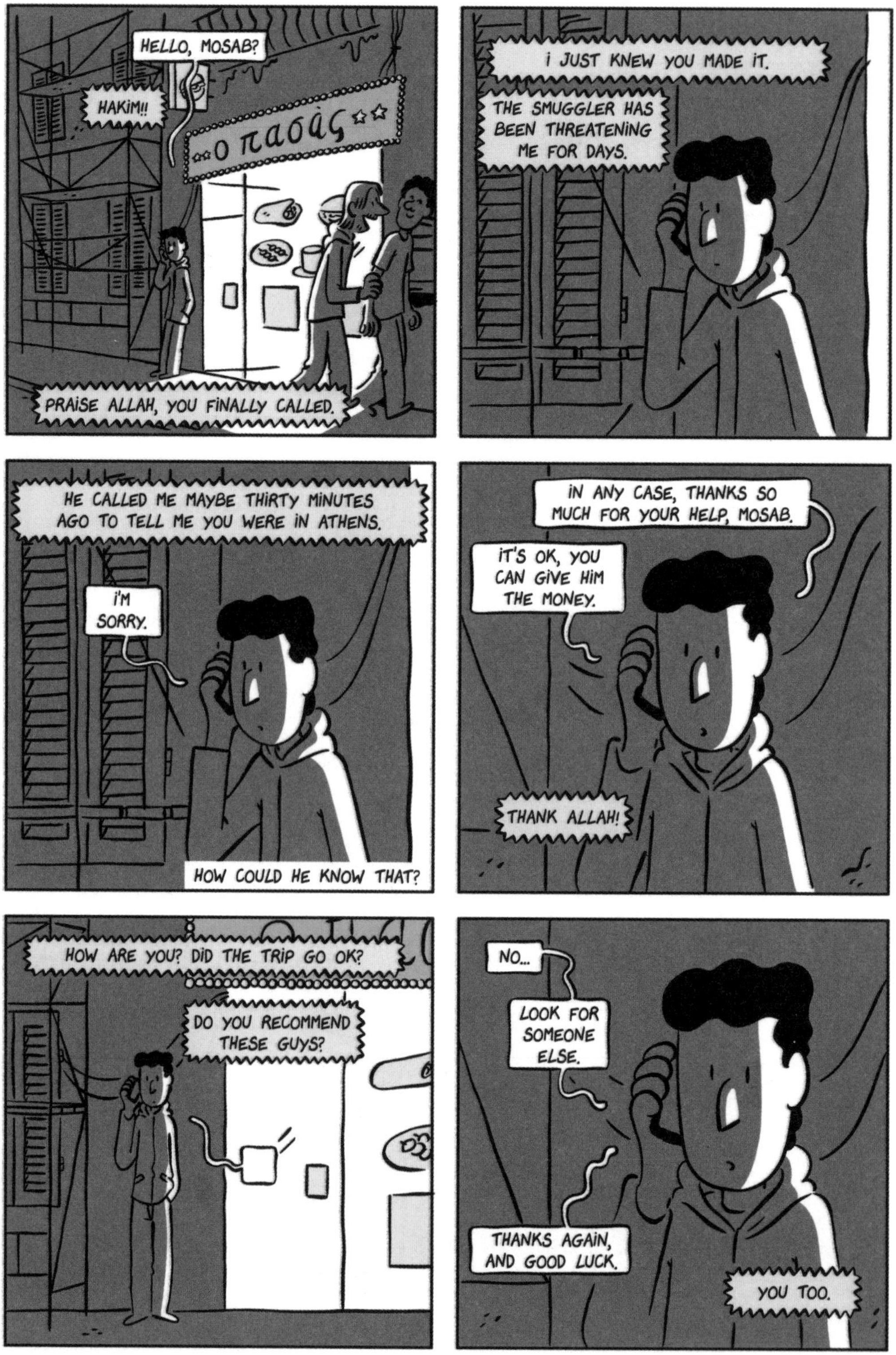
HELLO, MOSAB?
HAKIM!!
ο πασάς
PRAISE ALLAH, YOU FINALLY CALLED.
I JUST KNEW YOU MADE IT.
THE SMUGGLER HAS BEEN THREATENING ME FOR DAYS.
HE CALLED ME MAYBE THIRTY MINUTES AGO TO TELL ME YOU WERE IN ATHENS.
I'M SORRY.
HOW COULD HE KNOW THAT?
IN ANY CASE, THANKS SO MUCH FOR YOUR HELP, MOSAB.
IT'S OK, YOU CAN GIVE HIM THE MONEY.
THANK ALLAH!
HOW ARE YOU? DID THE TRIP GO OK?
DO YOU RECOMMEND THESE GUYS?
NO...
LOOK FOR SOMEONE ELSE.
THANKS AGAIN, AND GOOD LUCK.
YOU TOO.

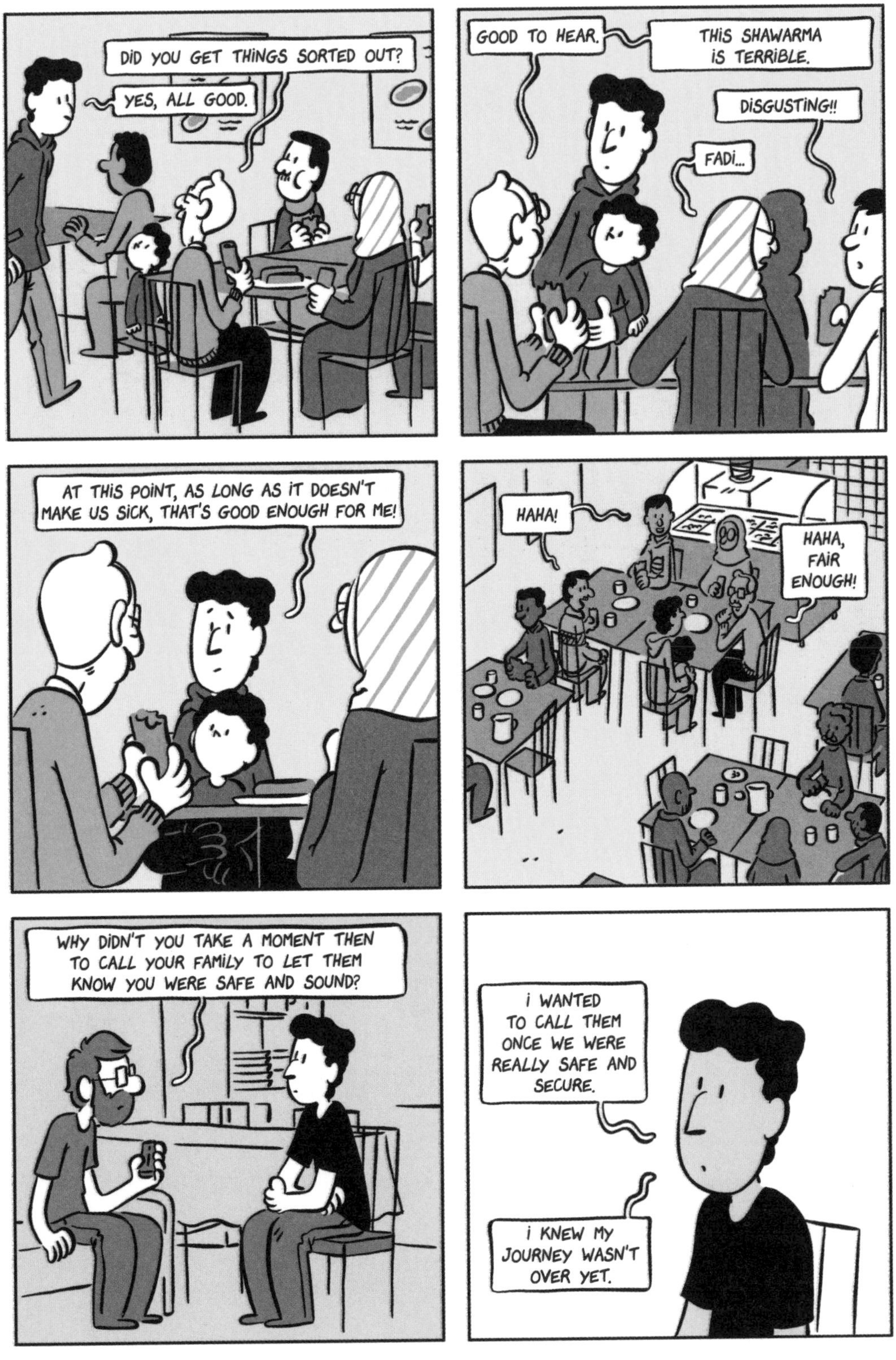
DID YOU GET THINGS SORTED OUT?
YES, ALL GOOD.
GOOD TO HEAR.
THIS SHAWARMA IS TERRIBLE.
DISGUSTING!!
FADI...
AT THIS POINT, AS LONG AS IT DOESN'T MAKE US SICK, THAT'S GOOD ENOUGH FOR ME!
HAHA!
HAHA, FAIR ENOUGH!
WHY DIDN'T YOU TAKE A MOMENT THEN TO CALL YOUR FAMILY TO LET THEM KNOW YOU WERE SAFE AND SOUND?
I WANTED TO CALL THEM ONCE WE WERE REALLY SAFE AND SECURE.
I KNEW MY JOURNEY WASN'T OVER YET.

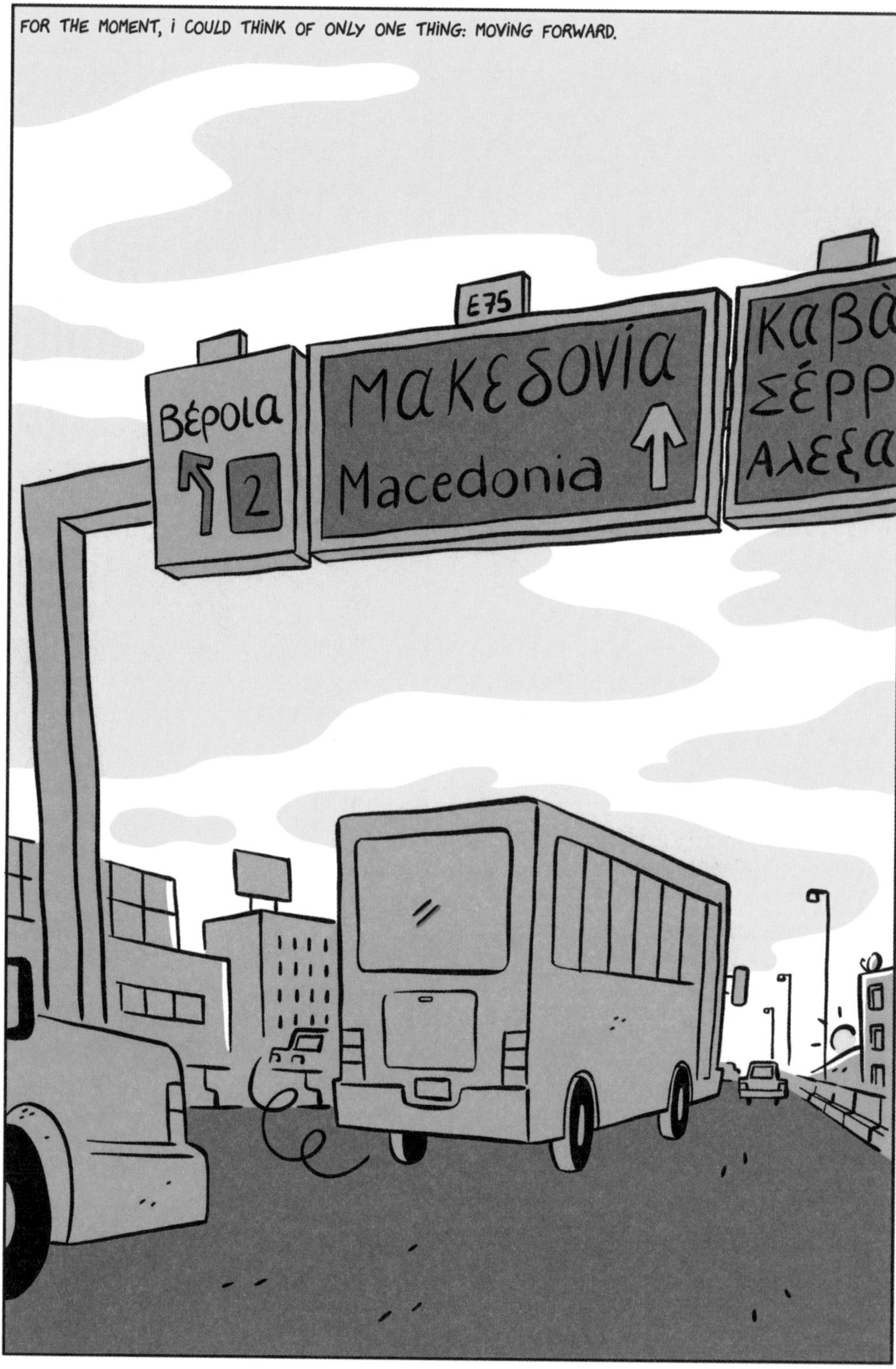
FOR THE MOMENT, I COULD THINK OF ONLY ONE THING: MOVING FORWARD.
E75
Βέροια
2
Μακεδονία
Macedonia

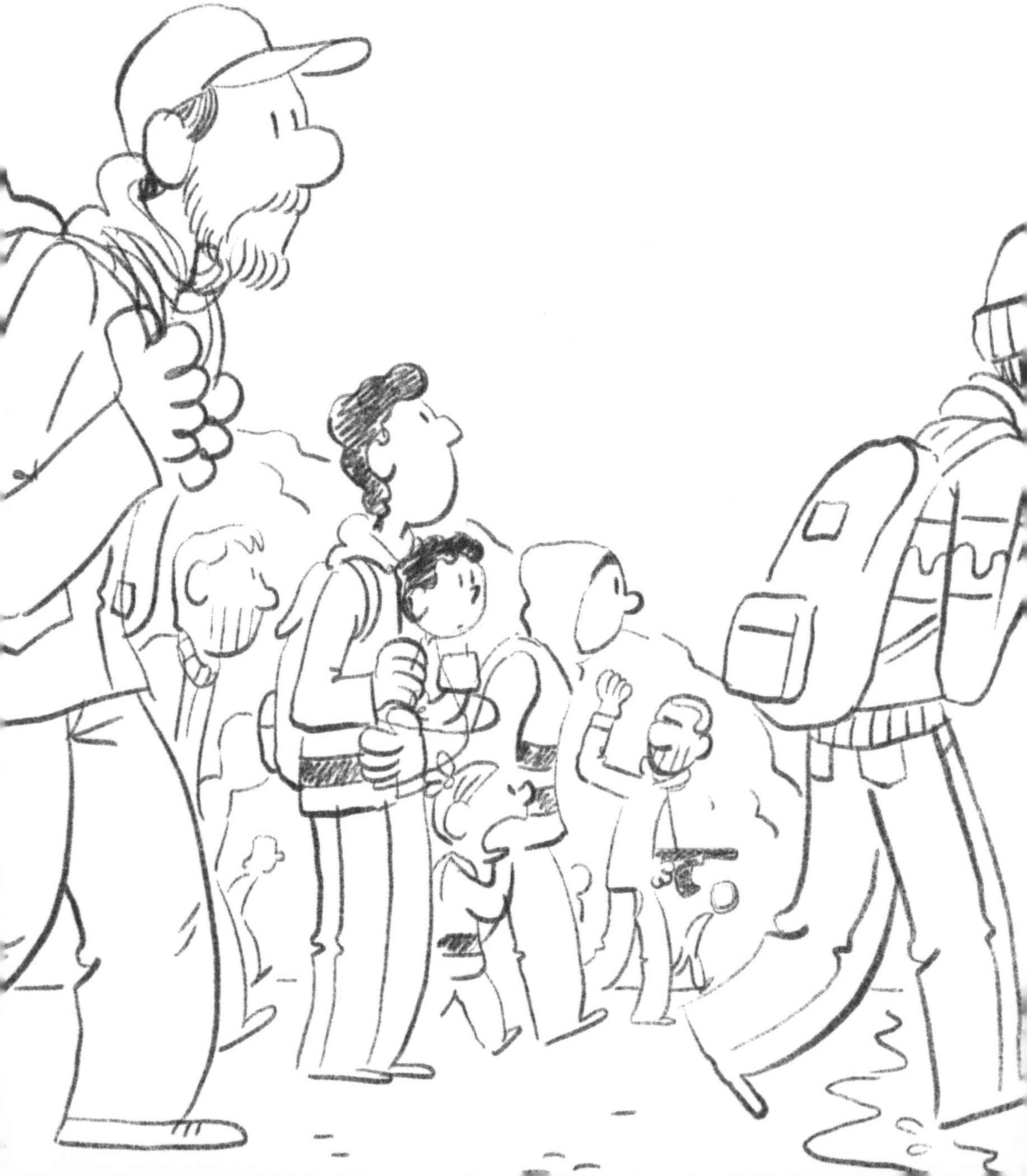

Thanks to my editor, Yannick Lejeune, for his help and advice; thanks to Patricia Haessig-Crevel and Laura Crevel-Floyd for connecting me with Hakim and for their help when the project ran into issues; thanks to interpreters Manuel, Bouchra Petit, and Michel Nieto for their indispensable aid; thanks to the teams at Delcourt (especially Leslie) who helped this book see the light of day; and my heartfelt thanks to Hakim, Najmeh, Hadi, and Sébastien for their patience and generosity.

Library of Congress Cataloging-in-Publication Data

Names: Toulmé, Fabien, 1980– author. | Chute, Hannah,
    1992– translator.
Title: Hakim's odyssey / Fabien Toulmé ; translated by Hannah
    Chute.
Other titles: Odyssée d'Hakim. English
Description: University Park, Pennsylvania : Graphic Mundi,
    [2022]– | "Originally published as L'Odyssée d'Hakim,
    volume 2 by Fabien Toulmé, Editions Delcourt, 2019."—
    Book 2. | Contents: Book 2. From Turkey to Greece
Summary: "An account, in graphic novel format, of a young
    Syrian refugee and how war forced him to leave everything
    behind, including his family, his friends, his home, and his
    business. This narrative follows his travels from Turkey to
    Greece"—Provided by publisher.
Identifiers: LCCN 2021017308 | ISBN 9781637790083
    (hardback)
Subjects: LCSH: Refugees—Syria—Comic books, strips, etc. |
    Forced migration—Syria—Comic books, strips, etc. |
    Syria—History—Civil War, 2011—Refugees—Comic
    books, strips, etc. | LCGFT: Graphic novels.
Classification: LCC PN6747.T68 O3913 2021 |
    DDC 741.5/944—dc23
LC record available at https://lccn.loc.gov/2021017308

Copyright © 2022 The Pennsylvania State University
All rights reserved
Printed in Lithuania by BALTO print
Published by The Pennsylvania State University Press,
University Park, PA 16802-1003

graphic mundi
drawing our worlds together

Graphic Mundi is an imprint of The Pennsylvania State
University Press.

Translated by Hannah Chute
Additional lettering and art reconstruction by Zen

Originally published as *L'Odyssée d'Hakim*, volume 2
by Fabien Toulmé
© Editions Delcourt – 2019

The Pennsylvania State University Press is a member of the
Association of University Presses.

It is the policy of The Pennsylvania State University Press to
use acid-free paper. Publications on uncoated stock satisfy
the minimum requirements of American National Standard
for Information Sciences—Permanence of Paper for Printed
Library Material, ANSI Z39.48–1992.